To Keep the Republic

GOVERNING THE UNITED STATES
IN ITS THIRD CENTURY

To Keep the Republic

GOVERNING THE UNITED STATES IN ITS THIRD CENTURY

David J. Olson

INDIANA UNIVERSITY

Philip Meyer

KNIGHT NEWSPAPERS, INC.

McGraw-Hill Book Company

NEW YORK ST. LOUIS SAN FRANCISCO AUCKLAND DÜSSELDORF JOHANNESBURG
KUALA LUMPUR LONDON MEXICO MONTREAL NEW DELHI PANAMA PARIS
SÃO PAULO SINGAPORE SYDNEY TOKYO TORONTO

This book was set in Garamond by Black Dot, Inc.
The editors were Robert A. Fry, Robert Weber, and James R. Belser;
the designer was J. E. O'Connor;
the production supervisor was Sam Ratkewitch.
The drawings were done by Vantage Art, Inc.
Cover photograph by Roy Volhmann; inset by Harry Naltchayan.
The printer was The Murray Printing Company;
the binder, Rand McNally & Company.

To Keep the Republic
GOVERNING THE UNITED STATES IN ITS THIRD CENTURY

1234567890MURM798765

Library of Congress Cataloging in Publication Data

Olson, David J
    To keep the Republic.

    1. United States—Politics and government—Handbooks, manuals, etc.
I. Meyer, Philip, joint author. II. Title.
JK274.038   320.4'73   74-31395
ISBN 0-07-047690-X

Contents

ABOUT

To Keep the Republic

It wasn't expected to be easy. The Founders had enough troubles of their own without trying to reach ahead two centuries to protect us from *our* crises. We feel their presence, nevertheless, and the question of whether we can keep the Republic is still open. The continuing crises of today—racial discord, environmental deterioration, energy shortages, simultaneous inflation and recession, food scarcity, and unprecedented exposure of corruption—threaten the viability of democratic institutions and the Republic itself. Writing a textbook on American government in the midst of such disarray has made us aware of the need to do two things: identify the major shortcomings in the performance of the political system; and celebrate those institutions and structures which have enabled us to cope with the staggering events never forseen by those who took up arms to secure their independence two centuries ago.

Such a writing task requires a stance somewhat different from those found in recent American government textbooks. The teaching of American government has gone through two major changes in the past decade, beginning with the trend toward texts written under the "behavioral" label with the announced purpose of correcting traditional interpretations of American government found in the "civics textbooks." The new texts emphasized political behavior rather than institutional structures; informal norms instead of formal rules; and political processes, not legal arrange-

ments. While this approach provided healthy adjustments to prior understandings of American government, it also lost or underplayed what was
best in the traditional approach it replaced. The behavioral texts pictured
American politics as an extremely successful enterprise, gave only scant
attention to political conflict, ignored the inequitable status of "have-not"
groups, and—most important—all but dropped the traditional concern for
assessing the practice of American government against its democratic
ideals.

A second shift in American government textbooks was stimulated by
the tumultuous politics of the late 1960s, the rise of a youth counterculture,
and violent protest on the campus and in the ghetto. Now the texts drew
attention to protest, conflict, violence, and Third World politics; they
featured an attack on establishment-oriented biases implicit in the earlier
behavioral texts. As its target of attack had done earlier, this new approach
provided a healthy corrective to deceptive orthodoxies, but it also underplayed the best in the behavioral texts it sought to replace. Analytic rigor
was sacrificed to ideological commitment, comprehensiveness gave way to
policy prescription, and student readers went unexposed to hard-nosed,
tough-minded empirical research and realities.

When we began writing this text, it was our conviction that traditional,
behavioral, and ideological approaches each suffered from weaknesses that
made them unsatisfactory introductions to American government. Yet each
offered valuable perspectives. We set out, therefore, to write a book based
on the strengths provided in the three traditions without becoming caught
up in differences that separated them. Accordingly, our text includes
traditional and behavioral perspectives, historical and contemporary materials, theoretical and empirical bases, conventional and nonconventional
topics, and interpretations of controversial subjects without, it is hoped,
compromising comprehensiveness of coverage.

Four general objectives guided the writing of this book. We wanted:

1. *To fashion a book that would be readable and understandable.* With the
student audience in mind, we desired to provide a text laced with
contemporary illustrations, organized around several major themes, featuring brief and clear presentations that would capture and retain the reader's
interest throughout.

2. *To produce a comprehensive introduction to American government.* We
aimed to treat not only the core features of American government, but also
various topics of importance ignored in other texts. And we tried to do so in
a manner that reflected alternative viewpoints held by political scientists.

3. *To stimulate creative and critical thinking among student readers.* We
view the form of government under which we live and the kind of politics it
produces as subjects for provocative discussion, debate, and criticism. We
attempted to address the most pressing issues confronting the nation,
suggest information and theories about them, and challenge readers to

engage in their own resolution of questions about American government raised by these issues.

4. *To examine alternative roles students can play as citizens in a democratic republic.* We wanted to describe and analyze both "usual politics" and "unusual politics," and to provide assessments of the consequences each is likely to have.

To fulfill these objectives, we have developed several distinctive features for this text. We begin in *Part One* by discussing contemporary issues in relation to their historical settings. The best and the worst in our two-hundred-year experiment in self-government are examined within a historical context often ignored at the price of missing the lessons the past has to offer. We believe, instead, that readers who understand where the nation has been will better understand where it is and where it might go. With similar reasoning, we link the bicentennial theme to the precipitous decline in confidence in American government and its institutions and the repeated crises accompanying this decline. In Part One we also include a discussion of the federal system and state and local government, believing they expose significant ties to the past and are important enough to merit more than appendant examination. *Part Two* is a critical analysis of traditional methods used by citizens to influence their government, concluding with an examination of unconventional modes of political participation. In *Part Three* we review traditional decisionmaking institutions, the decline of citizens' confidence in them, and their ability to cope with current crises. This section concludes with a discussion of the significant impact private power centers have on the lives of most citizens. *Part Four* indicates the differences politics can make through an examination of the political outcomes, in four illustrative policy areas, resulting from the interaction of citizens' demands and decisionmaking by public and private elites. The reader's attention is invited to critical questions and issues in brief essays introducing each part. An annotated list of additional readings follows each chapter for those readers interested in further pursuit of a subject.

Implicit in the title of this book is our conviction that the Republic merits preservation; that to preserve it, major alterations in some of its institutions are probably required; that to enhance its democratic performance, even more significant changes in numerous structures are in order; and that—resoundingly, in the 1970s—an informed and active citizenry is critical in deciding what to keep and what to change. Such considerations of preservation and change are incomplete without some reference to Watergate. Our position is that Watergate, together with the disposition of its related crimes through the political and governmental processes, offers important illustrations of the successes as well as the failures of the American system. The drama of such events often tempted us to focus on them as a central theme. But Watergate is not central. It has highlighted weaknesses in our institutions, but it has not changed essential features of our form of government. Those officials associated with the Watergate crimes have left public office, leaving us with an enigma: Our governmental institutions—some of which allowed Watergate to happen—remain unchanged. The Republic has survived, and if the enigma of Watergate is to be untangled, an understanding of the mechanisms described in this book which have worked to assist that survival—just as they have worked to greater or lesser degrees in the past—will be essential.

As we go to press, the wounds of Watergate are already healing, the scar tissue is forming, and the Republic should be stronger for it. The denouement has left us with many pedagogical opportunities and the reader will find these woven into the traditional, behavioral, and ideological aspects of the texts without departure from our central theme: The Republic is in a process of eternal challenge, revision, and adjustment; yet, it survives.

Now that the work is done, we can confess to occasional fears—most often felt at three in the morning—that our form of government might indeed change in ways favored by the Watergate conspirators, even as we studied it. Thus we have shared in the neurosis of our time. But the ailment is not terminal, and, given the wisdom of the Founding Fathers, it may even be self-limiting. We no longer fear that this will prove to be the last honestly optimistic textbook written about United States government.

We have shared with those who assisted our work on this project a neurosis produced by a different set of pressures, albeit at the same hour of the morning. Meeting deadlines for the several drafts would have been impossible without the resourceful assistance provided us by several people who sometimes also shared our views on American government. Our chief research assistant from beginning to end was Richard C. Rich, and his contributions to this project have been substantial. When we needed research support and the insight of persons who were in the front lines of the quest for information about the current state of the Republic, Robert S. Boyd and W. Davis Merritt, Jr., chief and news editor, respectively, of the Washington Bureau of Knight Newspapers, were always willing to avail us with their advice and their library. Pat Evans of the Supreme Court's own law library cheerfully helped us keep current our citations of recent cases. When the task of obtaining often obscure information, citations, and data needed to be performed, it usually went to Robert Goehlert, who also enlisted the valuable retrieval skills of Thomas Michalak. David Cox and Robert Bowers spent the better part of one summer providing information for the chapters dealing with public policy. When we began, Jan Froman organized our filing system, and Wanda L. Nicholls and Caroline Meyer helped to complete that and other aspects of the project. Marion Lovelace typed the first draft of this text, and Marianne Platt put her considerable skills to the remaining work. Ronald Wurm performed the art research. We are deeply grateful to all of these people, as well as to a host of student readers of the text, unknown to us by name.

Our indebtedness extends equally to the following political scientists who read and provided us comments on the text in earlier drafts: David J. Danelski, Cornell University; Kenneth M. Dolbeare, University of Massachusetts at Amherst; Edward S. Flash, Jr., Cornell University; John A. Gardiner, University of Illinois at Chicago Circle; John P. Lovell, Indiana University; Paul E. Peterson, University of Chicago; Ronald I. Rubin, Manhattan Community College; and James R. Soles, University of Delaware. We have been saved from many omissions, oversights, and errors by their comments, and we have benefited from their helpful observations. The end product is, of course, our own, and for errors, omissions, and distortions we willingly accept the responsibility—and the blame.

A TIME TRAVELER'S GUIDE TO THE THIRD CENTURY

When the Nixon Administration began the first preparations for celebrating the nation's bicentennial year, 1976, the mood was desultory, the organization casual. Given the strains the Republic was then under, no one felt much like celebrating. That changed, of course, but for a time it was hard not to see the artificiality of such a celebration. While two hundred years is a round number, it is linked to nothing in the laws of nature that gives it significance beyond the accident of our decimal system. Two hundred years is approximately seven generations, three human lifespans, or half the life of *Ulmus americana,* the American elm, that high-arched shade tree still found in parts of the Northeast not ravaged by Dutch elm disease.

And two hundred years is almost the age of the world's oldest written constitution still in effect—our own. Indeed, there is reason to argue that our real bicentennial year is 1989, the anniversary of the ratification of the Constitution of 1787. Only then will the United States have existed under the same form of government for two centuries.

On the other hand, the idea of the United States is much more than the contents of any document, however revered. Before the Revolution of 1776 could take place, a revolution of thought had to occur; and fixing a date for that is not easy—it was more process than event. In this sense, 1943 might be seen as the bicentennial year, because it was in 1743 that Samuel Adams first asserted in writing that the rights enjoyed by the American colonists were theirs not by virtue of British citizenship but as free members of the human race.

IS OUR GOVERNMENT OBSOLETE?

However the timing is reckoned, the ideas and symbols which underlie the organization of our society today were formulated roughly two centuries ago by men who could not possibly foresee the environments in which those ideas would survive or be forgotten. It is no small coincidence that

1776 was also the publication date of Adam Smith's *Wealth of Nations,* which drew the optimistic equation of happiness with property which would later haunt us in many different forms. And 1776 is also the approximate date of the dawn of the Industrial Revolution, which altered the happy comingling of self-interest and public interest envisioned by the merchants and shippers of Smith's time. Adam Smith's dream became, for some, a justification for profit seeking at all costs, including a rationalization for poverty and oppression. For others, it became a dream of freedom lost but still recapturable.

The times, in short, were growing more complicated, even as the Founding Fathers were preparing the charter for the new government. But while the physical and social environment changed, human nature did not, and the genius of the Founders lay in designing their system around that single constant human factor. The governors no less than the governed were selfish and deceitful. And the trick was to harness unpleasant forces and use them to make the system work, just as modern environmental engineers, knowing that garbage will always be with us, seek ways to turn it into fuel. Human beings can also be courageous and faithful to high purpose, and the system left room for those factors, too. But it did not assume the good and the wise would always prevail. The Founders understood human behavior, and they wrote the rules accordingly.

Several times their system has been severely tested. Before the first hundred years had passed, the mechanism for resolving sectional disputes failed completely, and the Civil War resulted. In 1933, the near collapse of the economic system, which still blindly followed the vision of Adam Smith, led to a strengthening of government's role in determining the social order. And in 1974, findings of criminal behavior directed from the highest levels to enhance the position of the persons in power provided a crucial test of the Founders' foresight. By objective standards, the system passed the test and did what it had been designed to do. The Watergate episode and related criminal matters amounted to what the Founders had feared most and had therefore been most careful about countering: the abuse of power to perpetuate the power of the abusers. They did not trust a king, and so they created an executive who is subject to a variety of checks. Not all the checks work all the time; but in their multiplicity, they cannot all be easily suppressed at any one time, for the mere act of suppressing triggers other parts of the checking mechanism. The White House decision to buy the silence of the Watergate burglars did indeed buy silence for a time, but it also created ripples which were noticed and attended to by more actors in the system than one ruler or party could control: a persistent judge; an alert newspaper; a convicted burglar angry at seeing others go unpunished. Whether these actors were motivated by fortune, revenge, self-esteem, or some higher purpose was not material to the test. The Founding Fathers had gotten it right, and a system designed in the eighteenth century could still disclose wrongs of the twentieth.

While the response to Watergate lends credibility to the system's ability to cope with certain blatant misuses of power, it does not constitute sufficient cause for smugness and self-satisfaction with our way of government. Checking power is only one side of the equation. The other side is using power. The Founders knew what they wanted there, too, and the six goals of government expressed in the Preamble to the Constitution of 1787 are still goals for government today. We have, however, perfected the definitions. Equal rights for women is now and was not then considered one of the blessings of liberty. The abolition of poverty was not then but is now considered an attainable contribution to the general welfare. As more things become possible our expectations about government increase, and we face the continual task of redefining our goals. Unanticipated complications and subtleties arise, as modern affluence and technology diversify the possible. For example, we are now forced to think about whether, in seeking social equality, we want to achieve equality of opportunity or equality in the end result. We are forced to think about this for the first time; the choice never seemed available before.

These choices become available not only because of technology, but because the social system which underlies government is shifting from a stratified class system, where wealth and power are inherited, to a more mobile system, approaching a meritocracy, which rewards the talented and the energetic. Every government rests on a social system in which some persons consent to be ruled by others. The Founding Fathers were members of such a ruling class, and the position of this class was sustained long after the Founders' time by an expanding economy and a continuing immigration of newcomers who obediently filled the lower ranks of the system. But the gates have shut, and the children and grandchildren of the immigrants were not content with such a humble position. The new people took the rhetoric of equality at face value, and those in power could no longer expect obedience automatically.

Yet, as Andrew Hacker argued two decades ago, the average American may be no more free. He or she may simply be manipulated in a different way by a different kind of ruling elite. Consent is engineered through public relations techniques, rather than habits of deference. "The average American of our day," said Hacker, "gives his consent not to prescription and the works of men long dead, but to a system of power which is controlled by men who are alive and among us. Both deference and manipulation are similar in that they are control. Both permit a few men to rule many men."

Hacker was writing in a time of exceptional calm, when leadership was trusted and major social conflict had not yet openly developed. Much of government's energy is now devoted to resolving social conflict and mediating (and sometimes promoting) the competing demands of groups which seek goals that were not seen even as remote possibilities a generation ago. The political stage is more crowded now, social conflict is less muted, and the variety of competing actors is greater. Partly due to these changes, the consensus and legitimacy needed to keep the Republic are more difficult to sustain. Broadened political participation and increased scope of governmental involvement ironically have contributed to the erosion of consensus and legitimacy at the same time they point toward a fuller realization of the democratic-republic ideal than the Founders dreamed of.

THE MANAGEMENT OF CONFLICT

Politics, as Harold Lasswell has said, is the process of deciding who gets what, when, and how. The benefits and costs of the social and economic systems, both material and psychological, are finite. Not everyone can have as much joy or as little sorrow as he or she would like. Every modern and industrialized society, therefore, no matter what its form of government or its economic system, must necessarily be competitive. The problem from the standpoint of governing is to manage the competitive forces, promote those receiving broadest popular support, keep the potentially most destructive in check, and, as a maximum hope, make them a productive and beneficial force. Gaining control of the government which manages the competitive environment is itself an object of competition.

Given finite resources and limited productivity, one person's gains in this system are most often someone else's losses. But not all the distributive decisions of government need involve such dismal choices. There are situations where successful management of a problem can put everyone ahead. If oil and gas for heating homes is in short supply, it makes sense for everyone to turn down the thermostat if that will ensure stretching the supply to last the winter. But it only works if everyone does it, and if you cannot be sure that others will do it, you may prefer to forgo the near-term discomfort of a cold house in the belief that the only way to assure yourself of your fair share of heat is to consume as much as you can while it is available. Many government problems involve the manipulation of incentive and disincentive systems so that the short-term motives of citizens will enhance, not impair, long-term gains for the society. The solutions are not always apparent or straightforward. And the distribution of gains is seldom even or fair.

MUDDLING THROUGH

Today, halfway through the lifespan of *Ulmus americana,* the process of designing the system of government continues to go forward. The restful eye that observes only the settlement of past questions (and thereby perceives the architecture of government to be fixed) is focused on the wrong target. Recast toward the dynamic center of current governmental activity, it would see the continuing evolution of new power arrangements, alternative instrumentalities for governing, and changing sets of recipients of the rewards and deprivations this political system produces. Although often painfully slow to develop, change is perhaps the only constant to be observed in American government. And those design changes are not always guided into being by enlightened craftsmen, nor is their impact uniformly progressive. The ebbs and flows that characterize the consequences of governmental reform are comparable in some respects to antidotes for the Dutch elm disease: Some are beneficial to the longevity of its recipient, others are not.

Constantly tampering with the instruments of government is unsettling to nearly everyone. Those who have been particularly blessed by established ways of doing things resist attempts at changing governmental structures for fear of losing their advantageous positions. The oppressed, or at least those who trace their disadvantages to the same structures, reject piecemeal modifications and adjustments to the system, preferring instead comprehensive change sufficient to alter their unequal status. And others in between simply tire of the endless tinkering, hoping in futility that such "political" maneuvers will end once and for all. The uniformity of opposition to muddling through as a way of deciding and redeciding questions about the form of government is surpassed nevertheless by the consistency with which muddling through has been used historically and is being used currently as the method for deciding what structures will be used to govern. And this is so for several very good reasons: the vastness of the land, the diversity of the population, the many competing sectional interests, the horizontal and vertical fragmentation of authority, the legacy of regional distinctiveness, and the radical decentralization of political structures all tend to promote marginal refinements that haultingly adjust governmental structures in what appear as step-by-step increments.

In its present state, the political system remains hardy and flexible. At the same time it continues to produce imperfect results. The civil liberties of some citizens are infringed, and the civil rights of others are still denied. Gaps between the "haves" and "have nots" remain and periodically widen. Deference is shown to the strong and the powerful, who thus become even stronger and more powerful. Devotion to the public good is not always rewarded. Villians go unpunished.

Events of the past decade show that the government and those who run it are responsible for many of the discrepancies between professed ideals and actual policies. Yet it was the wisdom of the Founders to repose power among the governed over those who govern. In the end the potential for having the form of government we choose to have is there, and the evils that attend to existing practices endure because they are tolerated. Whatever shadow falls between the dream and the reality is no more than the dusky pattern of popular indifference.

Part One

Foundations

OUR IMMEDIATE CONCERN IN PART ONE IS TO DISCUSS THE EIGHT-eenth century events and documents that constitute the foundations of American government. In Chapter 1, the historical events leading to nationhood and the constitutional document that put in writing a set of rules for governing the new nation are considered; constitutional guarantees ensuring individual liberties and civil rights are examined in Chapter 2, and Chapter 3 reviews the nature of the federal system launched by these events and documents.

In an era when obtaining food to eat and clean air to breathe are the major preoccupations, readers may fairly ask why any government textbook would begin by reaching back through two hundred years of musty history to analyze the parched scrolls recording our eighteenth-century origins. The simple answer is that records of such events and documents do exist and are worthy of review for their own sake. To take too lightly the experiences of those who preceded us in the experiment of self-government is to run the risk of incurring a peculiar form of ignorance about lessons the past may offer.

We are persuaded that the founding events and documents warrant examination. But is past history instructive? Does it repeat itself? Are there lessons for today to be learned from it? The following chapters reflect our affirmative answer in each instance. Yet the subject of historical recurrence and instructiveness is problematical and students of the American experience may well disagree with us. Because of such well-grounded uncertainties, our discussion throughout Part One is cast in a broad framework so that the meaning of the foundations of American government may be assessed for the twentieth century as well as for the eighteenth. The contemporary application of the founding principles of government is as much our concern in what follows as is tracing the origins of these eighteenth-century principles.

This approach provides us with the opportunity to pursue a major theme; namely, that self-government in America is a constantly evolving process with shapes and forms that take on new contours over time and represent significant adaptations to changing conditions, beliefs, and customs. The formation of the nation, for example, can be fixed in time at a specific date, but the meaning of nationhood has changed in important respects from what the Founding Fathers intended by it. The antagonists in the Civil War placed different constructions on it, as Native Americans and blacks continue to do today. The different situational contexts surrounding government partially explain why the founding principles meant one thing to one age and something quite different to another. And understanding why things are as they are today requires some appreciation of how they once were.

A somewhat related perspective on the importance of reviewing these foundations grows out of our conviction that contemporary proposals for reforming basic aspects of the governmental apparatus stand to benefit from knowing what consequences have followed past attempts at revision. The current debate over the relative merits of greater or lesser governmental centralization has ample historical precedents throughout the country's national existence. Present controversies about the proper scope of individual liberties and civil rights have similar antecedents, and the political consequences resulting from expansion or withdrawal of these basic guarantees can be determined by examining the historical record. Because many of the most visible disputes of the 1970s strike familiar notes from the past, our discussion weaves the strands of the historical development of the foundations into the structural fabric of contemporary American government.

The repeated crises in recent American politics, some of which threaten the viability of democratic institutions themselves, give us another reason for dwelling on the foundations of American government. The sometimes harrowing events of the last decade forced citizens to search soberly the collective understandings that originally bound a disparate people together for clues to the resolution of contemporary differences. Put more graphically, the Watergate crisis alone did more to engender respect for the institutional checks on the abuse of power than all the writings on the subject in recent civics textbooks. Part of this reflective behavior may simply be a longing for a return to a time when calmer passions prevailed. But one means for setting current disputes is to turn to the founding era to determine what is appropriate and allowable and what is not. Our examination of the motivations, aspirations, and behavior of the Founding Fathers reveals considerable wisdom in the form of government they created. It also shows areas where their self-serving acts produced governmental institutions beneficial to themselves. The warts and blemishes deserve attention as well as the achievements and triumphs.

Chapter 1

Historical Bases and Constitutional Foundations

DEFINING DEMOCRACY

Democracy on the Move: Three Cases

On the day that President Nixon was inaugurated for the second time, Embry Rucker chartered a bus. Mr. Rucker was the vicar of the Episcopal Congregation of the Church at Reston in northern Virginia, and as many of his parishioners as could crowd into the seats and the aisle rode the twenty-four miles to the Washington Monument grounds to protest the President's Southeast Asia war policies. The bus cost $72. Mr. Rucker paid the driver in cash from a wad of ones and fives passed forward during the ride down the George Washington Memorial Parkway. There was $29 left over. He gave it to the Washington Area Peace Action Coalition, a sponsor of the protest.

Two days later, the Democratic Conference of the House of Representatives met to change a long-standing rule dealing with the selection of committee chairmen. Under the new rule, committee chairmen would no longer be chosen solely on the basis of the number of years they had served in the House. The purpose of the change was not to be fair to younger men but to put new vitality into the House leadership, for Congress was struggling to regain the power some of its members thought they had lost to the Presidency.

3

While the House Democrats were holding their caucus, the Supreme Court, a block away, issued its decision in the case of *Roe v. Wade.* It said the right of privacy implicit in the Fourteenth Amendment prevented a state government from interfering with a woman's decision to terminate an early pregnancy. Forty-six state antiabortion laws were overturned by the decision. Mr. Justice Byron White, dissenting, called the action "an exercise of raw judicial power." But, he acknowledged, "the Court perhaps has authority to do what it does today."

Power: What Is It?

In a way, each of these events was commonplace. The citizens in the bus, the elected representatives, the judges with lifetime tenure were all participating in the continuing process of struggle and adjustment by which the power of the state is defined and applied. The nation was nearing the beginning of its third century, but the process was not new. It was the chief preoccupation of the founders, as evidenced by the things they read and wrote. "The theory of politics that emerges from the political literature of the pre-Revolutionary years rests on the belief that what lay behind every political scene, the ultimate explanation of every political controversy, was the disposition of power," says historian Bernard Bailyn (1967). "The acuteness of the colonists' sense of this problem is, for the twentieth-century reader, one of the most striking things to be found in this eighteenth-century literature: it serves to link the Revolutionary generation to our own in the most intimate way [p. 55]."

Presidential Inaugural, 1972: Defining the power of the state. *(Wide World Photos.)*

Power to the colonists meant the dominion or control of some men over others. They saw power as aggressive and expansive. In its simplest and most direct form, power is physical. Indeed, Bertrand Russell (1953) has speculated that technological developments, such as gunpowder, which made the concentration of physical power possible, are responsible for the rise of the modern state in the fifteenth and sixteenth centuries. Mao Tse-Tung (1938) put it more forcefully when he said, "Political power grows out of the barrel of a gun [p. 224]." In everyday life, power grows from more subtle sources, even though the threat or fear of physical coercion may lie behind every government act. But such an underlying threat was far removed from the thoughts of the peaceful marchers at the monument grounds, the congressmen yearning for fresh ideas, and the Supreme Court justices reversing state abortion restrictions. Sometimes the power of the state does manifest itself in a direct, physical way. Most of the time, where most of us are concerned, it does not. The reason we are so lucky is that we live in a society which is highly successful in managing its internal power relationships.

Power may be defined as the ability to attain one's ends despite resistance (Etzioni, 1968; Dahl, 1970; Olsen, 1970). If we ask you for your wallet, you may resist, but we can overcome that by displaying a handgun. Political power is the ability to obtain the symbolic or material values of society despite the opposition of others, and to do it, not by displaying a gun, but by manipulating one's position in society so that the resistance is overcome through authority that is recognized as legitimate. By "legitimate" we mean more than merely being legal. Authority is legitimate if it is recognized as proper and just even by people who may not like the uses to which it is put. Legitimate power commands consent. Groups which seek political power face not only the problem of getting it in the first place but the longer-range problem of legitimizing it, i.e., convincing others that the power is justly held. The methods which the tax collector uses to relieve you of the contents of your wallet may ultimately be as coercive as those of the mugger with a Saturday-night special. But you are more likely to consider the former legitimate, and so you consent.

Playing the Power Game

Resistance need not be active for a power relationship to exist. Some of the most crucial forms of political power involve the ability to squelch potential opposition before it ever achieves self-awareness. You can do this by concealing your acts or by hiding their effects upon the distribution of rewards. You can do it by invoking previously established symbols of legitimacy so that the "rightness" of what you do is never questioned. You can suppress opposition by invoking other symbols that define the opposition as illegitimate. The trick is to manipulate the flow of information and the use of symbols so that you control the agenda, deciding what issues will enter public debate and what will fail to surface.

The power to prevent others from recognizing their interests in decisions or to keep issues off the agenda as unimportant, nonpolitical, or not legitimate is crucial. You will recognize the code words: "not in the public interest," "national security," "traditional American values." The ability to manipulate these symbols to further one's own interests is perhaps the greatest source of power in a nonauthoritarian political system where the use of force is minimized and political acts are legitimated by the formal rituals of popular participation or the claim of majority rule. Peter Bachrach and Morton S. Baratz (1970) have called this the "other face of power." It poses a great problem for the student of politics because non-decision making is difficult to observe. One way to get a grip on the subject is to pass over the system of power relationships and look instead at the outcomes of those relationships. The way resources are distributed, the way values are allocated through public policy can give us clues to how and why power is exercised. We shall take that approach in later chapters. But first we must introduce some basic concepts.

Social Control

One of the earliest theoreticians of democracy, John Locke, recognized that government's role in creating standards of conduct is relatively minor. Government is "the coercive arm" of society, but the underlying moral structure which it supports is society's creation, not government's (Sabine, 1952, p.458). The everyday mechanisms of control do not involve government at all, and they are exceedingly subtle. They are informal and often unconscious, existing independently of codified rules and regulations. Custom and tradition are built and enforced by the emotional need to be accepted by peers, the psychological need to have guideposts for behavior which relieve the individual of evaluating every act and moment of his days. The pattern of responses that is conditioned by society is called *personality*, and it is the foundation for social order. The formal rules and procedures of the state are based on these more fundamental controls. "In simple societies," says Landis (1939), "there is a relative absence of the more formal controls which exist in the modern world [p. 21]." But the everyday applications of the controls are not too different. And the informal controls, because they reach nearly everything we do, are, in the long run, far more

Fire and Water

For liberty and authority they die
though one is fire and the other water
and the balances of freedom and discipline
are a moving target with changing decoys.

—Carl Sandburg, from *The People, Yes*

powerful than those the state can impose by force. A formal law which is contrary to generally accepted social convention will not be obeyed, and the conflict between the law and social convention becomes more of a threat to the system of law than to the specific social convention which it opposes. Thus the unenforceable prohibitions against the use of alcoholic beverages in the 1920s and the use of marijuana in the 1960s and 1970s did more damage to the ability of the law to elicit obedience than they did to the customs of drinking booze or smoking dope. In a sense, then, even the most tyrannical government exists by consent of the governed. No monopoly of physical power is great enough to monitor and control all the details of daily existence. Nevertheless, there is wide variation in the amount of control which a particular government may try to impose and a similarly wide variation in the amount of obedience with which a citizenry will respond. There are finite limits to government power, although modern technology might extend those limits to the degree envisioned by George Orwell in his chilling novel, *1984.* There are also finite limits to the freedoms of individuals who have to associate with other individuals, whether the association be in a family, a dormitory, a commune, or a formal system of government. The same technology which makes it possible to expand the power of the state also can be used to expand the freedom of the individual. If we define freedom as the ability to choose between alternative things to have and strive for, we find we have many more choices than our grandparents enjoyed—whether to spend the weekend watching television, hitchhiking to Los Angeles, or listening to the Bolshoi Theater Orchestra performing *Carmen*, for example. So while the nature of the debate in the nation's third century may be much the same, the situational context is not. The ranges and uses of power and the advantages and possibilities of freedom are greatly expanded. The problem grows more complicated. To understand it we must start with some essentials. We shall return later to the problems of the Reverend Mr. Rucker, the House Democrats, and Mr. Justice White.

Control by the State

By state, we mean a politically organized community located in a definite territory which monopolizes the physical power of that territory. It is not always the same as a nation, which can exist as a feeling of group identity in people's minds rather than being tied to a particular tract of territory. Indeed, the problem of linking nationhood with territory has been a leading cause of war. There is no set rule or eternal guiding principal which connects a given nation to a given piece of territory. "The moment you start to discuss factories, mines, mountains or even political authority as perfect examples of some eternal principle or other," says Walter Lippman (1922), "you are not arguing, you are fighting [p. 86]."

Whether and where a state exists is less arguable. There is or is not a sovereign power, and it does or does not control a given territory. The "nation of Israel," however, existed in the minds of Jews and others long before the state of Israel was finally carved out of what was formerly Palestine by David Ben-Gurion's declaration of Israeli nationhood of May 14, 1947 and the United Nations Partition Resolution of November 1947. Though dispersed about the globe, the members of this nation had cultural and religious ties, reinforced by a common experience of persecution, that bound them together in a condition that could be thought of as nationhood. The same claim might be made for the displaced Palestinians after 1948 or the Cherokee Indian Nation which retained its identity with great difficulty after being driven from its Georgia lands by federal soldiers carrying out the provisions of the Treaty of New Echota in 1838 (Filler and Guttmann, 1962). The Rev. Jesse Jackson of Chicago has used the phrase, "Nation-time is coming" to prophesy the eventual liberation of blacks. And blacks may think of themselves as a nation, whether or not they carve out a specific piece of land and exercise in that territory the powers of a state. Similarly, the Navajos, spreading out from the borders of their reservation and growing in population, can think of themselves as a nation, and there has been discussion of turning this nation into a political entity by creation of an independent state or a fifty-first state of the United States (*Society*, 1973, p. 15).

But the state and the nation can be and often are the same thing. A nation may be defined (White, 1947) as "a large group of people who generally form a state and who are welded together by common traditions and culture and usually by a common language. A nation regards itself and is regarded by others as being distinct from other nations [p. 191]."

The Idea of Progress

In the eighteenth century, the time was ripe for the idea of nation building. It was the age of Enlightenment and the rebirth of the idea of progress. "This idea," says Hallowell (1950), is "a secularized version of the Christian concept of Providence [p. 131]." It was one of the dominant ideas of the time. "Science at last had provided the certain means whereby man by his own efforts might successfully assert his own divinity, achieve the perfection of his being and the establishment of the perfect society on earth. The dream was as old as Adam, but never did it seem as likely of realization as it did toward the close of the eighteenth century [pp. 131–132]." The notion that nation building is a continuing task is still with us today; and it is a valuable one, because it reminds us that we are looking at a *process*, not a finished product. People who become disillusioned with the process are sometimes prone to announce that, having discovered the flaws, they are "turned off" of politics. If only politics could be done with, if politicians could be convinced that they have had their day and should retire from the scene, they seem to say, things would be better. We could then enjoy the finished product of statehood. But the product is

The warmest friends and the best supporters the Constitution has do not contend that it is free from imperfections; but they found them unavoidable, and are sensible, if evil is likely to arise therefrom, the remedy must come hereafter; for in the present moment it is not to be obtained; and as there is a constitutional door open for it, I think the people (for it is with them to judge), can, as they will have the advantage of experience on their side, decide with as much propriety on the alterations and amendments which are necessary, as ourselves. I do not think we are more inspired, have more wisdom, or possess more virtue, than those who will come after us.

—George Washington, from a letter to Bushrod Washington, November 10, 1787

"The Remedy Must Come Hereafter"

illusory, it is never finished, and only the process has reality. Even the progressive nature of the process may be an illusion. Instead of always pressing forward toward some imagined perfection, it may move in cycles. It is true that much of the process involves learning from the mistakes of the past and making continual accommodations and adjustments—fine-tuning the machinery to fit with the rest of the world. The problem is that the external world is always changing, and the fine-tuning gets out of phase. Instead of progressive improvement, there are sometimes setbacks, particularly when the process is viewed from the perspective of particular groups. For blacks, the period after the Reconstruction in the South certainly represented a setback. History may decide that the period between the Kennedy inaugural in 1961 and the second Nixon inaugural in 1973—when America's stance as protector and inspiration for the oppressed of the world was sharply attenuated by the Vietnam war—was a general setback. The mental picture of the kind of nation we want to be may be different for different groups, and the same groups may hold different versions of the ideal at different times. Even so, the process by which we move toward the mythical perfect condition—or fall back from it—remains a reality on which we can get a grip. Men and women *choose* the kind of government they will have, and the myth of perfection can serve as a guide in selecting the political acts which express that choice.

The Social Contract
The nation builders of colonial America were primarily concerned with the process of controlling and restraining power. This concern was not entirely the result of their immediate problem of dealing with a distant and oppressive ruler. If there were no new nation about to be born, it would still have been a problem they would have had to face as Englishmen. And it was English common law and political thought which set the stage for what would only later be viewed as a process of nation building. The basic idea

was the social contract, and it was expressed succinctly by an English vicar's son, Thomas Hobbes, when he published *Leviathan* in 1651 (Oakeshott, 1947). Without execution of the social contract, he said, men live in a natural state of war "of every man against every other man." He described it vividly:

> In such condition, there is no place for industry, because the fruit thereof is uncertain; and consequently no culture of the earth; no navigation nor use of the commodities that may be imported by sea; no commodious building; no instrument of moving, and removing, such things as require much force; no knowledge of the face of the earth; no account of time; no arts; no letters; no society, and which is worst of all, continual fear, and danger of violent death; and the life of man, solitary, poor, nasty, brutish, and short [p. 82].

To avoid this condition, each man, in Hobbes' version, gives up his natural right to govern himself to a sovereign power whom he is then obliged to obey. Hobbes saw no possibility of a limit on the power of the sovereign. That came from a more refined formulation of the theory of the social contract by John Locke a few years later. Writing as a theoretician of the English Revolution of 1688, Locke viewed the state of nature as one of confusion and inconvenience but not anarchy. There is a natural law of reason which exists prior to the social contract, and the contract is the community's means of mustering the power to enforce this natural law. Unlike Hobbes' absolute contract, Locke's is limited and specific. The only natural right given up is the right of enforcing the law of reason. The remaining natural rights are reserved to the people, and they limit the power of the sovereign (Carpenter, 1924). This is no obscure academic point. The idea of immutable natural rights found its way into the Declaration of Independence and then into the Ninth Amendment to the Constitution where it was cited as part of the argument for denying states the power to prohibit abortion in *Roe v. Wade* in 1973.

Even if the state of nature is not empty and brutish as envisioned by Hobbes, a social contract is needed in Locke's scheme of things to do three things:

1 Create an entity to define and interpret the natural law
2 Settle controversies
3 Wield the power to carry out these decisions

But while the lockean view contributed the most to English and colonial tradition, Hobbes' absolutism cast a long shadow. If it was untrue that power had to be absolute, as Hobbes believed, the threat of absolute power was ever present. In reading the Revolutionary pamphlets, Bailyn (1967, pp. 56–57) was struck by what seems almost a sadomasochistic fascination with power and the human control of human life. They wrote of power with vivid language: "encroaching," "grasping," "like a cancer it eats faster and faster every hour." And its prey was the liberty of individuals retained under the natural law. They knew that power was created legitimately by the social contract and that it was a practical necessity. But, says Bailyn, power was "the possession and interest of those who controlled government, just as liberty, always weak, always defensive . . . inhered naturally in the people and was their peculiar possession and interest [p. 59]." So it was a contest of the people against the government.

Democracy Today

The notion of a contest between government and people still survives in current definitions of democracy. But democracy is also seen as a way to manage contests that different groups of people have with each other. This function is emphasized by political theorists who favor what is called the "process" theory of democracy. E. E. Schattschneider (1969) calls democracy "a process for the resolution of conflict in which majority rule is an integral part [p. 68]." E. F. M. Durbin (1940) says democracy is "a method of making political decisions, of compromising and reconciling conflicting interests [p. 272]." Joseph A. Schumpeter (1950) defines it as "that institutional arrangement for arriving at political decisions in which individuals acquire the power to decide by means of a competitive struggle for the people's vote [p. 269]." All look to the procedures of government to test whether it is democratic or not. Popular participation, free and competitive elections, the right to form opposition parties, freedom to criticize those in power, freedom to seek public office are all indicators of democratic procedure. This procedure-oriented approach does not ask what use is made of the political power thus gained, although a wide range of outcomes is possible. For example, democratic procedures may be found in both socialist and capitalist nations. Theorists who define democracy in procedural terms argue that the people can do anything they want with their power and that so long as the process is preserved and the people retain the right to change their minds, the system remains democratic no matter what they do.

Other theorists prefer a broader definition of democracy, thinking of it as a way of life, a socioeconomic as well as political system. The reason for valuing democratic forms, they argue, is the outcomes that such forms make possible, outcomes such as liberty, equality, individual development, and civility. If you have democratic forms and do not get these outputs, they say, you don't really have democracy. Anthony Downs, Leslie Lipson, and Jack Walker are among the current advocates of this view. Although this concentration on outcomes has been associated mainly with radical values, it could also be a powerfully conservative tool. Entrenched interests could claim that outputs they didn't like were undemocratic, and keep them off the policy agenda. But something like this already happens under the dominance of the democracy-as-process school, as we shall demonstrate later in this book.

The advantage of concentrating on process is that procedures can be considered in the abstract, separately from specific and transient issues. If you are truly concerned with preserving democratic process, for example, you will be as quick to defend the procedural rights of someone you disagree with as someone on your own side. The work of the American Civil Liberties Union, which seeks to maintain democratic procedures on behalf of a wide variety of unpopular causes and individuals, is an example. But it is hard for even the best of us to be so consistent, and few ever fight for a procedural point without a specific substantive outcome in mind.

These two ways of defining democracy stem in part from the differing traditions from which the American Revolution borrowed. The English tradition, as interpreted by Locke, concentrated on the processes of liberty and was not inconsistent with the rigid separation of social classes which existed in England. "Except in America the democratic tradition that stemmed from Locke implied very little of social equality," says Sabine, "and the American version was due to America and not to Locke [p. 460]." The concern with outcomes—with equality as well as liberty—was strong in the French Revolution, which paralleled our own in time. That Revolution was "a revolt against status and its ideal was to destroy every status except one—namely, citizenship in the state. . . . It put at the center of modern politics the concept of equal national citizenship. . .[Sabine, p. 462]." American society, drawing on both traditions, became increasingly egalitarian. But a conflict persists. It is probably not possible to have both liberty and equality. One way to resolve the conflict is to define equality in a limited fashion and concentrate on equality of opportunity. But even that, as we shall see when we examine recent national policy in a later section of this book, is extremely difficult to achieve.

The ultimate definition of democracy probably needs to be formed from both procedure and substance. There must be self-governance in the sense of participation in the formal procedures of government and also in the wider sense of having the power to exercise choice. This latter criteria means having access to resources—the classic example being the black who won the right to be served at the lunch counter of his choice, but lacked the dime for the cup of coffee. In studying democracy, then, we must look not only at the formal procedures, but at their end results.

THE AMERICAN POWER STRUGGLE

Liberty's Last Outpost

The colonists' view of democracy was concerned with both procedures and substance, with both liberty and equality, but the immediate preoccupation was with procedures. The government was exercising powers against them which it ought not to have had. This way of looking at things was inherited from the English experience. Long before the idea of an American nation arose, the power struggle was seen as a contest of the English people against the English government. The rights which they wished to guard were English rights. From the vantage point of the colonists, England was a last stronghold of freedom in a world where the lights of liberty were winking out or had never shone—and things in England were not going too well. The view even became conspiratorial; dark connections were seen between encroachments on individual liberty in England and similar events in the colonies. The English people had won their Magna Carta, their elected parliament, and the Bill of Rights; and these victories could in turn be traced to ancient traditions brought by the Saxon settlers. Now, in the corruption of Parliament under King George III, the libertarian tradition was again threatened. And so the idea of America as the last outpost of liberty in a darkening world became one of the forces impelling it to nationhood. Bailyn (1967) cites two illustrative statements of the time: John Adams began to see the building of America as "the opening of a grand scene and design in providence for the illumination of the ignorant and the emancipation of the slavish part of mankind all over the earth." And Jonathan Mayhew expressed a prophetic vision. With liberty once established in America, he said, "we or our posterity may even have the great felicity and honor to . . . keep Britain herself from ruin [p. 140]."

King George III: A darkening world. *(National Archives.)*

Two forces were thus converging. The organic sources of nationhood were already there: large numbers of people occupying a specific territory with shared customs and a common language. This by itself is enough to create a sense of community, of belonging, a joining of interest. Add the other ingredients—the oppression from outside, the shared experience of limited self-government, the injustices inflicted by a common enemy—and the motivation for collective action becomes irresistible. Out of it came nationhood. Thinking about it today, we may find these forces vaguely abstract. But they grew from quite specific cases and problems.

Squeezing the Colonies

The trouble began in 1763, when, having ended the French and Indian War, the British government turned its attention to the Colonies in search of a solution for its pressing economic problems. From the viewpoint of England, America was still a business. Although the colonists had sailed for the New World with a variety of personal motivations, the money that sent them was put up by investors seeking profit. The original investors were disappointed—The Virginia Company, for example, never paid a dividend. But a system of trade regulation was maintained to ensure that whatever economic benefits developed would go to Great Britain and nowhere else. The plan was for America to produce raw material and sell it to England while providing a market for goods produced in England. The restrictions, in the form of duties and outright prohibitions, were only partly successful. The Colonies developed their own manufacturing industry anyway, and were not content to be an economic satellite. Pressure in England for short-term economic gain made clash inevitable. England's "hard, unimaginative concept ignored the real basis of successful Imperial connection: affection and loyalty," wrote British historian Eric Robson (1965). "It looked ever to the present gain; it overlooked colonial aspirations and needs; it took too much for granted [p. 3]."

The new British restrictions came at a time when the Colonies were anxious for less restriction. When England finally had the resources to apply the colonial system, it found it was too late. The Colonies had a political and economic life of their own. In the Colonies, the hope persisted for a while that this new stance of the British government was temporary and reversible. The hope was fed with the repeal of the Stamp Act in 1766, which seemed to vindicate the colonial argument that Parliament could not levy direct, internal taxes on the unrepresented colonies. But the Townshend Acts of 1767, which imposed duties on imports and enforced them, made it impossible to argue on such narrow grounds as internal versus external taxes. The colonists began to speak less of their rights as Englishmen and sought their justification instead in a higher, natural law. Benjamin Franklin noted in 1768 the difficulty of maintaining the ambiguity: Either Parliament had the power to make all law for the Colonies, or it had power to make no law. James Wilson quoted Blackstone, "The law of nature is superior in obligation to any other." And the arguments attained sudden pertinence in 1773 when Parliament sought to rescue the failing East India Company by giving it a virtual monopoly of the American tea trade. Bostonians responded with violence, destroying a shipload of tea in Boston Harbor. Parliament reacted to the Boston Tea Party by passing the Coercive Acts, providing, among other things, the quartering of British troops in private homes. The division, once healable, began to widen.

Underlying these points of confrontation was a basic economic contradiction. Forced to buy more from Britain than they sold to it, the Colonies had a balance-of-trade deficit. This deficit forced them to go into debt. To service the debt, they needed an expanding economy. But the expansion would compete with British enterprises. Fearful of competition from the Colonies, Britain sought to restrain their manufactures, their foreign trade, and their westward settlements to protect her own commerce, industry, and investments and to "reserve the West as a field for British enterprise [Nettels, 1963, p. 619]."

High Purpose and Fast Bucks
The evils suffered were so specific that the question arises whether the Revolution was motivated by an idealistic quest for freedom or by the

The Boston Tea Party: Widening the division. *(Bettmann Archives.)*

pursuit of narrow materialistic ends. Historians in the early part of this century generally accepted the materialistic theory. When Charles A. Beard published *An Economic Interpretation of the Constitution of the United States* in 1913, he drew a portrait of the Founding Fathers as men of property protecting and expanding their interests which contrasted sharply with the idealized nineteenth-century view. He applied new economic and psychological theory to historical interpretation and led many to dismiss the idealistic justification of the American Revolution as mere propagandizing—interesting and perhaps even logically coherent but not really important in considering the motivation of the revolutionaries.

More recent historians, especially Bailyn (1967, 1968), have restored the high moral purpose of the Revolution by pointing out that the change in American self-concept was great even though the change in social and political institutions was slight. John Adams (1818), writing forty years after the Revolution, could see this perspective: "The Revolution was effected before the war commenced. The Revolution was in the minds and hearts of the people; a change in their religious sentiments, of their duties and obligations. . . . This radical change in the principles, opinions, sentiments, and affections of the people was the real American Revolution [p. 248]."

The ideals and the material factors were, of course, interacting. From the viewpoint of the colonial elite, the advantages of membership in the British empire tended to outweigh the problems until around 1760. But then the French and Spanish military threats to the Colonies disappeared and there was no clear compensating benefit in return for the burden of taxation and regulation. The masses could see the disparity between English constitutional tradition and the inefficient and corrupt practices in the colonial administration, and their unrest made the elite insecure. As Lipset (1960) has observed, a test of the legitimacy of a political system is its success in meeting the needs of the ruled. For the landed, articulate, economically privileged among the colonial public, the British administration was no longer successful; it was no longer protecting their interests.

It is possible to think of the Revolution, then, as a preemptive strike by colonial conservatives to preserve traditional liberties and to restore order to social and economic relationships that were being disrupted. Their alienation from British authority was real, and their invocation of principles of virtue, liberty, and political equality was more than propaganda. Gordon S. Wood (1966) believes the ideas had "real personal and social significance for those who used them. . . . It was indeed the meaningfulness of the connection between what the Americans said and what they felt that gave the ideas their propulsive force and their overwhelming persuasiveness [p. 31]." If the ideas had not had this value to many Americans, the revolutionary elites would not have been able to mobilize a large segment of the population for war. These ideas became a unifying theme which overrode the many sources of internal conflict. Newly settled Western regions complained that older coastal areas were favored by colonial administrations. There were frontier disputes among the Colonies and class struggles within. The slavery issue was already dividing North and South. Efforts to set up some kind of central authority to deal with such common problems as defense against the French, Indian relations, and land development were unsuccessful. But by 1774, all these problems yielded in importance to the one of coping with the increasingly undesirable British control.

The Continental Congress

It was no coincidence that the call for the First Continental Congress came from Massachusetts. Its leaders were informed, active, and sometimes daring as evidenced by the dumping of tea in Boston Harbor. Their prosperity had brought them more than their proportionate share of repression from the Crown and they had put up more than their proportionate share of resistance. The meeting was called on June 17, 1774, and it convened at Philadelphia on September 5 of the same year.

Twelve Colonies—all but Georgia—sent delegates, choosing them in hastily formed conventions and meetings. These meetings were organized by anti-British elements, but the sentiment was for moving cautiously. Thomas Jefferson became ill on his way to the Virginia convention, but sent by messenger his position paper outlining an argument for the basic illegality of British efforts to legislate for the Colonies. The time was not quite right. "Tamer sentiments were preferred, and, I believe, wisely preferred; the leap I proposed being too long, as yet for the mass of our citizens,'' said Jefferson (Becker, 1922, p. 117). In Philadelphia, the talk was mainly of ways to make the British government back down, as it had done before. The meeting's main contribution may have been to open the lines of communication among the Colonies and set the precedent for future joint efforts. But it did act. An ambitious Declaration of Rights was adopted and resolutions were drafted to be forwarded to the colonial legislatures. In this tactic, the Continental Congress was displaying caution. Its acceptance and effectiveness depended on these local units of government. Its authority was still tenuous. But before it adjourned, it set a deadline. It would meet again the following May if the Colonies' grievances had not been redressed. If hostilities broke out, it would meet earlier. Meanwhile, there would be a Continental Association, with members organizing in town meetings and county conventions, to enforce a boycott of British goods. The Revolution now had momentum. The Association was everywhere, and people suddenly were forced to take a stand on the question of resistance. The shifting coalitions and factions divided cleanly now so that the activitists formed just two groups: loyalists and patriots (Nettels, pp. 650, 651). By now, the colonists were no longer limiting their quarrel to the specifics of British policy. They were challenging the form of government itself.

When the Second Continental Congress met in Philadelphia on May 10, 1775, the first shots had already been fired at Lexington, where British troops tried to seize armaments and arrest the leaders of the First Congress, Samuel Adams and John Hancock. The British were opposed by armed

Battle at Lexington, 1775: They could not pacify the countryside. *(National Archives.)*

colonists, and they found they could not pacify the countryside. Adams and Hancock escaped. At the Second Congress, all thirteen Colonies were represented; and it quickly declared war, named George Washington Commander in Chief, and began the final, year-long debate over whether this was to be the final separation. A faction led by John Dickinson of Pennsylvania held out for conciliation and engineered a last appeal to England. It was called the Olive Branch Petition. George III rejected it.

The Declaration of Independence

In January of 1776, Thomas Paine's pamphlet, *Common Sense*, became a best seller. Before the end of 1776, nearly every literate man in America had read it, either in the original pamphlet or in newspaper extracts (Mott, 1941, p. 91). It crystalized public support and, on June 7, 1776, Richard Henry Lee introduced his resolution for independence, foreign alliances, and American federation. Although a vote was postponed, a committee of five was formed to draft the Declaration of Independence: Jefferson, Franklin, Roger Sherman, R. R. Livingston, and John Adams. According to Adams's later recollection, Jefferson first proposed that Adams should write the first draft. "I will not," Adams said. "You shall do it. . . . I am obnoxious, suspected and unpopular; you are very much otherwise." Besides, Adams told Jefferson, "You can write ten times better than I can [Adams, 1856, p. 514]."

John Adams: Obnoxious and unpopular. *(National Archives.)*

Thomas Jefferson: Very much otherwise. *(National Archives.)*

Jefferson was then thirty-three, a Virginia aristocrat, graduate of the College of William and Mary, proprietor of 10,000 acres of plantation. For every 100 acres of this land, he kept one or two black slaves, whom he later freed but who meanwhile gave him the leisure to write informed tracts about human liberty. Jefferson was a product of the Enlightenment, whose world view had been profoundly shaped by the birth, with Sir Isaac Newton, of modern science. "They renounced the authority of church and Bible, but exhibited a naive faith in the authority of nature and reason," says Becker (1932, p. 30). If Newton could discover the natural mathematical laws which governed the movement of the planets, then all the laws of nature should yield to the human mind. The newtonian universe was basically mechanical and free of the uncertainties and ambiguities that overtook science in the nineteenth and twentieth centuries. The world was seen as a chain of causes and effects, whose principles could be deduced by observation and common sense.

The social contract theory of John Locke was the result of such common sense. Practical men already had examples of the lockean model in charters of the Colonies. Governments had confined themselves to the protection of the people, who, under conditions only slightly removed from the wilderness, had a good deal of personal liberty. There was no disagreement on the purpose of government. "Security to the persons and properties of the governed," said John Hancock, "is so obviously the design and end of civil government that to attempt a logical proof of it would be like burning tapers at noonday to assist the sun in enlightening the world [Randall, 1940, pp. 345–346]." Thus, the language in Jefferson's draft: "We hold these truths to be sacred and undeniable; that all men are created equal & independent; that from that equal creation they derive in rights inherent & inalienable, among which are the preservation of life, & liberty, & the pursuit of happiness; that to secure these ends, governments are instituted among men, deriving their just powers from the consent of the governed; that whenever any form of government shall become destructive of these ends, it is the right of the·people to alter or to abolish it, & to institute new government, laying its foundation on such principles & organizing its powers in such form, as to them shall seem most likely to effect their safety & happiness."

Jefferson's rough draft is on public display at the Library of Congress, filled with lines and brackets and insertions where Jefferson and others improved the style and made substantive changes to conform to decisions reached in debate. "Sacred and undeniable" became the more direct "self-evident." After bitter debate, an antislavery clause was struck out at the insistence of Georgia and South Carolina. The final language was approved two days after the unanimous approval of Richard Henry Lee's resolution on July 2. The engrossed parchment copy, signed by the delegates four weeks later, is on display, next to the Constitution, in the Exhibition Hall of the National Archives Building in Washington. To squeeze it onto the single piece of parchment and leave room for the signatures, the engrosser used dashes to indicate the beginning of paragraphs. His punctuation was faulty. But it is one of America's most treasured documents.

A Declaration for Today

If the Revolution was essentially a conservative protection of existing rights and interests; and if Thomas Jefferson, as he himself acknowledged, was merely trying "to place before mankind the common sense of the subject," why is it such a significant document? Besides its literary merit, it symbolizes what eventually proved to be a fundamental transition from an old order to a new. Though the aims of the Revolution were immediate and specific, the ultimate outcome was not. "The conservatives who began the revolution merely to preserve became innovators despite themselves; and the reluctant rebels who fought to free themselves only, in the process liberated all the world [Klein, p. 227]." The great moments in history come when ideas and action are fused. The idea of the social contract, of the right and duty of the ruled to "throw off such government and provide new guards for their security" could be authenticated only through action. The action, in turn, was legitimated by the idea. That the idea was so eloquently expressed is important, too; it made the link between thought and action

Scene in Independence Hall, 1776: A link between thought and action for all to see. *(National Archives.)*

clear for all to see. Having defined their action as a response to abuses of power and as an effort to put limits on the central authority, the former colonists moved ahead to do just that in ways that were unprecedented. While they built on a foundation of English law, they soon broke new ground, freed by what seemed to the more radical spokesmen to be a clear psychological break with the past. "We see with other eyes," said Thomas Paine (1782). "We hear with other ears; and think with other thoughts than those we formerly used."

The example and the rhetoric caught the imagination of other revolutionists. It still does. Simon Bolivar cited it in support of South American nationalism in the nineteenth century. Patriots in such radically different countries as Czechoslovakia, Indonesia, and Rhodesia have invoked Jefferson's language to support their own causes in this century. "The Declaration of Independence," says Milton M. Klein (1972), "is a more dangerous document today than it was when first written." Its warning that any form of government which fails to assure the life, liberty, and happiness of its citizens stands to be altered or abolished "is a challenge equally to dictators abroad and insensitive establishments at home [p. 229]."

The use of civil disobedience by Americans in the 1960s—to protest the war in Vietnam or to seek equality for oppressed minorities—was sometimes justified with a parallel argument. But there is an important difference between civil disobedience, which challenges a specific act of government without attacking that government's basic right to rule, and outright rebellion against the government itself. Locke's philosophy required men to rebel when the government became so oppressive that it was necessary to void the social contract. But as long as that contract was in force, he held that the laws should be obeyed. The modern justification for civil disobedience rests on other grounds, derived in part from the physical fact that technology has greatly increased the concentration of power available to the government to a point not foreseen in Locke's day. The protesters of the sixties believed, like the colonists, that the ruling establishment was failing to serve and protect their interests. They wanted it to change its ways. But they did not have the means to replace it. Insofar as eighteenth-century thought provides moral justification for disobedience—a subject to be discussed in a later chapter—its parallel with modern dissidence may be apt. But the contemporary dissidents have lacked the community of interest and the wide popular support necessary for a closer parallel to be drawn. While there was overlap, for example, between supporters of such causes as peace in Asia, women's liberation, and civil rights, there was no unified set of priorities and no ideological coherence to match that of 1776. Modern protest suffers from a greater complexity of themes.

In 1776, the theme was simple: restrict the power of the sovereign. In the 1960s and 1970s, the demands were more complicated. Moreover, they often sought substantive goals instead of mere procedural restrictions on the power of government. The Indian radicals who in 1973 occupied Wounded Knee, South Dakota, site of the 1890 massacre of a ragged band of Minneconjous and Hunkpapas, were echoing Locke when they announced that they were severing their ties with the sovereign. But the severance was only fleeting and symbolic. Technology has made the world smaller and enlarged the power of the rulers to command and control it, so that there is no way to force a new social contract, no virgin land left to which dissidents can flee. The issues of making the rulers responsive to the needs of the ruled and keeping limits on the arbitrary power of government are still fought within the framework established two centuries ago. The illustrations cited at the beginning of this chapter, all from the first week of the second Nixon administration, fit this framework. The lawmakers refurbishing their internal rules for tactical advantage in the system of checks and balances believed that the system was still capable of checking and balancing. The citizens so alienated by the war that they protested a ceremony which traditionally stands for a reaffirmation of independence and constitutional government were exercising the natural and constitutional right of peaceable assembly. And a conservative Supreme Court, yielding to the radical demand of the Women's Liberation movement, did it

Occupation of Wounded Knee, 1973: A fleeting and symbolic severence. *(Wide World Photos.)*

on conservative, power-limiting grounds. The Revolution begun in Philadelphia on July 4, 1776, was still being fought.

A DESIGN FOR POSTERITY

The Real Bicentennial

Although the year 1976 was, by popular acclaim and act of Congress, designated the bicentennial of the United States, the true two-hundredth birthday of the nation will not be until 1989. In that year, the United States will have completed 200 years under the same form of government. Most forms of government do not last nearly that long. Ours is already the oldest written constitution in the world. It was written in 1787, enacted in 1789, and it has set the ground rules for the contests for power that have been waged since then.

A Cushion against Future Shock

One reason for the Constitution's durability is that the Founding Fathers did not attempt to solve all questions for all time. They built a good deal of ambiguity into the new government, some of it consciously and deliberately, and some of it because they could not agree among themselves on all the specifics. Yet it was precise enough to serve as a starting point for all the debates that were to follow over the national government's proper role and the distribution of powers among its different elements. Debates over intensely vital current issues still rest on chains of logic that lead back to Independence Hall in 1787. The value of such a foundation increases with time. In a world of rapid change, we cherish the few things that remain constant. The day when a person could define himself in terms of his geographic location, his social status, and his occupation, and expect that identity to last a lifetime, is gone. Cues for national identity are shifting, too. One of the strategies for coping with the rapid pace of change, as Alvin Toffler (1970) has said, is to isolate and treasure the few things that can be held constant. One constant is the past. In emotionally troubling times, when uncertainty prevails, we can look to the past and anchor ourselves in its reliable, nonthreatening foundations. Thus the reverence with which the Constitution is regarded today provides a psychological cushion against the repeated shocks of change.

Life in the United States in the twentieth century seems to have been . . . "just one damned thing after another." The conditions under which the American system has been operating ever since 1914 have been those of emergency rather than routine, strife rather than stability, tension rather than serenity. Threat of war, total war, inflation, deflation, boom, panic, depression, recession, industrial conflict, and cold war with hot flashes have followed one another in bewildering succession. Four decades of crises have left many Americans convinced that there is nothing quite so normal as abnormality.

—Clinton Rossiter (1951, p. 60)

Tension, Emergency, Strife: Our Way of Life

Living by Eighteenth-Century Rules
Operating in today's world by rules that are nearly 200 years old can present some practical problems. When substantive issues lead to debate over constitutional procedures, the problem usually fits one of four basic categories of conflict arising from the structure of the constitutional system:

1   The sharing of powers and responsibilities between the state and federal government is often inefficient and sometimes encourages obstructionism. On the other hand, it sometimes blocks hastily conceived and unnecessary action.

2   Checks and balances within each level of government can produce stalemates at times when action is needed. But this structural bias against action can also be healthy in some situations.

3   Majority rule is often thwarted by structural arrangements. However, these same arrangements sometimes protect minority rights.

4   There are points of potential confrontation among the separate branches where no mechanism for the resolution of conflict exists. In most

situations, ways are found to avoid these showdowns, but in times of crisis they may be unavoidable. Accidents of circumstance then determine who prevails, and usually it is the executive branch, because it is geared for decisive action. There is thus a bias in favor of concentrating power in the executive in times of crisis.

How serious are these problems? A specific evaluation must await our examination of the Constitution itself and how it came to have its special place in our history. But Leland D. Baldwin (1972) has taken a backward look to note how successful the Constitution has been in weathering major social changes and incorporating them as political change. He cites four changes that can be classed as basic:

1   The national government has extended franchise rights and become more democratic.

2   Slavery has been abolished.

3   Federal sovereignty has become more dominant, moving into areas where the states were sovereign before.

4   Protections for citizens against abuses of state power have been imposed through federal power.

Each of these basic changes has been incorporated into the constitutional framework designed in 1787, although not always easily nor always without bloodshed. But the Constitution survived.

GETTING STARTED: THE ARTICLES OF CONFEDERATION

"Between These Colonies"

The Constitution, as Clinton Rossiter (1951) has said, is both "a grant of power" and "a catalog of limitations [p. 66]." Defining both the power and the limitations came very early in the order of business as the Revolution was secured.

The Second Continental Congress waited only a day after appointing the committee to write the Declaration of Independence before turning to concerns about what would follow the Revolution. A second committee "to prepare and digest the form of a confederation to be entered into between these colonies" was appointed. It was a somewhat audacious act, but no more so than the existence of the Congress itself, an ad hoc body which would float from place to place and stay in session as the only national governing body for six years. The Declaration of Independence, while clarifying and legitimating the separation from England, did not clarify the question of what was to be left after the separation. Was it thirteen independent and sovereign states? Or was it one sovereign nation composed of thirteen states? An immediate working solution for the colonists did not come easily.

They began, as did the writers of the Declaration, with British and colonial experience and the logic of the eighteenth-century Enlightenment thinkers to guide them. The British background provided a limited example of the use of separation of powers as a restraint on the sovereign. The British constitution—not a written document, but an organic body of law, custom, and judicial precedent—included three estates working together. There was the royalty, the nobility, and the commons, capable respectively of tyranny, oligarchy, and mob rule unless each element entered into government simultaneously to balance the others. The balance was not necessarily symmetrical, nor were the mechanics so straightforward as to provide for a separate branch for each estate. All shared in the legislative function, according to the theory, but the executive function was mainly for the monarch. However, the commons shared in the executive's enforcement function through the provision of trial by jury. Finally, the common people had the additional protection of the independent judiciary. Judges with lifetime tenure, independent of the whims of the executive, could see that the laws were enforced with impartiality (Baily, 1967).

Each Colony in America, whether chartered as a trading company, as a subsidiary of the monarchy, or as a private concern, had some system of representation. These assemblies gained increasing control over their sponsors. Members were elected, although voting was limited to property owners or taxpayers. The assemblies became a series of experimental laboratories in which arose a skillful political elite. They formed the pool from which the leaders of the Revolution were drawn. Their assemblies served as models, to be revised and refined, for the principles of representative government. They reflected in microcosm the struggle going on in Britain between the King and Parliament by initiating their own struggles between the King's agents and the elected assemblies.

The first tasks of writing the King out of the basic law and writing the people in were accomplished quickly. New Hampshire, South Carolina, Virginia, and New Jersey adopted new constitutions before Independence Day. Rhode Island and Connecticut kept their colonial charters but deleted all references to the King. In most cases, provincial congresses, which also served as legislative bodies, wrote new constitutions. Massachusetts, in 1779–1780, was the first state to call and hold a special convention to write a constitution and submit it to a popular referendum. All went to unprecedented lengths to extend the idea of popular sovereignty. Distrust of the executive was manifested in provisions for limited powers and short terms. The elected assemblies were based on a right to vote that was still somewhat limited, but what would become a two-century trend to expand the franchise was already set in motion. And these assemblies were given power to check the executive.

Getting Together in "Perpetual Union"

At the national level, some mechanism was needed beyond the aging improvisation of the Second Continental Congress. That body was coordinating the war effort with the tacit consent of the newly independent states, but without any basis in law, tradition, or constitution. And there were problems beyond the war: commerce among the states, taxation to support the troops, relations with other nations. (France recognized the new nation in 1778; The Netherlands did so in 1780. Both were hostile to England at the time.) Nevertheless, it took nearly five years to establish the beginning of a national government. The establishing charter was called The Articles of Confederation and Perpetual Union. Congress approved it on November 15, 1777, and eleven states had joined by 1778. Delaware and Maryland waited two more years. When the Articles finally took effect on March 1, 1781, the war was coming to an end.

Although later viewed as an overreaction to the colonists' fear of government in any form, the new system was an improvement on the Continental Congress. It placed all national powers in a unicameral (one-house) legislature which met each year and was composed of delegates appointed by state legislatures. Each state had one vote. There were no separate executive or judicial branches.

Ultimate sovereignty was left with the states. Congress had only "expressly delegated" powers and even these could, in most cases, be exercised only by vote of nine of the thirteen states. There was no provision for any direct national control of the people in the states.

This arrangement had the seeds of the two-party system. The weak general government was supported by small farmers and Southern planters who remembered how the British government had used its authority to support British merchants and landlords at their expense. They did not want new American institutions which might be capable of taking their place.

Opposition to the weak-government concept came mainly from merchants, investors, and men whose business interests crossed state lines. They saw that for maximum economic development they needed central regulation of trade, a national currency system, and a uniform navigation code. They also wanted a national army and navy to suppress whatever domestic disorder might endanger property rights. And they foresaw the need for a national government to supervise the orderly development of the Western lands.

Supporters of the Articles eventually formed the anti-Federalist party under the leadership of Jefferson. Their opponents organized the Federalist party as followers of Washington, Hamilton, and, later, John Adams. The debate between advocates of centralization and of dispersion of power continues to this day.

Probably the main achievement of the government under the Articles of Confederation was simple survival. But besides keeping the nation together until a more viable form of government could be established, it managed to put the new nation on a sound economic footing. The war debt was substantially reduced and the postwar depression largely overcome. The executive departments of the Post Office, Treasury, War, and Foreign Affairs were organized. And the Northwest Ordinances of 1784, 1785, and 1787 were passed. Besides setting boundaries for new development, these acts marked another fundamental break with the British way of doing things. They ensured that the new states in the land north of the Ohio River would be admitted on a basis of full equality with the original states. The new nation, having been itself the victim of a colonial power, was not going to create the same situation on its own continent.

Some Flaws in the Plan

However, there were other things that needed doing and could not be done under the Articles. Most of them involved money. The new government was unable to levy taxes and could not pay its bills. It could not make the states comply with its resolutions in areas which fell beyond the narrow boundaries of the "expressly delegated" powers. Finally, the internal trade problem got out of hand. States began erecting trade barriers against one another, and their dealings were complicated by an enormous currency problem with different jurisdictions issuing different forms of paper money which fluctuated wildly in value. The economic problems led to civil disorder in Massachusetts, where farmers were being evicted for failure to pay debts. Their only hope of relief seemed to lie in inflation-prone paper money, which Massachusetts did not have, easier credit, and, most immediately, a moratorium on foreclosures. In August 1786, a band of farmers led by a war veteran, Daniel Shays, tried to seize the government arsenal at Springfield. Merchants and landlords financed a militia so that the state could meet the emergency. The farmers succeeded in closing some of the courts temporarily, but the rebellion was crushed. Proponents of a stronger central government cited the incident as evidence that the nation risked anarchy if the system was not revised. The national government had no power to raise troops beyond forces donated by the states, and the states were inclined to keep their forces at home.

Meanwhile, concern over tariff barriers among the states led to the call, by Virginia, for a new convention to discuss that issue. It was held at Annapolis, Maryland. Nine states intended to send delegates, but those of only five arrived on time. Not much of a national scope could be accomplished with so sparse an attendance, and so the convention called another meeting, to be held in Philadelphia in 1787. Congress approved. The Annapolis delegates' untimely sacrifice of their own meeting was probably calculated. The decision not to wait for more delegates, who were known to be on the way, "was taken with an impatience which seems unusual for the eighteenth century [Feer, 1969, p. 392]." But they knew

How Shays' Rebellion Sparked Constitutional Reform

Jefferson, from his snug retreat in the Paris legation, remarked, "A little rebellion now and then is a good thing . . . the tree of liberty must be refreshed from time to time with the blood of patriots and tyrants." But most American leaders were alarmed. "But for God's sake tell me what is the cause of all these commotions?" Washington implored. "I am mortified beyond expression that in the moment of our acknowledged independence we should by our conduct verify the predictions of our transatlantic foe, and render ourselves ridiculous and contemptible in the eyes of all Europe." When Massachusetts appealed to the Confederation for help, Congress was unable to do a thing. That was the final argument to sway many Americans in favor of a stronger federal government.

—Samuel Eliot Morison, Henry Steele Commager, and William E. Leuchtenburg
(1969, p. 242)

they had focused public attention on the problem and believed that a later meeting with broader powers might go the whole distance to constitutional revision.

THE CONSTITUTIONAL CONVENTION

Philadelphia in 1787 was the most exciting and attractive city in the Republic. The census of 1790 would find 28,522 people living along the clean streets and symmetrical squares within its boundaries along the western bank of the Delaware River. It was the center of a metropolitan area of more than 170,000 with a well-designed system of great highways that brought people in for commerce, learning, and the arts. It was also hot in the summer. The convention met from May 25 to September 17, and the muggy weather tended to make tempers short. George Mason said he "would not, upon pecuniary motives, serve in this convention for a thousand pounds a day [Rossiter, 1966, p. 42]."

The Delegates

Thomas Jefferson was ambassador to Paris and did not attend. Neither did the revolutionary firebrands, Thomas Paine and Patrick Henry. Those who did attend, however, represented the best, the brightest, and the most influential: "An assembly of demigods," said Jefferson after he saw the list. They came from the population centers. None were dirt farmers, though some had heavy investments in land and slaves and some lived on plantations. They were also lawyers, merchants, state government officials, and physicians. More than half were college graduates, with degrees from such already venerable institutions as Harvard, Yale, William and Mary, Columbia, and Princeton. Their main academic fields were law and political philosophy. Forty-two of the fifty-five had served in the Continental Congress.

They tended to be well-traveled. The names of James Madison, Alexander Hamilton, Elbridge Gerry, and Roger Sherman were nationally known. George Washington and Benjamin Franklin had international reputations.

It was a youthful group. The average age was forty. Hamilton was thirty-three, Madison thirty-seven, William Paterson thirty-four, and Charles Pinckney twenty-four. Franklin, at eighty-two, was the oldest. There was a visible gap between two generations:the older men had formed their political outlook in the pre-Revolutionary period. They tended to view matters from the standpoint of the states. The younger members had gained their knowledge and political experience in the Revolutionary period, and their orientation was more centrist.

While the meeting was not exactly rigged in favor of a strong government, the decision of potential delegates to attend or stay home provided a self-selection process biased in favor of a constitution with increased national powers. By the same token, this process gave the struggle toward consensus a head start. Virginians Patrick Henry and Richard Henry Lee, who wanted to put the interests of their own state above all else, were elected as delegates but refused to attend. Henry said he "smelt a rat," and, from his perspective he was right; by agreeing to send delegates at all, a state assigned legitimacy to the convention and its aims. Rhode Island, anxious to protect its port revenues from any national government, sent no delegates at all. Antifederalist delegates from New York left before the convention was over. "Thus a group already predisposed in a national direction could proceed unhampered by the friction of basic opposition in its midst [Elkins and McKittrick, 1961, p. 181]." Those remaining shared a continental view that gave them more in common with each other than a group more fully representative of state attitudes and opinion might.

An Antidemocratic Plot?

This centrist, elitist cast of the group provided support for Charles Beard's (1913) thesis that the Founding Fathers had their own narrow monetary interests primarily at heart. In keeping with turn-of-the-century muckraker tradition, he based his argument on old Treasury records, never before opened, which showed that a number of federalists owned Continental securities which stood to rise in value with a stronger central government. But later scholars took a closer look and found the picture wasn't all that clear. Robert E. Brown (1956) found there was no correlation between the delegates' behavior in the convention and their property holdings.

The delegates did, of course, have a stake in the economic well-being of the country. But so did everyone else. Beard went so far as to argue that their concern for the protection of property rights prompted them to take a counterrevolutionary move to transfer power from the people to the nonrepresentative branches of government. A more recent scholar, David G. Smith (1965), argues that a desire to minimize conflicts among dissenting groups explains their actions more than any narrow economic interest. By providing for the protection of contractual obligations and the regulation of interstate commerce, they hoped to remove or reduce some of the sources of dissension among the states. They wanted to remove such subjects from "the most quarrelsome and heated centers of political dispute [p. 27]." Having lived under both the colonial governments and the Articles of Confederation, the delegates knew that the government might not survive the disruptions of factionalism and parochial outlooks. Their reason for meeting was to make the competing interests operate together as one country. And their checks on power—while explicitly supported by some delegates as restraints on the majority—were also attempts to restrain legislative and executive authority. Beard himself acknowledged that the framers worked from a variety of motivations. But the question of motivation does not seem so important today as the question of whose interests were being guarded or promoted. And the issues were not those of propertied versus propertyless classes. That property should be protected was taken for granted. The problem was to remove the sources of discord and build a system with room and tranquility enough for economic development to proceed. The interest in economic development was not, of course, equally shared. As major property holders and leaders of commerce, the delegates had a greater interest in economic growth and stability than most citizens. But the debate did not reflect the views of elite versus nonelite. The arguments were among competing elites, as for example, when landed interests lined up against those whose money was in commerce and manufacturing.

Another factor which seemed to lend weight to the theory of an antidemocratic plot was the decision of the convention to meet in secrecy. The purpose of the closed meeting was to allow for free exchange of opinion, to maximize the incentive for compromise, and to keep delegates from getting prematurely locked into positions they might later wish to change. Even so, they were somewhat inhibited at the beginning. James Madison, who took the best set of notes, quoted John Rutledge as complaining about the shyness of his fellow delegates. "He said it looked as if they supposed themselves precluded by having frankly disclosed their opinions from afterwards changing them, which he did not take to be at all the case [Madison, 1840, p. 241]." It was only a temporary problem. Behind closed doors, knowing that their product would be judged in its finished state, they argued freely.

The Virginia Plan

Despite the many common objectives, there were some built-in areas of conflict. The elites of different states had competing interests to protect.

And although the emergence of a strong central government was practically a forgone conclusion, it had to be brought forth in a way that would maximize its chances for adoption. John P. Roche (1961) has put the problem bluntly:"The Constitutionalists had to induce the states, by democratic techniques of coercion, to emasculate themselves." The main problem was overcoming inertia, keeping up the pressure for change, maintaining the initiative so that opponents were always off balance and defensive. The Virginians moved quickly to do this. While waiting for a quorum to gather, Madison drafted an agenda. Somebody had to open the meeting, and it might as well be Governor Randolph, and he might as well use the opportunity to put some proposals on the table for discussion. The boldness was masked by a self-effacing presentation.

The Virginia Plan called for a national executive, a system of national courts, and a legislature over both of them. The latter was to be of two houses, one elected by popular vote, the other chosen by the first house from nominees picked by the state legislatures. Voting strength in each house would be proportional—either to each state's nonslave population or to the amount of money it contributed to the national government. The powers of the national legislature would be broad. It could enact laws "in all cases to which the separate states are incompetent." It could negate state laws that were in conflict with the Constitution. It could invoke "the force of the Union" against disobedient states, choose the executive, and appoint the judges.

Although Virginia was a large, wealthy state, and this plan clearly benefitted the states in that category, some of these ideas were approved with no trouble at all. The proposal for a bicameral (two-house) legislature was quickly approved. Popular election of at least one branch was approved by a vote of six states to two, with two delegations divided. It was also agreed, by a narrower vote, that the two houses would be apportioned by population.

The New Jersey Plan

Then the convention took a different turn as the small states fought back. New Jersey asked and got an adjournment so it could prepare its own plan. The antifederalists were asserting themselves now, but they were already locked into a situation that was going to produce a stronger central government. As Roche (pp. 803–804) has noted, they could have torpedoed the whole thing by simply walking out. Instead, "they returned day after day to argue and to compromise." They could have taken their case to the people; there was no way to enforce the secrecy rule. But the rule was observed.

William Patterson introduced the New Jersey Plan on June 15, 1787. It called for keeping the structure of the Articles of Confederation but strengthening it with a national executive. The money problem would be solved by giving Congress the power to levy duties on imports and a stamp tax on documents. A supreme court would be appointed by the executive and it could hear appeals on federal questions.

The New Jersey Plan was not strictly a weak-government plan. One clause, whose importance was not immediately appreciated, called for all treaties and acts of Congress to become the supreme law within each state, enforceable in state courts. This would later become the key to federal dominance (Kelly and Harbison, 1958, p. 127).

If New Jersey had been as aggressive as Virginia and gotten the floor first, its view might have prevailed. Its plan was more in keeping with the stated purpose of the convention, which was to repair the defects of the Articles. But it gained the support of only two other states, New York and Delaware. Its advocates made an important point, nevertheless. The big states would have to compromise or risk ending with a plan that could not gain national acceptance. The votes already taken toward approval of the Virginia Plan would have to be reconsidered.

The Great Compromise

Despite disagreements, there were four broad areas of concensus:

1   The powers of the national government were going to be increased.

2   The machinery of government would have to be expanded to manage these powers.

3   The national government should operate directly on the people through its laws and its own court system rather than filter through the state governments.

4   The new Constitution should be the supreme law of the land.

Not even the overall structure was in serious dispute. The example of the rough separation of powers in the English constitution and their reading of the French jurist, Baron de Montesquieu, had convinced the delegates of the need for dividing power into three separate branches. And even most of the hard-core antifederalists were for giving the national government power to tax imports and regulate foreign and interstate commerce. By separating the functions of making law, enforcing the law, and interpreting the law, they hoped to keep any person or group from monopolizing government power. The separation could not be complete, of course. Each branch would participate in the functions of the other, thus assuring communication among them and providing checks and balances. For example, the President was given a role in law making with the veto power; the legislature could check the executive through the power to impeach; judges could review the actions of the executive and the Congress; and the President could appoint judges with approval of the Senate. While designed chiefly to prevent tyranny, such a system also provides multiple routes of access to the government. A group which finds its wishes blocked in one branch still has hope of getting action in another.

None of these devices proved to be particularly controversial. Nor was there much debate over the need to give the national government substantial economic power, including authority to tax imports and regulate foreign and interstate commerce. The major sticking point came instead over the question of representation in the legislature. The small states wanted equal representation. Large states wanted representation in proportion to size. Neither group trusted the other, and the convention was caught in an excruciating deadlock. During discussion of the Virginia Plan, a despairing New Jersey delegate, David Brearley, said they'd never work it out unless they erased all the existing state lines and started over with a new map dividing the nation into states of equal size.[1] Madison told the small-state delegates that they were worrying about the wrong things; the large states could not combine against them because their own interests were too diverse—Massachusetts was dominated by fishing interests, Pennsylvania by flour, Virginia by tobacco. Benjamin Franklin suggested that a daily prayer might help. Without "imploring the assistance of Heaven and its blessings," he warned, they would continue to be "divided by our little, partial interests [Boorstin, 1966, p. 95]." The suggestion was rejected; the members were unlikely to be able to agree on the mode of prayer. But Franklin, no longer as sharp of mind as in his youth, yet still capable of generating respect, changed the mood. An accommodation could be made between the large and small states, he said. "When a broad table is to be made, and the edges of the plank do not fit, the artist takes a little from both and makes a good joint."

Benjamin Franklin: Beware of "little, partial interests." *(National Archives.)*

The compromise committee was composed of one man from each state. The members were either moderates or hard-line states' righters. Their compromise was reported on July 5 and, as the weather cooled a week later, it was approved with one minor change. The committee recommended:

1 Representation in the lower house would be based on population with one member allowed for every 40,000 population.

2 Bills to raise or spend money would have to originate in the lower house.

3 Each state would get an equal vote in the upper house.

The last provision was changed after discussion. At the suggestion of Elbridge Gerry of Massachusetts, it was decided to let Senate votes be cast

[1]The idea still lives. In 1973, Prof. G. Etzel Pearcy of California State University, Los Angeles, proposed revising the boundaries of the 50 states to create 38 states which would be of similar size, with boundary lines avoiding major population centers (*Washington Post*, Sept. 9, 1973, pp. K18–19).

by individual members, not by states, although each state would be equally represented.

The outcome is a case study in the futility of trying to control the future through rules made in the present. Few of the questions that nearly broke up the convention turned out to have any lasting impact. As Madison had foreseen, the large versus small-state issue never has become important in American politics. Where geography has been a factor in our great controversies, the boundaries have been drawn along regional, not state, lines, as in the Civil War. The Senate did not become the guardian of states' rights, and small states have often been more forceful in advocating strong national government than the large ones. Smaller states have had the greater need for the kinds of government assistance that can only come from a liberal construction of power.

The other major disputed provision, for originating money bills in the House, remains as something more than a historical curiosity. The Senate has full freedom to accept, reject, or amend all legislation, but the House initiative gives it a tactical advantage in this field.

Gouverneur Morris, a Pennsylvanian whose oily savoir-faire aroused distrust in some delegates, did make one correct and dire prophecy. By giving states equal standing in the upper body, they were conceding some measure of sovereignty to the states. The encouragement of state sovereignty would create a source of future dissension. "This country must be united. If persuasion does not unite it, the sword will," he said. The composition of the Senate did not prove to be a factor in the ultimate armed conflict that was still three-quarters of a centry away; but, as Kelly and Harbison (1955) have noted, the fears of Madison, Morris, and others, that the retention of some measure of state sovereignty would lead to trouble, were presciently on target. The Civil War was a direct result of state autonomy.

Other Compromises

Other compromises came more easily. Southerners wanted slaves counted in the population for the purpose of apportioning the House. Northerners said that if, as the South contended, slaves were mere property, then slaves could not be counted unless other forms of property were also counted. There was available an arbitrary but visible cue which led to compromise: Congress had already faced the problem of what to do about the slaves while assessing the taxes it could not collect. It counted slaves at 60 percent or three-fifths of their actual numbers. Now the convention voted to keep that ratio, both for apportionment and for taxation purposes.

Another issue that divided North and South was slavery. This, too, was compromised; slave trade would continue until 1808, giving the South twenty years to build up its supply of slaves. Connecticut cast a key vote for this provision in exchange for support for land claims it held against Pennsylvania.

When the Convention turned to the executive branch, the issue of whether the central government should be strong or weak evoked the now-familiar conflicts. Alexander Hamilton bemused the delegates with his plea for "a strong, well-mounted government" headed by a monarch elected for life. His extreme fear of the passions of the mob was not shared by the other delegates. At the other extreme were proposals to divide the office among three men and to elect them for short terms with no right to succeed themselves. The strong-executive men, including Madison and Morris, wanted the President chosen by direct popular election to enhance his independence from the other branches and levels of government. The weak-executive group, including Roger Sherman and John Dickinson, wanted him chosen by Congress. The compromise was the electoral college, which left it to the states to decide how to choose electors. Each state was given a number of electors equal to its total representation in the two houses of Congress. States could, if they wished, choose electors by popular vote. And, in fact, nearly all the states did take that course within the very first years of the Republic. So the advocates of a nationally based executive eventually prevailed. The term was set at four years with no limit on succession.

There was little disagreement over the judicial branch. A Supreme Court whose members would have lifetime tenure was agreed to early in the convention. But the delegates did not decide whether questions of federal law should be decided by state courts or by a separate system of lower federal courts. Congress was given the power to create lower federal courts if it wanted to, and that gap was quickly filled by the Judiciary Act of 1789. (See Chapter 11.)

The question of providing a federal veto over state laws was raised in the convention as part of the original Virginia Plan. Randolph's original proposal to let Congress negate state laws which violated the Constitution was, when it came up the second time, after the great compromise, rejected. Instead, what seemed to be a fairly weak step was taken by adopting language similar to that in the New Jersey Plan: The Constitution, treaties, and acts of Congress would be supreme over state law, and state judges would be "bound thereby, anything in the Constitution or laws of any state to the contrary notwithstanding." Since state judges would decide what was constitutional and what was not, it seemed a clear victory for the champions of states' rights. But, in the words of Robert H. Birkby (1966), they "provided the potential for the development of a centralizing force far greater than the one they feared [p. 135]." The key would be the Judiciary Act of 1789, providing for appeals from state courts to be taken to the federal judiciary. Its ultimate effect, developed gradually over the years, would be to give a branch of the national government, the Supreme Court, the final veto over state and national legislation. The framers evidently never considered the possibility. "Like most of the rest of the Constitution," says Birkby, "the Supremacy Clause emerged as a response to immediate problems with little thought given to future developments."

Alexander Hamilton: "A strong, well-mounted government." *(National Archives.)*

Our greatest possession is not the vast domain; it's not our beautiful mountains, or our fertile prairies, or our magnificent coastline. It's not the might of our Army or Navy. These things are of great importance. But in my judgment the greatest and most precious possession of the American people is the Constitution.

—Sen. Sam Ervin, from a speech at Davidson College, 1973

The Ratification Problem

The delegates were practical men, and the practical problem at hand was to get the new document adopted. Mindful that it had taken nearly five years to accomplish the adoption of so benign a document as the Articles of Confederation, they decided, without any particular authority, to specify in the ratification clause that the instrument would take effect upon approval by conventions in nine of the thirteen states. This was a superb political stroke—the test being that they got away with it—and it has some justification in legal theory. A constitutional convention is, by definition, the highest ranking law-making body in the land, capable of creating and altering the basic institutions with a stroke of a pen. Answerable to no other organized institution, it can go as far as its ability to command obedience and the necessary popular support or acquesience will take it. (That is one reason there has not been a constitutional convention since 1787, although the Constitution itself provides an easy means of calling one, through requests from two-thirds of the state legislatures. Power holders of the past two centuries have found no problem so great that they would risk the legal framework of their own offices to solve it.) The decision to call for ratification by special conventions instead of the legislatures was also politically astute. Members of the legislatures had too much interest in the status quo. Conventions would let the people speak more directly, generate

Ratification of the Constitution of 1787

STATE	DATE	VOTE
Delaware	Dec. 7, 1787	Unanimous
Pennsylvania	Dec. 12, 1787	46–23
New Jersey	Dec. 19, 1787	Unanimous
Georgia	Jan. 2, 1788	Unanimous
Connecticut	Jan. 9, 1788	128–40
Massachusetts	Feb. 6, 1788	187–168
Maryland	Apr. 28, 1788	63–11
South Carolina	May 23, 1788	149–73
New Hampshire	June 21, 1788	57–46
Virginia	June 25, 1788	89–79
New York	July 26, 1788	30–27
North Carolina	Nov. 21, 1789	184–77
Rhode Island	May 29, 1790	34–32

more popular support, and confer greater legitimacy on the new government.

Ratification went quickly. Eight states ratified in eight months, and the vote was close only in Massachusetts. But more than just one more vote was needed to put it into effect. Because of their size and geographic position, New York and Virginia had to join the new government for it to exist at all. The federalists won a heated debate in Virginia and orchestrated their campaign carefully so that by the time the New York convention voted, ten states were already in the union. This seemed to reduce the question from the New York point of view to one of staying in or staying out, although a decision to stay out would have brought down the whole plan. Despite heavy antifederalist sentiment, New York stayed in. The new government opened for business with eleven states on April 30, 1789. North Carolina entered before the year was over, and Rhode Island followed in 1790.

One of the first acts of the First Congress was to keep a federalist promise made to concerned state convention delegates anxious to limit the authority of the central government in more specific ways than were stated explicity in the Constitution. Madison, on June 8, 1789, introduced a series of amendments in the House of Representatives, establishing the Bill of Rights. Although added at the end instead of being inserted in the text, as Madison intended, they are, in effect, part of the original Constitution.

James Madison: Keeping the promise. *(National Archives.)*

Why It Still Works

The framers proved to be right about some things, wrong about others. Their greatest gift to the nation may not have been the document at all, but rather the spirit of pragmatic compromise which set the precedent and tone for most of the future conflicts. In seeking practical solutions to relatively short-term conflicts, they were forced to be flexible. Their structure, which they thought of as regulating power in mechanical terms (this was the age of Newton), was loose enough so that it could bend and conform to changing social institutions and political tempers. They were distrustful of the passions of the ruled and the rapacity of rulers, and would have avoided so much flexibility if they could have. But the actors in the system turned out to be not so evil after all. The Founders were reasonable and well-motivated persons, and so, for the most part, have been the voters and officials who followed them. Benjamin Franklin, after the convention, was asked what form of government it had designed. His answer: "A republic, if you can keep it." It has been kept.

SUGGESTED READINGS

Bailyn, Bernard. *The Origins of American Politics.* New York: Knopf, 1968. A sensitive and insightful study of the roots and development of colonial political thought.

Boorstin, Daniel J. *The Americans: The Colonial Experience.* New York: Random House, 1958. A vivid and readable description of the colonial experience and its impact on the unique development of American political ideals.

Buel, Richard. *Securing the Revolution: Ideology in American Politics, 1789–1815.* Ithaca, New York: Cornell University Press, 1972. Examines how the political ideas of the revolutionary elite changed with the transformation from colonies to a nation.

Lipset, Seymour Martin. *The First New Nation.* New York: Basic Books, 1963. A historical and sociological study of the United States as an example of nation building. A significant contribution to the study of building political institutions.

Maier, Pauline. *From Resistance to Revolution: Colonial Radicals and the Development of American Opposition to Britain, 1765–1776.* New York: Knopf, 1972. A new portrayal of the causes of the revolution; looks at the radicalization of political opposition.

Rossiter, Clinton L. *Seedtime of the Republic.* New York: Harcourt, Brace, 1953. An invaluable analysis of the social and political history of the colonial and revolutionary periods. Provides an exciting picture of the men who founded the republic.

Smith, David G. *The Convention and the Constitution: The Political Ideas of the Founding Fathers.* New York: St. Martin's, 1965. A concise commentary on the political theories upon which the Constitution was constructed.

Chapter 2

Individual Liberties and Civil Rights

PROTECTING THE CITIZEN FROM THE GOVERNMENT

"To Be Secure in Their Persons"

Patrick Balistrieri walked briskly, because he was late for his 10 A.M. history class. It was May 3, 1971, and he had been delayed by a traffic jam caused by the May Day antiwar demonstrations. As he turned the corner, he saw that the street was full of policemen. He stepped around one group, which ignored him. Then three other uniformed men, none wearing badges, grabbed him, knocked the books from his hand, and slammed him against a bus. "I was flabbergasted," he said much later, "I didn't have time to get my thoughts together."

Balistrieri was held on the police bus and later taken with other arrestees to the Washington Coliseum. He was charged with disorderly conduct. It was early the next morning before he was able to post collateral—a form of bail—and go home. Like nearly all the 13,000 people arrested in three days of demonstrations, he was never prosecuted. He had commited no crime, and his arrest was illegal. The police sweeps of May 3 to 5 were, according to the American Civil Liberties Union (1972), the "largest mass arrest in our country's history." To cope with war protesters who had vowed to disrupt traffic, the police simply arrested everybody in sight at key intersections: bystanders, tourists, government workers,

Arrested May Day Demonstrators: So that traffic would move. *(Michael Abramson, Black Star.)*

whoever happened to be there. When the jails were filled, the arrestees were kept in a sports arena and outdoors in a fenced-in field, their release barred by administrative delays so that they would stay off the streets and traffic would move.

The right of the people to be secure in their persons . . . against unreasonable searches and seizures shall not be violated and no warrants shall issue but upon probable cause.

—Constitution of the United States, Amendment Four

"Freedom . . . of the Press"

When readers of the *New York Times* opened their papers on the morning of June 16, 1971, they looked in vain for the fourth installment of Neil Sheehan's analysis of a secret Department of Defense study of the Vietnam war. A federal judge had enjoined its publication. On June 30, after the material had been examined by government authorities, a divided Supreme Court ruled that publication could continue.

In the interim, the *Times* articles had been withheld from the public for fifteen days.

Congress shall make no law . . . abridging the freedom of speech or of the press.

—Constitution of the United States, Amendment One

Precedents dating from the seventeenth century hold that freedom of the press means, as a *minimum*, that there must be no restraint prior to publication.

"The Privilege of the Writ of Habeas Corpus"

The town of Cockeysville, Maryland, was reputed, in 1861, to be full of Southern sympathizers. This possibility presented a military problem to the North because of the little town's proximity to Baltimore and the railroad link between New York, Philadelphia, and Washington. Union soldiers went to the home of a rebel sympathizer, John Merryman, entered it forcibly, and arrested him.

His lawyer applied to Chief Justice Roger B. Taney for a writ of habeas corpus, which is an ancient device to bring a prisoner physically before a judge to determine if he is being lawfully held. Chief Justice Taney issued the writ. The military ignored it. Taney wrote to President Lincoln. Lincoln did not answer. Merryman was held until, after a year, the Army decided Baltimore was no longer in danger.

The privilege of the writ of habeas corpus shall not be suspended, unless when in cases of rebellion or invasion the public safety may require it.

—Constitution of the United States, Article One, Section Nine

While Congress may suspend the right of habeas corpus, it had not done so at the time of Merryman's imprisonment.

"Due Process of Law"

"Many thanks for your patronage," said the sign in the store window in the "Little Tokyo" section of Los Angeles. "Hope to serve you in the near future. God be with you till we meet again."

The sign had a signature: "Mr. and Mrs. K. Iseri [Lingeman, 1970, p. 338]." Its sad message was from two among the 110,000 persons of Japanese descent, most of them American citizens, who were moved from their homes, their jobs, and their businesses under the terms of Executive Order No. 9066. Signed by President Franklin D. Roosevelt on February 19, 1942, this order authorized military commanders to designate areas where the rights of persons to enter, leave, or remain might be restricted. The FBI had already rounded up those Japanese-Americans whom it had reason to believe might be security risks. For the rest, the only thing that distinguished them from other Americans was their race. "A Jap," explained one military commander, "is a Jap." The displaced Americans were detained in concentration camps for up to four years. In 1944, the concentration camp procedure was approved, albeit lamely and apologetically, by a divided Supreme Court (*Korematsu v. United States*, 323 U.S. 214). The precedent still stands.

No person shall be deprived of life, liberty, or property without due process of law.

—Constitution of the United States, Amendment Five

American Concentration Camp, 1942: The precedent still stands. *(Wide World Photos.)*

The Constitution Is Not Enough

The incidents illustrated here each involved a challenge to rights which are formally and explicitly protected by the Constitution. Such events demonstrate that constitutional language is not, in and of itself, a protection. Some of the most totalitarian societies have written constitutions with clear provisions for civil liberties. But some things are more important than the basic written law: among them are custom, legal tradition, the social and political climate prevailing at the moment, the extent to which individuals will defend their civil liberties, and their success at mustering popular support for this defense.

Nevertheless, the written constitutional provisions are a stabilizing force, for they provide the foundation on which all arguments over specific applications of civil liberties must rest. They have been the anchoring point for the evolving American legal tradition. The evolutionary process is, of course, as old as civilization. The ancient Greeks believed in freedom of discussion for citizens; even the feudal systems of the Middle Ages assumed some basic legal rights; and the Magna Carta was not viewed as a new achievement by the barons at Runnymede, but as a restoration of traditional immunities that had been temporarily and wrongfully denied them.

Civil Liberties and Civil Rights

The concept of civil liberty sometimes overlaps with that of civil rights. The distinction, for our purpose, is this: Civil liberties restrain the power of government to abuse individuals. Civil rights invoke the power of government to prevent individuals from being abused by other individuals, by private organizations, or by the government itself. Our civil liberties are spelled out mainly in the Bill of Rights. Our civil rights rest for the most part in other sections of the Constitution.

This affirmative-negative distinction is obviously slippery. For example, sometimes one branch of government is asked to take affirmative action to restrain another branch. Another distinction is that civil rights generally involve the treatent of groups. Persons hold the rights as individuals, but when they are denied them, it is usually because of some group characteristic which makes them readily identifiable and therefore susceptible to stereotyping. Examples of such characteristics are race, sex, age, religion, national origin, sexual preference, physical stature, economic condition, and geographic location. The variety of civil rights issues is enormous; but they nearly always involve discrimination of some sort, such as the case of the Topeka restaurant which used to display a sign "Mexicans served in bags only," or the more recent case of women complaining that it costs them a dime to urinate in public toilets while men may urinate free. The kinds of problems that come under the heading of civil liberties rather than civil rights are much more limited in scope. However, that scope has been widening.

Facility for Women, 1974: A variety of issues. *(Linda Strompf.)*

If God had meant us to have pay toilets, we would have been born with exact change.

—Sign at Feminist Party Convention, Cambridge, Mass., 1973

Modern Developments in Civil Liberty

In the modern world, three main developments have strengthened the benefit of civil liberties:

1 It has become generally accepted that persons have rights simply by virtue of being human and not as a consequence of class, social status, or contribution to the community. This development is more recent than you might think. We are only a little more than a hundred years away from slavery, and its aftereffects are still with us.

2 Increasing attention has been paid to *substantive rights* as opposed to *procedural rights*. The former are defined as ends in themselves, establishing

boundaries across which government may not trespass. Freedom of speech is a substantive right; Congress shall make *no law* abridging it. However, despite the absolutism which the language of the Bill of Rights seems to express, substantive rights tend to be ambiguous in application. Procedural rights, on the other hand, set out certain specific steps which government must take when it exercises its power against the individual. Trial by jury is a procedural right. Because the procedures are easy to define, procedural rights are relatively straightforward. You either have a jury or you don't. On the other hand, it is the ambiguity of the substantive rights which has left room for their expansion. The weakening of legal definitions of obscenity has broadened the substantive right of freedom of speech.

3 Human rights are increasingly defined in a positive context. Traditionally, civil liberties are, as we have seen, defined by what they prevent the government from doing. But there is growing use of affirmative government action to protect the exercise of these liberties. For example, your right to free speech prevents a policeman from arresting you for making a speech on the steps of the Student Union. But if a rock-throwing mob tries to chase you off the steps, the policeman may have to intervene on your behalf to protect your right to free speech. At another level, freedom of the press prevents the government from concealing its actions by telling editors what they may or may not print. But the government may still conceal its actions by refusing to give reporters access to them. For complete freedom of the press, the government must take affirmative action to disclose information about its activities.

The Constitution as Anchor

Some rights are considered so basic that they need no explicit statement in written law. They are, in the words of Associate Justice Benjamin N. Cardozo, "implicit in the concept of ordered liberty [*Palko v. Connecticut*, 302 U.S. 319][1]." They are "so rooted in the traditions and conscience of

[1]Supreme Court cases are cited by volume number, edition, and page number in that order. Cases before 1882 were privately published, and each edition bears the name of the reporter, e.g. Cranch. Later cases are available in three main editions. The government publication is *United States Reports*, abbreviated as U.S. Privately annotated versions are *Supreme Court Reporter* (Sup. Ct.) and *Lawyer's Edition* (L. Ed.).

"An Unflattering Estimate"

To believe that patriotism will not flourish if patriotic ceremonies are voluntary and spontaneous instead of a compulsory routine is to make an unflattering estimate of the appeal of our institutions to free minds. We can have intellectual individualism and the rich cultural diversities that we owe to exceptional minds only at the price of occasional eccentricity and abnormal attitudes.

—Associate Justice Robert H. Jackson, *West Virginia Board of Education v. Barnette*, 1943.

our people as to be ranked as fundamental." Cardozo was using this distinction in 1937 in an effort to decide which rights may not be infringed by state action. Alexander Hamilton used it in *The Federalist*, No. 84 to explain why there was no need for a bill of rights in the original Constitution. "Why declare that things shall not be done which there is no power to do?" he asked, "Why, for instance, should it be said that the liberty of the press shall not be restrained when no power is given by which restrictions may be imposed?" And John Adams said, one might as well try "to rule hell by prayer" as seek to restrain government abuse of power with philosophical "aphorisms."

Nevertheless, the authors of the Constitution did include an explicit statement of rights in Article I, Section 9, which limits the powers of Congress. Probably motivated by the Federalist concern over potential abuses of popular rule, they provided that:

1   Congress could not suspend the writ of habeas corpus except in case of rebellion or invasion, and only then when "the public safety may require it."

2   No bill of attainder nor ex post facto law could be passed. A bill of attainder provides for punishment of an individual for a specific crime and amounts to trial by legislature; an ex post facto law makes an act punishable even if it was committed before it became illegal.

Treason against the United States shall consist only in levying War against them or in adhering to their Enemies, giving them Aid and Comfort. No Person shall be convicted of Treason unless on the Testimony of two Witnesses to the same overt Act, or on Confession in open Court.

—Constitution of the United States, Article III, Section 3

In Article III, Section 3, the Constitution limits the power of the judiciary branch by providing procedural and substantive limits on conviction and punishment for treason—a political crime which officials had often used to abuse their opponents. Article XI provides that no religious test may ever be required as a qualification for public office. And Article I, Section 10 extends to state action the protection against bills of attainder and ex post facto laws.

The resistance to a fuller statement of rights was finally overcome out of political necessity. The Federalists were a minority in the Massachusetts ratifying convention, and when it appeared that the Constitution would be defeated, they promised a bill of rights. This move swung the support of John Hancock and Samuel Adams, and ratification narrowly passed. From that point on, acceptance of the Constitution was based on the promise of the coming amendments, although that was never made a formal condition of ratification. Had the promise not been promptly kept, however, the new government might have undergone a fatal crisis of confidence.

PUTTING IT IN WRITING

The Bill of Rights

Federalists and anti-Federalists formed a temporary coalition strong enough to get the ten amendments of the Bill of Rights swiftly adopted. Two other amendments, dealing with apportionment of representatives and congressional salaries, failed. An effort to extend the coverage of the Bill of Rights to state governments was blocked by the anti-Federalists.

Of the ten amendments, the First specifies the most basic of the fundamental freedoms, and it does so succinctly. In only forty-five words, it lays the groundwork for separation of church and state by denying Congress the power to establish a religion or prohibit "the free exercise thereof." It provides for freedom of speech and press, the right of peaceable assembly, and the right to petition the government for redress of grievances.

The Second Amendment covers the right "to keep and bear arms" for the sake of having "a well regulated militia." The Third and Fourth, which sprang from some of the specific grievances that led to the Revolution, bar the quartering of soldiers in private homes and prohibit unreasonable searches and seizures. A reasonable search or seizure is given a procedural definition: It can come only after a warrant issued upon probable cause, supported by oath or affirmation, and specifically describing what is to be seized and where it is to be sought.

The Fourth together with the Fifth, Sixth, and Eighth Amendments constitute the main protections for persons accused of crime. The Fifth Amendment requires grand jury indictment before a person can be tried for a major federal crime, prohibits the government from appealing acquittals or otherwise trying a person twice for the same crime, bars compulsory self-incrimination, provides for compensation when private property is taken for public use, and requires "due process of law" before a person is deprived of life, liberty, or property.

The right to a speedy and public jury trial, to be informed of the charges, to confront one's accuser, to subpoena witnesses, and to have counsel are provided by the Sixth Amendment. The Eighth bans excessive bail, fines, and cruel and unusual punishment.

The Seventh Amendment is obscure and rarely invoked. It provides for jury trials in suits at common law where more than $20 is in controversy. The Ninth and Tenth respond to the fears that a specific listing of rights might undermine the doctrine that all governmental power flows from the people. The Ninth says that the enumeration of certain rights does not imply that the list is exhaustive; other basic rights are retained by the people. The Tenth is the reserve clause: Powers not delegated by the

Constitution nor prohibited to the states are reserved to the states or to the people.

Later Amendments

The subsequent development of civil liberties has come mainly through changing customs, laws, and court decisions, although the formal amending process has also continued to play a role. Barriers to voting were eliminated by Amendments Fifteen (race, color, previous condition of servitude), Nineteen (sex), Twenty-three (residents of the District of Columbia in presidential elections), Twenty-four (poll tax), and Twenty-six (age, if 18 or older).

The Thirteenth barred slavery; and the Fourteenth, in language whose interpretation was to shift sharply over a century of constitutional development, barred states from denying their citizens the privileges and immunities of United States citizens, due process of law, and the equal protection of the laws.

A keystone for the protection of civil liberties, as perceived by the eighteenth-century political philosophers and borne out before and since in practice, is the presence of an independent judiciary. The courts can correct the arbitrary actions of officials. They can also check the power of laws which unjustly conflict with the Constitution. As Alexis De Tocqueville (1835) noted, "it is . . . by minor prosecutions, which the humblest citizen can institute at any time, that liberty is protected [p. 77]."

Limiting the States

The protection of persons accused of crime was one of the chief concerns of the authors of the Bill of Rights. Yet, throughout most of the Constitution's history, this protection has been limited by a paradox. The Bill of Rights was not intended to apply to state action (*Barron v. Baltimore*, 7 Peters 243). Yet, it is the states that have the primary responsibility for making and enforcing criminal law. Murder, for example, is a federal crime only if it is committed in a federal jurisdiction, such as a territory, aboard a vessel in U.S. territorial waters, or in the District of Columbia. Persons accused of crime had to look to state laws, customs, and constitutional provisions for their protections, and these have been quite uneven in their substance and in application.

There is strong historical evidence that Congress intended to extend the protections of the Bill of Rights to state action when it proposed the Fourteenth Amendment. The "privileges and immunities" of citizens of the United States which the states were bound to observe could have meant the privileges and immunities of the Bill of Rights. But the Supreme Court foreclosed that possibility in the 1873 Slaughterhouse cases (16 Wallace 36). A group of New Orleans butchers claimed their privileges and immunities as U.S. citizens were violated by a state law giving one company a monopoly on all slaughtering operations in the city. The Court said it could not be a "perpetual censor" of state legislation. For the federal courts to try to protect citizens from violations of their rights by the states would be a step "so serious, so far-reaching and pervading" as to make radical changes in the relationship of state and federal governments. The Court instead kept to the doctrine of dual federalism, holding, in the words of Associate Justice Samuel F. Miller, "that there is a citizenship of the United States and a citizenship of a state, which are distinct from each other." In effect, the Court was saying that the Fourteenth Amendment had not changed a thing. The privileges and immunities of citizens with respect to their states were just what they had been before.

But in the next two decades, the Court developed a new constitutional theory which did let it restrict state legislatures. The theory was called substantive due process, and it was developed not to protect individual liberties from state governments but to protect business from regulation by reform movements in the legislatures. The "privileges and immunities" clause of the Fourteenth Amendment had been rendered meaningless by the Slaughterhouse cases, and so the new doctrine turned to another phrase from the same section of the same amendment: ". . . nor shall any State deprive any person of life, liberty, or property without due process of law." Any unreasonable form of state regulation, the court said, in a series of cases around the turn of the century, amounted to deprivation of property without due process.

This theory (whose derivation is discussed in more detail in Chapter 3) eventually provided civil libertarians with the new Fourteenth Amendment handle they needed to restrain state violations of individual liberties, although the transition from property rights to individual liberties took more than thirty years. The development was gradual. A major turning point came in 1925 in the case of *Gitlow v. New York*, 268 U.S. 652, when the Court held that ". . . freedom of speech and of the press . . . are among the fundamental personal rights and liberties" protected by the due process clause of the Fourteenth Amendment from impairment by the states. . . ." Although Gitlow won that point, he lost his case. The Court decided that putting a man in jail for circulating communist literature was not an undue abridgement of freedom of the press. It did not have to face the issue squarely until 1931 when it decided the celebrated prior-censorship case of *Near v. Minnesota*, 283 U.S. 697. The Minnesota legislature had passed a law providing for court injunctions against the publication of scandalous, malicious, defamatory, or obscene matter. This law was used to suppress a weekly newspaper whose publisher was charging local officials with failing to act against organized crime. Chief Justice Charles Evans Hughes, speaking for a 5 to 4 majority, ruled that the injunction was prior censorship, and freedom of the press requires "principally, although not exclusively, immunity from previous restraint or

Benjamin Gitlow: A major turning point. *(Wide World Photos.)*

censorship." Near thus became the first citizen to have a First Amendment freedom protected from state infringement by the federal judiciary.

Expanding the Fourteenth Amendment

The Court's action in interpreting "due process" in the Fourteenth Amendment to mean that states could not limit freedom of speech opened the door to the gradual incorporation of most of the rest of the Bill of Rights into that restraint on the states. In 1932, the procedural guarantees of a fair trial and right to counsel in capital cases were included (*Powell v. Alabama*, 287 U.S. 45). The precedent was reinforced in 1936 when the murder convictions of three Mississippi blacks who had been tortured into confessing were overturned (*Brown v. Mississippi*, 297 U.S. 278).

Freedom of religion came under the substantive due-process umbrella in 1934 in one of those digressions the Court sometimes makes where it announces new principles of law without really affecting the case at hand. A student at the University of California skipped compulsory military drill as a conscientious objector and was thrown out of school. The Court agreed with him that freedom of religion was protected from state violation by the Fourteenth Amendment, but said his religious freedom had not been violated because he attended the school voluntarily (*Hamilton v. Regents of the University of California*, 293 U.S. 245).

This piecemeal expansion of restraints on the states in behalf of civil liberties continued in 1937 when freedom of assembly was included (*De Jonge v. Oregon*, 299 U.S. 353). But this bit-by-bit approach was somewhat unsettling to orderly judicial minds because no one had enunciated a unifying principle which would define with clarity what the states could do to their citizens and what they could not. Later in 1937, Associate Justice Benjamin N. Cardozo gave it a try in *Palko v. Connecticut*. Connecticut had convicted Palko of second-degree murder. The prosecutor appealed, won a new trial, and secured a first-degree murder conviction on the second try. Under the Fifth Amendment, the federal government may not have a person "twice put in jeopardy" for the same offense. But could the state of Connecticut do it? Cardozo said it could, and it therefore fell to him to rationalize the distinction between those provisions of the Bill of Rights that applied to the states through the Fourteenth Amendment and those which did not. Substantive due process, Cardozo said, covered only those rights so basic that they were "implicit in the concept of ordered liberty." By his reasoning, freedom of speech, religion, press, peaceable assembly, and the right to counsel in criminal trials were all implicit in "ordered liberty." The right to a jury trial, freedom from double jeopardy, freedom from self-incrimination were not, unless the defendant could show that special circumstances made his treatment fundamentally unfair. Palko was eventually executed. Cardozo's distinction stood for a generation before it was finally eroded. This erosion was foreshadowed by Associate Justice

Mr. Justice Cardozo: A concept of liberty. *(Wide World Photos.)*

Hugo Black who argued in 1947 that the entire Bill of Rights should be covered through the Fourteenth Amendment. That, he said, was the historical purpose of the amendment. But he was in the minority in that case, and the power of a state to require an accused person to be a witness against himself was affirmed (*Adamson v. California*, 332 U.S. 46).

A new expansion of the meaning of the Fourteenth Amendment came during the tenure of Chief Justice Earl Warren, although it never adopted Black's sweeping proposal. Instead, it reasoned on a case-by-case basis, extending the self-incrimination restraint to states in 1964 (*Malloy v. Hogan*, 378 U.S. 1). And in 1969, the Court finally admitted that it had been wrong to let Connecticut execute Palko. In *Benton v. Maryland*, 395 U.S. 784, Associate Justice Thurgood Marshall wrote:

> Our recent cases have thoroughly rejected the Palko notion that basic constitutional rights can be denied by the States as long as the totality of the circumstances do not disclose a denial of "fundamental fairness." Once it is decided that a particular Bill of Rights guarantee is "fundamental to the American scheme of justice" . . . the same constitutional standards apply against both state and Federal governments. Palko's roots had thus been cut away years ago. We today recognize the inevitable.

What States Can and Cannot Do

The case-by-case approach eventually brought these liberties under federal protection from state infringement through the Fourteenth Amendment:

Protection from Unreasonable Search and Seizure. Evidence obtained by illegal searches has been inadmissible in federal courts since 1914 (*Weeks v. U.S.*, 232 U.S. 383). However, the Court refused to impose this exclusionary rule on the states, arguing that lesser remedies would suffice (*Wolf v. Colorado*, 338 U.S. 25). As a practical matter, however, police had a strong incentive to use illegal means to gain evidence. The Court changed its mind in 1961 after police, without a warrant, forcibly entered the home of Dolree Mapp of Cleveland. They failed to find the fugitive and the supply of gambling equipment they were looking for, but they did find some "obscene materials." Ms. Mapp was convicted for that by the state of Ohio. In overturning her conviction, the Supreme Court ruled that since the right of privacy had been extended to the states through the Fourteenth Amendment, the exclusionary rule was applicable to both state and federal courts. There was a reaction. Alan H. Schechter (1972) recalls that, "policemen and prosecutors in half the states let loose a tirade of abuse directed at the Supreme Court [p. 91]." The protests soon faded when it became apparent that police did not need to violate the Constitution to do their jobs.

Right to Counsel. The Court held as early as 1932 that due process required states to make lawyers available to indigent defendants in capital cases. For less serious crimes, the right to counsel depended on whether the specific facts of the case made it clear that lack of counsel put the defendant in a position so disadvantageous that it was fundamentally unfair. In a generally popular decision in 1963, the Court erased this fuzzy distinction and decided that *any* indigent accused of a felony had a right to a court-appointed lawyer (*Gideon v. Wainwright*, 372 U.S. 335). Most states had already provided such a guarantee, and the others quickly did so. Florida, where Gideon's case originated, passed a public defender law within two months of the decision (Lewis, 1964).

Further Extension of the Right to Counsel. Being entitled to a lawyer does not do a defendant much good if he does not know about it. In 1966, the Court held that a suspect must be informed of his right to counsel before he is questioned by police (*Miranda v. Arizona*, 384 U.S. 436). In 1972, the right to counsel was extended by the Burger Court to all cases which could result in a jail sentence, whether or not the offense was a felony. Congress sought to soften the effect of the new rules by giving trial judges more discretion in deciding on the admissibility of confessions. But the effect of that provision of the Omnibus Crime Control and Safe Streets Act of 1968 remains to be fully tested. Meanwhile, the Burger Court decided that the *Miranda* rule did not apply in the special situation where a prisoner made damaging admissions without knowing of his right to counsel and then elected to testify in his own defense. The damaging statements, while not admissible as direct evidence, could be used to attack the credibility of his testimony. Dissenting justices complained that this left police free to "interrogate an accused incommunicado and without counsel" and still have the statements thus obtained used in court "if the defendant has the temerity to testify in his own defense." The five-man majority held that the possibility of exposing false testimony was more important than the "speculative possibility that impermissible police conduct will be encouraged [*Harris v. New York*, 28 L. Ed. 2d 1]."

Limiting the Death Penalty. In 1972, the Court ruled that the death penalty because of its uneven application by the states was a cruel and unusual punishment in violation of the Eighth and Fourteenth amendments (*Furman v. Georgia*, 408 U.S. 238). Some state legislatures sought to frame a death penalty that would be upheld by making it mandatory for certain crimes, thus eliminating the arbitrary and infrequent application.

A Uniform Criminal Procedure? As a result of the decisions since *Palko*, just about all the provisions of the Bill of Rights with contemporary applicability have been made binding on the states. Some portions of the Fifth Amendment have not been included, and trial by jury with the requirement of a unanimous verdict by twelve jurors does not apply to the states. Yet, the Court has come very close, says Herbert Weschler (1969), to "drawing from the Constitution a national code of criminal procedure, its content governed by the Supreme Court for both the Nation and the states, subject alone to constitutional amendment [p. 19]."

THE FIRST AMENDMENT

A Preferred Position

Although the distinctions which Mr. Justice Cardozo tried to make in the *Palko* case did not stand, he was on solid ground when he assumed that some liberties are more immutable than others. Associate Justice Harlan F. Stone may have put it better in 1938 when he singled out the First Amendment freedoms as requiring special protection because they represent "those political processes which make all other rights in our society possible [*United States v. Carolene Products Co.*, 304 U.S. 144]." The roots of this argument go back to the Federalist authors of the Constitution who believed that some liberties are so basic that it matters very little how they are expressed in written law. Other rights put limits on government power, but the First Amendment withholds certain powers completely. Freedom of speech and press may, in the words of Archibald Cox (1968), be thought of as "really reserved powers totally withheld from the government by the people, who are the ultimate rulers [p. 10]." The preferred-position theory was discarded after the death of Stone in 1946, but it was revived in effect by the liberal expansion of First Amendment freedoms by the Warren Court in the 1960s. This development has been less steady, though not clearly reversed, by the Burger Court in the 1970s.

One problem in interpreting the First Amendment is that it deals with the substance of liberty rather than its procedure. Its rules are difficult to define when they are applied to specific cases and controversies. Procedural liberties come closer to being absolute in application simply because they are easy to define: The policeman who knocks on your door either has a warrant or he does not. Moreover, the procedural liberties, because of their narrow scope, are less likely to conflict with other liberties or with the basic powers of government. Getting the warrant may be an inconvenience to the policeman, but it does not inflict a disabling handicap in the performance of his job. But the substantive rights of the First Amendment present many opportunities for conflict. For example, it is difficult to leave a person free to practice his religion if that religion bars him from paying taxes to support government activities which his religious code defines as sinful. Much of the history of the development and definition of the substantive liberties depicts the struggle of the Court to trace a path among such competing ambiguities.

Chief Justice Stone: Putting it better. *(Wide World Photos.)*

Archibald Cox: Power totally withheld. *(Dennis Brack, Black Star.)*

Freedom of Speech and Press

A few authorities, such as Associate Justice Hugo L. Black, have taken a fundamentalist view of the Constitution: that it means just what it says. "No law" means *no* law—for any reason or in any circumstances. To Black, freedom of speech "is the heart of our government" and vital to the healthy, continuing function of the government. But this absolutist position has always been the minority opinion. The majority has been able to find exceptions. Deciding just what these exceptions are has been troublesome. For example, it has long been assumed that the First Amendment did not protect obscenity. This assumption presented no special problem so long as people could agree on what constituted obscenity. With changing public standards, that has been quite impossible. By the time Ralph Ginzburg had exhausted his appeals and began serving his jail sentence for violating an obscenity statute with his magazine, *Eros*, the courts were permitting far more explicit sexual material than he had published. Ginzburg's crime turned on the marketing of his product; obscenity was the feature emphasized in his sales pitch, and this barred him from claiming the defense of redeeming social value. If the sexually explicit material was only incidental to the redeeming social content, the latter would have been advertised. The Supreme Court first had to face the obscenity problem in 1957 in the combined cases of *Roth v. United States* and *Alberts v. California*, 354 U.S. 476. The crucial test for measuring whether or not a particular work was obscene was framed by Associate Justice William Brennan. It is obscene, he said, if "to the average person, applying contemporary community standards, the dominant theme of the material, taken as a whole, appeals to prurient interests," and, further, if the material is "utterly without redeeming social importance." To these two tests of pruriency and social significance, a third was added by the court in 1962. In *Manual Enterprises v. Day*, 370 U.S. 478, the justices approved the sending of photographs of nude males through the mail because the pictures lacked "patent offensiveness," being no more "objectionable than the many portrayals of the female nude that society tolerates." A further clarification came in 1964 when the Court decided that the test of meeting "contemporary community standards" referred to national rather than local standards. This broadened interpretation plus the threefold test of patency, pruriency, and redeeming social significance left obscenity rather narrowly defined. The wave of sexually explicit art and entertainment during the 1960s and early 1970s was unhampered by the Court. But the issue is far from resolved. In 1973, the Burger Court widened the definition of obscenity somewhat to require the redeeming social content to be of "*serious* literary, artistic, political or scientific value." And the Court returned to the use of local community standards rather than national attitudes as the guide to prurience. The new test stimulated a new round of attempts by local lawmakers to ban the publication of material regarded as obscene and

Mr. Justice Black: A fundamentalist view. *(Wide World Photos.)*

Ralph Ginzberg: No redeeming social value. *(Associated Press.)*

"One thing about these film-obscenity cases—you get to see a lot of great movies!"   (Playboy.)

caused Mr. Justice Douglas to warn that the decision "would make it possible to ban any paper or any journal or magazine in some benighted place [*Miller v. California*, 413 U.S. 15]."

A further complication of the obscenity problem is the fact that no one knows for sure just what, if any, harm it does. The Burger Court left this question to state and local lawmakers, noting only that a connection between obscenity and antisocial behavior could reasonably be assumed. Congress tried to resolve that ambiguity by creating a special research commission to demonstrate the harmful effects of obscenity. But the commission could not find any. In 1970, it recommended that "federal, state, and local legislation prohibiting the sale, exhibition, or distribution of sexual materials to consenting adults, should be repealed." President Nixon rejected the recommendation, and Congress did nothing.

Conflicts with Government Power
Other barriers to freedom of speech and press are potentially much more complicated. The First Amendment needs most the protection of its

preferred status when the government sees its very survival threatened by free utterances. The conflict has always been with us.

Libel.   Laws against libel represent a very old form of restraint on freedom of speech and press. Historically, there is a distinction between criminal or seditious libel, which punishes speech damaging to the government, and civil libel, which permits recovery for damage which speech or publication has done to a citizen. The basic defense is truth—a precedent that was anticipated in the famous trial of John Peter Zenger, printer of the *New York Weekly Journal*, in 1735. Zenger's newspaper was a vehicle for the opposition party, and Governor William Cosby decided he had had enough of its attacks. Zenger was charged with seditious libel. The Governor's opponents got him a good Philadelphia lawyer, Andrew Hamilton, who made the then novel argument that truth was a defense. There was no precedent for this in English law, but Hamilton argued that the American situation was different: the rulers and the ruled were closer together, and the people needed the right to criticize the government to insure that it did its job of protecting their security. The jury accepted that argument, Zenger was acquitted, and the case "has served repeatedly to remind Americans of the debt free men owe to free speech [Katz, 1963, p. 35]." When the Federalists violated their new Constitution with the Sedition Act of 1798, they restored prosecutions for criminal libel, but they incorporated the views of Zenger's counsel; truth was made a defense, although the Federalist-dominated judiciary generally refused to observe it. That law's constitutionality was never tested, judicial review not yet having been established, and the law expired after the Federalists lost the election of 1800.

Criminal libel has faded as a threat to freedom of speech and press, although its ghost has been seen in some modern government actions. (A prosecution for criminal libel was pending in Sharp County, Arkansas, as recently as 1973.) Public officials attacked by the press have resorted mainly to civil libel, suing to recover monetary damages for publication of injurious material. Truth is an absolute defense. In 1964, the Court made the successful conduct of a libel suit even more difficult where public officials are involved by requiring them to prove malice. In *New York Times Co. v. Sullivan*, 376 U.S. 254, the Court held that libel laws may not be used to "cast a pall of fear and timidity on the press." The Birmingham, Alabama commissioner of public affairs had won a $500,000 award from an Alabama jury over a *New York Times* political advertisement which contained some misstatements of fact. They were minor errors, e.g., that the police had encircled the campus of Alabama State College during a civil rights demonstration when in fact they had merely been deployed near it. The Supreme Court reversed the Alabama decision, holding that "debate on public issues should be uninhibited, robust, and wide open" and that for a public official to recover libel damages he would have to show actual malice by proving that the false statement was made "with knowledge that it was false or with reckless disregard of whether it was false or not."

Subversion. The government's inherent authority to protect its own existence presents no First Amendment problem so long as those who would overthrow it are content with mere talk. But it quickly gets more complicated than that. Learned Hand, a U.S. Circuit Court of Appeals judge in New York who had a gift for epigrams, said in 1917 that "words are not only the keys of persuasion but the triggers of action [*Masses Publishing Co. v. Patten*, 244 Fed. 535]." The Espionage Act of 1917 punished attempts to interfere with the war effort, including those involving only speech. The Court upheld the conviction of a Socialist party official who had urged young men to resist the draft. Justice Oliver Wendell Holmes, seeking a clear rule that would define the line between protected and unprotected speech, expressed it this way:

> The question in every case is whether the words used are used in such circumstances and are of such a nature as to create a clear and present danger that they will bring about the substantive evils that Congress has a right to prevent. . . . When a nation is at war, many things that might be said in time of peace are such a hindrance to its effort that their utterance will not be endured [*Schenck v. United States*, 249 U.S. 47].

Mr. Justice Holmes: Seeking a clear rule. *(Wide World Photos.)*

Or, putting it even more succinctly, Holmes said the First Amendment does not protect a man "falsely shouting fire in a theater and causing a panic." However, the Court was slow to adopt the "clear and present danger" test. In 1919, it upheld the Sedition Law of 1918, which punished any "disloyal, profane, scurrilous, or abusive language about the form of government, the Constitution, soldiers and sailors, flag or uniform of the armed forces." Pamphlets expressing opposition to American intervention in Russia after the Revolution were held to be in violation (*Abrams v. United States*, 250 U.S. 616). Publication of a Socialist antiwar leaflet was held punishable in 1920 because it had "a tendency to cause insubordination, disloyalty, and refusal of duty [*Pierce v. United States*, 252 U.S. 239]." And New York was allowed to punish Gitlow for the distribution of communist literature in 1925. In none of these cases was the danger clear or present. It was not until 1937 that the Court remembered Holmes' rule and struck down a Georgia law banning communist literature and membership (*Herndon v. Lowry*, 301 U.S. 242). By World War II, "clear and present danger" was the accepted test.

However, as the stresses on government grow more complicated, so does the application of the rule. The "Red Scare" after World War II led to passage of the Smith Act, which made it a crime to willfully advocate and teach the overthrow of the government by force and violence. Eleven leaders of the Communist party of the United States were convicted and the convictions upheld by the Supreme Court despite some questions about the clarity and presence of the danger they represented. The Court made Holmes' formula somewhat more complicated: It considered the "gravity of the evil" discounted by its improbability. In other words, the greater the danger, the more murky and remote it could be and still be prosecuted (*Dennis v. United States*, 341 U.S. 494). That was in 1951. The Court moved back six years later toward the simpler Holmes construction when it decided that the mere advocacy of a revolutionary philosophy would not justify impairment of free speech. The prosecution must show that the speech in question incited other persons to specific action toward overthrow of the government by force.

David Paul O'Brien: Not-so-pure speech. *(Wide World Photos.)*

Protests. The complications of the 1960s were even greater. Protests against United States military action aimed not at overthrow of the government but at provoking official reaction and enlisting the sympathy of the uncommitted. This called for a strategy of calculated and sometimes imaginative civil disobedience. Irritated congressmen reacted by introducing legislation to create some new and exotic classes of federal crimes. Some of it, such as Ohio Sen. Frank Lausche's bill to make it a federal crime to lie down in front of a troop train, never passed. Legislation making it a federal crime to burn one's draft card did pass and was signed into law by President Johnson in August 1965.

David Paul O'Brien burned his card on the courthouse steps in south Boston and was arrested by the FBI, which promptly photographed the card's charred remains. O'Brien admitted the facts of the case and was convicted in U.S. District Court, but his conviction was reversed by the Court of Appeals which said the law violated the First Amendment because it singled out protesters for special treatment. The functioning of the Selective Service System, it said, was already protected by law, and O'Brien could have been punished for not having his draft card in his personal possession. The Supreme Court did not agree. Chief Justice Earl Warren said the law served "a legitimate and substantial purpose" in keeping the draft going. Associate Justice John Marshall Harlan, concurring, said that O'Brien's First Amendment rights were not impaired because he "could have conveyed his message in many ways other than by burning his draft card [*U.S. v. O'Brien*, 391 U.S. 367]."

Harlan's emphasis on the manner in which the defendant communicated his message reflects a comparatively recent distinction. In 1965, the Court said that the First Amendment does not "afford the same kind of freedom to those who would communicate ideas by conduct such as patrolling, marching, and picketing on streets and highways, as these amendments afford to those who communicate ideas by pure speech [*Cox v. Louisiana*, 379 U.S. 536]." It thus implied two categories, pure speech and not-so-pure speech, one protected and the other not. In 1969, it decided that for children to wear black arm bands protesting the Vietnam war was close enough to pure speech to be protected (*Tinker v. Des Moines School District*, 393 U.S. 503). But in *O'Brien*, the act of protest included more not-pure components, and it was therefore not protected. This confusing distinction restricts the available avenues of antigovernment expression.

Conflicts with the Rights of Others

First Amendment protections do not provide an automatic defense for committing a crime, defrauding another, invasion of privacy, or provoking a lynch mob. But even in instances where one right is pitted against another, the Court has, in recent years, tended to give preference to the First Amendment. The balance which must be weighed is often delicate.

Invasion of Privacy. The Constitution does not specify a right of privacy, but a common-law right to be left alone has begun to be recognized in a fairly recent series of developments. According to the American Law Institute, it is possible to recover civil damages when a person "unreasonably and seriously interferes with another's interest in not having his affairs known to others." The law on this point is likely to be developed further as the dangers inherent in private and public dossiers kept by schools, hospitals, credit bureaus, insurance companies, welfare agencies, and law enforcement organizations become more widely apparent (Wheeler, 1969). Meanwhile, the First Amendment takes precedence. In 1967, the Court ruled against a family which had won a $75,000 judgment against Time, Inc., under a New York right-to-privacy law. The family's history was bizarrely newsworthy. In 1952, while living in suburban Philadelphia, its seven members had been held hostage in their home by three escaped convicts. A novel was based on the incident, a play based on the novel, and a movie based on the play. After they had moved away and escaped the notoriety, *Life* magazine published an inaccurate account of the incident under the headline, "True Crime Inspires Tense Play." The Court ruled that the magazine's First Amendment rights would prevail in such a situation unless it published the report "with knowledge of its falsity or in reckless disregard of the truth [*Time, Inc. v. Hill*, 385 U.S. 374]." Time, Inc., did not have to pay the $75,000. But the right-to-privacy issue is by no means settled. The Burger Court expanded this right significantly when it decided the abortion question on the basis of right to privacy in *Roe v. Wade* (410 U.S. 113).

Free Press versus Fair Trial. Two of the most fundamental rights come into conflict when exercise of the First Amendment freedom of the press interferes with the Sixth Amendment right of an accused person to a fair trial. One of the most flagrant examples of disregard of the latter was the case of Samuel Sheppard, the Cleveland physician convicted in 1954 of

Dr. Samuel Sheppard: Trial by newspaper. *(Wide World Photos.)*

murdering his wife. Newspapers practically demanded his arrest, and the trial judge permitted a circus atmosphere in the courtroom, allowing reporters to wander at will between the bench, the counsel table, and the clerk's desk. The judge contributed to the publicity by discussing the case himself for the national press, granting an exclusive interview to Hearst columnist Dorothy Kilgallen. The Supreme Court deplored the "Roman holiday" conditions and granted Sheppard a new trial (*Sheppard v. Maxwell*, 384 U.S. 333). At the second trial, twelve years later, he was acquitted.

For the most part, courts have been able to protect an accused person from the effects of pretrial publicity without any direct restraints on the press. They can restrict the statements made about the case by officers of the court, including attorneys. They can move the trial to a jurisdiction unaffected by the publicity; they can continue the case until the publicity dies down; they can see that prospective jurors are questioned to determine whether exposure to information about the case has prejudiced them; or they can sequester the jury to shut out external influences while the trial is in progress.

On April 27, 1966, in his only appearance before the United States Supreme Court, Attorney Richard Nixon rose to argue for the individual's right to privacy.

His clients, the Hill family, had brought suit against Life magazine regarding its review of a play, "The Desperate Hours," in which a family was terrorized by escaped convicts. The Hills had gone through the ordeal in 1952 that inspired the play; they had turned down television and magazine offers at the time and moved out of state to escape further notoriety, but the magazine put the spotlight on them again, and in a sensational and inaccurate way, so the Hills took Time, Inc. to court.

The constitutional issue that went to the Supreme Court pitted press freedom against what Louis Brandeis and Samuel Warren had called in 1890 the individual's "right to be let alone."

Mr. Nixon lost the case. In a 5-4 decision, the Court extended the power of the press and diminished the right of privacy.

Surprised observers noted that as a lawyer, Mr. Nixon had argued the case with great skill; not only was his written brief cogent, but in oral argument he more than held his own before the Court with former Judge Harold Medina, the opposing counsel.

Mr. Nixon thought he could have done better. In a lengthy memorandum written the next day to law partner Leonard Garment, Mr. Nixon critiqued his own effort, exploring in detail what other points he might have raised using the Ninth and 10th Amendments "to give redress to private citizens where they are injured by other private citizens."

Mr. Nixon, a genuinely private person, chose to represent this client in this case out of his personal conviction that Justice Brandeis was right—that there was a "right to be let alone," and that it must be vigorously asserted.

—William Safire, *New York Times,* May 21, 1973.

To Be Let Alone

Recent Threats to Freedom of the Press

To print a book, pamphlet, or paper in seventeenth-century England, you had to first obtain a license for the specific thing to be printed. John Milton was arguing against this form of government restraint *before* publication when he wrote *Areopagitica*:

> And though all the windes of doctrin were let loose to play upon the earth, so Truth be in the field, we do injuriously by licencing and prohibiting to misdoubt her strength. Let her and Falsehood grapple; who ever knew Truth put to the wors, in a free and open encounter [Modern Library edition, 1950, p. 719].

Milton's plea for unlicensed printing was successful, and when the Founders wrote the First Amendment, the principle was already in the common law as expressed by Blackstone, who said:

> Every freeman has an undoubted right to lay what sentiments he pleases before the public; to forbid this is to destroy the freedom of the press; but if he publishes what is improper, mischievous and illegal, he must take the consequences of his own temerity [Corwin, 1963, p. 196].

In other words, no matter what restraints government might impose on expression, it could not exercise *prior* censorship. It could act only after the unwanted publication.

Nearly all subsequent argument over defining freedom of speech has involved the question of imposing sanctions after the disputed utterance or publication. Immunity from prior restraint has been taken for granted, as did the Court in the 1931 *Near* decision, where it quoted Blackstone on the basic nature of this immunity. The 1971 *New York Times* case may, however, prove to be a turning point away from that historic absolute.

Paul M. Branzburg: Protecting the source. *(Wide World Photos.)*

The *Times* has been criticized for not making a more vigorous contest of the original District Court injunction, which halted publication of information from the Pentagon papers. The first injunction was for four days to let the government examine the 7,000 pages of documents whose information the *Times* wanted to reveal. A *Times'* editor said he thought that was "reasonable." One injunction led to another. As other newspapers obtained copies of the documents and began publishing information, they were enjoined too. No editor risked a contempt citation—although reporters have routinely done that to protect news sources—to force a basic test of the immunity from prior censorship. Although the Supreme Court soon lifted the injunction, the precedent was established. Jack Landau (1971) noted that the government had succeeded "in an endeavor which no previous government had even dared to suggest. It had silenced four of the most respected newspapers in the nation: the *Times* for 15 days, the (Washington) *Post* for 11 days, the (Boston) *Globe* for eight days, the St.

Louis *Post-Dispatch* for four days.'' Although a six-member majority voted to lift the injunction, only three agreed with Associate Justice William J. Brennann, Jr., that ''The error which has pervaded these cases from the outset was the granting of any injunctive relief whatever.'' The main opinion was framed on narrower grounds.

Another freedom-of-the-press issue involves the protection of a reporter's sources. Many investigative reporters rely on confidential sources to develop information likely to lead to criticism of the government. If they cannot guarantee these sources complete protection of their anonymity, the reporters say, the damaging information will not be available. This was the argument of a former staff reporter for the *Louisville Courier-Journal* who was convicted of contempt of a grand jury for refusing to identify the young drug users and sellers he had interviewed for two newspaper articles. ''The First Amendment,'' said the Court in 1972, ''does not relieve a newspaper reporter of the obligation that all citizens have to respond to a grand jury subpoena and answer questions relevant to a criminal investigation. . .[*Branzburg v. Hayes*, 93 Sup. Ct. 2624].'' Paul Branzburg left Louisville to join the *Detroit Free Press*, and the governor of Michigan refused to extradite him to Kentucky. Others have spent varying lengths of time in prison rather than reveal their sources. Some states, Kentucky included, have ''shield'' laws which protect reporters from such a possibility in some circumstances, but they are ineffective in application. The problem is that the reporter's duty to remain silent may conflict with an injured or accused person's right to compel testimony on his behalf. Moreover, in determining who is protected by the shield, the state may find itself, in effect, imposing licensing requirements on reporters.

There have been more direct forms of coercion. In Philadelphia, the executive editor of the *Philadelphia Inquirer* received an anonymous letter containing out-of-context excerpts from the hospital record of a reporter who had criticized the mayor. Investigation revealed that the record had been subpoenaed by the city medical examiner, an appointee of the mayor, who, in order to get the record, had falsely certified that the reporter was dead. In Washington, Les Whitten, a reporter for United Features columnist Jack Anderson, was arrested by the FBI and charged with receiving stolen documents while covering the prearranged return of those same documents to the FBI. ''The FBI,'' said Anderson, ''had been emboldened, we now know, by word from the White House to make a case against us. . . . Our real crime, in other words, was to dig out stories that made the government look bad [1973].'' Whitten was saved, not by the First, but by the Fifth Amendment. A grand jury refused to indict him.

The effect of coercion on freedom of speech and the press is difficult to measure. More serious than the jailing of reporters, in a Los Angeles editor's view, is the fact that ''some elements of the press already are avoiding the kind of story that might cause them trouble [Thomas, 1973, p. 12].''

Les Whitten: Making the government look bad. (*Wide World Photos.*)

Freedom of Religion

The history of religious freedom in the United States has been full of ambiguity and contradiction, although recent years have seen a tendency toward interpretation that is fairly straightforward. Obviously, religious freedom cannot be invoked as a defense for violating laws which injure community welfare: you may not, for example, include human sacrifice in your religious rites. The Supreme Court made an interesting distinction here in 1878 when it upheld a federal law banning polygamy in the territory of Utah. A Mormon who had more than one wife was convicted, but the court held that he had the right to believe in polygamy if not to practice it (*Reynolds v. U.S.*, 98 U.S. 145).

More recent cases have shown a trend to require the government to make special allowances for religious beliefs when they conflict with ordinary duties of citizenship. In the Jehovah's Witnesses cases during World War II, children won the right to be excused from flag-salute exercises. That decision was made on broad, freedom-of-expression grounds rather than as a special religious exemption (*West Virginia State Board of Education v. Barnette*, 319 U.S. 624). The right of a conscientious objector to avoid military service has been expanded. Since 1970 (*Welch v. U.S.*, 90 Sup. Ct. 1792), the Court has defined any deeply held humanistic conviction as a religion qualifying for the protection; it is no longer necessary to show a formal religion, belief in God, or a comparable belief. However, the conviction must be general rather than particular. The objection must be to all war, rather than a specific situation such as the Vietnam war (*Gillette v. United States*, 28 L. Ed. 2d 168, 1971).

Such special provisions to accommodate unusual religious views may, if carried very far, encounter an important theoretical problem. By granting privileges or exemptions to persons because of their religious beliefs, the government may be giving official sanction to those beliefs, effecting the very establishment of religion which the Constitution prohibits. The two basic rules, that government may neither establish a religion nor prohibit the free exercise of religion, may thus, in some circumstances, be incompatible. To Jefferson, in the age of eighteenth-century rationalism, all that was needed was "a wall of separation between Church and State." But establishing the wall in theory and putting it into practice are not the same thing. Church and state were closely intertwined in the eighteenth century; and the building of that wall, mostly through judicial action, is still in process. Occasionally, a window is left.

Jefferson had reason to feel strongly about this issue. The Holy Roman Empire was not the only repressive church-state combination in recent history. England's 1689 Bill of Rights put religious restrictions on the royal family, requiring every successor of the Crown to be either a Protestant or married to a Protestant. The Founding Fathers shut off that precedent with the Article VI prohibition of any religious test for office. English law also established the Anglican church as the officially preferred religion with special privileges, and some states still imitated this practice when the Constitution was written. All the New England states, except for Rhode Island, gave preferred status to the Congregational Church. Pennsylvania and Delaware barred non-Christians from public office. And only Protestants could be office holders in Massachusetts, North Carolina, New Hampshire, and New Jersey. Massachusetts was the last state to drop this restriction, acting in 1833. It was not until a century later that the Court began to require the states, through the Fourteenth Amendment, to erect the wall between church and state.

Traces of government-established religion remain. The motto "In God We Trust" appears on our coins; the Senate opens with a prayer by the official chaplain; and the Supreme Court opens its public sessions with the words "God save the United States and this honorable Court." Divinity students had draft exemption. Government workers get religious holidays off. Much property owned by churches is exempt from taxes. Church services, conducted by clergy of various denominations, are sometimes held in the East Room of the White House. Of these practices, the most vulnerable to challenge under the wall-of-separation doctrine is the tax exemption for church property. But the Court approved it in 1970 on the ground that the church-state connection was slight (*Walz v. Tax Commission of the City of New York*, 397 U.S. 664).

Aid to Parochial Schools

Since the end of World War II, the Court has struggled with the problem of deciding what kind of government financial aid can be extended to parochial schools. Free bus transportation for parochial school students was approved in 1947 on the theory that it benefits the child, not the religion (*Everson v. Board of Education*, 330 U.S. 1). Arrangements to give public school children time off for religious instruction were approved, provided the religious teaching was not conducted on school property (*Zorach v. Clauson*, 343 U.S. 306).

As federal aid to education has grown and as Roman Catholic schools have faced increasing financial difficulties, pressure has grown for the government to find some way of providing them with relief. The Court approved the use of government money to build facilities for nonreligious instruction in private colleges, including those that are church related (*Tilton v. Richardson*, 29 L. Ed. 2d. 790, 1971). But it struck down a Rhode Island plan to spend state money on the salaries of parochial school teachers, even though it only covered the time they spent on academic subjects (*Lemon v. Kurtzman*, 29 L. Ed. 2d. 745, 1971). There were several key distinctions between these two cases. For one, college students were deemed less susceptible to religious indoctrination than elementary and secondary students. Another was that the secular purpose of physical facilities could be established in college, while secular and religious teaching are closely intertwined at lower levels.

SUMMARY OF THE ARTICLES AND AMENDMENTS OF THE CONSTITUTION OF THE UNITED STATES OF AMERICA

The Preamble: Declares the purposes of the Constitution and establishes it as a document of popular government which derives its authority from the consent of the people.

Article I: Vests the legislative power of the nation in a Congress composed of two houses and establishes its basic organization, powers, and limitations.

Article II: Vests the executive power of the nation in the office of President, establishes the means of election to that office, and enumerates some of its powers and duties.

Article III: Vests the judicial power of the nation in a Supreme Court and inferior courts established by Congress, and establishes their jurisdictions.

Article IV: Declares the states to be legally equal members of the Union whose interrelations are subject to regulation by the Federal government.

Article V: Establishes the procedures for amending the Constitution.

Article VI: Declares supremacy for the national government over those activities covered by its assigned powers and establishes the duty of state and federal officials to support the Constitution and the supremacy of the national government.

Article VII: Sets forth the conditions under which the Constitution initially went into effect.

Amendment I (December 15, 1791)*: Prohibits Congress from passing laws which interfere with the public's freedom of religious exercise, speech, assembly, or communication with government for the purpose of making demands on it.

Amendment II (December 15, 1791): Declares the right of the people to "keep and bear arms" as a corollary of the nation's need for defense by a citizen militia.

Amendment III (December 15, 1791): Forbids the housing of soldiers in private homes except by consent of owners or provision of war-time legislation.

Amendment IV (December 15, 1791): Forbids the government from subjecting citizens to unreasonable searches and seizures of their property or persons without proper warrants duly issued.

Amendment V (December 15, 1791): Establishes the grand jury system of criminal indictment, and prohibits the Federal government from the practices of multiple prosecutions for a single offense, forced self-incrimination, and deprivation of life, liberty, or property without due process of law.

Amendment VI (December 15, 1791): Declares the right of all accused persons to rapid, public trial by jury, to access to information necessary for a defense, and to the assistance of legal counsel in all criminal cases.

Amendment VII (December 15, 1791): Establishes the right to jury trial in common-law cases.

Amendment VIII (December 15, 1791): Prohibits the imposition of excessive bail requirements and extraordinary punishments for criminal acts.

Amendment IX (December 15, 1791): Declares that all rights not mentioned in the Constitution are still held by the people and are to be afforded full recognition.

Amendment X (December 15, 1791): Reserves to the people or their state governments all powers not delegated exclusively to the national government or denied to the states by the Constitution.

Amendment XI (January 8, 1798): Prohibits private individuals from sueing states in the federal courts without the state's consent except for violation of the Constitution itself.

Amendment XII (September 25, 1804): Changes the procedure for electing the President and Vice President.

Amendment XIII (December 18, 1865): Prohibits slavery.

Amendment XIV (July 28, 1868): Extended U.S. and state citizenship to all persons born or naturalized in the U.S. and prohibits the states from passing laws which abridge the privileges or immunities of U.S. citizens, while making the guarantees of due process and equal protection of the laws good against the state governments.

Amendment XV (March 30, 1870): Forbids the state and national governments from restricting the right of citizens to vote on the basis of their race, color, or previous slave status.

Amendment XVI (February 25, 1913): Gives Congress authority to levy and collect a federal income tax.

Amendment XVII (May 31, 1913): Provides for the direct popular election of U.S. Senators and for a means of filling vacancies in the Senate.

Amendment XVIII (January 29, 1919): Prohibits traffic in alcoholic beverages.

Amendment XIX (August 26, 1929): Guarantees citizens of both sexes the right to vote.

Amendment XX (February 6, 1933): Changes the dates of the terms of President, Vice President, Senator, and Representative, and made provisions for filling vacancies in the Presidency and Vice-Presidency.

Amendment XXI (December 5, 1933): Repeals the Eighteenth Amendment.

Amendment XXII (March 1, 1951): Limits Presidential tenure to two terms or ten years.

Amendment XXIII (March 29, 1961): Gives the District of Columbia representation in the Electoral College.

Amendment XXIV (January 23, 1964): Prohibits imposition of the payment of any tax as a precondition to voting in the election of federal officials.

Amendment XXV (February 10, 1967): Establishes a line of succession to the office of President and a means for filling vacancies in the office of Vice President.

Amendment XXVI (June 30, 1971): Extends the right to vote to all citizens eighteen years of age and older.

Proposed Amendment XXVII: Would ensure equal treatment under the law for members of both sexes.

*Date when amendment went into effect.

The issue remains politically sensitive. In the 1972 presidential race, Richard Nixon and George McGovern promised to find some way to help parochial schools. In the states, legislatures began trying tax credit plans to compensate parents who pay tuition to parochial and private schools. According to the American Civil Liberties Union (1972), legislators tend to treat the issue cynically. Knowing that the courts will strike down measures to aid parochial schools, legislators vote for them anyway in order not to offend constituents.

Prayer in the Schools

Some states used to require their public schools to open with prayer or readings from the Bible. The Court ruled in 1963 that this was an establishment of religion contrary to the First and Fourteenth Amendments, because it used the power of the state to compel attendance at worship. During the litigation, the Pennsylvania Legislature changed its law to allow dissenters to leave the classroom during this exercise. That, said the Court, made no difference. A subtle but effective compulsion remained. A child may, of course, still say a prayer in a public school. But officially organized religious activity was banned in 1963 (*Abington Township School District v. Schempp*, 374 U.S. 203).

THE PRICE OF LIBERTY

More than Vigilance

As this brief outline has shown, it takes more than vigilance to secure and maintain liberty. It also takes assertiveness. Ours is a government of laws *and* men, and the meaning and effectiveness of the laws at any given time depend on how men respond to them.

At the heart of the system of testing and defining the Constitution on a case-by-case basis are citizens with specific controversies who go to the trouble of pressing the issue. Often their victories or defeats are only symbolic. Ellory Schempp was a high school junior when his family challenged the Pennsylvania school prayer law, and the benefit that he personally derived from the victory was probably slight compared to the opprobrium he received. Few of those unlawfully jailed in the antiwar May Day demonstrations bothered to try to recover damages; the moment for making their political point had passed. And if the *New York Times* precedent stands, a newspaper may soon find that its effort to disclose a controversial situation can be delayed until the issue is moot. The Pentagon papers were history; but the injunctive delay could just as readily be used to forestall the speedy mobilization of public opinion in time to affect some current issue.

Because the law moves with slow, small steps, the effect of a precedent being set in a particular case or controversy may not be noticed by the general public until the case is long finished. The person who is battling for his or her rights must often do it without public support or recognition that the individual's cause is ultimately the public's cause in the unending struggle to hold the power of government in check. Moreover, the precedent-setting point may be a small one that would not seem to most people to be worth struggling over. With little direct gain and not much chance of public recognition, the only remaining reward is the satisfaction that a stubborn person receives from sticking to a principle until the resistance is overcome.

Such persons tend to be more peculiar or less likeable than the average citizen. But we owe them and the organizations which sometimes support them a good deal. By being stubborn and obnoxious enough to assert their liberties even when the personal benefit to them is far less than the cost, they are protecting us all and reaffirming the belief of the Founders that one human idiosyncracy could be checked by another.

PROTECTING CITIZENS FROM EACH OTHER

The Stereotyping Problem

The civil rights problem, as we have seen earlier in this chapter, involves considerations that differ from those in traditional civil liberties. Rather than imposing restraints on government, the problem in civil rights is to gain fair and equal treatment for everyone; this often requires the use of government power to keep citizens from being unfair to one another. The Founders saw government as inherently greedy, rapacious, and oppressive and gave us safeguards against it. But these very human qualities can also exist outside the formal structure of government and still be deeply ingrained in the social system. The victims are generally groups, usually minorities, which are susceptible to stereotyping. All of us tend to think in stereotypes. We have to in order to make any sense at all out of a rather disorderly world. "For the attempt to see all things freshly and in detail, rather than as types and generalities," said Walter Lippman (1922), "is exhausting, and among busy affairs practically out of the question [p. 59]."

But it is a habit easily abused. The combined qualities of minority status and susceptibility to stereotyping create a social situation in which a person is especially vulnerable. He or she may be assigned an inferior position in the social and economic hierarchy simply because the dominant members of the society agree to accord such treatment to the disadvantaged groups. The agreement may be explicit or tacit. Social convention thus creates a collective mental picture of a "place" in the hierarchial order of things for blacks, women, teenagers, homosexuals, Catholics, short people, or Appalachian mountain dwellers, to name just a few, and imposes sanctions on them when they fail to stay in their place. Sometimes these sanctions acquire the force of law. The power of the stereotype and social convention is so great that the law can thus become quite unfair, inhumane, and fundamentally indecent without the dominant majority ever being aware of it. The case of slavery in America is an obvious illustration—obvious because we can now view it from the perspective of more than a century's distance. The case of women takes more effort to see because we are so close to it. The institutionalized discrimination on the basis of sex is so much a part of the social conventions which govern our daily lives that many of us, male and female, have to be reminded that it exists. Its relative invisibility does not, of course, justify it.

When Social Sanctions Become Legal Sanctions

Part of the struggle for civil rights is the struggle to remove the sanction of law from discrimination. Some of it involves efforts by the federal government to curb discriminatory actions by the states. Sometimes one branch of the national government works to overcome discriminatory practices by other branches. In either case, the disadvantaged group is being extended a measure of protection *from* the government. But racism, sexism, or other forms of discrimination are not confined to public institutions. A large measure of the civil rights struggle has been to gain positive action by government against private discrimination. Thus the struggles acted out upon the stage of government reflect conflicts within the society. The conflict in society is between the generally accepted abstract principle that all men and women are created equal and the reflexive, often unconscious, attitudes and practices toward certain groups that deny them that equality.

In this section, we shall deal mainly with the case of blacks. This does not imply that the problems of Chicanos, American Indians, women, senior citizens, college students, or any other oppressed group are necessarily less important. The black case has simply been more intricately involved with the process of governing America than that of any of the others. It has been the most visible problem for the longest period of time; its victories and defeats, battles and skirmishes, supply the analogies for the other struggles.

Slavery

The first twenty Negroes who landed at Jamestown in 1619 were brought there as slaves under no precedent of English common law. Yet, Virginia law recognized the new institution as early as 1662. By the year of the Revolution, half a million blacks—one-sixth the total population —were in servitude. Those who survived the trip from Africa (one-third died between the interior and the African coast; another third died at sea) were mostly destined, as were their progeny, to be servants for life. They were deprived of their African traditions, dispersed among the plantations, forbidden to own property or enter contracts, including marriage. Their condition was worse than that of slaves in Latin America, where the slave-owning traditions of Spain and Portugal were transported to their colonies. The slaves of the Southern hemisphere had rights. They could marry and, once married, could not be sold separately. Laws encouraged the emancipation of slaves. It was possible to buy one's freedom.

In the United States, legal obstacles were erected against freeing slaves; an owner had to pay a tax to do so. In Virginia, a slave once freed could become a slave again. Free blacks were not really free. They faced legal restrictions on where they could live, how they could travel, the kinds of jobs they could hold.

The slavery issue was a momentary barrier to the framing of the Declaration of Independence. Jefferson's rough draft blamed the King for violating "the persons of a distant people who never offended him, captivating & carrying them into slavery in another hemisphere, or to incur miserable death in their transportation thither." The King, of course, had not had much to do with it. And the interests of Northern shipping and Southern agriculture were strong enough in the Congress to eliminate the antislavery phrasing without much argument. The declaration that "all men are created equal" remained. But neither that language nor anything like it was included in the Constitution of 1787. At the Constitutional Convention, the main concern was whether slave states or free states would get the upper hand as the nation expanded westward. Those provisions that did refer to slavery were protections of property rights: slave trade could continue for twenty years, and a slave could not rid himself of bondage by seeking refuge in a free state.

By 1819, the Union had twenty-two states—eleven slave and eleven free. Missouri applied for admission as a slave state. Northerners wanted to ban the importation of slaves into Missouri. The Missouri compromise gave the state its slaves but balanced Missouri with Maine: the latter was originally a part of Massachusetts and could form another free state. Other provisions banned slavery in the rest of the Louisiana Territory north of the Arkansas-Missouri border. The compromise was a fragile thing, and the controversy was only temporarily silenced—"like a firebell in the night," in Jefferson's words.

The Missouri compromise was repealed in 1854 by the Kansas-Nebraska Act, which provided for letting the residents decide the issue for themselves by popular vote. This was advocated as a peaceful solution. But since most of the land was not yet settled, it resulted in a bloody struggle for physical possession of the territory. In 1857, even popular sovereignty was threatened by the Dred Scott decision, in which Chief Justice Taney, in a digression, said that Congress (and, by implication, a territorial legislature)

Chief Justice Taney: A judicial digression. *(Wide World Photos.)*

could not exclude slavery from a territory. It was a deprivation of property "without due process of law [*Dred Scott v. Sanford*, 19 Howard 393]." When Abraham Lincoln ran for President in 1860 on a platform of restoring the Missouri compromise, he was less concerned with the rights of blacks than with preserving the Union. Even the Emancipation Proclamation, two years later, was a short-term political and propaganda weapon. It applied only to slaves in areas controlled by the Confederacy. Since the Union was, by definition, powerless to enforce it, it freed no slaves immediately. It did, however, clearly establish abolition of slavery as a goal of the war. Meanwhile, blacks in the border states of the Union remained in bondage.

Segregation

When the South lost the war and before Reconstruction could begin, Southern legislatures passed "black codes" to control the freed slaves and deny them civil rights. Outraged Republicans, firmly in control of Congress, passed the Thirteenth, Fourteenth, and Fifteenth Amendments. But their mood was not long sustained. Reconstruction ended with the compromise in 1877 over the contested Hayes-Tilden election (Vann Woodward, 1956) of 1876. Southern Democrats supported Republican Hayes in return for the withdrawal of Federal troops from the South. White conservatives controlled the South; and, while they did not go back at once to the black codes, the stage was set for the enactment of the Jim Crow segregation laws of the 1890s. The last, weak blow for freedom in that period was the Civil Rights Act of 1875. It provided that blacks should have the equal use of public accommodations, including transportation, inns, theaters, and amusement places. But, like other civil rights acts of the period (passed in 1866, 1870, and 1871), it lacked an effective enforcement mechanism. There was no provision for educating the former slave class. A promise of economic help through "forty acres and a mule" went unfulfilled. The Republican party became discouraged by the difficulty of building the hoped-for Southern apparatus and contented itself with its domination in the North and West, which gave it control of Congress and the White House most of the time. And in the Civil Rights cases (109 U.S. 3) the Supreme Court invalidated the Civil Rights Act on the ground that it covered violations of civil rights by individuals while the Fourteenth Amendment was only a prohibition against state action. "This was another way of saying that the system of 'white supremacy' was mainly beyond federal control, since the Southern social order rested very largely upon private human relationships and not upon state-made sactions [Kelly and Harbison, pp. 491–492]."

The voting rights provisions of the Fifteenth Amendment were quite visibly effective during Reconstruction. It was ratified in 1870; blacks used it; and they were elected to every Southern legislature, the U.S. Senate and House of Representatives, and the governship of Louisiana. But as soon as

Federal troops were withdrawn from the South, voting by blacks became the first target. The measures were swift and effective. In 1896, before Louisiana rewrote the franchise provisions of the state constitution, there were 130,344 blacks registered to vote. After the revision in 1900 only 5,320 were registered. The main vehicle of that day—to be replaced by more imaginative devices later—was the grandfather clause: only those eligible to vote in 1867, their sons, or grandsons could vote. Because of frequent miscegenation, some blacks had grandfathers who voted in 1867 and could prove it. Otherwise, the disfranchisement was nearly complete.

Also in 1896, the Supreme Court ruled against a Louisiana railway traveler who had a black great-grandparent but refused to sit in the section of the train designated "colored." Associate Justice John M. Harlan dissented. "The constitution," he said, "is color blind." That view would take nearly sixty years to prevail. Meanwhile, the Court's decision (*Plessy v. Ferguson*, 163 U.S. 537) was taken to mean that the Constitution would not stand in the way of a state's extension of racial segregation to all sorts of public accomodations, whether publicly or privately operated. The only requirement was that the separate accommodations be equal. The law could recognize a difference in color, the Court said, without having a "tendency to destroy the legal equality of the two races." If segregation stamped blacks as inferior, it was only because "the colored race chooses to put that construction upon it."

Removing the Barriers

Although the separate but equal doctrine was to prevail for more than half a century, the reversal, when it finally came, was not a sudden and unexpected action. When the first major blows were struck, the field had shifted from transportation to education. "This was not accidental," said one observer, British journalist Godfrey Hodgson (1973, p. 36). The foes of segregation "well knew that education was so firmly associated with equality in the public mind that it would be an easier point of attack than, say, public accommodations or housing."

In the early legal challenges to school segregation, the Court sidestepped the constitutional question, denying relief to the black plaintiffs on

We boast of the freedom enjoyed by our people above all other peoples. But it is difficult to reconcile that boast with a state of the law which, practically, puts the brand of servitude and degradation upon a large class of our fellow citizens, our equals before the law. The thin disguise of "equal" accommodations for passengers in the railroad coaches will not mislead anyone, or atone for the wrong this day done.

—John Marshall Harlan, dissenting in *Plessy v. Ferguson,* 1896.

"The Thin Disguise"

narrow technical grounds. The first finding that separate schools are inherently unequal came, in a limited application, in 1936. The paintiff was an applicant to the University of Maryland Law School. The state couldn't afford to maintain separate but equal professional schools, so it offered blacks scholarships to out-of-state schools that would accept them. The lawyers who sat on the Maryland Supreme Court immediately recognized the inequity here. The study and practice of law tends to be specific to a given state. By sending the black out of state, Maryland was denying him a first-hand exposure to the law of his own state, as well as to the professional associations that begin in law school. When he returned home to practice, he would be at a disadvantage (*Pearson v. Murray*, 182 U.S. Atl. 590).

When the U.S. Supreme Court had to face that issue, in a Missouri case two years later, it made the same finding. "The out-of-state tuition system," said Chief Justice Charles Evans Hughes, "does not remove the discrimination [*Missouri ex rel Gaines v. Canada*, 305 U.S. 337]."

The Court did not say, however, that separate law schools for blacks within the state would not be acceptable. Therefore six states, including Missouri, tried it. When the Court reached that question in a Texas case in 1950, it said, unanimously, that a separate black law school at the University of Texas was obviously unequal. "It is difficult to believe that one who had a free choice between these law schools would consider the question close," said Chief Justice Fred M. Vinson (*Sweatt v. Painter*, 339 U.S. 629). On the same day, the Court found that separation was inherently unequal for a black graduate student at the University of Oklahoma. This student was allowed to attend the same classes and eat at the same cafeteria as whites, but he had to sit in a special section of the classroom marked "reserved for Colored" and eat at a special table. Education, said Chief Justice Vinson, involves more than reading books and hearing lectures. The Oklahoma restraints impaired the black student's "ability to study, to engage in discussions, and exchange views with other students."

Linda Brown at Sumner School, 1954: Separate was not equal. (*Carl Iwasaki, Time-Life.*)

The Brown *Case*

The time was now ripe for a frontal attack on the legal structure of segregation. The National Association for the Advancement of Colored People, guided by its general counsel, Thurgood Marshall (who later became the first black Supreme Court justice), led a number of cases toward the Supreme Court. Five reached it at the same time. They were based on different facts and different local conditions but shared one common contention: separate was not equal. The Court considered them together. *Brown v. Board of Education* covered the Fourteenth Amendment argument raised in Kansas, South Carolina, Virginia, and Delaware. *Bolling v. Sharpe* dealt with the same questions under the Fifth Amendment in the District of Columbia (347 U.S. 483, 497). Linda Brown was an eight-year-old who rode a bus twenty blocks to an all-black school when her parents first challenged Topeka segregation in 1951. Her home was only four blocks from all-white Sumner Elementary School. But the two schools were basically equal in physical facilities and qualifications of teachers. A sympathetic federal district court in Topeka agreed that the mere fact of segregation had a detrimental effect on school children, but said it was bound by the precedent of *Plessy*. On May 17, 1954, the Court reversed that precedent. Said black historian Louis Lomax (1962):

> It would be impossible for a white person to understand what happened within black breasts on that Monday. An ardent segregationist has called it "Black Monday." He was so right, but for reasons other than the ones he advances: that was the day we won; the day we took the white man's laws and won our case before an all-white Supreme Court with a Negro lawyer, Thurgood Marshall . . . and we were proud [p. 84].

Chief Justice Earl Warren noted the difficulty of guessing what the framers of the Fourteenth Amendment had in mind with respect to education. Free public schools had not yet been widely established in the South. For blacks, there was virtually no education. "In approaching this problem," he said, "we cannot turn the clock back to 1868 when the Amendment was adopted, or even to 1896 when *Plessy v. Ferguson* was written. We must consider public education in the light of its full development and its present place in American life throughout the Nation."

Warren quoted, with approval, the finding of the lower federal court in Kansas that segregation per se had a detrimental effect on blacks.

> "The impact is greater when it has the sanction of the law," that court had said, ". . . the policy of separating the races is usually interpreted as denoting the inferiority of the Negro group. A sense of inferiority affects the motivation of a child to learn. Segregation with the sanction of law, therefore, has a tendency to retard the educational and mental development of Negro children and to deprive them of some of the benefits they would receive in a racially integrated school system."

Added Warren:

> Whatever may have been the extent of psychological knowledge at the time of *Plessy v. Ferguson*, this finding is amply supported by modern authority. Any language in *Plessy v. Ferguson* contrary to this finding is rejected. We conclude that in the field of public education, the doctrine of "separate but equal" has no place. Separate educational facilities are inherently unequal.

The Court then waited a year to announce its specific decree. After further hearings, it rejected Marshall's plea for "immediacy" and instead ordered desegregation "with all deliberate speed." Linda Brown went to Sumner school and won a scholarship to college. But in the South, there

Thurgood Marshall: The time was ripe. *(Wide World Photos.)*

was trouble. The decision opened a long period of Southern maneuvering and evasion. State legislatures passed "interposition" resolutions which sought to invoke the old doctrine of dual federalism. School boards adopted pupil assignment schemes which gave authorities maximum leeway to keep blacks out of white schools under the pretense of nonracial qualifications, such as aptitude, achievement, health, moral character, and residence. Virginia Governor J. Lindsay Almond, who as attorney general was a defense attorney in the Virginia companion case, launched a "massive resistance" program whose ultimate weapon was to close the schools. And that's what they did in Prince Edward County. After five years of legal battles, the Supreme Court found the Virginia law discriminatory in purpose and ordered the schools reopened (Smith, 1965).

The Court frequently expressed impatience with the pace of desegregation as the years went by and finally abandoned the all-deliberate-speed test. In 1968, it rejected a school board plan to let parents decide where to send their children as "intolerable" buck passing. "The burden on a school board today is to come forward with a plan that promises realistically to work and that promises realistically to work now," the opinion said (*Green v. County Board of New Kent County*, 391 U.S. 430).

Southern hopes that the Burger Court would turn back the clock proved to be without foundation. In 1971, the court rejected an attempt by the North Carolina state legislature to prevent local school boards from busing students on the basis of race to create racial balance in the schools. At the same time, it upheld the efforts of the school board in Charlotte to achieve racial balance by busing (*North Carolina State Board of Education v. Swann*, 28 L. Ed. 2d 586; *Swann v. Charlotte-Mecklenburg County Board of Education*, 28 L. Ed. 2d 554).

The Court's impatience was slow to develop, considering the open and flagrant nature of Southern resistance. In Arkansas, in 1957, Governor Orval Faubus called out the National Guard to prevent desegregation. President Eisenhower had to federalize the Guard and call in the regular Army to enforce the court order. President Kennedy sent troops to the University of Mississippi in 1962; and in 1963 Governor George Wallace of Alabama stood in the schoolhouse door in a confrontation with Deputy Attorney General Nicholas Katzenbach to keep two blacks out of the state university. Again, the National Guard was federalized, and Wallace backed down.

The De Facto Problem

Then, slowly, came the realization that there were also segregation problems in the North and that they were much more subtle. There were no laws requiring segregation, no transparent legalistic ploys, no schoolyard confrontations. And yet the North was segregated too. It was caused by

Wallace at the Schoolhouse:
Testing the Court's patience.
(Steve Shapiro, Black Star.)

residential patterns. Blacks moving up from the South looked for the
cheapest housing, which tended to be in the older sections of the central
city. These areas rapidly became ghettoes for blacks and soon were no
longer cheap as slumlords raised rents. As blacks spread out from the core,
whites fled to the suburbs. The result was all-black schools in the center of
the city, all-white schools in the fringes and suburbs. By 1965, Washington,
D.C., Cleveland, Philadelphia, Baltimore, Detroit, and other major cities
had black majorities in their school populations.

The *Brown* decision held that segregation imposed by law—de jure
segregation—was unconstitutional. Now the question of segregation imposed by other circumstances—de facto segregation—was raised. The first
hint that this, too, might be unconstitutional came in a New Rochelle, New
York, case. The school board there gerrymandered the attendance zones to
follow shifting residential patterns in order to keep blacks in predominately
black schools. A federal district court ruled that this practice was as illegal as
formal segregation (*Taylor v. Board of Education*, 191 F. Supp. 181, 1961).

Achieving Equality

The evidence in the *Brown* case included testimony by psychologists and
sociologists that segregation by law had a damaging effect on the child. By
the latter half of the 1960s, evidence began to accumulate that segregation
of any kind was harmful; this finding began to influence legislative and
judicial thinking. A massive study of school facilities and achievement,

commissioned by Congress to document the inequality of school facilities, turned up two very surprising findings. The differences between black and white school facilities were not nearly as great as had been supposed; and, even more surprisingly, school factors did not make much difference in pupil achievement, except for one: the social class climate of the school. Lower-class students in middle-class schools did better than lower-class students in lower-class schools. Since race and social class were closely related, it seemed to follow that a positive program of integration, not mere elimination of legally imposed segregation, was the only road to equality of educational opportunity (Mosteller and Moynihan, 1972).

That report, *Equality of Educational Opportunity* (also known as the Coleman report after its senior author, James S. Coleman), was published in 1966. In 1967, the U.S. Commission on Civil Rghts published its own analysis of the Coleman data, *Racial Isolation in the Public Schools*, in which it recommended that alternatives be found to the neighborhood school so that residence-based school segregation could be overcome. While the Supreme Court avoided facing the problem of de facto segregation directly, some lower courts began to take notice of the new findings. Federal courts in Massachusetts, Michigan, and Washington, D.C., ruled that de facto segregation violates the due process and equal protection guarantees of the Constitution.

This action raised new complications. In a city with a predominantly black school population, it is impossible to overcome segregation imposed by residential patterns without consolidation or cooperation among different political jurisdictions. In the District of Columbia, pupils would have to be bused in and out of neighboring Maryland and Virginia. The judge in that case said he had no authority to create such an area-wide school system. This judicial restraint was supported by the Supreme Court in a case involving Detroit schools in 1974. The district court in 1972 had ordered the Detroit school board to merge with fifty-three white suburban districts outside the city limits and to bus pupils across school lines. The Supreme Court reversed this decision in 1974 when it ruled that the Detroit plan was constitutionally improper. The Court allowed that illegal segregation had been proved to exist within Detroit, but not among the suburban districts, which prompted Chief Justice Warren Burger to write in his majority opinion: "Disparate treatment of white and Negro students occurred within the Detroit school system, and not elsewhere, and on this record the remedy must be limited to that system [*Milligan v. Bradley*, 418 U.S. 717]." This decision left unresolved the question of whether cross-district busing might be mandated where both innercity and suburban school districts engaged in illegal segregation schemes.

Some Southern school boards voluntarily adopted busing programs, reasoning that planned racial balance would at least stabilize their situation and spread the burden of integration equally. But there was bitter opposition in the North to busing. Whites could now sympathize with the parents of Linda Brown for not wanting their child barred from a nearby school to be bused to a more distant, segregated one. In an ironic parallel, whites found it difficult to accept busing from nearby de facto segregated schools to distant integrated schools. Finally, educators and social scientists began to wonder if too much was being asked of the schools. The Coleman data and related studies raised the question of whether education tended to be an equalizing force or whether it was merely a means of certifying social status to which children were already born. If the main determinants of success are family and social factors, then the civil rights battle could be reaching a point of diminishing returns where schools are concerned (Lipset, 1972).

Public Accommodations

The civil rights struggle has been most successful in dealing with short-term problems: specific categories of discrimination that can be attacked one at a time. And much of the civil rights struggle for blacks has followed such an incremental strategy. While the main thrust was on education, developments in other areas followed close behind.

The public accommodations struggle began only a year after the *Brown* decision. Where facilities were publicly owned, legal victories came easily. Segregation was banned in public housing in 1955 (*Detroit Housing Commission v. Lewis*, 226 F. 2d 180). Segregated public recreation facilities were outlawed in the same year (*Baltimore v. Dawson*, 350 U.S. 877; *Holmes v. Atlanta*, 350 U.S. 879). Intrastate buses were covered in 1956 (*Gayle v. Browder*, 352 U.S. 903). But enforcement was not always available, and there remained the problem of facilities which were open to the public but under private ownership. In 1955, Rev. Martin Luther King, Jr., led a boycott against the segregated buses in Montgomery, Alabama. It took two years, many arrests, and thousands of sore feet, but it was successful; blacks were allowed to ride in the front of the bus. King's tactics had a theoretical base in the nonviolent philosophies of Gandhi and Henry David Thoreau. Under an unjust government, Thoreau had said, "the true place for a just man is . . . a prison [1950, p. 646]." The litigation strategy of the NAACP began to yield to the civil-disobedience strategy of the Congress of Racial Equality (CORE) and the Student Nonviolent Coordinating Committee (SNCC). Under their leadership, blacks and whites began to assert a right to nonsegregated accommodations. They sat in at lunch counters until they were either served or hauled off to jail. They held wade-ins at public beaches. Sometimes they succeeded, and sometimes they met massive resistance. In most cases, they were convicted of criminal trespass, and this opened the door to a new legal argument for opening privately owned facilities to blacks.

The Supreme Court had ruled in 1948 that the power of the state could not be used to enforce a real estate contract in which the buyer agreed

Riding in the Front of the Bus: Martin Luther King, Jr., and Ralph Abernathy in 1956. *(Wide World Photos.)*

never to convey the property to a member of a minority group (*Shelley v. Kraemer*, 334 U.S. 1). While this decision did not make such covenants illegal, it did make them impossible to carry out. Some of the sit-in cases proceeded toward the Supreme Court, framed with a parallel argument: By arresting blacks for sitting at a white-only lunch counter, the state was aiding private discrimination and denying the blacks equal protection of the laws.

The legal argument was weak, since the discriminatory action was private in the case of the lunch counters. But the moral momentum of the time was on the side of the blacks. A decision sustaining the convictions of the demonstrators might have damaged the civil rights movement and ruined whatever confidence blacks had in the legal system. Political leaders began to see that it was too formidable a job for the judicial branch alone. Accordingly, President Kennedy submitted to Congress a bill to outlaw racial segregation in public accommodations. It also had provisions against discrimination in jobs, housing, and voting. The legal authority was based on the power of Congress to regulate interstate commerce, and the bill was passed on July 2, 1964. The Supreme Court upheld it almost immediately (*Katzenback v. McClung*, 379 U.S. 294), circumventing the limitations set in the civil rights cases of 1883. Ollie McClung, the proprietor of Ollie's Barbecue in Birmingham, had no out-of-state customers that he knew about. But much of the meat he barbecued came from non-Alabama herds, and so he was involved in interstate commerce. And the civil rights movement was bolstered by the fact that all three branches of the national government had participated in the historic action (Cox, 1968).

Voting

Of all the efforts on behalf of black civil rights, the drive for voting rights met the least resistance after the *Brown* case heightened consciousness of black problems. In 1957, Congress passed the first of the modern series of civil rights acts. It created the Civil Rights Commission and gave it subpoena powers to investigate voting rights violations and report them to the President and Congress; established the Civil Rights Division of the Department of Justice to enforce the new law; empowered the Attorney General to seek injunctions against state officials who denied voting rights to blacks; and it reaffirmed the right of a citizen to get injunctive relief on his own.

Though moderate steps when compared to later action, they were appropriate weapons against the patterns of administrative delay and purposive fumbling which had become the chief ways of keeping blacks from registering. After the grandfather clause was ruled illegal in 1915, Southern states resorted to a series of legal stratagems to keep blacks from the polls. The most effective, until it was finally struck down in 1944, was the white primary. In the one-party South, the only important elections were the party primaries. Since a party was a private organization, it could admit whom it pleased to membership, and so Democratic party organizations in the South passed regulations denying membership to blacks. The Court toyed with this mechanism in a long series of cases starting in 1927 before finally ruling in 1944 in *Smith v. Allwright*, 321 U.S. 649, that the Democratic party had such an essential role in the electoral process that it was acting as the agent of the state and could therefore not deny membership to blacks without violating the Fifteenth Amendment. That helped. The NAACP estimated that black voting participation increased from one million in the 1940 presidential election to three million in 1948.

There remained barriers which were not inherently discriminatory but could be administered in a discriminatory way—which made anything but a piecemeal, case-by-case attack very difficult. The poll tax and the literacy test were the main devices. A sample question from the Alabama literacy test: "If it were proposed to join Alabama and Mississippi to form one state, what groups would have to vote approval in order for this to be done?" To be effective against only blacks, it had, of course, to be administered selectively. The principle of selective enforcement could also be applied to other aspects of the registration process: limiting the times for registration to inconvenient periods, purposive clerical errors, unreasonable demands for proof of age or residence. Threats of physical or economic reprisal were not uncommon.

A Heavier Weapon

It soon became apparent that the 1957 Act was too light a weapon, and so it was supplemented by the Civil Rights Act of 1960. The new act gave courts the authority to appoint referees to assist persons to register and vote. It provided for injunctive relief to be sought on a wholesale basis when a "pattern or practice" of discrimination could be proved.

In the Civil Rights Act of 1964, the increasing subtlety of discriminatory practices was countered by a provision barring unequal application of voting requirements. And the effectiveness of the literacy test as a barrier to blacks was greatly weakened by establishing a sixth grade education as presumptive evidence of literacy—meaning that the burden to rebut it was placed on the state. Meanwhile, the poll tax was eliminated as a voting requirement in federal elections by the Twenty-fourth Amendment in 1964 and in state elections by a Supreme Court ruling in 1966 (*Harper v. Virginia Board of Elections*, 383 U.S. 663).

But the most comprehensive action since the Fifteenth Amendment came the next year in the Voting Rights Act of 1965, passed after the brutal repression of demonstrators petitioning for the right to vote in Selma, Alabama. It was designed to turn the federal government around from passive protector of voting rights to active battler. Under its provisions, the Attorney General could appoint a federal examiner to take over the registration procedure in any state which used a literacy or related qualifying test and where voting participation was markedly low. The latter condition was met if fewer than 50 percent of the voting age residents in the state were registered or had voted in 1964. This applied to seven deep-South states: Alabama, Georgia, Louisiana, Mississippi, North Carolina, South Carolina, and Virginia. It also made interference with voting rights a federal crime. States were barred from exercising the white officeholder's seemingly limitless ingenuity to invent ways to circumvent these measures; any new voter qualification laws would have to be approved by the Federal District Court for the District of Columbia.

That act, with its aggressive machinery, was scheduled to expire in 1970, but Congress extended it for another five years over the opposition of the Nixon administration. The Department of Justice estimated in 1970 that 900,852 blacks had been registered in Alabama, Georgia, Louisiana, Mississippi, and the Carolinas under the 1965 Act. That was almost as many as had been registered in those states in the entire century before (*Congressional Quarterly*, 1971). There was not, however, a corresponding dramatic increase in black voting. According to Bureau of the Census surveys, black voter participation in the South increased only from 33 percent in 1966 to 37 percent in 1970. Among white Southerners of voting age, participation was 45 percent in 1966 and 46 percent in 1970 (Department of Commerce, 1971). The long tradition of nonvoting was still to be overcome.

Jobs and Housing

Efforts were made to use the power of the federal government to end racial discrimination in employment practices as early as the Franklin Roosevelt administration when A. Philip Randolph threatened to hold a massive march on Washington to protest segregation in defense industries. Roosevelt lifted barriers to black employment by executive order. But the first major step came when Congress added a fair-employment provision to the 1964 Civil Rights Act. This provision makes it illegal to deprive anyone of equal employment opportunity on account of race, color, religion, sex, or national origin. The Equal Employment Opportunity Commission was established to investigate complaints. Though not directed specifically at blacks, the Manpower and Development Training Act of 1962 and the Economic Opportunity Act of 1964 were aimed at improving job opportunities for all economically disadvantaged groups.

National open housing legislation was first requested by President Johnson in 1966 and enacted in 1968 to take effect in 1970. It barred discrimination in the sale or rental of most housing; single-family homes sold without a broker, and owner-occupied dwellings with up to four rental units were exempted. Enforcement was left to private civil actions in the courts, except that the Attorney General could sue in cases where there was a pattern or practice of discrimination.

Enforcement: The Unkept Promise

By the 1970s, it had become apparent that the impressive array of legal tools put together in the 1960s was not enough to solve the problem of systematic discrimination against blacks. Much of the legislative weaponry was directed at de jure segregation in the South. The de facto segregation and discrimination problems in the North were less susceptible to legislative intervention.

Moreover, the enforcement of the new cluster of laws was less than vigorous. The Rev. Theodore M. Hesburgh, appointed chairman of the Commission on Civil Rights by President Nixon, began criticizing the lethargic enforcement in a series of annual reports beginning in 1970. His efforts did little good. In the last report covering Hesburgh's tenure, issued in January 1973, two months after his resignation, the commission said that the situation was still "dismayingly similar" to the one that had aroused its initial criticism. The executive branch was not doing its job:

> The enforcement failure was the result, to a large extent, of placing the responsibility for ensuring racial and ethnic justice upon a massive Federal bureaucracy which for years had been an integral part of a discriminatory system. Not only did the bureaucrats resist civil rights goals; they often viewed any meaningful effort to pursue them to be against their particular program's self interest.

Many agency officials genuinely believed they would incur the wrath of powerful members of Congress or lobbyists—and thereby jeopardize their other programs—if they actively attended to civil rights concerns. Moreover, since nonenforcement was an accepted mode of behavior, any official who sought to enforce civil rights laws with the same zeal applied to other statutes ran the risk of being branded as an activist, a visionary, or a troublemaker. Regrettably, there were few countervailing pressures [U.S. Commission on Civil Rights, pp. 2–3].

With its legislative victories, the black civil rights movement lost its momentum. The urban riots between 1965 and 1968 crystalized some of the more extreme forms of black nationalism and contributed to a splintering of the movement. CORE and SNCC parted company with their white liberal supporters. Advocates of violent reform enjoyed a brief period of media attention and then faded from view. Some blacks began to question the original goal of integration and to view it instead as a form of cooptation. "We cannot predict what the ultimate significance of these separatist impulses within the black community will be," said Angus Campbell (1971), whose Institute for Social Research at the University of Michigan has been monitoring long-term trends in racial attitudes. "They undoubtedly have influence and it may be a growing influence [p. 161]."

Other ethnic minorities have passed through a militant stage as they gained middle-class status. "We may ask," said Campbell, "whether the black population of this country will in its turn pass beyond militancy and achieve a secure sense of American identity. Even if one takes the uncritical view that the black minority will follow the pattern of the others, it seems clear that it will not be an easy passage . . . [pp. 161–162]."

PARALLELS TO THE BLACK EXPERIENCE

Voting Rights for the Young

Parallels to the black struggle can be seen in the problems of an extensive variety of other groups. Young people, eighteen to twenty years old, could be taxed and drafted but were not allowed to vote in most states until the Voting Rights Act of 1970 gave them the vote in national elections. The Twenty-sixth Amendment extended this franchise to state and local elections. Even then, they faced some of the same registration problems incurred by blacks in the South. These problems were particularly acute in college towns where the potential student vote was large enough to control the local government. And, as in the case of blacks, the exercise of the newly won right was disappointing. Fewer than half of the persons in the eighteen-to-twenty age group actually voted in the 1972 presidential election.

Earnings Comparison of Males and Females Aged 25–64
Working a Full Year in 1969

INCOME	MALES	FEMALES*
0–$2,999	4.2%	18.3%
$3,000–$5,999	15.2	49.6
$6,000–$9,999	40.9	27
$10,000–$14,999	26.2	4
$15,000 or more	13.5	1
Median	$10,150	$4,873

*Total is less than 100% because of rounding.
Source: 1970 Census.

Equal Rights for Women

In 1972, forty-nine years after it was first introduced, a constitutional amendment guaranteeing equal rights for women—and men—was passed by Congress. By the end of 1974, 33 states had ratified it. Although Congress specified that the states would have seven years to approve it, no amendment has ever been adopted after failing to gain the necessary three-fourths of the states within two years.

Its language is simple: "Equality of rights under the law shall not be denied or abridged by the United States or by any state on account of sex." Although laws already in effect require equal pay for equal work and prohibit job discrimination by sex, a number of inequities remain which would be reached by the amendment. It would remove barriers which keep women from gaining admission to some publicly supported schools and colleges, from getting credit and transacting business in their own names when married. It would also make them equally subject to the draft and eliminate the one-sided obligation for family support which compels men to bear the main burden of alimony and child support in divorce cases. Proponents consider it an important psychological step in granting new dignity to women while conceding that—as the case of blacks has illustrated—the law can have only a limited effect on long-established social patterns of discrimination.

Native Americans

Although American Indians were never the victims of a formal system of slavery, their deprivation of civil rights has been almost as flagrant. And their legal standing has been even slower to improve than that of blacks. The Fourteenth Amendment granted citizenship to all persons born in the United States after 1868, and the Fifteenth Amendment removed race restrictions on voting rights after 1870. But these measures were never interpreted as applying to Indians. Their citizenship rights were not recognized until a special act of Congress in 1924. Several states continued to deny them the right to vote until the 1950s.

The historic conflict, of course, was over the ownership of land—considered a free good, like air and water, in the Indian culture. Although there were negotiations and treaties, the ultimate resolution was for the Indians to be removed by physical force from whatever territory the white man wanted to settle and was able to control. The Indian Removal Act of 1830 made it legal.

Throughout the past century and a half, government policy has wavered between assimilation and separation of the Indian minority. Both were applied to the Indian's disadvantage. Assimilation into the melting pot of the larger society forced him to give up his traditional fishing and hunting in favor of unfamiliar means of livelihood and to lose his distinctive culture, life style, and political forms. It did, however, enable whites to claim lands occupied by Indians. The General Allotment Act of 1887 encouraged assimilation by allowing individual Indians to claim specific holdings in their collective territory and then dispose of them.

In 1934, the Indian Reorganization Act provided a change to a policy of enlightened separation. Indian land holdings were allowed to increase, tribal organizations and customs were recognized and reinforced, and some economic help was extended. Recent policy has emphasized separation, except for a brief return to assimilation during the Eisenhower administration. Either way, the Indians were losers, because there was no easy way to restore even a vestige of their ancient land and treaty claims.

Measuring the Gap

There are many different ways to define progress in civil rights: by changes in attitudes, by the replacement of old social customs with new ones, by success in achieving legislative goals, and by economic gains. The latter is the most carefully watched barometer of social change. The data are hard, the things measured are meaningful, and enough facts exist to make comparisons among groups and across time. By the economic standard, the box score indicates that the various civil rights movements still have a good deal to overcome. For minority groups, direct economic aid may be the only viable strategy left, but whether the political climate of the United States in the 1970s can make that possible remains an open question. We shall deal more fully with that subject in Chapter 15.

SUGGESTED READINGS

Casper, Jonathan. *The Politics of Civil Liberties.* New York: Harper & Row, 1972. A short study on civil liberties, covering theoretical issues as well as the historical dimension.

Deloria, Vine. *Custer Died for Your Sins.* New York: Avon, 1970. A historical treatment of Indians and their fight for civil rights.

Franklin, John Hope. *From Slavery to Freedom.* 3rd ed. New York: Knopf; 1967. A classic study of the history of the blacks in America, written by a prominent black historian.

Kelly, Alfred H., and Winifred Harbison. *The American Constitution: Its Origins and Development.* New York: Norton, 1963. An excellent history of constitutional developments, with great attention to the issues of civil rights and liberties.

Krislov, Samuel. *The Supreme Court and Political Freedom.* New York: Free Press, 1968. A study of the activities of the Supreme Court in respect to the major cases involving the right of free speech.

Roche, John P. *Courts and Rights: The American Judiciary in Action.* New York: Random House, 1961. An introduction to and history of the role of the courts in maintaining civil rights and civil liberties.

Westin, Alan F. *Privacy and Freedom.* New York: Atheneum, 1968. A current study of the new dangers posed to individual privacy by the technological developments in electronic surveillance.

Chapter 3

Federalism: Linking National, State, and Local Governments

THE THEORY OF FEDERALISM

Organizing a Large Republic

When the proposed new Constitution was debated, the name of Montesquieu kept coming up. A French lawyer and social observer, Baron de la Bride et de Montesquieu was widely respected for the thoroughness of his attempts to apply scientific method to the study of society. "He alone," said John Herman Randall, Jr. (1940), "realized that human societies are exceedingly complex, and that what suits one set of conditions will by no means satisfy another. He alone was impressed by the necessity of scholarly historical investigation to suggest real principles [p. 319]." Although other thinkers formed the ideology of the French and American revolutions, it was to Montesquieu that practical men turned for guidance when the fighting was over and it was time for specific action.

In New York, Montesquieu was quoted by opponents of the Constitution on the problem of arriving at the ideal size for a government. "If a republic be small," he had written (1748), "it is destroyed by a foreign force; if it be large, it is ruined by internal imperfection [p. 126]." The problem was to maintain diversity and local control while still presenting a united front to the world outside. New York opponents of the Constitution thought their state struck about the right balance in size and that they could therefore do better as a separate republic. Alexander Hamilton responded with an effective debating ploy: he quoted Montesquieu back at them. Although Montesquieu's best-known contribution to American political thought was the principle of separation of powers, he had, Hamilton found, also anticipated the federal system by recommending that a group of small states form a larger association to which they would yield a limited amount of their power. "As this government is composed of small republics," says Montesquieu in the quotation used by Hamilton while writing for the *Independent Journal* (Lodge, 1888), "it enjoys the internal happiness of each; and with respect to its external situation, it is possessed, by means of the association, of all the advantages of large monarchies [p. 49]."

The Founding Fathers' application of that principle turned out to be their creative tour de force. Although the *unitary* system of organization was generally taken for granted in their day, they saw that there are at least two other possibilities. These three methods of organization are possible regardless of whether the form of government is a dictatorship, a democracy, or something in between. In a unitary system, all authority pyramids to a single central source which controls all the territory and political subdivisions within its boundaries. This form of organization remains the most common today. Great Britain, Italy, Japan, and France are examples.

The Founding Fathers already had experience with a second possibility: a *confederate* system, which may be defined as a league of sovereign states whose members delegate a limited range of powers to the central authority but retain their own autonomy. The United Nations is a confederation. Other examples in history are the League of Nations, the Confederate States of America, and, of course, the United States under the Articles of Confederation.

The Convention of 1787 designed something in between, unitary in some respects, confederate in others. We call it a federal system. For a federal system to be distinct from the other two basic forms, three conditions must be present:

Layers of Government. At least two levels of government must rule the same territory and the same people.

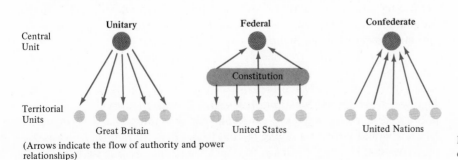

(Arrows indicate the flow of authority and power relationships)

Figure 3–1 Systems of Government Organization

Autonomy in Each Layer. Each of the levels must be autonomous in some specific way, that is, free from interference from the other levels in at least one clearly defined area.

Guarantees. To keep one layer from eventually dominating another, a way must be provided to guarantee this autonomy for each level of government.

"Publius" and the Federalist Papers

When Hamilton invoked the name of Montesquieu in support of federalism, he was taking part in a concerted propaganda campaign to win over the state of New York. A by-product of this campaign was the development of a carefully reasoned body of political theory to explain the Constitution and the operation of the federal system as intended by the framers. The newspaper articles were written by Hamilton, James Madison, and John Jay and later collected as a series of papers titled simply *The Federalist*. Each writer used the pen name of "Publius," but authorship of most of the papers is known. Although their points are sometimes conflicting, they remain a primary source for discovering what the Founders had in mind. One of their ardent readers, for example, was John Marshall, perhaps the most influential Chief Justice of the Supreme Court, who cited them in some of the decisions which set the direction of the new government.

In Madison's contributions to *The Federalist*, there is eloquent recognition of the fact that majority rule does not wash away all the problems of government. We now know that situations sometimes exist in which a decision by majority rule is mathematically impossible—for example, when there are three alternatives from which to choose and three groups of voters equal in size, each of which has a different ordering of preferences. This paradox may not have occurred to the political theorists of the eighteenth century, but they did recognize another danger in overreliance on majority rule: that a tyranny of the majority is as much to be feared and guarded against as other forms of oppression. Madison noted that organized society is primarily a contest among factions of men organized in groups to pursue common self-interests. "It is in vain to say that enlightened statesmen will be able to adjust these clashing interests and render them all subservient to the public good," he said in *The Federalist*, No. 10. "Enlightened statesmen will not always be at the helm."

The Benefits of Bigness and Diversity

Madison's—and the Constitution's—remedy was to provide an *extended* political society, so vast and far-flung that the number and diversity of factions would prevent any one faction from gaining a majority. It was too much to expect human virtue to check vice, but in a system of many different interests and many different ways of seeking power, vice could check vice. A rage for any "improper or wicked project" would "be less apt to pervade the whole body of the Union than a particular member of it . . . such a malady is more likely to taint a particular county or district than an entire state."

And Hamilton, who was more of a centrist, argued in *The Federalist*, No. 9, that the very size of the union would provide both internal and external security. It would have the resources to defend itself from enemies abroad and to put down the insurrections of domestic factions.

In *The Federalist*, No. 51, Madison noted further barriers against abuses by the popular majority in the system of checks and balances: ". . . so contriving the interior structure of the government as that its several constituent parts may, by their mutual relations, be the means of keeping each other in their proper places." Because the different branches of government would tend to serve different constituencies, it would be possible to "guard one part of the society against the injustice of the other part."

The internal checks, together with the federal principle, were designed to consolidate divergent interests, yet preserve the divergencies. The task of Constitution writing was to specify the relationships up to a point and, beyond that point, leave some flexibility as a hedge against changing situations and changing power relationships. The process of change and adjustment is still going on, as the different levels of government compete and change and form new relations with one another.

FEDERALISM AS PROCESS

To Concentrate or to Disperse?

One way to look at the process is to watch the ebbs and flows of centrism. The question of concentration or dispersion of power was a major preoccupation of the Constitution writers, and it continues to be a major preoccupation of policymakers today. As in 1787, which side one joins tends to be a function of how his specific interests of the moment are affected. One general rule has been that sections whose value systems deviate from those of the rest of the country tend to favor the side of decentralization in the hope of gaining protection for their deviant values. The relationship of the South to its black population has been a case in point throughout the life of the Republic. Federalism did not create the race issue, but the race issue has had a good deal to do with creating federalism. The South's vocal defenders of federalism have used it to promote states' rights. They have ranged from John C. Calhoun with his elegant theory of the concurrent majority (1851), which held that democratic decisions should be made only with the concurrence of all major segments of society, to George C. Wallace and his regionally based candidacies for the Presidency. Both held that, lacking unanimity among major groups, a decision should not bind the group whose interest it violates. For a more ephemeral example of situational factors affecting ideology, consider this reaction of the lobbyist for the U.S. Conference of Mayors to the revenue-sharing features of President Nixon's "New Federalism": "The mayors are big for this if it has money in it. But if it is to be underfunded, they're scared to death of it [Clark, 1972, p. 1912]."

The Courts and Federal Supremacy

One of the first and most important steps in the continuing process of defining federalism was the passage of the Judiciary Act of 1789. It created the basic court structure which the federal government has today: district courts with original jurisdiction in most cases, circuit courts of appeals, and one Supreme Court. But it was Section 25 of the act that secured the cornerstone of national sovereignty. This section provided for appeals to be taken to the United States Supreme Court from the highest state courts whenever the state court did one of three things: ruled against the constitutionality of a federal treaty or law, upheld a state law which had been challenged as contrary to federal law or the Constitution, or ruled against a right or privilege claimed under federal law or the Constitution. In other words, the Supreme Court would have the last word whenever state judges failed to yield to the supremacy of the national government as provided by Article VI—the supremacy clause. This closed an ambiguity left by the Constititional Convention and foreclosed the possibility that the Constitution would have as many different interpretations as there were states. The first case in which a state law was declared unconstitutional was *Fletcher v. Peck* (6 Cranch 87) in 1819. An attempt by the Georgia legislature to undo a fraud by its predecessor by repealing a large grant of land was judged to be an impairment of contract and invalid under Article I, Section 10.

The Bill of Rights was anticentrist in its effect. Although the ten amendments made no actual changes in the state-federal power relationship, they made explicit what had already been implied or generally taken for granted. All limit the national government and not the states. The Tenth Amendment provides the explicit statement of states rights: "The powers not delegated to the United States by the Constitution, nor prohibited by it to the States, are reserved to the States respectively, or to the people." The principle that the Bill of Rights limits only federal action and not state acts was established by the Court in 1833 in *Barron v. Baltimore* (7 Peters 243). Barron was a wharf owner who was left high and dry when a city-street-paving project diverted streams that fed his part of the harbor. He claimed that his private property was taken for public use without just compensation in violation of the Fifth Amendment. Chief Justice John Marshall reasoned that since the Constitution was designed to grant powers to the national government, "the limitations on power, if expressed in general terms, are naturally, and, we think, necessarily applicable to the government created by the instrument" and not to state governments. Barron's wharf stayed dry.

Chief Justice Marshall, a Federalist leader from Virginia appointed to the Court by President John Adams in 1801, served for thirty-four years, and wrote many of the landmark opinions which established the early nationalist interpretations of the Constitution. It was Marshall in *Marbury v. Madison* (1 Cranch 137; see Chapter 11) who first asserted the power of the Court to nullify unconstitutional acts of Congress, although the existence of this power had been implied in decisions as early as 1796 and was generally accepted by the legal profession by the time Marshall became Chief Justice.

McCulloch v. Maryland

Marshall's greatest contribution to national sovereignty came in 1819 during the presidency of James Monroe. At issue was the power of Congress to charter the Second Bank of the United States, which it had done in 1816. Largely controlled by the Federalists, the bank began under corrupt management and was blamed for a period of financial depression. Eight states passed laws aimed at restricting it, and the first tested was that of Maryland, which required the bank to pay a heavy annual tax. The cashier of the Baltimore branch, James McCulloch, refused to pay, and Maryland sued him. Because a state was a party, the Supreme Court had original jurisdiction under Article III of the Constitution.

The array of legal talent in *McCulloch v. Maryland* (4 Wheaton 316) was formidable. Daniel Webster was one of the lawyers for the bank. Luther Martin, an Anti-Federalist leader at the Constitutional Convention nearly three decades earlier, was among counsel for Maryland. The arguments turned on two basic questions: whether Congress had the power to establish the bank—a power not explicitly granted in the Constitution—and, if so, whether Maryland had the power to tax it.

The Supreme Court ruled, and Marshall wrote, that the Congress did have the power under Section 18 of Article I, which is now known as "the elastic clause." It empowers Congress "to make all laws which shall be necessary and proper for carrying into execution the foregoing powers and all other powers vested by this Constitution in the government of the United States or in any department or officer thereof." Establishing the bank, Marshall reasoned, was necessary and proper to carrying out the expressly granted powers of taxing, borrowing, and appropriating money to raise and support armies. He summed his test of congressional authority in one sentence: "Let the end be legitimate, let it be within the scope of the Constitution, and all means which are appropriate, which are plainly adapted to that end, which are not prohibited, but consist with the letter and spirit of the Constitution, are constitutional." And Maryland could not tax the bank because, "The power to tax involves the power to destroy." The states could not "retard, impede, burden, or in any manner control the operations of the constitutional laws enacted by Congress."

The Commerce Power

Marshall's other great contribution to congressional authority came with his liberal interpretation of the power to regulate interstate commerce—a line of reasoning which, much later, became greatly extended. This, unlike the bank case, was a popular decision. New York, to encourage development of the steamboat, had given Robert Livingston and Robert Fulton an exclusive right to navigate by steam in New York waters. The case of *Gibbons v. Ogden* (9 Wheaton 1) arose when this monopoly was challenged by a steamboat operator acting under a federal license. Marshall rejected the argument that commerce should be narrowly defined and ruled that the congressional power reaches interstate commerce even when it is carried on within the boundaries of a state. This finding set the stage for swift expansion of steamboat and railroad transportation free of the restraint of state-created monopolies. "The importance of national control of commerce in the rapid economic development of the country," say Kelly and Harbison, "is almost incalculable [1955, p. 296]." Monopolies were unpopular because they stifled economic growth, and the decision removed much of the pressure for a curb on the Court's authority which had resulted from its repeated invalidation of state laws.

Dual Federalism

Marshall's clear-cut statements of national sovereignty were eroded after his death in 1835, and the judicial trend began to move toward states' rights, a concept which became tangled with the defense of slavery. The ensuing conflicts were more than the system could handle. Issues postponed by the writers of the Constitution for the sake of compromise finally could be neither resolved nor postponed any longer, and the Civil War was fought over them. As a result, new rules defining federalism were written into the Constitution: the Thirteenth, Fourteenth, and Fifteenth Amendments. The Thirteenth abolished slavery and the Fifteenth gave blacks the right to vote. The Fourteenth was more complicated. The key words were "No state shall . . . deprive any person of life, liberty, or property, without due process of law; nor deny to any person within its jurisdiction the equal protection of the laws."

This amendment proved to be another illustration of the impotence of legal language, even when embedded in the Constitution. The words above would not overcome the prevailing forces of custom, social pressure, and the power division of the moment. With respect to civil liberties, the

Fourteenth Amendment was a time bomb whose force would not be felt for nearly a century. Meanwhile, another application was found for it.

Beginning with Chief Justice Roger B. Taney, Marshall's successor, the Court gradually embraced the doctrine of "dual federalism." This theory held that the Tenth Amendment had reduced federal supremacy to a condition of coequal sovereignty with the states. Federal power to encroach where states could act was limited; federal powers could not be reconstrued only because of new problems not foreseen by the authors of the Constitution. Taney also used the due-process clause of the Fifth Amendment as a restriction on the federal government from interfering with property rights. The phrase, "due process of law," dates from English law of the fourteenth century and, until the middle of the nineteenth century, was assumed to refer, as its language indicates, to procedural rights rather than to restrictions on the substance of what government could or could not do. Its main application was in criminal cases. The government could not put a person in jail without first following certain procedures, including trial by jury, allowing the accused to hear the evidence against him, and granting right to counsel. These protections were to prevent officeholders from using government power to persecute political enemies. But beginning around 1850, due process began to be invoked as a substantive protection for property rights—even though the question of proper procedures as such was not involved. Chief Justice Taney referred to this novel doctrine in the *Dred Scott* case, saying that due process prohibited the federal government from restricting ownership of property, that is, slaves, in the territories. Federal power was rolled back; Marshall's vision of national sovereignty was to be lost until its rediscovery more than a hundred years after his death.

In the middle of the nineteenth century, the laissez faire economic theory was at its zenith. Adam Smith had published *The Wealth of Nations* in the year of the American Revolution, 1776. But another revolution was already underway. James Watt had constructed his piston steam engine in 1769, and the industrial revolution would soon end the simpler agrarian society envisioned by Smith. But as the process of industrial growth became apparent, especially after the Civil War, the prevailing view was that government should stay out of the way while development of the nation's natural resources proceeded as rapidly as possible.

State legislatures generally agreed with this view until agrarian reformers began to have an impact toward the end of the century. Around 1890, the Court shifted from a constitutionally conservative position of protecting the separate spheres of state and federal power to a more activist stance of protecting industry from regulation by state governments. The legal theory used to deprive the states of some of their police power was substantive due process—but with the argument refreshed and applied to state action through the Fourteenth Amendment. A Nebraska law regulating intrastate freight rates was declared unconstitutional under this theory in 1898 (*Smyth v. Ames,* 169 U.S. 466). The Court did not say the state could not set rates. It said the rates set in this particular case were so low as to be unreasonable and therefore deprived the railroads of property without due process of law.

The fact that there was also a due-process clause applying to federal action in the Fifth Amendment was not lost on corporation lawyers, and the theory was soon applied to a federal statute. In 1908, a federal law barring "yellow dog" contracts in labor negotiations—contracts which keep workers from joining unions—was overturned as a violation of due process (*Adair v. United States,* 208 U.S. 181). In a way, it was a reaffirmation of dual federalism. The Court was holding back legislative power in both the separate state and national spheres. But in doing so, it was assuming for itself a measure of power that had belonged to the state and national legislatures. And it was flashing a green light for the development of great corporate wealth and power.

The Court Turns Around

The Court held to this stance long after it had ceased to be fashionable. It was not until the 1936 Democratic landslide inspired the second New Deal and a switch in sides by Associate Justice Owen Roberts that the Supreme Court ceased its systematic restraint of government intervention and permitted the other branches to regulate business and attack social problems. Beginning in 1937, the Court resurrected the centrist views of John Marshall and permitted broad uses of congressional power through the authority of Article I, Section 8, "to regulate commerce . . . among the several states." In a series of decisions, it drastically altered the federal-state relationship by specifying that Congress could regulate any activity, however local, that affects interstate commerce; that it would not question a congressional determination that a local activity affects interstate commerce if "there are any data affording rational support for that determination"; and that it makes no difference if the connection with commerce is remote or that the purpose of the legislation is local and noncommercial (Cox, 1968, pp. 52–53).

THE SHARED BURDEN

Mixing Up the Layers

The separation of the layers of government has never been sharp enough for a precise fit to the popular analogy of a layer cake. But it was only in the middle third of this century that the "marble cake" model became inescapable. Through the commerce power and grants-in-aid, the functions of the national government expanded in such a variety of ways that easily perceived lines of demarcation between state and federal authority became

Table 3-1 Shares of Domestic Direct Expenditures, Percent

	1902	1927	1948	1954	1962	1967	1969
Federal	17	15	23	26	27	34	32
State	10	15	26	24	24	24	25
Local	73	70	51	50	49	42	43

Source: Reagan, Michael D., *The New Federalism*, New York, Oxford University Press, 1972, p. 46.

harder to find. "There is no neat horizontal stratification," said Grodzins and Elazar (1961) in support of the marble-cake analogy. "Vertical and diagonal lines almost obliterate the horizontal ones, and in some places there are unexpected whirls and an imperceptible merging of colors, so that it is difficult to tell where one ends and the other begins [p. 4]."

One way to track the shifting relationships of federal, state, and local government is to note how much money they raise and spend. A straight-forward comparison would show that the proportionate share of local government has been declining in this century while the federal role has grown and that of the states has remained nearly constant. But much of the growth in federal spending is accounted for by national defense. When domestic functions are considered separately, it can be seen that the federal increase and the local decline have both been leveling off in recent years (see Table 3-1. Remember that the table shows only relative expenditures). All levels of government have been doing and spending more. Local expenditures, for example, increased from $45 billion to $67 billion between 1962 and 1967, even though the proportionate share at the local level was dropping.

The balance among the three levels is even greater than indicated in Table 3-1 if a slightly different method of accounting is used. Much of the money spent by local governments is given them by federal and state governments. If these grants are treated as expenditures by the level of government which makes the grant—instead of the level which ultimately spends it—the three are almost equal. Michael D. Reagan (1972) calculated that nondefense shares in 1968 were 35.3 percent at the federal level, 31.3 percent at the state level, and 33.4 percent at the local level.

These grant programs have arisen in part because of some basic problems with raising money at the lower levels of government. State and local taxes tend to be *regressive*, that is, they take a higher proportion of lower incomes. They are so regressive in fact that they effectively cancel the progressive effect of federal taxes so that the net result for taxpayers at most levels is that they pay the same proportion of income in total taxes—a bit more than 25 percent of total family income in 1966 (Pechman and Okner, 1974). The pressure for expansion of government services has led to demands on the more flexible federal tax structure. Tapping the federal revenues also has the advantage of equalizing the level of services among the richer and poorer sections of the nation.

96

Foundations

In tracing the history of federal grant programs, John M. DeGrove (1970) found only ten that had been approved before 1930 and seventeen during the period between 1931 and 1945. From the end of the war to the close of the Eisenhower administration there were nineteen. Then came the great grant explosion of the 1960s. These grants, many of them bypassing the states to go directly to cities, were aimed primarily at social and environmental services: air pollution in 1963, the Neighborhood Youth Corps, equal employment opportunity programs, community action programs, preschool education for deprived children, and solid waste disposal in 1964; water and sewer programs and law-enforcement assistance in 1965; and the Model Cities program in 1966. "The outburst of activity," says DeGrove (1970), "meant that grants-in-aid as a proportion of total national government spending rose from 4.6 percent in 1955 to over 10 percent in 1968 [p. 144]." This growth contributed to a pattern already established in the twentieth century: a sharing of government activity which leaves few functions as the sole responsibility of any one level of government.

Something for Everyone

The grants-in-aid system adapted nicely to the pluralistic qualities which the creators of federalism had envisioned. Competing and shifting coalitions of interest groups found that the system's flexibility made it possible for nearly everyone to gain something sometime. Some serious ideological resistance

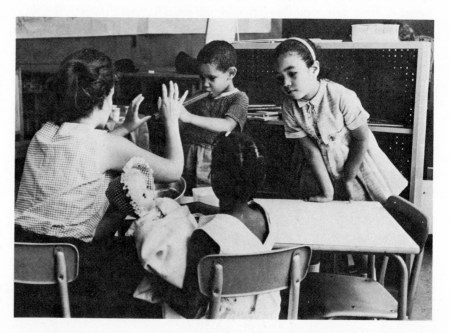

Head Start Program in 1965: An outburst of federal grant activity. *(Wide World Photos.)*

to federal support for local functions remained until after 1964. Then President Johnson's firm control of the Eighty-ninth Congress led to enactment of a large-scale federal aid program to elementary and secondary education—a field traditionally considered a primary responsibility of state and local governments.

Opposition to federal aid to education had been based on the belief that the national government ultimately controls what it pays for and that education might become centrally managed and politically manipulated. But grants-in-aid have not shifted all power over local decisions to Washington. Nor do they necessarily make the structure of government top-heavy. Between 1950 and 1970, the number of state and local government employees increased by 137 percent; federal employment in the same period increased only 36 percent (*Statistical Abstract*, 1972, p. 430).

Attaching Strings

Grants-in-aid, however, do deprive local authorities of some of their freedom to set local priorities. Grants-in-aid are made for specific purposes, and local authorities must account for the money, usually match it with some local funds, and demonstrate that it is spent for the national purposes intended by Congress. Local priorities tend to be organized around these congressionally defined national goals, which may not always correspond to immediate local needs. Furthermore, in bypassing the state governments in many cases, to make local governments the direct patrons of federal largesse, the structural relationship of state and local government is weakened. Cities and states do not exist in a federal relationship; the former —except where state constitutions provide a large measure of home rule—is an administrative subdivision of the latter. Governors sometimes become irritated when they see the money and the power it represents flowing past them, directly to city halls. Former Governor Nelson Rockefeller of New York expressed his frustration to a reporter in 1972:

> The federal categorical system has weakened the ability of state government to govern and it's getting worse all the time. In education alone, we have to file 21 state plans in different phases of education to get three categorical grants. Now, I honestly don't think that these plans really have anything to do with the way the programs are run. We just fill out these forms, write these papers, tell about these plans, but we just have to make all the stuff up, and then try and fit it into our program. I can't believe that anyone reads the plans when they get to Washington . . . [Clark, 1972, p. 1915].

Each program develops a constituency which tries to protect its vested interest in the continued flow of dollars. Because many of these interests tend to develop champions in Congress and because the inertia of the bureaucracy administering the programs tends to resist change, the commitment of money becomes difficult to dislodge or revise. President Eisenhower, early in his second term, decided that federal involvement in state and local affairs had already gone too far, and he appointed a high-level committee to identify those jobs "which the States are ready and willing to assume and finance that are now performed or financed wholly or in part by the Federal Government [1957, pp. 137–138]." The co-chairmen of the committee were Robert B. Anderson, Secretary of the Treasury, and Lane Dwinell, Governor of New Hampshire. It was well staffed and had plenty of time. But "never," says Grodzins, "did good intent, hopes, and labor produce such negligible results. The committee could agree on only two activities from which the federal government should withdraw in favor of complete state responsibility. One was the federal grant for sewage-treatment plants; the other was federal aid for vocational education [1961, pp. 5–6]."

These programs cost only $80 million or about 2 percent of all federal grants for 1957. The states could get this money, the committee said, by a juggling of state and federal shares of taxes on telephone calls. President Eisenhower recommended the entire package to Congress. The beneficiaries of vocational education and sewage-treatment grants included mayors, professional groups, outdoorsmen, educators, and governors. They all objected. No part of the program was ever enacted.

Revenue Sharing

A new idea began to develop about 1964. Walter Heller, who was chairman of the Council of Economic Advisors under President Kennedy, proposed a plan of giving away federally collected money without strings to state and local governments as a means of disposing of the budget surpluses then anticipated from the rising national income. The no-strings feature was called "revenue sharing." He thought it would strengthen state government and ensure that the new national income would be used for socially desirable ends (Opperman, 1968, pp. 43–44). But the Vietnam War wiped out the hoped-for surplus, and when revenue sharing was revived by the Nixon administration, it had a different slant: instead of supplementing the existing network of grants, it would replace them.

The idea of revenue sharing had bipartisan support, although some Democrats wanted to keep federal strings on the money that would go to states. Representative Henry Reuss proposed "one big initial string—that the state prepare in good faith a modern-governments program setting forth what it proposes to do in the years ahead to invigorate and modernize its own and its local governments [Reuss, 1970, p. 124]." This proposal was not successful. Most of the congressional debate was over how the money should be divided. The extent to which revenue sharing might become a substitute for grants-in-aid was not fully appreciated by the Democratic Ninety-second Congress.

Walter Heller: Cutting loose the strings. *(Wide World Photos.)*

The House and Senate divided somewhat along the lines of 1787 in their allocation formulas: the House gave the greatest weight to population; the Senate gave the greatest protection to the sectional interest of the South with its disproportionate share of poor people. Both formulas were complex. The compromise was for each state to receive the amount of money provided by the formula which is the most generous for it.

President Johnson liked to call his ballooning grants-in-aid program "creative Federalism." Nixon (1972) named his revenue-sharing plan the "New Federalism." He borrowed radical rhetoric to describe it, including the phrase, "Power to the people." It could, he told Congress in his 1971 State of the Union message, begin "a New American Revolution—a peaceful revolution in which power was turned back to the people—in which government at all levels was refreshed and renewed, and made truly responsive."

To emphasize his point that this was both a new departure and a renewal of historic values, Nixon chose Independence Hall in Philadelphia for the ceremonial signing of the General Revenue Sharing Act of 1972. In the chamber where the Declaration of Independence was adopted, where the Constitution was drafted, he invoked the myth and symbolism of the Presidency to surround his new program with the legitimacy of the past:

As we sign this historic document today, we are carrying on the work which started here in Independence Square—where independence was declared,

Nixon Signing the Revenue Sharing Act: An attempt to restore a balance. *(Wide World Photos.)*

where the Constitution was written, and where the Bill of Rights was formally added to the Constitution. . . . They came here in the Eighteenth Century to establish the federal system. We return here in the Twentieth Century to renew the federal system. They came here to create a balance between the various levels of government. We come here to restore that balance . . . [p. 1535].

The parallel is inexact, of course. The Founding Fathers were anxious to raise revenue for the central government and strengthen it to meet needs of the states that could only be managed by a more powerful central effort. President Nixon identified more with the Jeffersonian concept of democracy: bringing government closer to the people, avoiding the dangers of a large, unwieldy, inefficient central bureaucracy.

Reversing the Flow

The act signed in Independence Hall provided for $30.2 billion to be distributed over state and local jurisdictions in the next five years. Ten regional revenue-sharing offices were set up around the country to transfer the money from the Revenue Sharing Trust Fund, whose source was, of course, the federal income tax. Only three important restrictions were placed on the use of this money. Local governments could not use federal revenue-sharing funds as matching local funds to qualify for other federal grants. Revenue-sharing funds could not be used to reduce state aid to local governments. And, most importantly, revenue-sharing funds could not be used for programs or projects which discriminate by race or sex.

The hoped-for display of state and local efficiency and ingenuity did not immediately appear. Instead of the "new American Revolution," things went on about as before. State and local governments used the money to maintain prior patterns, stabilize local taxes, and hold down local debt. Perhaps the lack of visible change meant only that the change was evolutionary, not revolutionary. But local officials did not immediately show themselves to be any more imaginative than planners from Washington. They displayed a preference for highly visible capital-improvement items such as new police cars, streets and roads, and public buildings. Some communities consciously chose luxuries they could not afford before: golf courses, tennis courts, or bridle paths. The governor of Mississippi bought a jet plane with $600,000 of revenue-sharing funds. Corpus Christi, Texas, spent $100,000 on tennis courts. Burlington, Vermont, spent $300,000 on uniforms for the city band.

Conflicts of the 1970s

One problem with revenue sharing is that spending money without centralized direction opens up more opportunities for waste, duplication, and mismanagement. Corruption has historically been greater at lower levels of government which are less closely scrutinized by the news media. In that sense, these lower levels are not closer to the people at all. Moreover, the problem of faction, stated so eloquently by Madison, suddenly reappears. Competing interests are less diverse at the local level, and there is greater risk of a dominant interest gaining control of the available wealth and power to inflict the tyranny of the majority upon the helpless few. Local governments have generally been less responsive to the problems of the poor and the needy, for example, than has the national government.

By the middle 1970s, the New Federalism seemed likely to produce another of the periodic conflicts and adjustments within the structure of the national government. This time, it was the executive branch against the legislative. Congress saw, in the decline of grants-in-aid and the rise of stringless grants, a loss of its role as policymaker. Without the power of the purse, it would have less power to compel lower levels of government to follow national commitments—as it had, for example, in the widespread use of grant conditions to end the systematic discrimination against blacks by state and local government and private industry doing business with all levels of government. The New Federalism also threatened to diminish the influence of individual members of Congress who had maneuvered themselves into the leverage points of the grants-in-aid system. By manipulating formulas, conditions, and guidelines, they had important powers within the government and a power base of interest-group constituencies without. It was not something to be given up gladly.

President Nixon, facing a hostile Congress controlled by the opposition party, tried, before Watergate sapped his prestige and power, a strategy of expanding the authority of the executive branch. Though paradoxical, in the light of his expressed commitment to the Jeffersonian pattern, this strategy may have been the only way to effect the radical changes he had in mind. A key tactic was to assert the power to impound funds for grants-in-aid appropriated by Congress. The refusal to spend the money as directed by Congress was defended as consistent with the provision of Article II, Section 3, that the President "shall take care that the laws be faithfully executed." This language implies, it was argued, that the President should decide what is faithful execution of the law. The President's leading congressional critic on this subject, Senator Sam Ervin of North Carolina, argued that impoundment "merely provides a means whereby the White House can give effect to the social goals of its own choosing by reallocating national resources in contravention of Congressional dictates [Weaver, 1973, p. 16]."

Ervin's view prevailed in the early court tests. Meanwhile, other battles in the continuing evolution of federalism were fought at lower levels in the structure which raised questions about the role of the states.

Senator Sam Ervin: Preserving congressional dictates. *(Fred Ward, Black Star.)*

Two Views

Are the states capable of performing in ways that will meet the needs of the last fourth of the century? Do the states meet new problems with new programs that are responsive to the desires of their citizens? Should the states—and federalism itself—be abolished in favor of a unitary system of government?

Critics of state government do indeed suggest that the states may have outlived their usefulness. Defenders of state government maintain, on the other hand, that accomplishments still flow from the state capitals. To put the question in terms of keeping or abolishing the states is perhaps too extreme, and yet it helps in striving for a clear view of the contributions and deficiencies of state government. By facing squarely the prospect of taking the states out of the United States we can illuminate the strengths and weaknesses of the federal principle itself.

The States as Key Arch

To preserve the states means to preserve effective democracy, in the minds of many students of state politics. The states are seen as the keystone in democracy's archway. Although the initiatives of the national government are highly visible, what goes on in less-publicized capitals such as Dover, Topeka, Albany, Augusta, Cheyenne, Olympia, and Bismarck is said to be just as significant as the developments in Washington.

The governments headquartered in these relatively obscure cities are responsible for delivering vital services: education, highways, correctional and recreation facilities, public welfare, hospitals, and regulation of banking, labor, commerce, utilities, and industry. Thomas R. Dye (1969) has summarized the scope of state and local government:

> Despite the glamour of national politics, states and communities carry on the greatest volume of public business, settle the greatest number of political conflicts, make the majority of policy decisions, and direct the bulk of public programs. They have the major responsibility for maintaining domestic law and order, for educating the children, for moving Americans from place to place, and for caring for the poor and the ill. They regulate the provision of water, gas, electric and other public utilities, share in the regulation of insurance and banking enterprise, regulate the use of land, and supervise the sale and ownership of property. Their courts settle by far the greatest number of civil and criminal cases [pp. 3–4].

And even national programs, whether advanced as block grants or through revenue sharing, are more often than not administered by states and their localities.

There are other reasons to continue and strengthen the states. State governments are at least physically closer to their citizens than the distant national government; they have the chance to be more innovative than a lethargic federal bureaucracy. They can be less bogged down in red tape. They can serve as a proving ground for experimental programs and for future national leaders. Their boundaries preserve regional differences that were at the heart of the federal bargain in the first place. And they are the base around which political parties organize. For these and other reasons, Ira Sharkansky (1972) in *The Maligned States* adopts the theme that "state governments should be our heroes and the subjects of our hopes instead of our whipping boys [p. 12]."

The States as Fallen Arch

Critics of the states see them not as a keystone upholding the federal arch but as the fallen arch, crumbled by incompetence and corruption, lacking positive response to citizen needs. From this perspective, the reason for the prominence of national government has been the inability and unwillingness of state government to respond to urgent problems and modern conditions. The unwillingness of the states to act during the Depression led some observers to urge abolishing them. Luther Gulick (1933) concluded that states had already ceased to function: "It is a matter of brutal record. The American state is finished. I do not predict that the states will go but affirm that they have gone [p. 421]."

More recently, even those who care deeply for the states are among the first to point out their inadequacies. Former Governor Terry Sanford of North Carolina in *Storm Over the States* (1967) concedes that the states are indecisive, antiquated, timid, and ineffective, unwilling to face their problems, uninterested in cities, and unresponsive in general. These conditions, he says, "are true about all of the states some of the time and some of the states all of the time [p. 1]." Such problems have led some imaginative students to propose not the abolition of the states but redrawing state lines. Figure 3-2 shows the plan of G. Etzel Pearcy, a professor of geography, for reducing the number of states from fifty to thirty-eight to produce a better balance in size and population and, according to Pearcy, to improve government efficiency and effect fiscal economies. Such plans receive little attention. We are used to the states as they are.

How Well Have the States Performed?

The public evaluation of the states' performance is not very high. In 1973, the Senate Subcommittee on Intergovernmental Relations of the Committee on Government Operations commissioned the Harris Survey to

Figure 3–2. Pearcy's Plan to Reduce the States to Thirty-eight

measure confidence in government. Only about one person out of four (see Table 3-2) expressed a great deal of confidence in state government. The states fared somewhat better than the White House and the federal executive branch, but this was at a time when both were caught up in the Watergate scandals. Furthermore, public confidence in state government

Table 3-2 Public Level of Confidence in the People Running Various Institutions in the United States, 1973

INSTITUTION	LEVEL OF CONFIDENCE			
	Great deal	Only some	Hardly any	Not sure
U.S. Supreme Court	33%	40%	21%	7%
U.S. Senate	30	48	18	4
U.S. House of Representatives	29	49	15	7
Local Government	28	49	19	4
State Government	24	55	17	5
Executive Branch of Federal Government	19	39	34	7
White House	18	36	41	5

Source: United States Senate Committee on Government Operations, Subcommittee on Intergovernmental Relations, *Confidence and Concern: Citizens View American Government,* Government Printing Office, 1973, part 2, pp. 77–84, and part 3, pp. 40–47.

had declined from what it was five years earlier. In the public mind the states indeed appeared to be the "fallen arch."

Such attitudes, however, are not deeply held. In 1967, the Gallup Poll put the question in terms of money: "Which do you think spends the taxpayer's dollar more wisely—the state government or the federal government?" This time, the public sided with the states, 49 percent to 18 percent, with the remainder saying neither or having no opinion [*Congressional Record*, February 15, 1967]. Such sensitivity to the question wording suggests that most people simply do not pay much attention to state government, a suspicion that has been confirmed by M. Kent Jennings and Harmon Ziegler (1970). They found that citizens are most attentive to the national government, then local government. "International" government is third, and the states are last. The performance of the states may have to be judged by more specific criteria.

Institutions and Legal Structures

Most of the formal institutions and the legal structures of the state governments were adopted during the eighteenth and nineteenth centuries, a fact which leads critics to suggest that these institutions and structures cannot cope with today's problems. Urbanization and industrialization have created conditions that require flexibility, innovation, and initiative by state governments on a scale that was not envisioned earlier. Several institutional and structural features tend to make the states more rigid than the times seem to demand:

Constitutionalism.   Charges of obsolescence among the states usually begin with the state constitutions, the highest form of law after the Constitution of the United States. They vary considerably. The oldest was adopted by Massachusetts in 1780, and the newest, that of Montana, was enacted in 1973. Rhode Island was able to write its highest law in 6,650 words, whereas Louisiana required more than 350,000. State constitutions tend to suffer from anachronisms and excessive detail. Some contain deadwood provisions on dueling, slavery, and hereditary privileges. Louisiana's constitution names two Mississippi River bridges for Huey P. Long and proclaims his birthday a holiday forever. Such detailed and particular provisions set state policy on matters that reformers and critics say should be handled by elected officials.

State constitutions erect barriers to modern government to the extent that they are documents of *limitations* rather than *permissions*. Because of the Tenth Amendment to the U.S. Constitution, states have the power to constitutionally delegate vast amounts of authority to their own officials and to local government. Instead, most have chosen to pack their constitutions with limitations on authority. Eighteenth-century distrust of the executive led to limits on the governor; fear of generalized governmental activity resulted in limits on the fiscal authority of state and local legislatures; and the tendency to impose restrictions led to specification of the types of operating rules and procedures for lesser governmental units (counties, townships, municipalities). Cumulatively, these prohibitions impose severe constraints on state government activity.

State constitutions are also difficult to change. Two methods are available: *revision* by amendment and *replacement* by calling a constitutional convention. Both are difficult to effect. Amending the constitution requires action by both the state legislature and the electorate in some states, sometimes in two consecutive legislative sessions. Other states require more than a majority vote in the state legislature: two-thirds or even three-fifths. Replacing the constitution through constitutional conventions is provided for in forty-six states; yet this procedure usually involves cumbersome steps. Legislatures submit to voters the question of calling a convention; if the voters approve, the convention convenes, formulates a revised document, and then again submits the new document to the voters for approval.

But despite such unwieldy methods, much change has occurred in state constitutions in the 1960s and 1970s. Ronald E. Weber (1975) counted 322 amendments to state constitutions in 1972 alone. Between 1969 and 1973, five states (Florida, 1969; Illinois, North Carolina, Virginia, 1971; and Montana, 1973) adopted new constitutions by calling constitutional conventions. These newer documents, Weber says, are shorter and more refined than their predecessors. When the flaws become obvious—and painful enough—constitutional change is possible.

State Executive Authority. In what many describe as "the age of the executive," the current period has not seen an assignment of authority to state governors consistent with expectations about gubernatorial leadership. Most of the constraints on executive leadership are imposed by state constitutional limitations. Originally, these limitations arose from colonial distaste for policies pursued by governors appointed by the King of England. More recently, they reflect a more general reluctance to concentrate authority and power in the executive.

Such limitations on the governor tend to preclude dynamic, forceful, and creative action by the states. However, the historic limits on the governor have gradually been eroded through such changes as lengthening the term of office, direct popular election, allowing governors to run for reelection, and granting governors the veto power. Among the most common remaining restrictions, perhaps the most important is the popular election of the governor's subordinates, such as the attorney general, secretary of state, treasurer, and state school superintendent. In the extreme cases of Louisiana and Oklahoma, no fewer than thirteen separate executive officials are popularly elected. These officials are not accountable to the governor. Neither are members of independent boards and commissions, constitutionally mandated in most states to preside over administrative agencies.

One consequence of this "plural-executive" system is that the governor is faced with checks and balances not only from state courts and legislatures, but also from within his own executive branch. "Administrative policy" on any particular item may turn out to be conflicting administrative policies pursued by multiple executives with different bases of political support. Once enacted, the policy of a state administration may or may not be implemented according to the original intent, depending upon how the independent executive departments view the policy. Nevertheless, the governor is the most visible state executive and tends to be associated with policy accomplishments and failures and may suffer electorally from it. Thus Austin Ranney (1971) sees a new "political vulnerability" among governors. In 1966 and 1968, 88 percent of incumbent U.S. senators were reelected, but only 67 percent of incumbent governors were reelected (p. 116).

With so much unquestioned formal power, we might expect state legislatures to be the action centers of state government, taking the decisive and bold initiatives when needed. But, in general, they do not. The Citizens Conference on State Legislatures recently analyzed the decision-making behavior of the fifty legislatures and decided they are only "sometime governments." Decisions go unmade, the Conference said, "because our principal instrument of decision making—our fifty state legislatures—are in disarray [Burns, 1971, p. xi]." Some, of course, are in more disarray than others. The Conference scored each legislature on five basic qualities which a citizen has a right to expect of his or her legislature: it should be functional, accountable, informed, independent, and representative. By these criteria, California and New York were judged to have superior legislatures, with Illinois, Florida, and Wisconsin also among the top five (see Table 3-3). The higher-ranking legislatures, said the Conference, "tend to be generally innovative in many different areas of public policy, generous in welfare and education spending and services, and 'interventionist' in the sense of having powers and responsibilities of broad scope [Citizens Conference on State Legislatures, 1971, p. 77]." The wide variation suggests that the theoretical *ability* of state legislatures to act may not be as important as their *willingness* to act.

Apportionment.   Critics of state government, prior to the mid-1960s, pointed to unequal systems of representation in state legislatures as one of the more debilitating anachronisms. The manner in which legislative districts were drawn (apportionment) gave rise to inequality of representation (malapportionment) requiring redrawing of legislative district lines (reapportionment) if the states were to function responsively. Up until the

Foundations

Table 3-3 Overall Ranking of State Legislatures

RANK	STATE	FUNC-TIONAL	ACCOUNT-ABLE	INFORMED	INDE-PENDENT	REPRE-SENTATIVE
1	California	1	3	2	3	2
2	New York	4	13	1	8	1
3	Illinois	17	4	6	2	13
4	Florida	5	8	4	1	30
5	Wisconsin	7	21	3	4	10
6	Iowa	6	6	5	11	25
7	Hawaii	2	11	20	7	16
8	Michigan	15	22	9	12	3
9	Nebraska	35	1	16	30	18
10	Minnesota	27	7	13	23	12
11	New Mexico	3	16	28	39	4
12	Alaska	8	29	12	6	40
13	Nevada	13	10	19	14	32
14	Oklahoma	9	27	24	22	8
15	Utah	38	5	8	29	24
16	Ohio	18	24	7	40	9
17	South Dakota	23	12	15	16	37
18	Idaho	20	9	29	27	21
19	Washington	12	17	25	19	39
20	Maryland	16	31	10	15	45
21	Pennsylvania	37	23	23	5	36
22	North Dakota	22	18	17	37	31
23	Kansas	31	15	14	32	34
24	Connecticut	39	26	26	25	6
25	West Virginia	10	32	37	24	15

mid-1960s gross imbalances in the number of voters represented by legislators characterized the states. Grant and Nixon (1968) provide the following stark example in Maryland:

> A state senator from one Eastern Shore county (Kent) in 1961 represented 15,481 Marylanders, but one from Baltimore County represented 492,428. Over three-fourths of Maryland's population in 1961 lived in the four largest counties plus Baltimore City, but they elected only one-third of the members of the upper house of the state legislature [p. 282].

Not only did such unequal representation schemes violate democratic norms, but it was also widely believed that the plight of city dwellers originated from the dominance of state legislatures by rural representatives. Change the apportionment criteria to a strict population basis, the argument ran, and the cities' problems would decrease because of more responsive state legislatures.

U.S. Supreme Court decisions in 1962 and 1964 ordered reapportionment on the basis of population alone. In *Baker v. Carr* (369 U.S. 186,

Table 3-3 (continued)   109

RANK	STATE	FUNC-TIONAL	ACCOUNT-ABLE	INFORMED	INDE-PENDENT	REPRE-SENTATIVE
26	Tennessee	30	44	11	9	26
27	Oregon	28	14	35	35	19
28	Colorado	21	25	21	28	27
29	Massachusetts	32	35	22	21	23
30	Maine	29	34	32	18	22
31	Kentucky	49	27	48	44	7
32	New Jersey	14	42	18	31	35
33	Louisiana	47	39	33	13	14
34	Virginia	25	19	27	26	48
35	Missouri	36	30	40	49	5
36	Rhode Island	33	46	30	41	11
37	Vermont	19	20	34	42	47
38	Texas	45	36	43	45	17
39	New Hampshire	34	33	42	36	43
40	Indiana	44	38	41	43	20
41	Montana	26	28	31	46	49
42	Mississippi	46	43	45	20	28
43	Arizona	11	47	38	17	50
44	South Carolina	50	45	39	10	46
45	Georgia	40	49	36	33	38
46	Arkansas	41	40	46	34	33
47	North Carolina	24	37	44	47	44
48	Delaware	43	48	47	38	29
49	Wyoming	42	41	50	48	42
50	Alabama	48	50	49	50	41

Source: Burns, John, and the Citizens Conference on State Legislatures, *The Sometime Governments*, New York, Bantam, 1971, pp. 52–53.

1962), the Court ruled that apportionment of state legislatures on any basis other than population violated the equal protection of the laws provision of the Fourteenth Amendment. In *Reynolds v. Sims* (84 S.Ct. 1362, 1964), the Court specifically applied the same population criteria to the apportionment of upper houses in state legislatures. Chief Justice Earl Warren put the issue squarely for the Court:

> Legislators represent people, not trees or acres. Legislators are elected by voters, not farms or cities or economic interests. . . . The complexions of societies and civilizations change, often with amazing rapidity. A nation once primarily rural in character becomes predominantly urban. Representation schemes once fair and equitable become archaic and outdated.

The combined decisions had an immediate and significant impact, as is shown in the equality of representation systems prevailing in state legislatures by 1967 in Table 3-4.

But the anticipated improvement in the status of cities did not

Table 3-4 State Legislative Apportionment in 1962 and 1967 by Degree of Malapportionment*

	1962	1967
Number of states with malapportioned legislatures	49	6
Number of states with well-apportioned legislatures	1	44

*A state legislature is categorized as malapportioned if less than 45 percent of its population can elect a majority of the legislators in either chamber of the legislature.
Source: Boyd, William J. D. (ed.) *Apportionment in the Nineteen Sixties,* National Municipal League, New York, 1967.

materialize. Rural areas lost some weight after redistricting; but they were replaced in the halls of state legislatures not by inner-city representatives (which, by the mid-1960s had begun rapidly to lose population), but by representatives from suburban areas which had become the new population growth centers. Conservative representatives from wealthy suburban areas formed alliances with remaining conservative rural representatives and the new coalitions have generally proved hostile to the interests of inner-city residents.

In terms of abolishing the states or viewing them as the key to American democracy, this review of the institutions and structures of the fifty states reveals a mixed picture of state performances that fails to justify either of the extreme positions. Rather, deficiencies in state constitutions, executive organization, legislative activity, and past patterns of malapportionment are balanced to greater or lesser extents by the amendability and changeability of state constitutions, checks on executive authority, and the significant degree to which state legislatures are currently representative of state populations.

Moreover, the institutions and structures of the fifty states do not constitute the whole of state politics. Any assessment of the viability of the states must necessarily take into account less formal aspects of their politics. Political behavior, like the formal structures, also varies from state to state.

Sources of State Variations

The United States is a large and diverse nation, with regional variation within the country almost as marked as differences between this nation and other nation-states. Daniel Elazar (1966) suggests that political culture is an important factor in determining differences among the states, and he identifies three pure types: moralistic, individualistic, and traditionalistic. Moralistic political culture views government as a positive instrument with which the general welfare is secured and politics is seen as righteous activity. The individualistic culture stresses limitations on government and the centrality of private concerns. Traditionalistic culture desires government to maintain existing relationships, and politics becomes the caretaker of established interests. Figure 3-3 shows Elazar's distribution of political cultures within the states, with traditionalism dominating the greater South, individualism stretching from the middle sections of the country toward the Southwest, and moralism primary in the North, Northwest, and Pacific Coast.

But the concept of political culture is less than precise when one attempts to explain such specific differences as why more voters in certain states turn out on election days; why certain states enact right-to-work laws, open-occupancy statutes, and handgun-registration laws; or why some states spend so much more money on education, welfare, and health care than others. Other students of state politics have examined the different levels of socioeconomic resources available to the states in their search for explanations of state-by-state variations. Per capita income, degree of industrialization and urbanization, and education are the most frequently used measures to explain differences in state policies and expenditures (Dye, 1966). Generally these investigators have found that greater state expenditures for education, welfare, and health care are the product of higher income, greater industrialization and urbanization, and higher educational levels.

THE LOCAL COMMUNITIES

A Vote of Confidence
When the architects of the 1972 general revenue-sharing plan decided to give three-fourths of the money to local communities, they were reasserting

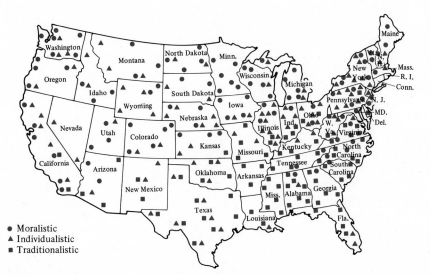

● Moralistic
▲ Individualistic
■ Traditionalistic

Figure 3–3 The Distribution of Political Cultures within States (From Elazar, 1966)

Table 3-5   Forms of Local Government

TYPE OF GOVERNMENT	1972	1967	1962
Counties	3,044	3,049	3,043
Municipalities	18,517	18,048	18,000
Townships	16,991	17,105	17,142
School districts	15,781	21,782	34,678
Special districts	23,885	21,264	18,323
Local governments, total	78,218	81,248	91,186

Source: "Finances of Special Districts," vol. 4, no. 2, *1972 Census of Governments*, Government Printing Office, 1974.

the belief that the people would be best served if the money were spent at a point close to home in a decentralized program. This belief rests on some assumptions that need examining: that local governments are in fact close to their citizens; that local communities have wisely allocated their financial resources in the past; that local governments are sufficiently independent to govern effectively; and that local political forces will tend to ensure that the money is spent fairly.

In the 1960s, attention given to the problems of cities made it easy to forget that the cities are not the only forms of local government. The cities were suffering the most pressing financial problems, losing population and their tax bases just at the time when protests and sometimes violent disorders were increasing the pressure on them to solve their social problems. But in fact, cities represent a minority of local governments: about one-fourth of the total (Table 3-5). Counties, townships, school districts, and an increasing number and variety of special districts also form the network of local government.

The Dependency Problem

Local governments are creatures of the states to which they are subordinate. The Constitution of the United States makes no mention of cities, counties, townships, or special districts. Each of these forms exists by virtue of state action. Cities are chartered by the state, and counties are administrative subdivisions of the state, created, as Elazar (1966) has noted, "without the particular solicitation, consent, or concurrent action of the people who inhabit them [p. 166]." County functions are state functions: recording of deeds, supervision of elections, and some quasi-judicial functions of the sheriff's office. Some counties are exceptions to this general rule, but only because their states have granted them broad charters to provide municipal services where rapid urbanization has made these services necessary. Dade County, Florida; Fairfax County, Virginia; and Los Angeles County, California, are examples.

The relationship of local government to the states is therefore not analogous to the relationship of the states to the national government. It is not a federal but a unitary relationship. Associate Justice Pierce Butler put it clearly in his opinion in *Trenton v. New Jersey* (262 U.S. 182, 1923): "In the absence of state constitutional provisions safeguarding it to them, municipalities have no inherent right of self-government which is beyond the legislative control of the state."

This legal dependency on the states is not a mere formality. It imposes real restrictions and erects solid barriers within which local governments must operate. The ease or difficulty with which local governments may be created, expanded, consolidated, or divide functions among one another is all controlled by the states. Even their finances are closely controlled. Their near-exclusive reliance on property taxes for revenue is state-mandated. So, in some cases, is the rate of taxation which may be levied and the ceiling on debt obligations. Grants-in-aid from states to localities tend to be highly specific about how they may be used. To engage in activities not specifically authorized in their state-framed charters, local governments must obtain state-enabling legislation. Lacking powers of their own, they must turn to the state governments whenever new and pressing problems arise.

This dependency status of local governments is at odds with the easy rhetoric about returning government to "the people" through revenue sharing. The most decentralized units of government in America are incapable of allowing citizens to control their own affairs, choose which programs they want, and fund projects most meaningful to them, as long as local governments are hostage to state-imposed prohibitions.

"Home Rule"

Reformers interested in breaking local governments out of dependency status have urged "home rule" since the middle of the nineteenth century. In theory home rule means allowing local units of government to exercise all power not specifically forbidden in state constitutions or statutes, but in practice the reformers' ideal is rarely, if ever, achieved. Missouri pioneered acceptance of home rule in its constitution of 1875 by allowing St. Louis and other cities over 100,000 population a measure of self-government. By 1960 half the states had incorporated similar provisions in their constitutions.

Constitutional delegation of state authority is one form of home rule; the other is conferral by state legislatures of a degree of self-government on localities by statute. Either way the principle is the same—local governments under home rule can change their powers, operations, and even their form of government through referendum vote without having to seek state legislative approval to do so. Where strong home rule is allowed (clearly the exception), it has had the effect of increasing the discretion of local decisionmakers, and of enhancing the flexibility of local government structures. Perhaps most important to state officials, it has decreased the petitioning of local officials and the number of detailed "nuisance bills" with which state legislators are confronted.

As so often happens, the reformers won the battle over home rule but lost the war over local self-government. The battle was won when half the states wrote home-rule provisions into their constitutions and all but about ten of the remaining states provided degrees of home rule by state statute; but the war was lost when the home-rule provisions were applied. Constitutionally provided home rule has been significantly diluted by court interpretations that restrict the authority of local governments, the power of the decisionmakers, and the degree of discretion allowed. Home rule based on state statutes has proved to be even more precarious, for the same state legislatures that grant local self-government can, and do, as quickly withdraw it. Banfield and Wilson (1963) see the home-rule issue as ultimately irresolvable:

> The problem seems to be inherently insoluble on any general and lasting basis. It is one that must be worked out by friction, and worked out anew every time it arises. What cities are to do or not do will in the last analysis always have to be decided on the basis of concrete political issues [p. 67].

And the most recent political issue around which the controversy of local self-government centers is, of course, the revenue-sharing program. Cities want the power to decide how the money should be spent. States are reluctant to grant it.

Fragmentation of Local Authority

The vertical dependency of local governments on the states imposes limits on what localities can do and how they can do it, but an equally important constraint is the horizontal fragmentation (division and sharing) of authority at the local level. State-imposed constraints limit local governmental autonomy; fragmentation of authority is a consequence of the need for local governments to adapt to state control. In part, that adaptation has resulted in the creation of multiple governmental units exercising authority and providing services in political jurisdictions that geographically overlap.

One device for showing the degree of fragmented authority is simply to list the sheer number of local governments. Table 3-5 indicates that in 1972 there were over 78,000 local governments and that the number of municipalities (cities) and special districts continues to rise. Only the number of school districts has declined markedly, and this is due to school consolidation in the last two decades. In any given locality these governmental jurisdictions overlap, creating a situation where multiple units of local government share responsibility in some of the same areas and over some of the same services. In metropolitan areas there may be tens, hundreds, or even thousands of governments. Special districts constitute the largest category. They are state-created units having financial autonomy and political independence from other local governments. For the most part they provide services in the form of airports, fire protection, water supply, housing, cemeteries, sewerage, parks and recreation, hospitals, libraries, and even mosquito abatement.

The picture of local government, especially in metropolitan areas, is thus one of a maze of interlocking and overlapping units; each has different degrees of independent authority and functional autonomy. Horizontal fragmentation gives rise to a series of identifiable problems. Daniel R. Grant (1970) lists six problem areas taken from 112 different surveys of metropolitan areas over a thirty-year period:

1   Unequal distribution of fiscal resources

2   Significant inequities in services provided

3   The absence of area-wide authority to cope with problems that spill over jurisdictional lines

4   Wasteful duplication of services and inefficient use of resources

5   Inability of citizens to fix responsibility and hold officials accountable for governmental action or inaction

6   Political segregation of suburbs, their residents, and their leaders from central-city problems

That these problems have endured and even become more intense over the last three decades is not surprising given the degree of governmental fragmentation already identified. But fragmentation of local government takes other forms as well.

Horizontal fragmentation of authority in localities also occurs through the principle of separation of powers and the doctrine of checks and balances. More-or-less separate executive, legislative, and judicial branches of local government within the multiple jurisdictions discussed above disperse authority among elected and appointed officials. Whether such officials act in concert or conflict depends upon local conditions, but the existence of various officials in different branches and chosen from multiple jurisdictions virtually ensures that coordinated assaults on local problems are difficult at best and impossible at worst. Moreover, within executive branches of local government there exists a degree of bureaucratic independence unmatched at state and national levels. Many county and municipal departments, agencies, and bureaus have been structurally removed from the elected executives' control and operate independently. The heads of such bureaucracies are often insulated from control by public officials through civil service laws, terms of office outlasting the mayor or county executive, or commissions and boards protecting them against "political interference."

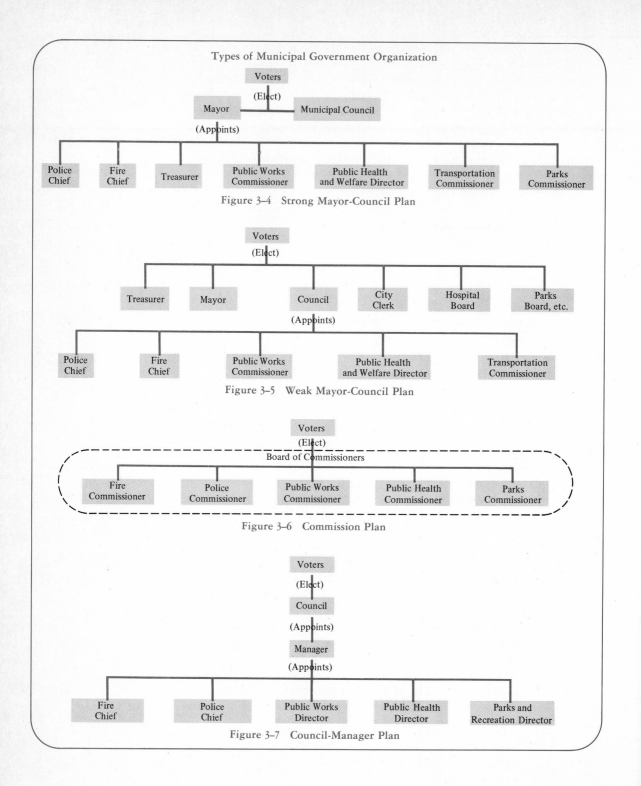

Types of Municipal Government Organization

Figure 3–4 Strong Mayor-Council Plan

Figure 3–5 Weak Mayor-Council Plan

Figure 3–6 Commission Plan

Figure 3–7 Council-Manager Plan

The different forms of municipal government illustrate how extensive horizontal fragmentation within just one local jurisdiction (the city) may be. Figures 3-4 through 3-7 diagramatically show the four common types of relationships between municipal executives and legislatures. These diagrams understate the extent of municipal fragmentation due to the exclusion of the judiciary and independent executive agencies.

Strong Mayor-Council. This form of municipal organization has the most centralized authority. The mayor is the undisputed chief executive with appointment and removal power over heads of executive departments, and he thus is more responsible for administrative matters than under the other plans. The mayor also shares legislative powers with the city council by preparing the budget, possessing veto power, and proposing legislation to the council. Boston and Cleveland are among the better examples of the strong mayor-council plan, and it has proved to be most attractive to large cities with most cities over 500,000 population adopting it.

Weak Mayor-Council. If the city council prepares the budget, appoints the heads of departments, is solely responsible for proposing legislation, and if the mayor lacks a veto and is only one of several elected executive officers, the weak mayor-council plan is in effect. This plan dates back to early American history and once again reflects the fear of a strong executive in the post-colonial period. The executive was indeed controlled, but one consequence of the plan was to fragment authority among a host of elected executive officials and between the mayor and council. It is still popular in small towns, especially those under 5,000 population. Yet it may periodically be found in large cities as Dye (1969) indicates is the case in Minneapolis:

> Minneapolis is perhaps the prime example of a weak mayor system: voters elect a library board, the parks board, a board of estimate and taxation, 13 aldermen, a treasurer, and a comptroller; the council, not the mayor, appoints the city attorney, city engineer, city assessor, and city clerk; the mayor makes only one major appointment—the city chief of police [pp. 213, 215].

The difference between the strong and weak mayor-council systems is not always clear-cut, and the best rule of thumb to distinguish the two is that a strong mayor-council system is present when the mayor's authority exceeds that of the council. Otherwise, it is a weak mayor-council system.

Commission Plan. Under the commission plan, authority is fragmented to such an extent that executive and legislative functions are merged as one. Here a small number of commissioners, usually five, are elected, and each assumes responsibility for managing a specific city department such as public works or police. One commission member may be symbolically designated mayor. Because of the extreme fragmentation of authority, when commissioners disagree on policy matters, the commission form of government results in the near absolute absence of coordination, becoming instead a government of independent fiefdoms each going their separate ways. For this reason the plan is the least popular of the four government forms, yet it remains in effect in Jersey City, Memphis, Omaha, Portland, St. Paul, and other cities. Interestingly, it was originally proposed by reformers who were appalled by the division of authority between the mayor and council. In 1960 it was even abandoned by Galveston, Texas, where it was first instituted in 1901.

Council-Manager Plan. Reformers also proposed this form of city government, convinced that principles of professional management could be incorporated into city government. Here the voters elect a city council—usually small in number and elected on a nonpartisan ballot from at-large districts—which selects a professionally trained administrator called the city manager. The council is responsible for legislating policy, the manager for carrying it out. City managers typically prepare the budget and administer it after council approval, appoint and remove heads of city departments according to criteria specified in civil service codes, and are ultimately responsible for the smooth operation of city departments and their delivery of services. The only administrative role for the council is selecting and dismissing the manager. Through this structure the reformers believed that community "politics" could be separated from "administration." The plan has been widely adopted in medium-sized cities (25,000 to 250,000 population). Administrative aspects of government are, however, inherently caught up in political questions about who should receive which services under what conditions. Managers are repeatedly involved in policy making when they urge certain budgetary priorities over others and when they render professional advice to city councils. Critics of the plan suggest that the professionally trained manager merely replaces, with some important differences, previously popularly elected executives. As Banfield and Wilson (1963) conclude: "However great the achievements of the plan in providing government that is honest, impartial, and efficient 'in the small,' it is not clear that it has always accomplished what its inventors mainly intended—namely by centralizing authority to make local government an effective instrument for carrying out the popular will [p. 186]."

There is nothing particularly new or unique about the fragmentation of authority in local governments, yet more than one observer has pronounced large American cities ungovernable. Why is this so? Are the local problems of race, class, air and water pollution, transportation, health, employment, and tax resources so much greater today than, say, fifty or seventy-five years ago? Banfield (1974) argues that just the reverse is true.

The plain fact is that the overwhelming majority of city dwellers live more comfortably and conveniently than ever before. They have more and better housing, more and better schools, more and better transportation, and so on. By any conceivable measure of material welfare the present generation of urban Americans is, on the whole, better off than any other large group of people has ever been anywhere [pp. 1–2].

Perhaps an answer to the governability of localities is not found in the problems confronting authorities, but in the manner in which authorities exercise power.

The Machine as Centralizer

The political machine dominated local governments from the Civil War through the first third of the twentieth century. The problems of cities during that time period—crime, poverty, disease, gang warfare, illiteracy, and so forth—were many times greater than today. Local government authority was at least as fragmented. Yet the machine governed. It got things done. It facilitated the rapid expansion and physical development of cities. And it did so largely by concentrating blocks of power in the organized machine to overcome formal governmental fragmentation.

A machine is simply a highly organized political party that seeks to control a sufficient number of votes to capture public office. Eugene Lewis (1973) provides a description of the machine organization:

> The structure of machines was nearly always similar to the formal structure of the political party or representational system. It was decidedly hierarchical. The lowest level of organization was the precinct. A number of precincts made up the next unit, the ward. Ward organizations were represented by party committees that usually consisted of the more powerful ward leaders. One of these was usually the city boss [p. 55].

The hierarchical organization Lewis speaks of is pictured in Figure 3-8. City bosses or district leaders preside over the organization, rewarding lesser

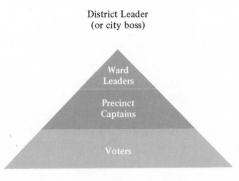

District Leader
(or city boss)

Ward Leaders

Precinct Captains

Voters

Figure 3–8 The Machine Organization

members who perform well and dismissing those who do not do so well in turning out the vote for machine candidates. Ward leaders are responsible to the city boss for the size of the vote turned out for machine candidates, in return for which they receive favors and jobs, and they themselves are often slated as candidates. Precinct captains do the doorbell ringing and footwork for the machine to ensure that voters favorably inclined toward its candidates make it to the polls, in return for which the precinct captains receive appointive public jobs and other favors.

At the base of the machine rest the voters. They are offered favors and services the machine has to dispense in return for their votes. In the era when cities were populated by teeming masses of recently arrived immigrants, the machine effectively controlled a sufficient number of votes to dominate municipal politics. In a classic volume, John T. Salter (1935) describes how it was done in Philadelphia:

> While I observed, 177 men and women voted. Of that number, 11 people voted without assistance; the 166 were assisted—partly because the machines were new to these people, but more truly because Nick (the machine politician) was their friend, and they wanted to show him that their vote was his [p. 149].

The Party Machine

The Hawk and Sam, as precinct captains, are basic parts of the Machine. There are some thirty-five hundred precincts in Chicago, and every one of them has a Democratic captain and most captains have assistant captains. They all have, or can have, jobs in government. The better the captain, the better the job. Many make upwards of fifteen thousand dollars a year as supervisors, inspectors, or minor department heads. They aren't the lowest ranking members of the Machine. Below them are the people who swing mops in the public buildings, dump bedpans in the County Hospital, dig ditches, and perform other menial work. They don't work precincts regularly, although they help out at election time, but they do have to vote themselves and make sure their families vote, buy the usual tickets to political dinners, and in many wards, contribute about two percent of their salaries to the ward organization. Above the precinct captain is that lordly figure the ward committeeman, known in local parlance as "the clout," "the Chinaman," "the guy," and "our beloved leader."

—Mike Royko, from *Boss: Richard J. Daley of Chicago*, New York, E. P. Dutton, 1971, p. 6.

Although lower-class ethnic voters supported the machine in return for favors, friendship, and assistance, the machine at the same time struck a symbiotic relationship with big business. Businessmen desired franchises, licenses, and permits to conduct their building programs, and in the age of the robber barons they were more than willing to pay machine politicians for them through bribes, kickbacks, and yielding to extortion schemes. Thus the machine accumulated political power from the lower and upper classes, captured and retained elective office, all the while skimming boodle from the city treasury.

But the machine did more than this. In a radically decentralized political system lacking central authority, it overcame fragmented authority structures to govern. It did so by concentrating power in the hands of those at the top of the machine hierarchy. And in a limited number of cases it still does so today, as Banfield and Wilson (1963) indicate for the city of Chicago:

> Chicago is a city in which an extreme decentralization of authority has been overcome by an extreme centralization of power, the power being based mainly on specific inducements. The mayor of Chicago is a boss. That is to say, he is a broker in the business (so to speak) of buying and selling political power. He performs an entrepreneurial function by overcoming the decentralization of authority that prevents anything from being done, and in this his role is very like that of the real estate broker who assembles land for a large development by buying up parcels here and there. Much of what the political broker gathers up is on speculation: he does not know exactly how it will be used, but he is confident that someone will need a large block of power [p. 104].

Although the corruption, exploitation of the ethnic immigrants, and partiality of the machine do not recommend it as a model to be emulated,

Mayor Daley: Gathering power on speculation. *(United Press International.)*

perhaps the manner in which it assembled power bases to overcome fragmented structures and govern is worth consideration.

Reform Politics and Fragmentation

Appalled by municipal corruption, inefficiencies, graft, and abuses, reformers began to organize at the turn of the last century and increasingly saw their goals for changing local governmental structures realized. The adoption of reform measures has tended to increase the degree of fragmentation in municipal authority. Reform advocates were drawn largely from the middle class which had been excluded from the machine's constituency, and reformers sought to alter precisely those political structures that allowed the bosses to pyramid blocks of power in overcoming fragmented authority.

Two of the four forms of municipal government just reviewed are the direct offspring of the reform movement. The commission plan and the council-manager plan were motivated in part by reformers' desire to curb executive authority in the form of strong mayors who also happened to be city bosses. The hierarchical organization of the machine most closely matched and was clearly harmonious with the strong mayor-council form of government. Both the commission plan and council-manager plan precluded an ambitious and powerful executive that the machine required.

The machine's vote buying, skirting of election laws, and trading of influence led reformers to attack the electoral base of machine organizations. Several well-known electoral devices emerged from the reform movement's attack on the machine's ability to control the vote. Nonpartisanship—the removal of party designation from the ballot—became a watchword of reform, and its adoption decreased electoral participation of the lower class which no longer had a "signaling device" about how to vote. Nonpartisanship also lessened the machine's ability to accumulate power along party lines. Reformers urged adoption of the initiative, referendum, recall, and nomination by petition as electoral mechanisms for removing power from the hands of machine bosses and placing it instead in the hands of an active, informed, and involved electorate. Again these measures curbed the accumulation of power by those presiding over the machine's hierarchy. Staggering local election dates so that they occur at times other than state and national elections also served to undermine the ability of a single party faction to control blocks of power and further decentralized the electoral process.

A series of reform measures designed to remove municipal bureaucracies from local politics and to make them more efficient contributed greatly to the fragmentation of local government. The machine had used city agencies as a source of jobs for its workers and as a device for rendering services to its supporters. To preclude such favoritism the reform movement stressed measures to politically "neutralize" city agencies by removing them from politicians' control. One means was to create independent departments presided over by boards and commissions that insulated the bureaucracy from mayoral influence. Another method removed city agencies from patronage politics by adoption of civil service laws which required appointment to and promotion within agencies according to merit rather than party service. The recruitment of professionally trained administrators for positions in city administrations applied this same principle to the top levels of city departments.

The reform movement has had a significant impact on local government in the twentieth century. Efficiency has increased, electoral systems are more democratic, and corruption and graft are more difficult, but at the same time the ability of any one elected official or coalition of officials to assemble sufficient power to overcome fragmented local units of government has been undermined. If anything, the structures incorporated into local government as a consequence of reform have increased the degree of fragmentation.

Reform has not entirely removed the machine from urban politics, as the continued dominance of Chicago politics by the Daley organization testifies. Even the merit system under civil service laws can be overcome, as Mike Royko (1971) indicates:

> There were more patronage jobs under the old Kelly-Nash Machine of the thirties and forties, but civil service reform efforts hurt the Machine. Some of the damage has been undone by Daley, however, who let civil service jobs slip back into patronage by giving tests infrequently or making them so difficult that few can pass, thus making it necessary to hire "temporary" employees, who stay "temporary" for the rest of their lives. Even civil service employees are subject to political pressures in the form of unwanted transfers, withheld promotions [p. 63].

In other communities reformed municipal bureaucracies may themselves be forming a new style of machine politics. Independent, professionalized city agencies behave according to principles of scientific management that professional associations of the employees create. Autonomous status has come to mean that only those professionally competent, that is, professional employees themselves, are qualified to judge the performance of city employees. Theodore J. Lowi (1968) argues that the legacy of the reform movement has created a new machine in the form of city bureaucracies:

> The modern city has become well-run but ungoverned because it has, according to Wallace Sayre and Herbert Kaufman, become comprised of "islands of functional power" before which the modern mayor stands denuded of authority. No mayor of a modern city has predictable means of determining whether the bosses of the New Machine—the bureau chiefs and the career commissioners—will be loyal to anything but their agency, its work, and related professional norms. . . . These modern machines, more monolithic by

far than their ancient brethren, are entrenched by law, and are supported by tradition, the slavish loyalty of the newspapers, the educated masses, the dedicated civic groups, and, most of all, by the organized clientele groups enjoying access under existing arrangements [pp. x–xi].

Whether the style of politics in localities is old machine, new machine, or reform, local governmental fragmentation imposes significant barriers to the governability of the most decentralized jurisdictions in American government. Local governments' unitary relationship to the states explains part of the barriers, but the interplay between machine and reform styles of politics accounts for other aspects of fragmented authority.

Given the size and diversity of American society, it is beyond question that the federal system of organization has considerable merits. But federalism imposes costs too. Whether the balance sheet of benefits and costs argues for retaining or abolishing federalism is a question beyond answer here, but one worth keeping in mind as we analyze other aspects of American government in its third century.

SUGGESTED READINGS

Elazar, Daniel J. *American Federalism: A View from the States.* New York: Crowell, 1966. An excellent general survey of American federalism. The book is good in pointing out the issues and problems surrounding intergovernmental relations.

Grodzins, Morton. *The American System: A New View of Governments in the United States.* Chicago: Rand McNally, 1966. A broad assessment of federalism in the United States. Covers many aspects of federal relations.

Maass, Arthur. *Area and Power: A Theory of Local Government.* New York: Free Press, 1950. A general discussion of the problems involved in the federal system of government. The theoretical and analytical approach makes the book very useful.

Prewitt, Kenneth, and Alan Stone. *The Ruling Elites: Elite Theory, Power and Democracy.* New York: Harper & Row, 1973. An introduction to the debate between elitism and pluralism and how it relates to democratic theory.

Riker, William T. *Federalism: Origin, Operation and Significance.* Boston: Little, Brown, 1964. A historical treatment of American federalism which is highly critical and provocative.

Wildavsky, Aaron B. (ed). *American Federalism in Perspective.* Boston: Little, Brown, 1967. A collection of essays by leading authorities on numerous aspects of federalism.

Wright, Deil S. *Federal Grants-in-Aid: Perspectives and Alternatives.* Washington, D.C.: American Enterprise Institute, 1968. Provides an extensive evaluation of the federal grants program.

Part Two

Politics

POLITICS TODAY IS INFLUENCED BY THE STRUCTURAL FOUNDATIONS discussed in Part One. On the other hand, many of the agencies through which American political negotiation is conducted go beyond the intentions of the Founders and the cornerstones for self-government which they designed. You may search the Constitution in vain for any mention of interest groups, public opinion, or political parties, let alone for guidelines about their proper governmental role. In the next five chapters we turn to the basic forms of participation in American politics. We look at the extent to which citizens have popular control over their government through public opinion and political socialization, interest groups and political parties, campaigns for public office, elections and voting, and a series of unconventional devices. The degree and kind of democracy citizens enjoy depend largely on the extent to which these devices advance or retard popular control.

Few would challenge what we assume in the next several chapters: that American democracy involves the ability of the governed to control their governmental institutions through available means of political participation. But how should we evaluate popular control? Should we simply examine the opportunities for citizen participation? If so, the issue turns on such global principles as the right to exercise the franchise, to express opinions freely, to choose between competing parties, and to associate freely and assemble in groups which petition and try to influence government officials. Without denying the importance of these *principles* of popular control, the following chapters assume that democratic self-governance often depends in the end on how well more subtle and often obscure *mechanics* of popular participation function.

Examination in detail of the mechanics of various forms of political participation makes it possible to distinguish the idealized image of American democracy from its practice. Popular control may hinge on such specific features of the political system as registration requirements for voting, the use by officials of opinion sampling techniques, the textbooks from which children learn in elementary grades, public disclosure of interest group contributions to political parties, and the potential for subliminal seduction in new campaign technologies. Such detailed consideration also covers the possible consequences for greater or lesser democratization inherent, in proposals to reform these mechanics of participation.

Our concern about the contribution of each form of the participatory process to democratic control should not obscure our concern for the end product. Taken together, do the various means of citizen input result in a democratic system of governing? Our review of recent trends may justify some pessimism. Declining rates of voting participation are all too apparent. Other forms of participation are also declining. And there are systematic differences between those who participate and those who do not. The nonparticipants are disproportionately drawn from the young, the less educated, and the poor. We relate these recent findings and trends to questions about the resources required for effective participation, the costs and benefits of participation, and the implications of declining participation for the legitimacy of government.

Groups, parties, opinions, campaigns, and elections are important forms of political participation. Yet these conventional forms do not span the entire spectrum of participation. A variety of unconventional forms of participation has been used to influence government and its officials. Protest, civil disobedience, rioting, and rebellion have been employed by the groups that are least active in the conventional forms and for whom conventional participation has yielded the fewest benefits. We conclude our discussion in Part Two with an examination of the nature, causes, and impact of unconventional forms of participation which sometimes represent a crucial dimension in American politics.

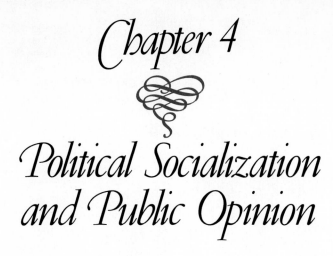

Chapter 4

Political Socialization and Public Opinion

LEARNING THE RULES

Thoughts on an Operating Table

When a delegation from the American Society of Newspaper Editors visited China in 1972, it stopped at Friendship Hospital in Peking to witness an acupuncture operation. The society's president, J. Edward Murray (1972), asked a seventeen-year-old patient who was on the operating table what he was thinking about when the incision was made.

"I was thinking how much the doctors are helping me so I can go back to work and help build socialism," said the youth.

"Were you thinking about anything else," persisted Murray, "anything more personal about yourself and the operation?"

"Yes. I was thinking that if the operation gave me pain, I would be resolute, fear no sacrifice, and overcome all difficulties to achieve victory for Chairman Mao."

Later, visiting Middle School 31, the editors listened to twelve-year-olds who were in their second year of studying English. "We love our great socialist motherland. Chairman Mao is the founder of New China. We love Chairman Mao," said one. "Chairman Mao leads us from victory to victory," said another.

Chinese Nurseryschool Children: Information at an early age. *(United Press International.)*

The seeming political precocity of the Chinese children amazed some visitors and disgusted others. Some were startled to find children with so much information at such an early age—impressive even without the consistent recitation of the party line. Some were repelled by the way the children's statements mirrored the thought of Chairman Mao indoctrinated into impressionable minds by an authoritarian regime.

But the Chinese practice is not as deviant as it might first appear. Practices that are easy to take for granted at home tend to stand out sharply when they assume unfamiliar configurations in a strange land. The fact is that every political system tries to implant attachments and loyalties into the hearts and minds of the young in order to gain the support of future generations. It is easy for a Western observer to dismiss as "political indoctrination" the image of Chinese youth parroting the party line, singing hymns about the triumph of the proletariat, and chauvinistically waving the little red book of Mao's thoughts. It is just as easy for observers from communist nations to label as "bourgeoisie propaganda" the stated ideals of American democracy found in our own civics textbooks, the flag salute and Pledge of Allegiance to the flag in school ceremonies, and in the retold tales of George Washington's cherry tree and Abe Lincoln's log cabin. Whether we think of it as indoctrination or education, the practice is universal. Children are everywhere taught to hold certain values and beliefs about politics and appropriate political behavior.

The opinions that adult Americans have about politics obviously do not spring fully developed into their minds as soon as they reach voting age. They are the result of a long and important process of acquiring attitudes, beliefs, and values which began quite early in life. Alexis de Tocqueville (1835) suggested, when he observed American politics in the nineteenth century, that an understanding of adult attitudes and beliefs had to begin with observation of childhood learning experiences:

> We must begin higher up; we must watch the infant in his mother's arms; we must see the first images which the external world casts upon the dark mirror of his mind, the first occurrences that he witnesses; we must hear the first words which awaken the sleeping powers of thought, and stand by his earliest efforts if we would understand the prejudices, the habits, and the passions which will later rule his life. The entire man is, so to speak, to be seen in the cradle of the child [p. 39].

Other political theorists considered this phenomenon before de Tocqueville. Plato (1908) recognized in the fourth century B.C. that what children were taught had an important impact on later adult behavior. He devoted a good deal of attention to methods of training for citizenship that would lead to a stable government and orderly politics.

The Power of Socialization

Modern interest in the phenomenon of political socialization was stimulated by the rise of authoritarian regimes, best exemplified by Nazi Germany in the 1930s. As a general rule, the better educated a society, the more libertarian it tends to be. Nazi Germany was an exception, and it got that way partly through the manipulation of the opinions and behavior of youth.

American Schoolchildren: Acquiring beliefs and values. *(Werner Wolff, Black Star.)*

Under the Nazi Banner, 1935: Building support for the system. *(Wide World Photos.)*

Political scientists began to realize that socialization—the process by which a child learns to come to terms with the expectations of the society around him—has an important political component. It is implicit in the nature of socialization, a process which has been colorfully described by John W. Whiting and Irvin L. Child (1963):

> In all societies, the helpless infant, getting his food by nursing at his mother's breast and, having digested it, freely evacuating the waste products, exploring his genitals, biting and kicking at will, must be changed into a responsible adult obeying the rules of his society [p. 63].

Political socialization, then, in the definition of Edward S. Greenberg (1970), is "the process by which the individual acquires attitudes, beliefs, and values relating to the political system of which he is a member and to his own role as citizen within that political system [p. 3]."

The process builds support for the system that is "diffuse" rather than "specific" in that the support is directed at the political system itself rather than individual actors in it. David Easton (1965) notes that this underpinning of diffuse support acts as a cushion against the ire of the public when things go wrong. Citizens are able to endure such mistakes and lapses of morality as the Vietnam war or the Watergate affair because they see the fault lying with the people who occupy the government positions at the time rather than with the underlying system. People come and go, but the form and structure of government remain, and so even the worst outcomes can be viewed as temporary aberrations. The legitimacy of the system remains unchallenged. Political parties as well as the total system can benefit from this effect. The Democrats lost some votes and some offices because of the Vietnam war. The Republicans lost some support because of Watergate. But most voters maintained their party loyalties throughout these crises (Converse, Miller, Rusk, and Wolfe, 1969; Gallup, 1973).

A Phenomenon Worth Watching

Socialization is such a powerful process that its effects on politics cannot be ignored. We are all subject to various learning experiences as we pass through different phases in the life cycle. Some of these experiences have to do with politics. Some of them have important consequences for how we view politics and how we behave with respect to the political system. There are three primary reasons for paying attention to this process of acquiring attachments and loyalties to political objects.

Potential for Manipulation. All governments want the support of future generations, and, to that end, they try to manipulate the kinds of values to which children are exposed. Certain American elites may call for an end to permissiveness, renewed attention to the virtues of private enterprise, and deference to the flag. The governing elites of other nations may manipulate with other kinds of symbols and information, but the object of the manipulation is the same: to produce support for the political system. This attention to what some may consider superficial or simpleminded is not as naive as it seems. It works.

Effectivensss. Children do become informed about politics at a very early age, and they are able to make choices. Table 4-1 shows how political

"A word to the wise, Benson. People are asking why they don't see Old Glory on your bike."

(Playboy.)

The Young as Invading Barbarians

During the first *two* years of the decade of the 1960s we added more young persons (about 2.6 million) to our population than in any preceding *ten* years since 1930.

The result of this has been provocatively stated by Professor Norman B. Ryder, the Princeton University demographer: "There is a perennial invasion of barbarians who must somehow be civilized and turned into contributors to fulfillment of the various functions requisite to societal survival." That "invasion" is the coming of age of a new generation of young people. Every society copes with this enormous socialization process more or less successfully, but occasionally that process is almost literally swamped by a quantitative discontinuity in the numbers of persons involved: "The increase in the magnitude of the socialization tasks in the United States during the past decade was completely outside the bounds of previous experience."

—James Q. Wilson and Robert L. DuPont, "The Sick Sixties,"
The Atlantic Monthly, October 1973.

knowledge increases with age among elementary school children in New Haven, Conn. The increase is steady and consistent. That this is a critical age period is demonstrated by the ability of seventh and eighth graders— twelve- and thirteen-year-olds—to know the name of the President or mayor and to provide informed answers about the duties and roles of each office. The New Haven study also shows that school children have political preferences. Of the ten-year-olds 63 percent identified themselves with a political party—far more than knew the President's or mayor's duties. Therefore, choice among political objects comes before knowledge about those objects. New Haven is not the world; but if this phenomenon is even close to being universal, political elites have good reason to be concerned with the kinds of political information that is made available to young people.

Explanatory Power.   The political choices made by children tend to stay with them when they become adults. Socialization is a continuing process,

Table 4-1   Accuracy of Information Given by Schoolchildren:
Fourth through Eighth Grades

	GRADE				
	4th	5th	6th	7th	8th
President's name	96%	97%	90%	99%	100%
Mayor's name	90	97	89	99	97
President's duties	23	33	44	65	66
Mayor's duties	35	42	50	66	67
Governor's duties	8	12	23	36	43
Role of state legislature	5	5	9	24	37
Number of cases	111	118	115	135	180

Source: Greenstein, Fred I., "The Benevolent Leader: Children's Images of Political Authority," *American Political Science Review*, December 1960, p. 937.

and some people may undergo several basic attitude shifts in the course of a lifetime. But, on the whole, early childhood attitudes remain among the strongest predictors of adult behavior. For example, V. O. Key (1961) noted that four out of five people whose parents supported the same party stayed with their parents' party in their first election. Later in this chapter, we shall look at the impact that adult opinions have upon American government and politics. But understanding adult opinions requires us to consider how they come to exist. The socialization process covers a complete generational cycle. Society forms attitudes in the child, who retains them as an adult and who forms part of the next generation's society which passes them on to its children. This does not mean that the same attitudes are always passed on from generation to generation unchanged. Too much goes on for that kind of static situation to exist. But the basic belief systems of Americans do show consistency over time (Campbell, Gurin, and Miller, 1954), and this is partly explained by the socialization process.

What Children Learn and How

The New Haven study showed that children have a high level of trust in public officials and support for American institutions. Political leaders were viewed as good, benevolent, and deserving of affection because of their competence and the services they provided (Greenstein, 1960, pp. 934–943). Much the same thing was found in another study (Easton and Hess, 1962) where 700 Midwestern school children were examined: "The sentiments of most children with respect to their political community are uniformly warm and positive throughout all grades, with scarcely a hint of criticism or note of dissatisfaction [pp. 236–237]." These studies, which

A study of children's attitudes toward the office [of the presidency] by Political Scientist F. Christopher Arterton of Wellesley College indicates . . . that the Watergate scandal already has profoundly altered at least one small group of the younger generation's perceptions of the presidency.

Writing in the current issue of *Political Science Quarterly*, Arterton cites a national 1962 study that indicated that children in the third, fourth and fifth grades overwhelmingly idealized the President, viewing him as "benevolent, omniscient, omnipotent, protective, infallible, diligent and likable." The professor's own much more limited current study of 367 children in the same grades in an upper-class Boston suburb (whose parents voted almost 2 to 1 for Nixon in 1972) shows a complete reversal. The President is now seen as what Arterton calls "truly malevolent, undependable, untrustworthy, yet powerful and dangerous." Where only 7% of the fourth-graders said of President Kennedy in 1962 that "he is not one of my favorites," 70% of Arterton's fourth-graders now hold that negative opinion of Nixon.

*The Effect of Watergate
on Children*

—*Time* Magazine, July 1, 1974.

pioneered in this relatively untapped field, showed how children enter the political world at an early age with the roots of strong and uncritical patriotism well implanted.

This same early research revealed that, by the age of seven or eight, children develop preferences for a political party in much the same way that they acquire an attachment to a religious denomination. Just as Methodist homes produce children whose religious preference is Methodist, so do Republican homes produce children who think of themselves as Republicans. The attachments to political parties tend to stick in much the same manner as denominational ties do. The data in Table 4-2, from a national election study in 1952, show how pronounced the effect can be.

Although the family seems to be the major socializing agent, the impact of schools, religious institutions, peer groups, and the mass media is important too. Robert D. Hess and Judith V. Torney (1967) argue that the school is even more important than the family because it reinforces the child's emotional attachment to his nation and teaches him to obey and conform. At the same time, they say, it de-emphasizes citizens' rights to participate in government and the power which individuals have to influence government. While this view asserting the primacy of schools over family is not shared by most students of the subject, there is agreement that educational institutions have a role in the process. About one-fifth of all school-age children attend parochial schools, and members of religious institutions may also be influenced when church officials take strong positions on political issues; for example, Jews favoring military protection for Israel, Catholics opposing legal abortion, and Jehovah's Witnesses refusing to salute the flag.

Just as much of a child's education takes place outside the classroom, so does the political socialization effect of schools occur partly in informal ways. Kenneth P. Langton (1967) has traced political attitudes to the kinds of friends one has in school. Studying students in Jamaica and Detroit, he found that working-class students have less positive attitudes toward voting and are less politically cynical and less economically conservative than middle-class and upper-class students. When lower-class students form friendships and associations with other students from the lower class, they come to hold attitudes that are accurate reflections of the lower class in

Table 4-2 Party Preference of Children as a
Function of Parental Preference

CHILD'S PREFERENCE	BOTH PARENTS DEMOCRATS	BOTH PARENTS REPUBLICANS
Democratic	82%	22%
Republican	15	73
Other	3	5

Source: Campbell, Angus, Gerald Gurin, and Warren E. Miller, *The Voter Decides*, Harper & Row, New York, 1954, p. 99.

(*Playboy.*)

general. But Langton found that these attitudes are not frozen. When lower-class students form friendships with students in higher social classes, they tend to adopt that group's political attitudes.

Socialization to Protest

When young people consciously reject the political system, as many have since the turmoil over race, poverty, and war in the 1960s, they are overcoming some very powerful internal forces. Hess and Torney (1967) have summed it:

> The young child's involvement with the political system begins with a strong positive attachment to the country; the U.S. is seen as ideal and as superior to other countries. This attachment to the country is stable and shows almost no change through elementary school years. This bond is possibly the most basic and essential aspect of the socialization into involvement with the political life of the nation. Essentially an emotional tie, it apparently grows from complex psychological and social needs and is exceedingly resistant to change or argument [p. 213].

Why, then, did young blacks riot in the streets, young whites protest the war in Vietnam, and young people of both races become disaffected with the system? For one thing, those who found expression in this way were not typical of young people in general. The so-called "generation gap" was largely a creation of the media generalizing from interesting but nonrepresentative cases.[1] It is more apparent than real, and differences within the younger generation are probably greater than differences between young and old (Adelson, 1970). The extent of youthful dissent nevertheless led students of political socialization to reexamine some of their evidence. One flaw which they found was that most of the subjects in the earlier studies were children in white, middle-class, and mostly suburban communities. It may have been wrong to assume that children from these communities were representative of young people in general and ignore the possibility that differences in race, income, or geography might be related to different views toward the political system.

In an effort to explain some of the behavior of the 1960s, researchers started looking elsewhere. One study chose an impoverished lower-class white area of eastern Kentucky to ask many of the same questions used in

[1]The "generation gap" was best defined by anthropologist Margaret Mead, who was talking about a one-time situation. Those born before World War II and those born after, she said, were socialized in grossly different circumstances.

Table 4-3 Fifth- to Eighth-grade Children's Evaluations of the President

		RESPONSE	KNOX COUNTY	CHICAGO AREA
1.	View of how hard the President works compared with most men	harder	35%	77%
		as hard	24	21
		less hard	41	3
2.	View of the honesty of the President compared with most men	more honest	23%	57%
		as honest	50	42
		less honest	27	1
3.	View of the President's liking for people as compared with most men	like most everybody	50%	61%
		likes as many as most	28	37
		doesn't like as many	22	2
4.	View of the President's knowledge compared with most men	knows more	45%	82%
		knows about the same	33	16
		knows less	22	2
5.	View of the President as a person	best in world	6%	11%
		a good person	68	82
		not a good person	26	8

the earlier research. Table 4-3 shows how these Appalachian children viewed the President as less hard working, less honest, less friendly, less knowledgeable, and not as good a person as did the middle-class Chicago suburban children. The Appalachian children were also more cynical about politics generally. These attitudes tended to endure over time.

Studies of black children also contest the early view that support for the political system remains strong among all children. Paul R. Abramson (1972) has summed their findings:

> Socialization researchers, having studied a wide range of political attitudes among American school children, agree upon the following two findings: Finding 1: Black school children tend to have lower feelings of political effectiveness than white children do; and Finding 2: Black school children tend to have lower feelings of trust toward political leaders than white children do [p. 1244].

Black school children's distrust of political leaders increased after the summer of rioting in 1967. A hypothesis to explain the greater distrust of black and Appalachian children is not hard to find. Both groups are relatively disadvantaged in terms of the opportunities they have for success in American society, and both are relatively powerless. These factors have

Young Voters in Berkeley, California, 1971: A rapid growth in interest. *(United Press International.)*

created subcultures of discontent. Conversely, the affection with which American middle- and upper-class whites view the political system and its institutions is an accurate reflection of the way the system treats *them*. This approval of the system is not necessarily an indicator of the system's democratic virtues (Weissberg, 1972).

The Duration of Socialization

In the early studies, it seemed that the work of political socialization was largely completed by the late grammar school years. Easton and Hess (1962) could see little substantive change during the four years of high school; attitudes seemed already frozen by then. Later work has shown that socialization is a lifetime process. Political knowledge and political interest are particularly susceptible to change in the high school years. M. Kent Jennings and Richard G. Niemi (1970) looked at national election studies by the Survey Research Center of the University of Michigan and found that "there is a major acquisition of knowledge" about differences between the political parties during the high school years (p. 149). And they found that interest in public affairs tends to grow rapidly among young adults as they enter the electorate, climbs for a while and then levels off, and finally in the retirement years, starts to decline. In our highly mobile society, there are many opportunities for exposure to new peer groups which result in changes in beliefs. Attending college, joining a trade union or a business association can have that effect. Upward or downward social mobility can change political ideas along with class identification. Finally, special situations can and do arise which override the effect of early socialization. As Greenberg (1970) has said,

> One need not be overtly oppressed or deprived to manifest nonsupport [for leaders of the political system]. Certainly, a significant number of the young and highly educated are beginning to bring into question the legitimacy of political, social, and economic arrangements. In a sense, the Vietnam war and the civil rights movement may be the most significant socializing events of our time, playing as powerful a role as did the Depression for the parents of the present generation [p. 12].

In other words, what the political system does to you or for you has an important impact on your political values, expectations, and beliefs. Government action or inaction always produces advantage for some and disadvantage for others. It is perfectly rational for both groups to adjust their beliefs, values, and attachments accordingly; and political socialization is, in part, a rational process. The socialization process in the adult years, therefore, both affects government and is affected by it. For one of the most important and visible products of adult political socialization is that fascinating force known as public opinion.

What Public Opinion Is Not

Scholars who have tried to arrive at a concise definition of public opinion have not been very successful. But one thing is fairly certain: It is not what you think it is. We make this assertion with some assurance because of the easy way the concept is used in casual conversation about political matters. "People won't stand for it." "People want the candidate to say where he stands." "People would rather have inflation than unemployment." In none of these statements is it specified just which people are referred to. Nor is it specified in just what form or intensity their views are held. Will the people who "won't stand for it," whatever "it" may be, riot in the streets if "it" is thrust upon them? Or will they merely complain mildly and turn their attention to something else? The difficulty is that there are many different publics, and opinion takes many different forms.

Some of the confusion exists because of the precise way public opinion *seems* to be measured. The Gallup Poll reported in August 1974, that 71 percent of the voting-age public approved of the way President Ford was handling his job as President, 3 percent disapproved, and 26 percent had no opinion. This suggests a situation in which nearly everyone has information on which to judge the President's performance, nearly everyone cares how well he is doing, and nearly everyone is able to reflect on one's feelings and one's information and arrive at an overall verdict of approval or disapproval. This image departs from reality in several respects.

For one thing, most of the respondents probably would not have thought about the President at all if the Gallup interviewer had not brought up the subject. The President's performance, while of concern to all of us, does not normally rank high on the list of daily worries. And among those who do think about it some are more concerned and better informed than others. For those who do feel a pressing concern, the issue is said to have salience. But the poll does not measure salience.

Another departure from reality comes from the unspoken assumption made by the use of the simple percentage breakdowns that every given person's opinion is as valuable as any others. For examples of why this is not so, we need think no farther than the college students who worked for Eugene McCarthy in the 1968 New Hampshire primary. Each of them, through his or her work on the Senator's behalf, was worth a great many votes—even though most were too young to cast votes of their own. Or, for another kind of example, consider the 100 largest donors to the 1972 presidential campaign. Together, they contributed one-third the total cost of reelecting the President (Polk, 1973). Obviously, their opinions count for far more than those of members of the public who are of average means.

Interest, intensity, and the ability to act are all qualities which make one person's opinion different from another's, even though both may give

Table 4-4   President Nixon's Popularity, January 1973 to August 1974.

Question: "Do you approve or disapprove of the way Nixon is handling his job as President?"

DATE	APPROVE	DISAPPROVE	NO OPINION
Jan. 12–15, 1973	51%	37%	12%
Jan. 26–29	68	25	7
Feb. 16–19	65	25	10
Mar. 30–Apr. 2	59	32	9
Apr. 6–9	54	36	10
Apr. 27–30	48	40	12
May 4–7	45	42	13
May 11–14	44	45	11
June 1–4	44	45	11
June 22–25	45	45	10
July 6–9	40	49	11
Aug. 3–6	31	57	12
Aug. 17–20	38	54	8
Sept. 7–10	35	55	10
Sept. 21–24	32	59	9
Oct. 6–8	30	57	13
Oct. 19–22	27	60	13
Nov. 2–5	27	63	10
Nov. 30–Dec. 3	31	59	10
Dec. 7–10	29	60	11
Jan. 4–7, 1974	27	63	10
Jan. 18–21	26	64	10
Feb. 1–4	28	59	13
Feb. 8–11, 15–18	27	63	10
Feb. 22–25, Mar. 1–4	25	64	11
Mar. 8–11, 15–18	26	62	12
Mar. 29–Apr. 1	26	65	9
Apr. 12–15	25	62	13
Apr. 19–29	26	60	14
May 10–13	25	61	14
May 31–June 3	28	61	11
June 21–24	26	61	13
July 12–15	24	63	13
Aug. 2–5	26	64	10

Source: Gallup Opinion Index.

the same response to the interviewer. These factors are measurable to some extent, and the more sophisticated public opinion research, some of it Gallup's, tries to get at them.

Getting Information about Public Affairs

The interest level of most people about public affairs is lower than you might think. You may (like most members of the minority who attend college) suffer from the egocentrism fallacy—the belief that most people see things pretty much the same way you do. But the single fact that you are reading this book marks you as a member of an incipient educated elite

Presidential Performance, 1974: The polls do not measure salience. *(United Press International.)*

which is quite peculiar and deviant when compared to the population in general. If, for example, you know the name of the congressman from your district, you are better informed than 54 percent of the adult population. "Even among the people who have had some college education," reports Louis Harris (1973), "only 55 percent could name their Congressman and 49 percent the party he belongs to [pp. 76–77]." Nearly all Americans can name the President, and nine out of ten can name their governors. Ignorance about state and local officials varies with size of community—the larger the community, the greater the ignorance. People are, however, capable of quickly becoming informed once an issue touches them directly, as when, for example, they are asked to vote on school bond issues which affect their taxes.

Broadcasting

The main source of information about public affairs is television, according to surveys sponsored by the Television Information Office (Roper, 1969). However, not even the major network news programs are well attended to. An average fall weekday will find about one adult out of four watching an evening news broadcast of one of the three major networks. Most of these viewers are quite regular about it. John Robinson (1971), who has done extensive research on how people spend their time, estimates that about one adult in five is a regular news viewer while the remainder are irregular viewers or don't view it at all. The latter category is surprisingly large. In one large-scale study cited by Robinson, a majority of the national sample went two weeks without seeing one national news program. The regular news viewers tended to be less well educated and included more persons over fifty than those who did not watch regularly. These are characteristics associated with people who watch more television in general.

Television Newscast: One in four is watching. *(Wide World Photos.)*

Newspapers

Nearly four out of five adults read a newspaper on an average weekday. Not all read for information about government, of course. The comic section is the most widely read section of the newspaper. The weather report gets high readership, as does information about war, defense, and major crime. State government is among the least read-about categories. News about the national government falls between these extremes, attracting about one adult reader in five (Swanson, 1965).

The influence of newspapers on public opinion is not evenly distributed. Officials in Washington are more likely to be influenced by the *Washington Star-News* than by the *Kansas City Star* simply because they have more access to it. Other elites tend to follow the Washington newspapers, the *New York Times*, and the *Wall Street Journal* because they know that government officials read them. The editors and publishers of these newspapers are aware of their special role, and this in turn influences the content of their papers. One result is that these newspapers become part of the apparatus by which the government communicates with itself. John Connally did not learn that President Nixon looked upon him favorably as a potential Republican presidential candidate by hearing it from the Pres-

Helping the Government Communicate with Itself

In late 1965, lower-level China-watchers within the State Department became alarmed over certain Pentagon targeting plans for the bombing of North Vietnam; the plans called for strikes against sites so close to the China border that the Chinese might feel compelled reluctantly either to intervene or at least to shoot down some of our off-course aircraft and thereby perhaps trigger a much wider war. These specialists had tried to make their case to the higher-ups, but in vain; the message had not got through to Messrs. Dean Rusk and Robert McNamara, nor to the White House. The worried officials therefore chose to alert a New York *Times* correspondent, on his daily rounds at State, that things were looking poorly; they did so carefully and obliquely. . . . The result was a front-page *Times* story the next day saying that China specialists in the Government were being locked out of Vietnam planning and were alarmed by impending escalation. McNamara called McGeorge Bundy in a fury; Bundy called some of the rest of us in a fury, and there was much hell to pay. But the upshot was that Rusk, McNamara and Bundy called in the China-watching community for a special Saturday morning session—and that the targeting plans were at once modified as a result of what the China types said.

—James C. Thomson, Jr., *New York Times Magazine*, Nov. 25, 1973.

ident's own lips. He read a secondhand report of the President's thoughts in a newspaper. This was a way of giving him the word while leaving the President free to change his mind. It also illustrates the quasi-governmental function of the elite press. The press is a kind of bulletin board where elites of the government, the media, and the private sector can keep track of one another, send signals to each other, and test ideas and proposals while they are still in a tentative form. Members of diverse and shifting factions use this medium to find out who is on whose side, to sort their friends from their enemies as situations and issues change.

We would expect, then, that the elite press has an elite readership, and the audience profile of the *New York Times* bears this out. In a 1967 study, 20 percent of the *Times* readers had incomes of $20,000 a year or more, compared to only 5 percent of the nonreaders, and 10 percent of its readers, but only 2 percent of nonreaders, held advanced degrees. The paper was read by 36 percent of all corporation executives in the United States (New York Times Company, 1968). It is known as "a proud, almost arrogant, newspaper whose daily circulation . . . goes to a special leadership audience around the world [Merrill, 1968, p. 263]."

Most people, however, do not have regular, easy access to the elite press. Their information about national affairs comes from wire service reports by overworked writers who are constrained by time and the need to satisfy a politically diverse clientele. Interpretative accounts are rare. There is a trend toward consolidation of newspaper ownership which can make the resources of large organizations available to small newspapers. In 1950, newspapers owned by groups accounted for 43 percent of all daily circulation. In 1972, groups had 60 percent of the total. At the turn of the century, most cities had competing newspapers. Now fewer than 4 percent do (Bishop, 1972). While consolidation produces economies of scale and an opportunity for product improvement, this benefit has not been consistently passed on to the consumer. Gerald L. Grotta (1971) made a time-series study of 154 daily newspapers and concluded that "consumers pay higher prices under consolidated ownership with no compensating increase in quality or quantity of product received and perhaps a decrease in quality [p. 250]."

Participation

Between broadcast and print media, the public has more information available than it is prepared to consume. The generally low level of interest in and information about public affairs is reflected in the rate of participation in the political process. The highest turnout for a presidential election since World War I was 64 percent, achieved in the 1960 election between Kennedy and Nixon which was atypical for a number of reasons. The election was close, neither candidate was an incumbent, both were young, and, in different ways, appealing. Turnout was 56 percent in the 1972 presidential election, the lowest since 1948. Lack of interest among the newly enfranchised eighteen-to-twenty age group was one factor. Among nonvoters interviewed in the Gallup Poll, the largest group, 38 percent, said they failed to vote because they either had not bothered to register or were prevented by residence requirements from registering. Twenty-eight percent said they were not interested in politics, 10 percent didn't like either Nixon or McGovern, and another 10 percent were sick or disabled on election day. The remainder were away from their home precincts on election day or couldn't get time off from their jobs (Gallup, 1972). Whatever the reason, nearly half of adult Americans were public-opinion dropouts on election day 1972.

Changing Minds

Anyone who tries to affect public policy by arousing public opinion must first cope with the apathy problem. In a classic study of why campaigns to inform the public about foreign affairs usually fail, Herbert H. Hyman and Paul Sheatsley (1947) examined attitudes toward five major issues. They found that 12 percent of the population was unaware of any one of the five issues and another 18 percent had heard of no more than one. The people most likely to acquire new information are those who already know something about the subject. Ignorance and apathy go together. Apathy and ignorance are not necessarily the fault of the citizen. They might be the fault of the government for failing to serve and stimulate the interests of the citizen by making itself available and understandable to him. If the issues

Presidential Candidates in 1960: Afterward, a dwindling of interest. *(Philip Drell, Black Star.)*

Combat in Vietnam: The public's attention was selective. *(United Press International.)*

are beyond the citizen's understanding or control, apathy is a perfectly sensible response.

While having some knowledge to start with makes it easier to acquire new information on the same subject, it can also create other problems. Hyman and Sheatsley found that people who already know something about the subject tend to be drawn to information that is consistent with the attitudes they already hold. When confronted with information that conflicts with these existing attitudes, they may simply misperceive it. Psychologist Leon Festinger (1962) has explained this process in his "theory of cognitive dissonance," which says that a person who is confronted with conflicting information will try to resolve the conflict, either by changing his opinion, by changing his behavior, or by distorting his perception. Often misperception is the easiest of these alternatives. Ralph K. White (1968) has attributed the high level of acceptance of the Vietnam war in its earlier years to "selective inattention" to the brutal facts of the war as a dissonance-reducing device (p. 202).

Instant Electorate?

Already, it can be seen that managing a democracy is more complicated than simply providing what the people want. "Your representative owes you, not his industry only," said Edmund Burke in 1774, "but his judgment; and he betrays instead of serving you if he sacrifices it to your opinion [1949, p. 447]." Or, as put by a contemporary observer (Sherrill, 1968), "If Congressmen decide their votes by following the leader as the best alternative to flipping a coin, they nevertheless display sheer brilliance compared with the electorate . . . [p. 176]."

Technically, it is possible to attach a button to the telephone of every voter so that an instant referendum could be held on every issue, from dropping bombs on a foreign capital to hiring an assistant dog catcher for the District of Columbia. But public opinion is too formless, uninformed, and inconsistent to make such a system desirable.

The deliberative process of representative government smooths out the inconsistencies, and it also builds in a time lag that tends to smooth the emotional peaks and valleys in the public response to events. A majority might be mustered to approve the bombing of a foreign capital in retaliation for some insult on Monday but not on Tuesday or Wednesday. A system that reacts slowly to public opinion is in less danger of giving disproportionate weight to the earliest and least considered opinions. And it provides better continuity in public policy.

Consensus and Clustering

Public opinion becomes less formless if we probe its structure for clusters of attitudes that have a bearing on specific issues. Systematic investigation that looks beyond the one-man, one-vote model of public opinion is a fairly recent development. Philip Converse noted in 1963 that much of what survey researchers thought they were measuring could only be called "non-attitudes." He decided this when he discovered that there were very low correlations between responses given by the same people to the same questions on political attitudes in successive surveys. Their opinions were so unstable they could hardly be called opinions at all. Later, he argued that people without any meaningful beliefs at all on a given issue ought to be "set aside as not forming any part of that particular *issue public*." What we are accustomed to thinking of as the mass public is really a "plethora of narrower issue publics [1964, p. 245]."

These issue publics are many and diverse. They defy classification along simple dimensions such as liberal-conservative. Whether a person belongs to any given issue public depends less on any kind of ideological bent than on how much information about the issue he has (Natchez and Bupp, 1968). Unfortunately, most opinion polls do not give us these data, and we are tempted to think of the public as more committed to strongly held views than it really is.

This point is illustrated by a question used in polls taken in the 1960 election campaign. Respondents were asked if the United States should defend the islands of Quemoy and Matsu against a hypothetical Chinese attack. Few Americans had heard of these islands before candidates Nixon and Kennedy began arguing about them. Few have thought about them since then. The deserved obscurity which this issue has attained with the passage of time suggests that the most rational responses were those of voters who said they didn't know or didn't care. But the contrived nature of the issue was not so apparent in 1960, and the polls played a part in the contriving. The problem is that the polls can create the kind of situation they seem to describe. Leo Bogart (1972) speculates that the public polls become a reference point around which individual beliefs are formed. "When polls are published and widely discussed, what people say they want is likely to be what they are told they want by the polls. Thus yesterday's perceptions govern tomorrow's expressions of the public mood [p. 20]."

A GUIDE FOR OPINION WATCHING

How Public Opinion Is Measured

The techniques of measuring public opinion are fairly straightforward. A small sample will be representative of the total population within predictable ranges of error provided it is drawn so that each member of the population has a known chance of being included in the sample. This is easy enough to visualize if you imagine a barrel containing 25,000 black marbles and 25,000 white marbles. If the marbles were thoroughly stirred so that you could draw from the barrel blindfolded with each marble having an equal chance of being drawn, you would not have to pull out very many before realizing that the distribution of black marbles and white marbles was about equal. From the well-established laws of probability theory, we can calculate that a sample of 370 marbles drawn in such a manner would reflect the true 50/50 division within a 5 percent margin of error nineteen times out of twenty. A larger barrel requires only a slightly larger sample: Increasing the marble population to infinity would require increasing the sample to no more than 384 for the same level of accuracy.

Sampling the electorate is somewhat more complicated than sampling barrels of marbles, only because voters won't hold still. But the same mathematical rules apply. The best way to draw a national sample of voters would be to put the names of all the voters in a barrel and draw out a sample large enough to assure the desired level of accuracy. Another way to accomplish the same result would be to assign each voter a number and then draw the sample by consulting a table of random numbers.

But there is no master voter list, and so pollsters base their samples on housing units instead. The Bureau of the Census can provide the number of housing units in every county, minor civil division, and census tract in the nation, and, in urbanized areas, in every block. Therefore it is possible to draw a sampling of housing units with each unit having a known probability of being included. Selection of respondents within the chosen housing units can also be left to chance. Refinements have been developed in recent years, some to reduce costs and others to improve accuracy. The result, in the case of the Gallup Poll, is a system which provides accuracy within 3 or

4 percentage points 95 percent of the time, using a national sample of 1,500 respondents.

Spotting a Bad Poll

A poorly designed survey can often produce the right answer so long as its bias does not correlate with the thing being studied. You could sample the well-stirred barrel of marbles by skimming the sample from the top of the barrel and still infer the true distribution of black and white. You could do this because there would be no correlation between position in the barrel and color of the marbles. But if the black marbles had been poured in first and if the barrel had not been thoroughly stirred, then position would correlate with color, and skimming the top would produce a sample biased in favor of white. In the same way, a newspaper survey of voters encountered in shopping centers can successfully predict the election as long as there is no correlation between candidate choice and tendency to frequent shopping centers. If stay-at-homes tend to vote a different way, the survey will be biased. There are only two ways to discover if this is so: Conduct another survey, using probability sampling, or wait for the outcome of the election.

The *Literary Digest* used a biased survey design with considerable success between 1912 and 1932. It began quite informally by soliciting volunteer reports from readers on voter sentiment in their areas and then became somewhat more systematic by sending ballots in the mail to the largest lists of names it could find, mainly automobile registration and telephone subscriber lists.

This procedure worked well enough. Errors were often large, but they were always in the winning direction, and so the magazine could claim to have predicted the outcome. And in 1932 there was virtually no error at all; the poll called Roosevelt's winning margin within a fraction of a percentage point. Its telephone and car-user lists were biased in favor of the affluent, but affluence did not correlate with presidential preference in 1932.

Four years later, it did. The New Deal coalition of farmers and workers gave the parties a new division along economic lines, and the *Literary Digest* bias, unknown to its editors, suddenly became crucial. From a mailing of 10 million ballots it received 2 million and predicted a landslide victory for Alf Landon. The landslide went the other way. The poll's error was 19 percentage points. It and the magazine were abandoned (Mosteller, 1949).

In that same year, Gallup and other poll takers with a better understanding of sampling theory correctly foresaw Roosevelt's victory. Gallup performed another impressive feat. On July 12, 1936, he published the result of a sampling of the *Literary Digest* sample. Using a mailing to only 3,000 names from the same list which produced the magazine's 10 million names, he predicted, within a percentage point, what the *Digest* poll would show and explained why it would be wrong. "While this may seem to have

Election Winner, 1948: For Gallup, a change in method. *(Wide World Photos.)*

been a foolhardy stunt, actually there was little risk,'' Gallup (1972) recalled later, ''. . . because of the workings of the laws of probability, that 3,000 sample should have provided virtually the same result as the *Literary Digest's* . . . which, in fact, it did [pp. 66–67].''

Quota Sampling

Probability sampling did not become the standard method until after the great polling debacle of 1948. Gallup and other pollsters divided the electorate into categories according to social and economic characteristics and assigned each interviewer a quota of respondents within each category. The interviewer could select the respondents so long as each quota was filled. This method worked reasonably well, but it contributed to a five-point error in favor of Thomas E. Dewey in 1948. Another factor in the error was a last minute shift of disaffected Democrats back to their own party. The Gallup interviewing ended in mid-October, too soon to catch this movement. Since then, the major polls have used probability sampling and have continued interviewing until the last minute. And their accuracy has been notable. In recent elections, the Gallup Poll and its younger competitor, the Harris Survey, have produced results well within the statistical tolerance for sampling error in national election surveys.

Hubert Humphrey in 1968 Campaign: A case of mistaken judgment. *(United Press International.)*

Bandwagons and Underdogs

When a politician is losing an election and the polls show him behind, he may come to believe that he is losing *because of* the poll. The voters, he reasons, are flocking to his opponent because they want to climb aboard the winning bandwagon.

Voters make their choices among competing candidates for a variety of reasons, some more rational than others, which will be explored in Chapter 7. There is no evidence that voters are motivated in their selections by a desire to be on the winning side. If that were the case, then election campaigns in which a series of polls are taken should show the front runner getting farther and farther ahead as the campaign progresses. In fact, the early front runner is just as likely to lose ground as to gain during the campaign. So if there is a bandwagon effect from polls, there must be an equal and opposite underdog effect which impels voters to choose the losing candidate because he is a loser.

The true bandwagon effect operates not on public opinion but on planning and morale of campaign workers and potential contributors. Hubert Humphrey, who had the support of only 30 percent of the potential voters at the start of his 1968 presidential campaign, had trouble raising the badly needed early money for television commitments (Alexander, 1971). Would-be donors were reluctant to back a loser. Had they realized that Humphrey's low September standing was only temporary and that the polls would show him in a dramatic last-minute resurgence, they might have made the early donations that would have changed the outcome of the election. While many campaign workers blamed the polls, the judgment of the donors, who mistakenly assumed that early voter attitudes are frozen for the duration of the campaign, must also be questioned.

Sometimes, a favorable showing in a poll can be bad news for a candidate. Robert J. Huckshorn and Robert C. Spencer (1971), in a study of losing campaigns for Congress, believe there is a reverse bandwagon effect on campaign workers. "If the candidate is shown by a poll to have a reasonable chance of success, his campaign workers may slacken their efforts on the assumption that their services are not really needed to assure victory [p. 184]." A well-managed campaign counters this tendency with exhortations to the workers.

A related concern over feedback effects of public opinion on the election outcome is raised by the practice of broadcasting early election returns from the East while polls are still open in the West. A number of studies have sought to learn whether Western voters who are exposed to these broadcasts exhibit measurable differences in candidate choice from those who are not. No such difference has yet been found (Tuchman and Coffin, 1971). However, in a very close election, such an effect might be too small to measure by conventional survey methods and still change the outcome.

News Management

Because information is so important in the formation of issue publics, the information-processing and distributing media play a key role. Skill in manipulating the media is therefore important to politicians. The overtly staged or pseudo-event is a common device. It may be a speech in the Senate, a radio broadcast by the President, a press release from the Federal Bureau of Investigation, or the appearance of a Cabinet secretary at a breakfast of newspaper reporters. In each case, the target is not the immediate audience but the potential issue public whose attention can be focused on the staged event by the media. News media are conditioned to respond to objective facts and tend to react to such stage-managing uncritically. "The problem in this fast-moving society," says Washington correspondent James McCartney (1970), "is to put hundreds of these pseudo-events, staged daily, into a context that bears a relationship to their importance [p. 41]." A failure to provide the needed perspective on the Vietnam war left many newspapermen with deep feelings of guilt over having passively abetted President Johnson in his quiet escalation of the conflict. "We knew what the Government was up to," said Tom Wicker of the *New York Times*. "I suppose I was one of the few people in Washington who could get the President of the United States on the phone if I had to, to check an important point. But that wasn't enough. I'm not sure in looking back now that sometimes we didn't do more harm than good by just telling it as the Administration said it was [McCartney, 1970, p. 36]."

When public opinion finally turned against the war, it was not because of moral revulsion or heightened awareness of the extent of the killing and suffering. It was reaction to a staged event, the Tet offensive on Saigon in January 1968. The official American military interpretation of that event was that it was a military defeat for the Viet Cong and the NorthViet-namese, but for the relevant issue publics, it was "new and dramatic evidence that the war was far from over and far from being won [Schuman, 1972, p. 516n]." That spring, the U.S. military establishment's plea for more intensive war making was rejected, President Johnson announced his retirement, and the ultimate winding down of the war was begun. Don Oberdorfer (1971), a reporter who followed events in Washington and in Asia, recalls what happened:

> . . . the fundamental decision . . . [to end the war] was made outside the government. Large segments of the American public and particularly the non-governmental elite of businessmen, lawyers, bankers, editors and publishers and the like, the influential leaders of "private opinion" in the United States, had lost confidence in the war. These people had approved and then tolerated the ever growing commitment of American troops and resources to South Vietnam, but time and events had strained their patience to the breaking point. After Tet, the promise of success had faded, the sense of futility and frustration had grown. The country would not go deeper into the quagmire without a clear and believable vision of success [pp. 296–297].

Another news management tool is the calculated "leak" of information. Leaking can have several functions beyond mere communication. One

President Johnson Meeting Reporters: An uncritical reaction to stage management. *(United Press International.)*

is the "trial balloon" in which a contemplated decision is floated to test what the public or interest-group reaction will be. President Johnson's conspicuous interviews with Senators Eugene McCarthy, Thomas Dodd, and others before he announced a vice-presidential choice for the 1964 election campaign are an example. In some cases, the President may have been carrying the subtlety of his manipulation one step further: perhaps he only wanted to give the *appearance* of floating trial balloons for old friends such as Dodd simply to give the flattering impression that he considered them qualified and to help them with their own constituencies.

A different function of the news leak is to block an unwanted policy move before its advocates in the administration can effectively launch it. If one group of advisors seems about to convince the President that he should propose a tax increase, an opposing group may leak the news that a tax increase is imminent in order to mobilize public opposition and kill the plan before it ever leaves the White House. In this case, the President is the object of manipulation. President Johnson, with his passion for secrecy, was particularly susceptible and was known to withdraw planned appointments when news of them leaked prematurely.

Opinion and Leadership

The Vietnam case illustrates how different issue publics can have different effects. The morally concerned, student-based opposition to the war began around 1965 and had very little effect on either mass opinion or on the nation's political leaders. Another segment of the public, more concerned with pragmatic outcomes than morality, supported the war so long as it was possible to believe that an evil was being avoided or a good was being obtained. This belief became increasingly difficult to sustain: the proportion of the public who said yes to the Gallup question, "In view of the developments since we entered the fighting, do you think the United States made a mistake in sending troops to fight in Vietnam?" increased. It went from 24 percent in 1965 to 61 percent by May 1971. The two months after Tet produced "the largest and most important change in public opinion during the entire war [Schuman, p. 515]." And this shift was led by the turnaround in elite opinion.

Leaders manipulate public opinion and public opinion manipulates leaders. The effects are difficult to sort out. One thing that seems clear is that leaders find it much easier to change their own minds about an issue than to change the public's mind. In part, this may be due to a conditioning effect of the media: new events are interpreted in old contexts simply because the interpreters lack the imagination to see the new context. Throughout most of the 1960s, any prominent officeholder who spoke in favor of diplomatic recognition for Mainland China risked being treated as a comical aberration. When President Nixon finally went to Communist China in 1972, the pundits who criticized him for lack of substantive

President Nixon in China, 1972: Breaking the old media mold. *(United Press International.)*

accomplishment did not realize that his main achievement was a domestic one: breaking the old media mold which reflexively held that any contact with the Chinese was laughably unthinkable. In doing this, the President was not entirely bold. He was accelerating a trend begun some years before. According to the Harris Survey, the sentiment for admitting China to the United Nations increased from 10 percent in 1964 to 48 percent in 1971, just before the President's trip was announced. And support for diplomatic recognition of China rose from 43 percent in 1966 to 55 percent in 1971. This trend went largely unnoticed by the media because it was not an "event." The President's trip was a reportable event, and it helped legitimate and consolidate approval of more realistic treatment of China.

The Echo Chamber

Very early in the Vietnam war, President Johnson made a calculated decision not to put the nation on a full-scale war footing with patriotic propaganda, atrocity stories, and other trappings of an all-out effort. He wanted to leave open the possibility of changing his mind and getting out, and this would have been difficult if a deep-seated hate-Hanoi attitude had taken hold. President Nixon was the beneficiary of this restraint when he began to bring the troops home and wind down the war. But he still had difficulty in selling Congress and the public on the desirability of a massive program of economic aid for the former enemy. A public conditioned to believe in the evil ways of the other side could not be converted overnight into believing that the former enemy was deserving of gifts from hard-pressed American taxpayers.

A similar problem existed on a much larger scale as the government sought to unload the burden of years of cold-war propaganda which had educated the public into accepting a simplistic view of international tensions as a struggle between good capitalists and bad communists for control of the globe. Sociologist Amitai Etzioni (1967) has observed that several presidents might have liked to support the admission of mainland China to the United Nations but did not because, "the American public was educated against it, and the administration believed that no amount of short run explanation could change public opinion to make the political costs low enough [p. 380]." President Kennedy tried to reduce cold-war tensions through a series of gestures that he hoped would produce similar reactions from the Soviet Union and which, in turn, would soften American public opinion toward the Soviets. Such an attitude change would increase his own range of options.

Not all heads of state have been so cautious. Winston Churchill publicly disdained public opinion polls, followed his own judgment, and counted on history to prove him right. V. O. Key, Jr. (1966), warned of the danger posed by leaders who develop an obsessive concern for public opinion, a concern which tends to grow as the opinion-measuring devices become more sophisticated:

> If leaders believe the route to victory is by projection of images and cultivation of styles rather than by advocacy of policies to cope with the problems of the country, they will project images and cultivate styles to the neglect of the substance of politics. They will abdicate their prime function in a democratic system, which amounts, in essence, to the assumption of the risk of trying to persuade us to lift ourselves by our bootstraps [p. 6].

The voice of the people, Key said, "is but an echo." What the leaders hear coming out of the echo chamber depends on what they put into it. "Even the most discriminating popular judgment can reflect only ambiguity, uncertainty, or even foolishness if those are the qualities of the input into the echo chamber [pp. 2–3]."

SUGGESTED READINGS

Bogart, Leo. *Silent Politics: Polls and the Awareness of Public Opinion.* New York: Wiley, 1972. A careful examination of the formation and changes in public opinion. Discusses the nature of polls and their relationship to public policy.

Dawson, Richard and Kenneth Prewitt. *Political Socialization.* Boston: Little, Brown, 1969. A good introduction to the subject of political socialization. The work utilizes numerous research studies conducted in this area of inquiry.

Greenstein, Fred. *Children and Politics.* New Haven, Conn.: Yale, 1965. A pioneering study of the process of political socialization of elementary school children.

Hennessy, Bernard. *Public Opinion.* Belmont, Calif.: Wadsworth, 1965. A good introduction to the theories and methods of public opinion, with an emphasis on the relationship between public opinion and democratic theory.

Key, V. O., Jr. *Public Opinion and American Democracy.* New York: Knopf, 1961. An excellent analysis of the dynamics between public attitudes and the operations of the government. Gives a detailed analysis of issues and concepts.

Lippmann, Walter. *Public Opinion.* New York: Free Press, 1965. A classic work on the psychological aspects of public opinion.

Rivers, William L. *The Opinionmakers.* Boston: Beacon Press, 1965. A critical study of the interaction between the government and the press and the effects of the press on the formation of public opinion.

Chapter 5

Interest Group and Party Politics

THE ROLE OF SPECIAL INTERESTS

A Bow From the Gallery

On an October afternoon in 1965, Rep. William H. Ayres of Akron, Ohio, stood up in the House of Representatives and denounced a bill to accelerate the collection of excise taxes from tiremakers. This bill, he said, was the work of "one gentleman who has been primarily interested in pushing this legislation, and some concession has been made to appease him."

Up in the gallery, George Burger leaned over, beamed at Ayres, nodded, and made a gesture to tell the rest of the gallery, "That's me."

Burger was enjoying the opprobrium because he had been lobbying for this minor change in the tax law for twenty-three years. His clients were independent tire dealers who thought the existing tax collection system was unfair, because they paid the tax when they bought the tire from the tiremaker, while the manufacturer's own store could wait until the tire was sold to the motorist and put the cash to other use in the meantime. George Burger had grown old in many small battles, and now, at the age of 77, he was winning one.

Your Man in Washington

There is more than one way to be represented in Washington. The most obvious way, of course, is through the formal election process which sends a member of Congress from your limited geographical area to look after that area's interests. But behind that formal system is an informal and extraconstitutional structure of political parties which determines how that person is selected and what combination of groups and interests he will represent. Less formal still is the role of organized interest groups (also called ''pressure groups''—we prefer the less pejorative usage) which keep their own men in Washington to monitor and influence the constitutional representatives. All have a part in the ''linkage'' process—connecting the desires of citizens with the actions of government.

The one-man lobby with an extremely narrow interest is still a common Washington phenomenon. George Burger operated an association with an impressive name: the National Federation of Independent Business. He had a newsletter which often featured photographs of himself talking to well-known members of Congress. For a small yearly fee, a tire dealer could learn about such pitfalls as the excise tax payment schedule and help support Burger as he identified and fought for the tire dealer's causes.

But, today, interest-group representation is becoming slicker and more systematic. The number and diversity of groups have become so great that some of the smaller ones band together under common management to maintain efficiency. Thus, in 1972, the American Ladder Institute, the Facing Tile Institute, the Instant Potato Products Association, the Sterile Disposable Device Committee, and forty other associations were all operated by the same professional management company. That company, Smith, Bucklin & Associates, provided the associations with account executives, Washington representatives, news letters, and promotional campaigns. Its client organizations used its telephone number and its mailing address in Chicago. ''Associations have grown so much'' explained a Smith, Bucklin founder, ''they are involved in so many complicated and expensive promotions, and so many things that the Government does affects them, that they need expertise and management services [King, 1972, p. 1].''

Other interest groups are large, cover more general areas, and support large staffs and publishing operations of their own. Some, such as the National Rifle Association, the American Institute of Architects, and the American Pharmaceutical Association, have their own office buildings in Washington.

The Factious Temper Problem

The problem of fitting interest groups into the operation of American national government has existed ever since James Madison warned in *The Federalist*, No. 10 (1888) about ''men of factious tempers, of local prejudices, or of sinister designs [p. 57]." Interest groups are not inherently sinister, although they do all have designs. Their successes and failures in influencing the operation of government affect the rest of us, whether we belong to groups or not.

An *interest group* for the purpose of this discussion is any group of people sharing an attitude or point of view and which organizes and competes with other groups to get the protection, assistance, or freedom from interference that it needs to enable its members to behave according to this shared viewpoint. Because this is a world of limited resources, one group often has claims against another group, as in the case of the independent tire stores who wanted manufacturers' stores to pay their taxes sooner. As soon as any institution of government is involved in this claim, the interest group becomes a *political* interest group (Truman, 1951).

Political interest groups may be organized and active or they may only exist as potential actors on the political scene. When Congress authorized the Army Corps of Engineers to build a reservoir in the valley of the Blue River in northeastern Kansas, the farmers who lived in the valley underwent a dramatic transformation from a potential to an active interest group. They organized the Blue Valley Study Association which succeeded in upsetting the normal political alignments of the area, electing a member of Congress sympathetic to their point of view, and temporarily halting construction of the reservoir (Davis, 1953). Such potential groups may, if

Meeting of the Blue Valley Study Association: A dramatic transformation. *(Philip Meyer.)*

the existence of the potential is recognized, carry considerable weight without ever taking direct action. Officials know that if such groups are disturbed, they may lose their inchoate, diffuse, fragmented, and apathetic status to achieve formal and potent organization. Alert policymakers may shape policies in anticipation of this possibility. They may do this by following the wishes of the potential group or by concealing the effects of their acts so as not to arouse the slumbering giant. Yet another variation is to consciously try to rouse such a group to gain support for things the policy- makers want: the Nixon administration's recruitment of the "silent majority" in support of its war policies is an example. And during the Watergate hearings, a National Committee for Fairness to the President was organized to operate a publicity campaign to defend the President from the charges raised in those investigations. A *potential group*, therefore, is an unorganized body of citizens with shared interests needing only some outside stimulus affecting those interests to convert it into an *organized interest group*.

A political party is not an interest group. A party seeks to gain control of the government by putting its people in public office. An interest group only wants to influence government in those limited areas where its interests apply, without bearing the responsibility for public office. The distinction holds most of the time, although there can be overlap when a party is organized around a single issue. (The Prohibition party still fields candidates for President.) But the successful political parties must mobilize coalitions of majorities of the electorate. The concerns of interest groups are almost always too narrow for such an objective; therefore, they must try to manipulate government from the outside, looking for the leverage points where they can alter, enact, amend, or veto the public policies that affect their limited goals. Such a process of trying to influence the decisions about who gets what, when and how is what politics is all about. Systematic, peaceful settlement of the conflicting claims made by groups on society is one of the main reasons for having government in the first place. People who get morally distraught about the machinations of "pressure politics" fail to recognize these essential truths.

Group Interactions

A lot of the tugging and hauling among different groups takes place outside of government—which saves the government a lot of trouble. Collective bargaining by labor unions is an example of how one group can act on another in a very formal way without any necessary intervention by government. The International Institute of Synthetic Rubber Producers can encourage a rattlesnake festival in Oklahoma because rattlesnake fanciers will consume rubber while driving to this event (Meyer, 1965). The Amalgamated Transit Workers Union, looking for new sources of jobs, can join with the National Council of Senior Citizens to urge owners of bus companies to give free rides to elderly persons.

Internal group negotiations are also important. By agreeing upon when and how to press their demands, the groups do much of the early processing and filtering and compromising that government would otherwise have to supervise. Before the Parent-Teachers Association of Shepherd Elementary School in Washington, D.C. petitioned Congress for a classroom addition to the school building, it first had to resolve conflicting desires within the association over the design, location, and use of the proposed addition.

The function of associations, says David Truman (1951), "is to stabilize the relations among their members and to order their relations as a group with other groups [p. 56]." All this movement represents a drive toward equilibrium, like water seeking its own level. But the equilibrium is always being disturbed by outside forces, and the pressure for equilibrium is continually renewed.

This motion has some value, although there is disagreement over just how important it is. Basically, five useful things may happen when groups process their problems internally.

1 Countless individual problems are pulled together and presented to leaders in an organized way so that they can be considered when policies are made. This process of *interest aggregation* allows an individual to pool his power with like-minded individuals and gain enough strength to be influential.

2 A two-way transfer of information takes place between the individual and his government. Without George Burger, the independent tire dealers might not have known that the manufacturers' outlets were getting a tax break. And Congress might not have known that the independent dealers resented it. Moreover, there is a spillover effect; the information exchange is public, and the public gets educated in the process.

3 Individuals can become more integrated into the political system. Popular participation in government is increased and alienation is reduced. The tire dealer can look at George Burger's newsletter, see the picture of George Burger talking to Senator Aiken, and feel that he, the tire dealer, has a place in this system.

4 Interest-group activity burns up energy that might otherwise be put to destructive and antisocial use. Antagonistic interests can fight their battles within the group, moderate their demands, and avoid extreme conflict and possible violence. The interest-group activity is a stabilizing force.

5 Groups also serve as a source of political cues and values for their members, helping individuals to relate to the political system. Thus through the influence of other group members, a white-collar employee may learn a negative attitude toward business regulation by the government from his management-oriented fellow workers. Or a labor-union member may learn a positive attitude toward import restrictions from his fellow union members who want protection from the competition of cheap foreign labor.

Lobbyist Burger and Quarry: For the individual, a place in the system. *(National Federation of Independent Business.)*

The extent to which all this happens in a way to make democracy run more smoothly depends, of course, on how power relationships are organized within the groups, on the amount of access that citizens have to organized political interest groups, and on the degree of success that citizens have at using groups for these ends. While access is fairly high—about as many people belong to organized interest groups as vote—their effective utilization appears to be quite low. Belonging to the PTA and having your interests truly and fully considered in the higher councils of government are not automatically the same thing. Something gets lost in the process. To find out how this happens, we must take a closer look at the process.

Opening the Doors

The basic requirement of an effective interest group is that it have access to the people in government who make the decisions with which it is concerned. Whether the tactic is writing letters or burning down government buildings, it does no good if it doesn't get the decisionmakers' attention. In fact, getting access implies a bit more. It means that the "*attentive interest* of the relevant decisionmakers" can be gained (Scoble, 1966).

There are, of course, various degrees of access, ranging from none at all to a situation in which the decisionmakers never make a move without taking the group's position into consideration. Access is ordinarily the most important thing that a large campaign contribution can buy. It doesn't guarantee that the group's position will prevail. But it does mean that the giver can at least get past the outer office to have his problems viewed with "attentive interest."

Who You Know. Access also depends on the group's *social status*. If its executive director dines in Georgetown with a key committee chairman, he is improving its access. If a group representing defense contractors is more likely to manage this than a group representing welfare clients, then the former has an advantage.

An overlap of personnel between the group and the target government agency is another way to manage access. Retired generals can find ready employment in the defense industry, and former members of regulatory agencies often go to work for the industries they used to regulate. A congressman who is defeated for reelection but does not want to leave Washington can find work as a lobbyist or trade association representative.

What You Know. Well-developed technical and political information is another asset in gaining access. Besides knowing just where to go, a well-informed group can use its technical expertise as bait for gaining attention. When legislation for medical care for the aged was drafted, the insurance industry automatically had access to decisionmakers in the executive and legislative branches because its technical knowledge was needed.

How Well You Play. Although access is gained by informal procedures, there are definitely rules of the game, and the only groups which can knowingly and logically violate them are those for whom access is shut off anyway. Some groups are handicapped by the fact that their claims are not considered expressions of legitimate interest, and so they will not be seriously listened to. The struggle to gain this recognition of legitimacy is the major goal of some groups. They face a paradox, because the tactics used to gain recognition may undermine the claims of legitimacy. Sleeping on the White House sidewalk, burning crosses on officials' lawns, creating a physical nuisance such as pouring blood on the draft board's files or capturing Wounded Knee are all tactics that do get attention. They do not always lead to access, for they run counter to the way the game is expected to be played.

There are, of course, other rules. Public threats or offers of remuneration are proscribed. An official cannot afford to be placed in the position of seeming to respond to either. Nor can he afford to deal with people who do not tell him the truth or who fail to keep their promises. Access is a highly civilized concept.

The Strategic Position

Group power has other ingredients. A group's leadership skills and its numerical, financial, and informational resources make a difference. So does its unity. Groups which expend most of their energy on internal struggles over policy or leadership have little left over for the outside world. Those with few members find it hard to make a credible impact unless they can compensate for numerical weakness by being well-endowed with some other resource such as money, knowledge, or access.

From this it follows that the most effective groups are those that can concentrate heavy resources on narrow goals. Keeping the goals narrow has three main advantages:

1 Members don't waste time arguing over sweeping issues, such as whether equal pay for women is more important than property tax reform.

2 They can concentrate their resources on a limited number of targets.

3 They have a reduced risk of pressing causes which will draw counterpressure.

Thus the American Farm Bureau Federation with more than 2 million member families and goals limited mainly to farm policy is likely to be more effective in the long run than Common Cause with only about 200,000 members and virtually unlimited goals.

The nature of the problem with which a group has to cope is also an important factor in determining how much success it has. The Blue Valley Study Association, formed to oppose the construction of Tuttle Creek Reservoir on its members' farmland in Kansas, could survive only one defeat. When the dam was built, the land ownership that was the basis for the group's existence was quickly dissipated.

Other special circumstances which a group often cannot control are whether it must take an offensive or defensive position and what kind of opposition it has. A defensive position is easier, and a very large share of group activity is directed at preserving the status quo. When a group is forced by circumstance into an offensive stance, it may try to manipulate the symbols so that it seems to be in a defensive position. For example, an interest group seeking legislation to weaken the strength of labor unions calls itself the National Right to Work Committee, implying that its purpose is to defend a basic right.

But the mere appearance of being on the defense is not nearly as advantageous as being a genuine defender of the status quo. It is always easier to keep something from happening than it is to make something happen. If a group's aims require positive action, then it risks stirring up counterpressure from groups who have grown accustomed to and developed interests in the existing situation. And defenders of the status quo have many potential roadblocks available to prevent action. If a threatening bill does pass the legislative gauntlet, it may be vetoed. If enacted, it may be enforced selectively, ineffectually, or not at all. If actively enforced, it may be countered through judicial action.

The classic case of a group with the advantages of both a defensive position and the absence of any organized opposition is the National Rifle Association, which has successfully resisted effective gun control legislation in the face of a clear majority of public support for such legislation. Even a majority of gun owners has told Gallup (1972) interviewers that they would favor a law which would require a person to obtain a police permit before he or she could buy a gun. But whenever a law to tighten control of guns is proposed, the National Rifle Association can, on short notice, produce half a million letters in support of its position while the unorganized proponents of gun control can do virtually nothing. Their interest is less intense, and they can't even make it an interesting fight.

What does make an interesting fight is a conflict between two or more strong, well-organized groups. When the ground rules for collective bargaining were being hammered out into the Taft-Hartley Act and its more recent refinements, the National Association of Manufacturers and the United States Chamber of Commerce were pitted against the large labor organizations, including what is now the AFL-CIO. When such giants clash, the whole array of pressure-group weaponry is broken out, and a citizen has to be very much out of touch not to know that a fight is going on.

Inside Tactics

The most obvious and best-known tactic for promoting group interest is lobbying. The term is derived from the practice by some representatives of interest groups of frequenting the lobbies in the Capitol hoping to talk to members of Congress, and has been in use since at least as early as 1830.

Congress first tried to control this activity with the Federal Regulation of Lobbying Act of 1946. The law requires lobbyists to register and file quarterly reports telling which bills the lobbyist is interested in, where the money for his activity comes from, and how he spends it. But its severe penalties (up to five years in prison and $10,000 fine) are not enforced. This law has been very narrowly interpreted to avoid conflicts with freedom of speech and the right of a citizen to petition his government. The only lobbyists who clearly have to register are the free-lance operators who represent a number of clients on a fee-for-service basis. This helps congressmen to keep track of who is promoting whom for pay. An interest-group's full-time employee who lobbies in the course of his work, such as James L. Robinson, director of government liaison for the United States Catholic Conference, is not required to register. Most labor-union lobbyists are exempt, although many register anyway. Indirect lobbying through attempts to influence public opinion is outside the law's scope (*United States v. Harris*, 347 U.S. 612). A more effective regulatory effort is a provision of the income tax law which says that a tax-exempt organization may not include lobbying among its "substantial" activities. Insubstantial lobbying is okay. The Sierra Club, a nonprofit group devoted to promoting conservation, was deprived of its tax-exempt status after the courts determined that it lobbied to a substantial degree. This provision is a fairly powerful inhibitor of lobbying activity by public-interest groups, even though the direct financial threat to them is minor. If an organization is truly nonprofit, it has no income on which to pay taxes anyway. The indirect financial threat is more important if the group is financed by voluntary contributions; an organization which loses its tax-exempt status may no longer receive contributions which are tax-deductible by the giver.

Like the congressman whose lapel he grabs, the lobbyist is someone's man in Washington. And so, in a way, he provides a contribution to representative government. It is highly specific representation and is beneficial in that it provides officials with a way of getting technical information and finding out about points of view that they might not otherwise attend to. It is, however, a benefit that is unequally distributed. Because of lack of organization, knowledge, money, and other resources, the points of view of many groups do not get attended to in this manner. A congressman who relies on lobbyists for his view of the world will see it in a distorted manner.

Lobbying is not the only interest-group tactic that can be carried on directly with government. Most Washington representatives of interest groups also have extensive dealings with administrative agencies as well. The Farm Bureau program for 1973 reflected, in addition to a long list of legislative objectives, a careful monitoring of the activities of the executive branch, some of which are fairly obscure to most of us. It urged the Plant Quarantine Service of the Department of Agriculture to step up its watch over imported vegetation. It promoted a switch to automation in the grading of cotton. It urged the Public Health Service to "use discretion" in regulating the construction of maple sugarhouses and dead bird disposal

Border Inspector with Confiscated Corn: An interest group wanted a closer watch. *(Wide World Photos.)*

units so that maple sugar and poultry producers would not suffer hardship. It asked the Internal Revenue Service to follow appraisal practices which would encourage farm heirs to keep the land in agricultural production (American Farm Bureau Federation, 1972). This attention to detail reflects the fact that the way administrators put the law into effect depends upon the kinds of problems that enter their field of vision. An alert interest group does not leave the exposure of its problems to chance.

Moreover, it looks for those areas where the law gives administrative officials a great deal of discretion in putting the law into effect. Where the subject matter of the law is complicated or technical, Congress must often leave it to the administrator to decide how the act will be implemented, the speed of implementation, which provisions to give priority, which tasks to give the most effective people, and what nongovernment groups to ask for help.

Interest groups also provide a good deal of work for lawyers. Besides engaging directly in litigation, as the NAACP did in the school segregation cases, they watch for court cases whose rulings will affect their members and file amicus curiae (friend of the court) briefs on behalf of the side whose interest coincides with theirs. The U.S. Catholic Conference supported fundamentalist preacher Billy James Hargis in his effort to keep his tax exemption, not because it favored his religious views but to protect its church's own tax exemption.

Interest-group lawyers are also kept busy with activity of a quasi-judicial nature before the various regulatory agencies. When these agencies exercise their rule-making functions, interest groups need to muster a blend of legal and technical expertise. When the Federal Communications Commission formulated the rules for expansion of cable television, it heard extensively from the National Association of Broadcasters and the National Cable Television Association as well as a wide variety of groups whose interests were indirect, such as the American Newspaper Publishers Association. All these groups presented both legal and technical arguments for regulating cable development in ways that would favor them.

Corruption

One problem inherent in systems that attempt to influence the government through direct contact is that they provide opportunities for corruption. Although the lobbyist, lawyer, or agency liaison man may base his appeals on compassion, sense of fair play, and his clients' voting power, the nature of the one-on-one, private-interest contact makes it amenable to secret dealings and private gain as well. This risk is smaller at the national level. Policy making there is more closely watched by a greater variety of interests

Former Vice President Agnew Leaving the Courthouse: Less visible officials are more susceptible. *(Wide World Photos.)*

and observers, including the national news media, than at the state and local level. As a general rule, the less visible a public official, the more susceptible he is to corruption. State and local officials, as the public opinion polls have shown, have very low visibility. If former Vice President Agnew, who took money from government contractors, had remained a lowly county official and paid his federal income taxes, he might never have been caught. When he was finally convicted and forced to resign, it was because of the work of federal investigators. States and cities usually have less stringent regulation on methods of choosing contractors, less professionalism in the bureaucracy, and less independent law enforcement.

Outside Tactics

It is possible to have an effect on government without ever making contact directly. Public relations campaigns, ranging from the broadly educational to the narrowly specific, aim to influence voters in the hope that they will in turn influence their congressmen. Their effectiveness is often difficult to pinpoint, given the general low level of interest in public affairs. An effective public relations operator does for news media what a lobbyist does for a legislator. He provides knowledge of a group's point of view and quick, easy access to technical information. A journalist seeking to inform his readers about the legislative struggle for national health insurance will

Consumer Advocate Ralph Nader: Human drama and technical expertise. *(Wide World Photos.)*

normally consult both the American Medical Association and the committee for National Health Insurance for the basic opposing points of view. For detailed variations, he will also visit with public relations people representing associations of hospitals, insurance companies, labor unions, nursing, and other health-care professions.

Ralph Nader's work on auto safety is a rare example of an effective, one-man public relations campaign that produced significant legislation. His book, *Unsafe At Any Speed* (1965), helped focus public attention on an already known but little-appreciated fact: Modifying vehicles is a much more productive route to highway safety than attempts to modify driver behavior. The impact of the book was enormously enhanced by Nader's image as a lone crusader battling the corporate giants—an image which the auto industry unwittingly helped him cultivate through clumsy attempts to intimidate him. He also became a reliable source of technical information for newsmen who followed the auto safety debate. This combination of human drama and technical expertise made his message hard to resist.

Most public relations campaigns do not produce such visible results, but interest groups engage in them anyway. When Chrysler Corporation (1973) bought full-page newspaper ads to urge readers to write their congressmen in opposition to clean-air standards, it probably produced more in the way of psychic benefit for company managers than it did in legislative effect. "There is some magic involved in the demand for public relations services," says one student of the process (Kelley, 1956, p. 205). But even if a public relations campaign fails to produce or forestall action directly, it may at least create legitimacy for the group's position in the public mind.

Interest-group involvement in partisan politics and election activity must also be classified as an outside-of-government activity. It can be quite efficient. Milk producers won price-support concessions from the Department of Agriculture after their trade groups gave large sums to the reelection campaign of President Nixon (Lardner, 1973). Labor unions customarily endorse candidates, although the AFL-CIO endorsement for the Democratic presidential candidate is normally regarded as automatic. When the organization refrained from any endorsement in the 1972 campaign, that amounted to tacit support for President Nixon. When it actively resisted attempts in state and local units to endorse McGovern, there was no doubt which way the national organization wanted the election to go.

At the state level, an interest group can sometimes succeed in getting its official spokesman elected to the legislature. At the national level, the connection between legislators and home-state interest groups is necessarily more vague. At the presidential level, it can even be counterproductive. Thus, the first Catholic to be President, John F. Kennedy, gave no support to advocates of federal aid to parochial schools for fear that he would be perceived as serving a narrow interest. But Quaker Richard Nixon could afford to be an open, albeit ineffective, advocate of such aid.

Two Popular Models

It is difficult to observe, let alone describe, just what effect interest-group politics has on a democratic system. To think about the problem at all, social scientists have developed tentative models that portray the way they imagine it works. There are two popular, competing models, both starting from the premise that interest groups are involved in a process where power is unequally distributed.

The most popular is called the *pluralist* model, and it views interest groups optimistically. It sees their power as dispersed rather widely, crossing class lines, and subject to change over time. When power moves from one group to another, it is a reflection of new conditions and new demands. Later, we shall discuss the *elite* model, which pictures a cohesive, autonomous few in the upper economic and social strata who dominate all the key decisions. Finally, we shall offer a revised and in some ways more realistic model to explain what happens.

The Pluralist Pot

Pluralist theorists, who dominate contemporary political science, see the system as a bubbling pot whose ever-moving currents bring first one group and then another to the top. While not everyone gets to wield power, at least everyone gets a fair shot at it. In addition to arguing that this is the way the system really works, most pluralists say that this is how it ought to work; while not the best of all imaginable systems, it is the best of all available systems.

The dispersal of power among interest groups is seen as a kind of extension of the more formal separation of powers in the three branches of government and the different levels of the federal system. The wider the

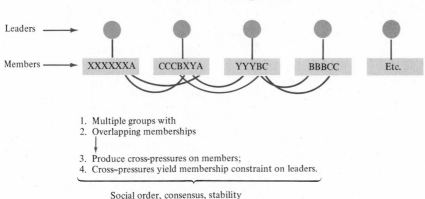

Traditional Interest Group Model

Leaders ⟶

Members ⟶ XXXXXXA   CCCBXYA   YYYBC   BBBCC   Etc.

1. Multiple groups with
2. Overlapping memberships

3. Produce cross-pressures on members;
4. Cross–pressures yield membership constraint on leaders.

Social order, consensus, stability
(Pluralists affirm this model; elitists deny it.)

dispersal, the less chance there is for control by any single center of power.

This argument gains plausibility if you step back from politics for a moment and look at the entire social system. Most decisions of who should do what to whom are privately made and executed. (See Chapter 13.) Social convention, not legislation, sets the rules for most of the games that we play with one another. Where formal rules are required, the rule making is often in private, not government, hands. School accreditation, certification of a physician's speciality, bestowing athletic titles, determining religious doctrine, newspaper delivery service, and apprentice training programs are all examples of organized activity which is governed by private decision and is therefore beyond the reach of popular control. Its private nature tends to keep it dispersed.

With so many separate units making decisions and bargaining with one another, the pluralist argument goes, everyone can pursue self-interest with a reasonable expectation that the ultimate outcome will serve the public interest. If the immediate goal is not reached, there is still hope. A battle that is lost can always be fought at another time, another place. And because no one can seize enough power to make swift and sweeping changes, the system is stable. Changes come in small increments that add up to comprehensive and fundamental change only after a long, evolutionary process.

The Elitist Iceberg

Elitist theory grants that most of the things the pluralists see in the system really are there. But it questions their importance, because the power to make the few decisions that really matter is invisible, like the hidden part of the iceberg and just as frozen. This power, the elitists say, is wielded by small, stable groups which are not affected by the desires of others. Nor do they have to report, explain, or justify these decisions to all those people bubbling around in the pluralist pot. They are not, in short, accountable.

The most cited example of such a power elite is the military-industrial complex. When it is caught in corruption or stupidity, such as the $2 billion cost overrun on the C-5A cargo plane, nothing much happens. When a nonelite power center is guilty of misspending some minor funds—the Office of Economic Opportunity for example—it may be put out of business.

"Undue attention to the middle levels of power," said C. Wright Mills (1956), "obscures the structure of power as a whole, especially the top and the bottom [p. 245]." At the top, the elites are frozen into power; at the bottom, the masses are frozen out. The pluralists view the social structure as the end product of attitudes and behavior, but the elitists see just the opposite process: A preexisting pattern of social stratification controls behavior, and attitudes follow from that behavior.

Wheel Falling Off C-5A
Cargo Plane: For elite mis-
takes, a different standard.
(United Press International.)

The Unrepresented

Who is right? One empirical test is to find out how many people belong to how many groups and with what effect. The number of belongers turns out to be quite large, but the number who see their organizations as having any political value is quite low. Not counting church groups, the number of people who are at least nominal members of organizations is between 40 and 60 percent of the adult population—which means that joining is about as common as voting. But it is by no means universal (Blackwell, 1950). If you count only occupational, business, or professional organizations, the number is much smaller. In a Philadelphia study, 74 percent did not belong to any of these kinds of groups (Bone and Ranney, 1963). Those who do belong to such groups represent the upper social and economic levels (Lazarsfeld, 1948). Many members probably belong in name only, paying little attention to what the group does. "The flaw in the pluralist heaven," said E. E. Schattschneider (1960), "is that the heavenly chorus sings with a strong upper-class accent. Probably about 90 percent of the people cannot get into the pressure system. . . . Pressure politics is a selective process ill designed to serve diffuse interests. The system is skewed, loaded, and unbalanced in favor of a fraction of a minority [p. 35]."

Many who do not belong to organized interest groups can, of course, if the need arises, form or join such groups. The fact that they do not belong may simply mean that the political system already adequately serves their needs. But there are other possibilities. Citizens may be unaware that their interests have something to do with politics. They may lack the skills or other resources necessary to organize. They may feel that the system is so biased against them that nothing they could do would be of any use. The available evidence indicates that the possibility of pursuing their interests through organized groups just does not occur to most citizens. When a national sample was asked about things that citizens could "do to try to influence their national government," the most frequently mentioned possibilities were individual acts such as writing letters. About three out of ten mentioned informal organizational strategies such as getting friends to sign petitions. A tiny minority of only 4 percent said they would work through a formal interest group. "In short," says Richard Hamilton (1972), "only a very small part of the population thinks in the terms assumed by the pluralists. The majority is prepluralist in outlook, still oriented to individual petitioning [p. 36]."

Revising the Model

For a better picture of reality, it may be necessary to invent a third model, many-sided like the pluralist image, but relatively frozen in structure like the elitist model.

In this model, the group a person belongs to is not important so long as it is a dominant group. The important question is the level to which he rises in the group. Individuals at any given level, looking across the dominant

Revised Interest Group Model

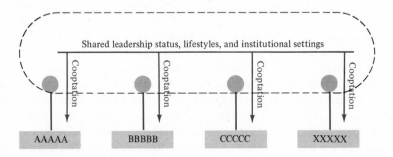

1. Yes, there are multiple groups in society;
2. No, membership does not overlap (except at high levels).
3. Homogeneous ideology among group members produces

    4. Leadership cooptation
    5. Similar elite social status
    6. Parallel lifestyles
    7. Common institutional settings

Social order, consensus, stability

Picket Line at General
Motors: Struggles may not
be as straightforward as they
seem. *(United Press International.)*

groups, have more in common with one another, in terms of power and
privilege, than they do with people who are members of their own groups
but at different levels. The president of General Motors and the president
of the United Auto Workers enjoy similar status, parallel life styles, and
move in the same institutional settings. All group leaders develop a stake in
preserving the amenities of office regardless of what particular group they
represent (Serrin, 1973).

Struggles between groups, in this model, are not as straightforward as
they seem. Leaders engage in them not to win but to preserve their
leadership positions. The appearance of a struggle can be more important
than the reality; the function of a strike may be not to persuade management to come to terms but to persuade the workers that the terms its
leaders got for them were truly hard-won gains. In this model, those at the
bottom of the organization's hierarchy are only slightly better off than those
who belong to no organized interest group at all. Nevertheless, they will
continue to support the organization so long as it provides some benefits,
real or symbolic, that are not available to nonmembers.

One empirical fact supporting this model is that the leadership of a
group often takes more extreme defensive positons than the rank and file
really want. The American Bankers Association and the American Medical
Association took much harder lines against truth-in-lending and medical-
care-for-the-aged legislation than was supported by their general memberships of bankers and doctors. In part, this may be because the persons most

commited to preserving the status quo work the hardest in the organizations and therefore rise to the top. But it may also be true that the purpose of a fight is not so important to the leadership of an organization as the fight itself. Their elite status is conferred upon them because they do battle for the membership, and so they must find battles to do and then persuade the membership that they are worth doing. So behavior flows from structure, as in the elitist model. And attitudes are the final effect, not the first cause.

A revised model should also take into account the fact that there is wide variation in the resources available to different groups. Even if some groups do succeed in serving the political interests of individuals by pooling their resources, giving them a hearing before government, providing a sense of control over public affairs, they usually perform these functions for the more affluent members of society who are less in need of this assistance. For the groups that never organize effectively around their shared interests (such as consumers of telephone service) or whose goals are not accepted as legitimate (such as the American Indian Movement) the availability of group activity does not guarantee political influence. Moreover, if the major power struggles are generally won by the same groups, and if these groups nominally represent the majority but are undemocratically controlled, we have an odd-looking hybrid of the plural and elitist models. We might call it a system of majority-sanctioned, plural-elite governance. This system shuts out the relatively powerless with what William Gamson (1969) has called "stable unrepresentation."

The shortcomings of the traditional elitist and pluralist models of how the system works are probably due to the limitations of the customary research techniques. Until better ways to study the problem are found, no one model, elite, pluralist, or hybrid, will be satisfactory as a description of interest-group politics.

POLITICAL PARTIES

The Quest for Office

The aim of a political party is to gain control of the government. This by itself is enough to distinguish it from an interest group, which seeks to affect policy without the responsibilities of running the government. For members of an interest group, control over official decisions is only the means to an end. For the party, that control is the end. And policy views that stand in the way of gaining office are likely to be abandoned or modified as necessary to maintain the quest for office.

In other times and places, parties have had strong ideological or issue orientations to promote. The British Labor party after World War II and the American Prohibition party are examples. While ideological and issue differences have sometimes been found between the two major parties in contemporary America (Miller, Miller, Raine, and Brown, 1973), their promotion is not the parties' reason for being. A party's function is more like that of a broker or intermediary between the people and the government. To gain and hold power, it must translate public desires into government action. Such a function requires flexibility.

Parties: One, Two, or Many?

This pragmatic character of parties in the United States is partly the result of structural peculiarities of the two-party system. To maintain a hope of winning control of the government, each party must shape itself into something with wide appeal to the voters. This requirement pulls each party to a centrist position and leaves little room for extreme elements. In close elections, both strive for the support of the same uncommitted, middle-of-the-road group of voters; and so both end up tending to be pretty much alike. When, on occassion, a divergent group gains control of the party's presidential nominating machinery—as did the Goldwater Republican right in 1964 and the McGovern Democratic left in 1972—the result has been electoral disaster. In close elections, like those of of 1960 (Kennedy-Nixon) or 1968 (Nixon-Humphrey), critics of the system may complain that the voters are not getting a real choice. But what has happened is that the parties have succeeded in performing one of their main functions: compromising different and conflicting points of view before the election. This success contributes to the stability of the system. Such a blessing is mixed, however. The same forces that keep the two major parties from becoming widely divergent also operate to shut out groups whose interests are so different from the mainstream that their claims are viewed as extreme. These tend to be the same groups which, as we have seen, are shut out from representation through the interest-group process.

It is possible to get by with only one party and still observe democratic principles. The one-party systems of the Deep South prior to the 1960s were able to give voters effective choices on many issues. The action, of course, took place in the Democratic primaries where nomination was—to borrow a favorite phrase from election night broadcasters—"tantamount to election." In some races, where the minority party fails to enter a candidate, it still is. Although the voters in such a situation cannot choose between total party platforms, they can, if they belong to the dominant party, choose between personalities and, to a lesser extent, principles.

Systems with more than two parties can flourish in parliamentary government where the compromising is done after election, not before. It flourishes where there is some kind of proportional representation or multimember district scheme, found in some United States cities and states and many European democracies. Minority interests are encouraged to form parties in such a system because it is not a case of winner-take-all. With proportional representation, a party with 10 percent of the vote can get 10 percent of the seats in the legislature and, once there, try to become part of a governing coalition, joining other minority parties to form a majority. This arrangement gives party membership more ideological or issue importance. The task of negotiating compromises is performed in the legislature, not in the parties, and so it takes place after the election. Governing is therefore conducted with more open turbulence of conflict and compromise.

Party, Not the Man

In recent years, the party system has been in poor health. One indicator of the low regard for political parties is a 1968 Gallup poll (October 1968, p.26) finding that 84 percent of the voters claim to choose the man, not the party. Laudable as such discriminating behavior may seem, it is not how the system is supposed to work. If parties were doing their jobs properly, you would choose the party, not the man. An advantage of having the parties do most of the major work of adjudicating differences among groups before the government side of the process is ever reached is that it also enables voters to fix the blame or the praise when things go wrong or right. When things go wrong, it is difficult or impossible for the voter to figure out who is to blame and direct his wrath at that person or agency. Government is too big and complicated. But because government is controlled by a party, it can hold the party responsible and vote to throw the rascals out when the occasion requires it. If voters are reduced to the frustration of trying to evaluate the performances of all the individual candidates they vote for, then the party is neither providing strong leadership nor serving the important function of guiding the voter in his political decisions.

The news is bad. "Modern democracy is unthinkable save in terms of the parties," says E. E. Schattschneider (1942). "As a matter of fact, the condition of the parties is the best possible evidence of the nature of any regime [p. 1]." David Broder (1971), noting the weary sameness of issues and problems from one election to another, argues that:

> American politics is at an impasse; that we have been spinning our wheels for a long, long time; and that we are going to dig ourselves ever deeper into trouble, unless we can find a way to develop some political traction and move again. I believe we can get that traction, we can make government responsible and responsive again only when we begin to use the political parties as they are meant to be used [p. xvi].

What Parties Are For

The way parties are meant to be used is not something we can ascertain by looking at the Constitution or the law. Parties grew to fill a structural vacuum, and so we must look at their historic functions from the perspective of the whole system.

From this viewpoint, the party's function is quite straightforward: to solve social problems by identifying and choosing from alternative courses of action, getting voter approval, and then executing these decisions. For carrying out that broad assignment, Walter Dean Burnham (1967) lists four main things that parties have to do. Paraphrased slightly, they are:

1 Integrate conflicting group interests through party mechanisms, such as the platform debates at national conventions
2 Recruit candidates and try to fill offices
3 Politically educate and socialize the masses
4 Make policy

These tasks involve some subtle benefits which become more apparent when we look at them from the separate vantage points of the citizen and the government.

The Citizen. From the citizen's point of view, the party provides a handy way to participate in government. The party label is a reference point around which he can organize his opinions—and most of us use it in this way from early childhood, as seen in Chapter 4. And the party label—despite poll respondents' claims that they vote for the man—remains the handiest cue to how to vote and the best predictor of voting behavior. In an uncertain world, this is a highly valuable quality. Issues and candidates come and go, but the two major parties are always with us, stable reference points on a stormy horizon.

When it makes citizens feel that they have some control over their government, a sense of party loyalty has some healthy side effects. This loyalty tends to increase voter turnout. And it gives citizens a sense of the legitimacy of power, so that they will accept actions even when they do not always agree with them. Also, in their competition for control of the government, the parties are forced to stir up interest in public affairs and add to the public's store of information.

The Government. At the government level, parties perform a lot of the work that government would otherwise have to do. Most of the nomination and election process is in their hands. Once in control, they often coordinate the management of government, both within and among the separate branches. The key leadership positions in Congress are party positions. The key administrators in the executive branch are faithful members of the President's party. Most new judicial appointees are recruited from the party of the President.

And, as we have noted, the parties in our system relieve government of much of the burden of moderating differences between opposing groups. Many conflicts are defused in a peaceable, institutional but nongovernmental setting. This institutionalization of party conflict has the happy effect of making the government more secure. Conflict and strife are expected, patterned, and moderated as the price for the chance to gain control of governmental offices in future elections. We don't need revolutions when the system operates effectively.

Why They Are Not More Effective

If, as we have suggested, the main function of political parties is to solve social problems, one is compelled to ask why they have such a spectacularly low success rate. Party activity is highly visible and intense. So are the social problems. What goes wrong?

The answer is simple. Before the election, the out party must spend its efforts almost totally on the pursuit of office if it is to entertain any hope of ever reaching a position where it can exercise enough control to attack the problems. But once it attains office, the governmental system does not automatically and instantly respond to the new hands at the controls. Much of the vast machinery of government must be reorganized and rebuilt whenever a change in the ruling party occurs. Such a rebuilding job requires coherent, unified direction. But the unity that a party displays at election time is hard to sustain afterwards. Individual and parochial concerns displace efforts to carry out a unified program. The party machinery must be tended to and maintained to be ready for the next election. (An advantage of the British system is that no one is sure when the next election will be, and so it is easier to set such fence-mending chores aside.) What Frank Sorauf (1968) calls "demands of the party" tend to displace the needs of the government (pp. 370–371). Electoral victory and the holding of office are not enough to provide the centralized control of government that is needed to make major policy changes.

How the Party System Began

In his farewell address, George Washington warned against the "baneful effects of the spirit of party." But he was already involved in party politics himself. He supported John Adams when the Federalists chose a candidate for his successor. Washington's valedictory was used as a campaign document for the Federalist ticket in the 1796 election, and Adams won over Thomas Jefferson, the candidate of the Democratic-Republican party.

The two-party mode came naturally, without forethought, as a result of certain structural features of the American system. Three are especially important:

1 Independent election of the executive, as opposed to multiparty systems where the executive is elected from within the ruling party or ruling coalition

2 A presidential system, as opposed to a parliamentary system

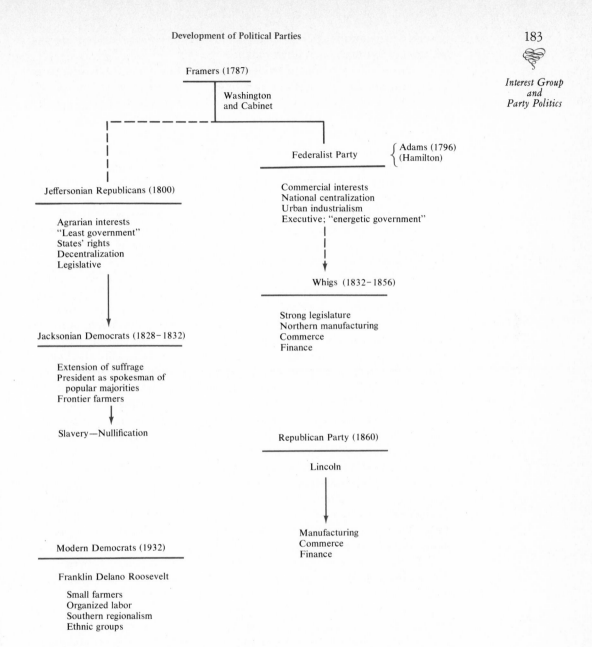

3   The use of winner-take-all single-member districts as opposed to schemes that allow for various forms of proportional representation (Rae, 1971)

In addition to these structural features, there was the influence of American habits of thought and social patterns. There were no class lines around which multiple parties might form, and there was no diverse array of ideological approaches to government.

The dichotomy was self-evident from the beginning. Only one party could control the government at a time, and so there were always two categories: the ins and the outs. The Federalists were in. Built by Alexander Hamilton, Washington's Secretary of the Treasury, this was a businessman's alliance: merchants, bankers, traders, and manufacturers who wanted a strong central government to promote economic development. The Democratic-Republicans were out. They were small farmers and their workers, small businessmen and their workers, cotton planters, and slave owners organized by Jefferson. But they were not out very long. Jefferson won election in 1800, and the Democratic-Republicans—whose name was later abbreviated to the Democratic Party—remained in control for most of the first half of the century. Their majority coalition came apart over the issues that eventually led to the Civil War.

The Federalists, in disarray, became the National Republican party; then, in the early 1830s, the Whig party (after the name of the patriot group during the Revolution whose name came in turn from the reform party organized in England in the seventeenth century). The Whigs were an alliance of Southern slave owners with Northern manufacturing, financial, and commercial interests. They contested national offices with the Democratic party from 1832 to 1856, electing two military heroes to the Presidency, William Henry Harrison in 1840 and Zachary Taylor in 1848. In the 1850s, the slavery issue tore the party apart with Southern members going to the Democrats. The Northern remnant formed the nucleus of the Republican party, organized in 1854. Its new majority coalition, put together under Abraham Lincoln's candidacy in 1860, was based on opposition to slavery. This coalition included commercial and professional groups in the North, farmers outside the South, and workers. The outcome of the Civil War left it the dominant party until 1932—except for temporary deviations that elected Cleveland in 1884 and 1892 and Wilson in 1912 and 1916. The Republican alliance included business, agriculture, the professions, blacks, white-collar workers, and the Grand Army of the Republic.

This coalition was not strong enough to reelect Herbert Hoover in the face of the Depression; and, in 1936, Franklin D. Roosevelt achieved the realignment that made the Democrats the new long-term majority. Two important changes made it happen. Organized labor reached new heights of political consciousness and made an all-out effort that turned the unions into effective political machines (Link, 1955). And black voters ended their historic connection with the Republicans and, for the first time, gave a majority of their vote to the Democrats. The failure of the Republicans to respond effectively to the Depression still stigmatized their efforts. Other ethnic and religious groups were part of the new alliance, as well as small farmers, farm workers, and Southern white Protestants.

The Roosevelt Acceptance Speech, 1936: A new alliance. *(Wide World Photos.)*

The Coming Realignment

The Democrats have been the majority party ever since, although events have forced them out of the White House for two 8-year periods. Eisenhower's victories in 1952 and 1956 were a tribute to his popularity as a war hero. Richard Nixon won in 1968 and 1972 because the Democrats were in disarray over the war and social issues. Throughout, a strong majority of voters with party attachments identified themselves with the Democrats, and the Democrats retained almost unbroken control of Congress.

This historic pattern shows the usefulness of political parties in holding stable coalitions together over long periods of time. When shifts in alignment come, they move great masses of voters. Watching for the next great realignment is a favorite pastime of journalists and political scientists. Recent election trends suggest that one is about due.

A realignment does not necessarily mean that the minority party becomes the majority. It means that a new kind of coalition will be formed, but the party in power may still be able to keep its majority. That was probably the case in 1896 when the Democrats formed a new sectional coalition of the South and West but failed to gain a majority. It is hard to tell just what happened because of the lack of reliable survey data for elections prior to 1936. "If we had had the Gallup poll since 1860, for example," said V. O. Key (1952), "we should know much more exactly the nature of the shifts among voters that make for party cycles [p. 213]."

The main requirement for realignment is a new issue which is forced to the point of electoral decision and on which members of existing coalitions cannot agree, e.g., slavery in 1860 and economic policy in 1936. When it happens, there is a brief period of innovation and creativity, then a longer time of gradual development and consolidation. The latter period may include some brief flares of reaction when the opposition party gets control. Then, before the next realignment, there is a period of drift and confusion while the new relationships are sorted out.

Through survey research, Teresa E. Levitin and Warren E. Miller (1972) have defined the outlines of a political division within the electorate which could become the basis for the next realignment. On one side is a group which strongly favors law and order, even at the expense of other values; has positive feelings toward the police and other agents of social control; and dislikes the youth counterculture and political protest. They call this group the "reactive silent minority." People with the opposite views—sympathetic to protesters and the counterculture, suspicious of agents of social control and demands for law and order—are labeled the "new liberal coalition." These are new dimensions; members of these two groups contain similar distributions of Republicans and Democrats, and they are not greatly different in their attitudes toward older policy questions such as government intervention to control inflation.

If the parties were to divide along these moral and social issue lines instead of the economic division that has prevailed since 1936, they would look quite different. The Republicans would gain working-class people and those with low incomes and limited educations who dominate the "reactive silent minority." Democrats would become more middle class, and their existing association with young and urban voters would be strengthened. In such an arrangement, Republicans would be at least a near-term majority. But as education increased and the young voters got older, the Democrats might prevail.

Third Parties

Besides the structural difficulty which the winner-take-all system presents to third parties, there are some additional legal barriers. Republicans and Democrats alike want no serious threat from third parties, and so it has been made difficult for them to get a place on the ballot. Rules vary from state to state. Usually, a party must have received a certain percentage of

Theodore Roosevelt in 1912
Campaign: Coming in sec-
ond. *(United Press International.)*

the vote in a previous election or else obtain the signatures on a petition of a
substantial fraction of the electorate to gain a place on the ballot.

Third parties have therefore been numerically small. They have also
been short in life span except where some firmly set doctrine holds them
together, as in the case of the Prohibition party or the Communist party, or
when they graduate to major party status as the Republicans did with
Lincoln's election. They are strongest when they form a dissident faction of
an existing major party. The only third party ever to come in second in a
presidential election was Theodore Roosevelt's Progressive party which
divided the Republicans and allowed Woodrow Wilson to win in 1912.

But they do have an effect. They can be innovative. For example, when
the major parties established their national nominating conventions, they
were copying a third-party idea; the first convention was held in Baltimore
in 1831 by the Antimasonic party (Hesseltine, 1962).

And they can serve as an incubator for new ideas and issues for which
there is not yet room in a major party. Socialist party programs such as the
minimum wage, regulation of working hours, and child labor laws were
later adopted by major parties and enacted into law. Even if their specific
programs are not adopted, they can make the major parties aware of
minority needs: The Black Panther party at least makes blacks more visible.
And George Wallace's American Independent party served as an outlet for
the dissatisfaction that Southern voters and working classes in general felt
with the major parties.

Parties at the State Level

Because the organization of political parties began as a private effort, it took a while for lawmakers to see that they were performing an essential public function. After the Civil War, widespread corruption in party machinery led states to begin regulating them. All elections for national office, including President, are state elections; and so the states, rather than Congress, are the designers of the system. There is considerable variety.

Here are some of the things the states make rules about:

Getting on the Ballot. While a party can field a slate of candidates in a write-in campaign, it needs the formal recognition of the ballot to get very far. Some regulation is needed to keep the ballot from being crowded with frivolous efforts at party formation, and these regulations tend to make things difficult for third parties.

How to Join. You join a party by voting in its primary. In some states you have to register as a member of that party first. Either way, the state decides who may vote.

Organization. The structure of officials, committees, and conventions and the rules for selection are now made by state law.

Choosing Nominees. State law dictates whether nominees will be chosen by party caucuses, conventions, or primary elections. Most nominations in most states are now made by primaries.

Keeping Track of the Money. Most states have laws regulating some aspect of party finances: how much may be spent in election campaigns, who may contribute, what public reports of receipts and expenditures must be made (Ranney, 1971).

Austin Ranney and Willmoore Kendall (1956) looked at state election returns for President, senator, and governor between 1914 and 1953 and concluded that only twenty-six had competitive two-party systems—defined as those in which the weaker party wins at least a fourth of the time. Analysis of more recent periods, however, indicates an increase in the number of states with competitive systems (Hofferbert, 1964).

Parties are not monolithic organizations with chains of command and control running from top to bottom. The national party is little more than a loose aggregation of state and local parties. These state and local organizations tend to be highly independent and capable of resisting attempts at national control, which aggravates the problem of using parties as instruments of national social reform.

Parties at the Local Level

Party organization is tightest at the local level. The big-city machines of the late nineteenth century were a functional response to specific needs. They channeled immigrants—with their language, employment, and housing problems—into the political system, attacking their problems in exchange for their votes. Jobs, both in and out of government, were placed through the machines. While not a model of honesty, impartiality, and efficiency, this system did serve to humanize and coordinate the fragmented operation of local government; and it gave lower-class immigrants access to government that they would otherwise lack (Banfield and Wilson, 1963).

When reformers gained control, they concentrated on structural change, both inside and outside the political system. On the outside, they organized citizens associations and research bureaus to keep watch on the activities of local government. They evaluated candidates and made recommendations as a guide to voters who were disenchanted with party labeling. Inside the system, they organized reform parties which tended to be issue-oriented and short-lived. Without the material inducements of patronage and kickbacks enjoyed by the corrupt regimes, their "blue-ribbon" candidates tended to lack the motivation to hang in and take control of the party even when elected. Nor could they form the coalitions of unofficial power necessary to govern the cities.

A typical reform package included a shorter ballot to simplify the voter's task, a professional executive (see Chapter 3), electing council members at-large to weaken the power of neighborhood interests, holding elections in odd years to separate them from state and national politics, and, in many cases, abandoning party altogether by holding elections on a nonpartisan basis.

But the machines found they could live with the structural changes. And while local government has become more honest, efficient, and democratic, the reform measures may have had little or nothing to do with it. The disappearance of the immigrant class, whose votes could be bought cheaply, may be a basic reason for old-style corruption's weaker hold. At the same time, issues which concern disadvantaged groups have been handled more and more at the national level.

Party Structure

The framework of the machine organization still provides the local basis for national politics. In its classic form, it starts at the bottom with the *precinct captain* who gets out the vote for his party. He is chosen by the *ward leader* who may be responsible for thirty to forty precinct captains. The ward leader is in charge of patronage and other favors for his part of the city. He is a sort of ombudsman who mediates between the voters and the bureaucrats. Next in the hierarchy are township or *district leaders* who may also hold formal office, such as city councilman. A powerful district leader might dominate an entire city as did Carmine De Sapio, the leader of Tammany Hall in New York, until reformers threw him out in 1961.

While systems vary widely below the county level, the structure is fairly standard from there on up. Ward, district, city, or other leaders form a *county committee*. And the county committees send *delegates*, either directly or through another intervening level, such as a state legislative district, to the *state central committee*. These committees, whose form and functions are controlled by state law, vary widely in their influence.

The national party structure, which is only a loose coalition of state and local parties, is based on *one national committeeman and one committeewoman from each state*. The national committee makes the formal selection of the *national chairman*, although in practice he is chosen by the presidential nominee. Even so, his influence may not be great. President Nixon's highly successful 1972 campaign was run not by the Republican National Committee but by an ad hoc group, the Committee to Re-Elect the President. Republican National Chairman Bob Dole had to yield to the chairman of that committee, first John Mitchell and later Clark MacGregor. And, since the candidate was already in office, most of the key strategy, where campaigning and governmental activity overlapped, was handled by members of the White House staff. On the Democratic side, McGovern's personal campaign manager, Gary Hart, was more influential than Democratic National Chairman Lawrence O'Brien.

IS THE PARTY SYSTEM OUT OF DATE?

Looking Ahead

Traditional political party functions are still changing. At the higher levels, candidates for office are much less dependent on the party machinery to appeal to the voters. The mass media, especially television, make it possible for the candidates to go directly to the public. However, it is difficult to sort out the effects of television and related social change from those of the normal cyclical changes in the party system. If we date the current cycle from the Franklin D. Roosevelt administrations, then television and its effects have been with us for only the latter half of the current cycle. If the parties seem less often issue-oriented than they once were, it may be because television fosters a preoccupation with style and imagery rather than substance; or it may be simply that the prior alignments of interest groups in each party have become out of date. They may no longer reflect the major political divisions in the public which they are supposed to represent.

Fitting New Groups into the System

As the parties have lost their focus, new interest groups which do not always share the middle-class value system have become increasingly mobilized. Their viewpoints are too narrow to be adopted and articulated by parties, which must base their appeals on issues broad enough to attract a wide spectrum of voters while trying to avoid alienating specific groups. But

Carmine De Sapio: An entire city dominated. *(United Press International.)*

the specific groups will not go away, and if they cannot find representation in the parties they will turn elsewhere. We may find a system of increasingly diverse interests and viewpoints all clamoring for attention while the parties grow increasingly amorphous and sluggish, unable to organize and moderate that diversity. If the parties do not organize the electorate, other political institutions may increasingly assume the responsibility.

Special-purpose Groups

We may see the development of a new kind of organization which is too broad to be classified with traditional interest groups but which still does not seek control of government and is therefore not a political party. Using the new communications technology—computer mailing lists and sophisticated advertising appeals—such a group can mobilize public opinion and perhaps compel candidates to take positions on the issues they raise. The study groups organized by Ralph Nader might be forerunners of this new hybrid. Common Cause, Environmental Action, the National Committee for an Effective Congress all exemplify what may be a growing trend. Since they do not need to maintain the hope of controlling government in order to survive, they may be much more durable than third parties. Because their appeals are broad and are directed at public rather than private interests, they may prove to be enormously successful.

Table 5-1 Self-described Party Affiliation, 1960–1974

	1960	1962	1964	1966	1967	1968	1969	1970	1971*	1972	1973	1974
Republican	30	29	25	27	27	27	28	29	25	28	25	23
Democrat	47	48	53	48	44	46	42	45	44	43	43	44
Independent	23	23	22	25	29	27	30	26	31	29	32	33

	TRENDS	
	1960–1970	1971–1974
Republican	−1	−2
Democrat	−2	0
Independent	+3	+2

*Eighteen-year-olds were included in the Gallup sample for the first time in 1971.
Source: Gallup Opinion Index.

Ticket Splitting

As traditional party organization has weakened, ticket splitting—the practice of casting votes for members of different parties—has increased. In surveys before World War II, more than four out of five voters were straight-ticket voters. Their number declined to the 60 to 70 percent range in the 1950s. By 1968, a majority of voters was splitting the ticket. Meanwhile, party identification has been growing weaker. The number of voters who classify themselves as independents in response to a standard question asked by the Gallup poll has increased from 23 percent in 1960 to 33 percent in 1974. In the decade prior to 1960, it was fairly stable around the 22 percent level.

Walter DeVries and V. Lance Tarrance (1972) think the ticketsplitters with their new independence are forming a "third force" which offers "the best hope for the revitalization of our unique American democracy [p. 122]." On the other hand, the ticketsplitters may only be Democrats on their way to becoming Republicans in the approaching realignment.

The Problem of Popular Control

Even if the parties have to appeal to increasingly discriminating independent voters, they will still be appealing to the same independent voters with candidates chosen by the party elites. Most people, despite recent reforms in the presidential nominating procedure—to be discussed in the next chapter—do not have a voice in that process. Those who do work for parties or candidates or who belong to political clubs or organizations form no more than 3 to 5 percent of the adult population (Robinson, Rusk, and Head, 1968). As long as voting is the only form of mass political participation, candidates will continue to be marketed to the voters in about the same way as before. If large numbers of voters cut themselves loose from party ties, that will be of interest to campaign strategists; but it may not necessarily make the system more democratic.

The power to choose candidates is every bit as important as the power to choose among candidates, and the selection of candidates remains a highly elitist affair.

The New Activism

People used to get involved in party politics for specific material gain in the form of patronage or favored treatment. Party organizations now tend to attract better-educated, part-time leaders motivated by their own personal visions of a better world. Sorauf (1972) sees these new activists as seeking "payoffs in the triumph of principle or program" and increasingly rejecting "the politics of compromise, accommodation, and pragmatism [p. 410]." The ideologically committed members who gained temporary control of the Republican party in 1964 and the Democratic party in 1972 may have been more interested in promoting their respective ideologies than in winning the elections. Having lost, they left the party arena for other kinds of political organizations. This makes for rapid personnel change and a good deal of instability as first one faction gains control of a party and then another. Parties may be becoming more responsive to short-term influences—which may or may not be good. Sorauf warns that the lack of party continuity and predictability could make voters more susceptible than ever to manipulation by those who have the knowledge, the money, and the organizing strength to do so. DeVries and Tarrance (1972) are more hopeful. They believe that voters who do not follow party cues are "the most discriminating voters in our democratic system [p. 122]." It may be some time before we know who is right.

SUGGESTED READINGS

Broder, David S. *The Party's Over: The Failure of Politics in America.* New York: Harper & Row, 1972. A critical examination of the party system and role of political participation.

Key, V. O., Jr. *Politics, Parties, and Pressure Groups.* 5th ed. New York: Crowell, 1964. An extensive study of both political parties and interest groups. Examines the role that parties and interest groups play in the political process and their impact on the operations of the system.

Lowi, Theodore J. *The End of Liberalism.* New York: Norton, 1969. A critical study of the theory and practice of interest groups since their development during the New Deal era.

Ranney, Austin, and Willmoore Kendall. *Democracy and The American Party System.* New York: Harcourt, Brace, 1956. Views political parties as instrumental to the process of democratic government.

Sorauf, Frank J. *Party Politics in the United States.* Boston: Little, Brown, 1968. A detailed analysis of political parties in the United States, examining the parties as political structures within the overall political process.

Truman, David B. *The Governmental Process.* New York: Knopf, 1951. A comprehensive study of interest groups in America, emphasizing the theoretical aspects of group behavior.

Zeigler, Harmon. *Interest Groups in American Society.* Englewood Cliffs, N.J.: Prentice-Hall, 1964. Provides a good analysis of the role of formal interest groups in the policy-making process.

Chapter 6

Political Campaigns

THE TECHNOLOGY OF CAMPAIGNING

Selling the President

It became the most remembered political message of that campaign, and it caught most of its audience by surprise as they sat at home watching NBC "Monday Night at the Movies." The picture that night, September 7, 1964, was "David and Bathsheba," starring Gregory Peck. Suddenly, there was a little girl, in a field flooded with sunlight, plucking the petals off a daisy and counting. As she counted and the camera zoomed closer to her, a man's voice was heard, gaining in loudness and counting backward. His cadence matched the girl's. She reached ten, and he reached zero. Then there was no girl, no voices, but an atomic explosion. The next sound was the voice of President Lyndon B. Johnson: "These are the stakes. To make a world in which all of God's children can live or go into the dark. We must either love each other or we must die." On the screen was a two-line message: "Vote for President Johnson on November 3."

Behind the Pitch: Two Views

President Johnson was not the first political candidate to be accused of letting himself be sold like soap, but his 1964 campaign did achieve new heights of slickness and impact. The TV spots were created by members of Doyle Dane Bernbach, Inc., a highly creative advertising agency which first gained attention with a low-key advertising campaign for Volkswagen. Besides using the little girl with the daisy, they attacked Republican candidate Barry Goldwater with such imagery as a torn-up social security card and a map of the United States with the eastern seabord floating off to sea. Critics of such campaign advertising fretted that it was potentially damaging to the democratic system, because it asked voters to follow their emotions, not their reason. James Graham, who headed the advertising agency's effort, denied it. He said the spots were only communicating the genuine issues of the campaign. "Advertising is just an intelligent way for a free political party in a free country to get the issues across," he said. "Besides, we have a free press in this country, and if unscrupulous types ever did get involved, they wouldn't get very far [Hamill, 1964, p. 130]."

But after the election, there emerged a somewhat different picture of the way the advertising men viewed their job. Several years later, reporter David Broder (1971) revealed:

> . . . a conversation I had at a lunch shortly after the 1964 election with some people who were involved in devising the media campaign for the successful presidential candidate that year, a man named Lyndon Johnson. They described, with what I can only call lip-smacking glee, the way in which they had foisted on the American public a picture of Barry Goldwater as the nuclear-mad bomber who was going to saw off the eastern seabord of the United States and end everyone's social security benefits. At the end of an almost sensual description of how they had manipulated and maneuvered all this, one of them apparently thought that an ethical comment was called for. "The only thing that worries me, Dave," he said, "is that some year an outfit as good as ours might go to work for the *wrong* candidate [p. 222]."

The effectiveness of the political advertising men should not, however, be judged solely by their own arrogant cynicism. Advertising and public relations men were portraying themselves as masterful manipulators of public opinion long before the age of television. As long ago as 1928, Edward L. Bernays, a pioneer in public relations, declared that "the sincere and gifted politician is able, by the instrument of propaganda, to mold and form the will of the people [p. 92]." Ithiel de Sola Pool (1971) finds "many similar alarmist theses about the magical powers of the hidden persuaders [p. 243]" in the literature on propaganda after World War I. The view that clever men could mold entire populations persisted until researchers began looking for the propaganda effect in election surveys. They found that voters formed "a fairly intractable population not easily moved from its fixed prejudices. Much of the alarmist literature had come from the practitioners of advertising themselves, who quite sincerely vastly overestimated their own effectiveness [pp. 234–244]." Pool thinks this early view has a parallel today as persons with technical expertise inflate their power to sell candidates on television.

The parallel, however, may not be exact. For one thing, much more than the addition of a new communications medium is involved. There is a genuinely ''new politics'' in the sense that the traditional tactics and strategies of the old politics now employ new technical devices. The tactics and strategies do not as yet seem to be basically different. For example, one function of the old-style political machine was to condition voters to identify themselves with a particular faction or party (as noted in Chapter 5), tag them, and deliver them to the polls. All those functions remain intact in the new technology. The direct inducements—a bucket of coal, a turkey, a job—have been replaced by mass audience appeals. The tagging and delivery functions are being taken away from the precinct captain, who once knew the voters personally; and they are becoming centralized and automated.

Professional Managers

This work requires skills which are not to be found among volunteers or people who hang around the courthouse. Dedication to a candidate or a political ideal is not a prerequisite. Theodore H. White (1973) has given an impression of Fred Malek, who ran the voter-contact operation for the 1972 Nixon campaign, which is illustrative:

> Malek's mind was managerial, not political. The structure, not the purpose, held him in thrall. How things worked—whether in storefronts or in government—was the measure of achievement. Men lived in boxes; they performed or they disappeared. The men in the boxes might be warm, easy-going, enthusiastic or thoughtful. But the neat charts, the criss-crossed boxes pegged them all to their tasks [pp. 323–324].

Malek was a Harvard Business School graduate who applied business techniques to the problem at hand, which happened to be winning a presidential election. Such skills are also becoming available to political candidates on a free-lance basis. There are now people whose fulltime profession is campaign management—political mercenaries who work on a fee-for-service basis like the hired gunslingers of the Old West. Some concentrate on specialized services, such as polling or computerized mailing lists. Others supply the total package. ''You just go to this firm and they throw a few switches and you go off in a corner and do what they tell you to do,'' said Oliver Quayle (1967) with some sarcasm. ''It may be nothing— just keep quiet, and come election day you'll have more than 50 percent of the vote [p. 165].''[1] The prototype for the total-management service was

---

[1]Keeping the candidate off in a corner is no innovation in political strategy. ''Keep Warren at home. Don't let him make speeches,'' said an astute Harding adviser in 1920. And Nicholas Biddle, managing Harrison's 1840 campaign, advised, ''Let him say not one single word about his principles or his creed—let him say nothing—promise nothing . . . Let the use of pen and ink be wholly forbidden as if he were a mad poet in Bedlam.''

```
                          TARGET '72

            TURNOUT INSTRUCTION & CONVERSATION SHEET

     Thank you for volunteering to turnout favorable voters for our crucial
     TARGET '72 Election Day Program.

     1.  Read thoroughly the Turnout Conversation Sheet and study the information
         on your list of favorable voters to contact before beginning your assignment.

     2.  Contact your first favorable voter approximately four hours before polls
         close.

     3.  Knock on the door of each assigned home on the block(s) assigned to you.
         Step back from the door a foot or two.  Remember to be pleasant and
         smile.

     4.  Remember, you are interested in the turnout of only our "favorable"
         voters (those persons whose "For" column is checked).  The Democrats
         will take care of their own supporters.

     5.  Immediately upon completion of your assignment, return to the Blitz
         Headquarters with your completed kit.

     6.  A sample conversation for your use is as follows:

         a.  "Hello, Mr. (Mrs., Miss) _____, my name is _____
             and I am a volunteer working for President Nixon's re-election."

         b.  "I want to remind you that today is Election Day and we really do
             need your vote.  Have you (and other members of your household) had
             a chance to vote yet?"

                                 IF YES
         _____

         c.  "Wonderful!  We need every single vote that we can get.  Thank you.
             Goodbye."


                                  IF NO

         d.  "Please do so before the polls close at ___ p.m., because we need
             every single vote that we can get."

         e.  "Do you need any assistance in getting to the polls?"  (If yes,
             note it on your turnout sheet and phone the appropriate information
             in to the Headquarters.)  "Thank you.  Goodbye."
```

Instructions for Republican Canvassers, 1972: The design was more managerial than political.

Campaigns, Inc., organized in California in 1933 by Clem Whitaker and Leone Baxter, a husband-wife team. He was a newspaperman, she a chamber of commerce manager. Their first project was to discredit Upton Sinclair's Democratic candidacy for governor. They succeeded admirably with a series of cartoons, displayed in newspapers and on billboards, which mocked Sinclair's muckraking, socialist views (Perry, 1968). "In their glory days, from 1933 through 1955, Whitaker and Baxter . . . managed seventy-five political campaigns in California and won seventy of them. . . . They

The room was windowless, and might have been sunk deep in the ground, as is the Pentagon's subterranean triple-depth war room. It glistened in the brilliant overhead lights. Fifty-three glassined panels, seven feet high, bordered in red-white-and-blue, swung on their hinges from high ceiling posts, so that one could turn them with a touch of a finger as one walked down the U-loop circuit. Each state had one panel, except for Texas, which, with 254 counties, had two; there was a panel for the District of Columbia; and a summary panel for the entire nation made the total of 53.

The panel for each individual state listed all the state's counties on their own lines and then was vertically cross-cut with canvassing, telephone and polling results. The Committee could, in sum, report to the White House that some direct personal contact had reached 15,932,000 American households—by phone or visit. . . . More people, we were told, had been reached in these households than actually voted for the President in 1968. The households were now coded as to (1) those which would surely vote for the President, (2) those inclined but not sure to vote for him and (3) those which needed just a bit more urging, contact, or a mailgram to tip them to the President.

—Theodore H. White (1973), describing the Situation Room of the Committee to Reelect the President (pp. 328–329).

were the first to find the way to the voter in the absence of a party machine [pp. 10–11].''

Their technique was large-scale research on both the client candidate and the opposition, from which they produced a simple, catchy theme. Then they pushed that theme in the media:

> In a campaign in 1948, Whitaker & Baxter distributed 10,000 pamphlets and leaflets, 4,500,000 postcards, 50,000 letters to important individuals; it placed 70,000 inches of display advertising (through its own advertising agency), contracted for 3,000 radio spots and twelve 15-minute radio programs. It put up 1,000 highway billboards and 20,000 smaller posters; it prepared slides and trailers for showing in 160 theaters. The campaign was no more than average Whitaker & Baxter. And, of course, successful [Perry, pp. 12–13].

Despite their success, Whitaker and Baxter had no imitators for nearly a generation. Perhaps only California, with its rapid growth and lack of an established machine or long-entrenched interests, could support such an operation in that day.

The Electronic Age

Professional management began to spread in the 1960s, as a result of two technological developments: television and data processing. Theodore H. White (1961) reports that when Richard Nixon came out second best in his

Nixon's "Checker's" Speech: The coaching was expert. *(Wide World Photos.)*

opening television debate with John Kennedy, he was largely the victim of inadequate professional guidance. Overscheduled and slowed down by a recent knee infection, he spent only ten minutes with a TV adviser in the car that took him from his hotel in Chicago to the CBS studio. His makeup was too light to conceal his late-afternoon beard growth. Someone let still photographers approach the set and leave the carefully planned lighting scheme, designed to erase his eye shadows, in disarray. Surveys after the broadcast "indicated that the Vice President had come off poorly and, in the opinion of many, very poorly," said White. "It was the picture image that had done it—and in 1960 television had won the nation away from sound to images, and that was that [p. 348]."

That was an ironic development for Nixon, who had been among the first beneficiaries of the use of TV as a political tool. During the 1952 election campaign, when he was running for Vice President, newspapers disclosed the existence of a private expense fund of $18,000 put up by wealthy Californians for Nixon's use as a senator. The ensuing uproar led the presidential nominee, General Eisenhower, to consider dropping Nixon from the ticket. Nixon made a direct television appeal to the public under the expert coaching of Edward A. Rogers, who had been producer of "The Lone Ranger." Even though television was still in its infancy, 9 million sets were tuned to that broadcast while he talked with emotion about his wife's cloth coat, his dog named Checkers, and how the money had been used to pay "political expenses of getting my message to the American people . . . this one message of exposing this administration, the Communism in it, the corruption in it [Kelley, 1956, p. 181]." His position on the ticket was saved.

In 1952, the radical changes in communication that television was bringing were not yet fully appreciated. Nixon saw it as a way of avoiding interpretive bias in the print media. It was viewed also as a highly cost-effective method of reaching voters. Nixon was able to reach an estimated 18 million viewers for only $75,000, or about .004 cents a person. Writing letters to the same number of people would have cost $1,260,000 (Kelley, 1956). But by 1968, the image-making power of television had become appreciated. Nixon's advisers in that campaign frankly concerned themselves more with the image than the man. Joe McGinnis (1969) quotes speech writer Raymond K. Price on the importance of personal factors:

> These tend to be more a gut reaction, unarticulated, not-analytical, a product of the particular chemistry between the voter and the *image* of the candidate. *We have to be very clear on this point: that the response is to the image, not to the man.* . . . It's not what's *there* that counts, it's what's projected—and carrying it one step further, it's not what *he* projects but rather what the voter receives. It's not the man we have to change, but rather the *received impression*. And this impression often depends more on the medium and its use than it does on the candidate himself [p. 38].

The analogy between promoting a political candidate and marketing a consumer good had been drawn before; but the 1968 Nixon campaign, vividly described from the inside by McGinnis, demonstrated that the comparison was surprisingly apt. "McGinnis said in 1968 they were selling the President the way you would sell toothpaste," said a member of the 1972 Nixon advertising campaign. "Well, that's exactly true, because the skills are transferable, whatever the product [Witcover, 1973, p. E4]."

The November Group

Dwight Eisenhower was the first President to openly employ the services of an advertising agency; he kept Batton, Barton, Durstine, and Osborn on retainer while he was in office. But political advertising became more circumspect after McGinnis joined the Nixon forces early in the 1968 campaign to write his devastating participant-observer account, *The Selling of the President, 1968*. H. R. Haldeman, a career advertising man who became Nixon's chief White House aide, and Jeb Stuart Magruder conceived the idea of a special, single-mission agency to handle the image making. Called the November Group, its members were recruited from leading agencies which granted them leaves of absence for the duration of the campaign. This system put the agency completely under White House control, closed the security gap through which McGinnis had slipped in

We feel so strongly that the whole system is wrong that on Oct. 6 we announced to our employes that we would not accept any political candidates in the United States in 1972. . . . The system of presenting our candidates, avoiding discussion of issues, and mouthing slogans on television needs more than just minor repair.

We must eliminate the use of TV advertising to sell political candidates for any office by the use of glittering generalities, abject and blatant sloganeering, as if they came in a tube and without regard for the ability of the voter to quickly correct his decision if he discovers he has been misled.

Advertising of a product is a totally legitimate part of the selling process because the customer can usually quickly reject an advertiser who has misled him. The political process does not lend itself to such quick correction. . . .

—Edward N. Ney, president of Young & Rubicam International, Inc.

1968, and provided an all-star team at lower cost because no commissions had to be paid. Sixty specialists worked in New York and ten in Washington under Peter Dailey, who was hired by Attorney General John Mitchell to run the operation. The group produced two basic kinds of ads: selected portrayals of the President in action and hard-hitting attacks on George McGovern. The two approaches were never presented together. The latter, in fact, were always run under the sponsorship of an organization called Democrats for Nixon, headed by former Texas Governor and Secretary of the Treasury John Connally.

"The local TV advertising might vary from place to place as the computers and polls defined the varying concerns of the twenty major media markets in whose framework advertising was placed," says White (1973). ". . . But the national message, when it was launched September 25th, was sharpcut." McGovern had favored cuts in defense spending. TV viewers saw a hand wiping out huge sections of the Navy, the Army, and the Air Force. McGovern was for liberalizing the welfare system. The camera focused on a hard-hat talking about people who work for a living. McGovern had softened some of his early positions. Viewers saw his face on a weathervane, spinning with the wind.

Computerizing the Precincts

When Hubert Humphrey decided to return to the Senate in 1970, he hired Valentine, Sherman and Associates to computerize the phone book. Every name in every telephone book in Minnesota was entered on a punched card along with the telephone number. The total of 1.1 million names represented the households of 85 percent of the electorate. The computer printed these names and phone numbers on special forms which in turn could be read by other automated equipment after new information was entered by members of a 9,000-person army of volunteers.

VOTER INFORMATION SURVEY

State MINN. County HENNEPIN City MINNEAPOLIS Cong. Dist. 5 Page No. 1

LINE NO.	TELEPHONE	NAME (Head of Household)	STREET ADDRESS	ZIP	PRECINCT
120250 01	727-1570	MR & MRS JOHN JAMES	3050 347⊢ AVE N	55420	02-04
120250 02	727-1580	MR & MRS DAVID SLIC	3052 347⊢ AVE N	55420	02-04
120250 03	727-8436	M. R. PALMER	3054 347⊢ AVE N	55420	02-04
120250 04	727-2758	MARY CONOVER	3057 347⊢ AVE N	55420	02-04
120250 05	727-6437	MRS J. BLTZ	3059 347⊢ AVE N	55420	02-04
120250 06	727-1227	MR & MRS DAVID ABBAS	3060 347⊢ AVE N	55420	02-04
120250 07	727-1463	J. A. SMITH	3062 347⊢ AVE N	55420	02-04
120250 08	727-2712	B. M. OPPEL	3063 347⊢ AVE N	55420	02-04
120250 09	727-3969	T. A. TOLE	3070 347⊢ AVE N	55420	02-04
120250 10	727-2410	MISS J. B. JONES	3075 347⊢ AVE N	55420	02-04
120250 11	929-1015	MRS K. KAWISKI	3081 347⊢ AVE N	55420	02-04
120250 12	929-7360	BERTHA GOLDFINGER	3082 347⊢ AVE N	55420	02-04
120250 13	727-2530	JOSEPH PALLS	3083 347⊢ AVE N	55427	02-04
120250 14	929-1114	MR & MRS T. A. KONAS	3085 347⊢ AVE N	55427	02-04
120250 15	727-4116	D. V. ANDERSON	3087 347⊢ AVE N	55427	02-04
120250 16	727-9523	L. J. PETERS	3090 347⊢ AVE N	55427	02-04
120250 17	929-6189	MRS P. MAZZUSI	3095 347⊢ AVE N	55427	02-04
120250 18	929-7777	MARK DERRING	3100 347⊢ AVE N	55427	02-04
120250 19	929-1963	PETER JAMES	3102 347⊢ AVE N	55427	02-04

Additional survey columns (per line): HEAD OF HOUSEHOLD (MARRIED / SINGLE / Husband / Wife), REGIS. STATUS (REGISTRATION / SINGLE), PARTY PREFERENCE, '68 PRES. ELECTION (68 PRES. ELEC.), CAND. PREF. (C F U), YEARS AT ADDRESS (Yrs. at Add. / 1-3 / 4-7 / 8+), CHILDREN IN HOME (Child in Hm. / Pre-Sch. / Sch. Age), SPECIAL QUESTIONS, UNABLE TO INTERVIEW (No Coop / No Answer / Out of Sec.)

Excerpt from Computerized Voter List: New efficiency for old political chores.

These volunteers called these households to get the additional information: whether the people were registered, their party preference, whether children or old people lived there, union membership, whether it was a farm home. With such a data bank, it is possible to do the traditional political chores with new efficiency. Matthew Reese (1971), president of a campaign consulting firm, has expressed the problem succinctly:

> We have four political resources—time, money, manpower, and talent—that are always limited. You spend these limited resources on the four ways you contact the voter—media, visit, telephone, and mail. The computer helps you to decide where to spend these limited resources intelligently [p. 163].

The first task of a campaign is to identify the voters who are already on your side so you can get them to the polls. The Humphrey telephone calls accomplished that. In the last days before the election, the computer produced a list of the most likely Humphrey voters, and 430,000 phone calls were made to them to remind them to vote. Another task is to persuade those who are undecided. Because the computer made classification so easy, letters could be tailored to special categories, e.g., farmers, old people, union members. Special equipment can also print the letters so that they seem to have come from an electric typewriter; the computer can drop in personalizing touches, such as repeating the addressee's family name and street name in the body of the letter, e.g., ". . . and please, Mr. Grimes, tell your neighbors on Sunken Heights Ct., to support . . ." The Humphrey campaign sent 200,000 computer letters to different categories of voters (*Congressional Quarterly*, 1972).

When assisted by the computer, direct mail is a potent fund-raising as well as vote-getting device. Morris Dees, who ran the direct-mail fund raising for the 1972 presidential campaign of George McGovern, pretested purchased lists in advance of the campaign with a sampling procedure to find out where the potential McGovern dollars were. The subscription list of *Psychology Today* was one of his richer veins. The computer then noted who gave, and that list, when the election was over, proved to be the most solid and negotiable asset which McGovern carried away from his campaign.

Some states have assisted the trend to automation in politics by using computers to maintain and update their lists of registered voters. A computer tape is just as much a public record as an entry in a book, and anyone can obtain these lists for the small cost of reproducing them. In the 1968 California presidential primary, volunteer workers for Robert Kennedy were given computer-printed lists of Democratic voters to call on in a door-to-door solicitation. The computer was programmed to produce the lists with names separated by side of the street for the convenience of walkers.

The Ke
480, wh
lights a
America
That is i
yet to aj
mail for
be tailo
groups.
stress th
for high
Detroit
such ac
compari
relativel

Future
The ne
politicia
Yet, lik
change
  On
will und
fully in
meaning
presiden
image, l
persona
appeal
techniqu
  An
not be e
has alwa
factor. I
fringes
harder t
be polit
  The
candidat
his adva
create f
election
might re
create a

Exploiting the Echo Chamber

The new technology also uses political polls to develop information for planning strategy and to pretest possible issues and slogans. In 1966, Joseph Napolitan included polling as part of his management package for gubernatorial candidate Milton Shapp in Pennsylvania. A January survey indicated that voters were tired of existing state and federal officeholders and would be more inclined to favor someone with a business background. Shapp had such a background; so his campaign slogan, authored by Napolitan, became, "A businessman who means business . . . and jobs for Pennsylvania." That kind of planning plus heavy media spending assisted Shapp to an upset victory over the state Democratic organization in the primary election.

Polling can also tell campaign managers what groups or localities are likely to produce the most return for the candidate's scarce energy, time, and money. Republican polls taken in the 1968 presidential campaign showed Humphrey gaining on Nixon at the last minute, with some of the gain attributable to the Vice President's strong statements on Social Security and unemployment. Nixon's speeches and advertising were revised to turn those issues to Republican advantage (Oberdorfer, 1970).

The Potential for Abuse

Despite the "gee whiz" tone in some of the journalistic accounts of these developments, the technological innovation of political campaigning represents little more than the belated adoption of practices already common in business. After watching the first senatorial campaign of Edward M. Kennedy in 1962, Murray B. Levin (1965) worried that

> The techniques developed during the graphic revolution, the skill that is now devoted to fusing sham with reality, and the fact that millions seek illusion may well mean that the distinction between the true and the false, the real and the unreal, and the image and the ideal no longer can be made. . . . The Kennedy brothers and the men who help manage their careers and campaigns have mastered the art of creating shadows and taking advantage of substance [p. 304].

But no one has demonstrated that voters are in fact less aware of reality than they were when older methods were employed. An attractive profile and a skilled manager were important assets long before television or computers. Samuel J. Archibald (1971) has put that in perspective:

> If television and the television manipulators had been around in 1920, I can just imagine the sort of campaign they would have mounted. They would probably have elected some handsome man, with a nice smile and no brains.

The Anti-Masonic convention's presidential nominee, William Wirt, was quickly forgotten. But four basic precedents which that body set have survived much longer:

1 Each state decided the methods of choosing delegates. Within limits, they still do.

2 Each state was alloted as many convention votes as it had members of Congress. That still determines basic representation, although there are bonus seats for party strength as demonstrated by success in winning elections.

3 It took a special (three-fourths) majority to get nominated. Democrats, for most of their history, required a two-thirds vote. This rule was repealed in 1936, in favor of a simple majority.

4 A national committee was organized to conduct party business between elections.

By 1840, the emerging party system had developed enough to give the presidential nominating power to the national conventions. Their representative character and the separation of presidential nominations from presidential control were happy side effects. What made the convention especially useful for parties was the way it could bring a national party's diverse sources of strength under one roof to unite behind a presidential ticket. By formalizing and widening participation in party activity, it helped build grass-roots support (Davis, 1972). The show-business aspect was recognized from the very first, more than a century before television. The first conventions were held as public meetings so that they could double as campaign rallies. From then on, this function "grew in importance," according to Paul T. David, Ralph M. Goldman, and Richard C. Bain (1960), although it was "seldom openly remarked [p. 19]."

Allocating the Delegates

The number of delegate votes varies from one convention to another as rules change and party fortunes rise or fall. In 1972, the Republicans had 1,346 and the Democrats had 3,016. The number of votes is not always the same as the number of delegates; some delegates may get fractional votes in order to increase the number who can participate. Both parties base the number of votes each state may have on the size of its congressional delegation, which is, of course, roughly proportional to population. That would provide a fair distribution of convention delegates if party strength were uniform among the states. But it is not. And since delegates represent a party population, not the general population, the formula must be adjusted. The method of adjustment is to award bonus votes for success in recent elections, according to rather complicated formulas.

In recent years, both major parties have taken steps to open convention participation to the rank-and-file membership. President Nixon in 1972 endorsed reform efforts to make the Republicans the "party of the open door." The Democrats put new rules into effect in 1972 which greatly increased the opportunities for women, youth, and minority-group members to participate.

Before this reform movement began, much of the delegate selection process was under the control of party professionals. In states without presidential primaries—still a majority in 1972—there was a hierarchical convention procedure whose beginnings at the precinct level tended to be obscure. Votes at precinct meetings would determine action at district meetings which in turn would affect the outcome of the state convention. The only place for the ordinary voter to have an input was at that initial precinct meeting which might be held in someone's living room with the time and place known only to a faithful few. The extent of this problem was not precisely known until the Democrats, at their 1968 convention, created the Commission on Party Structure and Delegate Selection (1970), also known as the "McGovern commission" after its first chairman, Senator George McGovern.

This commission found that more than a third of the delegates to the 1968 convention had already been chosen before 1968, long before there could have been any substantial knowledge about either the issues or the possible candidates. And when President Johnson announced that he would not run again, it was too late for the great majority of ordinary Democrats to have any say at all about who would replace him. The delegate selection process was already under way in all but twelve states.

"In at least twenty states," the report said, "there were no (or inadequate) rules for the selection of Convention delegates, leaving the entire process to the discretion of a handful of party leaders. . . . Secret caucuses, closed slate-making, widespread proxy voting—and a host of other procedural irregularities—were all too common at precinct, county, district, and state conventions [pp. 10–11]."

Democratic Reforms.   As a mechanism for reform, the commission was highly efficient. Mindful of the fact that failure to comply with its guidelines could lead to a challenge to their delegations' credentials at the convention, most states quickly changed their ways. Some of them junked the state convention method of choosing national convention delegates in favor of the presidential primary. As a result, presidential contenders had to face an unprecedented number of these hectic contests: twenty-three compared to seventeen in the 1968 campaign. Convention states sought and got widespread participation. In Virginia, for example, the process began, not in obscure parlors, but at well-publicized mass meetings which elected delegates to county conventions. Any registered Democrat could attend and cast a vote at the mass meeting. This system confers new importance on organization because the winner is the candidate whose lieutenants can persuade the most people to take the necessary Saturday afternoon off and go to the meeting. It also encourages participation. Ordinary voters not only know when and where the meeting is—if they are known to favor a particular candidate, they are personally implored, by that candidate's workers, to attend and participate.

The McGovern commission also required state party organizations to take "affirmative steps" to encourage representation of minority groups, young people, and women. While there was no formal quota system, a serious underrepresentation in any of these categories could be grounds for a credentials challenge at the convention, and so strong efforts had to be made to recruit members of these groups. The delegates who arrived at Miami Beach in July 1972 were 40 percent female, 14 percent black, and 21 percent young (under thirty). This was a substantial change from the predominately white, middle-aged, male membership of the 1968 convention which was 13 percent female, five percent black, and had only an insignificant scattering of voters under thirty. (See Table 6-1.)

Republican Reforms.   The less-formal Republican open-door effort also led to greater participation by the underrepresented groups than before. Its 1968 convention at Miami Beach created the Delegations and Organizations (DO) Committee to revise its procedures. Unlike the McGovern commission, it was not empowered to implement rules for the 1972 convention, and that gathering rejected the DO Committee's more far-reaching proposals. But meanwhile, state party organizations, acting on their own, made considerable progress. Youth membership at the convention increased from 1 percent to 12 percent; blacks from 2 percent to 4 percent; and women from 17 to 37 percent.

The 1972 Republican convention moved toward further improvement by adopting a rule requiring the state organizations to take positive action to include "women, young people, minority and heritage groups, and senior citizens in the delegate selection process." In the case of sex, it was specific. States were told to have equal numbers of men and women in their

Table 6-1   Convention Delegates Compared to the Voting-age Population, Percent

	REPUBLICAN[1]	DEMOCRAT[2]	UNITED STATES[3]
College graduate	56	58	7
Income over $10,000	91	82	40
Under age 30	12	21	28
Black	4	14	11
Female	37	40	51

[1]*Miami Herald* survey, Aug. 20, 1972.
[2]Democratic National Committee and CBS survey, July 1972.
[3]Bureau of the Census, 1970.

delegations to the 1976 convention. States with convention systems for choosing delegates were required to hold open meetings, beginning at the precinct level.

Second Thoughts. The experience of the Democrats demonstrated, however, that mere numerical fairness may provide symbolic reward at too high a cost. Seasoned professionals were in many cases shut out in favor of amateurs who had the superficial representational characteristics. The party lost the use of some of its best talent, and the minorities found that numbers were not enough. Even if groups are represented in proportion to their number in the population, the quality of that representation is not assured. The knowledge and influence of skilled insiders can outweigh a numerical advantage held by amateurs in the complexities of convention maneuvering. The Democrats, in revising their rules for the 1976 national convention, reduced the emphasis on strict numerical comparisons of age, sex, and ethnicity.

The Presidential Primary

Every primary is different. There is no self-evident optimum system for serving what are really two functions: choosing delegates to the convention who will have some autonomy to respond to new developments when they get there, and expressing a preference for a particular candidate. On the one hand, a delegate who is legally bound to vote for a particular aspirant cannot adapt to an unexpected situation; on the other, a delegate who has total freedom of choice deprives the voters of expressing their choice.

States have found a variety of ways of resolving this dilemma, as these examples show.

New York. Delegates are elected directly, and they are not formally bound. The preferences of some of the delegates may become known through the news media, however; and backers of particular candidates may sponsor slates of delegates, creating an informal pledge system.

Pennsylvania. Unpledged delegates are elected directly, as in New York; and there is a separate "popularity contest" in which voters express a choice for nominee. That choice is not binding on the delegates.

Indiana. Just the reverse of the Pennsylvania system: voters choose a nominee, and that choice is binding on the delegate, but the delegate himself is not popularly elected.

Other states use different combinations of pledged and unpledged delegates and binding or nonbinding preference votes. They also differ in the procedures for listing candidates on the primary ballot. In some states it is relatively hard to get on the ballot, in some it is easy, and in a few it is impossible for a well-known candidate to stay off. Florida law does not leave it up to the candidate at all. State officials consult the news media to see who the talked-about candidates are and put them all on the ballot. Because the Florida presidential primary is held early in the campaign season, in mid-March, before weaker candidates have dropped out, the list tends to be long. The 1972 ballot had eleven names on the Democratic side, including three—Vance Hartke, Wilbur Mills, and Sam Yorty—whose hopes did not outlive winter. Florida, whose public relations men are among the boldest in the world, designed its primary with attention-getting aspects in mind. New Hampshire, with a primary held the first Tuesday in March, used to get all the winter visits by news media. Florida, with its balmier climate, wider ticket, and more diverse voter population, began in 1972 to upstage that preliminary Yankee sideshow.

States also differ in their rules for deciding who may vote in a given party's primary. The two broad categories are the *open primary* and the *closed primary*. An open primary permits any citizen to vote in any party's primary provided he is registered to vote in the general election. He merely tells the clerk at the polling place which party's ballot he wants. In some states, a record of his choice is made so that he is publicly identified as a member of that party. In others, no record is kept so that party membership can be as secret as the vote. An extreme variation is the *blanket primary* in which a voter can participate in one party's primary for some offices and another's for other offices.

In the closed primary, a person must declare his party choice at the time he registers to vote. Changing his party requires another trip to the registrar's office before some specified date in advance of the election. In its most extreme form, he may even be required to sign a pledge that he has supported the party in the past or that he intends to vote for its candidates in the future.

The closed primary discourages switching. The open primary makes it possible for party loyalists to cross over to the opposition temporarily for the purpose of nominating its weakest candidate. For example, a loyal Republican, knowing that Richard Nixon would be nominated in 1972 no matter what happened in the primary, might ask for a Democratic ballot and vote for George McGovern on the theory that McGovern would be the easiest Democrat for Nixon to beat. This tactic helped confuse the Democrats in another way by giving McGovern a misleading sign of support. Patrick J. Buchanan (1973) told the Senate Select Committee on Presidential Campaign Activities that Republican strategists worked to promote the McGovern candidacy at the expense of Sen. Edmund Muskie, whom they thought would be harder for Nixon to beat (pp. 30–31).

Strategic Considerations

Republicans did not, however, deserve the full credit for McGovern's nomination in 1972. Most Democratic candidates in that year were slow to appreciate the importance of the changes brought about by the McGovern commission. McGovern was an exception. His workers got their people out to the mass meetings. When he took the lead away from Senator Muskie, it was because he dominated the convention states. But primary states have importance beyond their contribution to the delegate count. Parties, remember, exist in order to win; delegates want to know who has the ability to win; and the primaries tend to be regarded as testing grounds for winning ability. This is not entirely reliable. A candidate's ability to get votes from members of his own party, in competition with other candidates from his party, may not be a very accurate measure of his vote-getting ability in a general election. But, as in all other processes requiring judgment, the delegates must look at the only indicator they have.

Where he has a choice, therefore, a strong candidate will stay out of a primary where he does not think he has a good chance of doing well. What constitutes doing well is highly subjective. Eugene McCarthy lost to a write-in candidate in a 1968 primary but did well because he got 42 percent of the vote. The write-in opponent was Lyndon Johnson, and the primary was the season's opener in New Hampshire. Doing that well at that time revealed a previously unknown weakness in the popularity of Lyndon Johnson and the potential for dissent. Muskie won in New Hampshire in 1972 but suffered a tactical defeat because his victory margin was not as large as expected. Candidates, like football coaches, try to minimize expectations by down-playing their chances, but it is a hard thing to control. And when they lose, they have rationalizations ready which, if successful, can make defeat seem like victory. McGovern's staff explained Wallace victories by claiming that the Wallace votes came from the same group of alienated voters that liked McGovern. Recent campaigns are replete with similar examples (Polsby and Wildavsky, 1971, pp. 132–133).

Convention Procedures

The party out of power generally holds its convention first. It needs the extra time to get mobilized and start its campaign. If the party in power is renominating an incumbent, it can concentrate on the convention as a media presentation, which the Republicans did with some success in 1972. They hired Alvin Cooperman, former producer of "The Untouchables," as creative consultant and got a professional scene designer to plan the physical environment. It was done with the TV audience primarily in mind. Delegates in the first six rows, in fact, were part of the TV audience. They could not see the podium, because it had been elevated for the best camera angle, and had to watch the proceedings on television monitors placed below. The speeches were augmented by multimedia presentations of slides, sound, movies, and live TV flashed on nine screens at the front of the hall. Grateful networks, still worried by criticism of their coverage of protest demonstrations at the 1968 Democratic convention, kept their cameras pointed mainly inside the hall (Duff, 1972).

But whether or not there is a contest for the nomination, some other essential business must always be conducted.

The Keynote Speech. Originally a tone-setting pep talk by the temporary chairman, it is now a made-for-TV event designed to brush up the party's image in the eyes of the public. New faces which look and sound good, such as that of Florida Gov. Reubin Askew, who did the job for the Democrats in 1972, are often recruited to depict a party of vigor and fresh ideas.

Credentials. Sometimes two delegations from the same state will lay claim to the same seats. Republican conventions used to have these fights regularly over seats allocated to Southern states where GOP organization was thin and delegations tended to be self-appointed. Democrat credentials fights have been mainly over civil rights issues. In 1964, it was over the exclusion of blacks from the Mississippi delegation; the Mississippi Freedom Democrats won token representation. In 1972, it was over the low (25 percent) representation of women in the South Carolina delegation. The women lost.

A credentials battle can sometimes determine the nomination. The 1912 Republican struggle between William Howard Taft and Theodore Roosevelt turned on disputed Southern seats. "Had Roosevelt received even half the fifty contested seats that probably belonged to him, he might have been nominated," says Eugene H. Roseboom (1957). "The slippery Southern delegates would hardly have remained loyal to Taft when the band wagon hove in sight. The Old Guard leaders were even fearful that the convention might be prolonged over the weekend, leaving them short of funds to pay the extra expenses of their Southern following [p. 364]." Roosevelt followers then organized the Progressive party, and their man lost to Wilson in the general election. Taft came in third.

Permanent Organization. Selection of the permanent chairman, secretary, and sergeant of arms has usually been engineered well in advance and is not controversial. The last time it was disputed was at the 1932 Democratic convention when the factions of Alfred E. Smith and Franklin Roosevelt fought for control of the chair. When Roosevelt's people won, it signaled that he had the strength to get the nomination, which he did—on the fourth ballot (Davis, 1972).

Rules. The Rules Committee deals with both delegate selection procedure and the procedures to be followed once the convention is in session. Procedures and precedents of earlier conventions are usually adopted anew. The last major procedural change was outlawing of the unit rule—where all of a state's votes were cast for whichever candidate gained a majority of its delegation—by the Democrats in 1968. Republicans in 1972 banned frivolous favorite-son nominations and limited all nominating speeches to fifteen minutes.

Platform. "The much maligned party platform," say Polsby and Wildavsky (1971), "is exceedingly important . . . not so much for what it makes explicit but for the fact that it is written at all [p. 118]." It is the culmination of the compromising function of the party system and stands as visible evidence that the diverse and competing factions can agree on something. In 1968, the Republican and Democratic platforms were hardly distinguishable. In 1972, they were quite different, with the Democrats moving away from their centrist stand of 1968 in the adoption of planks supporting such controversial proposals as amnesty for draft evaders. The parties tend to converge and diverge in long-term cycles as new ideas are tentatively adopted and then, if successful, copied by the opposition party, or if unsuccessful, rejected.

The Vice-Presidential Nomination. Balloting for the vice-presidential nominee is usually a formality after the presidential nominee has indicated his choice. The last nominee to depart from this procedure was Adlai Stevenson, who threw it open to the floor in 1956, adding interest to an otherwise dull convention. Estes Kefauver won over John F. Kennedy on the third ballot. The selection, often made hurridly, provides an opportunity to appease losing factions. That was a purpose of Kennedy's gesture to Senate Majority Leader Lyndon Johnson in 1960. Theodore White (1961) quotes an unnamed Kennedy staff member: "It was always anticipated that we'd offer Lyndon the nomination; what we never anticipated was that he'd accept [p. 209]." In 1968, Richard Nixon promised Southern delegates that if nominated he would take care to choose a running mate who was not offensive to them. His choice proved to be both inoffensive and unknown. When the *Miami Herald* sent a reporter out to ask people on the street, "What or who is a Spiro Agnew," he got such responses as "a nut with a special thread," "an insect," and "something to do with cloud formations in the sky."

There have been various proposals for making the race for vice-presidential nomination an open one. In 1972, Rosemary Ginn, chairman of the Republican DO Committee, proposed that balloting on the Vice President take place before the choice of the presidential nominee. This suggestion, which was not adopted, was designed to relieve the nominee of the need to make such an important decision under the pressure of time and avoid in the future such disasters as befell that year's Democratic nominee, George McGovern. His choice of Sen. Thomas Eagleton was not prefaced by the careful staff work and consultation which might have disclosed the senator's political liability, a history of mental illness. Nor, as it turned out too late to affect the election, was the 1968 and 1972 Republican choice of Spiro T. Agnew, who had participated in kickback schemes as a state official in Maryland. In contrast, the first two Vice Presidents designated under the terms of the Twenty-fifth Amendment to the Constitution, Gerald Ford and Nelson Rockefeller, were given careful and unhurried scrutiny by Congress.

Are National Conventions Necessary?

Critics of the convention system's rowdy manipulations have been hard pressed to explain why it usually produces fairly good candidates. It must be, said Moise Ostrogorski (1902), because, "God takes care of drunkards, of little children, and of the United States [p. 229]." The main arguments for dropping it in favor of a national primary system are that it is unrepresentative, responding to party elites rather than rank-and-file voters; that the atmosphere is undignified; and that minority factions can sometimes gain control, as in the case of the Republicans in 1964 and the Democrats in 1972.

But these are not very serious shortcomings, and they have compensating advantages. The minority factions, if they remain a minority, which occassionally take over are roundly beaten in the general election; meanwhile, the system has given them their fair chance to take their case to the people, and this is better than a system in which they would never have a hope of accomplishing that much. There is always the outside chance of converting a majority to their view. The rowdiness may be esthetically offensive to some, but it is good fun for those who get to attend a convention and it does no real harm except possibly some short-term tarnishings of the party's public image. And the machinations of the party leaders have the important side effect of building consensus. Without the convention, the party's function of accommodating diverse interests and testing power relationships would be much harder if not impossible to fulfill. And it does not have to be as unrepresentative as it has been in the past, as the door-opening efforts of both parties in recent years have demonstrated.

A National Primary?

From time to time, someone proposes that the ills of the convention system be cured by substituting a national primary to choose presidential candidates. Senator Mike Mansfield regularly introduces such a measure. It has the virtue of apparent simplicity. But as Judith H. Parris (1972) has pointed out (and as the 1972 Florida primary demonstrated), the results of a primary can be quite confusing. "Essentially, a primary is a means of measuring attitude distributions—and not a method of arriving at agreement [p. 176]." When many candidates are in the field, like the Florida 11, it is hard to discern a consensus from the vote count. Even a system with a runoff between the top two candidates is subject to the capricious distribution of candidates and attitudes. It would also be expensive and physically exhausting, restricting the field, as Polsby and Wildavsky (1971) have said, "to wealthy athletes [p. 236]." It might, however, have the advantage of forcing tighter organizational lines between state and national parties.

CAMPAIGN PROBLEMS AND STRATEGIES

Evoking an Image

When Norman Mailer was running for mayor of New York City, a member of his campaign staff, Jack Newfield, implored an audience of volunteers to join a "guerrilla graffiti squad." They would meet at headquarters, be issued chalk, and then scrawl the campaign slogan, "No More Bullshit," all over the city. "The slogan was innocuous enough," said campaign manager Joe Flaherty (1970) some time later. "But this was not my idea of how to employ workers [p. 109]."

Finding the right slogan and then promulgating it are key goals in any campaign. The idea is to evoke just the right images and issues that will motivate wavering voters to support the candidate. The more successful slogans are remembered long after the issues behind them have been forgotten, and a successful leitmotiv may enjoy several incarnations. "Rum, Romanism, and Rebellion," which backfired against James G. Blaine and cost the Republicans the Irish vote in 1884, was also used against Al Smith in 1928. It is the alliterative ancestor of "Korea, Corruption, and Communism," against which Eisenhower ran in 1952. Theodore Roosevelt's "Square Deal" and Woodrow Wilson's "New Freedom" foreshadowed Franklin Roosevelt's "New Deal," Harry S. Truman's "Fair Deal," and John F. Kennedy's "New Frontier."

Does It Make Any Difference?

Until the survey research of the modern era, candidates could only guess at how much effect their campaign efforts had. We now know that it has some effect—not much, but enough to make a difference. The pioneering Erie County, Ohio, study by Paul Lazersfeld, Bernard R. Berelson, and Hazel Gaudet Erskine (1948) found three kinds of effect.

Conversion. Some voters will change sides. Their number is usually very small, but since each switch makes a difference of two votes—one subtracted from the old commitment and one added to the new—they can have enormous consequence.

Reinforcement. Voters who have made up their mind can find justification for their choice in the campaign messages. This tends to keep them

Goldwater Campaign in 1964: "In your heart, you know he's right." (*Max Scheler, Black Star.*)

from being converted by the opposition campaign. Candidates therefore direct part of their effort at voters who are already for them.

Activation.   A campaign stimulates some people to vote who otherwise would have stayed home. And it helps people who have no choice to make one.

Getting Known

The first fact which a candidate must communicate to the voters is that he exists. If they already know about him, he has a head start. Adlai Stevenson and Spiro Agnew had to overcome the fact that neither's name was, in Agnew's phrase, "a household word." Candidates who have been prominent in other fields, i.e., General Eisenhower, Ronald Reagan, John Glenn, have a head start. A candidate who is less well known than his opponent will try to engage him in direct debate; he has nothing to lose and even if the debate is inconclusive, he will have planted the thought that he is the other man's equal. It was a tactical error for Nixon to agree to the 1960 debates with Kennedy for that reason. In his 1972 campaign, he avoided that sort of mistake, appearing to stay aloof from any kind of activity that would imply equal status with McGovern. A Nixon adviser explained the strategy (Meyer, 1972):

> Say a news magazine wants to do a piece [on pollution] with Nixon's picture on one side and McGovern's on the other. We don't want Nixon in that situation, telling how he feels about crud in the river. We'll give them [Environmental Protection Agency Administrator William] Ruckelshaus. We don't feel Mc-Govern is the President's equal, and we are not going to portray him to be when it comes to things over which we have control [p. 24A].

A good campaign strategy emphasizes the strong points. A candidate who is in the majority party will stress his affiliation while his opponent will not mention his. An incumbent will run on his record, citing past achievement, appealing to the status quo. This can be a fairly powerful appeal even when it is misleading. Oliver Bolton's campaign signs in Portage County, Ohio, in 1962 said, "Return Bolton to Congress," when in fact he was running *against* the incumbent, Robert E. Cook. It was not exactly a lie, because Bolton had served one term five years earlier. He won. And there are still voters in Ohio who confuse Sen. Robert Taft with his late father.

Alliances, Issues, and Timing

Some of the decisions a candidate must make involve highly complex optimization problems. While they are the sorts of problems that can be made to yield to mathematical decision theory, most campaign strategists solve them intuitively. One problem is how to make an alliance with a group that has voting power without alienating opposing groups that also have voting power. Ambiguity is not always the best strategy (Shepsle, 1972).

The case of Richard Nixon and the black vote in 1960 is an example. Nixon began with some hope for a share of the black vote and yielded to demands for more liberal platform planks on race relations. But on a trip to the South, he was impressed by the reception he got from white crowds. While he was trying to make up his mind whether to appeal to blacks or to white Southerners, Martin Luther King, Jr., was arrested in Atlanta for refusing to leave a restaurant table. Nixon did nothing. Kennedy called Mrs. King to express his concern. King's father had been a Nixon supporter, but he quickly switched to Kennedy, who won 68 percent of the black vote (compared to Stevenson's 61 percent in 1956). In close states like Illinois and Texas, it may have changed the outcome of the election (Polsby and Wildavsky, 1971).

222

Politics

Humphrey Campaign in 1968: Timing the peak is critical. (*Black Star.*)

Deciding what issue positions to take presents an equivalent problem. McGovern began his 1972 campaign with clear positions on such controversial questions as amnesty and abortion, then, under mounting pressure from the unfavorable reaction, moved toward vagueness, a change which left him seeming indecisive. Issues usually are not discussed in great detail. One consistent general issue is the record of the party in power which can be attacked or defended. This is not always a straightforward choice, as Hubert Humphrey discovered in 1968. He ran on the record of the administration in which he had served although, clearly, his heart was not always in it.

In a close election, timing is critical. A candidate seeks to orchestrate his campaign so that it peaks on election day. Nixon may have peaked too soon in 1960; whereas Hubert Humphrey probably would have won in 1968 if the election had been held a few days later. Television advertising is stepped up toward the end of the campaign to induce peaking; if there are any dramatic announcements to make, the candidate may save them for the end. In 1952, Eisenhower's promise to "go to Korea" came shortly before election day.

Pranks, Outrages, and Dirty Tricks

When Richard Nixon ran for governor of California in 1962, he made the obligatory tour of Chinatown with the traditional delegation: a Miss Chinatown, courtly elders, children bearing bilingual signs. The English inscriptions said, "Welcome Nixon." The candidate was smiling for the TV cameras when an elderly Chinese whispered to him that the Chinese characters said, "How about the Hughes Loan?"—a reference to a controversial financial transaction between Nixon's brother and financier Howard Hughes. Nixon, recalls Dick Tuck (1972), who perpetrated that prank, "tore the signs from the children's hands and ripped them to shreds. It was all on the evening news [p. A30]."

When criminal activity on behalf of the Committee to Re-Elect the President was disclosed in 1972 and 1973, some Republicans sought to compare the break-ins, telephone tapping, illegal contributions, misrepresentation, and subsequent perjury with Dick Tuck's famous antics. Tuck was indignant. The Republicans, he said, "have corrupted a great American art form and don't even know the difference [p. A30]."

The distinction is not too difficult. Patrick J. Buchanan of the Nixon White House staff offered the Senate Watergate committee a scheme of classification:

> My own view is that there are sort of four gradations. There are things that are certainly utterly outrageous, and I would put that in with the kind of demonstrations against Vice President Humphrey in 1968 which denied him an opportunity to speak for almost a month. Then, there is dirty tricks, then there is political hardball, then there is pranks. I think you will almost have to leave it to the individual and his own sense of ethics as to what is permissible [p. 31].

Where criminal activity is involved, of course, the law and not the individual's sense of ethics defines what is permissible. But it was not only the criminal nature of the acts uncovered in the various Watergate-related investigations that made them distinctive. It was the use of the government's resources by government officials to break the law to maintain themselves in office.

Prior to Watergate, Samuel J. Archibald (1971), executive director of the privately financed Fair Campaign Practices Committee, estimated that about one contest in eight produces a complaint about dirty politics. A sample complaint: In 1970, a television spot in behalf of Indiana Rep. Richard Roudebush's campaign for senator depicted a Viet Cong soldier receiving a rifle. A voice said the incumbent senator, Vance Hartke, had voted for trade with Communist countries. It concluded: "Isn't that like putting a loaded gun in the hands of our enemies?" The committee offered to arrange for arbitration of Hartke's charge that the linkage between Viet Cong weaponry and his vote was a lie, but Roudebush refused to cooperate. Hartke won anyway.

If a statement in campaign literature is clearly a lie, the liar risks federal criminal prosecution. Donald H. Segretti, hired by White House aides to direct undercover activity for the Nixon campaign, was convicted for having false charges about the sexual and drinking behavior of some of the

Political Funnyman Dick Tuck: An art form was corrupted. (*Wide World Photos.*)

Democratic candidates circulated to voters in Florida before the primary. The charges were made to appear to come from the Muskie campaign; the purpose was to promote bitterness among the Democrats. Members of the November Group helped write copy for an ad in the *New York Times* on May 17, 1972, which seemed to reflect a voluntary outpouring of public support for Nixon's decision to mine the harbor at Haiphong. The support proved to be spurious. "They say now they were duped," reported Jules Witcover (1973), who called the ad "apparently illegal" [p. E1].

Other tactics, while less outrageous, clearly fell in the "dirty tricks" department: planting of spies in opposition campaign staffs, canceling speaking engagements by anonymous phone call, hiring demonstrators to disrupt personal appearances. The Senate hearings and the criminal prosecutions exposed a previously unsuspected plethora of such activity, and there was hope that the disclosures would lead to new standards of morality in political campaigning. Dick Tuck was doubtful, noting that politicians tend to imitate one another. Joe McGinnis wrote *The Selling of the President, 1968* to expose the evils of becoming preoccupied with imagery. But, said Tuck, "some politicians took it as a textbook and hired the same people that McGinnis was ridiculing. I fear that as a result of Watergate, the same politicians will now want wiretaps, goon squads and faked letters [p. A30]."

Ways To Reform

The Ervin Committee, after hearing the evidence, proposed a number of reforms in a lengthy report issued in the summer of 1974. Its recommendations tended to be highly specific for the abuses uncovered in the Watergate scandal, but they did not point to any general restructuring of political procedures which could overcome the root causes of the Watergate problem. Restraints were proposed on intelligence-gathering activities by White House staff members; a prohibition on examination of individual income tax returns by the President, his staff, or his executive office was proposed; expansion of the Hatch Act to bar political activity by appointed officials, including the Attorney General, was suggested; and a proposal was advanced for a federal commission to supervise the enforcement of federal election laws. There was also a proposal to institutionalize the role of special prosecutor by the creation of a "public attorney" who would provide an independent check of the administration of justice in the executive branch.

The proposals tended to reflect the belief that the Watergate problem grew from the system and its rules, or at least the problem was amenable to some kind of technical fix through a change in the rules. But some thoughtful observers, such as Barber (1974), warned that the cure was not to be found in the laws but in the people who obey and enforce the laws. "No 'system'—constitutional or otherwise—can be relied upon for political rescue," said Barber. "The real rescuers were the men and women who were determined to hold the government to the law. Our future safety and progress depend on our success in choosing leaders who have the character and talent to preserve the Constitution [p. C1]."

MONEY

The Root of Some Evil

The dirty tricks and outrages of the 1972 Republican presidential campaign, says White (1973), came about in part because the fund-raising efforts were so spectacularly successful. "There was always all that money available from the Finance Committee to Re-Elect," he said; "there was the temptation to find ingenious ways to use it [p. 276]." Students of campaign finance like to contrast contemporary practices with the first campaign of Abraham Lincoln. When Lincoln ran for the House of Representatives in 1864, a campaign fund of $200 was raised for him. After the election, he returned $199.25 of it. The 75 cents, according to folklore, was used to buy a barrel of cider.

Table 6-2   Total Campaign Costs, 1952–1972

YEAR	COSTS
1952	$140,000,000
1956	$155,000,000
1960	$175,000,000
1964	$200,000,000
1968	$300,000,000
1972	$400,000,000

Source: Citizens' Research Foundation.

In 1972, President Nixon's campaign fund was 60.2 million dollars, including some large contributions which were accepted *after* the election. One postelection donor was given a diplomatic appointment.

Neither Lincoln's 75-cent campaign nor Nixon's enormous modern-day effort were typical of their times. But campaign spending has increased by several orders of magnitude, and the rising cost has raised serious questions about the election process. Much of the increase has taken place fairly recently. The Citizens' Research Foundation, a private group which monitors election financing, estimates that the total cost of all campaigns for elective office in 1952 was $140 million. Its estimate for 1972 was $400 million (see Table 6-2).

Big Spending's Side Effects

Although it seems like a lot, the amount is not, per se, exorbitant. Compared to the amounts spent on advertising for private purposes, it is trivial. The problem comes in the way the money is raised and, to a lesser extent, in how it is spent. Delmer D. Dunn (1972) has summarized the ways in which money undermines the system.

The Falsified Image.   A well-financed campaign can afford the techno-logical devices, discussed earlier in this chapter, which can be employed to give voters a misleading impression of the candidate.

Unequal Exposure.   The candidate with the most money can use it to buy the most publicity. This does not guarantee success, but it improves the odds. In the sixteen presidential campaigns from 1912 through 1972, the candidate with the most money won nine times and lost seven, not a significant difference. On the other hand, the biggest spender won in five of the last six presidential campaigns. However, the cause-effect relationship is not straightforward here. A candidate who is expected to lose has trouble raising money; the well-financed Republicans might have won without the pocketbook advantage.

The Pocketbook Veto. The high cost of campaigning could keep some worthy potential candidates from ever reaching the electoral arena. If so, this gives wealthy donors an effective veto power over the office. The veto can also be exercised, of course, at the campaign stage. Many traditional Democratic bankrollers withheld their money from the McGovern campaign. But in this case, technology can be applied to improve the standing of the small donor. McGovern's 1972 campaign raised nearly $23 million—a record for a Democratic nominee—and most of it came in small donations through the direct-mail drive of the McGovern Million Member Club. When the Democrats found themselves $9 million in debt after their 1972 defeat, they eliminated it with yet another innovation: a series of celebrity-laden telethons on nation networks to appeal for donations.

Obligated Officeholders. The large campaign donor, if he is rational, expects to get something for his money. It may be no more than the satisfaction of helping a worthy cause, but more direct rewards are not unknown. Sizable Nixon contributions in 1972 came from persons or organizations which had specific interests in pending government action, e.g., the targets of litigation by the Justice Department, beneficiaries of price supports from the Department of Agriculture, objects of regulation by the Commerce Department (Franklin, 1973). At the very least, large donors expect—and get—access to decisionmakers.

The amount of visible unfairness which the political system can tolerate is limited. If representation has to be bought, then popular acceptance of the basic authority of government is hard to maintain. Even the facade of democratic government requires that the bases of legitimacy not be flaunted openly. Dunn (1972) quotes a U.S. senator interested in campaign finance regulation: "The very integrity of the system is at stake. People have less confidence in the system than they have ever had. I think that one of the prime reasons is the distrust . . . of the present way of financing elections [p. 25]."

Where the Money Comes From

A wealthy candidate starts with a large advantage; he can be his own biggest contributor. Herbert Alexander (1972) has found that most candidates, regardless of wealth, spend some of their own money. North Dakota Gov. William Guy contributed $200 to his own campaign in 1968. Missouri Sen. Thomas F. Eagleton put up $21,254 to win his Senate seat. At the affluent end of the scale, Nelson Rockefeller dipped into his family fortune for $350,000 to help support his unsuccessful bid for the GOP presidential nomination in 1968. His stepmother, Martha Baird Rockefeller, provided another $1,482,625. This money is especially important because it is available for crucial but mostly invisible work that needs to be done well in advance of the campaign: research, staff building, organization, and plan-

I can recall in one instance going to a labor union who I knew was contributing $5,000 to a Senate campaign—to anyone they endorse—all above board, all honest, you know, by the numbers, and it was a check, the full works. And we walk in and we sit down and we start off the discussion very polite. He said, "Mr. Biden would you like a cup of coffee?" We go through that routine, we have a cup of coffee, and my brother, who was my chief fund raiser with great experience at age 24, sitting next to me, and he . . . goes through the social niceties with my brother, then he says, "Well, what are your chances of winning?" And I go through the litany that I've gone through, as everyone else has who has run, a hundred times, and you go through and you do that by the numbers, and then you really get down to it. Then, no one asks you to buy your vote or to promise a vote, but they say things like this to me anyway, . . . "Well, Joe, had you been in the 92nd Congress how would you have voted on the SST and while you're at it how would you have voted on bailing out Lockheed?" Now, I may be a naive young feller, but I knew the right answer for $5,000. I knew what had to be said to get that money.

—Sen. Joseph R. Biden, Jr., Democrat of Delaware, in testimony to the Senate Rules and Administration Subcommittee on Privileges and Elections, September 1973

ning. These are the activities that are necessary to gain recognition that the candidacy is a viable one.

Then there are the fat cats. In 1973, James R. Polk, a journalist who specializes in following the intricate trails of paper that tell who gave what to whom, reported that the largest 100 donors in Nixon's 1972 campaign gave a total of $14 million, close to a fourth of his total campaign cost. The "super givers" were W. Clement Stone, chairman of the Combined Insurance Company of America, who gave $2.1 million, and Richard M. Scaife, Pittsburgh heir to banking and oil fortunes, an even $1 million. Only a few organizations were on the list of the 100 largest. Most were individuals. "One common thread ran through the Nixon list," said Polk, "men now in their 60's and 70's who started their own businesses, sweated through growth through the years, then found themselves with awesome fortunes when their stock value soared on the market in the last decade. At a glance, it seemed almost as if Horatio Alger's heroes had all grown up and become Richard Nixon backers [p. A8]."

Corporations have long been forbidden by law to contribute to campaigns, but many have tried ways of getting around it. Business firms have supplied office equipment, the use of company airplanes, and postage to candidates. They can buy advertising in convention programs. Some give bonuses to employees who then make individual contributions. Some business contributions are filtered through trade associations. Despite the existence of such loopholes, some firms gave money directly from corporate funds in 1972. American Airlines, Ashland Oil, Goodyear, Minnesota Mining & Manufacturing, Gulf Oil, and Phillips Petroleum were among the first to admit it under the pressure of the Watergate investigations. Labor unions are also forbidden to contribute to campaigns directly,

W. Clement Stone: One of the supergivers. (*Wide World Photos.*)

but they still control large amounts of money through organizations set up for that purpose. Union members are urged to send their dollars to the Committee on Political Education (COPE) which aids candidates. But labor, too, sometimes bypasses the available loopholes.

When W. A. (Tony) Boyle was president of the United Mine Workers, he, like his later corporate counterparts, gave money from his organization's treasury directly to campaign funds. He was convicted of embezzlement of union funds, conspiracy, and illegal donation, sentenced to five years in jail, and fined $130,000. Polk (1973) noted that the charges against the corporate contributors were "relatively lenient compared to . . . a labor leader in disfavor [p. A-10]." The board chairman of Minnesota Mining & Manufacturing was fined $500. The former chairman of Goodyear was fined $1,000. They were charged only with misdemeanors in keeping with the announced strategy of the first Watergate Special Prosecutor, Archibald Cox, to encourage corporate violators to confess. Polk's observation, however, suggests an illustration of a point we made in Chapter 5: that the treatment groups get depends on their perceived legitimacy.

Trying to Reform the System

Most reform efforts have aimed at trying to switch the financing source from large contributors to small ones. It has not been easy. Small contributors were important in the Wallace campaigns of 1964, 1968, and 1972, as well as the 1964 Goldwater campaign. But only George McGovern came close to discovering the full potential of this source. The 634,000 contributors to McGovern in 1972 made his the most broadly based presidential campaign in history. A desire to blunt the effect of big contributors was behind the first attempt at regulation of campaign finance in 1907, when contributions by corporations were outlawed. The Corrupt Practices Act of 1925 and the Hatch Act of 1939 put ceilings on the size of campaign contributions and on the amounts that candidates could spend. Both limitations were easily circumvented by the creation of multiple committees which could each receive and spend the limit.

Another form of regulation is the federal gift tax, applicable to gifts of more than $3,000. To avoid it, large donors break their gifts into $3,000 segments and spread them over a number of paper committees. The end result is not to inhibit large gifts but to make it difficult to trace them through the reports of the myriad committees.

The Federal Election Campaign Practices Act, which went into effect on April 7, 1972, made some improvement, particularly in the reporting requirements. But it is still possible to move funds among candidates and committees in a way that makes them hard to trace. Some Nixon campaign money in 1972 was processed through a Mexican bank, where it was hoped federal subpoena power could not follow. The process is called "laundering." The 1972 law limited the sums that could be spent on advertising in campaigns for Congress or the presidency, but these limits were superceded by total spending controls scheduled to take effect for the 1976 election. The new spending limits for Senate candidates (and House candidates representing an entire state) were based on the number of eligible voters. House elections were limited to $70,000 and presidential general elections to $20 million per candidate. Meanwhile, reforms were also evolving on the contribution side of campaign finance.

Beginning in 1973, taxpayers were given several alternative ways of having the government subsidize their campaign contributions through tax credits, deductions, or a simple checkoff. It was hoped that this would reduce the reliance of candidates on large contributors, but the number of taxpayers who took advantage of the system was relatively small, the check-off box having been placed in an obscure section of the form. It was moved to a more prominent position for taxes paid in 1974.

Despite "some reservations," President Ford signed the 1974 amendments to the Federal Election Campaign Practices Act to make the check-off dollars available to presidential candidates. To obtain full public funding, candidates would have to forgo private contributions. Independent candidates or those from minor parties could qualify for partial funding, with the amounts keyed to their number of votes. In addition, matching public funds of up to $4.5 million were provided for presidential primaries, subject to some limits designed to shut out frivolous third-party efforts. And campaign financial reporting rules were tightened still more.

Prospects for Future Reform

A number of things could be done to open up the pathways of communication between candidate and voter and ensure all candidates a minimally fair chance. Congressional campaigns could be directly subsidized with public funds. Short of that, candidates could be given a subsidy to buy broadcast time. The Public Broadcasting System could be funded for special coverage beyond what the three commercial networks provide. Congress could give free mailing privileges to candidates. It could cut down some of the cost of the new technology by providing each candidate a computerized, up-to-date list of qualified voters.

All these measures would be costly; but, as Alexander (1972) has said, "The cost of American politics must be measured not only in terms of dollars, but in terms of impact on democratic values [pp. 38–39]." With or without reform, a lot of money will continue to be spent on election campaigns. The problem is to channel it in ways that will serve the voters.

SUGGESTED READINGS

Davis, James W. *Presidential Primaries: Road to the White House.* New York: Crowell, 1967. Gives history of the development of the primary system and the significance of primaries in the nomination process.

Dunn, Delmer D. *Financing Presidential Campaigns*. Washington: The Brookings Institution, 1972. An excellent analysis of the issues and problems concerning campaign financing and the impact of money on politics.

Heard, Alexander. *The Costs of Democracy*. Chapel Hill: The University of North Carolina Press, 1960. An excellent study of the relation between politics and money and of the effects of money on the political system.

Hiebert, Ray, Robert Jones, John Lorenz, and Ernest Lotito. *The Political Image Merchants: Strategies in the New Politics*. Washington, D.C.: Acropolis, 1971. The new methods described by the practitioners, often richly anecdotal, as they let down their hair in a postcampaign seminar at the University of Maryland.

McGinnis, Joe. *The Selling of the President, 1968*. New York: Trident Press, 1969. A colorful and critical account of Richard Nixon's use of television advertising in the 1968 campaign.

Nimmo, Dan. *The Political Persuaders: The Techniques of Modern Election Campaigns*. Englewood Cliffs, N.J.: Prentice-Hall, 1970. A detailed analysis of the impact of public relation firms and of all forms of mass media on political campaigns.

Polsby, Nelson W., and Aaron B. Wildavsky. *Presidential Elections*. 2d ed. New York: Scribner, 1968. An overview of the strategies and tactics involved in presidential campaigns.

Pomper, Gerald M. *Nominating the President: The Politics of Convention Choice*. New York: Norton, 1966. A comprehensive study of the nomination process from delegate selection to convention.

Chapter 7

Elections and Voting Behavior

OUR ELECTION SYSTEM

A Potential Trouble Spot

Our system for electing the President of the United States contains some ambiguities which periodically raise the possibility of serious trouble. Every few elections, someone comes forth with a plausible and legal scheme for tossing a monkey wrench into that system. The object of the scheme is to bring the whole procedure to a halt while concessions are exacted on behalf of the group or individual causing the problem. This kind of activity understandably produces alarm. As a device for transferring power, the presidential election system has almost always been smooth and functional—so much so that we tend to take it for granted. So it is jarring when we are reminded that a calculating and determined minority can jam the system.

Such a bitter scenario has not been fully enacted since 1876, when the South won a halt to Reconstruction in exchange for letting the minority choice, Rutherford B. Hayes, become President. But a similar possibility has been threatened, and the threat has been credible, quite recently. In 1960, a Republican elector, Henry D. Irwin of Bartlesville, Oklahoma, sent the following telegram to the other 218 Republican electors pledged to Richard Nixon:

I am Oklahoma Republican elector. The Republican electors cannot deny the election to Kennedy. Sufficient conservative Democratic electors available to deny labor Socialist nominee. Would you consider Byrd President, Goldwater Vice President, or wire any acceptable substitute. All replies strict confidence [Longley and Braun, 1972, p. 6].

Irwin figured that if the other Republican electors would go along with him, they could find enough Southern Democrats to violate their pledges and put Virginia Sen. Harry Byrd, Sr., or some other conservative in the White House. None went along with him. Later, Irwin told a bemused Senate Judiciary Committee that he just "could not stomach" Mr. Nixon. So he voted for Byrd, in violation of his pledge. The Senate was not sufficiently upset to enact any measure to keep such a thing from happening again.

Eight years later, another attempt was made through the third-party effort of Alabama Gov. George C. Wallace. By preventing either Nixon or Hubert H. Humphrey from winning an electoral majority, Wallace reasoned, he could trade the winning margin for a major concession, such as a shift in racial policy. He won 46 electoral votes. It was not enough. But enough people were worried by the Wallace performance to create a serious effort to change the system. And 81 percent of the persons interviewed in a Gallup poll at the time said they favored scrapping the Electoral College in favor of a direct vote for President. That is one possible

George Wallace in His Third-party Campaign, 1968: A cause for worry. (*United Press International.*)

reform. There are others, and we shall examine them after a closer look at the way the system works now.

The Ballot and the Democratic Ideal

The pressure for election reform is heavy in years when there are close elections and strong third-party movements. At other times, the worries are forgotten or replaced by more immediate concerns. This lack of consistent concern about election problems is not so alarming as it might seem, for most of the proposed reforms could bring new and possibly worse problems of their own. On the other hand, the problem is important because it involves the basic need to keep elections free, open, honest, and straightforward; voting is a key process in democratic government. If elections are fair and free and provide citizens a means of registering their preferences, then the chances that democracy will work are enhanced. If elections are not fair and free, then government can be democratic in no more than appearance. As a means of conveying the will of the people to institutions of government and deciding who will occupy its offices, elections are critical to the process of keeping democracy.

Modern democracy was an idea talked about by philosophers long before its real-life versions existed. Our beliefs and expectations about that reality are still shaped in large degree by the mental pictures created by thinkers of the sixteenth and seventeenth centuries, who held out high ideals for self-government. If we had today the fulfillment of their vision, American government would have four central qualities.

Involvement. All citizens would be deeply involved in community and political affairs, each approaching the chores of self-government with interest and vigor.

Information. Because the decisions made by the people would be directly translated into governmental action, the people would take the trouble to inform themselves about the affairs and issues of government.

Discussion. Informed citizens would know that most problems have more than one possible solution and, accordingly, would debate and discuss the alternatives freely and frankly among themselves before choosing.

Public Benefit. No problem of conflict between private and public interest would arise because voters would make decisions on the basis of their judgments of what is best for the whole community. The public interest would be the sum of all the private interests.

These four conditions of the democratic ideal come closest to realization in small, homogeneous bodies such as that classic textbook example, the New England town meeting. In a large nation with a diversity of interests separated by time and distance, the ideal is much harder to approach. Involvement, information, discussion, and public mindedness are present, but these qualities are sporadic and unevenly distributed. The difference between a town meeting and a nation of more than 200 million people spread from ocean to ocean is greater than a mechanical difference. But the mechanics of democracy nevertheless become highly important. The systems designed for overcoming the physical and psychological differences between a continent and a meeting hall can determine the success or failure in approaching the democratic ideal. And, as we shall see, even minor tinkering with the system can have drastic and unexpected consequences. If you set out to design a system for transferring the operations of the town meeting hall to the entire nation, a wide and bewildering array of alternatives would quickly confront you. Part of the physical problem could be solved by technology: Wire everyone's television set into a two-way network and hold a town meeting on a grand scale. But, some form of representation would still be necessary. Even fairly small deliberative bodies must use committee systems to spread the workload and to narrow issues to questions that can be voted up or down by the main group. And the wired nation would not solve the problem of psychological distance. Not all people would be equally involved or informed or interested in discussion. Decision making consumes mental energy, and to expect everyone or even a substantial number of citizens to consider all the alternatives and consequences of each act and moment of government is clearly unrealistic. Therefore a representative system is necessary, and the way in which those representatives are chosen becomes crucial. The American systems of representation are unique, and they illustrate how practical necessity must compromise the democratic ideal.

The Legal Machinery of Election

Despite the critical importance of elections, the Founding Fathers stopped short of designing the exact methods for conducting them. As a result, most of the procedural details are controlled by the states. Congress has the power, under Article I, Section 4, to make or alter the state regulations; but it has used this power sparingly. The extent of congressional action has been to:

1 Require secret ballots in national elections.

2 Set the dates for presidential and congressional elections: the first Tuesday after the first Monday in November of each even numbered year for congressional elections, with the President elected at the time of every other congressional election.

3 Enact laws to regulate campaign contributions and expenditures and to define and punish corrupt practices.

4 Limit the restrictions on voting which states may impose through registration requirements.

Within these boundaries, plus those found in the Constitution, either explicitly or through Supreme Court interpretation, states are free to make the rules. The system, therefore, has not one but many designers.

PRESIDENTIAL ELECTIONS

A Case of Function Following Form

The system for electing the President evolved—and still evolves—as the work of many designers, state and national, public and private. It is not what the Founders had in mind. They envisioned an electoral college that would be a deliberative body, which, after the election of George Washington, would usually succeed only in narrowing the list of candidates, thus leaving the final choice to the House of Representatives. But private action, through the organization of political parties, quickly changed that. The bones of that ancient structure remain, however, and they still shape the way the system operates. The system in brief:

Composition of the Electoral College. Each state gets as many electors as it has members of Congress. Each therefore has a minimum of three (one each for the two senators plus the minimum of one representative which every state has regardless of size). Electoral vote is therefore roughly proportional to population, because 435 votes (corresponding to the 435 members of the House) are distributed on the basis of population. However, there are some sizable distortions, reflecting the distortions in the apportionment of the House. The main source of distortion is the fact that there are no fractional votes, and small population differences can produce disproportionate changes in voting strength. North Dakota had nearly the same 1970 population as Montana—617,761 to 694,409. But Montana's voting strength in the 1970s was one-fourth greater—four electoral votes to three—because it had two House members to North Dakota's one. Alaska, with less than half of North Dakota's population, also had three electoral votes.

Choosing the Electors. States have different requirements for getting a candidate for elector on the ballot; but all systems require some degree of organized effort, which means that the job usually falls by default to the political parties at the state level. For the 1972 election, twenty-nine states chose their candidates for elector by state party convention, ten by state central committee decision, seven by direct primary, and three by some combination of convention and primary. In one state, Pennsylvania, the electors were appointed by the presidential nominees. In about twenty states, the names of the electors appear on the presidential ballot in the general election. In the others, you may never know who they are.

The Unit Rule.   The candidate who gets the most votes—not necessarily a majority—in a state gets all of that state's electoral votes. For example, although Nixon got 57 percent of the two-party vote in California in 1972 and McGovern got 43 percent, Nixon got all of California's 45 electoral votes. If the electoral vote had been divided proportionately, Nixon would have received 26 electoral votes and McGovern 19. This unit rule has tremendous strategy implications. It means that it is better to win by a little in a lot of states than to win by a lot in a few states. It has another effect which seems trivial at first glance but turns out to be important: The winner's margin is greatly exaggerated in the electoral vote. Nixon in 1972 won 62 percent of the popular vote and 97 percent of the electoral vote. In 1968, he won 44 percent of the popular vote (in a three-way race) and 56 percent of the electoral vote. Hubert Humphrey, who won 43 percent of the popular vote in that election, had only 36 percent of the electoral vote. The Electoral College, then, serves to translate a very close vote into a decisive one whose legitimacy is more readily recognized.

The Electoral Commitment.   Since 1796, electors have been pledged to particular candidates. In all that time, only eight have broken their pledges by voting for another candidate; none of them were in a position to change the outcome. Nevertheless, most electors could legally vote for anyone they pleased. Only four states make adherence to an electoral pledge a legal requirement.

The Formalities.   To the surprise of many—and to the occasional frustration of people who make election bets on the percentage point spread—there is no official count of the national popular vote in a presidential election, nor is there need for one. Winning electors are certified by their state governors, and each group meets in its own state on the first Monday after the second Wednesday in December to cast its votes for President and Vice President. The outcome is sent to the president of the Senate (the incumbent Vice President of the United States), who supervises the formal counting of the electoral votes and announces the result at a joint session of Congress in January.

Contingency Plans.   What if no candidate gets a majority of the electoral votes? The newly elected Congress does the job. The House selects the President from the top three candidates, with each state delegation casting one vote. A quorum of at least one member from each of two-thirds (thirty-four) of the state delegations must be present for the voting. Balloting continues until one candidate receives an absolute majority (twenty-six) of the states. Meanwhile, the Senate chooses the Vice President, with each senator having a vote and an absolute majority required. If the House cannot agree on a President by Inauguration Day, the Senate's vice-presidential choice becomes acting president until a President is chosen.

Suppose a candidate dies or withdraws between his nomination in midsummer and the November election? The law makes no provision, but both parties pass resolutions to cover this contingency at their national conventions. When Sen. Thomas Eagleton withdrew as the Democratic vice-presidential nominee in 1972, his successor, Sargent Shriver, was chosen by the presidential nominee and nominated by the Democratic National Committee. Party representatives for each state cast as many votes as the state had at the national convention. The Republicans typically provide for either a similar procedure or a new national convention. Such emergency plans may also be invoked *after* the November election. The election that counts, remember, is the one held in the second week of December at the various state capitals where the electors meet. If a party's candidate is elected in November and dies before the electors meet, the party may choose a new candidate and expect the electors to make him President when they do their ceremonial December duty. No new general election is necessary.

This contingency planning leaves just one little gap, and that was filled by the twenty-fifth Amendment in 1967. If a President-elect dies or drops out after the Electoral College has voted, but before inauguration, the Vice President-elect is inaugurated in his place. If on the other hand, the Vice President-elect dies or quits in that period, the job remains vacant until the new President nominates a replacement and that nomination is approved by a vote of a majority of both houses of Congress.

The Itch to Reform

Three things can conceivably go awry in this system:

1 The electors might decide to elect as President someone the voters did not choose. Though statistically unlikely, it is possible. Henry D. Irwin was real.

2 The candidate who gets the largest popular vote and the candidate who gets the electoral majority might not be the same. This was the outcome of the Hayes-Tilden dispute in 1876. After Congress decided on contested returns in four states, Hayes was declared elected with 185 electoral votes to Tilden's 184. Tilden never became President, despite a 52 percent popular majority. In 1888, Benjamin Harrison was elected with a sixty-five-vote majority in the Electoral College, but Grover Cleveland got more popular votes. And in 1960, John F. Kennedy was elected by

eighty-four electoral votes although Richard M. Nixon got more popular votes.[1]

3   A third-party candidate who deprived either of the two major-party candidates of a majority might produce unpredictable and unpleasant consequences by swapping votes for promises in either the Electoral College or the House of Representatives.

A number of plans have been proposed to revise the Electoral College system and do away with most or all these dangers. The problem with these plans is that they tend to have very strong political side effects. Changes that seem minor turn out to have consequences that could revise the whole strategic picture. To appreciate them, we must take a closer look at the effects of the existing system before turning to the possible consequences of reform.

Current Strategic Considerations

As now structured, the presidential election system favors the populous, two-party states. There is no need for a candidate to campaign in a state where the outcome is assured; the unit rule leaves nothing to be gained from cutting losses or adding to victory margins in those states. It is the pivotal states, and the largest of those, that are the most important to a presidential candidate and to which an incumbent President counting on reelection will pay the most heed.

Partly because of historical accident and partly because bigness fosters diversity, the pivotal states and the largest states tend to be much the same. Because urban minorities are concentrated in the large states, Presidents tend to pay special attention to their needs. Thus, an unplanned structural peculiarity of the election system has a profound and lasting effect. This is a major reason why U.S. Presidents, Republicans as well as Democrats, have been more activist, welfare oriented, minority oriented—in a word, more liberal—than their congressional party counterparts (Polsby and Wildavsky, 1971, p. 261).

The small states, are, however, compensated to some extent by a secondary benefit of the Electoral College system. Because every state gets three votes regardless of size, the less populous states pull some extra

[1]The *World Almanac* says that Kennedy won the popular vote by 118,550 votes, but the *World Almanac* is wrong. The confusion arises because Alabama had a mixed slate of Kennedy and unpledged electors, and voters marked their ballots for each elector individually. Wire service reporters counted the unpledged elector votes for Kennedy—even though these electors eventually voted for Byrd—and this is the source of the erroneous 118,550 Kennedy plurality. When the Alabama popular vote is apportioned according to the Electoral College outcome, Kennedy's vote is reduced and Nixon becomes the national popular vote winner by 58,181. For a discussion of this problem, see Peirce (1968, pp. 100–105).

weight in the Electoral College. An Alaskan's vote in the 1972 presidential election was worth the votes of 4.4 Californians; Alaska had one electoral vote for every 100,724 residents in the 1970 census while California had one for every 443,403. Whether fair or not, such considerations affect the balance of power to which we are accustomed, and changing the rules could upset that balance.

Reform Proposals and Their Consequences

Although there are many different proposals for reform, they fall into four basic classifications:

Direct Popular Vote.   This one sounds appealing, and it always does well in the Gallup poll: Abolish the Electoral College and let the candidate who gets the most votes become President. In its most recent version, this plan would provide a run-off between the top two candidates if no candidate got 40 percent of the vote.

Its appeal lies in its fairness. However, it deserves a sober second look. The strategic picture would change considerably, with the balance of power shifting from the swing states to the most heavily populated one-party states. Candidates hunt, as Barry Goldwater has said, where the ducks are. Without the unit rule, a candidate could make the most effective use of his resources by boosting the margin and increasing the turnout in the states that are already strongly on his side rather than contesting for small margins in the two-party states (except for those whose sheer size would keep them from being ignored). One-party states tend to be conservative, and so we could expect the present tendency to choose relatively liberal Presidents to end—an effect that would be good or bad depending on how you feel about things. But that might be the least important effect.

Because it would no longer be necessary to win an entire state to have an effect on the outcome, minor parties would be encouraged. These parties would probably be organized around special interests: a racial segregation party, a peace party, a war party, a consumer's party, a women's liberation party, a pot-smoker's party. Voters would have the benefit of finding issues more clearly articulated in the campaign, and they would have more candidates with more visible differences from which to choose. Such diversity would have a heavy cost. A proliferation of special-interest parties might effectively destroy the two-party system and force a runoff election every time. Besides greatly increasing the financial cost of electing a President, such a system would produce serious instability as groups clustered and reclustered in search of a winning coalition for the runoff. The work of compromise and accommodation that now takes place within the parties would have to occur in some other manner. Polsby and Wildavsky (1971) believe that "the simplicity, ease of comprehension, and inherent majoritarian rightness of the direct election solution would quickly disappear [pp. 265–266]."

Another possible danger is that in a close election, such as in 1960 or in 1968, there would be a long period of uncertainty, perhaps weeks or months, before the winner was determined. Temptations for fraud might be greater if a few thousand votes anywhere could make the difference. Demands for recounts and charges of tampering with the polls might become routine.

Finally, since the successful candidate would have built his initial strength on a relatively narrow base, we might have Presidents whose legitimacy as representatives of all the people would be harder to accept.

The Proportional System. Known in the 1950s as the Lodge-Gossett plan and sponsored more recently in the Senate by Sam Ervin of North Carolina, this plan would keep the voting structure of the Electoral College but abolish the College itself. Each state would have the same number of electoral votes it has now, but the electoral vote would be divided in proportion to the popular vote. For example, if this system had been in effect in 1972, California would have given President Nixon only twenty-six votes, representing his 57 percent of the popular vote, and McGovern would have received nineteen electoral votes, representing his 43 percent of the popular vote. At first glance, this proposal seems like a nice compromise between the existing system and direct popular vote. But it turns out to be an even more extreme solution. The one-party states (assuming there would still be a few) would be in just as favored a position as in the direct-vote plan because, for all practical purposes, the unit rule would continue to apply to them and not to states where the two parties compete. The large states not only would lose the leverage they now have but would be in danger of being dominated by the smaller states with their proportionately greater electoral vote.

Senator Sam Ervin: A plan closer to the Founders'. *(Fred Ward, Black Star.)*

Ervin's plan recognizes that minor party candidates would be encouraged and that a majority would be hard to obtain. It provides that if the leading candidate gets less than 40 percent of the vote or if there is a tie, the President would be selected from the top two by a joint session of Congress with each member casting one vote. Such elections would probably become routine; the traditional separation of presidential selection from the legislative branch would be ended; and we would have a system closer to that envisioned by the Founders with Congress making the final choice.

Electing by Districts. Former Sen. Karl Mundt of South Dakota, a Republican, was a longtime supporter of a plan to move the unit rule system of the Electoral College down one level, from states to special districts. Each state would choose two electors at large plus one from each district. The candidate receiving the most votes in his district would get all the district's vote in the Electoral College under this smaller-scale use of the unit rule. The candidate with the largest statewide vote would receive the votes of the two at-large delegates to the Electoral College. District boundaries would be drawn by state legislatures. In some versions of this plan, the electoral districts would be identical to congressional districts.

Conservatives like this plan best of all. It maximizes power of the small states, rural districts, and one-party areas where the conservative vote is concentrated. The decentralization of the unit rule system would ensure that votes in these areas would not be automatically offset by the more liberal voters in metropolitan centers. Moreover, the plan hands to state legislatures the power to design election districts to favor the party in control of the state government. Minor parties would be encouraged, because it is easier to campaign in a congressional district than an entire state. Deadlock would be just as likely, and the opportunities for minority third parties to capture the swing vote and negotiate for concessions would be unimpaired.

The nature of the Presidency would change considerably under this plan. If elected from the same kind of constituency as Congress, the President might be much less independent and more a captive of parochial attitudes. He might be little more than, in the words of Wallace S. Sayre and Judith H. Parris (1970), "master of a coalition of petty sovereignties [p. 114]." This is more than just a reform plan, they warn. "It is really a protest against the sort of Presidency that has developed during the twentieth century [p. 117]."

The Automatic Plan.   There is one reform measure that everyone can agree on but about which nothing has been done. It doesn't preclude third-party maneuvers, but it does take care of the Henry D. Irwin problem. It would keep everything just as it is now except for abolishing the office of elector and the December rituals. As a result, each state's electoral vote would *automatically* go to the winner of its popular vote.

Some proponents of this step want to add another provision that would deal with the third-party threat too, by revising the contingency plan for the unlikely occasion when no candidate gets an electoral majority. These range from keeping the election in the House, but basing it on population by giving every member one vote, to automatically designating the leader in the popular vote as the winner. In 1968, when it seemed likely that Wallace might tip the balance in the Electoral College, some House members announced that they would cast their votes for the popular-vote winner rather than take part in any kind of negotiation with Wallace or his supporters.

Of these four reform proposals, only the automatic plan has much chance for adoption. In endorsing the present system, Sayre and Parris (1970), who analyzed it for the Brookings Institution, noted, "It is not perfect. But its defects are known, and they are relatively minor. The defects of the proposed alternatives are uncertain, and they appear . . . to be major [p. 149].''

ELECTING THE LEGISLATIVE BRANCH

The Representation Problem

Compared to the problem of figuring out the best way to elect a President, the design of a method for electing members of the legislative branch ought to be fairly straightforward. But it's not. As in the case of presidential elections, small structural changes can make important differences.

The first question is whether to elect members at large or choose them from districts. If they are chosen from districts, a choice remains between single-member districts (with a single legislator chosen by a winner-take-all plurality) or a multimember system (with more than one legislator in each district). Representatives from multimember districts may be chosen either from the highest vote getters or on a proportional basis. The United States House of Representatives is based on the single-member district system while most European nations and many of our state and local legislative bodies use multimember districts.

Election at large in multimember districts has the virtue of simplicity; but, as usually applied in the United States, it fails to give minorities a voice. With every member running from the same constituency, all tend to become spokesmen for the same majority. "We expect the election system," says Robert G. Dixon, Jr. (1971), "to yield both a majority capable of governing and a minority sufficiently cohesive to be both critic and heir apparent. A further goal . . . is that there be room in the system for all significant interests to acquire spokesmen—preserving the right of all to be heard, if not to be in control [p. 11]."

Minority interests have a chance of getting a voice when members of a legislature are elected from single-member districts, provided that their interests are organized geographically and that district boundaries are drawn in a way that gives them control of some districts. This is true for some interests, but not others. Farmers, blacks, and blue-collar workers are examples of interest groups which can control some congressional districts. But many other interest groups—consumers, retail merchants, women, young people, war veterans—are too geographically dispersed to control congressional districts.

Complicated systems of proportional representation (PR) in multimember districts have been designed to get around this problem of special-interest or minority representation. In this country, such arrangements have been tried at the state and local level with mixed results. A PR system gives better representation of diverse interests, but it postpones the coalition-forming process until after the legislative body has been elected with a consequent sacrifice of government stability. The single-member district system puts the burden of coalition forming on the political parties and practically guarantees a majority party. This majority may, of course, be a false one since the party attracts voters who are there only because they have no place else to go.

In comparison to other possible methods, the single-member district is regarded as reasonably fair; it has the virtue of simplicity. Congressmen normally run from single-member districts except on rare occasions when a delay in establishing the district boundaries forces one or more seats to represent the state at large. Some state legislatures have a mixture of single-member and multimember districts, which further complicates the fairness problem.

Apportionment and Reapportionment

State legislatures draw the boundary lines for both congressional districts and their own legislative districts. After each decennial (every ten years) census, the President submits a report to Congress showing the number of persons in each state and the number of representatives to which each state is entitled. The arithmetic is somewhat complicated, since each state gets one representative regardless of size and the remainder are distributed in proportion to population. The Constitution says "Indians not taxed" don't count, but that provision has been construed to be obsolete since 1940. Members of the Armed Forces and federal employees serving overseas and their dependents are credited to their home states for purposes of determining each state's number of congressmen, but they are not allocated to particular places within the states.

Fifteen days after the President submits his report on the results of the population count, the clerk of the House of Representatives sends each state governor a certificate showing the number of representatives to which his state will be entitled for the next ten years. It is then up to the state to draw the congressional district lines.

Apportionment for state legislative districts has been a much more difficult task. Until a recent series of Supreme Court decisions many states did not do it at all, allowing old apportionment schemes to stay in effect for decades, long after population movement from rural to urban areas had made them obsolete. While most state constitutions called for regular reapportionment, there was no enforcement method and thus no way of compelling legislators to obey. Because they were more interested in the status quo than in reform, more loyal to one another than to the public, legislators often failed to act. Legislative districts thus remained the same while the population shifted from rural areas to the cities and suburbs. This shift, rather than spurring legislators to redistrict, caused the rural interests to see their outdated districts as the last outpost against the power of encroaching urbanization; and they resisted change all the more vigorously.

In 1962 some states had rural districts whose population had thinned out until it was less than a fifth of the statewide average, giving the rural residents five times the voting power to which they were entitled.

The Supreme Court rejected an opportunity to set things right in 1946 when it ruled against a Northwestern University professor who sued the Governor of Illinois for letting the Legislature get by without any redistricting since 1901 (*Colegrove v. Green*, 328 U.S. 549). Legislators in the down-state rural districts wouldn't redistrict because they didn't want to give up control to Chicago. They were equally unwilling to give the Chicago area its fair share of congressional seats. One congressional district in Chicago had 914,053 people compared to the population in a down-state district of 112,116. Professor Colegrove, a political scientist, asked the Court to enjoin the Governor from conducting the November 1946 legislative elections under the 1901 districting arrangement. Associate Justice Felix Frankfurter said, in the Court's opinion, "Courts ought not to enter this political thicket," and declared that the proper remedy lay in electing state legislatures that would not misbehave.

The paradox, of course, was that there was no way for the petitioners to elect enough right-minded legislators because the inequity being protested was a lack of voting power. Frankfurter's legal reasoning was perfectly sound; one branch of government ought not to intrude on the province of another. "But government is more pragmatic than ideal," says Archibald Cox (1968). "In a practical world there is, and I suspect has to be, a good deal of play in the joints. If one arm of government cannot or will not solve an insistent problem, the pressure falls upon another [p. 118]." And when the Court changed its mind in deciding *Baker v. Carr*, 369 U.S. 186, in 1962, it did so because there was no other remedy for the plaintiff, Charles W. Baker of Memphis. Tennessee's state legislative districts had also gone unchanged since 1901, and there was no prospect that they would ever be changed without some outside compulsion. In what Chief Justice Earl Warren later called the most important decision made during his tenure on the Court, it found that malapportionment was in violation of the equal protection clause of the Fourteenth Amendment.

Implementing Baker v. Carr

There remained the problem of how to implement redistricting. All a court can do is sit passively and say what is right and what is wrong. Mr. Justice Frankfurter, in the 1962 minority, noted that "The Court's authority—possessed of neither the purse nor the sword—ultimately rests on sustained public confidence in its moral sanction [p. 267]." The Supreme Court sent *Baker v. Carr* back to the Tennessee courts without saying how, when, or where redistricting had to take place. The specific guidelines came out only gradually in a series of cases, deciding one issue at a time, over more than a decade.

Associate Justice Felix Frankfurter: Avoiding the political thicket. (*United Press International.*)

Chief Justice Earl Warren: A most important decision. (*Fred Ward, Black Star.*)

One of the first questions was whether the ruling also applied to congressional districts. In *Wesberry v. Sanders*, 376 U.S. 1, in 1964, the Court ruled that it did. Another question was whether both houses of a state legislature had to apportion on the basis of population or whether one could, like the U.S. Senate, be apportioned on some other basis. Alabama wanted to draw a parallel between its counties and the states of the United States, giving counties equal numbers in the upper house and basing representation on population in the lower house. The Court said (*Reynolds v. Sims*, 377 U.S. 533) in 1964 that the analogy wouldn't hold; states were independent political units in a federal system while Alabama counties were only administrative subdivisions of the state government.

But the toughest problem of all was defining the exact degree of inequality that violated the Fourteenth Amendment. A district that deviated from the state average by 500 percent was obviously in violation, but what about a deviation of 5 percent? Or 0.05 percent? For several years, the Court seemed bent on splitting such hairs. In 1969, it overturned Missouri and New York congressional redistricting plans where the maximum deviation from average population was 3.1 and 6.6 percent (*Kirkpatrick v. Preisler*, 394 U.S. 526; *Wells v. Rockefeller*, 394 U.S. 542). When the 1970 election was held, New York had honed its districts so finely that the maximum deviation was only 0.12 percent.

This kind of mathematical precision produced some ironic consequences. To get that kind of equality, it was necessary to carve up existing political subdivisions and draw irregular boundary lines, putting just the right number of people in each. It was also necessary to place more faith in the accuracy of the United States census than it deserves. The census misses some people, particularly young black males, and makes other kinds of errors which amount to several percentage points in some areas. New York's 0.12 percent deviation was therefore largely a statistical fiction. Moreover, the plaintiff in that case found that the numerical result did not give him the result he had hoped. Dixon (1971) tells what happened:

> In its final outcome in 1970 this case had almost a quixotic quality. It will be remembered that, after a bipartisan revision of New York congressional districts was accomplished by a split legislature in 1968, Mr. Wells took a solo appeal. Even though the most deviant district was only 6.6 percent from ideal, the Supreme Court voided the plan and announced a precise equality rule. On remand, the New York legislature, then controlled by Republicans in both houses, produced a plan only 0.12 percent deviant at its extreme. This plan was not to Mr. Wells's liking for alleged gerrymander reasons. Accordingly, he returned to the federal district court in 1970 to plead that, if it did nothing else, it at least should restore the very plan which he had successfully contested the year before! The court refused . . . [p. 45–46].

Once freed of existing political boundaries, and with the aid of computer analysis of detailed census data, legislators could design districts for partisan benefit with an efficiency never before possible and still meet the most rigid equality tests. In 1973, the Court backed away from its simplistic, mathematical equality approach and ruled that strict observance of population equality could yield to a "rational state policy of respecting the boundaries of political subdivisions [*Mahan v. Howell*, 410 U.S. 315]." The Virginia legislative apportionment plan which it upheld had a maximum deviation of 9.6 percent from the average. The Court appeared to be pointing toward a position that apportionment plans would not be found unreasonable per se if they met some rule-of-thumb test, possibly a 10 to 15 percent deviation from average.[2] Meanwhile, it performed the useful service of focusing on the *gerrymander* as the main enemy of representative government.

The Sinuous District of Elbridge Gerry

It wasn't really Gov. Elbridge Gerry's fault that one of the Massachusetts legislative districts established in 1811 wound with reptilian form from Marblehead to Salisbury and in the process diluted the Federalist voting strength. Painter Gilbert Stuart penciled in a few details and said to Benjamin Russell, editor of the *Boston Sentinel*, "That will do for a salamander." "Salamander?" said Russell, "Call it a Gerrymander." And that has since been the word for the drawing of districts in a way to favor one party or faction over another (Safire, 1972).

In a sense, all districts are gerrymandered. You can't make any decision about drawing the lines without favoring one party or the other. For this reason, the fairest districting plans are created by bipartisan commissions. Ordinarily, however, districts are designed by the party that controls the legislature. The principle is simple enough: Concentrate the votes of the opposition party in as few districts as possible while giving your

[2]Measuring maximum difference from the average is the clearest test of deviance, although lawyers and judges have sometimes followed the journalistic practice of comparing the largest district with the smallest. That produces a larger percentage difference than deviation from the arithmetic mean, but its interpretation is ambiguous. The method can produce a large or a small difference depending on whether the percentage is based on the largest district or the smallest.

North Carolina Congressional Districts, 1949: Depriving the Republican counties.

own party a working majority in as many as possible. This operation can produce odd-looking districts. The Democratic Legislature of North Carolina, for example, used to deprive the Republican mountain counties of representation in Congress by drawing long, fingerlike districts that picked up enough Democratic voters in the central piedmont to offset them. Now, however, Republican strength has grown, so that plan no longer works; but the state still has some odd-shaped districts, such as the Ninth which puts southern, urban Mecklenburg County with northern, mountainous Wilkes.

Traditional tests of a fair districting plan ask that the districts be compact and contiguous as well as equal in size. But it is possible to meet both tests and still be grossly unfair. In the absence of any easily applied objective standards of fairness, gerrymandering is likely to remain a problem that cannot be reached by the courts and one that is best attacked by bipartisan groups, which can consider the political implications from the very beginning.

ADMINISTRATION OF ELECTIONS

Keeping Things Honest

States make the election laws and delegate the work to the counties. County officials are in charge of designing and printing the ballots, deciding whether to use paper ballots or voting machines, deciding whether to tabulate by hand or by computer, and choosing the local election supervisors.

But the real work is done at the precinct level. At this level, the population is small enough so that election officials can keep track of the voters, check their qualifications for voting, and count the votes with a minimum of delay. The size of a precinct may vary from 300 to 500 voters, where paper ballots are used, to from 500 to 10,000 voters, where voting is by machine.

The precinct level is important because it is at this point that the state rules are enforced. The precinct officials, usually selected by local parties, determine who may and who may not vote. When fraud takes place it is usually at this level. The main safeguard against fraud is the presence of representatives of both parties at the polling place; and ideally, every action gets checked twice, once by a member of each party. But in areas that are heavily dominated by one party this doesn't always happen. There are three time-honored methods of cheating:

Padding the Rolls. The list of eligible voters can be inflated by keeping dead people on the roll and getting somebody to impersonate them and cast their votes. The same can be done for people who have moved out of the precinct. Reverse padding is also done: keeping eligible voters off the rolls. Young people in college towns began complaining of this practice soon after the 18-year-old vote was established by the Twenty-sixth Amendment in 1971.

Stuffing the Box.   If paper ballots are used, a crooked precinct official can mark extra ballots for his candidate and put them in the box when no one is looking. If a machine is used, the counting mechanism can be tampered with to achieve the same result. Of course, if this produces a vote that exceeds the number of people living in the precinct, someone may get suspicious.

Miscounting.   The simplest way to cheat in an election is to report an incorrect total to county officials, but false figures can be discovered in a recount. Another way is to make marks on valid ballots to spoil them. (A ballot with an identifying mark on it is void. This rule is supposed to discourage vote buying on the theory that there is less incentive to pay a voter to vote a certain way if he can't prove that he did indeed vote as he was told.) Where ballots are counted by computer, more sophisticated cheating is possible; hard-to-detect changes in the computer program could cause ballots for one candidate to be counted for another.

Where there is collusion with election officials—and that is not unknown in American politics—all these methods can be used in combination. Robert Sherrill (1967) tells what happened in Texas when Lyndon Johnson appeared to be about to lose his race for the Senate in 1948:

> . . . the folks over in Jim Wells County got to scratching around in Box 13 and, by gosh, discovered another 203 votes—all but one for Johnson! Ah, strange things are done 'neath the south Texas sun. Some of this misty constituency had marched to the polls to vote in alphabetical order, all their names signed to the poll list in blue-green ink (the rest of the list was black ink), and, such was their regard for Johnson, some had even arisen from the grave to cast their ballots. . . . Before an official investigation could be completed, the votes were accidentally, they said, burned [pp. 113–114].

Outright buying of votes was effectively hampered by the adoption of the *Australian ballot* around the turn of the century. The Australian ballot is simply one that is supplied by the government and marked in secret. Before its adoption, the parties supplied the ballots, often making them large and colorful so that a poll watcher could note who took which ballot. Checking up on a bought-off voter is still possible, however, where paper ballots are used. The briber gives the voter a ballot which he has marked himself. After dropping it in the box, the voter brings back his blank ballot which the briber then marks for the next participant in this illicit maneuver.

Time and Manner of Elections

Parliamentary democracies such as England have flexible election schedules so that issues can be forced to a test at the ballot box. Our system uses fixed election dates which gives officials, once elected, a freer hand but makes it harder to establish the linkage between the voting decision and ultimate policy decisions. The timing of elections often falls when issues are not pressing, and so candidates and parties must create them, often by inflating minor issues. The arguments over the fate of Quemoy and Matsu (two small Nationalist Chinese islands) and the nonexistent missile gap of the 1960 presidential election are two examples of issues that were quickly forgotten after the campaign.

In the United States, elections are staggered so that in many places, almost every year is an election year. This contrasts with the European practice of holding a big general election where all officeholders come up for reelection. However, some states still elect governors in the same years as presidential elections. And the entire House of Representatives and one-third of the Senate is elected along with the President. So some coattail effect is present in U.S. presidential elections.

The coattail effect is enhanced by the *long ballot*. A reform of the Jacksonian era designed to give voters more detailed control over their public officials, it encourages straight-ticket voting simply because most people cannot keep track of all the candidates. In some places, the ballot is so long that not even the most interested voters can remember the names of the candidates. Newspapers sometimes help by printing sample ballots, with the papers' own endorsements marked, which voters can carry into the voting booth. The existence and nature of coattail effect has never been clearly isolated (Miller, 1955; Moos, 1952), but it seems clear that its importance has diminished with the increased tendency of voters to split their tickets and make independent judgments.

Ticket splitting can also be a function of the physical design of the ballot. In some states, a voter can mark one box or pull one lever to vote for a party's entire slate of candidates. This form is known as the "Indiana ballot," and its design was helpful in encouraging parties to go along with the adoption of the Australian ballot. In its original and basic form, it was like pasting the old party ballots side by side on one piece of paper. This was an improvement over the previous system in which a voter might not ever see the names of the candidates of the opposition party. Reformers who thought that straight-ticket voting was itself an evil designed the office-block ballot, also called the "Massachusetts ballot," in which candidates are grouped by office rather than party and the voter is forced to make each choice separately.

Even if straight-ticket voting is not explicitly provided for, the design of the ballot—or of the voting machine—can make a difference. Typographical or physical arrangements can enhance or minimize the party cue. In Florida, there is no straight-ticket lever on the voting machines, but a voter may cast a straight-ticket ballot by running his index finger from right to left along the levers in the row of the party of his choice.

VOTING BEHAVIOR

The Early Studies

The first applications of survey research to voting behavior produced a rather static picture of the electorate (Lazarsfeld, Berlson, and Gaudet, 1944). This finding may have been an accident of the particular time and place—Erie County, Ohio, 1940—chosen for the pioneering work, described in *The People's Choice*. That was an election whose personalities and issues were about the same as those in preceding campaigns. "I have often wondered," says Donald E. Stokes (1966), "whether the static social determinism of *The People's Choice* would have emerged from a campaign in which the tides of short-term change were more nearly at flood [p. 19]." The Erie County study found voters to be highly predictable. Party identification—a person's psychological attachment to a political party— was the most important predictor of vote, and that was itself predictable from just a few variables: socioeconomic status, religion, and place of residence. High-status rural Protestants were the most Republican; low-status urban Catholics were the most Democratic. Other combinations were neatly ordered between. These findings were repeated in later state and national panel studies of the same period (Berelson, 1954; Campbell, 1960).

Party Identification

The social factors isolated in the Erie County study are still considered important. One thing that makes them important is their stability. Candidates and issues may come and go, but a person's basic social characteristics—his religion, income, region of residence, and education level—do not change very much or very often, and neither does party identification. When party identification does change, it is usually because of a change in some social element. A moderate Republican moves from Nebraska to Florida and finds that he is in more substantive agreement with the Democrats there. A child of a blue-collar worker goes to college, enters a profession, and changes from Democrat to Republican. But that kind of social and geographic mobility is more exceptional than ordinary, and party identification is quite stable over time in individuals and, therefore, in the electorate as a whole.

Nearly everyone identifies himself or herself with a party and has done so since childhood, as we noted in Chapter 4. Most of those who call themselves independents will, when pressed, admit to leaning toward one party or the other. The Center for Political Studies at the University of

Michigan measures intensity of party identification in its biennial surveys and finds the distribution quite stable over time.

Generally, the more intense the partisan commitment, the greater the interest, likelihood of voting, and concern over the election's outcome. This comes as a surprise to amateur political observers. The 1964 Goldwater candidacy was sustained by a belief that the electorate contained a sizable bloc of conservative voters who consistently abstained from voting to protest the liberal stance of most presidential candidates. Goldwater's nomination, the theory went, would bring out this "silent" vote. But it never showed, never even existed. The conservative wing of the Republican party, survey research has shown, is more ideologically committed and more likely to vote—even for moderate candidates—than more liberal Republicans (Converse, Clausen, and Miller, 1965). Belief in the discerning, independent voter—not to be confused with the ticketsplitter, who represents a different concept—who rises above party to make his rational decision is likewise not sustained by the evidence, as Hugh A. Bone and Austin Ranney (1971) have noted:

> We have all heard about the "independent voter"—that noble old civics-textbook hero who is not contaminated by blind loyalties to any party, who always votes for the best man, and who is deeply concerned with public affairs and highly conscientious about doing his civic duty. But when we look for him in the actual electorate, he isn't there. The few self-styled "independents" we *do* find have no party preference because they have few political preferences of *any* kind, they simply are not much interested in politics and civic affairs. The ideal independent may be a man of proud and free conscience, but the real-life independent is likely to be a man who couldn't care less [p. 9].

Party identification may be more important in races at the congressional and state level than at the presidential level. Even though the Republicans have been the minority party since 1936, they have succeeded in capturing the Presidency in four of the six elections between 1952 and 1972. At the same time, they have been consistently weak in congressional elections, failing to control either house since 1952. Congress stayed Democratic even in the Republican presidential landslide election of 1972. Gerald M. Pomper (1973) believes that "this disjunction is part of a larger fission in which the Presidency is being separated effectively from partisan politics. . . . This perception goes beyond the act of splitting the ticket. Rather, in the voter's mind, there is no ticket. He has one ballot for president and another ballot for everything else [p. 15]." To explain how voters make up their minds about presidential choice, then, we must look beyond party identification and social factors.

Issue Orientation

Issue orientation—a person's view of a candidate or party's stand on issues—is usually a relatively weak predictor of vote. The mass media devote a lot of time and space to issue questions in a campaign, but this information tends to reach only the limited portion of the public which is interested, and even this portion usually has already made up its mind. Moreover, people who have opinions on issues tend to think that their favorite candidates agree with them—whether they do or not. This phenomenon was noticed quite early in the investigation of voting behavior. In 1948, the Taft-Hartley Act and price controls were much-debated issues; both presidential candidates took clear public positions. But among the voting-age population of Elmira, N.Y., only 16 percent knew the correct stands of both Harry S Truman and Thomas E. Dewey on these two basic issues (Berelson, Lazarsfeld, and McPhee, 1954).

But the politician who relies on low issue awareness may risk an unpleasant surprise. Voter inattention, as Walter Dean Burnham (1965) has observed, "can be replaced almost instantaneously under the right circumstances by an extremely pronounced sensitivity to an issue [p. 7]." Rep. Brooks Hays of Arkansas lost his seat in Congress to a write-in candidate when the race issue suddenly crystalized. Rep. Albert Cole of Kansas in 1952 became the first Republican ever to be thrown out of his district's congressional seat when he supported the federal dam project that was to ultimately displace his constituents in the valley of the Blue River.

At a somewhat less specific level, most voters do draw general

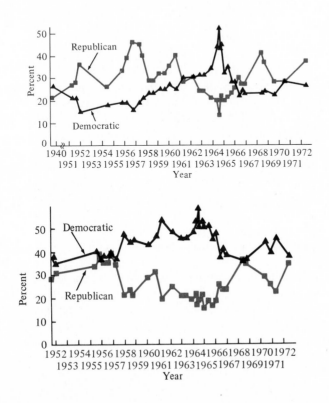

Figure 7–1 Which Party Is Best to Keep the United States Out of World War III?

Figure 7–2 Which Party Is Best to Keep the United States Prosperous?

connections between parties and very generalized clusters of issues. The Democrats, through most of the past forty years, have been associated with good times and war, the Republicans with strength in foreign affairs and economic trouble at home. These associations have risen and fallen with different combinations of circumstances and candidates (see Figures 7-1 and 7-2 on the previous page).

The Rise of Issue Politics

By 1973, it had become clear that issues and ideological concerns were assuming an importance in elections that had not been seen since the Depression years. Arthur H. Miller, Warren E. Miller, Alden S. Raine, and Thad A. Brown (1973) trace this development from the activist leadership of President Kennedy in trying to use the resources of the national government to attack social problems. Before that, the nation had been preoccupied with World War II and the post-war adjustments with political divisions following the 1930s pattern. Voters slumbered through the 1950s with a divided national leadership failing to define problems or argue over solutions with any sense of urgency. Kennedy's call to get the nation moving again changed that. Suddenly, "the very real problems of the society were being publicized by word and deed through the dramatic medium of national television. The political scientists' pleas for the elevation of issue politics and the creation of conditions that would permit or force responsible party government into existence were being answered [p. 3]." The behavior of national leaders since Kennedy has "brought the substance of issue politics into the public domain [p. 4]."

The Republican nomination of Goldwater in 1964 and the Democrat nomination of McGovern in 1972 reinforced this trend, as both men had clear ideological and issue differences from their incumbent opponents. Miller, Miller, Raine, and Brown, analyzing data from the Michigan Center for Political Studies for the 1972 election, found that the voters were clearly aware of these differences and behaved accordingly. Questions of handling the war in Vietnam, providing jobs and a good standard of living for minorities, and dealing with campus unrest were the most important issues; voters tended to choose the candidate whom they saw as closest to themselves on these questions. For most voters, that candidate was Nixon. The issue preferences, the Michigan investigators found, "were at least equally important as party identification" in predicting how individuals would vote (p. 69).

Furthermore, the issue preferences tended to cluster in a way that suggested new varieties of the old liberal-conservative ideological spectrum. That division has traditionally been applied to economic questions, but the Michigan study found it working in other ways on voters. For example, the war issue was divided along liberal-conservative lines, especially among independent voters, with liberals favoring the more dovish positions. Among young voters, the liberal-conservative split was most evident on cultural questions of individual morality symbolized by legalization of marijuana, abortion, and women's liberation. More voters considered themselves closer to Nixon on most of these issues than to McGovern, and that is an important factor explaining why his victory reached landslide proportions. However, the Michigan investigators observed that McGovern's supporters in the 1972 election may prove to be "the vanguard of a liberalizing trend occurring not only in the ranks of the Democrats but in the population as a whole. Thus, McGovern's principal error may have been in overestimating the speed of the population trend [p. 13]."

The Candidate Effect

Some voters look at issues and others look at the candidate. Depending on the situation, the personal qualities of the persons who are running may be the deciding factors. In 1972, they were of secondary importance. Nixon had less personal popularity in 1972 than he enjoyed in the 1960 election, but he was still far more appealing to most voters than McGovern. Indeed, much of the Republican party's success in winning presidential elections since World War II may be explained by the greater personal attractiveness of its candidates.

Candidate appeal has two basic components: what the person can do (instrumental quality) and what the person is or appears to be (symbolic quality). Richard Nixon rated very high on the instrumental dimension for specific things he had done, such as winding down the Vietnam war and trying to revitalize federalism. Dwight D. Eisenhower and John F. Kennedy had symbolic appeal. The former was perceived as a good, benign father figure, the latter as a charismatic figure who led with style and grace. When new candidates for the Presidency emerge, they sometimes create new pictures in voters' heads about what officeholders should be like and bring about very sharp fluctuations in voting behavior even while basic party loyalties remain unchanged. This, says Stokes (1966), is "quite out of keeping with the static perspective of the earliest studies of voting [p. 27]."

It also explains why the Democrats can be the majority party and still lose the Presidency so often. All other things being equal, party identification will win the election for them. However, Democrats, having more than a proportionate share of low-educated and low-income voters, have more difficulty in getting out their vote than do Republicans; this tends to equalize matters somewhat. If the Republicans can also get candidate orientation going for them, as they did with Eisenhower in 1952 and 1956 and with Nixon in 1972, or issue orientation, as in the case of Nixon in 1972, they can overcome the Democrats' numerical advantage. Table 7-1 shows how Nixon pulled voters across party lines in the 1972 election.

The Question of Obedience

Most forms of unconventional political participation require some kind of disobedience—to the law in the more intense forms and to prevailing social standards in the less intense forms. Disobedience incurs some fairly heavy costs: you can go to jail, you can lose your friends, you can make your family unhappy, you can suffer considerable psychological distress, or even lose your life. Psychologist Stanley Milgram has found, in a series of laboratory experiments, that people will go to surprising lengths to obey someone in authority, even when they think that their obedient action is inflicting severe pain and possible physical harm on an innocent person (Meyer, 1970). If you are primarily concerned with maintaining order, then obedience is among the highest virtues. If you value at least one thing more than order—and most participants in unconventional politics by definition do—then obedience becomes in some situations no virtue at all, because it is an obstacle to the greater value. In most cases, obedience is not the result of an abstract regard for the power of the state but simply a way of avoiding all the tiresome, mostly petty decisions that a truly autonomous person would have to make. We do as the law or society tell us because it would cost something to make waves, and we would rather not pay that cost. The subjects in Milgram's laboratory became extremely nervous, upset, and agitated, but many kept on obeying anyway. The alternative, disobedience, would have put even more psychic strain on them than obeying the directives of what seemed to be an abusive authority.

When people turn to unconventional forms of participation and decide

Kent State, 1970: The costs can be heavy. (*United Press International.*)

to disobey, it is usually because of a special situation in which the consequences of obeying are even more painful than the consequences of defiance of the established authority pattern. This was part of the message in Dr. King's letter from Birmingham jail:

> We can never forget that everything Hitler did in Germany was "legal" and everything the Hungarian freedom fighters did in Hungary was "illegal." It was "illegal" to aid and comfort a Jew in Hitler's Germany. But I am sure that, if I had lived in Germany during that time, I would have aided and comforted my Jewish brothers, even though it was illegal. If I lived in a Communist country today where certain principles dear to the Christian faith are suppressed, I believe I would openly advocate disobeying these anti-religious laws . . . [p. 105].

When King asserted that a person who breaks an unjust law is "in reality expressing the very highest respect for law," he was echoing a thought which is traceable to the social contract. It was Henry David Thoreau (1849), jailed for not paying his poll tax, who said, "Under a government which imprisons any unjustly, the true place for a just man is also a prison [p. 646]." And in his plea for John Brown, when Brown was being tried for his raid at Harper's Ferry, Virginia, Thoreau said the only government worth recognizing is "that power that establishes justice in the land, never that which establishes injustice [p. 699]."

The trouble with such logic is that there is no universal agreement on where and how it should be applied. What one person considers an injustice great enough to fight at the risk of hobbesian disorder may seem tolerable to another. Organized society does not require that everyone agree with the government's actions. It does require that everyone at least put up with them. And when government officials repress those who defy it, the government can justify its action with equal logic: The authority of the state must be preserved to keep us all from the brutish injustices of anarchy—Hobbes' state of nature.

Dr. King's resolution of the order problem—a resolution not adopted by all unconventional political participants—was to accept, even welcome, the legal penalties. "One who breaks an unjust law must do it *openly, lovingly,*" he said in his letter from jail (p. 105). By accepting the penalty, he was recognizing the power of the state. By defying the law, he was calling attention to its injustice.

For many other dissenters against the existing order, a more personal calculation has to be made. Most people operate most of the time under the assumption that the existing social and governmental authority is legitimate and should be obeyed. They do not think too much about the moral implications of the acts performed by that authority in their name. To do so is asking for a heavy burden. If, for example, before paying your income tax you calculated how each dollar would be spent and weighed each activity of government according to your personal moral code, you would be putting yourself to more trouble than most people can tolerate. So, for the sake of convenience, the presumption that most of us routinely make is on the side of obedience. It takes something that is flagrantly outrageous to override that presumption. In recent times, the Vietnam war was, for some people, such an overriding factor. For others, it was the denial of civil rights to blacks. In both cases, there were demands which seemed to have little prospect of being met through conventional participation and which were intense enough to impel some people to seek relief in unconventional participation.

Some Historical Antecedents

The seventeenth- and eighteenth-century apologists for political violence followed the individual decision-weighing model. John Locke was justifying the English revolution of 1688 when he developed his social contract theory, under which a government could be overthrown if it abused the authority given to it under the social contract. Jeremy Bentham put the equation on an individual basis: If you cause less evil by resisting the government than by submitting, then you should resist. Contemporary thinkers who have tackled the question have applied the same sort of approach to recent problems. Frantz Fanon (1968), justifying the Algerian nationalism, went farther by claiming that the catharsis of violence was necessary for the population's collective mental health after the degradations of colonial status. Albert Camus (1951) deplored violence but argued for resorting to it when present violence could bring about changes which would prevent worse violence in the future.

The existing order has its defenders. Spiro T. Agnew (1968), referring in the 1968 presidential campaign to civil rights protest activity, said, "You cannot even allow that kind of thing to take place because it still leaves the determination of what is right and what is wrong and which laws are unjust and can be broken for moral reasons and which are just to the evaluation of the individual [p. 44]." But choice is sometimes forced upon the individual because the law is not always clear. Early in the civil rights movement, leaders periodically argued that state and local laws enforcing segregation were in conflict with the federal law and the Constitution. The issues were eventually resolved by the courts, but in the meantime individuals had to decide. The Air Force personnel who refused to fly bombing missions over Cambodia avoided direct defiance of the law because they challenged the legality of their orders. So many cases of what seem to be civil disobedience may turn on legal rather than moral grounds.

There remains, however, a hard core of cases where the decision to obey or not to obey is based on fundamental morality rather than any assertion of legal right. Our own government has set a firm precedent for recognizing not only the right but also the duty of an individual to make his own moral evaluation of the law. The Nuremberg trials before the

Judgment at Nuremberg, 1946: A duty to violate the law. *(Wide World Photos.)*

International Military Tribunal led to the conviction of German military and civilian officials for their failure to disobey immoral orders. Under this precedent, a citizen may claim a duty to violate the law in certain situations.

A basic requirement of an orderly legal system is predictability. A citizen should be able to identify in advance those situations in which his duty to higher morality will be judged to outweigh his duty to obey the law. But the perspective of time is usually needed before such situations can be seen at all. Legal scholars who have tried to specify the operating conditions for lawful disobedience have been unsuccessful at achieving any degree of precision. Former Supreme Court Justice Abe Fortas (1968) may have come closest when he said that violence is defensible only when there are no alternative methods of getting change. But there is bound to be disagreement on whether the alternative methods exist and whether the desired change is worth the disruption caused by disobedience. In the United States, in Fortas's view, the alternatives to violence are always available, and violence is therefore never justified. Others disagree. Charles Frankel (1964) has noted that the Fortas argument is based on assumptions which will not always be true:

> The basic fallacy in the proposition that, in a democracy, civil disobedience can never be justified, is that it confused the *ideals* or *aims* of democracy with the

inevitably less than perfect accomplishments of democracy at any given moment. In accordance with democratic ideals, the laws of a democracy may give rights and powers to individuals which, in theory, enable them to work legally for the elimination of injustices.

In actual fact, however, these rights and powers may be empty. The police may be hostile, the courts biased, the elections rigged—and the legal remedies available to the individual may be unavailing against these evils.

Worse still, the majority may have demonstrated, in a series of free and honest elections, that it is unwavering in its support of what the minority regards as an unspeakable evil . . . [pp. 93–94].

The situation grows even more complicated when one tries to adjust the conditions to justify greater or lesser degrees of civil disobedience in their varying forms.

The question seems clearly unanswerable. The most eloquent and persuasive statements for order on the one hand and for disobedience on the other have been made in response to specific situations. It is much easier to be eloquent and persuasive when justifying or criticizing a particular action that has already happened than it is when trying to define and classify an abstract class of actions. A specific case has its special set of strengths and weaknesses on which the debater can base his point. The special circumstances can obscure what, in the abstract, is a paradox: The state should always require obedience; the individual should not always obey.

THE UNCONVENTIONAL ALTERNATIVE

An Underresearched Problem

Students of politics have tended to avoid systematically examining unconventional forms of participation, partly because the questions are difficult, and partly because they are unpleasant. Protest, rioting, disobedience, and other acts outside the conventional framework threaten the stability and precision of conventional political arrangements, and this can be unpleasant to think about. It is less unsettling to confine scholarly inquiry to the more predictable and less threatening phenomena of interest groups, parties, election laws, and the like. Exclusive concentration on these conventional forms of participation reflects social scientists' middle-class biases about what kind of behavior is important. Rioting, protest, and civil disobedience are usually engaged in by "outsider" groups in society while conventional forms have a distinct middle-class association. Investigators tend to be curious about activities with which they are familiar, and social scientists have not been primary participants in unconventional politics. Those few social scientists who have investigated the subject have found difficulty in obtaining useful data on unconventional political acts. Reports on interest-group membership and activity and on election outcomes are relatively easy to get. Information about persons who protest or commit violence is harder to obtain.

Nevertheless, unconventional participation is and always has been an organic part of the total political system. It does not happen in a vacuum. It does not go away if we avert our eyes. Unconventional participants interact with the system, are affected by the system, contribute to shaping it. Our statute books are filled with examples of laws codifying principles which could be promoted only through unconventional means before they were considered in the conventional legislative and political arenas. Labor organizers used disruptive measures to gain the rights later codified in the Wagner Act of 1935, agrarian reformers employed similar methods to secure regulation of rail shipping rates, and the Civil Rights Act might not have been passed in 1964 if Martin Luther King had not gone to jail in 1963.

Traditional Analysis

Because of the rich variety of forms and motivations in conventional political participation, attempts to explain and classify them are afflicted with a certain vagueness. And analysts who were not attempting to include unconventional participation under their classificatory umbrella have still left room for it there. Thus Herbert McClosky (1968) defines political participation as "those voluntary activities by which members of a society share in the selection of rulers and, directly or indirectly, in the formation of public policy [p. 252]." In the case of the protests against the Vietnam war, unconventional participants met both criteria: they spurred activity within the conventional system which caused President Johnson to suffer his disappointment in the 1968 New Hampshire primary and contributed to his decision not to seek reelection. And protestors focused public attention on the war itself, making it more difficult for policymakers to pursue the war for an indefinite period.

Conventional participation is sometimes classified as either instrumental or expressive. That categorization fits unconventional participation, too. *Instrumental* activities are those directed at specific, usually material, goals, such as enactment of a law, victory in an election, or personal gain for the participant. *Expressive* activities are those that just make you feel better. They usually deal with general, nonmaterial subjects. Talking politics with your neighbor is instrumental if you are trying to influence his vote, expressive if you are just venting your feelings. Voting is instrumental if you care who wins and you think your vote might influence the outcome. It is expressive if you do it merely to fulfill your notion of civic duty. Likewise, the urban riots of the 1960s were instrumental for some, expressive for others. The expressive rioters were venting their anger and frustration at the larger society. The instrumental rioters were more

Rioters in Detroit, 1967:
Instrumental for some,
expressive for others.
(*Dennis Brack, Black Star.*)

interested in specific goals, ranging from obtaining property by looting a store to changing the practices of local businessmen and government officials.

Broadening the Participatory Base

An unresolved question in political science asks whether apathy is bad for the system. Those who say it is bad argue that it deprives large numbers of people of the benefits of power, that it increases the probability of oppression by an elite, and that these factors produce tensions which could ultimately be explosive. Defenders of apathy do not entirely disagree: they simply maintain that it is better to preserve the apathy than risk the explosion that might result if it is overcome. Government is more stable and efficient, they say, when it is run by "those active minorities who, by virtue of their interest, knowledge, and judgment, have shown that they are capable of governing in a democracy [McClosky, 1968, p. 263]."

Both sides tend to discount the importance of unconventional participation. Include it in the equation, and the apathy problem is not quite so threatening. The traditionally apathetic groups—blacks, youth, poor people—have found expression through unconventional means, and the conventional system has responded without being forced to make basic structural changes. Finally, as we have suggested, nonparticipation in the formal system can be rational behavior; the participants have a stake in keeping the nonparticipants excluded; and the ways to do that are to see that either they are traumatized into withdrawing or kept reasonably comfortable. So nonparticipation can be a form of prepolitical participation.

UNCONVENTIONAL PARTICIPATION: STRATEGIES

Negative Inducements

The basic limitation of a powerless minority is that it has nothing to bargain with; bargaining requires power. Mass protest is a last-resort way of gaining some bargaining power, and accomplishes this end simply by inflicting pain on the other side and offering to stop in exchange for concessions. The pain may be economic, as in the case of a boycott, or it may be psychological and physical, as in the case of violence or the threat of violence. Either way, the inducement is a negative one. As James Q. Wilson (1961) has said, "a promise by one party *not* to act in a certain manner can be, relatively, a reward to the other party [p. 114]."

Rocking the Boat

The best argument against unconventional forms of participation is that everyone, no matter how disadvantaged, has some stake, however unequal, in the maintenance of order. If radical rhetoric became a reality and the existing system of controls was torn down, everyone, including the radicals, might suffer. Blacks in riot areas and students on campuses torn by disturbance have found that disorder can be quite painful for participants on both sides. Afterward, the gains may seem hardly worth the price. If both sides had been able to predict the costs of disturbance, they might have been able to come to terms without it. But such prediction is, of course, impossible.

The threat of disorder, if it is credible, can be as effective as the disorder itself. Black leaders, lobbying for federal aid to cities in the years after the riots, used it in a low-key but effective manner, talking about their effort to "cool it" and the difficulties of "controlling our people" when summer came. This strategy was effective in several ways. First, it was not a direct threat because the possibility of another riot was something beyond the control of the negotiators. If they were in control, there would be an incentive for the authorities to test their will and head for a confrontation. The more ambiguous situation left some room for bargaining, because officials could yield without giving in to lawless behavior. However, to be effective, the threat must be credible. It won't work unless there really is a threat of disturbance. Thomas Schelling (1960) has described the situation well in the context of international negotiations, a field where there is very little conventional structure and political participation is prone to follow lines paralleling the unconventional in a domestic context. He notes that a threat which would punish both sides can be effective if something is left to chance:

> "Rocking the boat" is a good example. If I say, "Row, or I'll tip the boat over and drown us both," you'll say you don't believe me. But if I rock the boat so that it *may* tip over, you'll be more impressed. If I can't administer pain short of death for the two of us, a "little bit" of death, in the form of a small probability that the boat will tip over, is a near equivalent. But, to make it work, I must really put the boat in jeopardy; just saying that I may turn us both over is unconvincing [p. 196].

The strategy of black protest in the 1960s was partly one of boat-rocking. For some the boat did sink, causing loss of life and property for both blacks and whites. It is not a strategy that can be followed on an everyday basis, and its effectiveness is still unclear.

Dramatizing the Issue

People who want to overcome the status quo have to conquer inertia. The political system has a considerable capacity for absorbing argument and controversy without anything happening to change things. One factor that operates to cushion conflict is the tendency of people not to pay attention to it. Psychologists call it *selective inattention*. Although looking the other way may not solve problems, it at least makes us feel more comfortable. Social psychologist Ralph K. White (1968) thinks that one reason the Vietnam war went on for so long was simply that most people were not paying attention. Bad things were being done in the war; our country does not do bad things. Thinking about that paradox causes discomfort; not thinking about it eases the discomfort. "Call it resistance, repression, ignoring, forgetting, non-learning, inhibition of curiosity, evading, card-stacking, perceptual defense, blind spots, or plain not paying attention," says White. "By whatever name, it is omnipresent [p. 198]."

One strategy of unconventional participation is to break through the perceptual defenses and pose the issue in a way that cannot be ignored. This was Dr. King's aim in Birmingham. "Nonviolent direct action seeks to create such a crisis and establish such creative tension that a community that has constantly refused to negotiate is forced to confront the issue," he said in his letter from jail. "It seeks so to dramatize the issue that it can no longer be ignored [p. 101]." In the month following his arrest, Birmingham police began their use of dogs, cattle prods, and fire hoses; and it was seen on national television. "White racial violence in the early 1960's contributed measurably to the success of the nonviolent direct action movement in winning the nation's sympathy and support," says Thomas R. Dye (1971, pp. 121–122). The black nonviolence, was, of course, calculated to provoke and display that white violence.

Birmingham in 1963: Establishing creative tension. (*Charles Moore, Black Star.*)

The guerrilla theater tactics of the Vietnam war foes were likewise designed to overcome inattention; pouring blood on draft board files, dressing in shrouds and death's heads and wailing outside the Fontainebleu Hotel during the 1972 Republican National Convention. But among the more effective antiwar demonstrations was the "last patrol" of Vietnam veterans who marched up Capitol Hill and threw their medals away. That bit of symbolism was all but impossible to misperceive.

Forcing a Decision

The governmental analog of public inattention is purposeful procrastination. In the case of administrators, this is a perfectly rational policy: a good proportion of problems will go away without administrative intervention. One purpose of unconventional political action is to keep problems on the agenda and force them to a stage where some sort of decision must be made. If the right psychological pressure point is found, the effect can be dramatic. When John Brown captured the arsenal at Harper's Ferry, Virginia, in 1859, he was playing upon Southern fears of a slave insurrection. His attack was not very threatening physically, but it frightened Southern leaders who had been wavering on the question of secession, hoping that it would go away, and moved them closer to a decision. Brown's action was important not so much in itself but in what it told the South about the North. Brown had received financial backing from prominent Northerners, he was glorified by Thoreau and Ralph Waldo Emerson, and his execution was publicly mourned in New England. After Lincoln's election the following year, says David Potter (1963), "proponents of Southern rights felt that the South must act before it slipped into the position of a hopeless minority, at the mercy of men who had approved of John Brown [p. 200]." Brown had made it difficult to think ambiguously about the issue.

UNCONVENTIONAL PARTICIPATION: FORMS

Violence

Rap Brown was not entirely inaccurate when he said that violence is as American as cherry pie. Public support for violent methods of social control is high. The University of Michigan Survey Research Center asked a national sample of American men about the use of violence in different circumstances. Two-thirds said police should shoot, but not to kill, when trying to stop a gang of hoodlums from a disturbance involving property damage. Almost as many, 61 percent, recommended the same procedure in

The Last Patrol: Symbolism impossible to misperceive. (*Wide World Photos.*)

ghetto riots, and 48 percent favored it where the disturbance involved white students. In each case, a large minority was in favor of shooting *to kill*: it ranged from a third who approved killing hoodlums to a fifth who endorsed killing college students. "Whether one agrees or disagrees with these sentiments," says Michigan's Robert L. Kahn (1972), "the data are unambiguous; American men are prepared to justify very substantial amounts of force and injury by the police for the sake of social control, and there is no requirement that the precipitating events have initiated personal violence. It is provocation enough if they are 'disturbances' and involve property damage [p. 164]." Political order is highly valued by most Americans, even when the cost of maintaining it is high.

As expected, fewer respondents favored violence to accomplish social change. But here, too, the size of the violent minority was surprising. About 20 percent said violence involving some property damage or personal injury is necessary for social change, and about 10 percent said that the violence would have to include some death and extensive damage. "This is prediction, rather than advocacy," said Kahn, "but it is sobering prediction and it is the belief of about five million men [p. 165]."

The two kinds of violence—from below in the form of protest, from above in the form of repression—have to be considered separately. The distinction has been noted by Elliott Currie (1970) who argues that the problem of violence from above has been overlooked by social scientists. Such things "are usually ignored because they are traditionally the concerns only of the powerless," he says.

> The FBI publishes statistics on the number of policemen killed in the line of duty, but not on how many people are killed by policemen. What evidence we have indicates that most of these people are ghetto blacks. How and why, exactly, were they killed? In the great majority of cases, you'll just have to ask the police [p. 15].

Situations where violence is employed for social control, Currie argues, may be useful indicators in locating the points of strain in American society; it is a sign that stability cannot be maintained through conventional means.

Robert Dahl (1968) has found a cyclical trend in violent conflict in American history. It becomes severe, he says, about once a generation. At some point in our history, nearly every section of the country has been the scene of violent episodes. And violence has played a role in virtually all the important social movements—where one group had far-reaching demands to make on others—including temperance, abolition of slavery, woman suffrage, and the labor movement.

Does it work? Kansas (where Carry Nation wielded her hatchet) no longer has saloons, Americans have no slaves, women have the vote, and labor has collective bargaining. Perhaps these ends would have been

Carry Nation: In Kansas, no more saloons (*National Archives.*)

achieved nearly as soon without violence. Perhaps not. It may not be a researchable question. The National Advisory Commission on Civil Disorders expressed the view that violence is counterproductive: "Violence cannot build a better society. Disruption and disorder nourish repression, not justice. They strike at the freedom of every citizen [p. 2]." On the other hand, the commission itself made sweeping recommendations for aid to cities and minority groups which it would not have made—indeed, the commission would not have existed—but for the Newark and Detroit riots of 1967. While those recommendations have, for the most part, been ignored, there has been more attention paid to the needs of urban minorities and there has been a pronounced change in the self-image of the blacks, with greater pride of race. "The historian is obliged to concede," says Arthur Schlesinger, Jr. (1968), "that collective violence, including the recent riots in black ghettos, has often quickened the disposition of those in power to redress just grievances. Violence, for better or worse, *does* settle some questions, and for the better [p. 22]."

Sidney Hook (1935), writing before this generation's violent episodes, said that without violence every social movement would fail. Where one group has to give up some of its privileges to another, he said, the privileged will give in only under duress. "Practically all movements of social revolt which have proved to be successful have been compelled to use violence at some point in the process of acquiring power [p. 265]." A contemporary scholar, Charles Tilly (1969), agrees:

> As comforting as it is for civilized people to think of barbarians as violent and of violence as barbarian, Western civilization and various forms of collective violence have always been close partners . . . Historically, collective violence has flowed regularly out of the central political processes of Western countries. Men seeking to seize, hold, or realign the levers of power have continually engaged in collective violence as part of their struggles. The oppressed have struck in the name of justice, the privileged in the name of order, those in between in the name of fear. Great shifts in the arrangements of power have ordinarily produced—and often depended on—exceptional movements of collective violence [p. 4].

However, Hugh Davis Graham and Ted Robert Gurr (1969), writing for the National Commission on the Causes and Prevention of Violence, argue that short of a situation where the initiator of violence has overwhelming force at his command and can physically subdue his entire opposition violent methods need popular support, both for their means and for the ends they seek to achieve, in order to succeed. Without this popular support, "their advocacy and use are ultimately self-destructive, either as techniques of government or of opposition [p. 813]." And given this kind of support, a social movement may not need violence except for temporary tactical aims. From this perspective, violence becomes a symptom of social change rather than a cause, and powerless minorities are better off using other forms of unconventional participation while they seek to build the necessary popular support.

Civil Disobedience

Nonviolent civil disobedience can contribute to some of the same strategic goals as violent behavior—negative inducement, dramatizing the issue, forcing a decision—but without as much risk. A protester who nonviolently submits to the blows of a policeman's club is a much more heroic and sympathetic figure than one who attacks the policeman or smashes a store window. Violence is part of the strategy; but it is government violence, provoked by peaceful demonstrators, which repels neutral observers, becomes counterproductive for the government, and promotes the protesters' cause. The trick is to promote the most violence by officials or opposition groups with the least amount of antisocial behavior. In the South in the late 1950s and early 1960s, it was easy: all you had to do was be black and sit at a white-only lunch counter or march with other blacks in a parade along a southern street. Respect for order is preserved by the protesters' willingness to accept the law's penalty. When violence results, the instigators hope that the opprobrium attaches to the opposition. Dr. King was indignant when the Alabama ministers blamed the danger of violence on his actions:

> Isn't this like condemning the robbed man because his possession of money precipitated the evil act of robbery? Isn't this like condemning Socrates because his unswerving commitment to truth and his philosophical delvings precipitated the misguided popular mind to make him drink the hemlock? Isn't this like condemning Jesus because His unique God consciousness and never-ceasing devotion to His will precipitated the evil act of crucifixion? We must come to see, as Federal courts have consistently affirmed, that it is immoral to urge an individual to withdraw his efforts to gain his basic constitutional rights because the quest precipitates violence. Society must protect the robbed and punish the robber [p. 105].

Another advantage of nonviolent disobedience is that it is a fairly cheap way to get attention in the media. However, a way must be found to make the confrontation as dramatic as possible. When there is no threat of violence, this requirement takes some imagination, and it often fails (Maynard, 1973). The Poor People's Campaign of 1968 got a good deal of media coverage by establishing a mud-surrounded tent city on the mall between the Washington Monument and the Lincoln Memorial. That had inherent drama, even without the sporadic conflicts between tent-city residents and the U.S. Park Police. The May Day antiwar demonstration in

1971 achieved drama with protesters using a minimum of violence through an audacious attempt to halt the operation of the federal government by creating a massive traffic jam. Protesters who tried to block traffic with their bodies were quickly carted off to jail or detention centers—along with just about everyone else on the scene—and the traffic jams were not much worse than those that occur in a heavy rain. However, the imaginative nature of the threat and the image of the nation's capital rendered helpless by bodies blocking the streets fascinated the news media, who gave it a good deal of space in advance. Officials became frightened and took the extreme action of the illegal police sweep, and this produced even more publicity for the demonstrators.

Demonstrators who marched on the Capitol toward the end of the May Day week worked out a civilized arrangement with police. The police indicated a line beyond which any trespasser would be arrested. Demonstrators lined up in an orderly manner to cross the line and accept arrest one at a time. Trespassing, while not a violent action in itself, at least produces a physical confrontation. It was the main technique of student demonstrations of the 1960s, beginning at Sproul Hall at the University of California at Berkeley in 1964. By forcing police to physically remove them from the property, the students called attention to their demands and conveyed the message that they felt strongly about them. Militant Indians adopted this technique in the 1970s, somewhat more spectacularly than the students, occupying first the offices of the Bureau of Indian Affairs in Washington and later the site of a historic Indian massacre at Wounded Knee, South Dakota.

Do such tactics work? As in the case of violence, they can be counterproductive if there is no broad public support for both the goals and the methods. It is somewhat easier to gain sympathy for nonviolent methods, although the distinction is sometimes lost when the methods provoke violence. Black nonviolence was successful. The students were generally successful in gaining a larger voice in the operation of universities, although major changes in educational policy were not forthcoming. The Indians gained some sympathetic attention; but their problems are so overwhelming that this gain may not yield much in long-term substantive value. The war protesters focused attention on the issue, but they failed to receive a sympathetic hearing from national officials. When a majority of citizens finally turned against the war, they did not do so out of the same moral revulsion which impelled the demonstrators who placed public debate on the war before society. The majority was motivated instead by the more pragmatic consideration that the high costs of the war were not justified by commensurate benefits (Schuman, 1972). The protests might eventually have had an even larger effect, but American involvement in the war was greatly scaled down before this possibility could be fully tested. At least the issue had been kept on the national agenda.

Passive Measures

Another category of unconventional political expression makes creative use of inaction rather than action. Participants hope to gain some bargaining power by refusing to do that which they normally do and which their opposition has some interest in their continuing to do. The Montgomery, Alabama bus boycott, inspired by the refusal of Rosa Parks, a black seamstress, to give up her seat to a white, is an example. Because of their passive nature, there is little personal risk to the participants unless they have a legal duty to perform the action being avoided. Boycotts have been organized on behalf of a wide range of political goals. Liberals have boycotted grapes and lettuce raised by nonunion workers, and conservatives have boycotted canned ham processed in Communist Poland.

Persons who avoid paying taxes or being drafted to protest government action are somewhat more daring because of their affirmative duty to pay taxes and serve when drafted. In both cases, the protester can regulate the intensity of his protest by his choice of measures. Avoiding the draft by fleeing to Canada was a less intense protest than going to jail. Persons who have protested government action by refusing to pay their income tax have in some cases managed to keep this a low-intensity protest through arrangements by which the refusal was little more than a bookkeeping device. The person would protect himself from criminal fraud by filing a return stating what he owed, then fail to pay it. The government would then attach his bank account and collect the money. At a higher level of intensity, tax resisters file no returns and do their best to keep their assets out of government reach. Karl Hess, a speech writer for Barry Goldwater in the 1964 presidential campaign, later became an ardent tax resister, living on a boat to avoid real estate tax and bartering his welding services for food to avoid the accumulation of seizable monetary assets.

Passive measures tend to be more expressive than instrumental. They help the individual to define his political self and to strike a symbolic blow for a cause which he thinks is right, and he can do this at little or no personal cost. The Montgomery bus boycott is an outstanding exception. It caused real economic hardship to the bus system, although even that was not by itself enough to force a change in policy. The boycott was still in effect when the Supreme Court outlawed racial segregation on public buses.

The successful group in American politics is not the polite petitioner who carefully observes all the rules. It is the rambunctious fighter, one with limited goals, that can elbow its way into the arena. But the willingness to fight is not enough. A group must be *able* to fight; it needs organization and discipline to focus its energies.

—William A. Gamson, "The Meek Don't Make It," *Psychology Today,* July 1974, p. 39

Petitioning with Elbows

Alternative Governments

There are some areas of human activity which require a measure of organization and disciplined conduct but which the government cannot regulate because the activities are illegal. The victimless crimes fall into this sphere: usury, gambling, prostitution, and use of drugs (including alcohol between 1919 and 1933). Providing these services to the public requires organization and rules of conduct which must be policed. Because the activities are illegal, the policing function takes place outside the conventional political system. This gap is filled by an unconventional system, the organized crime syndicate. It has many of the characteristics of a government: requirement for loyalty, a hierarchical structure, and a procedure for the redress of grievances. Mario Puzo's novel, *The Godfather*, opens with a poignant scene about an immigrant who petitions the Mafia for redress of a grievance when the conventional system has failed him. Criminal syndicates, many based loosely on Italian-American kinship ties, tend to be decentralized (Ianni, 1972). Violence is used as a method of social control, and their most violent episodes have involved jurisdictional or organizational disputes within the system.

For two governments to occupy the same territory, some kind of accommodation must be made, and the mechanism is usually bribery. "All available data," said the President's Commission on Law Enforcement and Administration of Justice (1967), "indicate that organized crime flourishes only where it has corrupted local officials. As the scope and variety of organized crime's activities have expanded, its need to involve public officials at every level of local government has grown [p. 191]." Moreover, the commission noted, as government regulation has expanded to manage the increasingly complex affairs of modern society, the opportunities for corruption have also expanded. But it is no new problem. In 1931, the National Commission on Law Observance and Enforcement said that "nearly all the large cities suffer from an alliance between politicans and criminals." In the 1950s, the Senate Special Committee to Investigate Organized Crime in Interstate Commerce (the Kefauver Committee) found links between public officials and organized crime in every city where it held hearings.

After Richard Hatcher was elected mayor of Gary, Indiana, in 1967, he reported that he had been offered $100,000 not to challenge an entrenched machine that was protecting criminal activity. After refusing and beating the machine in the Democratic primary, he was offered the same amount to continue the protection of gambling and other rackets. He declined (National Advisory Commission on Criminal Justice, Standards, and Goals, 1973). Underworld money was a source of campaign funds for Newark Mayor Hugh J. Addonizio. He was eventually convicted of sharing in money extorted from contractors who did business with the city. The National Advisory Commission on Criminal Justice, Standards, and Goals (1973) estimated that in one large eastern state, which it did not name, criminal indictments in the period from 1969 to 1973 reached "ten mayors, two judges, three state legislators, various local officials, and several state officials including two secretaries of state [p. 206]."

Several scholars have estimated that organized crime is the source of about 15 percent of the money spent on state and local political campaigns (Heard, 1960; Lasswell and Rogo, 1963; Cressey, 1969). In New York City, it is estimated that graft paid to city employees is the equivalent of a 5 percent tax on all construction costs paid to the alternative underworld government (National Advisory Commission on Criminal Justice, Standards, and Goals, 1973).

The extent of the power of organized crime was noted by Robert Kennedy when he was Attorney General of the United States in 1963. He told a Senate subcommittee that the task of providing physical protection for witnesses who cooperated with the government often required those witnesses to change their appearance, their names, and their residences. The President's Commission on Law Enforcement and Administration of Justice (1967) commented: "When the government of a powerful country is unable to protect its friends from its enemies by means less extreme than obliterating their identities, surely it is being seriously challenged, if not threatened [p. 1]."

AN ANTIDOTE TO RIGIDITY

Overcoming Cultural Lag

Every form of organization, including government, suffers from the "but this is the way we've always done it" syndrome. Structures and patterns are devised to cope with specific problems, and they tend to remain the same long after the problems have changed or gone away. When formal systems fail to respond to changing needs or demands, informal systems are created to meet these needs and demands. If they are successful, they may operate indefinitely outside the formal structure, like organized crime, or they may change and be incorporated into the formal structure, as in the case of black civil rights. Either way, the unconventional forms, whose effects may be malignant or socially useful, are part of the total system. They are the tools of social movements whose function, as Jack Walker (1966) has said, "is to break society's log jams, to prevent ossification in the political system, to prompt and justify major innovations in social policy and economic organization [p. 294]."

The use of coercive and unconventional methods when other methods fail to bring about change is not confined to minorities. Others can play this game. Journalist Arlen J. Large (1973) has drawn a convincing parallel between the use of illegal tactics by blacks, students, and Indians and illegal activity by the President. Late in his first term, President Nixon sought to cancel some long-entrenched and legally established federal programs, not

Striking Teamsters and Police in Minneapolis, 1934: Breaking society's logjams. (*National Archives.*)

by asking Congress to repeal them, but by simply refusing to spend the money which Congress had appropriated for them. Federal courts ruled that he couldn't do that. But he got results. Large provides an example:

> Budget directors of earlier Presidents beefed for years about the bargain interest rates on federal rural electrification loans, for example, but Congress always voted the money and the lending obediently continued. Mr. Nixon last December smashed that traditional interplay by simply ordering a halt to the loans. Congressmen screamed it was illegal, but the President at last had got their attention.
>
> The result has been a reluctant attempt to redirect the cheap loans to rural electric co-ops that really need them . . . no earlier President has forced this much motion with more conventional methods.
>
> . . . Cooperation is pleasant and statesmanlike. But "defiance of the law" calls more attention to neglected problems, whether on the campus or the musty chambers of the House Appropriations Committee. It's deplorable, but it works [p. 13].

Another sign of the integration of unconventional methods with the formal system is the way in which politically efficacious individuals are able to move back and forth between the two modes. Participants in protest marches tend to be more active in conventional politics than nonmarchers. The National Advisory Commission on Civil Disorders found that the typical rioter was "substantially better informed about politics than Negroes who were not involved in the riots [p. 129]." Later research for the commission disproved the theory that rioters were poor, uneducated "riff-raff" so low on the social scale as to be completely outside the system (Fogelson and Hill, 1968).

Creative Conflict

A traditional test of democracy's success has been its stability. If the system can mediate among conflicting desires so that consensus, or at least acceptance, can be maintained, then it is working. If groups have to settle their difference by coercion or force, as in the case of the Civil War, it is not working. This traditional analysis, however, tends to ignore the lesser episodes of force and coercion in American politics and their creative function in preserving and maintaining the larger system. "A certain amount of discord, inner divergence and outer controversy," says George Simmel (1955), "is organically tied up with the very elements that ultimately hold the group together; it cannot be separated from the unity of the sociological structure [pp. 17–18]." Seen in this light, unconventional participation is not a rebuke to the system; it is part of the system.

SUGGESTED READINGS

Bell, David V. J. *Resistance and Revolution.* New York: Houghton Mifflin, 1973. An inquiry into political conflict and violence that traces the source of this behavior to inequalities in society.

Binstock, Robert H., and Katherine Ely (eds.). *The Politics of the Powerless.* Winthrop, 1971. A collection of essays dealing with what it means to be powerless and the political limitations experienced by the poor when they attempt to achieve their goals.

Gardiner, John A. *The Politics of Corruption.* Chicago: Sage Books, 1970. An analysis of long-term corruption in an American city with assessment of its causes and consequences including the functions performed by municipal corruption.

Gardiner, John A., and David J. Olson (eds.). *Theft of the City.* Bloomington, Indiana: Indiana University Press, 1974. A collection of readings on municipal corruption, emphasizing works dealing with types, causes, and consequences of local corruption.

Hirsch, Herbert, and David C. Perry (eds.). *Violence as Politics.* New York: Harper & Row, 1973. Original essays written by scholars from various disciplines who discuss the political meaning and import of violent behavior.

Lipsky, Michael. *Protest in City Politics.* Chicago: Rand McNally, 1970. One of the best studies of peaceful, nonviolent protest focusing on the limitations inherent in the protest process when used by relatively powerless groups.

Pranger, Robert J. *The Eclipse of Citizenship.* New York: Holt, Rinehart and Winston, 1968. A brief discussion of the politics of power and participation, suggesting that traditional elements of citizenship are now on the wane.

Wolfe, Alan. *The Seamy Side of Democracy.* New York: McKay, 1973. An examination of how official policies and behavior have introduced political repression of dissident groups in America. Includes a forecast of likely future policies.

Part Three

Decisionmakers

THE VARIETY OF CONVENTIONAL AND UNCONVENTIONAL METHODS OF involvement in American politics is matched by the diversity of motives inspiring citizens to participate. Some no doubt become involved merely for the satisfaction of playing the political game. Others participate to comply with their perception of norms about civic duty. Still others are impelled to act because of pressure from friends and neighbors. Viewed in isolation, these and other motivations yield confusing portraits about what citizen participation means, ranging from ritualized play-acting for its own sake to atomized political acts unrelated to each other or to anything else. Placed in the context of the larger political system, however, citizen participation takes on crucial meanings, especially for questions about democratic self-government.

Democratic theory maintains that citizen participation is *the* means for ensuring popular control over elected and appointed officials and the governmental institutions they preside over. In the five chapters which follow, we examine the behavior of public officials and the institutional performance of the national government in order to assess the nature of the links between citizens and their government. How the legislative, executive, and judicial branches and the bureaucracy work is described, interactions between them are discussed, and the decisions coming from them are related to the preferences of citizens.

Governmental responsiveness and accountability to citizen preferences involves more than simply determining the concerns and desires of the majority and making decisions based upon them. Modern society is too complicated for such a pure and simple scheme to work. If we are to understand decisionmaking processes, modern complexities require that we probe the institutional structures and settings where decisions are made, the social and psychological forces influencing decisionmakers, who the decision makers are, the procedures and rules they follow, as well as the formal and informal norms they adhere to. Our focus on these intricate, detailed, and sometimes anachronistic processes should not obscure our equal concern for the larger questions dealing with popular control over government officials and institutions.

Ours is often described as a government "of rules and not men" and a system featuring "the separation of powers." Rules are important in American government as are the institutional arrangements for checks and balances. Yet one of the perspectives we advance is that power is shared across the separate branches, and the rules often leave unclear who has authority to act until such time as questions are resolved through the decisions of public officials. The shared responsibilities, jointly held authority, and overlapping functions among separate decisionmaking institutions account for the significant degree to which bargaining, concessions, and compromise characterize official decisionmaking processes within American national institutions. They are also the source of much popular dissatisfaction because of the difficulty, if not the impossibility, of fixing responsibility on errant public officials and holding them accountable for their deeds.

Dissatisfaction over the lack of responsiveness and accountability of decisionmakers is itself a primary source of the recent precipitous decline in confidence and trust that citizens hold for the national government. We explore the dimensions of this crisis as well as the proposals for reforming the Congress, Presidency, Supreme Court, and the bureaucracy spawned by the crisis. Regardless of which governmental branch is targeted for reform, one continuity running through most of the proposed changes is that the substantive interests of those who recommend procedural alterations will be enhanced by adoption of the reform. Our discussion of reforming decisionmaking institutions includes assessments about who will benefit and who will lose if such reforms are adopted and the likely impact they will have on the balance of power among the branches of government.

The concluding chapter in Part Three examines the nature and extent of private decisionmaking by nongovernmental power centers. Most of the decisions that affect the lives of citizens are not made by public officials; rather they are determined by elites who control or preside over large organizations in the private sector. This fundamental characteristic of decisionmaking in American society raises a series of questions about the degree and kind of democratic control citizens can exercise: Are the private organizations internally democratic? Does the clash of competing private decisions serve the public good? Can private organizations accumulate sufficient resources to control public officials? What are the sources of legitimacy for the concentration of vast private resources in the hands of a select few? Discussing these and other questions about private decisionmakers gives us the opportunity to assess the persuasiveness of three models of the decisionmaking process. The first maintains that private power centers dominate and control governmental officials; the second argues that governmental institutions are capable of controlling private power centers when necessary; and the third holds that governmental institutions are capable of dominating private decision makers but that they have abdicated this role. Which model is correct is more than an academic debate because the question of popular control gets to the heart of democratic self-government.

Chapter 9

Congress

THE POWER OF THE LEGISLATURE

A Problem of Balance

The design of Congress involved a delicate balancing act for members of the Constitutional Convention of 1787. Two memories were fresh in their minds. One was the bitter experience of living under the unchecked executive power of the British Crown during the colonial period. The other was the frustration of trying to make the government operate with the weak foundation of the Articles of Confederation. The problem faced in 1787 was finding the right mixture of strength and weakness. There was yet another level to the paradox: The dominant interests represented at the convention wanted protection from unruly masses. But they also wanted protection from the effects of unrestrained ambition on the part of any faction within their own dominant group. They were willing to place complete trust in neither the people nor in each other.

The now-celebrated solution reached by the Founders was to create centers of countervailing power, including an executive capable of acting and a legislature strong enough to block any extreme action or prevent any consolidation of power which the executive might attempt. An elite faction might control the executive branch, they reasoned, but there would always be a place in Congress for opposing elites. Factions that were temporarily out of power or whose interests were so narrow that they were permanent minorities could still maintain some leverage and visibility in the legislative branch.

The legislative branch was also designed with an internal contradiction in mind. Because members would represent the people, their actions would have the legitimacy of originating from the popular will. On the other hand, the popular will could not have unlimited expression. If radical or immoderate causes gained too-easy access to the government through this route, the dominant elites might withdraw their support, and the entire governmental experiment could come tumbling down. So the system was designed to keep out all but stable, responsible men. Its internal workings were intended to encourage deliberation, moderation, and compromise.

Some things have changed, but the rough outlines of that design can still be seen today. Changes in election procedures have opened membership to persons of more diverse character, some of whom the Founding Fathers might not have considered cool, responsible, or sound. Technology, the rapid pace of events, and the increasing importance of foreign affairs have multiplied the powers of the executive branch at the expense of Congress. But it is still a place where the clash of interests can be accommodated in a polite, civilized manner, where action can be slow and deliberative, where the rewards tend to go to the practical.

A Conservative Force

The Founders succeeded in their aim of placing checks on both the popular will and the executive branch. Congressional inertia has prevented the tyranny of aroused masses who might suspend the civil rights of minorities and slowed the tendency toward true popular control of government which would likely take power from economic elites. Greedy minority interests and broad popular movements alike have been frustrated. While sluggishness has been the normal condition of Congress, it has also demonstrated its ability to fulfill the other part of the Founders' intent: blocking excessive attempts on the part of the executive to consolidate power. Congressional assertiveness in the early 1970s began as a response to the Nixon administration's exercise of war powers abroad and redirection of social programs at home. As the Watergate scandals unfolded, Congress played a major role in curbing the abuse of executive powers through its investigations of the Nixon administration and the House Judiciary Committee's voting out articles of impeachment of President Nixon. By the mid 1970s, the reassumption of its constitutional prerogatives placed Congress on a more equal footing with the executive than at any time in the prior forty years.

But in normal times, how you feel about Congress and the way it does its job depends pretty much on how satisfied you are with the status quo. For most observers, any evaluation has to be mixed. Nearly everyone is conservative about something. Conventional liberals may chafe at the slowness of Congress to embrace social welfare programs, but they welcome its protection of civil liberties from executive infringement. Most proposals for reforming and modernizing Congress are aimed at making it more responsive to public demands, generally by making it more accountable to a majority of its own members. But measures that make Congress responsive to the public can also be manipulated for the benefit of special-interest groups, and the public is not always right, particularly in the short run. So pressures for reform tend to be limited to small increments: removal of a particularly sticky roadblock in the legislative process or overcoming the abuse of power by a committee chairman. This seemingly minor tinkering with the machinery determines where Congress stands on a broad spectrum of possibilities: from a vehicle for massive popular influence over government policy on the one hand to a stubborn tool of entrenched interests on the other. It is constantly fine-tuning itself for a more comfortable position along that scale. Understanding that process requires a look at some of the mechanics.

Formal Powers

The powers enumerated in Article I of the Constitution make Congress—in the formal sense—the most powerful national legislature in the world. Congress does not, however, often exercise the full scope of its enumerated power. While executive power grew steadily from the 1930s through the 1960s and the judicial branch took an activist stance under Chief Justice Earl Warren in the 1950s and 1960s, Congress remained comparatively passive. It initiated little action of its own and was content to respond to Court decisions and policy programs of the executive branch and various interest groups. Yet, it has been more than a rubber-stamp operation, and it leaves its distinctive mark on the proposals that flow through it. No proposal can become law without agreement by a great variety of elite interests reflected in the congressional makeup, and modification and compromise are often required. The survival rate of legislative proposals gives an indication of the obstacles involved: of about 10,000 bills introduced in a typical year, only around 500, or 5 percent, become law. Congress works hard at screening and modifying, and its work is important even when the initiative comes from other branches or private interests. It is the focus of much interest-group activity, and its specialized committees have become a major point of communication and mediation between governmental and nongovernmental elites.

Meanwhile, the potential for Congress to be the most powerful branch of government continues to reside in Article I. When Congress and the executive are controlled by different political parties, as they have been for most of the past quarter century, there is pressure in Congress to assert that potential. During the 1950s, however, the Democratic leadership in Congress worked out informal understandings with the Republican President, Dwight D. Eisenhower, and direct confrontations were avoided. Not until the second Nixon administration did Congress begin to use its considerable authority to resist executive initiatives. Among the formal tools of this authority are:

Control of the Purse Strings.   The taxing and spending powers are the key to nearly everything else that the government does, and they give Congress its most important leverage—when it chooses to exercise it—over the executive and judicial branches. Congress has refused to delegate the taxing power with one major exception: The Reciprocal Trade Agreements Act of 1934 empowers the President to raise or lower tariffs by as much as 50 percent in return for similar action by another nation. The present-day tariff is mainly a device for regulating trade. But until the first part of this century, it was the major source of federal revenue. After passage of the Sixteenth Amendment in 1913, the income tax replaced it as the main revenue source.

The Constitution requires tax legislation to originate in the House of Representatives. By custom, laws for spending money follow the same route. Congress has seldom considered taxing and spending as a unified package, and so the job of coordinating the two shifted in this century to the budget-making process of the executive branch. Another way in which Congress has forgone the chance to control spending has been its practice of acting on each department's appropriation separately. The temptation to increase spending is greater when small increments are considered independently than when the entire year's spending is planned as a single package. Such a unified approach was tried in 1950 when the House Appropriations Committee experimented with an omnibus appropriations bill. The experiment was a success: Congress finished work on appropriations two months earlier than it had in 1949 and trimmed the President's budget by $2.3 billion. But the specialists who chaired the subcommittees saw that they were losing their power to control departmental money requests in their areas of expertise, and the plan was abandoned.

Another effort at regaining control of the purse strings was initiated with the Congressional Budget and Impoundment Control Act of 1974, whose provisions were to become fully effective in 1976. If faithfully implemented, this law would leave time, after the individual department decisions had been made, for Congress to take a look at the result of its labors and then try to bring the total budget into line with what it had actually targeted for spending, taxing, and borrowing. To provide the time for this extra work, the act advanced the beginning of the fiscal year from July 1 to October 1, beginning in 1976. It also created a new structure to perform this coordinating work: a twenty-three-member House Budget Committee with rotating membership and a fifteen-member Senate Budget Committee, whose members would be allowed to serve on only one other major committee after 1976. These committees were to be backed up by a

Congressional Budget Office supplying the experts and the computers to analyze the President's budget and assist the committees in preparing an alternate congressional budget. The key to this plan lay in the scheduling. The law provided specific dates for Congress to complete each phase of the process (see Table 9-1), but it also allowed these procedures to be waived in special circumstances. Congressional self-discipline is therefore still required.

A Share in the Conduct of Foreign Affairs.   The Constitution gives Congress the power to provide for defense by raising and maintaining military forces and declaring war and to regulate commerce with other nations. In addition, the President's power to make treaties and appoint ambassadors is subject to the advice and consent of two-thirds of the Senate. There was disagreement among the Founders over whether Congress or the President should have the initiative in foreign affairs. But George Washington assumed it with his proclamation of neutrality in the war between France and England in 1793. And it has resided mainly in the executive branch ever since except for a few brief periods of congressional assertiveness over foreign affairs.

The Senate has rejected only eleven treaties, the most important of which was the Treaty of Versailles, incorporating German surrender in World War I and the establishment of the League of Nations. Nevertheless,

Table 9-1   Congressional Budget Schedule

CONGRESSIONAL BUDGET AND IMPOUNDMENT CONTROL ACT OF 1974

Mid-January	President's budget submitted
March 15	Committees send budget reports to the Budget Committee of each House.
April 1	Congressional Budget Office sends report to Budget Committees
April 15	Budget Committees report first budget resolution to House and Senate, setting overall targets
May 15	All authorization bills reported. Final action on first budget resolution
One week after Labor Day	Final action on appropriation bills
September 15	Final action on second budget resolution, affirming or revising the previous targets
September 25	Final action on budget reconciliation measure
October 1	Fiscal year begins

recent Presidents have relied increasingly on executive agreements which do not require Senate approval to do business with foreign countries. The armistice agreement ending direct United States participation in the Vietnam war in 1972 was an executive agreement. Congress has also yielded its constitutional war power to the executive branch over the past thirty years. The last declaration of war by Congress was against Germany, Italy, and Japan on December 8, 1941. Since then, American military forces have been used in Korea, North Vietnam, South Vietnam, the Dominican Republic, Lebanon, Cambodia, and Laos without prior consultation with Congress. There are pre–World War II precedents for executive-ordered military action as well, mostly in Latin America. Historian Henry Steel Commanger (1971) has noted that the objects of presidential military action have generally been "small, backward, and distraught peoples [p. 223]." He did not think that historical perspective showed the action in any case to have been necessary. In 1973, Congress required the President to obtain congressional approval before extending any executive-initiated military action beyond sixty days. President Nixon vetoed that plan, and the veto was overridden.

Congress authorized President Johnson to "take all necessary measures to repel any armed attack against the forces of the United States and to prevent further aggression" when it passed the Gulf of Tonkin resolution of August 7, 1964. President Johnson interpreted this resolution as authorization to conduct the war, although he did not wait for it to be passed before ordering a "retaliatory" air strike against North Vietnam. United States troops were already fighting in South Vietnam. The resolution was requested as a response to reports—whose accuracy was later disputed—that North Vietnamese patrol boats had attacked American destroyers in the Gulf of Tonkin. In January of 1971, Congress repealed the resolution; but direct American participation in the Vietnam war continued for two more years, indicating, once again, the President's independence of Congress in exercising the war power.

Approval of Appointments.   The Senate's power to approve presidential appointments resulted from compromise between executive and legislative advocates at the convention of 1787. Most appointments get routine approval. The exceptions tend to be notable. About one out of five Supreme Court appointments has been either rejected or stalled until it was withdrawn. The most recent failures were Abe Fortas and Homer Thornberry, nominated by President Johnson to be Chief Justice and Associate Justice, and Clement F. Haynsworth, Jr., and G. Harrold Carswell, both nominated for Associate Justice by President Nixon. Fortas's nomination was withdrawn, and he later resigned his Associate Justice seat when conflict-of-interest charges were aired at the nomination hearings. Congress adjourned without acting on Thornberry. Haynsworth and Carswell were nominated for the Fortas seat and both were rejected. Their opponents,

Roosevelt Asking Congress for Declaration of War, 1941: Prior consultation is the exception. (*Wide World Photos.*)

accused by the President of being prejudiced against Southern conservatives, raised questions of ethics in the former case and judicial competence in the latter.

Diplomatic, cabinet, and subcabinet nominations run into trouble less often since these posts are part of the executive branch where more deference is given to presidential preference. The Senate asserted itself several times when relations between the executive and legislative branches became abrasive in the second Nixon administration. It forced the withdrawal of Patrick Gray as the nominee to direct the Federal Bureau of Investigation in 1973 after committee hearings revealed that Gray had been lax in investigating the Watergate burglary and had destroyed evidence that could have implicated the White House staff. In confirming Elliott Richardson as Attorney General, the Senate demanded and got as a condition of his confirmation a written commitment to preserve the independence of Special Prosecutor Archibald Cox. Richardson resigned during the "Saturday night massacre" rather than obey a presidential directive to fire Cox. Confirmation of William H. Saxbe as Richardson's replacement as Attorney General required an even stronger pledge of independence for the Special Prosecutor's office under Leon Jaworski. The fact that the Senate could exact such commitments demonstrated the potential flexibility of its confirmation power.

For some appointments, mainly federal district judges, U.S. attorneys, and federal marshals, the senators of the President's party act as patronage agents, distributing the jobs as rewards for faithful party service. Until 1969, when the U.S. Postal Service was organized, this was also true of postmasters.

Under the unwritten rule of *senatorial courtesy*, a senator of the President's party can usually block any appointment to a federal job in his state. Until about 1930, he had only to declare the candidate "personally obnoxious," but he is now expected to explain his reasons for the objection. Senators also extend a special privilege when one of their own members or a former member is nominated for federal office: He is usually confirmed at once without prior committee action.

Impeachment.   The Constitution provides, in Article II, that "the President, Vice President and all civil officers of the United States, shall be removed from office on impeachment for, and conviction of, treason, bribery, or other high crimes and misdemeanors." But an impeachable offense may be something less than a crime. In 1936, Congress impeached and removed Judge Halsted L. Ritter of the Southern district of Florida. He was acquitted of specific criminal charges, but removed for bringing "his court into scandal and disrepute," which was not a specific crime. An impeachable offense according to Gerald R. Ford, then speaking as House Republican leader and advocating impeachment of Associate Justice William O. Douglas in 1970, is "whatever a majority of the House of Representatives considers it to be at a given moment in history." Most authorities, including Raoul Berger (1973), believe that the impeachment power is more limited than that but not limited to criminal conduct. Alexander Hamilton (1788) expressed the Framers' intent in *The Federalist*, No. 65: Impeachment is for "those offences which proceed from the misconduct of public men, or in other words, from the abuse or violation of some public trust. They are of a nature which may with peculiar propriety be denominated *political,* as they relate chiefly to injuries done immediately to the society itself [p. 407]."

The House Judiciary Committee did not try to resolve these conflicting views of the impeachment power when it voted to recommend impeachment of President Nixon in 1974. Each member, in explaining his vote, applied his own interpretation of congressional authority to the facts at hand.

Impeachment is analogous to indictment; it is a formal charge of a stated offense. The House impeaches by majority vote, and the Senate tries the impeached officer with a two-thirds vote of the senators present required for conviction.

While impeachment proceedings have been started in the House about fifty times, only twelve cases have gone to trial in the Senate. Four ended in conviction and removal. All those removed were judges. Two high-ranking officers were impeached in the nineteenth century: Supreme Court Justice

Judge H. L. Ritter after his impeachment, 1936: Scandal and disrepute, but not a crime. (*Wide World Photos.*)

Samuel Chase in 1805 and President Andrew Johnson in 1868. Both were acquitted in the Senate after bitter partisan struggles. The 1974 debate in the House Judiciary Committee over its recommendation to impeach Nixon was not polarized strictly along party lines. And when Nixon resigned in August 1974, it was clear that a majority of both parties was prepared to vote for conviction.

The power of presidential pardon does not extend to cases of impeachment, although it can be used to grant relief from criminal prosecution which might arise from the facts uncovered in an impeachment investigation—which President Ford did for former President Nixon in September 1974.

Regulation of Commerce. Congress, unlike the state legislatures, has no general power to legislate for the health, safety, and welfare of the citizenry. But it has gradually developed the equivalent of that power through application of the authority to regulate interstate and foreign commerce granted in Article I. This expansion has come mainly since 1937, when the Supreme Court began to uphold the economic regulations of the New Deal, beginning with the National Labor Relations (Wagner) Act of 1935. Chief Justice Charles Evans Hughes held that a steel company was subject to the act because it drew its raw materials from across state lines and shipped them back into interstate commerce (*National Labor Relations Board v. Jones and Laughlin Steel Corp.*, 301 U.S. 1). In succeeding decisions, Congress has been granted extremely wide latitude in deciding what kinds of activity affect interstate commerce and therefore may be regulated. The Civil Rights Act of 1964 represented another major expansion of the commerce power, applied this time to ban discrimination in hotels and restaurants. In 1968, the commerce power was the basis for a law making it a federal crime to incite or participate in a riot. Although enacted in response to ghetto riots, it was used in the Nixon administration to prosecute antiwar demonstrators.

Amending the Constitution.   The Supreme Court ruled in 1939 in *Coleman v. Miller*, 307 U.S. 433, that Congress controls the process of changing the Constitution by formal amendment. Under Article V, amendments may be proposed in two ways: by two-thirds of both Houses of Congress or by two-thirds of the state legislatures applying to Congress to call a constitutional convention. The latter procedure has never been employed. Amendments may be ratified by three-fourths of the legislatures or by conventions called for that purpose in three-fourths of the states. Congress chooses the method of ratification. The convention method of ratification was used only once, for the Twenty-first Amendment, when Congress was in a hurry to repeal prohibition and Prohibition party forces controlled rural-dominated state legislatures.

The Constitution leaves a number of questions about the amending process unanswered, and the Supreme Court has held that these are up to Congress to decide. Thus Congress sets the time limit for ratification, if any. And it set the precedent in the case of the Civil War amendments that a state legislature which has rejected ratification of an amendment may change its mind and ratify but that a ratification once enacted may not be withdrawn.

In 1969, a proposal for a constitutional convention to consider an amendment revising the one-man, one-vote ruling of *Baker v. Carr* (see page 108) came within one state of the necessary two-thirds. If a thirty-fourth state had passed the resolution, most observers believe that Congress would have found a way to avoid calling the convention—a gathering whose inherent power could have been greater than that of Congress itself. A convention, as the one in 1787 demonstrated, has no limitations. It could abolish Congress. A bill proposed by Senator Sam J. Ervin, Jr., would limit the life of state resolutions calling for a convention to seven years. The first resolutions on the reapportionment question were adopted in 1963 and would therefore be voided by the Ervin plan if it were to be enacted.

Conducting Investigations.   Although the Constitution does not specify a congressional investigating power, the Supreme Court held in *McGrain v. Daughterty*, 273 U.S. 135, 1927 that the "power to secure needed information'' is ''an attribute of the power to legislate.'' The specific issue in that case was the power of Congress to subpoena witnesses in the Teapot Dome scandal of the Harding administration and punish them when they failed to appear and testify. It was upheld.

Investigations have been held for purposes other than gathering information on which to base legislation: to inquire into the effect of past legislation, to inquire into the qualifications of members of Congress, to gather facts for impeachment proceedings. Some members have been criticized for using investigations as vehicles for personal publicity and political advancement. Some Presidents, including Harry S. Truman and Richard M. Nixon, first gained national attention as congressional investigators.

In 1973, Senate Resolution 60 created the Select Committee on Presidential Campaign Activities to determine whether improper conduct in the 1972 election indicated ''the necessity or desirability of the enactment of new congressional legislation to safeguard the electoral process by which the President of the United States is chosen.'' The committee hearings were presented on national television and, under the guidance of Chairman Sam Ervin, had little impact in generating new regulations on campaigns, but had the vastly more important function of informing the

Richard Nixon as a Congressional Investigator: A vehicle for advancement. (*Wide World Photos.*)

public about the attempted subversion of the electoral process by the Nixon campaign staff.

Judging the Qualifications of Members.   Both the House and Senate judge their members' elections and qualifications, and each may punish its members by censure or expulsion for disorderly behavior. The power to pass judgment on qualifications of members was sharply limited by the Supreme Court in the case of Rep. Adam Clayton Powell, who was denied the seat to which he had been elected in 1966. The charge against him was misappropriation of his travel and staff funds. The Court held that a properly elected member could be barred only for failure to meet a qualification spelled out in the Constitution, i.e., age, citizenship, or residence (*Powell v. McCormack*, 395 U.S. 550). Prior to the Powell case, a number of members-elect of both houses had been denied seats for other reasons, ranging from involvement in racial violence to polygamy.

The power of each house to decide contested elections is more clearcut. Challenges to election outcomes are fairly common, especially in the House; a formal procedure has been codified in the Federal Contested Election Act of 1969. A notable recent dispute was the attempt of the Mississippi Freedom Democratic party, which had challenged the regular Mississippi delegation to the 1964 Democratic National Convention, to prevent the seating of the five Mississippi congressmen in 1965. It was unsuccessful.

Congress has expelled members only rarely. Censure is a more common disciplinary measure; although its effect is almost as devastating, it leaves it to the voters to decide whether the offender should continue in office. The Senate censured Sen. Thomas J. Dodd in 1967 for converting campaign funds to his personal use. In 1954, it censured Sen. Joseph McCarthy, Republican of Wisconsin, for bringing the Senate into dishonor and disrepute, obstructing its constitutional processes, and impairing its dignity during his investigations into domestic Communism. A House member, Rep. Thomas L. Blanton, Democrat of Texas, was censured in 1921 for putting "foul and obscene matter" in the *Congressional Record*.

CONGRESSIONAL ROLES

The formal powers of Article I of the Constitution establish three roles for Congress in the national government: enacting legislation, finding and correcting administrative flaws, and representing the public.

The Legislative Process

Seen in the sterile language of the statute books, the legislative task looks like a relatively neutral act of deciding technical questions. In fact, law making involves a wide range of choices among competing claims and interests. It is therefore an *evaluative* job. Congress is a distributor of rewards and punishments which reinforce or discourage a variety of behaviors. The rewards are not always material. As you can tell from the thickness of the *Congressional Record* (45,000 pages in fiscal 1970 at $119 a page), members have a lot to say. And while much of what they say may seem irrelevant, extravagant, or useless, it all has some purpose. Consider the following extract from the *Record* of January 16, 1973:

MR. HARRY F. BYRD, JR.   Mr. President, I invite the attention of the Senate to a proposal for an American Revolution Bicentennial theme, which has more merit than any I have heard to date. The theme, which has been suggested by the Cultural Laureate Foundation, Inc., is "Let Freedom Ring."

This phrase captures the essence of our Nation. It applies to all Americans—in all walks of life, in all stations, high and low. It touches the pulse of our society.

I commend the Cultural Laureate Foundation for its perception.

This nonprofit, charitable organization, recently formed in Arlington, Va., is dedicated to the encouragement and stimulation of cultural achievements of mankind. . . [p. S 695].

Statements of this sort, found in the *Record* every day, can be inexpensive but highly valued symbolic rewards for a variety of groups. They are assurances that group interests are considered legitimate, and that their demands can be heard. The things said in Congress can bestow upon disturbed citizens some comfort that the values they hold dear are being saluted in the highest levels of government.

Symbolic payoffs are by no means always frivolous. The black civil rights movement of the 1960s owes part of its success to the things said about it in Congress. The favorable comments by national legislators amounted to a recognition of legitimacy. Leaders of the movement would have found it more difficult to maintain the enthusiasm of their followers without such symbolic reassurance. Even the enactment of the Civil Rights Act of 1964 may have had more symbolic value than tangible importance to the cause of black liberation.

There is, of course, a danger in this use of symbolic manipulation; it may become a substitute for concrete activity. Interest-group leaders can use symbolic rewards to keep their members in check without doing anything about their material needs. Large, unorganized sections of the public might get the symbolic rewards while tangible gains are shunted off at their expense to better organized, less visible groups (Froman, 1962).

Dispensing material rewards is, of course, also part of the legislative task of Congress. In its law making, it sets the general tone for national policy, deciding who will get what. The expansion of technology on the one hand and the nation's international role on the other have greatly increased the complexity of legislation, and the danger of drowning in technical detail sometimes seems very real to congressmen. Worse yet, the rapid pace of change raises a continuing danger that a law passed to solve today's problem will not work at all in tomorrow's situation. The result has been a trend toward more general laws and more dependence on the interpretation and discretion of administrators in the executive branch to fill in the details when legal theory is applied to real situations. In this way, Congress has lost some of its influence on national policy. At the same time, the importance of its monitoring the execution of its laws has increased.

Watching the Administrators

The process of keeping track of what happens to congressional intent after the laws are enacted is called the *oversight function.* It involves far more than harrassment of members of the executive branch by a weakened and jealous legislature—although that is sometimes part of it, particularly when the Congress and the White House are controlled by different parties. It provides necessary hindsight to the legislative process; congressmen have to know what effect the laws they have already passed are having so that they will know what to do about enacting new laws or altering the old ones. Hearings on the actions of administrators have other useful effects: They deter abuses of power, expose corruption, and detect incompetence. This watchdog role is uneven, however. Much depends on the intentions and the vigor of the committee and subcommittee chairmen conducting the hearings.

Yet another effect of the oversight function is the influencing of public opinion or executive action. Even if a committee knows most of the facts in advance and has made up its mind about legislative goals, airing the proposal in a public hearing can mobilize public opinion and executive support needed to get the legislation enacted. An important symbolic function is also involved here. Interest groups can state their cases in an official forum. Congressmen often testify as a means of assuring their constituents that they are taking care of them. Sometimes the ceremonial effect of a congressional hearing can serve to confer the mantle of legitimacy on a viewpoint not previously considered debatable. The Senate Foreign Relations Committee, for example, began its hearings into the conduct of the Vietnam war at a time when opposition to the war was still widely considered to be deviant, peculiar, and even unpatriotic. The hearings increased information about the war, undercut its legitimacy, and may have been a factor in turning public opinion around. Another example is the use of committee hearings to place the poverty problem on the national agenda in the early 1960s. The plight of the poor was no worse than before, but a decision had been made by certain leaders of the Democratic party to begin a major undertaking in that field. Congressional hearings helped give it visibility.

Ever since the origin of representative government, there has been an argument over the proper role of the legislator. Should he take the assignment of representation literally and try to serve as a transmission device for the attitudes and choices of his constituents? Or should he follow his own judgment and policy preferences? This is no mere academic.point. When Rep. E. G. Shuster of Pennsylvania was still unpacking after being sworn in to the House of Representatives in 1973, he had to choose between his personal conservatism on government spending and the desires of his constituents who were sending him angry letters complaining about cutbacks in farm programs. "I gave it a night's sleep," he said. "And then I knew the answer. I had to keep faith with my people [Hunter, 1973]." He opposed the fund cuts.

On most questions, however, learning the public's preference, if any, is not so easy. Public opinion, as we have seen in Chapter 4, tends to be ill-informed, diffuse, and hard to measure. If a representative were only a transmitting machine, he could be replaced with something much cheaper and more efficient in the form of an electronic device. A congressman who seriously tries to learn the wishes of his constituents—as many as half a million for a member of the House, more for senators from all but the smallest states—quickly discovers some problems. His large and heterogeneous constituency may be so divided that there is no majority opinion on many issues. Even if there is, opinion may be based on less information than is available to the congressman. In a fast-moving legislative situation where compromises are being worked out, there will be nuances that not even the most sophisticated constituents can understand without spending time and effort to study them—a cost that few are willing to pay unless they are members of a special-interest group directly affected by the legislation. Even then, they are likely to rely on someone else to do the studying and thinking for them.

Some members of Congress are careful to tabulate opinions expressed in letters and telephone calls to the office. But such expressions are not representative. University of Michigan election surveys (Converse, Clauson, and Miller, 1965) have found that only about 15 percent of the adult population reports ever having written a letter to a public official. "Of the total stream of such letters from the grassroots, two-thirds are composed by about three percent of the population [p. 333]." And the letter-writing public is disproportionately conservative. Other members use the privilege of free postage to send out opinion questionnaires. These, too, tend to draw a selective response, and the questions are often loaded to favor the congressman's predetermined view (Bogart, 1972). Even without these disadvantages, such surveys would still tap only the simplest division of opinion and be of little help in making the myriad series of more subtle decisions that enhance, impede, or revise a bill on its way to becoming a law.

So while congressmen may give lip service to the instructed-delegate model, they are more likely to follow Edmund Burke's advice by giving their constituents not their obedience but their judgment. Many times the end result is the same because a congressman tends to share the viewpoints of the people who elected him. Adam Clayton Powell never would have made it to Congress from western Kansas nor would his Harlem constituency ever have elected Kansas Sen. Bob Dole. Moreover, the distinction between obedience and personal judgment is fuzzy. If constituent opinion is vocal or when interest groups make their wants known, a member of Congress will often modify his judgment to conform to these intensely held constituent wishes. Different issue categories tend to produce different patterns. Domestic issues produce more of the sort of constituency opinion that influences Congress than foreign affairs issues, where more voters are inattentive or content to go along with the national leadership (Miller and Stokes, 1963).

On the whole, therefore, a member of Congress has a good deal of latitude. Issues likely to get him into trouble with his constituency are relatively uncommon. One resulting problem is that special-interest groups can exercise a lot of influence on a congressman without anyone noticing that real constituent interests are going unattended. Oddly enough, the problem is not nearly as severe as it might be. While constituent reaction is not a very great danger to members of Congress, most of them are in the habit of behaving *as if* it were. Elected representatives are, ironically, used to dealing with a highly unrepresentative sample of their constituencies; so they misperceive their true attentiveness.

Studies of congressional attitudes have shown that members tend to see the voters as alert, aware of their legislative records, and ready to reward or punish them on election day on the basis of those records. So they do have a reason, however erroneous, to follow public opinion (Kingdon, 1967).

This misperception might be healthy for guarding the democratic ideal if it went no further than an overestimate of the attentiveness of voters. But there are other errors of perception. Citizens who have the means and the know-how to get the congressman's attention are atypical. A member represents not so much his formal constituency, defined by a geographic area, as a group of issue constituencies, defined as those who can make their views known to him on specific matters (Jones, 1961; Clotfeler, 1970).

Many people, of course, will belong to no such issue constituency. Some may belong to "negative reference groups," organizations whose values conflict strongly with the majority. A politician can use such groups to manipulate the fears of other constituents. Or they may simply be part of a permanently powerless minority which withdraws from political participation altogether. If there are enough members in this inactive group, a politician might win election to office by arousing their interest, becoming their champion, motivating them to vote, and moving the other groups out of the functional constituency.

Another form of representation, following neither the obedient, instructed-delegate model nor the burkean independent-decisionmaker model, consists of sending a person to Washington who is just like the folks back home. In a homogenous district, this is quite possible. A member from a wheat-farming district of Kansas or an oil-producing district of Oklahoma doesn't have to think twice about reconciling his judgment with the interests of wheat growers or oil producers if he is one himself. There is no need for close communication between the member and his constituents, because his interests are coincident with their interests from the beginning.

INSIDE THE CONGRESS

The Representation Problem

If the problem of representation were simply one of reducing more than 200 million people to the 535 in Congress, the best way to choose members of Congress would be by lot. A probability sample of that size would have an excellent chance of being like the larger population on most dimensions within a few percentage points. About half would be female, one in nine black, half would have incomes below the median, and so on. But Congress is instead, and not surprisingly, an elite institution. It reflects not so much the nation in microcosm as the governing elite or the sum of many different local and regional elites. Compared to the general population, it is better educated, more affluent, more white, male, and native born. It also has a more prestigious employment history. Members tend to be the sons of professional or business leaders and to have practiced a profession or engaged in business themselves before election to Congress. The legal profession is highly overrepresented. Lawyers compose two-tenths of 1 percent of the labor force and about half of Congress. Blacks are still underrepresented, although they have made considerable progress since the civil rights movement of the 1960s. In 1966, Edward Brooke of Massachusetts became the first black elected to the Senate since Reconstruction. The number of black representatives increased from six in the Ninetieth Congress (1967–1969) to nine in the Ninety-first Congress, twelve in the Ninety-second Congress, and seventeen in the Ninety-fourth Congress (1975–1977). There is a parallel trend for improvement in the representation of women, which reached a record eighteen elected to the Ninety-fourth Congress. Moreover, there is a greater likelihood for the women who do reach Congress to be elected on their own rather than the earlier pattern of election or appointment to fill out the terms of their late husbands. Until recent years, this ''widow's mandate'' accounted for about half of the female representation in Congress. The women who served the longest, Sen. Margaret Chase Smith, Republican of Maine, and Rep. Frances P. Bolton, Republican of Ohio, were first elected to the House in 1940 to fill the unexpired terms of their late husbands. Mrs. Smith won

Senator Brooke: One in a hundred. (*Fred Ward, Black Star.*)

election to the Senate in 1948 and served four terms before being defeated in 1972. Mrs. Bolton was ranking Republican on the House Foreign Affairs Committee when she was defeated for reelection in 1968.

Young people are also underrepresented. A representative must be at least twenty-five and a senator thirty. But few ever reach Congress at such early ages. Building a career record impressive enough to convince voters that you should represent them takes time, and the average age in recent Congresses has been in the fifties—low fifties on the House side, upper fifties in the Senate. A century ago, members were younger: The average age in the Forty-first Congress (1869–1871) was 44.6 years. Partly because of their advanced age, today's congressmen reflect a geographic distribution of the past: They come from rural and small-town backgrounds at a time when more than half the population lives in metropolitan areas.[1]

Margaret Chase Smith: A widow's mandate. (*Ivan Massar, Black Star.*)

The Conservative Bias

It should be no surprise, then, that congressmen tend to feel supportive of the status quo. Before the decision in *Baker v. Carr*, it was widely assumed that the main cause of conservatism in the House was malapportionment of congressional districts with heavy overrepresentation of rural areas. But the effect of one-man, one-vote reforms on the overall conservative stance of the House has been minor. The source of the conservatism has merely shifted from sparsely populated rural areas to heavily populated, middle-class suburban areas. After the 1972 elections, more were elected from suburbs than from either the central cities or rural areas. Relatively affluent suburbanites are not particularly interested in having their tax dollars go to the solution of social problems in less prosperous rural areas or central cities.

Representation in the Senate, where every state has two votes regardless of size, was once considered a source of conservative bias because the representatives of a minority of the citizens could block action desired by representatives of the majority. In the most extreme possibility, the votes of the senators from the nine largest states, representing a majority of the population, could be canceled out by the votes of the senators from the nine smallest states, who represent less than 2.5 percent of the population. When political issues tended to divide along geographic lines, this inequity was more important than today when regional cleavages have become increasingly blurred.

How Congress Works

The Senate is the more prestigious of the two houses of Congress. It is also the more relaxed. Small enough to proceed without a great deal of

---

[1]House members must also have been United States citizens for seven years and be residents of the states (but not necessarily the districts) that they represent. Senators must live in the states they represent and have been United States citizens for nine years.

formality, it can manage to have virtually all its 100 members considered on scheduling and procedural matters. The House of Representatives, on the other hand, is so large that it needs tightly structured procedures and a careful division of labor to get the work done. Its organization is more hierarchical, power is less evenly distributed, and it takes a member many years to rise toward the top. Power in the Senate is more evenly distributed. Democrats, for example, through a reform instituted by Lyndon Johnson as minority leader in 1953, are guaranteed a position on at least one major committee no matter how new and inexperienced they are. Pressure to conform is greater in the House than in the Senate. A senator has a national forum at his disposal from the moment he is sworn in. A member of the House finds it much more difficult to attain any kind of national visibility. He is therefore more dependent on his seniors.

House members, because there are more of them to share the work, are more likely to become subject-matter specialists than senators. A senator must divide his time among several committees and relies to a greater degree upon his staff for substantive expertise.

A bill may be introduced by any member of either house. Both houses must pass it in identical form before it is sent to the President to be signed into law, as shown on the next page. Its actual origin may, of course, be somewhere outside of Congress: the executive branch in most cases and sometimes the legislative office of an interest group. Nelson Polsby (1971) points out, however, that Congress, particularly the Senate, plays an often unnoticed role in the earliest stages of legislative origination. Measures proposed by the President as ''new'' may have, in fact, been bouncing around the halls of Congress for years. Much of the chatter in the *Congressional Record* is about bills that are seemingly going nowhere. And yet, it keeps the ideas alive, gives interest groups a reason to stay interested, helps people who haven't thought about a new idea to get used to it. Then when a new President's intuition tells him there is something to be gained from innovation, ''desk drawers fly open all over Washington. Pet schemes are fished out, dusted off, and tried out on the new political leaders. There is often a hiatus of years—sometimes decades—between the first proposal of a policy innovation and its appearance as a presidential 'initiative'—much less a law [p. 67].''

Committees of Congress

The House has twenty standing committees, and the Senate has sixteen. Acting as legislatures in microcosm, committees make the most crucial decisions in the life—or death—of a bill. And the committee assignments a member gets may be equally crucial to his own career. Committee members are appointed by vote of the separate houses, but that is a mere formality. Party leaders agree upon the ratio of Republicans to Democrats in each committee (the majority is generous to the minority because it assumes that it will be a minority someday), and each party designates its own members'

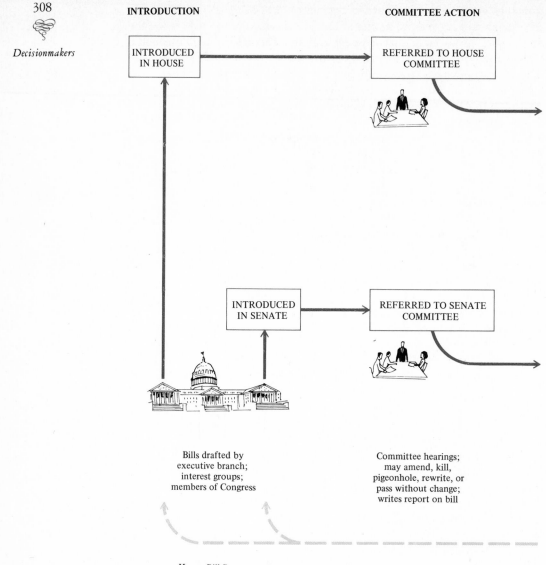

INTRODUCTION

INTRODUCED IN HOUSE

REFERRED TO HOUSE COMMITTEE

COMMITTEE ACTION

INTRODUCED IN SENATE

REFERRED TO SENATE COMMITTEE

Bills drafted by
executive branch;
interest groups;
members of Congress

Committee hearings;
may amend, kill,
pigeonhole, rewrite, or
pass without change;
writes report on bill

How a Bill Becomes a Law

committee appointments. This process usually amounts to filling vacancies, since members like to stay on the same committees year after year in order to advance in committee seniority. Vacancies are caused by death, retirement, failure to win reelection, and, occasionally, a decision to invoke the prerequisites of seniority to leave a low-status committee for one of higher status.

Committee assignments are determined by committees of party members which are structured in various ways, depending on the house and the

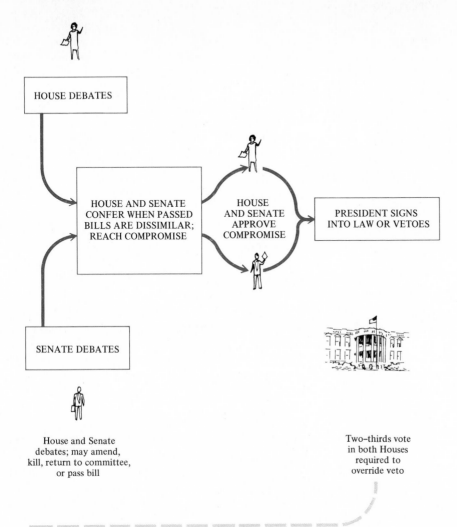

party. All the committees on committees have this in common, however: They are designed to reflect the choices of the older, more experienced party members. These design features tend to insulate the committee selection procedure from the capricious effects of electoral change. Younger members do not have much to say about it. Leaving it in the hands of the older, experienced members has a stabilizing effect, and they are not in all ways obstructionist. "After years of experience in a collective body," says Nicholas A. Masters (1961), "senior members are readier to recognize the need for compromise and adjustment if work is to be done [p. 350]." The old hands in the House will wait until they have had an opportunity to observe a younger member in action for several years before putting him on a major committee, such as Appropriations. On lesser committees, the possibility of helping a member win reelection is a major consideration. Farm-state members tend to get the agriculture committees, for example. When George McGovern was a House member from South Dakota, his membership on the Education and Labor Committee was criticized by his opponents back home; so he sought and gained transfer to the Agriculture Committee where he could look after his constituents' more immediate interests. Shirley Chisholm of Brooklyn, New York, appealed her freshman assignment to Agriculture and got Education and Labor instead in a reverse application of the same reasoning. Although the presence of urban members on the Agriculture Committee might be helpful in protecting the consumer interests of their constituents, they prefer more visible ways of serving their voters.

Committees vary in operating style, depending on their subject matter and the personalities of their senior members. Some, like the House Rules Committee in the 1960s, have been closely knit and well-coordinated groups with broad effective power; others, like the House Education and Labor Committee in the same period, are internally competitive and chaotic and thus less able to influence the entire House. Ideally, a committee should fall between these extremes, giving opposing interests fair hearings and arriving at reasonable compromises. The House Agriculture Committee has been cited as an example of this type (Rieselbach, 1973).

Congressional Subcommittees

Woodrow Wilson (1885) suggested that committees were where the real work of congressional decision making took place. Today, much of that work has shifted down one level to the subcommittee. A subcommittee may be created by the chairman of the full committee and its personnel and subject matter controlled by him. There are two types: ad hoc subcommittees to consider special questions or even a single bill and standing subcommittees which study some subject within the jurisdiction of the larger committee. A standing subcommittee can develop such a monopoly of information about its specialized subject that it exercises life or death power over legislation simply because other members are dependent on it for expertise. As the complexity of national issues and the scope of government activity have expanded, the number and the importance of subcommittees have grown: from 180 standing subcommittees in 1945 to 219 in 1970.

One effect of the committee system is to disperse power within the Congress, making it harder to produce coordinated legislative programs, more difficult to hold members responsible to their party leaders, and easier for special interests to gain access to critical decision points. The Legislative

Reorganization Act of 1946 reduced the number of committees, but its intent was erased by the proliferation of subcommittees.

The Seniority System

A wide range of benefits, from the choicest offices to the committee chairmanships, are allocated to members of Congress on the sole basis of who has been there the longest. This seniority system evolved as a conflict-reducing device. Faced with many internal decisions on individual privileges and assignments, leaders found it a troublesome chore to decide each case on its merits. Seniority is easy to define and it is sufficiently reasonable to justify a claim to legitimacy. The Senate has followed it since about 1846 and the House from shortly after the turn of the last century.

Neither a law nor a formal rule, the seniority system operates on two different levels. In Congress, it is the means of deciding who gets the most desirable office space and a factor in getting an assignment on a major committee. At the committee level, it determines who advances to chairman when a vacancy opens up and is a factor in getting subcommittee chairmanships or assignment to House-Senate conference committees which reconcile different versions of bills passed by both houses. The system has survived efforts to dislodge it. In 1971, for example, House Democrats provided for an automatic vote in their caucus on committee chairmen at the beginning of each new session. The balloting is secret if one-fifth of those present ask for it. In the Ninety-second Congress and again in the Ninety-third, the most senior members were elected chairmen, just as though there had been no rules change.

The strength of this custom may make arguments about whether it is good or bad merely academic. Offsetting the advantages of hassle-free selection and reaping the benefits of experience are four main problems:

Diffusion of Power. When a member reaches the top of his committee's seniority ladder, the leadership decision that put him on that ladder in the first place may have been made thirty years before. So committee chairmen are independent of leadership. As a result, power is scattered.

Obstructionism. While there are exceptions, old men often tend to be conservative and uninterested in the current goals of the party in power. They can use the power of the chairmanship to keep important legislation stalled in committee. For example, when Medicare was finally enacted in 1965, it was the turnabout of one man, Rep. Wilbur Mills of Arkansas, Chairman of the House Ways and Means Committee, which finally sprang it loose after being blocked for fifteen years.

Unrepresentativeness. To be around long enough to become a committee chairman, a member must come from a "safe" district, that is, one with no effective opposition party. Such districts are not typical of the nation as a whole and tend to be sheltered from the winds of change and political strife. They are often found in conservative one-party states of the South and Midwest.

Lack of Merit. Age is only slightly correlated with ability to do the job. Blind adherence to seniority sometimes elevates men who are incompetent or even senile to positions of power and shuts out better qualified younger men.

However, the rule is not inflexible; when any of these problems becomes unbearable to a majority of members, exceptions can be made. House Democrats have stripped some of their Southern members of seniority as punishment for supporting Republican or third-party nominees for President. Rep. Adam Clayton Powell lost his seniority and his chairmanship of the Committee on Education and Labor for misuse of congressional funds. Moreover, Reiselbach (1973) points out that some of the distortions induced by the seniority system are more apparent than real. Southern Democrats and Midwestern Republicans are so numerous that they would probably dominate the leadership positions even if committee chairmen were chosen by drawing names out of a hat. The predominance of Southern Democrats in recent years is a temporary phenomenon which can be traced to a 1946 Republican landslide in the North which removed many of the Southerners' intraparty competitors from the seniority race. And while it is true that the more senior Democrats are more conservative than their younger colleagues, this age difference does not seem to appear among Republicans. "Reform of seniority practice, in short," says Rieselbach, "might not make as much difference in legislative outputs as its critics seem to imply [p. 73]."

Wright Patman: Some go too far. (*Fred Ward, Black Star.*)

The Power of the Chairman

Although he can in theory be outvoted by his membership on procedural matters, an aggressive chairman can exercise near-total influence over the fate of legislation assigned to his committee through a wide variety of strategies available to him. Calling meetings, setting agendas, appointing subcommittees, channeling bills to particular subcommittees, hiring staff members, directing staff investigations, and influencing time for debate on the floor are all normal duties of the chairman. And all can be manipulated to help or hinder specific legislation. Committees which have exercised the majority power to overrule the chairman have found that for every action they take, the chairman can usually find a countermeasure. One trick is to call meetings on short notice when certain members are known to be out of town.

Sometimes a chairman will go too far. In 1967, Rep. Wright Patman's Banking and Currency Committee revolted over what members considered his arbitrary and oppressive leadership style and took away his authority to appoint subcommittee members and hire staff members. Members of the House Rules Committee, after years of yielding to the decisions of Chairman Howard Smith of Virginia, waited until he was defeated for reelection in 1966 before revising the rules to give the membership more authority over procedures. Even then, there were signs that the pressure for reform came not from within the committee but from the Democratic leadership (*Congressional Quarterly*, 1971).

Sometimes the chairman's position as the key to making or breaking legislation is more visible than real. No legislator likes to support a losing cause, and what appears to be a chairman's refusal to cooperate may simply be the outward symbol of the reluctance of Congress to act. Members who are opposed to change can tell constituents who feel otherwise that it is not their fault that Congress has not acted; it is the fault of the stubborn committee chairman. Since he is usually from a safe district, the chairman can take this heat.

Directing Traffic

The job of keeping things moving is much simpler in the Senate than in the House because of its smaller size. Nelson Polsby (1971) has described the difference:

> Whereas the House of Representatives is a firmly structured and highly articulated machine for processing bills and overseeing the executive branch, the modern Senate is, increasingly, a great forum, an echo chamber, a theater, where dramas—comedies and tragedies, soap operas and horse operas—are staged to enhance the careers of its members and to influence public policy by means of debate and public investigation [p. 67].

Any member of the Senate can speak for as long as he wants to on any subject. Since much of the business is transacted by unanimous consent, coordination is accomplished not so much through internal rules as through the party machinery. When the majority party leaders agree on what to do, they can be very efficient at setting the agenda and rounding up the votes. But the lowest-ranking senator also has a voice. He can block a unanimous consent motion or, in an extreme case, he can filibuster.[2] A determined minority can have a devastating effect on the Senate by invoking individual privileges in a manner calculated to prevent action. Since 1959, however, it has been possible to limit debate with a two-thirds vote in favor of a *cloture petition*, which is simply a request by one-sixth of the members to close debate on a measure. This rule was first successfully used to cut off a liberal filibuster against the Communications Satellite Act of 1962. It has since been used to cut off Southern filibusters against civil rights legislation.

---

[2]A *filibustero* was a West Indian pirate. A filibuster is any kind of delaying tactic, not limited to talking. The comparable Japanese word translates as "cow waddle," a reference to the desultory walk with which members of the Diet (assembly) approach the ballot box.

In the House, debate is sharply limited. Each bill has a specific time for debate set by the Rules Committee, which acts as traffic cop. Division of the time alloted is normally controlled by the chairman and ranking minority member of the committee having substantive jurisdiction over the bill.

The House Rules Committee. The traffic-directing function of the Rules Committee goes beyond mere procedure. It considers bills on their merits and hears testimony from members of the House. This committee can kill a bill by the simple expedient of not granting it a rule, a decision which has the effect of keeping it from being considered by the House. When Howard Smith was chairman, he was in the habit of killing liberal legislation single-handedly by disappearing to his Virginia dairy farm so that the committee could not be convened. Or he would put a disliked bill at the bottom of the agenda, invite a long list of witnesses, and ask them long-winded questions. This is the House version of the filibuster; the difference is that it is not available to every member.

Whether the committee acts as expediter or roadblock depends, of course, on its personnel. Between World War II and 1961, it was notorious for blocking presidential programs. In 1961, Democrats loyal to President Kennedy overcame the Republican–Southern Democrat coalition in the House and expanded the size of the Rules Committee to give Democratic leadership a working majority. It has had it ever since. This committee, says Polsby, which once "captured nationwide attention by its capacity—and willingness—to say 'no' to the best-laid plans of Presidents . . . now has all the fascination of an open valve [p. 103]." By 1973, under the chairmanship of Ray Madden of Indiana, the Rules Committee was more liberal than the House as a whole, and its efforts to expedite legislation were sometimes overruled by the House. For example, when the House wanted to avoid a controversial pay raise bill, it voted to kill the rule, refusing, in effect, to even consider the substance of the bill.

The Discharge Petition. The House has a general remedy for dilatory committee tactics. Any bill which has been in committee for longer than thirty days can be brought directly to the floor when a majority of members sign a petition to discharge it. The fact that it is not done very often suggests both respect for the prerogatives of the committee and the possibility that committees accused of bottling up legislation are usually in fairly close accord to the wishes of the House. When it appears that a discharge petition might be successful, the offending committee will usually get the bill moving by itself.

Some Congressional Styles

Within the institutional framework, a member of Congress can choose from among different styles of behavior. For a House member, a wide variety of approaches is possible. In the Senate, a member has two basic choices: He can be an insider or an outsider.

The Inner Club.   Some authorities doubt whether there really is an inner club in the Senate. It may just be a myth perpetuated by Lyndon Johnson to conceal and rationalize his manipulations when he was the majority leader, a "polite explanation for the exercise of his own discretion [Polsby, p. 69]." William S. White (1956) and Donald R. Matthews (1960) have both portrayed the Senate insider as an effective legislator who gets that way by observing the norms of the Senate, defending its institutions, proceeding slowly to assert himself. Ralph K. Huitt (1961), who pointed out the advantages of the outsider role in a case study of Sen. William Proxmire, Democrat of Wisconsin, has summed the portrait of the insider:

> He is courteous to a fault in his relations with his colleagues, not allowing political disagreements to affect his personal feelings. He is always ready to help another senator when he can, and he expects to be repaid in kind. More than anything else, he is a Senate man, proud of the institution and ready to defend its traditions and prerequisites against all outsiders. He is a legislative workhorse who specializes in one or two policy areas. . . . He has a deep respect for the rights of others . . . the senator as an ideal type is a man of accommodation who knows that "you have to go along to get along"; he is a conservative, institutional man, slow to change what he has mastered at the expense of so much time and patience [pp. 566–567].

According to Matthews, the insider is measurably more effective in getting legislation passed than someone who does not take this slow, gentlemanly route. Huitt argues, however, that other things are as important as getting one's bills passed. Proxmire spent the first half of his first full session (he was elected in 1957 to fill the unexpired term of the late Joseph McCarthy) playing by the rules. Then he got tired of that and began to do what came more naturally. He spoke frequently and immodestly. He offered amendments to a bill outside his specialty and pressed them to a vote. He even filibustered. All this was in support of lost causes. He got himself frozen out of the inner club.

Huitt, who was Proxmire's legislative assistant at the time, thought it worked out pretty well. Wisconsin voters approved his independent role. His fellow senators did not stop speaking to him. And he was at least getting attention for views which might otherwise not have surfaced. One of the functions of Congress, Huitt suggests, "might be to provide catharsis for fringe views which never will prevail." A gadfly like Proxmire, though an irritant in the Senate, "may serve as the psychological representative of all the Outsiders in the great society [p. 575]."

The insider-outsider division in the Senate has begun to erode recently. Every senator is a celebrity in his own right, and none is completely ineffective. The conformists may do better in getting committee assignments and leadership posts, and bills that they sponsor may have a

Senator Proxmire: For fringe views, a catharsis. (*United Press International.*)

better chance of getting passed. But there is more to legislative effectiveness than that. The role each senator plays is related not only to his personality but to the specific situations in which he finds himself. As Rieselbach (1973) has noted, each must choose for himself "the conditions under which he feels it necessary to behave in ways that his colleagues will not approve [p. 149]."

Taking Care of the District.   "Need help? Call Congressman Ayres." That was a message often seen on billboards in Akron, Ohio, when Rep. William H. Ayres was in Congress from 1951 to 1971. A Republican in a normally Democratic district, he stayed in office all that time by concentrating on the direct-service functions of a congressman. The number and kinds of contacts an ordinary citizen has with his government keep growing: a Social Security check is lost, a relative in the old country can't get a visa, a son is in trouble with the Army. Charles L. Clapp (1963) quotes a freshman House member:

> When I first came here, I was dumbfounded by the number of requests. I was inclined to think I didn't have time to take care of them, and that I would have no time for legislation . . . I now realize that one of my most important functions is to help these people. If they are entitled to go through a door they cannot find, it is my job to locate that door so they can go through [p. 54].

One of the congressmen interviewed by Clapp estimated that some members spent 90 percent of their time on "case work," as direct service to constituents is called. John S. Saloma III (1969) found in a sample survey that a more typical figure is 9 percent of the member's time and 19 percent of his staff's time spent on case work. When answering mail, receiving visitors, and responding to requests for information are included, service to constituents takes 28 percent of a member's time, on the average, and 41 percent of staff time. But there is a good deal of deviation around that average. A member who makes servicing his district his main preoccupation may have no time left for other congressional roles. A Ralph Nader study group (Green, Fallows, and Zwick, 1972) offered this description of Rep. William Barrett, Pennsylvania Democrat, as an example of a nearly full-time caseworker:

> He flies back to his district *every night* from Washington to hold office hours from 9 P.M. to 1 A.M. At the corner of 24th and Wharton Streets in south Philadelphia, in the shabby office of a building he owns, Barrett sometimes sees as many as 750 people a week "on marital matters, child welfare, foreclosures, evictions—everything that affects the human person," he says. For this, his constituents call him "the Reverend" and the night sessions "the confessional [p. 216]."

Developing a Specialty.   On the House side, one route to power, if not to prominence, is to learn more about one thing than anybody else.

Information is a valuable commodity in Congress, and it is unevenly distributed. Members who don't know about a particular subject tend to be guided by those who do. The combination of subject expertise and a subcommittee chairmanship can ensure a virtual veto power in a special field. For example, Paul Rogers, a Florida congressman of little national reputation, was cited by the Nader group as the key specialist on health. Nearly all legislation dealing with health must go through his Subcommittee on Public Health and Environment of the Committee on Interstate and Foreign Commerce.

The Distribution of Power

In both houses, the key positions are those of committee chairmen, majority and minority party leaders, and their assistants, or "whips." In addition, the Speaker of the House can, depending on his energy and aggressiveness, wield a good deal of personal influence aside from his formal power to interpret the rules, recognize participants in debate, and refer bills to committees. There is no comparable position in the Senate, whose presiding office is the relatively powerless Vice President of the United States. The Vice President normally yields the chair to the president pro tempore (for the time being) of the Senate, who, because the work is dull and unrewarding, generally finds a junior member to sit in the presiding officer's chair for him. In the less structured atmosphere of the Senate, the rulings of the chair are seldom crucial, and the post of president pro tem serves merely to honor the senior member who holds it.

To the extent that power is concentrated in a relatively few members, the representativeness of Congress is impaired. There would be more balanced representation over a period of time if the leadership positions changed hands more often. But turnover in Congress is quite low. Once elected, a member tends to keep winning reelection. Those states and districts where there is competition and turnover lose out in the contest for the committee chairmanships because of the seniority system. And they are disadvantaged in seeking the other leadership jobs because seniority is a strong factor, although not necessarily the deciding one.

On the other hand, there may be no inherent virtue in coming from a competitive district. A study by Roger Davidson (1969) suggests that the broadest national perspective tends to come from the safe-seat members. Freed from voter pressure to look after district interests, they can afford to develop a national orientation.

REFORM

Overcoming Sluggishness

The main complaint about Congress is that it does not move very fast to do the things that need to be done. In calmer days, Congress was often able to finish its year's work by summer, and members had time left over for renewing their home ties. The Legislative Reorganization Act of 1970 reflects some nostalgia for this situation by requiring that the Senate and House adjourn by July 31 of each year "unless otherwise provided by the Congress." But one session still runs up against another, with much important legislation crowded into the frantic last days. Of 498 bills reported out of committees in the House in the second session of the Ninety-second Congress in 1972, 80 came in the final 12 days. The session failed to act at all on appropriations for foreign aid and the departments of Labor and Health, Education, and Welfare. Much of the early time of a new Congress is taken up with internal organization. House Speaker Carl Albert complained in 1973 that "the leadership spends the first few months of almost every session contacting committee after committee, week after week, literally bird-dogging for enough bills to give the House a reasonably respectable program for three or four days a week [Russell, 1973]."

But there is more to the pressures for reform than that. Behind every desire for a procedural change, there is usually a specific policy goal. Because Presidents have generally been more liberal than Congress, liberals have favored reforms which would remove the power of minorities to block congressional action so that the President's program could speed through unhindered. Conservatives have wanted to preserve the power of the minority to block action, but they have also favored reforms that would improve the efficiency of Congress. A more efficient Congress, they reason, could initiate its own programs in competition with the liberal executive.

This traditional alignment began to shift as a result of events during the Johnson and Nixon administrations when executive initiatives threatened to encroach on legislative functions. Liberals found that Congress can be a conserver of minority interests, a protector of domestic welfare programs, a guardian of civil liberties, and a check on abusive use of the President's military powers. And conservatives found that White House-initiated legislation they badly wanted could be blocked by stubborn liberal committee chairmen, as when Rep. Emanuel Cellar turned back repressive anticrime legislation while he was chairman of the House Judiciary Committee.

Help-the-President Reforms

Reforms that would help the President get his programs through Congress range from major structural overhaul to removal of petty sticking points. Some examples:

A Four-Year House Term.   With their terms doubled in length, House members would be freer of pressure from the electorate, including interest groups and campaign contributors. If always elected in presidential years, they would depend more on the presidential coattails and, ultimately, on the President's leadership. This dependence would strengthen the President's hand in his dealings with Congress.

Centralized National Parties. If parties were better organized, they could keep their officeholders united behind a single program. A party's nonloyalists in Congress could be punished by being denied committee chairmanships or leadership positions. Congress and the President would work more closely together, and the party would get the blame or the credit for what happened (American Political Science Association, 1950; Kirkpatrick, 1971).

Weakened Committee Chairmen. Even when the committee membership can overrule the chairman, he has enough other powers to make members reluctant to do so because of the risk that he might retaliate. Therefore there would have to be a wholesale reduction of the prerequisites of the chair if the committees are to be made more democratic.

The Twenty-one-Day Rule. In 1949–1951 and 1965–1967, the House made it possible to bypass an obstructionist Rules Committee after the committee had sat on legislation for twenty-one days. In the more recent version of the twenty-one-day rule, the Speaker could recognize a committee chairman for the purpose of placing a bill before the House if the bill had been before the Rules Committee for twenty-one days without action. This procedure was used to bypass a Rules Committee roadblock only infrequently—eight times in 1965–1967. The more amenable Rules Committee of recent years has removed pressure for reviving the twenty-one-day rule.

An Easier Discharge Petition. Fewer bills would get stuck in committee if the number of signatures required for a discharge petition (see page 314) were reduced from 218 to 150 or some other number less than a majority.

Limitation of Debate in the Senate. Lowering the vote required for cloture from two-thirds to a simple majority would kill the danger of a filibuster. Sen. Joseph Clark, Republican of Pennsylvania, has proposed that no senator be allowed to talk for more than two hours unless he is the floor manager for a bill or has unanimous consent.

Fight-the-President Reforms

Reformers who want to strengthen Congress to counterbalance the President have historically been conservative, and this has led to a dilemma. Strengthening Congress usually means making it more efficient, improving its ability to act. But conservative reformers don't want to end the power of minorities to slow things down. A sampling of their proposals follows:

Better Information Resources. The executive branch, with its computers and its budgeting and systems analysts, has a huge advantage over Congress in the technology of decision making. One way for Congress to try to match it would be by increasing the staff size for both members and committees and developing modern information retrieval and analysis methods.

A Smaller Bureaucracy. One source of congressional frustration is the size of modern government. If federal programs could be reduced to a more manageable number, Congress would be in a better position to keep track of what goes on in implementing legislation.

Coordination of the Budget. A return to the ill-fated Omnibus Appropriations bill, in which expenditures are voted on as a single package rather than on a piecemeal basis, would help Congress to arrange priorities and make expenditures match income. The 1974 Budget Reform Act, taking effect in 1976, gave Congress new budgetary tools by creating budget committees in both houses, providing more information and staff expertise, and setting up a joint Congressional Office of the Budget to match the executive branch's Office of Management and Budget.

"Radical Incrementalism." Prof. Aaron Wildavsky (1966) has suggested that Congress stop trying to review every budget item every year and concentrate instead on small increments where radical change is needed. Most items could continue from year to year at the same level. This would leave Congress free to think more deeply about the most serious problems. By looking at a few things in detail, Congress would learn enough to make major change where it is warranted.

Executive Liaison Officers. The executive agencies all have legislative liaison officers who respond to congressional inquiries and generally try to smooth the agency's relations with Capitol Hill. If the liaison men could stay where they are but switch to the congressional payroll, they could become the eyes and ears of the legislature and help Congress keep the executive branch under control (de Grazia, 1966).

Elections as a Tool of Reform
Whether making Congress move faster also makes it better depends in large degree on how you feel about the policy outputs that are at stake. Speed of response and quality of response are not the same thing. Sometimes Congress seems to be frustrating a very clear public will by moving as slowly as it does. But the slowness can improve the quality of its response to that will by providing time for a wide variety of interests to be heard and considered. Calls for faster action often assume a public consensus that

either does not exist or would prove to be fleeting as more knowledge became available. Law making is a process of *conflict resolution*. The object is not only to pass the right law but to get the job done in a way that will bring the law the maximum amount of public acceptance and support. A hasty job can sacrifice these qualities. The Economic Opportunity Act of 1964 might have enjoyed a better fate if more time had gone into its framing and enactment. If it had gained the support of the local elites—who eventually demolished the program through the Nixon administration—the outcome might have been much different.

Organizational arrangements are not politically neutral. Each has advantages or disadvantages for different groups. Abstract arguments for specific reforms often mask the desire to use the reform to gain a specific policy output. Most reform proposals therefore have the disadvantage of being *time bound*. It is easy to see in a specific situation how one little rule change would save a desirable bill. But in another situation at another time, that same rule change might allow passage of a bill that is seen as highly undesirable. Today's reform easily becomes tomorrow's corruption.

One solution to this dilemma is simply to stop trying to change the output by tinkering with the processing machinery; instead, change the input by electing different men and women to Congress. It is easy to forget that Congress does what it does, not only because of what it is as defined by its rules but because of the people who sit in it. They are not the helpless victims of the rules. The power of individual members, while uneven, determines the end product. Changing the members can change the product.

Changes made through the election process are often slow, but they can work dramatically, as was demonstrated in the flood of legislation that followed the Democratic sweep of 1964. That was a special situation caused by a counterproductive Republican presidential campaign, but the 1964 Democratic landslide shows what a difference a change in personnel can make. A decade later another specific situation, created by the aftermath of Watergate and economic recession, demonstrated again the potential for reform through the ballot box. The 1974 congressional elections secured for Democrats control of three-fifths of the Senate and two-thirds of the House of Representatives without the help of presidential coattails as they had in 1936 and 1964. Even before the Ninety-fourth Congress (1975–1977) began, the Democratic majority adopted measures to reform its leadership structure by eroding the power of some committee chairmen and by giving junior members a greater voice on important committees.

If the public were to become sufficiently interested in Congress to manipulate it at the ballot box, there might be a corresponding change within the institution. If more seats were contested and turnover increased so that a member's expected tenure were no more than two or three terms, members might have much less interest in strict adherence to the seniority rule. Effects of the seniority system would be diminished without any

President Johnson with
Cabinet: Telephone or
mail would have been as
useful. (*United Press International.*)

the Senate in the negotiating stage. It did not work, and since then there has
been a divison of labor: The President negotiates a treaty and the Senate
ratifies or rejects it.

Appointments. The President nominates ambassadors, judges, and "officers of the United States" subject to the advice and consent of the Senate.
Congress may give the President exclusive appointive power where "inferior officers" are concerned, but it seldom yields its important check on
executive appointments. Even second lieutenants are confirmed by the
Senate. In President Nixon's first year in office, the Senate approved 72,635
presidential nominations. Members of the President's immediate staff are
not subject to Senate approval, but those in statuatory positions in the
Executive Office of the President—such as the director of the Office of
Management and Budget or the director of the Office of Economic
Opportunity—are scrutinized by the Senate.

The House of Representatives is consulted in only one kind of
presidential appointment: one to fill a vacancy in the office of the Vice
President. Authors of the Twenty-fifth Amendment required approval of
both houses of Congress in order to give the appointment as broad a base as
possible, because the President and the Vice President are the only officials
who are normally elected by all the people.

Reporting on the State of the Union. The President is required to report to Congress on the state of the Union "from time to time" and recommend legislation. By custom, the state of the union message comes early in the year, usually in a formal address to a joint session of Congress. Sometimes he sends it in writing. The state of the union message will usually cover the general outlines of the President's legislative program, but the specifics follow later in a series of special messages, including draft copies of the laws he would like enacted.

Special Sessions of Congress. A President may call a special session of either or both houses of Congress "on extraordinary occasions." He may also adjourn Congress if the two houses cannot agree on a time of adjournment. A call for a special session was a source of considerable dramatic effect in times when Congress was not in session the year around. In recent years, there has been no need to exercise this constitutional authority. In 1963, President Johnson, anxious to establish leadership, invoked his authority as chief of party to call the House of Representatives back from a Christmas holiday leave. On Christmas Eve, the House yielded to Johnson and approved a controversial measure to permit wheat sale on credit to the Soviet Union. At that moment, wrote Johnson (1971), power "began flowing back to the White House [p. 40]."

No President has exercised the power to shut Congress down.

Receiving Ambassadors. Here the Constitution bestows an important initiative on the President in the conduct of foreign relations. Receiving ambassadors is more than a ceremonial duty: it amounts to the power of granting or withholding diplomatic recognition of a foreign government. In the international community, diplomatic recognition by a major power can be an important factor in establishing the legitimacy of a new regime.

Executor of the Laws. Strong Presidents have taken the constitutional requirement that they "take care that the laws be faithfully executed" to be a general grant of implied power. When such power has been asserted, Congress has often been careful to limit it with specific legislation. For example, Lincoln seized the telegraph and railroad lines between Baltimore and Washington in 1861 without any specific authority to do so. In 1862, Congress passed an act to authorize such seizures, spelling out the circumstances when they would be permissible. In 1973, the clause was cited by President Nixon's legal counsel as the basis for a general authority to impound, i.e., not spend, funds appropriated by Congress. Federal courts held that no such broad power existed.

What Really Happens

The formal powers do not, of course, fully describe what the Presidency is all about. The informal powers which Presidents have assumed make it a much more lively and powerful institution than the Founders envisioned. One way of viewing the Presidency more fully is to examine the various roles which recent holders of the office have played. Such an examination is subject to the ambiguities of classification. Clinton Rossiter (1956) counted ten presidential roles. Others have found as many as forty-three (Bailey, 1966).

In Rossiter's imagery, the ten-hatted President is Chief of State, Chief Executive, leader of foreign policy, Commander in Chief of the Armed Forces, chief legislator, chief of party, voice of the people, protector of peace, manager of prosperity, and leader of the world's free nations. But it is possible to know all that and still be in the dark about what the Presidency is and does. Thomas E. Cronin (1970) provides insight when he looks at the Presidency not in terms of the many hats the President wears but with a view of the job's three "overriding functions." These are:

1   To recast the nation's policy agenda—which suffers from a chronic tendency to lag behind changes in social need—and bring it up to date

2   To serve as a "symbolic affirmation" of our basic national values

3   To make the machinery of government move to carry out his programs as well as those he has inherited from his predecessors

Most discussions of the problems of the Presidency end up, sooner or later, focusing on what Cronin calls "the slippage and gap" between the definition and the implementation of the national agenda (p. 574). The machinery does move, but its main propellant is inertia.[1] To accelerate it or to get it to change direction in order to cope with current needs requires the imposition of an outside force. It is the President's job to be that outside force. It isn't easy.

President Kennedy (1963) summed the difficulties in a television interview after nearly two years in office:

> . . . the problems are more difficult than I had imagined them to be. The responsibilities placed on the United States are greater than I imagined them to be, and there are greater limitations upon our ability to bring about a favorable result than I had imagined them to be. And I think that is probably true of anyone who becomes President, because there is such a difference between those who advise or speak or legislate, and between the man who must select from the various alternatives proposed and say that this shall be the policy of the United States [p. 889].

---

[1]Parallel axioms in the physical sciences and the social sciences are rare and worthy of being cherished when we find them. Newton's First Law of Motion defines inertia: It is the property of matter by which a body in motion continues in motion, at the same velocity and in the same direction, until acted upon by an outside force.

"The probabilities of power," Richard E. Neustadt (1960) has said, "do not derive from the literary theory of the Constitution [p. 43]." They derive instead from organizational and situational factors. A powerful President is one who can evaluate current reality, find the levers that will make things happen, and manipulate them toward his desired ends. Some of these levers are in the organizations he commands. A President operates as head of his party, as the top command figure over the executive bureaucracy, and as the chief spokesman for his party's representatives in Congress. Channeling the resources and support of these groups is one way of gaining and exercising power. The President's ability to persuade is also important. Neustadt quotes Truman on this point: "I sit here all day trying to persuade people to do the things they ought to have sense enough to do without my persuading them. . . . That's all the powers of the President amount to [pp. 9–10]."

The President's constitutional powers can, of course, be used as instruments of persuasion. So can the symbolic value of the office. In Neustadt's analysis, presidential power flows from three interacting sources:

1   The self-preservation drive of officeholders. This is a key motivating factor in government (or any large organization). The President can invoke the symbolic and real powers of his office to persuade other officeholders that what he wants them to do is what their own responsibilities and interests require them to do.

2   The expectation that the President is able and willing to use the advantages which lesser officeholders think he has.

3   The estimates of how the general public (or the relevant-issue publics) will react if the other government elites do what the President wants them to do.

"In short," says Neustadt, "his power is the product of his vantage points in government, together with his reputation in the Washington community and his prestige outside [p. 179]."

When a President goes on national television to explain an order he has just given or is about to give, explaining it to the public is only one of the purposes he has in mind. He is also trying to generate support and to make sure that the order is carried out. Widely publicized orders are more likely to be obeyed. Neustadt, whose primer on presidential power was carefully read by President Kennedy, lists four other conditions necessary to ensure obedience to the President: The fact that the President is involved directly in the problem must be clear. His order itself must be unambiguous. The persons who receive the order must have everything they need to carry it out. And they must be sure of the President's authority to issue the order.

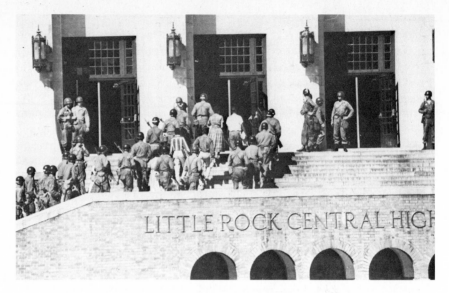

The National Guard in Little Rock, 1957: Widely publicized orders are more likely to be obeyed. (*United Press International*.)

If any one of these factors is absent, Neustadt warns, "the chances are that mere command will not produce compliance [p. 19]." Two examples of presidential orders that met that test are Eisenhower's sending the 101st Airborne Division to integrate Central High School in Little Rock in 1957 and Truman's firing of General Douglas MacArthur as Commander of the Armed Forces in the Far East in 1951. These directives were obeyed with exceptional dispatch.

But many tasks that need doing in the government cannot be handled so decisively. Many presidential orders have to be ambiguous, cannot be made public, and do not have his direct involvement. There are not enough hours in the day for the President to become directly involved in every executive action. And so the outside force needed to overcome bureaucratic inertia is often not there. Jonathan Daniels (1946), who served on Franklin Roosevelt's staff, explained the problem of getting cabinet members to carry out a President's wishes:

Half of a President's suggestions, which theoretically carry the weight of orders, can be safely forgotten by a Cabinet member. And if the President asks about a suggestion a second time, he can be told that it is being investigated. If he asks a third time, a wise Cabinet officer will give him at least part of what he suggests. But only occasionally, except about the most important matters, do Presidents ever get around to asking three times [pp. 31–32].

And Roosevelt himself once compared the problem of effecting a change in the Navy Department to punching a feather bed. "You punch it with your right and you punch it with your left until you are finally exhausted, and then you find the damn bed just as it was before you started punching [Eccles, 1951, p. 336]."

One cause of the Watergate fiasco may have been President Nixon's frustration at not being able to get the existing intelligence and law enforcement agencies to do his bidding. This frustration led to the creation of an intelligence force in the White House staff. The members of this force were relative amateurs, they broke the law, and they got caught.

Coping with Congress

The failure of Congress to organize itself to deal with complex and rapid change has pushed the President toward the role of chief legislator. After Lincoln and before Theodore Roosevelt, the President's legislative role was minor. In 1893, a Washington correspondent wrote of presidential attempts to influence legislation: "His message is treated always as a perfunctory document and while it is regularly and respectfully referred to the proper committees for consideration, it is very rare that any suggestion made by the Executive has any practical result [*Congressional Quarterly,* 1971, p. 576]." Roosevelt seized the legislative initiative with his "Square Deal," the first formal legislative program ever submitted to Congress by a President. After him, Woodrow Wilson, Franklin D. Roosevelt, and all the post-World War II Presidents took the legislative initiative, with Wilson, Roosevelt, and Lyndon Johnson being the most successful. A number of tactics have evolved for getting what a President wants out of Congress.

Direct Contact.   The symbolic value of the office is so great that the President can get much of what he wants simply by asking for it. "A private breakfast, a walk in the White House rose garden, an intimate conference—all duly and widely reported in the press—give a man a sense of importance that not only may flatter his ego but also may remind him of his responsibilities as a national legislator, as a trustee of the common weal," says Nelson Polsby (1971). "Congressmen and Senators generally find it hard to say no directly to the President of the United States, especially when he asks them nicely [pp. 137–138]."

Legislative Liaison.   Presidents since Eisenhower have had full-time White House lobbyists at work lining up votes for White House-sponsored

> We have no discipline in this bureaucracy. We never fire anybody. We never reprimand anybody. We never demote anybody. We always promote the sons-of-bitches that kick us in the ass.
>
> —Richard M. Nixon, 1970

A President's Frustration

legislation. Eisenhower's congressional liaison man was Bryce Harlow, who also served in the Nixon administration. Kennedy had a staff of lobbyists under his former campaign manager, Lawrence F. O'Brien, whose White House title was special assistant for congressional affairs. The aggressiveness of this staff proved disquieting to some of the members. Meg Greenfield (1962) wrote about one congressman who cited "the case of a young liaison man, the very sight of whom at the cloakroom door, he claims, is enough to cost the administration twenty-five votes. Under questioning, he lowered the figure to three, but this time he seemed serious [p. 30]."

The Public Opinion Backfire. If a member of Congress does not agree that what the President wants is also in his own best interests, the President is in a position to change that situation by going directly to the voters to put pressure on Congress. The presidential press conference can be used in this way, and John F. Kennedy excelled in its use with frequent, televised news conferences held in the State Department auditorium. Franklin Roosevelt made masterful use of radio with the intimate format of his "fireside chats." President Nixon used television for major announcements and appeals and radio for more routine messages. His press conferences were infrequent. In contrast, President Ford opened his administration with a promise to hold press conferences often.

The Nixon administration made an attempt to gain some central control of the public information operations of the various departments. When Mr. Nixon was seeking to cut back government spending on a variety of social and welfare programs, departmental information specialists were directed to dig out "horror stories" about failures in the application of the affected programs. This attempt to orchestrate government press agentry to fan a public opinion backfire was not notably successful and was probably counterproductive. Blatant attempts to manipulate public opinion may be resented. In 1938, when President Roosevelt sought to purge Democrat members of Congress who failed to support his program for enlarging the Supreme Court, his targets, in most cases, got reelected. By calling attention to their opposition, Roosevelt may have helped them.

The Veto Threat. An act of Congress becomes law when it is signed by the President. If he does not sign, it becomes law anyway after ten days unless he vetoes it.[2] Overriding a veto requires a two-thirds vote of both houses, which is difficult to muster. Nixon and Eisenhower, dealing with Democratic Congresses which sometimes sought a larger federal role in solving social problems than they did, used the veto or the threat of a veto

[2]If Congress should adjourn during the ten-day period and the President does not sign the bill, it dies. This is called a *pocket veto*. Its strategic advantage for the President is that Congress can't do anything about it.

to narrow the scope of Democratic programs. So did President Ford, who vetoed two spending bills in his first week in office. The congressional strategy to counter a veto threat is to package the legislation so that something the President badly wants is in the same bill as the thing he doesn't want. Advocates of a stronger Presidency have proposed a constitutional amendment to give him the *item veto,* which is the power (held by some state governors) to veto parts of a bill without sacrificing the remainder.

Impoundment of Funds.   Although the tactic is of dubious legality, some Presidents have achieved the effect of an item veto by impounding —refusing to spend—money which Congress has appropriated. In 1949, President Truman asked for money for a forty-eight-group Air Force. Airpower advocates in Congress were successful in getting an appropriation enacted for a fifty-eight-group Air Force. Truman refused to spend the money for the extra ten groups. President Nixon used impoundment in a major effort to roll back programs inherited from previous administrations. For example, in 1972 Congress voted $6 billion to help states clean up water pollution. President Nixon vetoed the bill. Congress overrode the veto. He then refused to spend the money.

Administration impoundment of pollution, highway, and antipoverty funds was challenged in a series of court cases in 1972 and 1973; federal courts in most cases ordered the money released. The administration's argument that the President's power to "take care that the laws be faithfully executed" amounted to a general grant of authority to withhold spending was not sustained. In the Congressional Budget and Impoundment Control Act of 1974, Congress provided procedures to counter presidential attempts to postpone expenditures or to reduce spending or terminate programs by refusing to spend the money. If a President refuses to comply with a congressional action to overrule an impoundment, the comptroller general may seek a court order requiring the President to spend the money.

Patronage and Preferment.   Although most federal jobs are now in the Civil Service system and most contracts are awarded by competitive bidding, there is still some room for administrative discretion; jobs and contracts can be given as rewards for members of Congress who are supporters of the President's program. Other weapons are the location of federal installations and the distribution of grants under special programs. When the first grants were announced under the Johnson administration's Model Cities program, there was a significant correlation between the success of certain cities in getting the early money and previous favorable action by their congressmen in the critical legislative battles to enact the program. No explicit deals need be made. A skilled executive merely plays upon hopes and expectations for preferment.

The Majesty and the Glory

As the foregoing enumeration indicates, the President's power to persuade has only a narrow tangible base. Most of it stems from the symbolic standing of the office. When the President is obeyed, it is often not because of his actual powers but because of his perceived standing and legitimacy as the elected chief of all the people. This standing makes him a natural reference point in the process of resolving major conflicts among groups. Those with competing demands are likely to give weight to a presidential proposal for a settlement simply because it is expected of them, and they expect one another to defer to the President.

The importance of the President's perceived standing is illustrated by the fate of President Nixon in 1973. After he was elected by a landslide in 1972, it was assumed that this expression by the voters amounted to a mandate to exercise extraordinary powers. When he ended United States military participation in the Vietnam war, the President's standing in the polls was relatively high, and he assumed that he could safely ignore Congress and go his own way. Some observers feared that his popularity and power would transform the Presidency into a monarchy. But in the next nine months, the disclosures associated with the Watergate burglary and subsequent coverup dropped his rate of approval among the electorate from 60 percent to only 27 percent (Gallup, 1974). The President became deferential in his dealings with members of Congress, and fears of a monarchy began to be replaced by fears that the Presidency had become weakened and disorganized to the point of impotence.

This reversal may have been no more than an isolated incident involving only one President, but it served to raise fresh doubts about the wisdom of conferring too much awe and respect upon the office. Barbara W. Tuchman (1973) argued for restructuring the Presidency into something more like a professional managerial job. But she noted that such a step would fail to

> . . . satisfy the American craving for a father-image or hero or superstar. The only solution I can see to that problem would be to install a dynastic family in the White House for ceremonial purposes or focus the craving entirely upon the entertainment world, or else to grow up [p. 37].

There were still some politicians who thought it was necessary to continue to believe in and even revere the Presidency at all costs, no matter what perceptual distortions were required. Former Secretary of Defense Melvin Laird, later a White House counsel, declared that if the President himself were involved in the criminal activity, it would be better not to know. But this view was not widely shared; the tendency to view the office in a new light, which had begun slowly after the death of President Kennedy, was accelerated. Of all the fading cliches of American political folklore, one in particular no longer seemed tenable: the belief that ordinary men could be made transcendent by the mystical aura of the office and acquire new wisdom and character. Bill Moyers (1973), a member of the Johnson White House staff, used the occasion of the Nixon scandals to point out that it is not necessarily so:

> In one sense [the Presidency] is nothing but an office, with chairs, desks, carpets, telephones, and marks in the floor left by Dwight Eisenhower's golf shoes as he stalked out to the putting green on the south lawn. Nothing there, not even the pictures of the few previous occupants who deserve to be called great, will suddenly nullify old habits or endow a man with virtues he never had.

President Ford: A monarch wouldn't fix breakfast.(*Wide World Photos.*)

In another sense, the Presidency is a depository of tradition and legal power. But even in this it is neutral. It will shrink to fit the most mendacious soul or grow to accommodate the most generous. The trappings of the office may enable a man to hide his petty faults (although in the long run I doubt it), but they contain no mystical power to change his character. A man given to extravagance, as Lyndon Johnson was, will go right on doing everything in excess. A man like Richard Nixon, who all his life played to win, isn't suddenly going to insist that his colleagues memorize Robert's Rules of Order [p. 43].

The demythologizing of the presidency was assisted by the folksy, down-home style of President Ford. Television viewers and newspaper readers saw him taking his own notes at meetings with economic advisors, and even fixing his own breakfast—something no monarch would do. The symbolic value of the Presidency, then, like nearly everything else about it, is neither more nor less than what the existing holder of the job is able to make it.

STAFFING AND STRUCTURE

The Swelling of the Presidency

Traditional organizational charts show the President at the top of a pyramid with lines leading to each of the cabinet departments, implying a clearcut chain of command from the President to the lowliest clerk. Such a chart is consistent with one of the main axioms of public administration: that an executive's "span of control" is limited and he loses effectiveness when he has more than about a dozen people reporting to him. In 1973 there were eleven departments: Agriculture; Commerce; Defense; Health, Education, and Welfare; Housing and Urban Development; Interior; Justice; Labor; State; Transportation; and Treasury. And so the system would seem, on paper, workable. And it might be if all the President had to do were to oversee those eleven departments. But he must also deal with more than forty independent agencies. And he is, it will be remembered, multihatted and has more to do than be Chief Executive. To help him do all the things a President is expected to do, a much more complicated system of organization has been developed. The standard pyramid-shaped organizational chart is no longer adequate. A better physical representation would be three-dimensional and many-layered, like an onion.

At the center of the onion is the President. Immediately surrounding him is his personal staff, whose membership divides roughly into six separate functions. First and foremost, he needs someone to guard the door to his office, deciding who to let in and who to keep out. He needs a political adviser to consult on questions of patronage and preferment, a legislative liaison person, a public relations operator to orchestrate his exposure to the outside world, advisers on substantive domestic and foreign policy questions, and miscellaneous counsels and consultants including a legal adviser. Each of these functions is filled not by one person but by a staff. In the Nixon White House, for example, the public relations function was filled by some 100 persons, including a communications director and, a press secretary—both of whom had assistants and deputies—as well as speech writers and people to make travel arrangements for reporters following the President and to fill other obscure specialties.

Lyndon Johnson had a staff photographer whose sole duty was to follow him around, snapping pictures of the presidential countenance. (Some 250,000 negatives are in the Johnson archive in Texas.)

Beyond the immediate White House staff is the Executive Office of the President, a group of specialized agencies which provides both substantive advice and coordination of executive branch activities. It includes the Office of Management and Budget, the National Security Council, the Council of Economic Advisers, the Central Intelligence Agency, the Office of the Special Representative for Trade Negotiations, and the Council on Environmental Quality. This is just a sampling of more than a dozen agencies attached to the Presidency.

Outside this structure, but orbiting around and through it, is a large scattering of ad hoc advisory groups and individuals. This array includes the President's personal friends and political allies whom he may consult informally from time to time. It also includes advisory and special study commissions both short and long term, interagency committees put together to try to keep the government from working at cross-purposes with itself, private consultants who are in the business of providing technical advice, and special conferences, such as the White House Conference on Children and Youth, held, by custom, every ten years.

Put it together, and you find that the White House itself is a bureaucracy nearly the size of the State Department. Thomas E. Cronin (1973) estimated its size at the start of Nixon's second term at between 5,000 and 6,000 people, not counting the CIA which has another 15,000. Between 1954 and 1971, the White House staff grew from 166 to 600 and the Executive Office of the President (again, excluding the CIA) grew from 1,175 to 5,395. "The Presidential Establishment," said Cronin, "has become, in effect, a whole layer of government between the President and the Cabinet, and it often stands above the Cabinet in terms of influence with the President [p. 31]."

How the Presidential Establishment Evolved

The onion analogy is not quite accurate because the layers are not clearly separated and there are shifting tunnels, sanctuaries, and lines of communication through and around the separate layers. Each administration has its own peculiar configuration. The last President to write all his own speeches was Herbert Hoover, and that was unusual even in his relatively uncomplicated time. "The very fact that he had a deep aversion to ghostwritten speeches," says his biographer, Eugene Lyons (1964), "seemed to the conventional politician as old-fashioned as his collars. . . . But his every address, article, or book . . . was the product of his own mind and hands [p. 193]." He also had the habit of involving himself in administrative detail. "One admires Hoover's industry," says Neustadt (1960), "but not his judgment of what to take upon himself and what to leave to others [p. 214]."

Jostling with Roosevelt.   The modern framework for White House staffing was an innovation of Franklin D. Roosevelt. Late in his first term, he appointed a Committee on Administration Management, known as the Brownlow Committee, after its chairman, Louis Brownlow. Out of its report grew Executive Order 8248 of September 8, 1939, the beginning of the institutionalized Presidency. It created the Executive Office. Roosevelt himself was careful, by acting as his own staff director, to maintain personal control of what went on in the White House. Nevertheless, he set in motion the process of growth so that presidential power has grown ever more diffuse. In Neustadt's (1963) words, "the phrase 'this is the White House calling' has less meaning every decade [p. 861]."

Roosevelt drew a critical distinction between his personal staff and the institutional staff. While he was in office, anyone who did say, "This is the White House calling" was either the President himself or somebody acting "intimately and immediately" for him. Tasks which did not require direct presidential involvement were staffed outside the White House itself. Physically, the separation remains. The Executive Office of the President is now concentrated behind the 900 doric columns of the former State, War, and Navy Building next door to the White House and in the two brick high-rise office buildings overlooking Lafayette Square across the street.

A presidential assistant who becomes known as the leading White House expert in a substantive policy area can quickly develop a power base of his own. Roosevelt wanted to stay personally in charge, and he did it by dividing the staff work along procedural rather than substantive lines. No one became a subject-matter specialist. "These men knew what their jobs were, but they could not do them without watching, checking, jostling one another. Roosevelt liked it so . . . he positively encouraged them to jostle [Neustadt, 1963, p. 857]." The perpetual ambiguity was Roosevelt's way of staying in charge. As the ultimate resolver of conflict, he remained the ultimate decisionmaker. And, during the prewar years, he was careful never to have more of these general-purpose staff persons than he could supervise himself.

Another feature of the Roosevelt White House was a fluid operating style that kept a number of alternative channels of information open so that he did not risk the limited view of the world that might be filtered through the White House staff:

Herbert Hoover: His own mind and hands. (*Eugene Smith, Black Star.*)

He also used Executive Office aides, personal friends, idea-men or technicians down in the bureaucracy, old Navy hands, old New York hands, experts from private life, Cabinet officers, "Little Cabinet" officers, diplomats, relatives —especially his wife—toward the end, his daughter—as supplementary eyes and ears and manpower. He often used these "outsiders" to check or duplicate the work of White House staff, or to probe into spheres where White House aides should not be seen, or to look into things he guessed his staff would be against [Neustadt, 1963, p. 858].

Truman's Improvised Staff System.   Roosevelt's highly informal system was not, of course, easily transferable; when Truman became President, he had to build his own system. It was more structured than Roosevelt's, at least on paper. But he was a natural improviser. "His office was decked out with many of the trappings of what later became known as a staff system, but he, himself, remained incurably informal and accessible [Neustadt, 1960, p. 172]." However, the process of institutionalization continued during the Truman administration with the creation of the Council of Economic Advisers and the National Security Council. He took a more direct hand in the budget-making process than Roosevelt had, using his affinity for facts and figures to "plunge deeply into the business of government [Truman, 1955, p. 59]," and this meant a larger role for what was then the Bureau of the Budget. And the delegations of work Truman assigned were specific.

Ike's Chain of Command. Under Truman, the President and the Presidency—the man and the institution—were still clearly separate with the man dominating. The institution had no life of its own without the presence of the man whose motto in office was, "The buck stops here." Under Dwight D. Eisenhower, that changed. Eisenhower established a formal, military-like staff system with clearcut chains of command running toward a chief of staff who was the only person who reported directly to the President. Under Eisenhower's passive administrative style, authority drifted downward. Staff director Sherman Adams (1962), in his memoirs, reports that Eisenhower left the basic foreign policy decisions, as well as the steps to carry them out, to his Secretary of State, John Foster Dulles. He liked to have difficult and complicated problems digested into one-page summaries. He could then make a straightforward yes-or-no decision. He held regular cabinet meetings and included members of the Executive Office and of the White House staff so that their size grew to from twenty to thirty regular participants. He established a systematic congressional liaison operation.

This machinery worked well enough to keep the White House going through three major Eisenhower illnesses. After his heart attack, he dispensed with much of the ceremonial and symbolic functions of the Presidency, and this turned out to be a useful precedent, as Neustadt noted in 1963:

> It is only thirty years since Hoover, once a week, received whatever citizens desired to shake hands. It is little more than a decade since Truman's days were crowded by obligatory interviews with Congressmen, with lobbyists, with spokesmen for good causes. One of Eisenhower's greatest contributions to the Presidency—and to the sanity of future Presidents—lay precisely in this: the gift of time [p. 862].

Critics of the Eisenhower Presidency have complained that he was overprotected by his large and formal staff system, that he was cut off from information and from the opportunity to make decisions. But Nelson Polsby (1971) argues that this is the way Ike wanted it. "His philosophy of government welcomed self-limitation [p. 25]." After the troubles that stemmed from the actions of his more activist successors, that self-limitation began to look better. In 1973, Rexford Tugwell, who had been a member of the Roosevelt staff four decades earlier, wrote this appreciation of Eisenhower:

> Roosevelt had fumbled toward executive expansion and a more effective office, but he never quite reached it. Perhaps Eisenhower's Presidential effectiveness came from his military experience. He regarded his governmental subordinates as field commanders. After being briefed, he had the art of making quick but informed decisions. He never undercut or second-guessed those who carried out his directions, but he sternly checked overreaching.

. . . His office was a quiet and efficient center of operations. When he had a scandal he cleared it away at once [p. 57].

The Competitive Kennedy Men.   President Kennedy dismantled the Eisenhower staff system but preserved the curb on strictly symbolic activity, kept the legislative liaison system, and allowed further growth in the Executive Office with the creation of the Office of Science and Technology. His White House staff was much on the order of Roosevelt's, though without as much clash of personalities. He did not bother with cabinet meetings. Like Roosevelt, he used various means to form independent contacts with the outside world. There were two entrances to the Oval Office: personal secretary Evelyn Lincoln guarded one and appointments secretary Ken O'Donnell the other. An adviser barred from one still had a chance at the other. Groups with different ideas were encouraged to fight for them.

Kennedy was not hesitant to cut through the bureaucracy to get what he wanted, and he frequently called medium-level personnel directly for information. In 1962, when Jack Rosenthal was manning the press office at the Justice Department during the University of Mississippi riots, he picked up the phone and heard the familiar Kennedy accent. Assuming it was Joseph Mohbat, then an Associated Press reporter who could do a good imitation of the President, he said, "Cut out the horseshit, Mohbat."

President Kennedy: No bureaucrat was safe. (*Black Star.*)

"No, no, this is really the President," said the voice. And it was (Wise, 1973, p. 208).

Because of Kennedy's casual approach, said Douglass Cater (1964), "No bureaucrat could feel safe from a Presidential phone call. Kennedy was remarkably cavalier in handing out assignments, frequently using the man who happened to be nearest at hand when a problem arose [p. 98]."

Domination by Johnson.   President Johnson's staff system was based not on interaction but on domination. The staff was large, responsibilities were not clearly fixed, and its mission was simply to display "complete conformity to his will—expressed and unexpressed [Barber, 1972, p. 80]." Press Secretary George Reedy (1970), once publicly addressed by the President as "you stupid son of a bitch," afterward characterized the White House operation as like the Japanese game of Go:

> . . . there is only one fixed goal in life. It is somehow to gain and maintain access to the President. . . . Consequently the President's psychology is studied minutely, and a working day in the White House is marked by innumerable probes to determine which routes to the Oval Room are open and which end in a blind alley [pp. 90–91].

Clark Clifford: Advice from an old friend. (*United Press International.*)

Preoccupied with the Vietnam war, unwilling to hear dissent—except from George Ball who had an institutionalized devil's advocate role and whose views were given hearing as a matter of form and then dismissed—Johnson gradually lost the advisers with whom he had built his lifetime political career. But it was finally the advice of an old friend, Clark Clifford, a Washington lawyer who replaced Robert McNamara as Secretary of Defense, that convinced Johnson that the Vietnam war was at stalemate.

Nixon's Isolation.   The largest recent expansion of what by now has become the White House establishment was during Nixon's first term. The increase in personnel was about 20 percent over the Johnson Presidency. He restored something like an Eisenhower staff system with H. R. Haldeman in the role of chief of staff. When Haldeman was forced by scandal to resign, as Sherman Adams had been in the Eisenhower Presidency, he was replaced by a general—as was Adams, and the staff system continued. Although much more active than Eisenhower, Nixon preferred to work in even greater isolation. Haldeman provided it, as R. W. Apple, Jr. (1973), has described:

> He set up what quickly became known as "the Berlin wall" around the Oval Office, and he would decide which among the "hundreds or perhaps thousands who want to see" Mr. Nixon, again in his own words, "have no legitimate claim." In general, there was no recourse from the potentially critical decision on access, taken by a man unknown to 99 per cent of the country, although his effort to move Rose Mary Woods, Mr. Nixon's long-time secretary, away from

her boss's side ended in abject failure. . . . Haldeman lorded it over the Congress, the bureaucracy, the Republican politicians, and the press, and many in those quarters came to see him as a Rasputin [p. 103].

345

The Presidency

In the beginning of his second term, Nixon tried to gain better control of the bureaucracy by creating a super cabinet, giving the secretaries of Health, Education and Welfare, Housing and Urban Development, and Agriculture second hats as counselors to the President. This design was to unify the roles of creator and executor of policy. But it depended for its coordination on Haldeman and John D. Ehrlichman, assistant to the President for domestic affairs, who also resigned in the scandal. When they left, the super-cabinet plan was abandoned. The overall burden on the staff within the Nixon style of decision making remained. He liked to receive the relevant information, have the alternatives presented, then withdraw for solitary pondering (often to a site remote from Washington), and finally emerge with a decision. Much depended on how things were formulated and presented and how time was organized for the lonely ruminations.

Managing the Presidential Establishment

The presidential establishment is supposed to help the President manage the government, but this establishment has grown to the point where just managing it is a full-time job. It has one virtue: its inner workings can be thrown out and designed anew every four or eight years when a new President assumes the office. But much of what has been created by legislation remains in existence from one administration to the next. And like the main bureaucracy it is supposed to control, the presidential establishment is subject to continuing pressures for growth which are not related to any substantive work that needs to be done.

One such pressure comes from the prestige of a White House job. People whom the President (as chief of party) wants to reward with jobs would rather be in the White House than in one of the departments or independent agencies. Cronin (1973) reports that when George McGovern was offered the directorship of the Food-for-Peace program by President Kennedy, McGovern objected to locating the job in a logical line department such as State or Agriculture. He wanted the prestige of a White House job, and Kennedy gave it to him, complete with the title of special assistant to the President.

Another pressure for swelling the Presidency comes from interest groups which want representation in the White House. By 1973, the Executive Office included such diverse units as the Council on Environmental Quality, Office of Telecommunications Policy, Council on International Economic Policy, Office of Consumer Affairs, and the Special Action Office for Drug Abuse Prevention. Less formal representation is achieved by including token minority-group members on the staff. "Once this foothold is established, of course," says Cronin, "interest groups can play upon the potential political backlash that could arise should their representation be discontinued [pp. 35–36]."

Finally, there has been the trend, which may or may not prove reversible in the long run, for Congress to avoid facing up to tough decisions and complicated problems by delegating increasing authority to the executive branch. When laws are passed in general terms and it is left to the President to fill in the details, it takes a bigger White House bureaucracy to do the detail-filling work which Congress does not want to do.

THE MAN AND HIS IMAGE

The President and the Media

Because presidential power is based largely on persuasion and expectations in the minds of others, much depends on the image the President presents to the outside world. The Nixon administration scandals, for example, quickly eroded the President's power base in all sorts of substantive areas which had no direct bearing on the scandals. Congress voted to curb his war-making powers because its members knew that a President with damaged personal prestige could not rally the voters to punish them at the polls. The economy, which is held together to a certain extent by psychological cement, began to reflect investors' worries about uncertain leadership. This is an extreme example and one that cannot be readily affected by a public relations campaign. But Presidents can and do try to engage in major manipulations of the image which the public receives. President Johnson began the practice of having executive departments with good news to announce send it to the White House press office so that he could take the credit for it. Cronin (1973) notes that more than the man is being aggrandized by such activity:

> This activity is devoted to the particular occupant of the White House, but inevitably it affects the Presidency itself, by projecting or reinforcing images of the Presidency that are almost imperial in their suggestions of omnipotence and omniscience. Thus the public-relations apparatus not only has directly enlarged the presidential workforce but has expanded public expectations about the Presidency at the same time [p. 36].

Public relations activity can cover a broad range from writing speeches to calling up editors and asking them to print articles giving the administration's point of view. Sometimes such articles are signed by members of the executive branch but ghostwritten by members of the public relations staff. The most effective device, in the hands of a President who is skilled at using it, is the presidential press conference. But as Presidents have relied increasingly on their staff public relations work, the tradition of direct confrontation with the press has diminished. Franklin D. Roosevelt had more than one news conference a week; Truman had them nearly every week. Under Eisenhower and Kennedy, press conferences became more formal institutions, announced well in advance and held in large rooms with, in Kennedy's case, live television coverage. Johnson tried to revive some of the Roosevelt informality and spontaneity by inviting reporters into the Oval Office on short notice, but became increasingly remote in the later years of his Presidency. Nixon in his first term was more remote than any of his three immediate predecessors, averaging only one news conference every seven weeks and relying on poorly informed aides to brief reporters. Stuart H. Loory (1973) noted that in staying so aloof from the press, the President was depriving himself of a valuable source of information. If he had been holding regular and frequent press conferences, Loory said, Nixon might have faced earlier the scandals that followed his 1972 reelection: "the storm warnings any politician must heed to save his skin would have been waving vigorously week after week [p. 45]." George Reedy (1970) had the same point to make about the Johnson administration:

> Of the few social institutions which tend to keep a president in touch with reality, the most effective,—and the most resented by the chief beneficiary—is the press. It is the only force to enter the White House from the outside world

Truman Press Conference, 1952: Keeping in touch with reality. *(United Press International.)*

THE PRESIDENT'S CONTACT WITH THE OUTSIDE WORLD

DIGEST OF WEEKEND COMMENT

January 7, 1974

ENERGY

The Agronsky Panel from Kilpatrick to Rowan was highly skeptical about the degree of the oil shortage w/much protest over the incomplete or inaccurate stix which come only from those w/self–interests, eg., oil industry. Both Rowan and Kilpo told of individual firms who say they have all the fuel they need and more. Lisagor, Drew and Agronsky, along w/<u>Post's</u> Berger on NET, all had high praise for Simon's openness. Lisagor praised Simon's weekly briefings, his acceptance of suggestions, his efforts to get info for press. "Refreshing," said Lisagor of the "one clear, fresh voice in DC, bar none." Lisagor said the way Simon's letting it all hang out is way govt. in free society ought to operate. Agronsky noted Simon's "fantastic" remark that it was his, Simon's business to spend time w/press. Simon won Rowan's recognition as an accurate prognosticator in view of the FEO chief's predictions on rising gas prices. Rowan also noted, re: long–term seriousness of situation, Simon's view that 1/2 of US oil in '78–'79 will have to be imported. Lisagor expressed belief in long–term seriousness of situation, saying W. Eur. and Japan aren't going to let the shieks cause those industrial economies to fall and war is very possible if situation worsens.

The way Knight's McCartney sees it, "hottest issue facing Hill will be spiraling oil profits and what to do about them." . . . "Utilities say public has done such a good job of heeding RN's appeal that electric company revenues are falling all over. And, to recoup these losses, companies say rate increases are inevitable." Thus, <u>Inquirer</u> reports, "either way the consumer loses."

<u>Star</u> welcomes the "reassuring" and "encouraging" news that RN will take the initiative to organize oil producers and consumers in effort to avoid energy–related depression in world. . . . But <u>Sun</u> wonders, as it did during Brezhnev summit, "whether a Pres. under impchmnt threat can conduct an effective foreign policy." In fact, the earlier summit had negative impact on W. Europe which contributed to problems of the alliance during M–E war and the alert. RN's initiative is welcomed by <u>Sun</u>, "yet from a psychological point of view, he'll have to engage in oil diplomacy at decided dis-advantage."

Nixon's White House News Summary: Instead of reading the papers.

with a direct impact upon the man in the Oval Room which cannot be softened by intermediary interpreters or be deflected by sympathetic attendants [p. 100].

The press is widely used as an informal means of communication among different power centers. President Kennedy knew this and played the game well, encouraging the release of "trial balloons" to test the response of the public and of other power centers to policies that were under consideration. Johnson, who had a compulsion for secrecy, did not; he often went to great lengths to shut off the trial-balloon phenomenon— going so far as to delay or cancel an announcement of an appointment or a program if word about it leaked out in advance. President Nixon's use of press reports for feedback received widespread criticism for his habit of relying on a staff-prepared news summary instead of reading the papers himself. The staff member in charge of preparing the summary, Patrick J. Buchanan, was also a principal presidential speechwriter. The President's source of information for the evaluation of the effect of his public statements therefore lacked independence from the origination of those same statements. That this closed system produced biased feedback has been indicated by press critic Ben H. Bagdikian (1973). In an analysis of a copy of Buchanan's report which fell into the hands of a *Washington Post* correspondent, Bagdikian found that, "It was full of inaccuracies about what the news media had actually said." Moreover, "It systematically omitted public condemnations of the President [p. 43]." President Ford relied both on his own reading of newspapers and a staff-written summary, prepared under the supervision of an old friend and former *Chicago Tribune* correspondent, Philip Warden.

President Johnson had another subtle way of avoiding unpleasant feedback. By holding his press conferences on short notice, he limited them to the White House regulars, correspondents who, in James Reston's (1967) words, are "subject to his system of punishments and rewards, which can be embarrassing to a reporter on a highly competitive beat [p. 52]." The specialists in the Washington press corps, persons who knew enough about foreign affairs or urban problems or political campaigning to ask the well-informed and penetrating questions, were shut out.

The Presidential Character

The problems of the Presidency, it can now be seen, are very human ones that tend to resist the institutional solutions previously favored by many political scientists. The kind of Presidency we get is highly dependent on the kind of President; man and institution are not so separable after all. Given this situation it becomes important for the voters, if they are going to exercise anything but a belated, ex post facto control over their government, to be able to predict the style and performance of the men they send to the White House.

James David Barber (1972) has initiated work in this direction. "Every story of Presidential decision-making," he says, "is really two stories: an outer one in which a rational man calculates and an inner one in which an emotional man feels. The two are forever connected. Any real President is one whole man, and his deeds reflect his wholeness [p. 7]." Barber hypothesizes that the basic qualities of presidential performance can

Q: Are we in direct contact, or any kind of contact, with the insurgent groups in Cambodia?

Ziegler: I am going to answer your question by saying not to my knowledge, and I would add to that by saying that we are not [*April 7*].

Q: What is the purpose, Ron, of the Cabinet meeting?

Ziegler: The purpose is to meet with Members of the Cabinet . . . [*March 18*].

Question: Is the President intervening in any way on the Wounded Knee crisis?

Ziegler: That matter is being commented on at the Justice Department and I have no comment on it from here.

Q: Ron, I called the Justice Department and they won't have any comment either.

Ziegler: Well, call again [*March 8*].

be predicted from just two variables drawn from the man's life history which, dichotomized, form a table with four property spaces. The variables are first, how active he is and second, whether or not he enjoys politics. The chart, with some sample Presidents listed in the appropriate property spaces, looks like Figure 10-1.

Barber's favorite type is the *active-positive* President, the one who works hard at his job and enjoys it. His personality is healthy, consistent, oriented "toward productiveness as a value and an ability to use his styles flexibly, adaptively . . . an emphasis on rational mastery, on using the brain to move the feet [p. 12]." The other internally consistent type is the *passive-negative* person who is in politics out of a sense of duty, though he does little and enjoys it less. He displays "old-fashioned virtue and honesty" and fills a need when voters tire of political rhetoric and hunger for the straight talk of an antipolitician. Coolidge restored confidence in government after the Harding scandals; Eisenhower cleaned up what in Truman's day was known as the mess in Washington. But, says Barber, under such a President, the nation drifts. "The body politic lapses into laxness, and the social order deteriorates as neglected tensions build up. Eventually some leader ready to shove as well as to stand fast, someone who enjoys the great game of politics, will have to pick up the pieces [p. 173]."

The *passive-positive* Presidents are among those with a restricted view of the office: they are happy doing little. Taft (1916) adhered to a strict construction of presidential power, arguing that overactive exercise of executive authority "might lead under emergencies to results of an arbitrary character, doing irremediable injustice to private right [p. 27]." Barber thinks such Presidents are starved for love. Politics gives them "mass love" but sometimes makes them pay for it by requiring them to take unwanted aggressive action to sustain that love. They tend to be nervous and fragile.

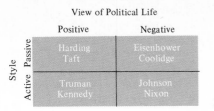

View of Political Life

Figure 10-1   Presidential Properties: Samples

Because of recent history, Barber is preoccupied with the problem of the *active-negative* President. We have already seen that Johnson and Nixon did have much in common—the secretiveness, isolation, and tendency to let the majesty of the office block their view of the outside world. The activity of such a man "has a compulsive quality, as if the man were trying to make up for something or to escape from anxiety into hard work. . . . He has a persistent problem in managing his aggressive feelings. His self-image is vague and discontinuous [p. 12]." The risk is rigidity. Like Wilson, who stood stubbornly by principle and let the Treaty of Versaille fail when a compromise might have saved it, he tends to hang on to a failing line of policy, come what may. In Hoover's case, it was failure to initiate direct government action for relief of the effects of the Depression. For Johnson, it was the war in Vietnam. Each played the role of "the lone hero bucking the tide of his times in favor of some eternal purpose [p. 447]." Barber is not being sardonic when he puts it that way. The stubborn cowboy is an archetype in many fields of American endeavor:

> . . . the temptation to stand and fight receives wide support from the culture. The most dangerous confusion in that connection is the equating of political power—essentially the power to persuade—with force. Such a President, frustrated in efforts at persuasion, may turn to those aspects of his role least constrained by the chains of compromise—from domestic to foreign policy, from foreign policy to military policy, for instance, where the tradition of obedience holds. Then we may see a President, doubtful within but seemingly certain without, huffing and puffing with *machismo* as he bravely orders other men to die [pp. 446–447].

The test of any hypothesis is its predictive power, and Barber's book, *The Presidential Character*, is subtitled, *Predicting Performance in the White House*. He was therefore obliged to include a prediction in it. This is what he said about Richard Nixon in the book published before the election campaign of 1972:

> The danger is that crisis will be transformed into tragedy—that Nixon will go from a dramatic experiment to a moral commitment, a commitment to follow his private star, to fly off in the face of overwhelming odds. That type of

reaction is to be expected when and if Nixon is confronted with severe threat to his power and sense of virtue. . . . As the election approaches, Nixon's Presidential fate will clarify itself. If the uncertainties fade in the light of the polls, and the probability of a defeat for Nixon rises sharply, this President will be sorely tempted to do what he feels he must do before it is too late. The loss of power to forces beyond his control would constitute a severe threat. That would be a time to go down, if go down one must, in flames [p. 442].

Barber's work contains useful insight, but it does not pretend to offer a total explanation of presidential behavior. As we have noted, there are institutional constraints which tend to act in a stubbornly consistent way, no matter what sort of personality characteristics the President brings to the office. And skill remains a most important variable which may be independent of character.

Toward Antiaggrandizement

After the Nixon election scandals, there was talk in Congress of cutting the Presidency down to size. This was a relatively new idea, although not brand new. Until the middle 1960s, beginning about with Lyndon Johnson's first (and only) term in his own right, the current generation of presidential scholars had generally equated strength with goodness. Lists of the "great" Presidents have favored the most active. Authors preoccupied with the many and demanding roles of the Presidency were concerned with ways to strengthen the office so that the President could do a better job of running the country. The assumption that giving him more responsibility and power would solve the country's problems was seldom questioned. But this kind of thinking, as we have seen in our examination of Congress, tends to be time-bound. It reflects the observer's policy preferences of the moment. If the observer identifies his policy interests with those of the urban, liberal constituency of the Presidency as framed by the election system and the issue structure of the 1950s, then he is likely to have felt frustrated by the lack of presidential power in opposition to a conservative Congress and a sluggish bureaucracy. But times change. David L. Paletz (1970) saw the change coming in an appraisal written at the start of the Nixon administration. Johnson's handling of the war had demonstrated "two things: first, that Presidents can make mistakes; and secondly, that the effects of such errors can be devastating. Accordingly, there has been a diminution in the enthusiasm for loading responsibilities onto the President and in the proposals for increasing his power [p. 437]." But this view, too, can be time-bound. Edward S. Corwin, who published a leading work on the Presidency in 1940, took an antiaggrandizement view that was probably a reaction to the growth in presidential power under the New Deal. Now, in the wake of Johnson's war and Nixon's scandal, the antiaggrandizement view will flower for another cycle.

Some presidential scholars, such as Schlesinger (1973), worried that

Nixon Defending Watergate Record, 1973: Institutional constraints can be stubbornly consistent. (*Wide World Photos.*)

the pendulum of antiaggrandizement might swing too far, permanently weakening the Presidency at a time when strong leadership is required. What is needed, Schlesinger said, is "a middle ground between making the President a czar and making him a puppet." The Nixon administration's failure was in losing sight of the fact that the great powers of government must be shared among the different branches in a spirit of accommodation, self-restraint, and respect for law. "We need," said Schlesinger, "a strong Presidency as much as ever—but a strong Presidency *within the Constitution*" [p. 10].

Concern over ways to weaken the powers of the office may miss the main point. It is not power that fosters presidential irresponsibility, says Paletz, "I suspect that presidential irresponsibility is more likely to be a function of the relationship between the office and the 'legitimate' demands placed upon it, with 'legitimate' being, as often as not, redefined from one problem to another." In other words, no amount of tinkering or fine-tuning the machinery will result in a configuration that is optimum for all situations.

Four More Years?

Nevertheless, proposals for changing the machinery are advanced with regularity. The idea of a multiple-person Presidency, considered and rejected in 1787, has been raised by Barbara W. Tuchman (1973). She proposes replacing the President with a six-man directorate serving as a unit for six years with each member taking the chairmanship for a year. George

Reedy proposed switching to a parliamentary system with the House of Representatives electing a "chief of government" who would serve only at the pleasure of the House. He did not pretend that it had any chance of ever being adopted, although the Nixon troubles later produced many wistful comparisons of our system with parliamentary government. Some new interest was kindled in the idea of restructuring the system so that a presidential government could fall and be replaced when it lost public confidence. But no serious effort was advanced for such radical change.

President Nixon, in the midst of the Watergate investigations, called for a commission to study campaign reform and give highest priority to the idea of a single, six-year term for the Presidency. He maintained that an incumbent who hopes for reelection must cope with too many pressures from narrow interests to pursue the larger public interest. A President in office for six years with no extension possible would be free of those pressures. The disadvantage, of course, is that such a President would be equally free to pursue policies that were counter to the public interest. "To extend the term of office to six or more years is to run unwise and unnecessary risks of prolonging the cost of mistaken judgment," says Henry Steel Commager (1973, p. 11).

A more plausible reform would subject the President to more electoral pressure rather than less. This could be done simply by eliminating the two-term limitation by repealing the Twenty-second Amendment. A President who had the option of running for a third term would be less likely to resort to extreme and unscrupulous measures to win his second term. In office for a second term, he would behave in a manner calculated to keep the third-term possibility alive. His authority would also be enhanced. Other centers of power are more likely to react favorably to a President who has a possibility of being in power for more than a limited span of time, as opposed to one who spends four years as a lame duck.

The two-term limitation, enacted by Republicans in response to Roosevelt's four elections, is a limitation on the voters rather than on the government, and one not envisioned by the Founding Fathers. The argument for keeping the ban on third terms is that an incumbent has a heavy advantage in the election and that without it a President could, like Roosevelt, become entrenched in the office for life. But Harry A. Bailey (1972) has shown this danger to be almost nonexistent if history is any guide. Roosevelt won his third and fourth terms because of the reluctance of the nation to change leaders in the middle of the world's greatest war. Only one other President ever seriously sought a third term: Ulysses S. Grant. He was rejected by his party. Even two-term Presidents are a historical minority. Only thirteen of our Presidents have been elected to two terms. No President who attained office by succession from the Vice Presidency ever served two full elective terms in his own right. "The American presidential tenure experience," says Bailey, "comes closer to being a one-term tradition [p. 106]." But the *possibility* of more terms can make a subtle but important difference in the nature of the office.

A Shadow Presidency

Power accumulating in the executive branch tends to negate the eighteenth-century system of checks and balances. The obvious solution—building checks and balances inside the executive branch itself—is hard to come by. Where they have existed, as in the cases of Kennedy and Roosevelt, it was because of the restless styles of the men in the office who habitually sought conflicting views. And even they suffered from the inhibiting effects of small group dynamics in the rarefied atmosphere of the White House. Reedy has summarized the problem:

> The fact is that a president makes his decisions as he wishes to make them, under conditions which he himself has established, and at times of his own determination. He decides what he wants to decide and any student of the White House who believes that he is making a contribution to political thought when he analyzes the process is sadly mistaken. At best—at the very best—he can only contribute to human knowledge some insights into the decision-making process of one man [p. 40].

One current student of the White House, James MacGregor Burns (1973), believes that its problems have to be solved from without. He proposes a better-organized opposition, a Shadow Presidency, that would keep an alternative view in front of the public and therefore in front of the President. "The greatest need," he says, "will be an opposition that challenges presidential values, presidential methods, presidential institu-

George Reedy: A President sets the conditions.
(*United Press International.*)

tions, that is eager to take power and to present its own definition of the national purpose [p. 341]." That task has traditionally fallen to members of the opposition party in Congress, but they are usually disorganized as each member pursues his own narrow interests or assauges his own petty irritations. Burns proposes a strengthened party apparatus that could hold conventions, perhaps annually, and tell the President and the country what he is doing wrong. It would be difficult to achieve because it would mean imposing a strong, centralized party structure on top of the loose coalition of state and local parties that exists now. But "the Shadow Presidency could offer relentless criticism in the free press, hold hard-fought elections at regular intervals, and thereby present an arresting and responsible alternative to the incumbent administration [p. xiii]."

The Importance of Being Lucky

In addition to the institutional forces on one hand and the effect of individual personality on the other, there is a third factor which few political scientists, with the exception of Nelson Polsby (1971), seem to have noticed: There is no very good connection between the kind of man who holds the office and the kind of luck he has. The Kennedy administration was full of impeccably credentialed men who gave some advice that turned out to be disastrous (Halberstam, 1972). The bad decisions which led to the futile war in Vietnam can be traced neither to stupidity nor to malice. If those in power could not see as clearly as we can now with hindsight, it was because of perceptual blinders beyond their immediate control. "So many circumstances that impinge mightily on the fate of nations are beyond the realm of presidential discretion," says Polsby. "If things turn out well, we praise the President; if badly, we blame him. But we can only guess at the differences he and his policies have made [p. 46]."

PRESIDENTIAL SUCCESSION

A Need for Clarity

For eight Presidents, luck has been especially bad; four of them died while in office and another four were assassinated. One of the most trying developments for any government is the loss of the head of state. When Joseph Stalin died in 1953, the Soviet Union witnessed a struggle for power caused by the absence of clear procedures for naming his successor. For twenty-five years speculation has abounded in and out of China about how Mao would be replaced upon his death and by whom. In the United States should a President resign, be removed, or die, there are clear lines of succession.

The Constitution provides that the Vice President succeeds to the office of President when it becomes vacant, as Gerald Ford did upon

Richard Nixon's resignation in 1974. The Vice Presidency itself, however, has been vacant ten times. This contingency is provided for through an act of Congress in 1947 which specifies that the Speaker of the House of Representatives is next in line for the Presidency, followed in turn by the President pro tempore of the Senate, then the Secretary of State, then the remaining cabinet officials in the order in which their departments were established.

Questions of succession are raised not only due to the death of a President, but also in cases of disability or when a President is not physically or mentally capable of carrying out his duties. When President James Garfield was shot by an assassin, he did not die until eight days later; Woodrow Wilson remained in office for eight months after suffering a stroke; and Dwight Eisenhower suffered a temporarily disabling heart attack. The Twenty-fifth Amendment, enacted in 1967, provides that in such cases the Vice President becomes acting President until the President indicates he is able to resume the duties of the office. This amendment also addresses the circumstance where the Vice Presidency is vacant. It provides that the President can nominate a Vice President who takes office after both houses of Congress have consented by majority vote. This procedure was first applied in 1973 when President Nixon named Gerald Ford to replace Spiro T. Agnew, who resigned upon his criminal conviction.

Upgrading the Vice Presidency

The frequency of presidential deaths and vacancies in the Vice Presidency has given the office of Vice President renewed attention. For much of the nation's history the office was little more than a ceremonial post. Presidential nominees selected their running mates on the primary criterion of "balancing the ticket." Richard Nixon's selection of Spiro T. Agnew and George McGovern's initial choice of Thomas Eagleton show the dangers inherent in selecting a Vice President to aid the ticket without due consideration for scrutinizing the fitness of the candidate for the office. Because few important responsibilities have traditionally been performed by Vice Presidents, the office has not attracted persons intrigued by power or higher ambition. Yet that situation has changed; increased responsibilities have been assigned to Vice Presidents. And four of the last six Presidents—Truman, Johnson, Nixon, and Ford—served as Vice President before becoming President. But the prime responsibility of the office is simply to exist in readiness for an orderly transition should the need arise.

SUGGESTED READINGS

Cronin, Thomas E., and Sanford D. Greenberg (eds.). *The Presidential Advisory System.* New York: Harper & Row, 1969. A revealing look at the men and new institutions of the growing Presidency.

Davis, James W., Jr. *The National Executive Branch.* New York: Free Press, 1970. A general analysis of the national executive branch as a whole.

Hirschfield, Robert S. (ed.). *The Power of the Presidency: Concepts and Controversy.* 2d ed. Chicago: Aldine, 1973. A balanced collection of essays dealing with the sources, limits, and responsibilities of presidential power.

Koenig, Louis W. *The Chief Executive.* rev. ed. New York: Harcourt, Brace, 1968. A general and comprehensive study depicting the numerous roles and facets of the Presidency.

Mueller, John E. *War, Presidents and Public Opinion.* New York: Wiley, 1973. A current study of the role of public opinion in the making of foreign policy, especially in regard to the President's war-making powers.

Reedy, George. *The Twilight of the Presidency.* New York: World, 1970. A critical and pessimistic analysis of the office of the Presidency, arguing that there is a decreasing ability for the institution to solve the problems of modern society. The book provides a vivid picture of the Presidency, giving the reader a sense of the complexities of the office.

Schlesinger, Arthur M., Jr. *The Imperial Presidency.* Boston: Houghton Mifflin, 1973. Eloquent alarm expressed by a former White House adviser over the monarchial reconstruction of the Presidency, neatly placed in historical perspective.

Tugwell, Rexford G., and Thomas E. Cronin (eds.). *The Presidency Reappraised.* New York: Praeger, 1974. A mixed bag of essays, including some on subjects too rarely considered. For example, see Milton Plesur's treatment of "The Health of Presidents."

Wildavsky, Aaron B. (ed.). *The Presidency.* Boston: Little, Brown, 1969. An excellent collection of essays covering all aspects of the functions and responsibilities of the institution of the Presidency.

Chapter 11

The Judiciary

THE LEGAL TRADITION

Judicial Persuasion

It is easy to forget that a judge is a politician. But like a member of the legislative branch or the executive branch, he is interested in certain policy results and has a limited amount of power which can sometimes be used to approach or achieve those results. And like members of the other branches, he comes to his role with a history of involvement in public affairs. Only 1 percent of Supreme Court justices reach that high position without having held some other public office (Schmidhauser, 1959). And only 20 percent of federal district judges attain the bench without service in a previous office (Jacob, 1965). But the political nature of the judge and his task is obscured by a setting which is quite different from the arenas occupied by congressmen and the President. The mythology surrounding the courts tends to veil the fact that judges are involved in politics at all. But it is a thin veil, and it has its uses.

The judicial branch of government, even more than the executive and legislative branches, depends for its authority on the power to persuade. It commands no army like the President and controls no purse strings like the Congress. It is obeyed only when its orders are perceived as legitimate by the other branches and by the public. The mystical trappings of the courtroom—the robes, the deference to "your honor," the bailiff's command to "all rise" when the judge enters—enhance this necessary perception of legitimacy. They are, in effect, a substitute for more palpable sources of power.

Much scholarship has been devoted to examining this phenomenon. The traditional view that a judge's robes made him the objective keeper of the mystical secrets of the law was challenged by what Robert G. McClosky (1960) called "legal realists." These investigators discovered that judges, like senators and Presidents, "may have prejudices and those prejudices may affect their understanding of the Constitution [p. 19]." But the realists, said McClosky, then created a myth of their own, that the trappings of the court concealed political functions no different from those of the legislature. Their functions are different, and the Supreme Court "blends orthodox judicial functions with policy-making functions in a complex mixture [p. 20]." Keeping the mixture in balance without offending a general sense of legitimacy is the key to the Court's power. It is also the source of the limitations of the Court's power.

A Quest for Precision

The behavior of the judicial branch is shaped by its primary function of interpreting the law, with all its stylized conventions. These conventions, the development of several centuries in the English-speaking world, define and rationalize the rules for conducting human affairs with as much precision as possible. One of the fundamental requirements of a workable system of law is that a person who is subject to it be able to understand it. A system capable of being understood is one whose effects are predictable with some reliability. If a given deed is going to subject the doer to punishment for committing a crime or a judgment to compensate someone for damages, he ought to be able to know that fact before he commits the act. Precision is also a requirement for consistency. If the same rules are to be applied to different persons in different situations, then the rules must be stated precisely enough so that uniformity can be defined. Without such uniformity, evasion would be easy. A law subject to different interpretations encourages a potential violator because he can hope that the interpretation applied in his own case will vindicate him.

The goal of precision is therefore crucial. It is also unattainable. The variety of human experience is so great, the contortions and permutations of human behavior so numerous, that the law can never attain anything like scientific precision. Unlike science, it has few quantitative definitions or rules. Its expressions are verbal, not numerical. But after much usage and long development, legal expression has at least achieved some feel of precision, if not precision in fact. And to legal enthusiasts, there is a kind of symmetry and order to the law, a sense of bringing form out of chaos, that satisfies the same kind of hunger for logic which must motivate mathematicians. That quest for order, precision, and continuity shapes the training of lawyers and judges, conditions their way of looking at the world, and affects the way they conduct themselves as members of the judicial branch in the political arena.

A key element which the training of lawyers seeks to develop is the "instinct for the relevant." Up until World War I, the legal tradition was perpetuated in nonacademic settings with aspiring lawyers learning the trade by apprenticing as clerks in the offices of practicing attorneys. When university legal training evolved after the Civil War, efforts to make it systematic led to reliance on the case-study method. Through the systematic organization of casebooks, the student was no longer limited to the kinds of cases which a clerk might encounter by accident in the course of helping his employer; he could study collections of cases to separate particular from general rules and master past precedents in the development of the law. This practice contributed to the coherence and continuity of the law, but it insulated students from exposure to different social settings within which they would later practice as lawyers. Herbert Jacob (1972) has noted that a fledgling lawyer is supposed to learn

> how to separate fact from rule, the governing facts from the incidental ones, and the *ratio decidendi* (the rule of the case) from *obiter dicta* (incidental comments), in order to understand the principles that underlie the common law and govern the development of case law . . . teaching students to understand the social context of legal work is not yet part of the mainstream of legal education [pp. 47–48].

The free use of Latin terminology in law, as in medicine, is a way of imparting a feeling of precision where actual precision may or may not exist. The rationale behind the case-study method is the rule of stare decisis, which literally means "to stand by things settled." In practice it means that new cases should be settled by the same principles established in earlier similar cases. This common-law rule goes a long way toward achieving the goal of making the law predictable. Yet, the world changes often enough and swiftly enough that it provides no more than short-run predictability. Many cases will find valid precedents on both sides of a question. Stare decisis produced a rationale for keeping whites and blacks in separate schools in the half-century between *Plessy v. Ferguson* (1896) and *Brown v. Board of Education* (1954). It did not prevent the Court in 1954 from adapting to a changing world, as Chief Justice Warren noted in his opinion: "Whatever may have been the extent of psychological knowledge at the time of *Plessy v. Ferguson*, this finding [that segregated facilities inflicted psychological deprivations on minorities] is amply supported by modern authority. Any language in *Plessy v. Ferguson* contrary to this finding is rejected [*Brown v. Board of Education* 347 U.S. 483, 1954]." The rule of stare decisis nevertheless remains a useful aphorism if not an eternal principle.

The Legal Structure

The legal system is organized around a few fairly straightforward distinctions which serve to channel the thinking of lawyers and judges. The most basic is the distinction between *statutory law* and *common law*. Statutory law is enacted by legislative authority (which is shared by the President), whereas the latter covers matters which the legislature has never gotten around to deciding but for which rules can be found in the body of precedent, preserved through stare decisis. It is thus possible to get into trouble today for violating a custom that originated in England in the twelfth century and has stayed alive in a chain of court citations reaching forward through the centuries. Statutory law takes precedence over common law when there is a conflict, but such conflicts are rare. Many statutory laws are based upon common law or are interpreted by the judiciary in terms derived from the common law.

A second basic distinction is between criminal and civil law. *Criminal law* defines what constitutes a crime and refers to rules imposed and enforced by government on its citizens to regulate individual conduct. Crimes are classified as *felonies* and *misdemeanors*. The former are more serious and receive more severe penalties. In criminal cases, the government is always the initiator and prosecutor, and the government may not be charged with a crime, although, as in the case of the Watergate affair, its agents may be so charged.

Civil law deals with controversies between individuals, although the individual need not be a person. It may be a corporation or the government itself. The substance of criminal law is spelled out almost entirely in statutes, mainly state statutes, although the number of federal criminal statutes is increasing. However, common law may govern some procedures used in the enforcement of criminal law. Civil law, because of its immense variety of problems, leans more heavily on common law.

Civil actions may be taken at *law* or *equity*. Originally, there were separate law and equity courts. The equity system goes beyond the traditional remedy of providing for payment of damages *after* a wrongful act has been committed by allowing for a remedy *before* the act is committed. In cases where irreparable harm may be done, equity law allows an individual to show the court why common-law procedures are insufficient and to seek relief by asking the court to require that something be done (specific performance) or to forbid certain actions (injunction). Such an order in advance of the oncoming damage is called *relief in equity*.

If I dump my sewage into the stream from which you draw your drinking water, you may recover, through action at law, the value of the lost drinking water. But suppose I find it cheaper and more convenient to continue to dump sewage in your water, and risk having to pay you the cost of getting water elsewhere, than to find some other way to get rid of my sewage. I would be forcing you into an inconvenient and dangerous situation since you would never know when to expect the first traces of sewage and you might die of the contamination. Your right to collect monetary damages after the fact is not of much use in that situation. But your right to seek equitable relief through a court order to stop my dumping would be of use.

Equity action covers a variety of remedies that are not provided in other legal concepts. The best known is injunction: a court order to prevent an act that would do harm which could not be repaired. The effect of injunction is to increase the penalty against the wrongdoer. He is not only liable to compensate his victim but also stands to be punished for disobeying the court. Another form of relief through equity is the *mandatory injunction*, which demands performance, usually of the terms of a contract, to prevent irreparable harm to a party. There is also the *writ of mandamus*, used to compel an administrative official to perform his legal duty.

The Adversary System

In its ideal form, the adversary system, around which American judicial proceedings are organized, solves many of the difficulties inherent in the settlement of controversy. Its theory calls for an impartial judge to leave the fact gathering to the two contesting sides. Because it is a contest, neither side should spare any effort to uncover all the facts that might support its case; however, the conditions of the ideal form are not always met. In the trial of the original Watergate burglars, the prosecution was content to limit its fact-finding efforts to the immediate and narrow charges at hand. Judge John Sirica abandoned the traditional judicial stance to manipulate his sentencing procedure to coax further incriminating testimony from one of the burglars. This initiative on the judge's part opened the investigative trail to new discoveries of wrongdoing, but his behavior was not in keeping with the ideal functioning of the adversary system.

The main advantage of the adversary system is that, when it works, it is self-propelled. The participants are highly motivated to develop and present their points of view. Yet, the system failed to produce indictments from the original investigation into the slaying of Kent State students by the Ohio National Guard in 1970, because the needed motivating force on the prosecution side was not present. The requirement that both sides must want to win also applies to civil suits in the adversary system. A friendly suit, organized for the purpose of making a point of law or challenging a statute, is ordinarily not allowed because the two parties do not have a genuine motivation to get both sides of the argument before the court.

Because the two sides are seeking opposite results, the adversary system requires rather strict procedures and rules of evidence to ensure fairness in determining the law and the facts of the case. These rules are intuitively sensible. When there is a jury trial, the judge is supposed to determine the law while the jury determines the facts. If there is no jury, the judge rules on both law and fact. In a criminal trial, the proceedings open with a presumption that the accused is innocent. This presumption

Judge John Sirica: Not the traditional stance. (*Black Star.*)

means that the evidence against him must establish his guilt beyond a reasonable doubt. In a civil trial, facts are established less stringently; a finding for one side or the other need be based only on the preponderance of the evidence. In criminal cases, the burden of proof is on the state. In civil cases, it is on the party seeking redress. In either a criminal or civil case, the burden of proof can be shifted to the other party if there is a prima facie (at first sight) case for a disputed fact. For example, if the border patrol finds marijuana in your hubcaps, there is a prima facie case that you are a smuggler, and the burden is on you to prove that somebody else put it there without your knowledge.

In application, the neutrality of judges, the antagonism of lawyers, and the strictness of the rules are often lacking. Prosecutors and defenders may be more loyal to the smooth running of the system than to their clients of the moment, and many defendants are not disposed to fight, perceiving that the odds against them are too great or the legal expenses too vast.

Constitutional Law

The Constitution is the highest law of the land, and constitutional law consists of the basic document and its two centuries of history. The document itself is brief. The statutes and cases which record two hundred years of interpretation are not. All constitutional officers—members of Congress and the President as well as judges—are sworn to uphold the Constitution, and this duty implies a power to interpret the meaning of the Constitution. But for the courts, this power has special significance. Since 1803 when Chief Justice John Marshall invoked *judicial review*—the power to declare legislative acts void when they conflict with the Constitution—the Supreme Court has had almost the final word when there have been disputes over what the law of the Constitution actually is. (The ultimate last word, of course, is through the amending process.) In attempting to apply the specific language of the Constitution to the endless variety of problems and cases never dreamed of by the Founding Fathers, the Supreme Court has used lawyerlike thinking to construct elaborate verbal frameworks of ratio decidendi, the "rule of the case." The sense of precision thus rendered is, however, lost upon close inspection, leaving a collection of aphorisms such as the "clear and present danger" rule limiting free speech (see Chapter 3) or the "separate but equal" test which justified segregation for so many decades. The aphorisms are useful signposts in the development of constitutional law, even though they are not engraved in tablets of stone.

Political Roles

A judge gets into politics in a number of different ways. Some of them are quite effective:

Creating Legitimacy.   Most of the things that are done by Congress, the President, or the federal bureaucracy are accepted as a matter of course. When they are not accepted, the issue often reaches the Supreme Court in the form of a specific case to be resolved by judicial determination of the legitimacy of an act by one of the other branches. This determination can contribute to the popular acceptance of the things the other branches do. Charles L. Black (1960) has emphasized the importance of this role:

> I have described the function of the Supreme Court in a way that turns the usual account upside down. The role of the Court has usually been conceived as that of *invalidating* "hasty" or "unwise" legislation, of acting as a "check" on the other departments. It has played such a role on occasion, and may play it again in the future . . . the most conspicuous function of judicial review may have been that of legitimatizing rather than that of voiding the actions of government [pp. 52–53].

Sometimes the goals of the two other branches of government will be at odds, and the Court must decide which to legitimate. For example, Congress wrote guidelines for setting the pace of school desegregation. The Justice Department, in the early years of the Nixon administration, decided to slow that pace down. But the Supreme Court in 1969 declared that "the time for mere deliberate speed has run out" and awarded the mantle of legitimacy to the congressional action (*Green v. County Board of New Kent County*, 391 U.S. 430, 1969). The executive branch reversed course and began enforcing it.

Resolving Conflicts.   When different groups have conflicting demands, that conflict, if not resolved by the other two branches, usually reaches the judiciary—something that Alexis de Tocqueville noticed in an often-cited observation.[1] In strict legal theory, the court is deciding only that specific case. In fact, it is making law and resolving a political dispute over what the law should be.

Generating Support.   The Supreme Court is careful to make its major decisions in a way that maximizes the use of its persuasive powers. When school segregation was overturned in 1954, the Court acted unanimously, thus depriving opponents of the chance to cite the opinion of even one dissenting justice to justify resistance or to raise hopes that the Court might later reverse itself. The intricate verbal trappings of the law are also employed for this purpose. Archibald Cox (1968) has said:

> Ability to rationalize a constitutional judgment in terms of principles referable to accepted sources of law is an essential, major element of constitutional

---

[1]"Scarcely any political question arises in the United States which is not resolved sooner or later into a judicial question" (*Democracy in America*, 1840).

adjudication. It is one of the ultimate sources of the power of the Court—including the power to gain acceptance for the occasional great leaps forward which lack such justification. . . . Their power to command consent depends upon more than habit or even the deserved prestige of the justices. It comes, to an important degree, from the continuing force of the rule of law—from the belief that the major influence in judicial decisions is not fiat but principles which bind the judges as well as the litigants and which apply consistently among all men today, and also yesterday and tomorrow. I cannot prove these points, but they are the faith to which we lawyers are dedicated [pp. 21–22].

Cox's use of the words "belief" and "faith" are not signs of cynicism. Obviously, there are no easily perceived rules for governing complicated human affairs which govern "all men today, and also yesterday and tomorrow." But it is sometimes necessary, in order to function at all, to act *as if* such unwavering codes existed. The quest for this mystical standard is something which can unite groups which differ on almost everything else, and so it helps make the system orderly and workable, generating popular and elite support for government acts.

Judicial Recruitment. The selection of persons to serve on the bench is explicitly political. Our Presidents often attempt to appoint men with views similar to their own, and senators, who confirm the appointments, take into consideration the political views of the candidates and the possible political consequences of their tenure on the bench. Even judges, casting impartiality aside, get into this process. Harold W. Chase (1972) reports that sitting judges are consulted by officials in the Justice Department and by committees of the American Bar Association about prospective nominees. The judges, says Chase, "give their opinions freely [p. 34]." Even the respected Judge Learned Hand was known to write a letter on behalf of a candidate for a judgeship.

Judge Learned Hand: A letter of recommendation. (*Wide World Photos.*)

COURTS IN THE POLITICAL SYSTEM

What the Framers Wanted

The system of checks and balances designed at the Constitutional Convention of 1787 was meant to do more than arrange the power relationships among the three branches of government. It was also designed to be a check on the power of the masses of citizens. Devices such as the indirect election of senators, the electoral college, and federalism were intended to protect the minority from the tyranny of the majority. But the most powerful force restraining the majority was to be—and still is—the Supreme Court. Consider its structure: it is independent; its members have lifetime tenure with appointment by the President and confirmation by the Senate, neither of which were originally directly elected. Furthermore, this Court, insulated from popular control, has the power to limit the actions of the two branches which were less removed from the need to answer in some degree to the public. This relatively independent institution was given the power to overrule the Constitutional interpretations of Congress and the President, although this power was not explicitly spelled out until Marshall seized it in *Marbury v. Madison* in 1803. It had, however, been foreshadowed in the arguments at the convention and in *The Federalist,* No. 78, where Hamilton (1788) said:

> By a limited Constitution I understand one which contains certain specified exceptions to the legislative authority. . . . Limitations of this kind can be preserved in practice no other way than through the medium of courts of justice, whose duty it is to declare all acts contrary to the manifest tenor of the Constitution void. Without this, all the reservations of particular rights or privileges would amount to nothing [pp. 484–485].

Judicial Conservatism

The Court was thus intended from the beginning to be more than an enforcer of statutes and settler of disputes. It was to be a key part of the policy-making apparatus of the nation. Different interests, however, held conflicting kinds of hopes for its role. Conservatives saw it as a curb on legislatures that might be captured by popular movements seeking to undermine the sanctity of private property. Liberals saw the Court as a restraint on the President, who they feared might develop a kingly standing that would lead to arbitrary action at the expense of civil liberties. The liberals hoped that judicial review could be limited to this one area. Times and the Court's personnel have changed, but the basic ideological ambivalence toward the Court has remained. Conservatives have looked to the Court for protection of property rights, and liberals tend to seek from it protection for individual liberty. Through most of the Court's history, the conservative application has prevailed. Glendon Schubert (1965) attributes this conservative impulse to the traditions of the legal profession:

> The common-law tradition looks backward to the problems of the past and to the accommodations for those problems that were contrived by judges of an earlier day. With very few exceptions, commentators upon and teachers of law have looked upon it as a great stabilizing force, the purpose of which is to improve the predictability of future outcomes of present human decisions rather than as an instrument for helping to bring about social, economic, and political change [p. 132].

But judicial conservatism is more than a side effect of stare decisis. A lawyer earns his money by performing services for fees. Supply and demand push the best lawyers to those clients who can pay the highest fees, and these tend to be members of the business and industrial community. Schubert sees this effect as a highly specific one: Those lawyers most likely to gain fame and fortune have been those with the luck and ability to successfully represent "the interests of whatever form of wealth was dominant at the time [p. 132]." Early in the nineteenth century, the best lawyers worked for the land companies and plantation owners. Later they represented the railroads, cattle ranchers, and lumber producers. In our own time, oil, transportation, manufacturing, and big labor have attracted the first-rate legal talent. It is possible, of course, for a lawyer to attain national prominence in a low-paying field, such as civil rights or the consumer movement. Thurgood Marshall did move from the legal staff of the NAACP to the Supreme Court, and the appointment of a Ralph Nader is not unthinkable. But the great bulk of successful lawyers and, hence, most of the judges and Supreme Court justices come from more conservative backgrounds.

Structure of the Court System

The federal system has produced a dual court structure in which the state courts do most of the work. At the lowest level are the minor courts, often headed by a justice of the peace who may or may not have had legal training, which hears minor criminal matters or civil cases involving small amounts of money. These minor courts have different names in different states. They are often called *municipal courts*. There are also specialized courts at this lower level, and the division of specialities also varies. *Probate courts* supervise the disposition of the property of dead persons. *Juvenile courts* deal with cases in which the criminal code makes special provision for minors. *Domestic courts* hear disputes on family matters, including divorce cases. *Traffic courts* deal with parking and driving violations. *Small claims courts* handle disputes involving small amounts of money without the need for the complaining party to hire a lawyer. Generally, the more urbanized the jurisdiction, the more specialized the court system. In small towns and rural counties all these functions may be performed by a single minor court.

At the next level are *trial courts* which handle more serious business, including major crimes and civil actions over large amounts of money. Usually, there is one to a county, and it may be called *county court*, although the nomenclature varies from state to state. In most states, any case requiring a jury trial will be heard at this level.

Every state has at least one court to which decisions of the trial courts can be appealed. Usually, it is called the *supreme court*.

Because there are comparatively few federal crimes, most of the criminal cases are heard by state courts. Federal courts try violations of federal law, such as tax fraud, kidnaping across state lines, or counterfeiting. Civil cases can come under federal jurisdiction if they involve interpretation of federal law or of the Constitution, although state courts may also consider such cases. A civil case may also be heard in federal court if the parties are citizens of different states. Usually, and for no very good reason except to hold down the number of matters that burden the federal courts, the amount in dispute must be at least $10,000.

The basic federal court system has three levels. There are ninety-four *district courts*, each with its own geographic jurisdiction, which are the basic trial courts. There are eleven *courts of appeals*, each with its own geographic area which is called a *circuit*. These courts hear appeals from the district courts and federal administrative agencies but not from state courts. At the top of the structure is the Supreme Court of the United States which may review not only the decisions of the lower federal courts, but also the decisions of the highest state courts when federal questions are involved.

If a case involves a key Constitutional question, as did some of the later cases on the speed and manner of school desegregation, it may be heard, at the request of the litigants, by a special three-judge court. At least one of the three judges will be a district judge and one a judge of a court of appeals. Its decision may be appealed directly to the Supreme Court. This procedure is used when the public interest is served by a fast and authoritative ruling. In 1974 the Court heard the *United States v. Richard M. Nixon,* a case questioning whether the President could refuse to honor a subpoena for sixty-four White House tapes. In a rapid decision, the Court unanimously (with one abstention) ruled against Nixon's refusal to comply.

Several specialized federal courts have original or appellate jurisdiction in certain kinds of cases. The *Court of Claims* has original jurisdiction in tax, contract, and other claims against the government where recovery for damages is not involved. It has a limited power to hear appeals from district courts in cases over damage claims against the government. The *Court of Customs and Patent Appeals* reviews the rulings of the Customs Court, the Patent Office, and the Tariff Commission. The *Court of Military Appeals* reviews court-martial decisions.

The potential overlap of state and federal jurisdictions is extensive. State courts may interpret federal law, and federal courts hear cases argued under state law and must apply the law of the state in question. Before 1938, there was an attempt to apply a general federal common law in cases which involved citizens of different states, but this attempt at uniformity failed. "A case that might be brought in a state court and there be decided one way might also be brought in a federal court where an opposite result could be reached," says Delmar Karlen (1964, p. 19). In 1938 the Supreme Court decided that the federal system required that there be no general federal common law overriding the common law of the states (*Erie Railroad v. Tompkins,* 304 U.S. 64, 1938).

The Making of a Judge

The Constitution says there shall be one Supreme Court and "such inferior courts as the Congress may from time to time ordain and establish." It says nothing about qualifications. A Supreme Court justice need not even be a lawyer, although all have been. He need not have had any prior judicial experience, and a look at the historical record shows that some of the most influential justices of the Supreme Court did not serve in lower courts prior to their appointment. For example, Earl Warren was governor of California, Felix Frankfurter a law professor, and Hugo Black a senator.

Senators are highly influential in the selection of federal district judges. The senators in turn consult with local interests. The American Bar Association and state bars also play a role. The American Bar Association is an interest group actively concerned with attempts to influence the President at the nomination stage. In recent years, it has been relatively successful. Since the Eisenhower administration, the ABA opinion of potential nominees has been formally sought by the Attorney General. President Eisenhower gave the ABA a virtual veto over possible nominees. Other Presidents have listened to the association's advice without always following it. The justification for an interest group holding this much power is that no one else is as well equipped to judge the honesty, intelligence, and legal training of prospective judges. This information is useful to a President, but if other criteria are used, the President may, without desiring it, have his options needlessly limited. John R. Schmidhauser (1960) has noted that it is hard to keep ideological considerations out of the judgment of a person's competence. A candidate who has argued cases for liberal or radical causes might be seen by conservatives as less competent than a lawyer with a conservative background.

An aggressive President can use the bar association to work around Senate pressures by spotting good candidates and building local support for them. President Kennedy, who got a windfall of district-judge appointments from an expansion of the federal judiciary, followed this procedure. Home-state senators were not in a position to oppose his choices when the local endorsements and bar-association support had already been gained.

The President has somewhat greater freedom in appointing judges of the Courts of Appeals because their jurisdictions span several states with diverse interests. Senate recommendations may or may not be effective depending on individual bargaining power, the specific situation, and the inclination of the President to seek senatorial advice. Franklin Roosevelt, for example, tended not to seek it at all.

At the Supreme Court level, the choice is entirely the President's, with the Senate exercising only its seldom-used veto power. When a nominee does run into trouble—as did Clement Haynsworth and G. Harrold Carswell in the first Nixon administration—ideological differences between the Senate and the President are often at the root of it. Although ideology was not raised in the debate on those two nominees, their rejection led Nixon to charge the Senate with bias against conservative nominees from the South.

To avoid that kind of problem, Presidents tend to look for nominees who have a record of noncontroversial public service. They also seek men whose ideological stance is close to their own, recognizing that, because of the lifetime tenure of judges, a President's Supreme Court appointments may be his most lasting mark on the nation.[2] Sometimes their guesses about an appointee's future judicial behavior prove to be wrong. Harlan F. Stone, who presided as Chief Justice from 1941 to 1946, was originally appointed as a conservative by Calvin Coolidge, but he began siding with the liberals almost from the beginning of his career. Such major deviations are rare, however. Most justices conform in broad outline to their past leanings, although they may develop tendencies to depart in a few unforeseen issue areas.

Selecting judges is highly political in that party affiliation is a key consideration. Nine nominations out of ten are chosen from the ranks of the President's party. When Abe Fortas failed to win confirmation as Chief Justice and Homer Thornberry lost out as his replacement, the successful effort to block a vote was supported by Republican senators. Because of the approaching 1968 election, which a Republican had a chance to win, they saw a chance to place Republicans in those positions. The strategy worked.

From the nature of the job, we would not expect the membership of the Supreme Court to reflect a social microcosm of the nation. Henry J. Abraham (1962) describes the typical Supreme Court justice as

> white; generally Protestant . . . 50 to 55 years of age at the time of his appointment; Anglo-Saxon ethnic stock . . . high social status; reared in an urban environment; member of a civic-minded, politically active, economically comfortable family; legal training; some type of public office; generally well educated [p. 58].

Persons of similar backgrounds tend to see the world in similar ways. One reason the Court has traditionally been a guardian of established interests is that these are the interests with which most members have always identified themselves. If the Court is the keeper of the American conscience, says John R. Schmidhauser (1960), it is a conservative, middle-class conscience. "While such influence cannot ordinarily be traced in cause-and-effect formulas in specific decisions, it frequently emerges in the careers of individual justices as setting implicit limits on the scope of theoretical decision-making possibilities [p. 58]."

Samuel Krislov (1965) suggests there is also some more specific chemistry that makes a subliminal match between the philosophies of appointer and appointee, exceptions such as Coolidge and Stone notwithstanding. He cites the Truman appointees—Harold Burton, Fred Vinson, Tom Clark, and Sherman Minton—as "reasonably liberal in their economic decisions but quite conservative in their civil rights and national security rulings." Truman's memoirs and statements after he left office showed that his personal beliefs fit this pattern even more closely "than had his activities as President [p. 7]."

[2]William O. Douglas became the justice to serve the longest term in history in October 1973 when he passed the record of thirty-four years and eight months set by Samuel Field in 1897. He was appointed by Franklin Roosevelt.

The selection of Supreme Court justices is, then, infused with political considerations, although it is cloaked in procedural and rhetorical custom which follows an abstract model of justice set apart from political strife. This conscious mispackaging may serve some useful function by enhancing the legitimacy of Court decisions, and there is little danger of its being taken so seriously as to cause interference with the Court's political role. "If justices were appointed primarily for their 'judicial' qualities without regard to their basic attitudes on fundamental questions of public policy," says Robert Dahl (1958), "the Court could not play the influential role in the American political system that it does in reality play [p. 285]."

Judicial Decision Making

You might, somewhere, still find someone who will argue that judges are strict interpreters of the law as written and exercise no discretion or policy decision making on their own, but it is a difficult argument to maintain. The school of "judicial realism" has taken this myth apart through empirical research (Frank, 1958). Judges are, of course, constrained by law and precedent and the need to make coherent, rational arguments to get from a premise to a conclusion. But they can do all that and still find a lot of latitude left, owing to the necessary imprecision of the Constitution, the statutes, and the common-law aphorisms.

In one landmark study, Sheldon Goldman (1966) treated votes in federal appellate courts to a kind of analysis usually applied to legislative voting to see what kind of influences might be at work. He found that the standard demographic variables—such as religion, socioeconomic background, education, and age—which correlate with most political attitudes, were "almost entirely unrelated directly to voting behavior" by judges in appellate cases. However, party affiliation was associated with voting behavior. When a case involved a conflict between liberal and conservative points of view on economic questions, the Democratic judges tended to take the liberal side more often than the Republican judge. (p. 382). A *Philadelphia Inquirer* (1973) study of criminal cases in that city found that Republican judges were somewhat more likely to find defendants guilty and to give long sentences than Democratic judges. Since political party is also the strongest correlate of legislative voting behavior, the theory of parallel political influences in these separate branches is supported. (See Chapter 5.)

THE SUPREME COURT IN OPERATION

Selection of Cases

The Constitution gives the Supreme Court original jurisdiction in cases in which a state is a party and in cases affecting ambassadors and other public ministers. In other federal cases, it has appellate jurisdiction with authority to review both the law and the facts of a case. The Judiciary Act of 1925 provides that cases from lower federal courts may reach the Supreme Court through either of two routes: certiorari or appeal. The appeal route is for a relatively narrow range of cases, usually involving a conflict of state and federal powers, where the need for resolution by the Supreme Court is obvious. Everything else gains access to the Court by writ of certiorari, in which the Court asks to review a case by vote of four of the nine justices. The Court thus has total discretion over most of the cases it hears.

Some 4,000 requests for certiorari are filed each year. Each of these goes to the office of the Chief Justice where his clerks prepare a list, sometimes called the dead list, which is circulated to the other eight justices. It takes the vote of just one justice to put a case on the discussion list. If no justice so requests, certiorari is denied or probable jurisdiction is not noted, and there is no further discussion or vote. It is not required that a reason be given for not granting certiorari. About 70 percent of the cases are rejected at this early screening stage. Many are frivolous or involve questions that are already going to be decided in other cases. This still leaves more than a thousand cases a year to be discussed in the weekly closed meetings of the Court and whose petitions for certiorari are voted upon. In the course of a year, fewer than two hundred are accepted for argument.

This wide-open selection process is an important source of the exercise and control of the Court's political power. At this stage, the Court is not so much concerned with gaining justice for individuals as it is for

The Supreme Court: The power to clarify or leave ambiguous.
(*Ronald Wurm.*)

classes of individuals. It is here that the finer points of the law are ultimately resolved and—when the Court feels the need—some of the broader points, too. Of course, lower courts resolve points of law and engage in law making. But the Supreme Court has the last word, and the lower courts are bound to follow its decisions. And one of its foremost powers is the power to decide what to clarify and what to leave ambiguous.

The Utility of Ambiguity

You have probably noticed by now that the Founding Fathers built a good deal of ambiguity—"play in the joints" is what Archibald Cox called it—into the system they designed. If you hoped, in tracing the various levers, gears, and pulleys of the machinery of government, to arrive eventually at a point where the ambiguity will finally be resolved, you probably expected that point to be the decision-making power of the Supreme Court. But, alas for those who suffer from low tolerance of ambiguity, it is not so.

In the first place, the Supreme Court cannot answer everything. Perhaps it could not do so even if it were composed of nine gods instead of nine men. Many conflicts in American life are simply not reconcilable, at any given time, and the best anyone can do is paper them over, patch them up, ignore them, or wait for them to go away. Ambiguous solutions are often better than precise ones, because they leave both sides of a conflict with some hope that when it gets down to a specific case of conflict, one where one side or the other has to prevail, there will at least be a possibility of winning. Perhaps the head-on confrontation will never take place. If it

The Growing Burden

At the Supreme Court, cases come now at triple the rate of twenty years ago and two-thirds more than the rate of a decade ago. In the past term, the nine Justices of the Supreme Court produced 327 written opinions totalling 5,000 pages, half again as many opinions as a decade ago, and double the number of pages of ten years back. Such tabulations, however indicative they may be, do not, of course, reflect the gravity of the issues now being posed. That may be suggested by a few references to the past. From 1803 to 1857 not one act of Congress was declared invalid because it was at variance with the Constitution. In the same 54 years only 36 state statutes were held unconstitutional. By contrast, fifty-seven of the 177 cases argued before the Court during the past year involved claims that a federal or state statute or a city ordinance violated the federal Constitution, and many of these claims were upheld. Fifteen of the first twenty-four cases which were argued before the Supreme Court in the current Term involved constitutional issues. All considered, this means that the burden resting now on the nine Justices is four or five times graver than that faced a generation or two ago by such giants of Court history as the great Taft, Holmes, Brandeis, and Hughes.

—Chief Justice Warren E. Burger, 1974

does, it may be under new circumstances that no one can foresee but which will in themselves introduce new ambiguities. Ambiguity is a kind of social lubricant and it can make the legal system run more smoothly and efficiently than it otherwise could because some problems are better left off the agenda. A classic example is the division in Kansas over the issue of prohibition before 1948. The state was sharply divided between wets and drys when national prohibition was repealed, and the drys succeeded in keeping a strict state law which banned the sale and consumption of alcoholic beverages. It was enforced strictly enough to give symbolic comfort to the dry majority but not so strictly as to deprive the large wet minority of its booze. Bootleggers flourished, liquor was served at country clubs and American Legion halls, and the conflict was nicely resolved with the ambiguity of Kansans, as William Allen White observed, staggering to the polls to vote the state dry. Kansas might still be dry today had not an ambitious attorney general, Edward Arn, taken a stand against ambiguity, which he unaccountably viewed as hypocrisy, and started raiding the country clubs and Legion halls. The mortified voters repealed prohibition and elected him governor.

Edward Arn of Kansas: The voters were mortified. (*Wide World Photos.*)

The Supreme Court is tolerant of ambiguity. Although the Court has operated under different philosophies of judicial restraint at different times in its history, it has often maintained the habit of deciding only what has to be decided and leaving as many questions open as possible. Many questions sloughed off in this way become moot with the passage of time. Many can remain suspended indefinitely. Some not in these categories can be resolved in future cases.

The Supreme Court and Self-Preservation

Some concern for self-preservation enters into the Court's calculations about what to resolve and what to leave ambiguous. By not entering into disputes that deeply divide the public, the Court conserves its power to command obedience for those few areas that it decides really matter. Whether it makes the right choices depends, as always, on your point of view. Because members come from elite backgrounds, they may tend to resolve those issues that elites want resolved and leave undisturbed what the elites want undisturbed. If such a process does operate, it is largely unconscious. The things that seem important to a person depend on that person's background and training. Although Supreme Court justices tend to have the kinds of backgrounds associated with economic conservatism, they also tend to be predisposed to an abstract appreciation of individual liberty, and on many issues this predisposition can counter the conservative leaning. "One wonders, indeed," says Cox (1968), "whether the gulf between the Supreme Court and the Congress is not partly a reflection of the closer kinship the justices have with the intellectual community [p. 120]."

When the Court elects to resolve an ambiguity and take a position that carves out a new line of social policy—as it did, for example, when it outlawed school segregation in 1954 and legalized abortion in 1973—it is doing things that Congress would not dare do, and it risks eroding its own power, for it undermines the myth of the absolute continuity and predictability of the law. The common and implicit agreement to observe that myth holds the system together. Effects of weakening the myth are hard to see, although the massive disobedience to the desegregation ruling in the South is at least of anecdotal significance. The benefit is easy to see and the cost is murky. This fact has troubled Cox, who observed, "The gains of decisions advancing social justice are evident when they are rendered; any costs in erosion of the power of law to command consent are postponed until the loss accumulates." The Court's long-range problem, he says, is to preserve "the power of judge-made law to command consent while at the same time changing it to serve the new and newly felt needs of the community and the demands of individual justice [p. 23]."

Getting Access to the Court

Popular accounts of the work of the Court tend to dwell on individuals such as Linda Brown and Clarence Gideon, who had their grievances redressed by the highest court in the land. But the fact that Brown got to attend a previously all-white school and Gideon received a new trial with a public defender are of relatively minor concern. Their participation was of more symbolic than material importance. Their cases were heard, not because they were deserving people or wronged victims of oppression, but because each represented a large and significant class of problems. The Court, said Chief Justice Fred M. Vinson in 1949, hears "those cases which present questions whose resolution will have immediate importance beyond the particular facts and parties involved." The Court is interested in the "consequences for other litigants and other situations [Vose, 1958, p. 20]." The law- and policy-making functions are therefore more important than the function of dispensing individual justice, which is left to the lower courts which lack the power to select the cases they will hear.

It comes as no surprise, then, that the image of a dauntless individual, fighting to right the unrightable wrong, working his way up the hierarchy of the courts with his unique and self-contained problem, is inaccurate. Litigation is more and more an interest-group activity. Cost alone makes this almost a necessity. *Brown v. Board of Education* (1954) cost the NAACP $200,000 when dollars were worth considerably more than dollars today. Groups not only can afford to pay costs that individuals are unable to bear, but by the mere fact of their participation can demonstrate to the Court that their case has importance "beyond the particular facts and parties involved." Another way for interest groups to use the judicial process is by the filing of amicus (friend of the court) briefs. The strategic value of these briefs is to raise arguments of moral or social significance that need to be brought to the attention of the justices without detracting from the strictly legal arguments of the main parties in the case (Krislov, 1965).

A group effort can also provide coordinating services that are beyond the reach of individual litigants. Out of all the pending court cases against school segregation, the NAACP was able to choose those which presented the issue most clearly and which minimized the opportunities for a decision on narrow grounds that might leave the main issue unsettled. The advantage of the *Topeka* case was that the separate schools there were in fact equal, and so the Court could not logically have granted relief to Linda Brown without overturning *Plessy v. Ferguson*, which had upheld the separate-but-equal standard.

Such coordinated efforts can also be applied to steer cases away from the Supreme Court when the Court's composition and current trends are deemed unfavorable. Lawyers for Joe Bell, a young black man from Mississippi, argued in the state courts that his arrest and jail sentence were the result of evidence obtained in illegal arrest procedures. The Warren Court had declared that such evidence could not be used against a defendant. Bell's conviction was upheld by the Mississippi Supreme Court, but his lawyers decided not to appeal to the U.S. Supreme Court as it was constituted in 1973. They feared that the less liberal Burger Court would use the case to relax the rules against use of illegally obtained evidence. Their interest group, the Lawyers Committee for Civil Rights Under Law, was anxious to deny the Supreme Court that opportunity and to keep the stricter rule in effect for the protection of the defendants in states which still observed it. The client's interests were secondary. He stayed in jail (Matthews, 1973).

Some groups have better luck in reaching the Supreme Court than others. In general, the larger the group, the greater its chance of reaching the Supreme Court. "Supreme Court cases involve interests which are significantly larger in size than most of the interests represented by litigants in cases that are finally disposed of by subordinate judges," observes Jack Peltason (1955, p. 19). Intensity of the conflict is also a factor, as the ongoing fight over pornography illustrates. Cases which make the front page of a newspaper at the trial level are the ones most likely to be carried to the Supreme Court. However, the intensity of a case may work against its acceptance by the Supreme Court if the justices feel that the nation is not likely to accept a judicial settlement under the prevailing conditions. Then, it may let the issue stew in the legislative and executive arenas in the hope that some resolution will be worked out there, or, failing that, that a gradual entry of the judiciary into the conflict can be effected. A series of cases involving higher education nibbled at *Plessy v. Ferguson* for several years before the Court finally grasped the issue firmly in *Brown*. A pattern of judicial gradualism is also evident in the voting rights cases, as Krislov (1965) notes:

Classic v. U.S., which merely indicated that the government could punish ballot stuffers in a primary election, was a good bridge to the decision of *Smith v. Allwright*, which held that white primaries were illegal. Inasmuch as both cases hinged on the principle that primaries were elections supervised by the government, the small departure in the Classic case and the surrounding circumstances were excellent in facilitating the much more controversial destruction of the white primary [p. 45].

Concurring and Dissenting Opinions

Like the other institutions of government, the Court changes its philosophical stance from time to time as its personnel change. Its minority views are allowed expression, go into the record, and sometimes emerge in later cases as part of a new majority. The Court seldom speaks with one voice. Once the decision in a case has been reached, the Chief Justice assigns a member of the majority to write the opinion. Those who agree with the decision and the reasoning by which it was reached may also sign this *majority opinion*. Those who agree with the decision but for different reasons may write *concurring opinions*. Each justice who disagrees with the outcome may write his own *dissenting opinion* or join in another's dissent.

The multiple record left in this way has a number of uses. A dissenting opinion gives symbolic reassurance to interest groups on the losing side, but it is more than that. It makes a record which preserves the possibility of forging a link to some future new direction which a differently constituted Court—or even the same Court in different circumstances—may choose to follow. Associate Justice Oliver Wendell Holmes, for example, wrote dissenting opinions in the first part of the century which set out a systematic legal rationale for allowing state regulation of working conditions, and they later became the majority view. His famous remark, "The Fourteenth Amendment does not enact Mr. Herbert Spencer's *Social Statics*," was made in dissenting from the Court's ruling that a state could not limit working hours in bakeries to sixty a week (*Lochner v. New York*, 198 U.S. 45, 1905). Soon afterward, the Court began reconsidering the power of the states to enact such social and economic reforms, and it specifically reversed itself on the sixty-hour week in 1917 (*Bunting v. Oregon*, 243 U.S. 426).

Concurring opinions serve somewhat the same effect because the reasoning by which a decision is reached may be more important than the substantive effect of the ruling itself. In the 1972 case which gave qualified approval of the right of the *New York Times* to publish the Pentagon papers (*N.Y. Times v. U.S.*, 403 U.S. 713), nine separate opinions were written—which in itself is an indication that the Court's thinking on the First Amendment is far from settled.

Behind the Closed Door

We know little about the forces affecting Supreme Court decisions. Its deliberations are not a matter of public record, and justices do not behave like other national officials. They do not announce their voting intentions in advance, and they do not always explain them afterwards. What little information we do have comes from biographical materials and from voting-record analyses. There are several parallels with the legislative process. Justices, like legislators, bargain to gain a majority of the Court to side with their positions on decisions that involve public policy. This bargaining is particularly important at the stage of writing opinions, where dissenters from the majority may attempt to influence the majority by circulating their opinions and strengthening or weakening the terms in which the dissent is put; however, the give and take is not so direct as in legislative "logrolling."

A persuasive justice, says Walter F. Murphy (1964), may try to argue "the merits of his policy choice, to capitalize on personal regard, to bargain, to threaten, and if possible to have a choice in the selection of new personnel [p. 43]." When a justice sees that he cannot get his way, he may try to minimize the damage by persuading the majority to frame the decision in ways which will soften the policy impact. Out of these very human interactions comes the Court's public stance. When the closed door is opened, the public sees only nine men in black robes and their written opinions. There is little information about who did what to whom to produce the outcome contained in those opinions. The Court, in the public's perception, remains a monolith. Thus most discussions of it, this one included, refer to "the Court" as though it were maneuvering on the political stage as a single nine-headed beast. The reality is obscure and the metaphor forgivable.

JUDICIAL ACTIVISM AND JUDICIAL RESTRAINT

A Matter of Phasing

Sometimes the Court sits passively, watching the world go by, taking great care to decide the matters that come before it in a manner that will disturb that passing world as little as possible. In other periods, the justices seem like men on white horses, fighting to set the world right. In this stage, they may be galloping forward or backward; forward to advance new policy ideas that the other branches of government are not yet ready to embrace—or backward to defend outmoded policies that the other branches want to abandon. The kind of Court depends mostly on accidents of timing.

Many abstract arguments are raised in favor of judicial activism or judicial restraint. But like most arguments about American government, they rest not on immutable philosophies but on whose interest or whose policy is being benefited or hindered at the moment. The Court is an elite institution. So are the executive and legislative branches, but because of the different ways in which members of the different branches are selected and empowered to operate, they sometimes represent different elites in competition with one another over the distribution of the symbolic and material benefits of government. At any given moment in history, the Court may be ahead of, in step with, or behind the attitudes of the dominant elites in control of the other branches. When the Court is in step with everybody else, the result is a period of judicial restraint. When it is either ahead or behind, a period of judicial activism results while the Court struggles to pull the other branches ahead or hold them back.

Through most of the nation's history, the Court has usually been in phase, and so judicial restraint has been the dominant tradition. There is often an interaction process which tends to push the Court into an in-phase stance sooner than it might reach it if left to itself or if it had power beyond its mere moral authority and persuasive ability. Stuart S. Nagel (1969) counted 165 instances of bills introduced to restrict judicial activity between 1802 and 1957. He found a pattern of stimulus-response in which the Court does something to disturb the elites in control of the other branches, they fight back, and the Court changes its behavior. Franklin Roosevelt's Court-packing plan was an attempt to stop the Court from knocking down his economic and social legislation of the first New Deal. After the 1936 landslide reelection of Roosevelt, the plan was drawn up in 1937. Then Associate Justice Owen Roberts switched from the conservative to the liberal side, and the Court-packing plan was no longer necessary.

Other Court-restricting measures have been based on the congressional authority—in Article III, Section 2—to make exceptions and regulations to the Supreme Court's appellate jurisdiction. As a practical device for curbing the Court, it is not very useful, for the curb would come at the price of a certain amount of chaos. Congress was unhappy with the Court's action in the reapportionment cases, but it did not enact legislation to withdraw reapportionment matters from its jurisdiction, because it might then have been left with different reapportionment standards in each of the ten appellate jurisdictions. But the mere fact that such legislation is introduced and taken seriously by important members of Congress serves as a signal to the Court that it is treading on the toes of other elites. Whether it trims its sails depends on its evaluation of the risk of losing its sometimes tenuous basis of power.

Mr. Justice Roberts: A message in the election returns. (*Wide World Photos.*)

Techniques of Sidestepping

The rationale for judicial restraint seems solidly constructed, perhaps because so much time and thought has gone into it. However, it does not always bear close inspection. For example, the Court will sometimes dodge an issue on the ground that it is a "political" as opposed to a legal or judicial question. What this means, beyond the fact that the Court would rather have elected officers of government tackle the question, has not been very well established. Jack Peltason (1955) searched the decisions in which the Court retreated on the basis of a professed desire to avoid political questions and tried in vain to find the consistent thread. Political questions, he concluded, are those which judges choose not to decide, and a question becomes political by the judge's refusal to decide it. The refusal to decide is itself interest activity and affects the outcome of the group struggle. For example, those anxious to retain the Georgia unit system for nominating their governor won a considerable victory when the Supreme Court refused to consider the constitutionality of the scheme because it was a political question. Judges, because they are judges, are involved in the politics of the people [p. 10].

That particular example of a political question has, of course, been discarded. But before the Supreme Court tackled the problem of representation in *Baker v. Carr*, the "political question" problem was its standard rationale for not facing that issue (*Coleman v. Miller*, 307 U.S. 433, 1939; *South v. Peters*, 339 U.S. 276, 1950).

Beyond the issue of whether a question is political or legal, there are any number of maxims for judicial self-restraint. The number depends on whose analysis is used and how detailed interest is in this rather academic question. Henry J. Abraham (1968) lists sixteen self-imposed "thou shalt nots." Louis D. Brandeis (1935) gave seven. Archibald Cox (1968) has boiled it down to three. The latter's succinct summary:

> First, the courts should avoid constitutional issues whenever possible. Such issues should be decided only when raised in ordinary litigation by one who could show that his own constitutional rights were violated and who could not prevail without a constitutional decision.
>
> Second, the courts should not invalidate laws unless they were inconsistent with some specific constitutional prohibition.
>
> Third, wherever there was room for rational difference of opinion upon a question of fact or upon the relative importance of different facts or conflicting interest . . . the doctrines of federalism and separation of powers would require the Court to uphold the legislation [pp. 3–4].

The theory of judicial restraint was developed in response to the backward-looking judicial activism that struck down first state and then federal legislative action to achieve social and economic reforms in the first third of the twentieth century. Judicial restraint put the Court back in phase with the other branches and levels of government from 1937 until the beginning of Chief Justice Earl Warren's tenure in 1953. Under Warren's guidance, the Court stepped out ahead, doing things that the other branches were reluctant to do in civil rights and civil liberties, beginning with school desegregation in the *Brown* case in 1954.

Under Chief Justice Warren Burger, appointed by President Nixon in 1969, the Court has wavered between activism and restraint, depending on the issue involved. The decision to overturn state abortion laws was an activist decision, because it did what state legislatures were not willing to do. The 1973 decision not to equalize school financing (*San Antonio Independent School District v. Rodriguez*, 411 U.S. 1) was one of restraint. That decision, by a 5 to 4 vote, returned the battle over reform of school financing to the legislative arena. Associate Justice Lewis F. Powell, Jr., who wrote the opinion, acknowledged that the policy outcome of ruling the other way would have been a desirable one. Because schools are financed through local property taxes and localities vary widely in wealth, there are severe inequities in the resources available to the public schools. But Powell said that he and the other justices in the Court majority were "unwilling to assume for ourselves a level of wisdom superior to that of legislators, scholars and educational authorities in 49 states, especially where the alternatives proposed are only recently conceived and nowhere yet tested."

This, then, was a Court that could go either way, one that could take the activist step or hold back in the self-restraining stance, depending on the circumstances. The one consistent thread is that it is the circumstances, not devotion to abstract principle, that determine the stance.

The Legacy of the Warren Court

When the Warren Court departed from the restraining notion that electoral inequities were problems restricted to the "political" arena for solution, it established a new and yet very sound rule of law. The Court said, in effect, that it makes no sense to send an aggrieved litigant to the other branches of government for redress when the very grievance that he is complaining about is denial of access to those other branches. That, of course, was precisely the situation in the reapportionment cases. Until *Baker v. Carr* in 1962, the Court had stood by the opinion of Frankfurter (1946) in *Colegrove v. Green* (328 U.S. 549), which reads like something from *Catch 22* by Joseph Heller (1955): "The remedy for unfairness in districting is to secure state legislatures that will apportion properly." Frankfurter and the rest of the Court knew, of course, that there was no way to secure such state legislatures as long as there was unfairness in districting. Yet they were not being cynical or stupid like the officers in Joseph Heller's mad army. They were simply afraid that the Court would be biting off more than it could chew, that it would give the command and nothing would happen, and that it would stand there naked and powerless. Frankfurter was still around in 1962 to express this fear explicitly in his dissent to *Baker v. Carr*:

> The Court's authority—possessed of neither the purse nor the sword—ultimately rests on sustained public confidence in its moral sanction. Such feeling must be nourished by the Court's complete detachment . . . from political entanglements and by abstention from injecting itself into the clash of political forces in political settlements [369 U.S. 267].

The Warren Court's contribution was the recognition that the Court had a special duty to take such a risk in cases where the nature of the problem at hand closed other sources of relief. It assumed a specific obligation to take the catches out of the system. This assumption led it beyond the apportionment problem to the reinforcement of the preferred position of basic political liberties, including speech and association. Without these liberties, the system works in ways never intended. If the executive or the legislative branches suppress them, it does no good to tell the silenced citizen to take his battle to the polls. If he is silenced, he cannot do that effectively. The Court has special responsibilities in those matters that involve keeping the system open and operating.

THE LIMITS OF JUDICIAL POWER

A Long-run Vulnerability

Felix Frankfurter's worried argument that *Baker v. Carr* would undermine the Court's authority turned out to be wrong for the time in which he made it. The Court made the audacious ruling and it got away with it. Reform was accomplished, attacks on the Court were repelled, and its prestige and authority were enhanced. But the Warren Court and the issues it faced met at a special time in history. It may be that in most times and situations, the Frankfurter impulse to tread softly would be the wise one. When it does seem to break new ground, the Court may be overcoming no more than a temporary snag in the operation of the other branches. Given time, the other branches might have come around. Meanwhile, if the Court succeeds at leading, it is because it has the tacit support of the public or at least the absence of any cohesive majority opposing the new step.

Mr. Justice Frankfurter: The worried view may be wisest. (*Wide World Photos.*)

John P. Roche (1955) argues that a main source of the Court's power is indeed such a negative one: the fact that in this diverse nation there is seldom a cohesive majority on any given question. "No cohesive majority . . . would permit a politically irresponsive judiciary to usurp decision-making functions, but, for complex social and institutional reasons, there are few issues in the United States on which cohesive majorities exist," he says, adding ". . . when monolithic majorities do exist on issues, the Court is likely to resort to judicial self-restraint [p. 771]."

What happens when the Court acts in opposition to a cohesive majority? Congress could withdraw the subject matter of its decision from the Court's jurisdiction. It could initiate a constitutional amendment to reverse the decision. It could change the size of the Court. But each of these strategies involves an attack on the Court as a highly regarded symbol of justice. Usually there is an easier way: just pass legislation which alters the effects of Court decisions without attacking the Court itself. This strategy is possible when the ruling is based on something other than direct constitutional interpretation, such as the meaning and intent of a statute or vague rules of law which Congress has the power to clarify. Congressional reaction to Court decisions enlarging the rights of persons accused of crime has followed this borderline path with results which have yet to be tested. For example, the Supreme Court ruled in 1966 in *Miranda v. Arizona* (384

U.S. 436) that the Fifth and Fourteenth Amendments required that a suspect's confession may not be used in evidence against him if it is obtained without informing him, prior to any questioning, that he has the right to remain silent, that anything he says could be used against him, that he has the right to the presence of an attorney, and that if he cannot afford an attorney, one will be appointed for him. In 1968, Congress altered the criminal code to provide that the conditions of the *Miranda* decision should be considered in determining whether a confession is voluntary and therefore admissible, but that "the presence or absence of any of the above-mentioned factors to be taken into consideration by the judge need not be conclusive on the issue of voluntariness of the confession [82 Stat. 210]." The effect, of course, was to reverse the main thrust of the *Miranda* decision, at least until the new law could be tested in the Court. Enactment of this provision was a defeat for libertarians in Congress, but they took some satisfaction in being able to block more drastic measures which would have restricted the jurisdiction of the Court in such cases. There is always the threat of these more drastic strategies, and the threat itself can be effective in modifying the Court's behavior.

Curbing the Court: The Attack from the Right

Segregationists and people who still thought Communists were taking over the national government launched an attack on the Supreme Court in the late 1950s. While citizens' groups erected billboards with the slogan, "Impeach Earl Warren," members of Congress introduced a wide variety of bills to limit the Court's jurisdiction in special cases involving subversion and schools. The large number of bills was a sign of the weakness of the attack. Members were introducing them, not in any hope of getting them passed, but to provide symbolic satisfaction to their constituents. It indicated, says Nagel (1969), "a lack of cohesive leadership by the anti-Court forces which kept these forces from centering on one or a few bills [p. 45]."

Herman Pritchett (1961) followed that battle from 1957 to 1960 and attributed the Court's ability to cope with the attack to four factors:

1   The widespread respect for the judiciary among the citizenry

2   The nature of the motives of the attackers who were out of step with the dominant views of that time

3   The obvious exaggerations in their charges against the Court

4   The Court's own moderation of its views (as, for example, when it allowed the interpretation of "all deliberate speed" in desegregation to become slower and slower)

California Billboard, 1963:
The attack was weak.
(Wide World Photos.)

The final point of this analysis supports the view of the Court's long-term weakness. The Court wavered even though the attack was very weak. If the charges had been better grounded or if the attackers had represented something approaching a cohesive majority, the Court easily would have been rendered helpless. Nagel suggests that cooperation of the President and Congress is a prerequisite for bringing the Court to heel, but that, of course, presupposes a cohesive majority.

The Court and Public Opinion

The Court's prestige, like that of other major institutions, began dropping in the decade of the 1960s, although it showed signs of recovery in the 1970s. In 1966 the Harris Survey asked, "As far as the people in charge of running the U.S. Supreme Court are concerned, would you say you have a great deal of confidence, only some confidence, or hardly any confidence at all in them?" The 51 percent who said they had a great deal of confidence in

Table 11-1 How much confidence do you have in the people running the U.S. Supreme Court?

	TOTAL	EAST	MIDWEST	SOUTH	WEST
A great deal:	33%	34%	37%	28%	32%

Source: Louis Harris & Associates, *Confidence and Concern: Citizens View American Government*, Committee on Government Operations, U.S. Senate, 1973.

the Court in 1966 dwindled to 28 percent in 1972 and then increased to 33 percent in 1973. Faith in government in general, particularly in the executive branch, was declining in the same period, and the Court's dip in prestige produced no noticable loss of its power to command obedience. As with other branches of government, it may not be the general attitude which matters so much as the attitudes of specific issue-publics. Walter F. Murphy and Joseph Tanenhaus (1969) reasoned that for the Court to draw its moral authority from public support, three conditions must be met: (1) the public must be aware of the issues involved; (2) it must know of the Court's action on these issues; and (3) it must be willing to accept the authority of the Court to decide the issue and agree with the correctness of a particular decision. Putting questions designed to test the existence of these conditions to a national sample, they found that only about one person in eight among the adult population met all three of their criteria. However, this one-eighth represented "a considerable share of the politically active public [p. 295]."

From what we have already found out about the relatively low level of public awareness of public affairs (see Chapter 4), this is not very surprising. It is nevertheless easy to forget. The Court's attentive audience is limited, but it is an important audience, and it probably varies from one issue to another.

Restraint as a Source of Power

In the long run, the Court maintains its power by being quite careful about how it uses it. This has been true since the days of John Marshall, who was crafty as well as careful. His decision in *Marbury v. Madison* (1 Cranch 137, 1803) is remembered for its assertion of the power of the Court to declare acts of Congress unconstitutional. But it is also the archetype of judicial politicking in its most cunning form. The case arose over the "midnight judges" appointed by President John Adams to fill newly created vacancies with persons sympathetic to the outgoing Federalists. Adams literally sat up the night before Jefferson's inauguration, signing the commissions of the new judges.

The Jeffersonian Republicans repealed the act under which the new judgeships had been created, and the Federalists complained that the repealing statute was unconstitutional. William Marbury's commission as justice of the peace in the District of Columbia had been signed by Adams on the eve of the inauguration but it had not been delivered. The Republicans, of course, refused to deliver it. Marbury sought relief under the Judiciary Act of 1789, which gave the Court power to issue a writ of mandamus to compel the public official to carry out his duty. He wanted the Court to make Jefferson's Secretary of State, who happened to be James Madison, deliver his commission.

Chief Justice Marshall's sympathies were with the Federalists. But it

Chief Justice Marshall: Separating fact from principle. (*Wide World Photos.*)

was clear that if he granted Marbury's plea, Jefferson and Madison would not obey it, and nothing would be gained except a demonstration of the Court's powerlessness and possibly his own impeachment. His solution, a standard one in politics, was to find a way to separate fact from principle. Marbury was right in principle, he said, for the Republican administration should have delivered the commission, and the writ of mandamus was the proper remedy. But although he was right in principle, Marbury must lose in fact, Marshall continued, because the section of the Judiciary Act of 1789 under which he brought his plea was unconstitutional. Congress—under Article III, Section 2—could regulate the Court's authority only in appellate jurisdiction. Therefore, the Supreme Court was powerless to grant Marbury the relief he deserved because its first duty was to the higher law: "An act of the legislature repugnant to the Constitution is void. . . . It is emphatically the province and duty of the judicial department to say what the law is."

Everybody was happy. Marshall had sidestepped a quarrel with Jefferson. Marbury had known he would never be a judge anyway. And Marshall had planted his judicial time bomb. An act of Congress would not again be declared invalid until the Supreme Court used the *Dred Scott* case to nullify the Missouri Compromise in 1857. Without *Marbury v. Madison*, the Founders' intent to grant that power to the Court might have been forgotten.

Reform by Consensus

Not even the activist Warren Court was powerful enough to carry out social reform by itself. Enforcement of the 1954 *Brown* decision was obstructed and delayed for more than fifteen years before compliance was finally effected on a meaningful scale. That was a case of overcoming defiance. Evasion is more difficult. "Thousands of policemen mumble the Miranda warnings about the right to counsel and the freedom to remain silent when they arrest suspects," says Jacob (1972), "but the circumstances are such that the warning does not ordinarily inhibit interrogation because the suspect does not comprehend its importance [p. 217]." The chief reason for the Court's success in gaining legal assistance for poor defendants in criminal trials is the widespread support among lawyers for the *Gideon* decision (see p. 51). And Archibald Cox (1968) has documented the Court's internal struggles with its collective conscience over the desegregation of public accommodations in the early 1960s. If that reform had come through the courts alone, it might have suffered a far worse fate than the *Brown* decision. Fortunately, the Court was able to sidestep the issue until President Johnson requested and Congress enacted the Civil Rights Act of 1964. The Court promptly upheld its constitutionality and that decision, having the participation of all three branches of government, had an irresistable force of legitimacy behind it. Like all political institutions, the Supreme Court is most effective when it expresses consensus.

Clarence Gideon: Support among lawyers. (*Wide World Photos.*)

SUGGESTED READINGS

Abraham, Henry J. *The Judicial Process.* 2d ed. New York: Oxford University Press, 1968.   An extensive introduction to the American judicial process, containing basic information on all areas of the judicial system.

Becker, Theodore (ed.). *The Impact of Supreme Court Decisions.* New York: Oxford University Press, 1969.   This volume gives an excellent analysis of the consequences and influence of Supreme Court decisions on the political system.

Blumberg, Abraham S. *The Scales of Justice.* 2d ed. New York: Transaction Books, 1974.   Examines the obstacles to change in the legal system and the unequal influence of groups in the judicial system.

Dean, Howard E. *Judicial Review and Democracy.* New York: Random House, 1967.   An in-depth analysis of the concept of judicial review and its place in the democratic process of politics.

Lewis, Anthony. *Gideon's Trumpet.* New York: Vintage, 1966. Unfolding the case that produced the declaration of the right to counsel for persons accused of state felonies, Lewis shows the workings of the Court in intimate detail.

McCloskey, Robert. *The American Supreme Court, 1789–1960.* Chicago: The University of Chicago Press, 1960.   A historical analysis of the role of the Supreme Court in the political process.

Richardson, Richard J., and Kenneth N. Vines. *The Politics of Federal Courts.*   A careful analysis of the lower federal courts, with useful information concerning their role in the policy-making process.

Schubert, Glendon. *Judicial Policy Making: The Political Role of the Courts.* Chicago: Scott, Foresman, 1965.   A good introduction to the functions of the judiciary in the political system and its place in the process of policy formulation.

Chapter 12

The Bureaucracy

THE IDEAL AND THE REALITY

Getting the Work Done

In the spring of 1972, with an energy shortage obviously developing, the Office of Emergency Preparedness made a strange decision. It refused to expand the amount of oil allowed to be imported into the country. This lack of action hastened the shortage. The Senate Committee on Government Operations assigned an investigator to find out why the action was not taken. The investigator (Duffy, 1973) interviewed the decisionmakers and came back with an answer. If large quantities of foreign oil had been allowed into the country, the bureaucrats in the Office of Emergency Preparedness would then have faced the job of allocating it fairly among the competing claims of the nation's refineries. They did not want to do that work:

> Federal oil planners were undermanned and overworked, and they didn't want to take on the new and quite demanding task of managing an expanded oil import program. So they refused to expand the level of oil imports sufficiently and created the shortage. This is a classic case of a bureaucracy setting a course of action, not in response to the nation's needs, but to secure its own comfort [p. 4].

Oil import quotas were finally abandoned, but not until April 1973, when the shortage was reaching crisis proportions.

If making policy seems complicated, carrying it out can be even worse. Viewed from afar, the national government of the United States seems to have a straightforward system of organization with separate functions assigned to separate branches. Congress makes the law, the courts interpret the laws, and the President executes the laws. We have found out by now that this division is not so clearcut and that the three branches are constantly performing functions ascribed to the others.

In this chapter, we shall encounter the problem of overlapping functions once more. Moving to more mundane levels than we have covered before, we shall see how the bureaucracy not only carries out the law but also interprets the law and sometimes even makes the law. For when the work does get done, it is the bureaucracy which performs it.

Bureaucracy as the Enemy

In some respects, the bureaucracy is like an unexplored continent. Many have penetrated it, but no one explorer has a clear idea of all that it contains or enough insight to predict how it will behave. An observer who examines some portion of it in detail may quickly be reduced to a condition of despair. Neil Sheehan, whose job with the *New York Times* required him to read the Pentagon Papers in their entirety, came away from that experience with an altered consciousness of the way the government works. Inside it, he said, was an inner government:

> . . . a centralized state, far more powerful than anything else, for whom the enemy is not simply the Communists but everything else, its own press, its own judiciary, its own Congress, foreign and friendly governments—all these are potentially antagonistic. It had survived and perpetuated itself, often using

Gasoline Lines, 1974: To expand imports was too demanding. *(United Press International.)*

the issue of anti-Communism as a weapon against the other branches of government and the press, and finally, it does not function necessarily for the benefit of the Republic but rather for its own ends, its own perpetuation; it has its own codes which are quite different from public codes. Secrecy was a way of protecting itself, not so much from threats by foreign governments, but from detection from its own population on charges of its own competence and wisdom [Halberstam, 1972, p. 409].

Sheehan was talking about the national-security bureaucracy of the Kennedy and Johnson administrations which, counting the Department of Defense and using the annual budget and number of employees as standards of measurement, was just about half the total federal bureaucracy. He also noted that this "centralized state" kept going, from one administration to another, with each group of newcomers careful not to expose the shortcomings of those before them. The Founding Fathers did not plan that a monarchy would rule in perpetuity. Yet, though there is no king, we have a presence which persists for long periods, capable at times of escaping the control of checks and balances.

This phenomenon is not restricted to the national-security field. On the domestic side, the Nixon administration, long before the political espionage scandals came to light, became locked in conflict with Congress over the President's use of extreme methods to make the bureaucracy do his bidding. Chief among these methods were impounding funds that Congress had voted and asserting a privilege of all members of the executive branch to refuse to discuss their actions with Congress. Mr. Nixon also put the key decisionmakers not in the departments, but in the White House. He placed in the departments some men who lacked substantive background for the jobs they held but whom he trusted to serve as watchdogs for the inside staff. Nelson Polsby (1973) observed that Nixon governed the executive branch "in the manner of a small army of occupation garrisoned amid a vast and hostile population." The President did this because he could not be sure that he could get the people who worked for him to do his bidding. Polsby explained:

> It is a fairly reliable rule of thumb that government agencies retain forever the political coloration that they have when they are founded, given their central missions and (the way they are) initially staffed. Undeniably, also, the great expansions of federal agencies have taken place under Democratic presidents. Thus a Republican president is bound to feel at least a little like he is surrounded by career-long Democratic bureaucrats, all hot in pursuit of the basically Democratic objectives of their housing, education, welfare, transportation, urban development and science programs [pp. C1–3].

The formless power of the bureaucracy can frustrate and at times assume the formal duties of all three constitutional branches of government. There is scarce evidence that the Founders foresaw this development.

Origins

Congress has authority, under Article I, Section 8, to make all the laws "necessary and proper" to carry out its enumerated powers. That gives it the power to create administrative departments and agencies. Once they are created, someone has to run them. The President is required by Article II to "take care that the laws be faithfully executed." That is his chief claim to power over the bureaucracy, but the claim is neither exclusive nor sufficient. Congress and the President have been in continuous contention for control of the bureaucracy, and one effect has been to give the agencies the opportunity to play one off against the other, thus remaining largely self-controlled.

On the typical organization chart, the President seems to be in control because he is at the top of the structure. It is true that he can hire and fire between 6,500 and 7,000 officeholders who are unregulated by the Civil Service. This power is important at the top levels, including Cabinet secretaries, undersecretaries, and agency heads, who chart the course of policy as it is carried out. Yet, despite the appearance of the chart, the greater share of formal power belongs to Congress by virtue of its uncontested ability to arrange the administrative machinery when it creates an agency. Congress can, and often has, set up agencies that are independent of the President. Through the power of the purse, exercised by committee specialists, it can maintain some degree of continuing control.

The Constitution has had a lot to do with the evolution of the bureaucracy even in the absence of specific provision for it. In addition to creating the two branches of government with operational authority over the bureaucracy, the Constitution created yet another source of conflict by guaranteeing individual rights against government abuse. This feature allows the courts to act as a check on bureaucratic actions. And the federal structure lends itself to decentralization in the organization of the bureaucracy. As a result, the bureaucracy is fragmented and subject to cross pressures; it reflects the diversity of the dominant elites. The bureaucracy's internal conflicts are the elite's conflicts (Woll, 1963).

George Washington began as President with only about 350 civilian employees. As late as 1801 there were only 2,100 working for Thomas Jefferson. By the start of the twentieth century, under William McKinley, there were 208,000. The civilian bureaucracy is now at about 3 million persons. Organizational complexity has also increased. In the beginning, there were only three departments, War, State, and Treasury, reflecting the basic needs of the new republic. These are now eleven, each formed to meet specific needs of its times.

For most of the first century of the bureaucracy's growth, there was no civil service system. If there had been, the party system might not have gained its initial foothold. Jobs were the parties' main currency. It was Senator William Marcy of New York, defending an appointment by President Andrew Jackson, who explained the patronage system with the simple phrase, "to the victor belong the spoils of the enemy [Safire, 1972, p. 630]." The system was attacked, first on moral grounds, then on the basis that a growing and industrializing nation needed more professional administrators. The assassination of President James A. Garfield in 1881 by a disappointed office seeker focused attention on the problem, and a limited civil service system was established with the Pendleton Act of 1883. From that time on, no President ever found any political advantage in cutting the Civil Service, and many found something to gain in expanding it, usually in response to some current abuse or political problem. About 85 percent of all federal employees are now included in the system.

From Spoils to Merit

Workers for the bureaucracy are recruited through competitive examinations administered by the Civil Service Commission throughout the nation on a regular basis. Anyone may take the tests, and the scores determine who is eligible for federal employment, with war veterans spotted extra points. An agency with a job opening notifies the Civil Service Commission and is given three names from which to choose.

Although fairer than the spoils system, this method of recruitment leaves some groups still discriminated against. Those with fewer educational opportunities are less likely to score well on the exams, which are imperfect predictors of job success. And the force of tradition has discouraged members of some groups, such as women and blacks, from seeking work beyond a limited range of categories. Jobs in the higher-paying categories are held primarily by white males.

To help insulate the system from political pressures and the evils of the spoils system, public employees in the civil service have their political activities limited by law. They may vote, make financial contributions, and express their opinions. They may attend political rallies or hold some local offices. But the Hatch Act, first enacted in 1939, bars them from taking an active part in party politics and campaigns. Nor may they hold any state or federal elective office. Another limitation to the activity of government workers is the agreement which a job seeker makes upon applying to the civil service not to strike against the government. In recent years, this pledge has not been a total barrier to collective bargaining. In 1962, President Kennedy recognized the right of government employees to organize when he signed an executive order to that effect. Today, a majority of civil service workers belong to unions. The no-strike pledge has not always been strictly observed. Postal workers walked off the job in 1970, and this action was followed by a "sick out"—workers calling in sick instead of reporting to work as a way of protesting their job conditions—among a substantial number of the Federal Aviation Agency's air traffic controllers.

The substitution of a merit system for a spoils system has produced a stable and capable bureaucracy, but one which absorbs a good deal of time and energy in internal administration. It also creates a conservative bias by insulating agency decisionmakers from electoral constraints and by discouraging innovation. Government policy has been removed yet another step from popular control. If law is what the judges say it is, policy is what the administrators say it is. And when administrators do not change with elective officials, political interests can continue to operate inside the government long after they have been repudiated by the voters.

Designing the Ideal System

As in most human endeavor, it is possible to design a system on paper that seems clear and efficient. But once it is in operation, things begin to happen that the designer did not count on. The design is still useful, however, if only as a standard for comparison with reality.

The complexities of the modern age require conscious coordination of effort, and so rationalized, large-scale hierarchial organization of human activity is one thing that sets off the modern age from all others. Older civilizations had their bureaucracies, of course. Max Weber, looking at practices in ancient China, Egypt, India, and Rome, and in modern Western Europe, found that the common elements were hierarchy, with a line of authority running from top to bottom; a rational division of labor; the formalization of duties according to rules of procedure; and the professionalization of the administrative class (Bendix, 1960; Weber, 1964). In Weber's ideal type, the bureaucracy is a passive, depersonalized, neutral instrument of government, organized to carry out policy and not to make it.

But our own bureaucracy acts on its own as well as at the behest of policymakers. It is neither neutral nor passive. It contains active representation of various interest groups in the society, and it is itself a powerful interest group with its own specific concerns to advance and protect. Our bureaucracy is also more fluid in terms of personnel than Weber's highly formal system would allow. Around the core of career personnel are many people who move in and out of the system, and the flow of power is affected by personal relationships among bureaucrats, private individuals, and elected officials.

If the executive branch merely carried out the policies set by Congress and the President, it would come closer to Weber's idealized design. But the bureaucracy gets its hand into the process at both the input and output stages. It develops and recommends policy proposals that go into the decision-making system and interprets and implements them after they come out (Woll, 1963). The range of possible actions is wide. Administrators can oftentimes ignore a statutory provision altogether and get away with it. The most famous example is the nonenforcement of the Sherman Antitrust Act from its passage in 1890 until its activation by Theodore

Roosevelt beginning in 1904. Administrators can also apply the law with a zealous exactitude well beyond the intentions of the legislature. There are always more things to do than administrators have the time or energy to accomplish. In deciding how to allocate their scarce resources, they are making policy. They must decide which rules to enforce with vigor, where to relax, which violators to prosecute, and which of the conflicting interpretations of the law to follow. The problems that most interest these working-level decisionmakers are the problems that are most likely to be handled. Between 1961 and 1969, a Ralph Nader study group discovered that the number of restraint-of-trade and deceptive-practice cases initiated by the Federal Trade Commission declined. But the number of such cases involving textiles and furs remained relatively steady, thereby accounting for an ever-higher proportion of all cases. Somebody, said the Nader report, had a wool and textile "fixation" (Nader, 1971). But someone must ultimately decide which kinds of cases to pursue, and such decisions are implicit in the bureaucrats' work. Additionally, administrators are often granted explicit power to make rules of procedure when Congress lacks the time or the knowledge to incorporate such rules into its legislation. Finally, bureaucrats are, like other agents of government, dispensers of symbolic rewards. A delegation of civic leaders seeking a new post office will visit not only its representatives in Congress but also the bureaucrats in the General Services Administration to receive assurances that their needs are understood and that their pleas produce a sympathetic response—if not an actual new post office.

The Structure of the Bureaucracy

The classification of executive organizations is fairly complicated because they are, in a sense, organic, that is, created in response to specific needs. These organizations evolve and grow in response to the demands of particular constituencies. Sometimes an agency and its constituency have a symbiotic relationship in which each needs the other to survive. The classic example is the case of the Army Corps of Engineers and the interests represented by the National Rivers and Harbors Congress (Maas, 1950).

A logical classification system would start by separating foreign affairs and defense from domestic matters. The former includes the Departments of State and Defense; the embassies and missions overseas; the quasi-independent Agency for International Development; and the Central Intelligence Agency. The domestic agencies include cabinet departments, such as the Department of Housing and Urban Development; agencies in the Executive Office of the President, such as the Office of Economic Opportunity; and independent agencies, such as the Interstate Commerce Commission.

The basic building blocks in the executive structure are departments or agencies, each with a single head—a cabinet secretary in the case of a department, or someone with the title of administrator or director in the case of an agency. The top-level functions in the cabinet departments are performed by political appointees with a bewildering array of titles: undersecretary, assistant secretary, deputy assistant secretary and—in the Department of Defense—principal deputy assistant secretary. Below the top executive level and at the highest career level, you find subdivisions with a variety of labels: *administration*, as in the Manpower Administration of the Department of Labor; *bureau*, as in the Bureau of Indian Affairs of the Department of Interior; *service*, as in the Community Health Service of the Department of Health, Education, and Welfare; *division*, as in the Civil Rights Division of the Department of Justice. These are further subdivided by specialized function into organizations which also have a variety of names: *office*, *division*, and *directorate* are among the most common. There is no uniform classification system which enables an observer to tell at a glance the relative level of jobs in different departments without resorting to the appendix of the budget to see what pay grades are programmed for each slot. Generally, the greater the specialization needed to do a job, the more intricate the organization.

Bureaucrats, like anyone else, tend to forget that the world of their immediate perception, containing the people they regularly serve and interact with, is not a representative sample of the real world. It tends instead to be a highly narrow, peculiar, and deviant sample of the real world. Forgetting this, they find it easy to assume that the immediate interests of the bureau and its clientele are synonymous with the national interest. Since different bureaus have different clientele who want different things, they cannot all be right, and the government frequently works at cross-purposes with itself. Bureaucratic conflict may arise when different departments have similar missions, as when social problems associated with urbanization are attacked by both the Department of Health, Education, and Welfare and the Department of Housing and Urban Development. Or two departments may find that different missions bring them into similar subject areas, which often happens with the Department of Defense and the Department of State. Both sorts of conflict may also arise within departments. Some units of the Department of Agriculture, for example, have spent money to increase crop yields while other units were paying farmers to cut yields back. The government has helped tobacco farmers to market their crop while urging consumers to stop using it because of the health hazard. Government employees in Washington have been given an incentive in the form of free parking spaces to drive their automobiles to work even when their work consists, as it does for some employees in the Department of Transportation, of finding ways to persuade Americans to stop driving their cars and use mass transit instead. Such conflicts illustrate the complexity of the tasks facing the federal bureaucracy and some of the built-in barriers to accomplishing its goals.

In biology, life forms evolve slowly to meet the demands of the environment. In government, there is also a process of adaptation in response to needs, pressures, and shifting power relationships. The most elementary organizational problem is the one of dividing the work. There are four different kinds of divisions by which work can be and is apportioned:

Geography.   This obvious division in a country as large as ours occurs at some level in most government operations: for example, the Alaskan Air Command, the Soil Conservation Service South Regional Technical Service Center, or the Appalachian Regional Commission.

Clientele.   Some organizations deal with a particular group, no matter where members may be located: the Bureau of Indian Affairs, the Veterans Administration, the Departments of Labor and Agriculture.

Function.   The most straightforward kind of organization centers on a specific task. The Bureau of the Census performs the constitutional function of counting the citizenry every ten years and runs a continuing, large-scale survey of current population characteristics.

Process.   Sometimes it makes sense to group people who utilize similar skills together, even though they perform different functions for different clientele. The Health Services and Mental Health Administration is an example.

Any or all these divisions of work could be incorporated into the traditional department system. But specific needs and problems have led to the creation of novel forms of bureaucratic life which have tended to proliferate in the past half-century. This development began on a very small and tentative scale with the act in 1846 that created the Smithsonian Institution in response to the bequest from James Smithson. The Smithsonian charter was the first attempt to mix private and public functions (Seidman, 1970). Its strange table of organization lists "The Establishment" at the top, consisting of the President, Vice President, Chief Justice, and department heads. "The Establishment" has no known functions. Business is conducted by a board of regents, composed of the Vice President, the Chief Justice, three senators appointed by the president of the Senate, three House members appointed by the speaker, and six private citizens appointed by joint resolution of Congress. This board chooses the Institution's secretary, who is its operating head. Although the President has no power to hire and fire Smithsonian officers, the Institution is treated as an executive agency, and most of its income comes from congressional appropriations. The secretary therefore tends to be "most discreet in asserting his prerogatives as the agent of an independent establishment [p. 219]." As the oldest scholarly organization in the federal government, the

Smithsonian would have been a good place to put such related functions as the National Archives and the National Foundation on Arts and Humanities, but this was not done because the President lacked direct power over the Institution.

The next big departures from departmental organization came with the establishment of two somewhat independent agencies, the Civil Service Commission in 1883 and the Interstate Commerce Commission in 1887. (The latter was linked to the Department of the Interior in its earliest years and then cut loose.) During World War I, the government corporation emerged as a new organizational form to enable the government to handle tasks that had previously been performed exclusively by private business. To conduct the war, it was suddenly necessary, as Seidman describes, "to construct and operate a merchant fleet, to build, rent, and sell houses, to buy and sell sugar and grain, to lend money, and to engage in other commercial enterprises [p. 227]." Traditional government organization did not fit these tasks for a number of reasons: users, not taxpayers, paid most of the cost of goods and services; expenditures fluctuated too greatly for annual appropriations; and it was necessary to conform to trade practices that were already well established outside of government. So Congress created the Shipping Board, Food Administration, and War Trade Board, maintaining federal control through the power to appoint directors and supervision by the cabinet officer who organized the corporation. The idea worked well enough to be employed again in the next emergency period, the Depression. Some of that period's creations, the Tennessee Valley Authority, the Commodity Credit Corporation, and the Federal Deposit Insurance Corporation, are still with us. When their proliferation seemed to be getting out of hand, Congress passed the Government Corporation Control Act of 1945 and the Budget and Accounting Procedures Act of 1950, which have narrowed the distinctions between government corporations and other government agencies. The main differences are that the corporations develop their own budgets and can borrow money in their own names without being affected by the public debt ceiling. And, unlike the agencies, they lack government immunity from lawsuits. Government corporations are subject to audit by the General Accounting Office.

Another form of organizational ambiguity is found in independent regulatory agencies which follow the pattern of the Interstate Commerce Commission. The functions of such agencies are partly judicial and partly legislative—they make regulations for specific industries, and they adjudicate controversies. Regulatory agencies are run by multimember commissions, and their members serve for fixed terms during which they may not be removed except for causes specified by statute. The President can control their operations indirectly, however, through the budgeting process, and by appointing new members to replace those whose terms expire.

There are now nine regulatory agencies. In addition to the ICC, they are the Federal Reserve Board, created in 1913; Federal Trade Commission, 1915; Federal Power Commission, 1920; Federal Communications Commission, 1934; Securities and Exchange Commission, 1934; National Labor Relations Board, 1935; Civil Aeronautics Board, 1938; and Atomic Energy Commission, 1946. All have suffered in some degree from what Seidman calls "the regulatory commission syndrome." (See Chapter 16.)

> The symptoms of this geriatric malady are disorientation and growing inability to distinguish between the public interest and the interests of those subject to regulation.
>
> Similar problems arise from a commission's intimate involvement with the legal profession and the practitioners appearing before it. The fact that lawyers have dominated the commissions can be seen in the case-by-case approach to regulation, emphasis on adversary proceedings, and complex judicialized processes and procedures [p. 224].

Yet another relatively new form of organization has resulted from the government's assumption of broad new functions without an existing organization to do the work. The National Aeronautics and Space Administration, the Veterans Administration, and the United States Information Agency are examples. The VA is larger than some of the smaller cabinet departments. Sometimes such an independent agency can advance to cabinet status, as when the former Housing and Home Finance Agency became the Department of Housing and Urban Development in 1965. Like departments, these agencies have a hierarchical structure with a single individual at the head.

Finally, one rather broad category of agencies, again with considerable variation in form, differs from all the others in that it serves not the public but the government itself, generally under direct control of the President. For example, the General Services Administration is in charge of the government's vast physical plant—from building the new post office in Akron to providing elevator operators in federal office buildings. The Civil Service Commission, a multiheaded independent agency, is in this category. So is the Office of Management and Budget in the Executive Office of the President.

Recent Developments

With such diverse agencies performing so many different tasks in such a variety of ways, problems of coordination are inevitable. One solution to the coordination problem has been to create still more agencies to keep track of what others are doing, improve communications among them, and try to reduce conflict. These coordinating agencies are organized around specific problem areas: the Water Resources Council, for example, or the Federal Interagency Committee on Education.

Another group of coordinating bodies has the more ambitious task of coordinating different levels and units of federal, state, and local government: the Appalachian Regional Commission and the New England River Basin Commission are examples. The traditional method for doing jobs that require the cooperation of several states is through interstate compact. In 1961, the first federal-interstate compact was made with the creation of the Delaware River Basin Commission to oversee water resource planning in the valley that includes the Philadelphia-New York metropolitan corridor. Water resources development has been an especially promising activity for such special-purpose units for the simple reason that watersheds follow the contours of the land in disregard of state boundaries. There was some initial fear that making the federal government a party to the Delaware Basin agreement would give the affected states an edge in competing for federal services. But so far, the commission has avoided this sort of controversy.

Another new and exotic species of organization is represented by the Communications Satellite Corporation (COMSAT). It is essentially private and for profit, with half the stock held by private communications carriers and half by public investors. Three of the corporation's fifteen directors are appointed by the President to look after the public interest. The National Home Ownership Foundation and the Corporation for Public Broadcasting are also private organizations, but they have a public connection by virtue of the power of the President to appoint directors.

In 1948, the Air Force sponsored the establishment of a private, nonprofit company for research and development called the Rand Corporation. Congress had nothing to do with its establishment, but the corporation was designed to work for no one but the government. Its advantages included the ability to hire and fire without regard to civil service restrictions, control of its internal budgeting, and the ability to attract capable personnel who were not particularly interested in lower-paying levels of government service. Eighty percent of government research and development work is now performed by contract with such nongovernment institutions. Not all of them are the government's own creations, although the Rand model has been repeated a number of times. Examples include the MITRE Corporation, the Institute for Defense Analysis, and the Urban Institute. One study has estimated that nearly 6 million people work in government activities through this indirect route without being government employees (Kilpatrick, Cummings, and Jennings, 1964). That is twice the number of civilians on the executive branch payroll.

The proliferation of government departments, agencies, and hybrid forms of organization has continued at an accelerating pace. With each new activity government attempts to perform, the need is created for new administrative instruments. As the number and kind of agencies continue to grow, so do complaints of bureaucratic "red tape," problems of conflicting jurisdictional responsibility, competing budgetary applications, and concern over the bureaucracy's accountability to the public through elected officials.

Filling the Jobs

The federal government is, of course, the largest employer in the nation. Not all of its workers are in Washington nor are all of them clerks. Federal workers are distributed throughout every state, and they include lawyers, scientists, and physicians, as well as welders and truck drivers. A national survey of the public image of the federal service has shown that the phrase "good personal character" comes closest to fitting the mental picture which most adults have of the typical civil servant. It also indicated that "security and fringe benefits" are the most attractive features of a career in the civil service. These are not, however, the qualities necessarily associated with a prestigious career. Job security, steady income, and retirement benefits are valued most by persons at the lower end of the occupational scale. So federal employment appeals most to those persons whom the government can most readily find. At the other end of the scale, recruiting is tougher:

> The appeal of federal employment is lowest among those kinds of employed adults for whom the government's qualitative needs are the greatest and for whom the competition will be keenest in the future. In general, those persons with better education feel that federal employment would seriously lower their occupational satisfaction [Kilpatrick, Cummings, and Jennings, 1964, p. 117].

In 1973, the Gallup Organization asked its national sample of respondents to rate the suitability of nine professions for a young person starting a career. The public rated government service next to last, ahead only of banking and far behind medicine, law, and engineering (Gallup, 1973). A Harris survey in the same year found a relatively high level of public confidence in such local government functions as garbage collection and police, but low confidence in the executive branch of the federal government (Senate Committee on Government Operations, 1973).

This problem of low public esteem for government workers is serious, because it aggravates the problem of recruiting the necessary experts and specialists. At the beginning of the Republic, the everyday tasks of public administration were fairly simple. But by the late 1950s, one of every seven white-collar jobs in the federal service required professional training. Government work requires, on the whole, more skill than work in the private sector. In 1960, for example, jobs in science or engineering were held by 7 percent of the federal work force, compared to only 2 percent of the national work force.

The Political Executives

More than two thousand political executives come and go with changing administrations. These persons make up the President's team as heads of departments, undersecretaries, assistant secretaries, heads of some of the independent agencies, and officers in the Executive Office of the President. The President's power to appoint them is shared with the Senate, with some exceptions. A careful President will also share the responsibility informally by taking into account the preferences of interest groups, party leaders, key members of the House of Representatives, his own advisers, and the public. While he wants persons with views similar to his own, he may place more importance on winning votes in Congress or the support of interest groups. Halberstam (1972) reports that President Kennedy, concerned by the narrowness of his 1960 election victory, tended to choose foreign policy advisers who were more conservative than he was. Specialized talent can also be a factor. Robert McNamara was appointed Secretary of Defense because it was thought that the managerial skill he demonstrated at Ford Motor Company could be used to bring that department's sprawling bureaucracy under control.

At the second echelon below the President, appointments may be presidential only in name, with the department heads given freedom to choose their own assistants. President Nixon, however, planted more than a hundred trusted White House insiders in these jobs to serve as "listening posts" in the bureaucracy (Woll and Jones, 1973). Influential interest groups have also been able to affect choices at this level, sometimes as a consolation prize for not having their desires met in the choice of the department head.

Political executives have difficult jobs. Besides commanding the day-to-day operations of their departments, they must develop policies and programs, defend administration positions before Congress and the public, and promote the party position. The job can be predominantly defensive; because of the scarcity of resources, any decision tends to disappoint more interests than it serves, and so the political executive must spend much of his time defending his department's programs and performance. In many ways, the job of a political executive is similar to that of an executive in business in that he must plan activities, see that the work gets done, and evaluate the results. But the political executive has some additional burdens. He is less likely than his business counterpart to have had extensive substantive experience in his department's field. There are exceptions, such as Wilbur Cohen, Secretary of Health, Education and Welfare in the Johnson administration, who had been a career man in that agency; and Nixon's third Attorney General, Elliott Richardson, who had been attorney general of Massachusetts. But most political executives come from backgrounds that make it difficult for them to deal in technical matters. They must therefore cultivate a secondary skill, the ability to work with staff technicians and benefit from their expertise without being put at their mercy. It is often difficult to distinguish between a policy question and a technical question.

The political executive must also have a greater tolerance for disagreement than a business executive. Since he deals with many conflicting interests, and is in some respects accountable to the public, he must put up with and even encourage disputes and ambiguity, debating some issues to a conclusion and leaving others unresolved. He spends more time justifying his programs and operations. And, hampered by regulations and civil service protection for employees, he must use more persuasion and less force than a business executive. The top person in the department may choose to concentrate on the task of manning the political defenses and delegate the operating tasks to the next level. At the second echelon, however, there is no escape. If policy is not to be defaulted to the career people, these appointees must take hold and run the department. But finding people who can do it is difficult. Dean Mann (1965) has taken a careful look at the problems at this level:

> The selection of men for the second echelon of the President's executive team reflects many of the basic characteristics and values of the American political system. Having responded over the years to the cross pressures of conflicting interest—executive and legislative, business and professional, public and private, the process appears haphazard, for no formal procedure has been devised for locating, classifying, and enticing qualified men into these positions. An even more important point is that no system has been evolved for preparing potential candidates adequately for their duties in office. As a result, the government is largely dependent on untrained people to fill its policy-making positions [p. 264].

The Career Executive

Because it is difficult to recruit qualified people for the political jobs, much important work filters down by default to the career civil service executives. At the highest level are from four hundred to five hundred bureau heads, office chiefs, deputies, and assistants. Some may rank as high as political executives and differ only in the way they are appointed. Below the top level are the heads of smaller bureaucratic subdivisions, in Washington and in field offices, for a total career executive force of about ten thousand. A version of the Peter Principle—that people who perform competently tend to be promoted until they reach a position for which they are not competent—operates against the government here. Capable executives tend to find tempting job offers outside the government. Those not so capable tend to stay, their tenure protected by the Civil Service. This problem would not be so serious if it were easy for executives to shift back and forth from public office to private life. But the financial and psychological barriers tend to inhibit this.

At any given time, only about one-fifth of the executives in the career service can be classed as "in-and-outers"—those who have interrupted their federal careers to work in business, education, or lower levels of government. Another one-fifth have extensive nongovernment experience and entered the government at a senior level. The remaining three-fifths are full careerists, executives who have had no or only very junior experience outside the government.

The Bureau of Executive Manpower (1972) offers this portrait of the typical executive. He is

> . . . male, 53 years old, and has 26 years of service. He entered the Federal service at grade 5 and received his first supergrade (executive) appointment at age 45. He holds a bachelor's degree which he obtained prior to his entry into the service and has acquired some further education during his employment. He has worked in one or possibly two agencies but has made no move since (approaching the executive level) . . . he will be eligible for retirement in four years [p. 8].

The Budgeting Process

The budget is the ultimate expression of the government's priorities, preferences, and values. Budgetary decisions determine who gets what. These decisions are the result of bargaining and negotiation among different segments of the government where different interests find expression. In other words, it is a political process, and no matter how sophisticated the analytic tools used to develop the budget become, the element of politics cannot be avoided or ignored. This process begins in the spring, more than a year before the start of the fiscal period which the budget covers; work on the 1976 budget, for the fiscal year beginning July 1, 1975, was started in the spring of 1974. In the traditional process, each agency which spends money looks at its programs and decides what it will need, taking into consideration any changes or reforms that are planned for its programs. These requests are reviewed by the Office of Management and Budget, which forces the agencies to justify their requests, determines whether the spending plans are in accordance with the President's program, and tries to reconcile requests from different agencies when they appear to be in conflict. The Office of Management and Budget then presents preliminary plans to the President. The President also gets estimates of available revenue, which are prepared jointly by the Treasury Department, the Council of Economic Advisers, and the Office of Management and Budget.

By midsummer, the President establishes his general budget and fiscal policy guidelines for the fiscal year whose beginning is still twelve months away. If he has important new programs under consideration, this is when he makes key, although still tentative, "go" or "don't go" decisions. The agencies are then given planning targets that enable them to prepare their budgets in detail. Their results are reviewed again by the Office of Management and Budget in the fall and early winter and again checked by the President, who by then has more up-to-date information about the economic outlook and expected revenues and can revise his decisions on what to leave in and what to take out. The plans are then printed in a paperback volume titled *The Budget of the United States Government*, and sent to Congress late in January. Although this is the point at which the process becomes public, most of the budget battle is already over. The most important influence on a budget is the previous year's budget with fairly predictable increases for higher costs and expanded activities. Next most important is the executive budgeting process. Congressional changes in the recent past have been relatively minor when compared to the total budget. However, the new procedures of the Congressional Budget and Impoundment Control Act of 1974 (see Chapter 9), including advancement of the start of the fiscal year to October, are intended to give Congress an opportunity to make more extensive modifications.

Once the budget is approved, central control of its enactment is maintained by the Office of Management and Budget, which distributes the money, usually on a quarterly basis. The OMB reviews reports of agency action and financial status to see that the money is spent for the purposes for which it was appropriated. As a further check, the General Accounting Office, which is an arm of Congress, not of the executive branch, conducts a continuing, roving audit, looking for careless or improper use of funds.

The Politics of Budgeting

Everyone has a slightly different ax to grind in this process. The agencies usually ask for as much as they think they can without provoking a backlash of congressional hostility. The Office of Management and Budget, trying to match outgo with income, tends to cut. The House, which sees itself as the Constitutional guardian of the Treasury, has an even greater bias for cutting. Richard F. Fenno, Jr.(1962), has noted how the language used by members reflects the intensity of this bias:

> Agency budgets are said to be filled with "fat," "padding," "grease," "pork," "oleagininous substance," "water," "oil," "cushions," "avoirdupois," "waste tissue," and "soft spots." The action verbs most commonly used are "cut," "carve," "slice," "prune," "whittle," "squeeze," "wring," "trim," "lop off," "chop," "slash," "pare," "shave," "fry," and "whack." The tools of the trade are appropriately referred to as "knife," "blade," "meat axe," "scalpel," "meat cleaver," "hatchet," "shears," "wringer," and "fine-tooth comb." Members are hailed by their fellows as being "pretty sharp with the knife." Agencies may "have the meat axe thrown at them." Executives are urged to put their agencies "on a fat boy's diet." Budgets are praised when they are "cut to the bone." And members agree that "You can always get a little more fat out of a piece of pork if you fry it a little longer and a little harder [p. 312]."

Against this harsh environment, it is necessary to counterpose something more sweetly reasonable. The Senate Appropriations Committee obligingly acts as an appeals court to which the agencies can take their wounds for healing. These balancing roles, say Otto A. Davis, M. A. H. Dempster, and Aaron Wildavsky (1966), tend to "fit in with one another and set up patterns of mutual expectations which markedly reduce the burden of calculation for the participants [p. 530]." In other words, no one group has to think about the whole process. The agencies know they must ask for more than they expect or need because someone—the Office of Management and Budget or Congress—will cut them back. At the same time, they must not ask for too much because that could lead to loss of confidence in their management ability. From the House Appropriations Committee point of view, a trimming job has been much easier than a total budget evaluation would be. Whether the new procedures would give Congress the discipline needed to perform a more coordinated task could be discovered only through experience. But they gave some promise of providing a more orderly system.

What You Pay Versus What You Get

One of the better ideas that Robert McNamara brought to the government was a budgetary method called PPBS, which stands for Planning, Programming, Budgeting System. It seeks to measure what the government gets for what it spends and find out whether there are cheaper ways to accomplish the same ultimate goals. Although this may seem like an obvious thing to do, it often goes undone once an agency stops questioning the basic assumptions underlying its budget requests. The idea of raising such questions was novel when McNamara introduced it to the Defense Department. The traditional budget system was entirely input-oriented. An agency figured how much it wanted to spend on salaries, how much on typewriter ribbons, and took the programs for granted. There was no basis, said William M. Capron (1968), who served in the Bureau of the Budget in the Johnson administration, for making such judgments as, "What will happen if I have to cut this agency's request by 10 percent? Since there was no relationship between the inputs and any kind of indication of the purposes or the output of that agency's activity, this was a decision that had to be made in the dark [p. 147]." PPBS is a way of measuring outputs in terms of dollars spent, getting, as they said in the Defense Department, a "bigger bang for a buck." McNamara's attempt to use PPBS to bring a runaway military spending program under civilian control led President Johnson to order it put into effect on a governmentwide basis in 1965. The budgeting process kept its traditional form, but each agency was required to develop in addition special analyses and evaluations of its programs and a "program and financial plan" looking farther ahead than the one-year budget period. This information is summarized each year in a "program memorandum" for each major program area of each agency to back up the budget request when it goes to the Office of Management and Budget.

The usefulness of PPBS is best explained by example. Robert N.

Robert McNamara: A better idea. *(United Press International.)*

Grosse (1968) has illustrated its application to disease-control programs in the Department of Health, Education and Welfare. The problem was finding where the limited amount of money would do the most good. One study compared the potential results of different cancer programs:

> We looked at cancer of the uterine cervix, breast, head and neck, and colon-rectum. We estimated cost per examination, the number of examinations that would be required before a case would probably be found. From this was derived the number of cases that would be found, and estimates of the cost per case found. An estimate was made of the number of deaths that could be averted by the treatment following the detection of the cancers. Then we calculated the cost per death averted, which ranged from about $2,200 in the case of cervical to $46,000 for colon-rectum cancer [pp. 163–165].

With this information and a limited amount of money to spend, it becomes apparent that to maximize the number of lives saved, the first dollars should be spent on cervical cancer, with spending on other forms of the disease held back until the high-return area can be fully exploited.

The HEW studies carried the process further, adding other disease and accident-prevention programs to the equation. Motor vehicle programs proved to save more lives per dollar spent than any other programs (Figure 12-1). But a more sophisticated measure of benefit than simple number of deaths averted is needed. Arthritis, for example, cripples but does not kill. Some diseases tend to strike the young, who would otherwise have many valuable productive years left, whereas other diseases attack persons whose remaining life expectancy is already short. Both of these factors were taken into account by estimating the lifetime additional earnings created by saving the people affected from death or crippling. Using that measure (Figure 12-2), the HEW studies showed that syphilis programs were even more effective than programs to cure cervical cancer. Arthritis programs were better than either.

If the PPBS system were strictly followed, the government would suspend all spending on the least effective programs and divert the money to the most effective ones. "But it remains a fact of life," said Grosse,

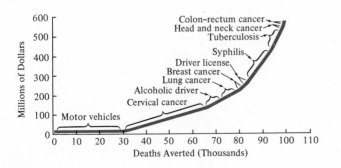

Figure 12-1 Resource Allocation Alternatives for Selected Diseases: Deaths Averted *(Source: American Enterprise Institute for Public Policy Research.)*

Figure 12-2 Resource Allocation Alternatives for Selected Diseases: Savings *(Source: American Enterprise Institute for Public Policy Research.)*

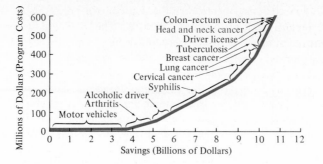

"that it is very hard to reduce an existing program with all the commitments that have been made [p. 169]." Instead of proposing to start afresh, the analysts merely recommended that new money should go to cervical cancer, syphilis, and arthritis programs before less effective programs were expanded.

Although the budgetary process remains the same, PPBS has some important effects, of which not the least is giving more influence to economists and other experts at quantification. With their slide rules and computers, these specialists make excellent shock troops in the fight against bureaucratic inertia. They can drive a wedge into agency autonomy and help upset the symbiotic relationships among bureaucrats, congressional committees, and interest groups. When well deployed, they can bring runaway departments under the control of their politically accountable heads.

Perhaps for this reason, the impact of PPBS has not been as great in other departments of government as it was in the Defense Department. Many defense applications involve the procurement of hardware, and the problems yield readily to cost-benefit analysis. In other government activities the relationship between expenditures and results is more difficult to chart—ambiguities result from political considerations and value judgments in the decision-making process.

By providing a way to relate inputs to outputs, PPBS may reduce some of the pressure for the proliferation of agencies. In the past, a President with a problem to solve was tempted to create a new agency to deal with it simply because he had no way of finding out why the problem was not being solved by existing agencies. PPBS exposes hidden possibilities for reform and revision. On the other hand, Aaron Wildavsky (1966) notes that the system ignores *political* costs and benefits. Although it might tell a policymaker that the nation as a whole gets more in benefit than it pays in costs from a given program, it does not address the question of who should pay and who should benefit. For example, the cheapest method of flood control is often flood-plain zoning: buying up the property in an area that floods periodically and converting it to park land or some other use which will not be badly hurt when the river claims its flood plain. But if the flood plain is occupied by powerful industrial interests which do not want to be forced to move, applying the solution that makes the most economic sense becomes very difficult politically. The more common solution, the one applied, for example, to the Kansas River Basin in the 1950s, is to build costly reservoirs, where the only land taken is that of the less powerful upstream farmers. Although more costly in dollars, that solution had a lower political cost. Another factor lowering the political cost was the fact that an existing agency, the Corps of Engineers, was organized and on hand to plan and build the reservoirs; flood-plain zoning could have been accomplished only by a basin-wide, interstate authority with extraordinary powers, and none existed. "If the costs of pursuing a policy are strictly economic and can be calculated directly in the market place," says Wildavsky, "then the procedure should work well. But if the costs include getting one or another organization to change its policies or procedures, then these costs must also be taken into account [p. 252]."

One of the main advantages of PPBS is that it forces analysis of government programs as opposed to mere justification. A budgetary decision must be based on more than the current price of typewriter ribbons. It must also be grounded in explicit and detailed policy objectives—the intended output. It must compare costs and benefits of alternatives. The ultimate result may be much better policy innovation and development. But negotiation, bargaining, and compromise, the familiar political components of the budgetary process, will remain an essential part of the way the budget is determined.

PLANNING AND THE POLITICAL PROCESS

To Budget Is to Plan

A planned society has generally been considered incompatible with the democratic process, particularly so in capitalist societies. Planning requires coordination and centralized decision making. Freedom, as usually defined, allows individuals to pursue their own interests in whatever portion of the total system falls under their control, whether it is a unit of government, a corporation, or only a single vote on election day. In capitalism, the hidden hand of the market provides the orderly allocation of priorities as rational people make their choices.

The growth of government, with its assumption of many services which were formerly handled by the private sector or left unattended, has complicated this question in large degree. Today the taxpayer pays the government to solve problems in such complicated fields as housing, transportation, education, and urban development. This transfer of resources involves the political questions of who shall pay and who shall benefit—as well as where, when, and how. Jobs on this scale cannot be done without an enormous amount of coordination and planning. Although the budgeting process is subject to the tugging and pulling of politics, it is also planning. Historically, however, it has been planning in a limited form. The decisions are *incremental*—as is illustrated by the case of the HEW decision to apply new-found knowledge about the effectiveness of different disease-control programs only to "new" money—while keeping old, ineffective programs going. The incremental approach—where change takes place only at the margins and not in a comprehensive manner—makes the system very slow to respond to changing needs and awareness. But its political cost is low. President Nixon, even before the Watergate scandals began to damage his effectiveness, was using politically expensive methods. He lost potential support for measures that might have been achievable because of his heavy-handed efforts to cut back on existing programs. Political capital is as limited as economic capital. "Those who continually urge a President to go all out—that is, use all his resources on a wide range of issues," says Wildavsky, "rarely stop to consider that the price of success in one area of policy may be defeat in another [p. 251]." It may be that the existing political structure simply cannot support a process that is truly efficient in the economic sense or comprehensive in the planning sense.

Building Support for Programs

One reason that budgeting is limited to incremental changes is that so much power resides within the agencies rather than being imposed from outside by the President. Presidents come and go, subject to varying interests and attention spans. No President can pay consistent attention to all the agencies all the time. So, to survive, an agency must find a power base somewhere else. The two logical places to look are to interest groups and to the Congress.

David Truman (1960) noticed that the administrator who depends on interest groups for his support has a precarious situation if the program is new. The interest groups who are active during the legislative battles over the program and those that stay active afterward do not exactly correspond. Those that become activated just for the battle will fade away, leaving only the best organized interests with which to deal when the administrator carries out the program. The usefulness of the organized interests is, of course, dependent upon their ability to influence the President or Congress or both to continue to support the agency and its programs.

The Case of the Corps of Engineers

The Army Corps of Engineers is a classic case of a government agency which has been so successful at building support that it seems to have a life of its own, independent of the government. Its clientele of interests seeking flood control and navigation projects is aggressively represented in Washington by the National Rivers and Harbors Congress. There have been efforts to bring the Corps under the control of a wider-ranging plan of water resources policy—a logical move because irrigation, water supply, pollution control, and soil conservation all involve the same water and the same geography as flood control and navigation. But the success of these coordination efforts has been limited. Members of the United States Congress like to maintain a good working relationship with the Corps because the benefits of its projects can be specific to their districts and highly visible there. These rewards can be obtained at fairly low political cost through *logrolling*, the process of tacit or explicit exchange of favors (you scratch my back, and I'll scratch yours; or, you vote to dredge my harbor, and I'll vote to dike your stream). The need to cope with a more economically rational master plan would reduce the rewards or increase the political costs or both. Arthur Maas (1950) wrote a classic case study about the King's River project in California. Two agencies, the Bureau of Reclamation of the Department of Interior and the Army Corps of Engineers, had prepared proposals for water development in that broad river valley. The President and most water resource experts backed the Bureau. Congress backed the Corps. The Corps won. The President's announced preference had no visible effect on his nominal subordinates in the Corps because they knew they had the support of Congress.

Agencies and Congressional Committees

The bureaucracy, says Richard E. Neustadt (1973), is "a projection of congressional committee jurisdictions—or, more precisely . . . of standing subcommittee jurisdictions [p. 120]." Congress, as we have seen in Chapter 9, is decentralized and disorganized. The committee chairmen are more concerned with their own jurisdictions than they are with Congress or the government as a whole. Bureaucrats have a comparable concern for their own agencies at the expense of the executive branch as a whole. From this self-concern grows the harmonious relationship between executive agencies and congressional committees, defending one another from threats by forces outside the bureau-committee alliance.

The Constitution provides a number of potential links between Congress and the executive bureaucracy, and members of Congress know how to exploit them. Agency decisions on how, when, and where to implement their programs have effects on congressional constituencies that are immediate and tangible. For a member of Congress, who was elected for the purpose of seeing that the government serves the interests of the people in his district, it can be frustrating to see this power wielded by the bureaucrats. It is he, not they, who must answer to the voters. And so with the proliferation of programs to provide direct services to the citizens, the efforts by Congress to increase control over the bureaucracy have intensified. Neustadt lists three basic forms which these attempts at control have taken:

Patronage.   Congressional interest in federal jobs used to be limited mainly to hometown appointments, such as postmasterships. But now influential congressmen like to get persons who will be sympathetic to the needs of their constituencies placed in the political executive levels of the departments. The Senate's power to confirm appointments is one mechanism for achieving this placement, but it is not the only one. Influential committee members can drop hints of trouble with legislation and appropriations if the desired candidate is not appointed.

Annual Authorization.   Most operations of the government have permanent authorization for the programs and need only the annual appropriations to keep going. But some newer agencies are given one-year authorizations which must be renewed. The effect of this is to give substantive committees of each house—in addition to the Appropriations Committee—a hold on the purse strings. For example, the House Science and Astronautics Committee must first authorize spending by the National Aeronautics and Space Administration before the Appropriations Committee can approve the actual appropriation. This requirement, plus the technical expertise of the Science and Astronautics Committee, increases congressional influence over the agency's operations.

Committee Clearance.   Various statutory provisions give certain committees the power to block some kinds of agency action. Before the General Services Administration could proceed with design and construction of the new federal courthouse and office building in Topeka, it had to submit a prospectus (including price, floor space, justification, and method of financing) to the Public Works Committees of the House and Senate. The committees on Agriculture, Armed Services, and Interior also regularly assert this kind of control. And the Joint Committee on Atomic Energy has been given a continuing responsibility for supervising the activities of the Atomic Energy Commission.

Each of these three forms of legislative involvement in administration causes some confusion and violates textbook principles of good management. Yet, says Neustadt, from the agencies' viewpoint the effect has been pretty good:

On balance, these assertions of control have compensations for officialdom. They sometimes produce good ideas and sensible improvements: congressmen are capable of being very helpful. They may produce a measure of political protection, which is never to be slighted by an agency official. Moreover, they permit an able operator to play his committee "masters" off against each other. Control by two committees of each house can mean control by none, while serving at the same time to dilute direction from above, from the administration [p. 123].

INFORMATION

The Costs of Not Knowing

"Knowledge," said James Madison (1822), "will forever govern ignorance; and the people who mean to be their own governors must arm themselves with the power which knowledge gives [p. 337]." In the twentieth century, his observation is even more true, because of the pace of change and the increasing variety and complexity of things to know. For the bureaucrat, maintaining a monopoly over the information that others need is a means of both self-preservation and enhancement of power. He can dole out closely held information to reward or punish those he seeks to influence; he can use secrecy to cover up his own mistakes; and he can even build up a mystique of expertise to intimidate a public that would not be nearly as impressed if it had the facts. Francis E. Rourke (1972) cites the case of some secret documents stolen from the FBI office at Media, Pennsylvania. It was at first supposed that the agency kept the material locked up in a safe so that its super-sleuth methods and exotic discoveries would remain protected. But it turned out that the exotic secret was that there were no exotic secrets. Publication of the stolen material "plainly revealed that much of the information gathered and stored by that organization can most charitably be described as trivial. This kind of secrecy helps an agency establish and reinforce a myth of expertise on matters about which it may be no better informed than the public [p. 117]."

Bureaucratic possession of secret information not only tends to intimidate a less informed public, but also can be used to influence the decisions of policymakers who operate with varying degrees of certainty about policy proposals. The most dangerous examples occur if policymakers defer to administrators who claim to base their choices on information beyond the reach or understanding of the policymaker. When President Nixon urged congressional leaders to support the plan for bringing oil from Alaska's north slope through a pipeline across the state to the port at Valdez instead of south through Canada, he cited "national security" reasons without further elaboration. Invoking "national security" as a substitute for explanation became a near ritual in the latter part of Nixon's Presidency.

President Johnson often justified his military adventures by claiming they were necessitated by secret information available only to him. But as

George Reedy (1970) has noted, when such basic policy decisions are made, a President generally has about the same kind of information as is available to the average citizen. When Johnson decided to send troops to the Dominican Republic, "He had no information advantage over his fellow Americans other than a brief telephone conversation with his ambassador [p. 37]." And when the innermost thought processes of that administration's Vietnam policy were exposed with the publication of the Pentagon Papers, they turned out to be surprisingly mundane. The only important secret was the extent of the government's own ineptitude, and that had been guarded not from the enemy but from the American public. The lack of that knowledge kept the public from turning against the war earlier than it finally did.

The Case of the Secret Tax Letters

Lack of information can be especially painful in a field as complicated as tax law. It involves more than figuring out what the statutes say. There are court decisions, regulations of the Internal Revenue Service, and statements of IRS policy in the form of letters to taxpayers who have written to inquire how an action they have taken or are contemplating affects their tax status. The statutes, the court rulings, and the regulations have always been public. The letter rulings have not. There are some 30,000 of them a year, representing the bureaucratic response to specific problems and situations, and the rule of stare decisis applies to them as to court decisions. Rulings are made to conform with those in earlier cases having similar characteristics.

The problem for taxpayers was that they had no way of knowing what was in the bulk of that vast body of precedent. Only a small sample of the letter rulings was made public: a few score each year before 1952, and after that, in response to pressure from Congress, from five hundred to six hundred a year. The agency had a self-protective advantage in keeping the remainder secret because if IRS rulings were inconsistent, with similar taxpayers getting different treatment, there would be no way for the taxpayers or the public to know. However, some of the secret letters did gain limited circulation. Lawyers specializing in taxes and taxpayers with similar problems set up their own informal exchange programs so that they could read each others' letters from the IRS. This arrangement gave the tax bar a vested interest in secrecy; their knowledge became a product of limited availability and high demand, and therefore it had artificially enhanced value. A citizen with whom they did not choose to share information was at a relative disadvantage.

The Freedom of Information Act of 1967 was successfully invoked in 1973 to end this secrecy. Tax Analysts and Advocates, a public-interest law and information organization, obtained an order from the United States District Court for the District of Columbia to require the Internal Revenue

Service to make the letters available for inspection and copying. "Publication would simply make available to all what is now available to only a select few, and subject the rulings to public scrutiny as well," said Judge Aubrey E. Robinson, Jr., in his opinion. "Such public availability and scrutiny are the very fundamental policies of the Freedom of Information Act."

The Freedom of Information Act

The successful application of the act was a rare victory. The pressures in favor of secrecy are so great that ways can usually be found to circumvent the rather sweeping terms of the Freedom of Information Act of 1967.

John Moss: Shifting the burden to the government. *(Wide World Photos.)*

Sponsored by Rep. John Moss (California Democrat and chairman, Foreign Operations and Government Information Subcommittee of the House Government Operations Committee), the act was an amendment to the Administrative Procedures Act of 1946 which had previously provided a large share of the justification for government secrecy. The 1967 act established four broad principles: (1) that disclosure of government records be the general rule and not the exception; (2) that all persons have equal right of access to government documents; (3) that in a dispute over releasing a document, the burden of justification be on the government agency that wants to withhold it, not on the person who wants to see it; (4) that persons denied access to government records have a right to seek relief through court action.

"I have always believed," said President Johnson when he signed the act, "that freedom of information is so vital that only the national security, not the desire of public officials or private citizens, should determine when it must be restricted." He then refused a request for the original draft of his speech (Rothchild, 1972, p. 17).

Application of the act has been infrequent. News media, thought at first to be the main beneficiaries, have lacked the patience or the sustained interest in any given document to fight the long legal battles needed to implement the act. Few citizens are aware of it. Interest groups have used it with some success, according to Rothchild:

> The real beneficiaries of freedom of information have been precisely those who needed the law least—lobbying groups and corporations who are self-interested in government studies. The *New York Times* did not think it worth the effort to sue the Renegotiation Board for material on an evaluation of defense contracts, but Grumman Aircraft, one of the interested subcontractors, did sue and finally won the case [p. 22–23].

The secrecy drive is so strong that agencies go to heroic efforts to escape the consequences of the act. They use a variety of techniques. Bureaucrats may mix national security material that is legitimately exempt with other material that is not—and then refuse to release the covered matter on the ground that it would compromise the security file. They may refuse to supply index files or master lists of the documents on hand and then refuse requests because they are nonspecific "fishing expeditions." If a specific request is made, they may claim that the material has never been compiled, or that it exists only as preliminary working papers whose content would be misleading. Fees for copying materials, permitted by the law, are sometimes set exorbitantly high. Possibilities for delay are plentiful; before you can sue, you must exhaust the administrative remedies, including submission of written requests. It may take weeks or months to get the official response. Once you sue, the government has sixty days to reply. Finally, the act has nine exemptions, including national security information, trade secrets, certain personnel files, and internal memoranda.

Keeping Secrets from Congress

In the quest for information, Congress has standing superior to that of the ordinary citizen. Its chief frustration has come through the claim of executive privilege, a doctrine not found in the Constitution or the statutes, but implied in the concept of separation of powers. It is one of those ambiguous points which both branches resist fully testing for fear of provoking a constitutional crisis. Congress claims absolute constitutional authority to demand information; the President claims discretion to withhold it. President Nixon invoked executive privilege to keep his confidential advisors from giving unlimited testimony to congressional committees. At one point in his administration, he claimed the privilege for the entire executive branch, but this claim was not pressed. He did press the claim to executive privilege in witholding sixty-four subpoenaed White House tapes dealing with the Watergate scandal. For the first time the Supreme Court in 1974 spoke to the issue, saying in *United States v. Richard M. Nixon* only that presidential claims to privilege were constitutionally based, but in this particular case the need for information on suspected criminal activities outweighed executive privilege and the tapes had to be turned over to prosecution authorities.Critics of the doctrine have argued that it is mere custom, not rooted in law at all. Arthur S. Miller (1972) argues that it stems from a misconception of the nature of the system of separation of powers, which he says is really a sharing of power, not a division:

> Once that minor but important point is seen, then the question of furnishing information to Congress from the bureaucracy takes on a different perspective. For the sharing of power implies access—full access—to all information relevant to making and administering public policy. It is impossible to perceive how Congress can perform its constitutional mission of formulating broad governmental policies, unless it is privy to all of the pertinent facts.

In much of the struggling between Congress and the bureaucracy, Congress is at a disadvantage for lack of information. Some of it stems not so much from secrecy but from the lack of staff resources and technical expertise on Capitol Hill. Some of the more promising proposals for improving the effectiveness of Congress involve better information support services. These proposals recognize that in government, information is power, and the best way to make the bureaucracy the servant of the public, rather than its enemy, is to maximize the distribution of information.

SUGGESTED READINGS

Altshuler, Alan A. (ed.). *The Politics of the Federal Bureaucracy.* New York: Dodd, Mead, 1968. Covers the various roles that the bureaucracy plays in the political system.

Cary, William L. *Politics and Regulatory Agencies.* New York: McGraw-Hill, 1967. Discusses the politics involved in the regulatory administration of several of the most important independent agencies.

Galbraith, John K. *The New Industrial State.* Boston: Houghton Mifflin, 1967. A critical discussion of the demands of technology and economics upon American society. Of special significance is the examination of the relationship between the government and the industrial corporations.

Jacob, Charles E. *Policy and Bureaucracy.* Princeton, N.J.: Van Nostrand, 1966. A concise work on the nature of administrative decision making and the formulation of policy.

Rourke, Francis E. *Bureaucracy, Politics, and Public Policy.* Boston: Little, Brown, 1969. A comprehensive introduction to the study of bureaucracy and its role in the policy making process.

Seidman, Harold. *Politics, Position and Power.* New York: Oxford, 1970. An interesting and important study of the politics of the federal bureaucracy. Especially good in pointing out the nature of power relationships between different organizations of the bureaucracy.

Wildavsky, Aaron B. *The Politics of the Budgetary Process.* Boston: Little, Brown, 1964. A detailed account of the dynamics of the federal budgetary process and how it relates to the making of public policy.

Chapter 13

❧

Nongovernment Power Centers

THE PRIVATE MAKING OF PUBLIC POLICY

Against the Corporate Giant

In 1965 an unknown lawyer published a book entitled *Unsafe at Any Speed*, cataloging the automobile industry's lack of concern for passenger and driver safety and the overemphasis on style and salesmanship. The book was built on a case study of design defects in one car, General Motors' sporty Corvair.

Overnight, Ralph Nader became the nation's leading spokesman for auto safety, and two months later he was invited to testify on the subject before a Senate subcommittee. Before he reached the hearing room, some strange events took place:

> His landlady was asked about his promptness in paying bills. An attractive girl invited him to her apartment to discuss "foreign affairs with a few of her friends." Two men followed him from an airport. His old law school friend, Frederick Condon, was asked questions by an investigator supposedly representing a client who was thinking of hiring Nader. Other friends and associates were asked all kinds of questions by investigators from different agencies, *including whether or not he led a normal sex life, possible anti-Semitism, and political affiliations*. A blonde in a supermarket asked him to help her move some furniture (and asked no one else when he refused) [Sethi, 1971, pp. 190, 191; emphasis in original].

It was later revealed that General Motors Corporation had hired a private investigator "to check his life and current activities to determine 'what makes him tick,' such as his real interest in safety, his supporters, if any, his politics, his marital status, his friends, his women, boys, etc., drinking, dope, jobs—in fact, all the facets of his life [Sethi, p. 198]." General Motors eventually apologized and settled an invasion of privacy suit out of court by paying Nader $425,000. Not every victim of the abuse of private power does as well, and the incident illustrates one means used to exercise that power upon public policy by inhibiting the free flow of public discussion. The various methods and the power centers which exercise them are the subject of this chapter.

Beyond the Web of Government

"The community," said R. M. MacIver (1947), "is more than the state [p. 441]." In terms of all that goes on in society, the range of government activity is fairly narrow. The government's first concerns are to preserve order and to provide services. But most social control is exercised by nongovernment means, and most goods and services are provided by the private sector. MacIver argued that society's creative juices are to be found mainly on the private side, that "in its spontaneous life and in the rich differences it breeds, there move the forces that create the future, and that for this reason the cultural values of men and groups must remain essentially free from the uniformizing activities of government [p. 441]."

However, persons and groups are not always willing to maintain a separation between public and private concerns. Any government decision about what services to provide to whom and what behaviors to regulate or prohibit invariably conflicts with the goals and values of someone. And many people seek to enlist the aid of government to achieve what are essentially private goals and values. The Eighteenth Amendment's prohibition of the drinking of alcoholic beverages is an extreme example of an attempt to use government's uniformizing power to affect social values.

Conversely, the uniformizing effects which MacIver warned against are sometimes achieved independently of government power. Decisions made by corporations, churches, labor unions, or voluntary and professional associations can be sufficiently coordinated to match and even exceed those of government in their sweep and effect. For example, the decision to base the nation's transportation system on high-performance, energy-wasteful, air-polluting automobiles had an impact on the quality of life that could be exceeded by very few government decisions. While no one entity decreed that effect in a single decision, it happened through a series of small, incremental decisions that were made mostly by private groups—although it was supported by some government decisions, most notably the adoption of the Interstate Highway program.

The impact of private decision making imposes some difficult philosophical problems for democratic societies. Democracy seeks to maximize both individual freedom and popular control. We have already seen how difficult it is to maintain popular control over government activities. If most or much of the power to affect the directions society takes is not in government hands at all, then we must look beyond government to understand the ultimate limits of popular control, something political scientists have traditionally not done. Many polemics have been written against the power of American corporations—mostly by neo-Marxists. But there has not been systematic study of how private decision-making processes operate, nor is there adequate understanding of the consequences for the larger society which result from these private decisions. Our examination of the broader picture of decision making must therefore be tentative and sometimes speculative.

Leviathan Revisited

In the seventeenth century, it was clear to Thomas Hobbes that government was necessary to protect man from the evils of the state of nature, where life would be "solitary, poor, nasty, brutish, and short." Citizens of twentieth-century democracies do not submit unquestioningly to Hobbes' all-powerful sovereign, but they do, in a parallel to the social contract, enter into ordered relationships in society which require them to submit to some coordination and control. The reward for this submission is the opportunity to provide for basic needs and to seek improved status in an orderly manner. These benefits come from a variety of social institutions, and most of them are large private organizations whose power is concentrated at the top. This concentration of power is no accident. It occurs as a functional response to the demands of a technological world. Sociologists explain it with what is called the *theory of functional integration*. Marvin Olsen (1971) has summarized the theory:

> Very briefly, this theory states that if a society is to remain unified in the face of growing role diversification and specialization (or division of labor), it must create elaborate mechanisms for coordinating, regulating, and controlling social activities. The more highly specialized the various parts of a society, the more interdependent they tend to become on one another through extensive exchange relationships. But such a complex network of interdependent exchange relationships can operate effectively only if it is coordinated and directed by some kind of over-all centralized authority. This central agency performs such activities as facilitating communication among all the involved parts, establishing and enforcing uniform operating rules and procedures, handling serious conflicts and disruptions, and ensuring that no one part gains enough power to exploit the entire system for its own benefit [pp. 231–232].

The need for coordination can be met by centralizing power in one agency, the national government. Or it can be provided by a number of power centers, each concerned with a different kind of activity. Decision making can be decentralized, Olsen suggests, while some central coordination is maintained. But whether there is one power center or many, some centralization of power must occur; the alternative is "fragmented, powerless social anarchy." The American system has many power centers. Government is one of the centers and one of the coordinating agencies. Its interaction with other centers is so extensive, and the actions of other centers are so important, that a study of government without an examination of these other power centers is incomplete.

The American system of multiple power centers is a by-product of the constitutional arrangements designed to provide freedom from oppressive government. But one of the prices paid for that freedom is the growth of decision-making centers which are less susceptible than government to popular control—although popular control may play a part and even prevail in the long run. The decisions made by private centers include choices which all societies must make in one way or another. Any decision is public, in effect, if it affects large numbers of people or involves the use of extensive resources for an extended time. Any decision affecting individuals and groups is political if it determines the allocation of society's rewards and punishments, both material and symbolic. When such decisions are made by private power centers, the questions of responsibility and accountability are largely beyond immediate popular control. No law of nature requires such an arrangement. The decision to place significant decision-making power in private hands is voluntary and revocable. Other nations have chosen other systems which concentrate the decisions in state officials to a much greater degree. But the pervasive liberal tradition in American politics, with its fear of government oppression and relative leniency toward private oppression, keeps the balance of power on the private side. Having examined the politics of public decision making, we must now, to complete the picture of government in America, turn to the inner workings of the private bureaucracy and try to assess the consequences which flow from the private-public decision-making apparatus.

The Private Bureaucracy

Scientific method, when applied to techniques of organization, can produce a bureaucratic technology that gives a modern organization extraordinary control over its members. The modern organization retains its power because it can bend to meet changing situations, as Nathan Glazer (1963) has observed:

> The technology of science permits the organization to become ever larger and more effective. And the steady rationality of scientific thinking applied to organizational problems seems to overcome some of the chief characteristics

and perhaps weaknesses of organizations in the past—their rigidity, their lack of dynamism, their stubbornness. Perhaps these characteristics once permitted us, like primitive mammals around a dinosaur, to outwit the organization, to achieve changes without the exhausting investment of unlimited energy that is now required. But we have suddenly arrived at a point when even the biggest organizations we have . . . can, by the power of a rational analysis, be made flexible [p. 227].

Anyone who has served in the Army or read Joseph Heller's *Catch 22* (1961) knows what Glazer is talking about. When a variety of situations are encountered, some always can be handled most efficiently and justly by violating regulations. The survival of the system depends on arranging things so that regulations can be violated when deemed necessary. This arrangement keeps the organization loose and not too threatening. But modern command-and-control technology makes it possible to approach the bureaucratic ideal of having a regulation for *everything*. The result is to take the looseness out of the system.

And all citizens are potential victims. Bureaucratic decisions made in private organizations are difficult to fight. Today's average citizen has more contacts with his government than ever before. He also has more contacts with private bureaucracies which enforce, in the words of Michael Walzer (1970), "a great variety of rules and regulations with the silent acquiescence and ultimate support of the state."

Commercial, industrial, professional, and educational organizations, and to a lesser degree, religious organizations and trade unions all play these parts—and yet very few of these reproduce the democratic politics of the state. They have official or semi-official functions; they are enormously active and powerful in the day-to-day government of society, but the authority of their officers is rarely legitimized in any democratic fashion. These officers preside over what are essentially authoritarian regimes with no internal electoral system, no opposition parties, no free press or open communications network, no established judicial procedures, no channels for rank-and-file participation in decision making [p. 225].

The legitimacy of private authority is indirect; government, operating through the consent of the governed, decides to leave it alone. The decision can, of course, be withdrawn, although that possibility is remote. Meanwhile, the citizen is the relatively helpless subject of a private reigning authority which he can barely identify, much less control. A well-informed person might be able to name the major elective and many of the appointive officials in his own political jurisdictions. He is less likely to be familiar with the names of the heads of major corporations, religious bodies, educational institutions, and other private groups that directly affect his life. Nor does he get much chance to judge their actions.

What is a power center? Kenneth M. Dolbeare and Murray J. Edelman (1971) have defined it in terms of resources. A power center is "any organization that is able to build up very large economic resources or political resources or both [p. 299]." This definition provides an analytic distinction from interest groups, which may or may not have significant economic and political resources. And a power center may be an individual. Joseph McCarthy in the 1950s and George Wallace in the 1960s were power centers because they controlled the very large political resources vested in blocs of voters sharing a common viewpoint for which they were the spokesmen. Stewart Mott and Clement Stone, millionaire contributors to the political left and right, respectively, became power centers because of their huge command of economic resources which they applied directly to achieve political goals.

Organizations can achieve the status of power centers by appeal to specialized value systems. For example, the National Council of Churches can translate the religious values of its members into a political resource. The American Civil Liberties Union does the same with the basic human sense of fair play and justice. Economic resources are, of course, easier to measure. General Motors is obviously a power center with its annual sales receipts of $30 billion—an amount greater than the gross national product of all but the top twenty-two nations of the world. Trade associations can be

Senator Joseph McCarthy in 1954: An individual can be a power center. *(King Features.)*

power centers: the American Petroleum Institute wields power based on economic resources; the American Newspaper Publishers Association has both economic and public-opinion resources. The National Association of State Universities and Land Grant Colleges has political resources based on educational values, as well as the strong economic interest which underlies these resources by virtue of the fact that state colleges provide research and training for their regions' main industries. The key is gaining the resources to influence and control others—and using them. To do so is to become a power center.

Private Power Centers and the Government

Much controversy surrounds the relationship of private centers of power to officials and agencies of government. Three basic viewpoints, often backed more by ideological predisposition than by empirical evidence, are predominant among social scientists. One holds that private power centers do and must necessarily dominate the government decision-making process under the existing constitutional and capitalist systems. A second view maintains that government institutions not only hold their own, but dominate the private centers when necessary. The third view argues that government institutions are capable of dominating the private power centers but that they have abdicated this role. Each of these three models of the relationship between government and private power is worth considering in more detail.

Model 1: Private Power Is Dominant

Analysts who argue this position see government officials as the agents, functionaries, or pawns of a tiny handful of the most powerful private groups and individuals in the society. These elites are the puppeteers who pull the strings that make public officials respond. (This is the *elitist* view.) While such observers agree that private power must always dominate, they reach that conclusion by various routes, some of which are familiar.

Economic Dominance. The classic argument that power stems primarily from private economic resources is found in studies of an Indian town by Robert S. and Helen M. Lynd (1929, 1937). They found that wealth was concentrated within a family-controlled business and financial network and inferred that the wealth shared by these few individuals was the primary source of power in the community.

Since this pioneering study, others have cited the growth and concentration of corporate wealth as evidence that there is a parallel dominance over government at the national level. This concentration follows the process predicted by the theory of functional integration—that coordination of power centers is a necessary consequence of modern life—and it seems to be accelerating. In 1965, Dr. Willard F. Mueller, a former chief economist of the Federal Trade Commission, warned the Senate Subcommittee on Antitrust and Monopoly that trends then operating would, if continued, leave the 200 largest manufacturing corporations controlling two-thirds of all manufacturing assets by 1975. Four years later, he was forced to revise that prediction. When he appeared before the subcommittee again in 1969, he reported that "Today the top 200 manufacturing corporations already control about two-thirds of all assets held by corporations engaged primarily in manufacturing [Mintz and Cohen, 1971, p. 35]." It had happened six years ahead of schedule. Another visible sign of the concentration of corporate wealth is the relatively recent phenomenon of the multinational corporation. Comparisons of the gross annual sales of the leading multinational corporations with the gross national products of the nations of the world show that the presidents of some corporations can supervise more total economic power than the presidents of many nations (Table 13-1).

Table 13-1 Comparison of Top
Economic Powers, 1969–1970

ECONOMIC POWER	BILLIONS OF DOLLARS
1 United States	974.10
2 Soviet Union	504.70
3 Japan	197.18
4 West Germany	186.35
5 France	147.53
6 Britain	121.02
7 Italy	93.19
8 China	82.50
9 Canada	80.38
10 India	52.92
11 Poland	42.32
12 East Germany	37.61
13 Australia	36.10
14 Brazil	34.60
15 Mexico	33.18
16 Sweden	32.58
17 Spain	32.26
18 Netherlands	31.25
19 Czechoslovakia	28.84
20 Romania	28.01
21 Belgium	25.70
22 Argentina	25.42
23 GENERAL MOTORS	24.30
24 Switzerland	20.48
25 Pakistan	17.50
26 South Africa	16.69

Source: National Observer, July 28, 1973.

Table 13-2   Share of Aggregate Income Before Taxes Received by
Each Fifth of Families
(Ranked by income, selected years, 1947–1972, percent)

INCOME RANK	1947	1950	1960	1966	1972
Total families[1]	100.0	100.0	100.0	100.0	100.0
Lowest fifth	5.1	4.5	4.8	5.6	5.4
Second fifth	11.8	11.9	12.2	12.4	11.9
Third fifth	16.7	17.4	17.8	17.8	17.5
Fourth fifth	23.2	23.6	24.0	23.8	23.9
Highest fifth	43.3	42.7	41.3	40.5	41.4
Top 5 percent	17.5	17.3	15.9	15.6	15.9

[1]The income (before taxes) boundaries of each fifth in 1972 were: lowest
fifth—under $5,612; second fifth—$5,612–$9,299; third fifth—$9,300–$12,854;
fourth fifth—$12,855–$17,759; highest fifth—$17,760 and over; top 5 percent—
$27,837 and over. Income includes wages and salaries, proprietors' income,
interest, rent, dividends, and money transfer payments.
Note: Detail may not add to totals because of rounding.
Source: Department of Commerce, Bureau of the Census, as published in *The
Economic Report of the President*, 1974.

This corporate wealth was amassed without a parallel concentration of
personal wealth, although impressive personal fortunes are still made. Over
time, the distribution of personal wealth changes little, with no clear trend
toward either equality or concentration of income. Most of the leveling that
has occurred took place before World War II. In 1929, the wealthiest 5
percent of families received 30 percent of the total personal income. By
1944, the share of the richest 5 percent was down to 21 percent of the total.
Since then, the share of the wealthiest groups has declined to 16 percent
(Miller, 1971). The offsetting gains have been spread through the middle
brackets, but the poorest groups have not increased their share of income at
all (Table 13-2). Another way to look at the concentration of wealth is to
examine the concentration of its various components, as in Table 13-3. The
top 1 percent has 31 percent of the total wealth. These data support the
argument that economic concentration is a fact of life in American society,
and these economic resources may be applied to the exercise of power. The
mere observation of the existence of concentration, however, is not
sufficient to document the actual exercise of political power. A weakness

Table 13-3 Distribution of Various Types of Personal Wealth, 1962

	WEALTHIEST 20%	TOP 5%	TOP 1%
Total wealth	76	50	31
Corporate stock	96	83	61
Business and professions	89	62	39
Homes	52	19	6

Source: Ackerman, Frank, et al., "Income Distribution in the United States," *The
Review of Radical Political Economics*, vol. 3, no. 3 (Summer 1971), based on data from
Dorothy S. Projector and Gertrude Weiss, *Survey of Financial Characteristics of
Consumers*, Federal Reserve System, 1966; and Irwin Friend, et al., *Mutual Funds and
Other Institutional Investors: A New Perspective.*

in many arguments that an economic elite maintains long-term control over governmental institutions is that the equating of wealth with power is often assumed rather than demonstrated.

Institutional Dominance. C. Wright Mills (1957) is the scholar most commonly associated with the view that institutional arrangements are the key in determining who rules. Wealth alone is not always sufficient. Mills saw power concentrated in three basic hierarchies: (1) a concentrated economic sector, as in the previous model, plus (2) a bureaucratic military, and (3) a centralized government with power concentrated in the executive. The ruling elite is formed from a network of interconnections at the top levels among these three hierarchies:

> The inner core of the power elite consists, first, of those who interchange commanding roles at the top of one dominant institutional order with those in another: the admiral who is also a banker and a lawyer and who heads up an important federal commission; the corporation executive whose company was one of the two or three leading war material producers who is now the Secretary of Defense; the wartime general who dons civilian clothes to sit on the political directorate and then becomes a member of the board of directors of a leading economic corporation [p. 288].

Leadership in the Mills model depends on more than money. Information and control of technological advances are resources which also enable one group to exploit another. Mills' leadership is centered in different hierarchies at different times. Which one takes charge "depends upon the tasks of the period as they, the elite, define them [p. 277]." In the latter part of the nineteenth century, rapid industrialization led to dominance by the economic sector. Economic chaos during the Depression and the resulting social crisis brought forth the dominance of the political institutions, especially the executive branch. In times of war or fear of external threat, the military ascends in importance. But the central "ruling elite" among the three hierarchies always interprets these needs and responds to them independent from popular direction or influence.

Technological Dominance. Where power ultimately resides may depend upon social forces that are more important than either wealth or institutions. John Kenneth Galbraith (1967) finds such a force in the explosive growth of modern technology. One consequence of the technological explosion is the creation of more knowledge than any single person can absorb and use. This knowledge tends to be unequally distributed, and power tends to flow to those who have the ability to perform the coordination and planning needed to gain and use knowledge. The primary reservoir of technological information is in industry, but Galbraith does not argue that this makes industry completely dominant over government.

Government shapes the uses of technology by its purchases. As government and industry work together, their interests are fused in a symbiotic relationship. The state provides the stable market and the system for planning so that industry can exploit technology. The decisions made in that process shape the goals of the society. Such a process puts the decisions beyond the reach of the ordinary citizen or consumer:

> The initiative in deciding what is to be produced comes not from the sovereign consumer who, through the market, issues the instructions that bend the production mechanism to his ultimate will. Rather it comes from the great producing organization which reaches forward to control the markets that it is presumed to serve and, beyond, to bend the customer to its needs. And, in so doing, it deeply influences his values and beliefs . . . [p. 6].

The industrial state, says Galbraith, is a machine which we have created to serve us, but, instead, we are becoming its servants, both in thought and in action.

Decisionless Decisions.   Not to decide is to decide. But this kind of negative decision making is difficult to study simply because the student does not know where to start looking. Peter Bachrach and Morton Baratz (1970) argue that the real power in society may be exercised simply by keeping certain questions from ever reaching the agenda for decision. If so, something is missing from studies of power that concentrate on the participants in various debates to see who wins. The real winner may be persons or interests so strong that they never find it necessary to enter the debate at all because they can see to it that the questions which would threaten them are never raised. Inertia is on their side. This inertia limits the news media, whose managers are conditioned to view matters in familiar perspective (see Chapter 4). The media thus are a power center in support of the status quo—most of the time. When the media do move, as the *Washington Post* did in the case of the Watergate investigation in 1972 and 1973, their anti-status quo effect can be devastating.

But most of the time, a powerless group which wants a question resolved must first overcome the problem of finding a way to get the question asked. Women's liberation leaders, for example, must talk about "consciousness raising" just to get others to see that there are roles for women besides those which have traditionally suited male elites. The first obstacle which the black civil rights movement had to overcome was to gain the simple acceptance of the *possibility* that blacks did not have to be relegated to an inferior position. Polluting industries were able to foul the air for decades simply because the assumption that smokestacks ought to emit smoke was taken for granted. Control measures never reached the municipal agenda (Crenson, 1971). Habits of thought are difficult to break, but they do not have the immutability of laws of nature.

Air Pollution in Gary, Indiana: Smoke was taken for granted. *(Tony Castelvecchi, Black Star.)*

Bachrach and Baratz suggest that the status quo supporting habits of thought consist of "predominant values, beliefs, rituals, and institutional procedures ('rules of the game') that operate systematically and consistently to the benefit of certain persons and groups at the expense of others [p. 43]." The rules are sustained by nondecision making: a process of suffocating potential demands for change before they can be voiced. The process of suffocation can be as direct as a lynching or as subtle as a false concession, as when, for example, a university administration responds to student grievances by creating machinery to hear the grievances, but without any intent to act upon complaints once they are aired.

Model 2: Government Power Is Dominant

A second school of thought about the relationships among government and private power centers looks at the the same institutions and the same behaviors, and sees no elite at all. Their view of the system pictures a multiplicity of competing decision-making centers outside the government. None dominates. Over time, they tend to battle each other to a standoff, and government, as another power center, mediates disputes and tips the balance. This is called the *pluralist* view.

Galbraith (1952) expressed this view early in his career with the publication of *American Capitalism: The Concept of Countervailing Power.* Looking at evolving patterns of economic power, he noted that the trend toward industrial concentration created not only strong sellers but an offsetting trend of strong buyers. "The two develop together," he said, "not in precise step but in such manner that there can be no doubt that the one is in response to the other [p. 118]." Some political scientists see a parallel development in terms of political power with big labor organizations and powerful consumer interest groups developing as a check on big business. Intramural competition within power centers also exists, as when coal competes with oil, aluminum with steel. In this model, whenever one of the private decision-making centers threatens to become dominant, the opposition groups petition the power of the government to restore the balance. The history of labor legislation is an example of such a seesaw process. After the Wagner Act of 1935 stripped employers of their major anti-union weapons and established a right of collective bargaining, the Taft-Hartley Act of 1947 moved the balance in the other direction, depriving the unions of some of their weapons, including the closed shop. Much farm legislation similarly represents an attempt to fine-tune the balance of power among the producers, processors, distributors and consumers of agricultural products.

David Truman (1950) has traced the way competing organizations attempt to turn government power to their ends through the various means of influence, including parties, elections, and contact with the institutions of government. The recent history of the black civil rights movement is illustrative. Failing to improve their conditions through state and local government, blacks tried at the national level, and, failing with Congress and the executive, eventually gained access through the judiciary. Their victory in the *Brown* case caused segregationists to look for those parts of the government where they could gain access and reverse the *Brown* decision. In some cases, segregationists succeeded in using state governmental powers temporarily to obstruct the Supreme Court's ruling. The competition for the use of government power on the race issue continues with struggles over busing, tax privileges for private schools, and the use of federal funds to encourage or discourage action by local officials. The process does not produce equilibrium instantly or even quickly. But proponents of this model argue that the long-run tendency is toward equilibrium. If so, the race issue should, in time, achieve relative stability.

Model 3: Government Abdicates Power

Some current students of American politics agree with Truman about the way competing power centers operate to balance one another, but they argue that the government has not been assertive enough to tip the balance, and power has gone to the private decision centers by default if not by conscious designs. Theodore Lowi (1969) argues that the previous model, with its competing powers in long-term balance, makes two assumptions which fail to stand up under scrutiny. One is that the various interests—blacks, farmers, labor, for example—are homogeneous with clear and easily agreed-upon ideas of just what their interests are. The other is that organized interests, the private power centers, "fill up and adequately represent most of the sectors of our lives [p. 71]." But the world is not that neat. Interests are quite heterogeneous, and a policy which aids one segment of a group may harm another, as, for example, when the interests of large and small farmers conflict. A potential power center whose needs are fragmented and conflicting spends most of its energy mediating its internal power struggle and has little left over to use to compete with outside interests and influence government. And some interests which are important to the lives of citizens are never organized at all. Consumer interests are a classic example from our recent past. Mass transit riders are a more specific and immediate case. More money has been spent on highways than on railroads and better bus service, not because the people who have to get to work asked to have it that way but because existing economic and political groups pushed transportation development in that direction. Consumers of health care, also unorganized, have had their interests take a low priority compared with the wishes of the medical profession and the drug industry, although that may be changing. Meanwhile, government delegates essentially public decisions about health care, such as how many doctors will be trained and graduated, the policing of the medical profession, and the distribution of health services to the population, to the medical profession itself. The profession is organized; the patients are not.

Interests which remain unorganized are systematically excluded from access to government power. According to the government abdication model, all that groups which have access need to do is work out their differences. Once that is done, the government will ratify their private agreements and adjustments. Such agreements will generally be to the disadvantage of those who are not thus represented, and the government will not help them because it has abdicated to the dominant interests and remains passive.

Who Has It Right?

The Lowi viewpoint in model 3 takes us almost full circle. Traditional elitists say that power rests in a few private centers (model 1). Pluralists (model 2) say that private powers are countervailing so that government can tip the balance. Lowi agrees with some of their premises but insists that government does not tip the balance. Why such a variety of views?

One problem is that there is no very good way to research the question of where power lies and how it flows. Those who do attempt systematic investigation tend to find the system working pretty much the way they expected it to work before they began their investigations. Even so fundamental an issue as the relationship of wealth to power has received very little study. Just about everyone agrees that a relationship between wealth and power exists, but how it works and what conditions enhance it and which diminish it are simply not known. Power in democratic societies needs continued analysis with a special focus upon its private forms.

interest whose effect would be directly apparent rather than on the remote and vague abstractions of the government in Washington. It would be something like the New England town meeting in a modern setting.

There are other possibilities for closer popular control of corporate activity. Edward Mason (1959) summed them up nearly a generation ago:

> . . . One possible route leads through court decisions to a rule of law designed to make equitable and tolerable the actions of inevitable private power. Another envisages an extended federalism, with corporations recognized as quasi-political entities properly legitimated. Still other routes move in the direction of public ownership or an expansion of the public-utility concept [p. 5].

Nader also suggests modifying criminal laws to make corporate officials personally responsible for violations of the law by the corporation. Criminal sanctions for corporate behavior are now rare and difficult to impose. Each of these measures designed to attach some legitimacy to corporate power would be difficult to achieve. But none of them is unthinkable. Corporate power is held at the sufferance of society. The existing way of dealing with it is not the only, nor necessarily the best, way.

Big Labor

Organized labor is sometimes seen as a counterbalance to the power of large corporations. It does represent people whose interests conflict, in many ways, with those of big business. However, nationally organized labor unions have themselves become nondemocratic power centers with substantial control over the lives of Americans. The most successful unions win their benefits for members by shifting costs to the unorganized sectors of society—of which there are many. Moreover, like their corporate and government counterparts, they tend to become self-perpetuating bureaucracies more interested in their own survival than anything else. Henry S. Kariel (1961) has described the labor movement as something that began as an effort "to protect individual members from outsiders" and "generally ended as one to protect the leadership from insiders." The decision-making power, he said, "has come to reside in well-protected, self-perpetuating incumbents whose prestige and skill . . . are such that the rank and file, perhaps gratefully unconcerned, only rarely challenges their word [pp. 46–47]." When rank-and-file members do assert themselves and gain control, it often requires a major upheaval, as was the case with the United Mine Workers when the leadership changed hands in 1972. The previous president was convicted in the murder of an earlier election opponent.

Disclosure of corruption in labor unions in the 1950s led to the Landrum-Griffin Act of 1959, which contained some reforms, including a requirement that unions file elaborate financial reports with the Secretary of

Arnold Miller Taking Oath as Mine Workers President: For the rank-and-file to assert themselves may take a major upheaval. *(Wide World Photos.)*

Labor, but enforcement proved difficult. "The government of the union," said Hans J. Morgenthau (1960), "has become in good measure an autonomous private government, making and enforcing its own laws and pursing its own policies, regardless of the public laws, the public policy, and the public interest [pp. 81–82]."

One obvious misuse of labor power has been the continuance of racial discrimination. Through control of apprenticeship programs, unions can determine who will get the better-paying jobs, and blacks have been systematically excluded, particularly in the building trades. Another example: the large industrial unions, such as the United Auto Workers, will readily admit blacks to the starting, unskilled jobs on the assembly line, but blacks meet resistance when they try to move up to jobs requiring more skill. National labor organizations have firm policies against racial discrimination but fail to enforce them on a local level (Knowles and Prewitt, 1969). Thus a group which gained significantly on the political scene was shut out of a private power center.

The rise of a rough equality of bargaining power between big business and big labor, plus the adoption of a conciliatory attitude by labor leaders and reduced hostility on the part of industry, has created a stable atmosphere. The relationship is based on cooperation, mutual understanding, recognition of common goals, and mutual acceptance of the legitimacy of the other side. But this happy state of affairs is of no help to the millions of Americans who are not part of big business or big labor. Nonunion workers, members of small, locally based unions, and thousands of small business owners and operators who compete with big firms are in fact disadvantaged by the collusion of large power centers. The gains of the organized have to come at a cost to somebody, and that cost is paid by the unorganized sector.

Private Foundations

Economic power wielded in the name of philanthropy also has an important influence in shaping our lives. By deciding what research to fund and what educational goals to support, foundations make choices which are political in effect. The fruits of their work are generally beneficial; society is probably better off than if the money were spent for private purposes. However, the charity of their intent does not ensure that the causes which foundations choose to support are the most pressing causes nor that the long-term effects are those that society would choose against other alternatives. For example, the fact that a student interested in a teaching career must spend the time and money to get a Ph.D. degree is because of a set of circumstances traceable in part to a foundation decision. The Carnegie Foundation helped establish the Teachers Insurance and Annuity Association; to be eligible for participation in its retirement plans, an institution must demonstrate its educational legitimacy. The easiest way to do that is to have department heads with Ph.D's. This small administrative step has been blamed for the shift in emphasis from teaching to research in graduate education (Lundberg, 1968).

Foundations consciously look for such ways to enhance the effects of their spending. The aim is to create broad ripples of reform with just the right amount of money applied in just the right place. The decision as to what constitutes reform is, of course, their own, and broad effects are not always good. An example is the case of the Ford Foundation whose early work on poverty helped to focus attention on the problem and inspire the 1964 Economic Opportunity Act. Stephen M. Rose (1972) has traced many of the shortcomings of the government's war on poverty to the service-oriented philosophy of reform which Ford Foundation personnel built into the very beginning of the program. Without the Foundation's role, the war on poverty might have taken a different and more successful direction.

Professional Associations

Professional persons such as teachers, doctors, and lawyers share common educational backgrounds and goals of service to society. When they organize to set and maintain standards for their professions, they quickly discover that they also share common economic interests. The fusion of economic and professional bonds, observes Joseph C. Palamountain (1955) in a study of the way goods and services are marketed, "can produce an unusually cohesive economic group with a strong sense of group purpose. It also tends to produce a conviction that their services should not be evaluated under solely economic criteria and that, accordingly, they should be protected from the rigors of the market [pp. 93–94]." Thus the American Medical Association sets standards which give some measure of protection from quackery, but, also by reducing competition, these standards ensure physicians a very secure and comfortable economic position. A hierarchy of medical societies, with the American Medical Association at the top, invokes a variety of private and governmental sanctions to control the ways doctors do business. State and federal laws regulating the practice of medicine have generally been written in collaboration with the medical establishment. As a result, medical associations have effective control over such matters as hospital affiliations, speciality accreditations, and, in some cases, the legal right to practice medicine. They even regulate to some extent the choice of a physician; there was a time when, if one needed an allergist, he could find that speciality listed among subcategories under "Physicians" in the classified section of the telephone directory. Classification by speciality is now barred in most places as "unethical" advertising. To find a specialist, one must call a local medical society. It is not likely to refer the patient to a nonmember.

Professional associations tend to define as "unethical" any practice that costs them money. When Lewis Goldfarb bought a home in Virginia, he wrote to a number of lawyers asking what they would charge to perform the title search. All quoted the same price. Some volunteered that it would be "unethical" to charge him less because it would violate the fee schedule set by the bar association. Goldfarb sued and won (355 F. Supp. 491, 1973). Federal courts are beginning to recognize that price fixing by professional associations is as illegal as price fixing by corporations.

Organized Religion

The power of churches stems both from their economic resources and from their ability to mobilize manpower and attitudinal support. They have a series of public privileges. Churches participate in the administration of such civil matters as marriage and divorce. They join with local government in the administration of educational and welfare programs. They enjoy special tax exemptions which not only enhance their economic power but have long-term influence on investment and development patterns.

Rules for tax exemption vary from state to state, but the usual principle is that a church need not pay taxes on its property if its use is church-related. Alfred Balk (1971) cites the case of the Catholic Archdiocese of Hartford, Connecticut, which bought 121.5 acres of land in New Britain for $23,500. The land was granted tax exemption as a cemetery. A body was buried on the property. When real estate development pushed the value of

*"I always think of the eleventh commandment as
'Thou shall not tax the churches.'"*

(Playboy, December 1969.)

the land to $607,000, the land was sold and the dead person was removed. A
private speculator making the same transactions would have had to pay
$200,000 in real estate taxes during the period of church ownership. The
church paid none. Balk reports that the total value of tax-exempt church
property is about $110 billion. In 1959, the general secretary of the World
Council of Churches said the churches, with "reasonably prudent management," might be able to control the nation's entire economy "within the
predictable future [Balk, 1971, p. 39]."

However awesome their economic power, churches have a more subtle
and fundamental power. By influencing basic values, they have a tremendous impact on the beliefs, attitudes, and expectations of citizens about
political matters. If the political system is controlled by an elite for its own
benefit, the system is easier to maintain and control if it is supported by
churches. If the system operates unjustly, the injustice will be harder to

defend if the churches mobilize moral indignation against it. Empirical studies indicate that the former situation applies more often than the latter (Hudson, 1970; Ellul, 1960). Religious institutions tend to reflect and reinforce whatever distribution of material wealth and prestige exists in society (O'Dea, 1966).

In addition, religion has a historic role of providing a safe outlet for the frustrations of powerlessness (Lanternari, 1963). Blacks in the old South were encouraged to look forward to "pie in the sky, by and by" rather than rewards in this world. A similar attitude is found among the Appalachian poor of the current period (Coles, 1972). Gary Marx (1967) found as recently as 1964 that among urban blacks, the stronger the religious feeling, the weaker the political militancy.

Like other large organizations which must attend to a variety of functions with different specialties, churches have become bureaucratized. Their power is not legitimated in democratic fashion, and their officials, like other bureaucrats, become preoccupied with self-perpetuation.

PRIVATE DEMOCRACY

Controlling Private Power Centers

Should government take over the private power centers or not? As we have seen, the government in its present form already has its hands full just trying to carry out its given functions. Hans J. Morgenthau (1960) notes that government power is too fragmented to cope with the functional concentrations of private power. Government power enters this arena with a basic fragmentation among branches and jurisdictions established by the Constitution, whose eighteenth-century authors intended it that way. When this fragmented government power engages in conflict with more tautly organized private power, the private power centers usually win in the long run.

When private power centers get the upper hand in conflicts with government, their victories are legitimated by our historic fear of the evils of government. That private power may be just as oppressive is a notion that tends to surface only after periods of extreme abuse. For Ralph Nader to be noticed, many people had to die in auto crashes. The fact that academic political science tends to ignore the political nature of power in private hands also contributes to this myopia.

The best hope for introducing some measure of popular control to the private power centers is probably through the democratization of the centers themselves. Such a goal is especially important in view of the increasing mutual penetration of public and private power centers. Personnel and information pass increasingly between the two, and private centers are being given more responsibility to perform governmental functions while the government enters areas once thought of as strictly private. Government subsidization of private activity is varied and growing. Private competitive enterprise, says Michael D. Reagan (1963), is "no longer either private or competitive in the traditional meaning of these words." His "realistic, if slightly cynical" definition:

> Private enterprise is a politico-economic system in which each private group seeks to direct public policy to the improvement of its competitive position, share of national income, or bargaining power vis-à-vis other segments of the society. The private elements in the system lie in the insistence by business that, in return for public benefits . . . no limitations be placed on resultant profits or managerial discretion, and that the public good is not to be planned for, but is to arise as a by-product of private planning for private purposes [pp. 209–210].

Galbraith (1967) has echoed a similar view in *The New Industrial State*, where he notes, "The industrial system, in fact, is inextricably associated with the state. In notable respects the mature corporation is an arm of the state. And the state, in important matters, is an instrument of the industrial system [p. 296]."

Corporate Responsibility

Very early in this book, we made the observations that any government to survive must have the support of its subjects over the long run, and that this is true even of totalitarian governments. No organization can maintain the physical force and presence necessary to govern for long periods of time without the consent of the governed. If this is true, and if private power centers often behave like governments, it must follow that private centers are also limited in their means of social control and must maintain the consent of the ruled. A look at the behavior of the most enduring private power centers bears this out. None can afford to alienate any significant portion of the public for very long. Here, as in government, information is crucial, and the most effective way to end behavior that is damaging to society is to expose it.

Raymond A. Bauer and Dan H. Fenn, Jr. (1972), have noted that the current concern among corporation managers over social responsibility is nothing new. Business has "Always, in a rough sense, reflected the values of the community in which it was imbedded [p. 4]." And if the profit motive has been held as the supreme and only goal, it is only because the rest of society has agreed that wealth is a positive good in itself and that material success is God's way of rewarding virtue. By getting rich, a businessman was, by definition, meeting his social responsibility.

Since World War II a broader view has taken hold. Its growth has been most vigorous in the past decade. No one is sure why. Population growth, improved education, better communication, new awareness of bypassed problems, and the end of the illusion of American omnipotence may have all contributed. Whatever the reason, corporate power centers have found it bad form to contribute to or ignore social problems; their "citizens"—consumers, stockholders, and employees—will not let them. Bauer and Fenn have cited the new mood of industrial restlessness:

> . . . a major insurance company was troubled by the questioning its employees were doing about the socially beneficial nature of much of its product; a utility was under great pressure from its workers who felt that it was not serving its customers adequately; company after company in the defense business has been attacked by its own employees for participating in the Vietnam War; Polaroid faced a deeply angered minority over its involvement in South Africa. In addition to their concern with the quality of their own lives on the job . . . many employees and managers are questioning the social usefulness of what they and their employers are doing in American companies today [p. 9].

A Social Audit

Ralph Nader's Project on Corporate Responsibility, which tried to gather proxies from General Motors stockholders and use them to influence company behavior, has led some institutional investors to question the social effect of their portfolios. For example, some liberal church groups stopped investing in companies with Vietnam War contracts. Special investment funds have been created to route money to companies that consider their long-run effects on society as well as short-term profits. This sort of activity may be more than a passing fashion. It is taken seriously enough so that some social scientists are turning their attention to the problem of measuring the effect of corporation activity on the larger community—a "social audit." Corporation managers need this information, say Bauer and Fenn, and so do the rest of us:

> If the institutional and individual investors are to separate the socially responsible from the irresponsible, if they are to bestow white hats and black hats, they need definition and measurement. If customers are to buy selectively from the good guys and bypass the bad guys; if graduating students are to respond to the job offers from the responsible and reject the irresponsible; if students are to select their business targets with maximum efficiency and level their rifles at real bull's eyes; if employees are to express their concerns meaningfully, they need definitions and measurements [p. 14].

Perhaps the nation needs a Social Accounting Office. It might audit the other private power centers as well. The Athenian statesman Demosthenes summed it as well as anyone: "There is one safeguard known generally to the wise, which is an advantage and security to all, but especially to democracies as against despots. What is it? Distrust." Freedom requires distrust of power wherever it is found.

Domhoff, G. William. *Who Rules America?* Englewood Cliffs, N.J.: Prentice-Hall, 1967. This book examines the sociological background of key decisionmakers in America and finds them to come primarily from the upper class, said to constitute a power elite.

Dutton, Frederick G. *Changing Sources of Power.* New York: McGraw-Hill, 1971. This book argues that a confrontation over power is inevitable in America and that the insurgent force in the clash will number among its members women, blacks, youth, and suburban voters.

Greenberg, Edward S. *Serving the Few: Corporate Capitalism and the Bias of Government Policy.* New York: John Wiley, 1974. A provocative and logically reasoned essay on the dominance of American society and politics by corporate elites whose position of prominence is ensured by the positive state.

Kolko, Gabriel. *Wealth and Power in America.* New York: Praeger, 1962. A study of income distribution among social classes that shows the persistence of inequality in American life and the concentration of resources in the hands of a small segment of the society.

Lundberg, Ferdinand, *The Rich and the Super-Rich.* New York: Lyle Stuart, 1968. An analysis of the structure of wealth in America and the political power possessed by a small number of families who are said to be able to control elected and appointed government officials.

Mintz, Morton, and Jerry S. Cohen. *America, Inc.* New York: Dial, 1971. Journalistic view of the interrelationships of public and private corporate powers.

Orren, Karen. *Corporate Power and Social Change.* Baltimore: Johns Hopkins University Press, 1974. A unique and systematic examination of the political role played by the life insurance industry and the power it wields.

Sethi, S. Prakash. *Up Against the Corporate Wall.* Englewood Cliffs, N.J.: Prentice-Hall, 1971. A collection of essays discussing how major social problems are likely to continue to arise because of the structure and influence of business corporations in America.

Part Four

Policy

IN THE FINAL SECTION OF THIS BOOK WE TURN TO THE SUBJECT OF public policy. in its simplest form, public policy is the cumulative result of interactions between the institutional foundations of American government, the influences of various kinds of political participation, and the decision-making processes presided over by elected and appointed officials. In short, public policy consists of the rules, decisions, and programs arrived at by government officials. We devote the concluding four chapters to domestic and foreign policies because they represent the end products and substantive results of the interplay we have described between various forces within the political system.

We have already observed some aspects of public policy formation in American politics. The eighteenth-century structural foundations and institutional arrangements reviewed in Part One have a continuing impact on the kinds of policies produced by the political system; the degree and intensity of involvement in the forms of participation discussed in Part Two affect to some extent the decisions of public officials; and the decision-making processes, structures, and officials examined in Part Three made the final determination about which policies are forthcoming. In the following chapters, our discussion is devoted explicitly to various stages in the formation of public policy. We examine the social and political origins of policy initiatives, the deliberations surrounding the policy formulation stage, the decision-making coalitions involved when policies are officially chosen, and the changes that are introduced when policies are actually implemented and carried out. This detailed discussion reveals how complex the policy formation and policy implementation processes are and how they, in turn, affect the substance of public policy.

Public policies contain important dimensions in their final implementation stage that are worth keeping in mind when reading the following chapters. Perhaps the most important dimension is that all public policies involve *rewards* for some people and *deprivations* for others. Who wins policy benefits and who loses and suffers policy deprivations are usually determined by the political strength and tactical skill displayed by those involved in the policy formulation and implementation stages. Another dimension of public policies is that their impact may be *symbolic* or *material* in nature. Symbolic rewards or deprivations provide their respective recipients with psychological gratification or costs, while material rewards or deprivations are tangible gains or losses for their respective recipients. The usefulness of these two dimensions is that they can be applied to a particular public policy and assessments can be made about who benefits and who does not.

Public policy encompasses too vast an array of rules, decisions, and programs to be dealt with comprehensively here. Our discussion therefore focuses on specific policy areas and is necessarily selective. Our criteria for deciding on policy areas require some explanation.

In Chapter 14 we deal with the issue of "law and order" and the anticrime policies intended to be responsive to it. We begin by examining the origins of law and order as a political issue and the distribution of public attitudes toward it. Then we trace public officials' responses to the issue, the governmental policies they adopted to attack it, and the consequences these policies had. As a relatively recent political issue, law and order allows us to explore whether it arose from expressed citizen concerns or from elite rhetoric and manipulation. Finally, we assess the effectiveness of anticrime policies and who the prime beneficiaries of these policies have been.

Chapter 15 deals with policies aimed at two basic, enduring contradictions in American society: poverty and race. In both cases explicit policies intended to redress past grievances and give full membership in society are analyzed to determine what impact the policies had.

In Chapter 16 we discuss a central issue in American political debate, both historically and currently: economic policy. The different fiscal and monetary policies and governmental attempts at economic regulation and promotion are related to recurrent cycles of inflation, recession, and prosperity. These three chapters dealing with domestic policies show the inherent political nature of the policymaking process and the inevitability of winners and losers in policy outcomes.

Chapter 17 examines American foreign policy in some depth; The process of making foreign policy is analyzed, as are the substantive policies resulting from that process. Conflicts are exposed between espoused goals and actual foreign policies. And the relationships of the United States to Europe, to Third World nations, and to emerging powers on the world stage are explored. In each case, foreign policy, like domestic policy, results from interplay of political forces.

Chapter 14

Law and Order:
The Making of an Issue

A President Speaks

In his first administration, President Nixon made a ringing public declaration of his approach to the problem of crime:

> The right of all citizens to feel safe on the streets and secure in their homes is fundamental to individual liberty and national progress. It is a right on which this Administration has placed a new and major emphasis. . . . Another key ingredient in the crime fight has been the development of a new, less permissive public attitude toward crime and criminals. The American public now is fully awake to the social menace of crime, and fully determined that criminals must be defeated if America is to make continued social progress [Law Enforcement Assistance Administration, 1972, p. 12].

At about that same time, agents of the White House and the Committee to Re-elect the President were breaking into the headquarters of the Democratic National Committee in the Watergate office building. The President's private response to that crime was to discuss payments of money and executive clemency for the burglars and to congratulate his aides for their apparent success in limiting the official investigation to the seven persons apprehended at or near the scene. The flavor of his attitude is captured in this extract from the transcript of Oval Office conversations released to the House Judiciary Committee:

> D (John Dean, III): Nothing is going to come crashing down to our surprise.
>
> P (President Nixon): Oh well, this is a can of worms as you know a lot of this stuff that went on. And the people who worked this way are awfully embarrassed. But the way you have handled all this seems to me has been very skillful putting your fingers in the leaks that have sprung here and sprung there. [*The White House Transcripts*, p. 61].

In the social context of the White House staff from 1972 to 1974, the Watergate burglary was embarrassing, but it was not a crime. It is quite conceivable that, in their own minds, Nixon and his staff were perfectly consistent when they demanded law and order on the one hand and resisted the inquiry into the burglary on the other. Crime is socially defined, and the definition changes from one society to another and even from one transient social situation to another. Because of this flexibility, the crime issue is an ideal one to illustrate a fundamental question about what really happens in the political process. The question, in brief, is this: when an issue comes to the forefront of the political arena, is it because the mass of citizens perceives a problem and demands action? Or is it because the ruling elites create the issue as an excuse to do the things necessary to maintain and improve their own positions?

Who Created the Crisis?

The traditional view of how public policy is made in the United States follows a simple stimulus-response model: The public feels a need and expresses that need to the system, and the system responds by forming and executing a policy. In this way, the political system eliminates undesired conditions and creates desired conditions. If the system fails to respond, the public has several possible remedies. New officials with more responsive policies can be elected. Changes can be made in the system itself to encourage a better response.

The other view, suggested by V. O. Key's metaphor of the echo chamber (see Chapter 4), holds that the public is not the initiator of policy at all. In this model, leaders can improve their own situations by sending forth messages of their own invention which are reacted to and fed back to them by the public. If the leaders are successful, this feedback strengthens their positions as ruling elites and helps them to channel the society's economic and symbolic rewards to themselves and to the groups which they favor. The process need not be consciously manipulative in order to work. The gasoline shortages of 1973 and 1974 generated support for measures long sought by petroleum industry elites. Yet the conditions that led to the shortage were sufficiently complicated so that no one has been able to

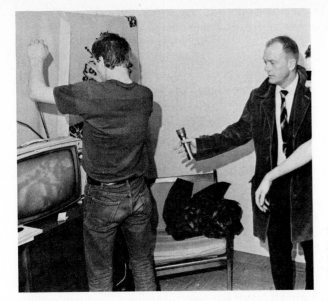

Drug Arrest in a Col-
lege Town, 1971:
Crime is socially de-
fined. *(Wide World*
Photos.)

isolate a specific elite decision to create the shortage to gain the desired
response. The model fits even without the imputation of particular
Machiavellian motives, for the energy crisis, if not consciously created, was
at least allowed to happen by leaders who could see it coming and did not
act to stop it or alleviate it until the public was prepared to reward them for
doing so.

The question is troublesome because if popular demand can be
generated by political elites and used to justify their self-serving actions,
then the system is not as democratic as its formal mechanisms and the
associated rhetoric make it appear to be. The treatment of the law-and-
order issue by the administrations of Presidents Johnson and Nixon appears
to fit this model's version of reality. It should be remembered, however,
that the stimulus-response model and the created-stimulus model are, like
all such models, only approximate representations of the way public policy
is made. Different cases may fit different models.

Was There a Crime Wave?

Both the number of reported crimes and the rate of reported crime per unit
of population increased in the 1960s. But the increase in fear of crime was
even greater. Tracing the events of a decade indicates that the growth in
popular fear of crime was not proportional to the increased risk of criminal
victimization faced by the average citizen. A plausible explanation for the
increased fear is found in the intensification of political rhetoric and the
statements of public leaders that crime was a menace about which citizens
should be fearful. What was behind this rhetoric? One way to begin to find

out is to examine the nature of the issue, the legislation that resulted, and the ultimate outcome in terms of who benefited and at whose expense.

The Reality of Crime

All crime, as the Watergate case so aptly illustrated, is socially defined. What one society considers a crime, another may not. And the same society may consider a form of behavior criminal at one time but not at another. We may therefore define crime as human behavior which the relevant society considers so undesirable at the time as to want official sanction. This usage is consistent with the suggestion of Herbert Jacob (1973) that "any activity may be criminal if it is so labeled. What distinguishes criminal from legitimate behavior is the label attached to it [p. 16]."

This idea that there are no universal standards to give crime an objective existence may seem difficult to accept at first glance. Yet not even lying, cheating, and killing are criminal in all situations. An undercover narcotics agent lies and cheats with the official sanction of the law. Killing is officially sanctioned in wars, in self-defense, and as punishment for certain crimes. What is considered a crime tends to reflect prevailing community standards of conduct, but in the end it is what the lawmakers and law enforcers want to define and label as crimes. Sociologist Richard Quinney (1970) has put it rather bluntly:

> By constructing a reality that we are all to believe in, those in positions of power *legitimize* their authority. . . . (The) reality of crime that is constructed for all of us by those in a position of power is the reality we tend to accept as our own. By doing so, we grant those in power the authority to carry out the actions that best promote their interests.
>
> This is the *politics of reality*. The social reality of crime in politically organized society is constructed as a political act. Both private and governmental groups have a vested interest in constructing particular criminal conceptions that instruct official policy. From beginning to end, then, the construction of the social reality of crime is a political matter [pp. 303–304].

When authorities extend their interpretation of what does or does not constitute a criminal act beyond what is publicly acceptable, they may quickly find that there are limits to their ability to manipulate this social reality. John D. Ehrlichman, former chief domestic affairs adviser to President Nixon, sought to justify the burglary of the office of Daniel Ellsberg's psychiatrist as a necessity for national security. He went beyond the limits of public acceptance and was not believed.

Measuring the Problem

The Uniform Crime Reports of the FBI document the steady increase in the incidence of *reported* behavior that is officially defined as criminal. These

John Ehrlichman before Watergate Committee, 1973: Going beyond the limits. *(Wide World Photos.)*

reports are constructed from accounts submitted by local law enforcement agencies. However, these records suffer from several deficiencies, making the reported crime rates less than the actual occurrence of crime in society. Long-term trends are confounded by lack of records for early periods and noncomparable record systems for different regions and historical periods (Bell, 1960). A great deal of crime goes unreported to police or is unreported by them. Local police departments voluntarily report crime figures to the FBI, and their reports are not audited. Only crimes falling within one of the seven crimes used in the FBI index (murder, forcible rape, robbery, aggravated assault, burglary, auto theft, and larceny) are used in compiling the rates. These seven crimes cover less than 10 percent of all arrests. There remains a "dark figure" of unreported criminal behavior, and Albert Biderman and Albert Reiss first reported in 1967 that this figure covers a majority of all criminal acts.

They reached this estimate by comparing the reported crime rate with the rate at which citizens reported being victimized in a sample survey of the general population. This finding was confirmed in 1974 when a very large sample survey conducted by the Bureau of the Census produced criminal victimization rates about twice as high as those reflected in the FBI

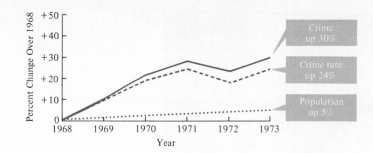

reports. The discrepancy varied from place to place. In Philadelphia, for
example, crime rates reported in the survey were nearly four times as high
as those reported from law enforcement sources. Because Philadelphians
were just as likely to report crimes as citizens of other large cities, the
inference was drawn that police in Philadelphia were less efficient at passing
on crime reports to the FBI. This survey, sponsored by the Law Enforcement Assistance Administration, was scheduled to be repeated so that a
reliable measure of changes in patterns of crime over time could be
developed. (See Table 14-1.)

However unreliable as an indicator of what is happening in the real
world, the FBI reports do make it clear that the incidence of crime that is
known to police authorities has been increasing. These figures form much of
the basis of the popular view of the reality of crime. It is therefore
worthwhile to consider a number of possible explanations for the reported
increase.

Population Trends. Only part of the increase in the number of reported
crimes is explained by the increase in the number of people. However, the

Table 14-1 Reported Crime Compared
with Actual Victimization
(*Frequency of crime reported in FBI Uniform Crime
Report versus LEAA survey*)

CITY	FBI	LEAA
Chicago	313,093	621,300
Detroit	167,701	345,600
Los Angeles	327,797	693,500
New York	649,785	1,100,100
Philadelphia	101,189	396,400
Total	1,559,565	3,156,900

Source: Law Enforcement Assistance Administration, *Crime in the Nation's Five Largest Cities,*
Washington, U.S. Department of Justice, Apr.
15, 1974, p. 4.

structure of the population increase had disproportionately swollen the ranks of the kinds of people who commit crimes: the young and city dwellers. Both of these trends have now peaked. The baby boom tapered off after 1958 (the year of birth for most members of 1976 high school graduating classes), and suburbs have replaced urban areas as the growth centers. As Table 14-2 shows, property crime rates are higher in population centers. A similar pattern exists for violent crime.

Economic Trends.   Growing affluence has put more goods in the hands of most Americans, who have been somewhat less careful with their belongings than in days when luxuries were harder to come by. Affluence has therefore made crime easier at the same time that it has become more tempting. Moreover, the gap between the affluent and the nonaffluent has increased, perhaps increasing the motivation of the poor to steal from the rich. Moreover, the greater share of the increase in crime has come from property crimes, and inflation has exaggerated the statistics. The dollar value of goods increased while the dollar definitions of serious larceny remained the same. More thefts thus became reportable quite apart from any actual increase in thievery.[1]

However, even after population trends and economic factors are taken into account, very little of the increase in reported crime is explained. Other factors, bearing more on the reporting of crime than its actual incidence, may contain the explanation. These factors may be summarized in the following two categories.

Sociocultural Trends.   Before the civil rights movement, police were inclined to be tolerant of crime in black neighborhoods on the theory that white society was not harmed by blacks committing crimes against one another. One of the improvements in the status of blacks has been

[1]Beginning in 1973, the FBI dropped the dollar definition of larceny in its index of serious crimes. From 1958 to 1973, larceny was counted in the index when the value of the goods stolen was $50 or more. Besides being distorted by inflation, this test made the figures subject to manipulation by overstated or understated valuations. The index now includes all larceny and theft, regardless of value.

Table 14-2   Crime Rates by Size of Community, 1973
(Reported crimes per 100,000 population)

CITY SIZE	VIOLENT CRIME	PROPERTY CRIME
Over 250,000	1003.4	5579.5
100,000–250,000	545.0	5606.2
50,000–100,000	371.5	4635.9
25,000–50,000	295.2	4124.0
10,000–25,000	220.7	3555.8
Under 10,000	199.0	3017.8

Source: Federal Bureau of Investigation, *Crime in the United States—1973*, U.S. Government Printing Office, 1974.

Police Catching Bank Robbers: Increased efficiency clouds the statistics. *(United Press International.)*

somewhat better law enforcement and more care by police in their record keeping on crime in black areas (Pettigrew, Summers, and Barth, 1970). In an unrelated but parallel development, women are becoming more assertive about protesting rape and more willing to report it.

Improved Police Efficiency.   The experience of blacks may have also occurred in the society at large. It makes sense to call a policeman only if you think he might actually catch the criminal. The better police get at catching criminals, the more criminals they are asked to catch, and the more crimes are placed on the record. This effect can be intensified by a good public relations campaign so that the rate of reported crime is less a measure of crimes actually committed than it is of faith in policemen (Bloch and Geis, 1970).

Police efficiency has a more direct effect as well. Donald F. Black (1970) has reported evidence that police handle many felonies informally without making reports. Shuffling papers is not consonant with a policeman's self-image, and many try to avoid it as much as possible (Rubin, 1972; Chambliss and Seidman, 1971). Moreover, low-level police administrators may find it advantageous to underreport crime in their districts to inflate their apparent effectiveness. But all of these pressures against accurate recording are being eroded by tighter organization and better law enforcement technology, so that the "dark figure" of unreported crime is edged evermore into the light (Bennett, 1964; Cook, 1968).

What can we now say with any certainty about how to explain the heightened public demand for crime control legislation in the 1960s? It is apparent from the foregoing discussion of population and economic trends that the heightened concern *cannot* be explained by changes in the characteristics of individual Americans. This conclusion is consistent with the findings of the President's Crime Commission (1967):

> Although the Commission concluded that there has been an increase in the volume and rate of crime in America, it has been unable to decide whether individual Americans today are more criminal than their counterparts 5, 10, or 25 years ago [p. 26].

More likely, what happened in the 1960s, especially in view of sociocultural trends and increasing police efficiency, was a crime-*reporting* wave rather than a massive and genuine increase in the actual instance of crime. But even here considerable uncertainty clouds the crime issue, giving it an Alice in Wonderland image that Fred J. Cook (1971) described with reference to the 1968 presidential campaign rhetoric:

> Unrealism haunts the whole issue. . . . There is unrealism in the expectations now being aroused by campaign oratory that something swift and sure can be done; unrealism concerning the public's own role and the price it will have to pay to get what it wants, and, finally, unrealism concerning the whole complicated system of American criminal justice [p. 32].

Public Attitudes about Crime

Although objectively unreliable, official statistics may be even more important than the reality of crime in determining how the public feels about crime. We derive our images about what is happening from our personal experiences and from what we are told by others. Criminal victimization is rare enough so that most of us, thankfully, have only second- or third-hand knowledge most of the time. Public perception of crime depends on the attention the mass media give to it and the statements made by public figures.

Public concern, once aroused, tends to be self-reinforcing. It leads to action, such as the creation of special investigating commissions, which in turn heighten the public concern. The Gallup Opinion Index (1972) reports that in 1949 only 4 percent of the residents of cities of 500,000 or more population listed crime as their city's "worst problem." In 1972, 22 percent said crime was the worst problem. In a national Gallup sampling in 1972, interviewers found 42 percent who said there were areas around their homes where they were afraid to walk alone at night. Four years earlier, the percent with this fear had been only 31.

However, it is significant that crime did not attain a high position on the national sample's list of most important problems until *after* the 1964 presidential campaign when Barry Goldwater used the issue to attack the

Democrats and *after* President Johnson created the first national commission to investigate the problem in 1965. Moreover, the Gallup-documented spurt in fear of crime during 1972 came at a time when the increase in reported crime was tapering off. The FBI was even claiming a victory of sorts because of the decreasing rate at which reported crime was increasing.

This experience tends to illustrate both the validity and the complexity of the created-stimulus model. An issue can achieve a kind of resonance in the echo chamber of public opinion so that an issue raised by officials produces citizen reactions which stimulate the officials to increase their rhetoric and activity which stimulates the public still further. The spiral is not infinite, however, because the parties in the process—the public, the media, and the politicians—eventually tire of the issue, become more knowledgeable about it, or find other issues to replace it. Crime gave way as public concern turned to inflation, the energy shortage, and corruption in government in 1973 and 1974. The percentage of Gallup respondents who listed crime as the nation's first or second most important problem faded from 22 percent in 1972 to 17 percent in March of 1973 to 13 percent in October of 1973. By February of 1974, crime was almost forgotten: only 3 percent listed it as one of the most important problems. Yet the actual risk of criminal victimization changed very little in this period.

The Political Response

Goldwater's theme of "lawlessness" in the 1964 campaign raised enough public concern so that President Johnson, despite his landslide victory over Goldwater, felt a need to react to it. By executive order, he created the President's Commission on Law Enforcement and Administration of Justice to study the problem and propose solutions. The commission had 19 members, a staff of 63 plus 175 consultants and hundreds of informal advisers. It held three national conferences, sponsored five national surveys, and held hundreds of meetings. It published several volumes of findings and made more than two hundred specific proposals. In general, these proposals followed the conventional liberal stance of the Johnson administration, calling for elimination of the basic social causes of crime and improvement of the criminal justice system. The report was "noncontroversial and clearly within the bounds of the established political and legal order [Quinney, 1970, p. 309]."

The Johnson administration's legislative answer to the problem was the Omnibus Crime Control and Safe Streets Act of 1968. This law was originally designed primarily to assist state and local governments in improving law enforcement and criminal court procedure. But it took some unexpected turns. In the political climate of that year, with a presidential campaign approaching and the memory of the April riots after the assassination of Martin Luther King still fresh, it was very difficult for an elected official to oppose any anticrime measure. And a number of amendments—whose substance we shall examine shortly—were added which went far beyond the original intent. Meanwhile, the 1968 presidential candidates each tried to carve out a position of opposition to crime. Candidate Nixon promised to get "a new attorney general" to "restore order and respect for law." Candidate Humphrey promised to end "rioting, burning, sniping, mugging, traffic in narcotics and disregard for law." Candidate Wallace called for freeing police of restraints, equating the crime problem with the urban riots: "That's right, we're going to have a *police* state for folks who burn the cities down. They aren't going to burn any more cities [Quinney, 1970, p. 313]."

HOW THE ISSUE WAS RESOLVED

Whatever the source of popular fears of crime and the demands for action, the outcome needs to be measured by a specific comparison: who was the most fearful of crime and who was the most vigorous in seeking governmental action? And who benefited the most? If the system follows the stimulus-response model, those who feel most aggrieved by crime should be most helped by anticrime legislation. If it follows some other model, a different set of beneficiaries may emerge. The history of the Omnibus Crime Control and Safe Streets Act of 1968 should be instructive on this question.

The Crime Bill

The conventional liberal view in America has been nicely (though skeptically) summed by Walter Lippman (1973) as "the belief that man is essentially good and can be made perfect by making the environment perfect, and that the environment can be made perfect by taxing the mass of people to spend money for improving it [p. 16]." The Johnson administration's approach to crime, according to Richard Quinney (1970), held that "with the expenditure of enough energy and money . . . crime can be abolished without any significant alteration in American institutions [p. 310]." The administration's crime bill was originally drafted to reflect the recommendations of the President's Crime Commission, published the previous year, which proposed sweeping changes in laws and social priorities to eliminate the *conditions* which contribute to crime. It also called for extensive reorganizations and upgrading of the criminal justice system to make it move more swiftly and effectively (Rice, 1968; Campbell, Sahid, and Stang, 1970).

As introduced in Congress, the administration's bill retained the preventive proposals and included strong gun control measures and a ban on all wiretapping and electronic eavesdropping except in cases of national security. Stressing the need to upgrade the criminal justice system, the bill

Senator Philip Hart: A difficult question, even if the bill is bad. *(United Press International.)*

called for establishment of the Law Enforcement Assistance Administration (LEAA) at the federal level to make grants and provide technical assistance for state and local police in a number of areas. These included programs to improve the recruiting, training, and pay of policemen; modernization of equipment and methods; reorganization of departments; development of advanced rehabilitation techniques and modernized correctional facilities; streamlining court systems; establishing crime prevention programs in higher education; and conducting research in all areas of law enforcement. Compared with previous approaches to the crime problem, it was "generally considered the most enlightened and most promising one ever developed [Harris, 1968]."

When Congress convened on January 15, 1968, the Associated Press said, "overwhelmingly, members reported that anger over riots and crime overshadowed all other domestic issues and, in many cases, even the war in Vietnam [Harris, 1969, p. 67]." The bill began to change. The original $150 million funding request was doubled with most of the increase earmarked for control of riots. Amendments were added to shift the emphasis from crime prevention to the punishment of criminals. Some members used the bill to try to reverse the effect of Supreme Court decisions defining the rights of persons accused of crime. For them, it was an opportunity not only to discredit the libertarian rulings of the Court but to try to undermine public confidence in its civil rights rulings. One amendment, enacted as Title III, gave state and local authorities broad powers to tap telephones and engage in other forms of eavesdropping. Gun control, a key crime-preventive measure recommended by the commission, was virtually ignored. All that was prohibited was the sale of handguns in interstate mail to nondealers and over-the-counter sales of handguns to minors and out-of-state residents.

The revised bill passed easily. The vote in the Senate was 72 to 4. Senator Philip Hart of Michigan, who voted against it, understood the position of those on the other side:

> . . . a . . . difficult question arises when it comes to voting in a way that will make the public feel that their government is against them. Some men in the Senate feel that if it is a real possibility that the people will lose their faith in the government's ability to protect them—in this case, against crime—then the vote must be cast to reassure them that the government is on their side, even if the bill is bad. I don't share that view, but it may be what happened here [Harris, 1969, pp. 99–100].

President Johnson (1971) called the wiretapping provision a "major disappointment." But he signed the bill anyway because he said, "We desperately needed immediate assistance for our local police forces, for our courts, and for our correctional system [p. 335]." Attorney General Ramsey Clark, who had supported the original version, disavowed the final result and warned against its effects.

Those effects were first fully felt during the Nixon administration, which was elected with a promise to restore "law and order." The LEAA administrators named by President Johnson were ignored by the Senate, and Nixon replaced them with nominees supported by the conservative coalition he was trying to maintain between Southern Democrats and Northern Republicans (Harris, 1969). He also accelerated the funding schedule so that the first money spent would go out in April rather than in June. What happened next can best be demonstrated by tracing the flow of the federal government's anticrime money.

Where the Money Went

Total federal expenditures in the war against crime, of which LEAA funds were an important, but by no means the only, part, increased significantly in the Nixon administration. In fiscal 1970, the last year budgeted by the Johnson administration, $856.9 million was spent on the reduction of crime. In the first fiscal year, 1971, over which the Nixon administration had full control, the federal effort increased to $1.4 billion. In 1972, it was $1.8 billion. By fiscal 1975, the amount in the President's budget for anticrime activity had climbed to $3 billion. The programs which gained the most were those directed to rehabilitation of offenders—up 90 percent from 1972 to 1974—and support for crime research and statistics and reform of criminal laws, both of which more than doubled in that period. By 1973, the national government was spending more money to help states and localities improve their correctional programs than it was spending on its own federal correctional institutions and rehabilitation activities. Thus the general anticrime expenditures showed some responsiveness to the targets singled out by the President's Crime Commission in 1967.

But the LEAA money, provided in specific response to the anxieties of 1968, was not so well balanced. The new concept of block grants gave states and localities considerable freedom in deciding how to spend the money,

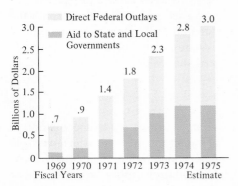

Figure 14-2 Federal Outlays for the Reduction of Crime (*Source: The United States Budget in Brief, Fiscal Year 1975*, U.S. Government Printing Office)

and there was relatively little interest shown in spending it on attacking the sources of crime or even on training police in more sophisticated and effective techniques. There was interest in using the money to stockpile heavy weapons and equipment, such as machine guns, helicopters, and sophisticated communications gear. In the competition among local groups for the federal funds, police tended to be the most influential (Bopp, 1971). This effect was especially pronounced after the 1970 amendments to the act increased the amount of control exercised by local officials. In Denver, Len Ackland (1973) wrote that the city's share of LEAA money "is going to fuel a program which is little more than a funding mechanism for the traditional agencies of the criminal justice system—including the police department, courts and correctional institutions [p. 651]." Some citizens of Denver had thought local control meant that community-based groups would have a voice in the anticrime program. But the police and other agencies had the advantage. The program, said Ackland, "boils down to a highly political game in which non-agency, community-based groups too seldom understand where the power resides and how to get to it [p. 651]."

Reviewing a breakdown of the early LEAA funding shows that upgrading law enforcement and prevention of crime were given much lower priority than detection and apprehension of lawbreakers. Without question, police agencies were among the main beneficiaries of the early grants. Their professional image has been enhanced in the eyes of the public, their personal salaries have been increased, the quality of their equipment and the scope of their programs have been improved. And the federal outlays have stimulated increased local effort. Municipal expenditures for police pay increased from $11.02 per citizen in 1965 to $36.43 in 1971 (Bureau of the Census, 1966, 1972). The size of police departments also increased. In 1966, there was an average of two police employees for each 1,000 citizens in American cities. Five years later, there were 2.4 police employees per thousand citizens (FBI, 1966). Because of the population increase, that per capita gain indicates an absolute increase in police of more than 23 percent. So the money to fight crime went in large measure to the existing law enforcement agencies. That this money would have a marked impact on abatement of crime was argued strongly by local police and LEAA officials, but data existing at the time might have raised serious questions about the relationship between police expenditures and the frequency of criminal behavior. The figures show that both crime and police expenditures have risen rather consistently in the decade of the 1960s.

How Did Crime Change?

Tracing the effects of the increased expenditures for crime fighting is difficult because of the unreliability of the crime statistics which we have already noted. If the money does make police more efficient, we might expect to find them probing deeper into the previously unreported "dark

Scene in a New Jersey Reformatory: The money went to the traditional agencies. *(Werner Wolff, Black Star.)*

figure" of crime and bringing more offenses to light—in which case the FBI index should show an increase. On the other hand, increased police efficiency might deter crime, in which case the number of reported crimes might fall. It is also worth considering what the record keepers, the police, have to gain or lose by changes in the rate. Political leaders and the public tend to take the FBI reports at face value, and it might be difficult to sell them the notion that an increase in reported crime is a sign of successful anticrime effort. On the other hand, a decrease in the crime rate might be a handicap in arguing for still more financial support for the crime-fighting agencies. The numbers could be interpreted to show that they are doing fine with the amount of money they already have. Clearly, the best outcome for maintaining the political advantage of the crime-fighting agencies would be an ambiguous one, that is, one subject to a great variety of interpretations.

Ambiguity was indeed the outcome. In the four years after passage of the 1968 act, crime continued to increase, but at a steadily *decreasing* rate of increase. The FBI index of serious crime (murder, forcible rape, robbery, aggravated assault, burglary, larceny of $50 and over, and auto theft) had shown a 17 percent increase in the starting year of 1968. In 1969, the increase was only 12 percent, and in 1970, it was down to 11 percent. In 1971, it increased by only 7 percent.

These figures refer to the crime *rate*, which is the number of crimes per unit of population. The decreasing rate of increase in the rate between 1968 and 1971 provided a nice picture for the law enforcement interests. The fact that the crime rate was increasing showed that they needed still more money. The fact that it was increasing at a slower rate shows that the money they had been given had been used effectively.

In addition to the basic problem that the ratio of reported crime to all crime may not be constant, another warning is in order. Reforms tend to be initiated when the evil to be overcome is unusually high. If it fluctuates over time, as the crime rate does, and if the attention of investigators and reformers is focused on it when the cycle is at an upward swing, then chance alone is likely to bring it down—no matter what the effect of the reform. Social scientists call this phenomenon "regression toward the mean [Campbell, 1969]." To put it in a somewhat simpler fashion, it would have been physically impossible for the crime rate to increase at an *increasing rate of increase* for very long after 1968. Even if that year's 17 percent increase remained constant, crime would double every four and a half years. For society to maintain such a furiously criminal pace, we would soon all have to become full-time criminals. The more likely trend, of course, is in the other direction.

Other statistical indicators can be checked for signs that the LEAA grants were effective in combating crime. If crime is increasing in the face of greater police efficiency, then that gain in efficiency should at least be reflected in a higher proportion of crimes solved. But the FBI records show that the rate at which reported crimes are "cleared" from police records by arrest has declined since LEAA went to work. (See Figure 14-3.)

Another way to test for evidence that the crime money makes a difference is to look for the different patterns of victimization that might develop as criminals seek new channels for illegal activity to replace those barred by the more efficient police work. Eventually, the victimization surveys conducted by the Bureau of the Census may give good information on these patterns. Meanwhile, it is necessary to rely on data from police sources, and they show no changing patterns. Rape, robbery, and burglary are still concentrated among low-income victims and decrease steadily as income goes up. Victimization for larceny is still most frequent in high-

Figure 14-3 Crime and Crimes Cleared (*Source: Uniform Crime Reports for the United States, 1973,* Washington, 1974)

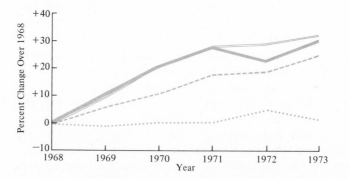

income groups. Age, race, and sex patterns are also unchanged. In one area, however, there has been a shift. An upward movement in the rate of crime in suburban and rural areas has, for some of the major categories, outrun the gains in the cities. The cause of this shift is unknown. One speculation is that greater police effort made possible by LEAA in the cities drove burglars and thieves out to the suburbs and countryside. The growth of a youth population in the suburbs; the greater wealth and accessibility of things to steal; or, conversely, the beginning of urban decay in the fringes and the older suburbs may also be causes of increasing suburban crime.

One thing does seem clear in this otherwise murky picture: the citizenry has not benefited in important respects from federal policy of the first four years of the war on crime. This failure may indicate the magnitude of the problem rather than reflect the competence of police or the intent of the political elites who formed the policy, but it also suggests something else. The policy was made in contradiction to professional advice that might have channeled it in more productive directions, and blatantly political use was made of it. A different policy might not have satisfied the popular demands about crime as they then existed. But we must remember to consider the possibility that these demands were the result of public officials sending out messages that they wanted returned to them. The messages the officials wanted to hear, if the created-stimulus model is accurate, were those which would legitimate the kind of anticrime policies they wanted to adopt, and these policies were inconsistent with serious attacks on the causes of criminal behavior.

Such an outcome suggests that there is a systematic bias in the political system against addressing the causes of civic problems when to do so would threaten the existing distribution of power and benefits or threaten the ideological basis for that distribution.

The National Commission on the Causes and Prevention of Violence warned that the solution lay in treating the criminal justice system—police, courts, and corrections—as a system rather than as a set of separate activities. But, LEAA became, in the words of James F. Ahern (1970), a former police chief, "a viaduct for the dissipation of federal funds into local political boondoggles. Its effect has been not to help local police departments but to create fifty separate state bureaucracies which channel money into local police departments that have proven through the years to be unworkable [p. 233]." Even if the money were helpful in catching criminals, that would not reduce crime so long as the rest of the system recycles the criminals to the streets.

Who Benefited?

The incidence of civil disorders has declined, possibly in response to a heavier police presence in the black, innercity neighborhoods. This is a mixed blessing. In a 1968 survey of fifteen cities, Angus Campbell and

Howard Schuman (1968) found that blacks are nearly twice as likely as whites to complain that police do not come quickly enough when they are called for help. On the other hand, blacks are more than three times as likely as whites to say that police are unnecessarily rough and abusive in making arrests. So, for some blacks, increased police presence might be viewed as repression rather than assistance (Baldwin, 1966).

Members of the law enforcement establishment have benefited by having increased income, manpower, weaponry, and prestige. So have the administrators whose job is drawing up grant applications. Businessmen who make and sell crime control hardware have benefited. The universities which received money for police-training programs (labeled "shallow and unimaginative" by Ahern) were certainly beneficiaries. Of course, so were the politicians who found crime a beneficial and risk-free issue with which to build their reputations and followings.

More broadly, established powers benefited by having their positions of power strengthened against potential challenges. The "crime crisis" was used to fashion tools of repression. When President Nixon told graduates of an FBI training academy for local policemen that "the era of permissiveness in law enforcement is over," he was signaling an official disregard for civil liberties. Some of this disregard came formally, through legislation to facilitate imprisonment without bail, forcible entry to gain evidence, and expanded wiretapping, but most of it came through a peculiarly perverted permissiveness toward the commission of crimes by the government against groups and individuals considered its enemies. The revelations during the Watergate investigation demonstrated how flexible the social definition of crime can be. The burglars who worked for the White House thought *they* were the law enforcers, and in the narrow social *milieu* of their operations they were, in a sense, right. But in the larger society, they and the men who sent them were criminals. How far this attitude trickled down to local police actions against citizens considered to be hippies, radicals, Communists, Black Panthers, or other persons they considered undesirable in local surroundings can only be conjectured. "In many ways," says Quinney, "the war on crime has become a substitute for the older war on internal communism. Crime today is similarly being billed as 'a threat to the American way of life.'" It is used to justify the unjustifiable.

The irony is that nonelites, whose exposure to many of the crime categories in the FBI index is the greatest, have been made less safe by recent anticrime policy. Resources which should have gone to crime prevention have been spent on expensive but ineffective showcase projects. The nonelites are in more danger both from police and from criminals than a more enlightened policy might have allowed.

The case of the law-and-order issue is therefore at least of anecdotal significance in support of the created-stimulus model. Elites and masses responded to one another, but the principal initiative came from the elites, and they were the chief beneficiaries of the outcome. The model, as we stated at the outset, does not fit all issues. But it fits enough questions of public controversy to lead the wary citizen to look twice at each new "crisis" and ask who raised the questions and who is likely to benefit from the answers.

SUGGESTED READINGS

Jacob, Herbert. *Urban Justice: Law and Order in American Cities.* Englewood Cliffs, N.J.: Prentice-Hall, 1973. An exploration into the complexities of the criminal justice system in urban America.

National Commission on the Causes and Prevention of Violence. *Law and Order Reconsidered.* Washington: Government Printing Office, 1970. A comprehensive review of the place of social order and the rule of law in America with particular attention to the institutions and agencies responsible for law enforcement.

Rubinstein, Jonathan. *City Police.* New York: Farrar, Straus & Giroux, 1973. This highly readable book focuses on the everyday work environment of policemen, the problems they confront, and the means they use in order to cope.

Schur, Edwin M. *Crimes Without Victims.* Englewood Cliffs, N.J.: Prentice-Hall, 1965. This book evaluates one type of crime where consenting individuals willingly engage in an activity prohibited by law. The author shows the unrealistic nature of many laws dealing with "deviant behavior."

Skolnick, Jerome H. *Justice Without Trial.* New York: Wiley, 1967. An intensive study of municipal police behavior, values, and organization as they relate to the larger criminal justice system.

Chapter 15

Poverty and Race:
Issues in Search of a Solution

If a free society cannot help the many who are poor, it cannot save the few who are rich.

—John F. Kennedy, 1961

We didn't spend time on the disadvantaged for the simple reason that there were no votes there.

—Jeb Stuart Magruder, 1973

GOVERNMENT AND THE POOR

The Visibility Problem

John F. Kennedy had rested in the sun at Montego Bay before arriving in West Virginia for the presidential primary campaign of 1960. His shock at the poverty he saw throughout the state, wrote Theodore White (1961), "was so fresh that it communicated itself with the emotion of original discovery."

> . . . he could scarcely bring himself to believe that human beings were forced to eat and live on these cans of dry relief rations, which he fingered like

artifacts of another civilization. "Imagine," he said to one of his assistants one night, "just imagine kids who never drink milk." Of all the emotional experiences of his pre-convention campaign, Kennedy's exposure to the misery of the mining fields probably changed him most as a man . . . [p. 127].

Why should Kennedy, whose party had been dominant for nearly three decades as the champion of the downtrodden, be surprised at the sight of poverty? The answer lies in the history of the social welfare issue as it evolved in the New Deal during the Great Depression of the 1930s.

A Dual Welfare Policy

The victims of the Depression were the working and middle classes whose savings and jobs had been adversely affected by the collapse of the financial system. The social programs that grew out of the New Deal were directed at maintaining job and financial security for these classes. Social Security, railroad retirement, workmen's compensation, unemployment benefits, veteran's disability compensation, and the insuring of bank accounts all had this goal in common plus one thing more: Their benefits were granted routinely, predictably, and as a matter of "right" to the eligible recipient. Such programs may be thought of as "social insurance" as opposed to "public assistance" which is the other side of the dual system. Public assistance programs, aimed at the underclass poor, are granted only to those who are willing and able to demonstrate economic need. They are not nationally centralized. Rather, they consist of a patchwork of state and local programs, operating with some federal funds, directed at different kinds of specific needy cases. The largest is Aid to Families with Dependent Children (AFDC). Two kinds of subtle but mostly unspoken judgments underlay this dual design. One class was composed of people who worked and therefore deserved to be aided. The other did not work and was therefore undeserving. Moreover, given the social disruption of the Depression, the importance of returning people to productive labor was so great and so obvious that the other problem was seen as relatively unimportant. It was necessary to stabilize the position of the productive people to keep the society functioning at all. In the pursuit of that concern, the plight of the underclass was easy to overlook. The nation came out of the Depression with a set of programs to maintain the incomes of workers and middle-class people, and the economic and industrial boom during World War II and afterward seemed to ensure a decent job and income for all. This goal was legitimated by the Employment Act of 1946, which created the Council of Economic Advisors to study and propose ways to keep the economy running at high levels of productivity and income. The problem of large-scale poverty was simply not on the agenda, and opinion leaders were inattentive. As recently as 1958, the innovative economists, such as John Kenneth Galbraith, were more interested in the problems of affluence—although Galbraith did note in *The Affluent Society* (1958) that pockets of "insular poverty" still existed. Michael Harrington published *The Other America* in 1962 and drew the attention of social workers and sociologists. The issue began to build, and by 1963 opinion leaders had begun to pay attention. A *New Yorker* article by Dwight MacDonald (1963) called attention to "Our Invisible Poor," and in 1964 the Social Security Administration helped make the problem visible by quantifying it. An official definition of poverty was established (for a nonfarm family of four persons in 1960, it was $3,022; in 1973, it was $4,550). The Social Security Administration calculated that nearly one out of every five persons in the United States was below the poverty line in 1964.

Poverty and Politics

The poor finally got their problems placed on the national agenda when the traditional coalition of support for the Democratic party began to come apart. The Southern and Northern wings of the party, bound together by pre-Civil War issues that had long ceased to be relevant, began to split on both the race issue and economic questions. The contradictions in the coalition of conservative Southern and liberal Northern Democrats were confirmed in the 1960 election. The newly arrived blacks in Northern cities were aggressive. They made claims on the policy positions of the Democratic party, and they used their increasingly important voting power to enforce these claims. The shifting voting patterns were reinforced by the civil rights movement. In the no longer solid South, the hold of the Democratic party began to weaken, and the party turned increasingly for support to voters in the large Northern cities, where blacks were still moving and establishing their voting power. John F. Kennedy was aware of these developments, and he appealed to the black vote, losing much of the South but winning the crucial cities (White, 1961).

Yet, during his first two years of office, Kennedy found little to do on the civil rights question. He signed an executive order to bar discrimination in federally subsidized housing, but he did little to carry it out. He needed a way to attract big city votes and solidify the urban minority without the direct involvement in civil rights that would further alienate the Democrats of the South. The War on Poverty was the ideal vehicle, and in October of 1963 he decided that it would be a central feature of the next year's legislative program to prepare for the presidential election of 1964. The strategy was outlined in a working paper, prepared at Kennedy's direction by the Council of Economic Advisors, called "Program for a Concerned Assault on Poverty." Its conceptual foundations had been laid in two earlier demonstration programs: the Ford Foundation Grey Areas Projects and a federal program called Mobilization for Youth (MFY). The Ford project established pilot programs in four large cities, Boston, New Haven, Oakland, and Philadelphia, to provide services to slum populations. Aimed at black and Puerto Rican youth in New York City, MFY tried to provide opportunities that would steer them away from delinquent behavior. Leaders of both programs considered the existing professional groups and agencies that rendered service to the poor as inadequate and self-serving and sought bold departures from past structures and assumptions. Their thinking played an important role in the shaping of the new government program.

Of all the programs that President Johnson inherited from his assassinated predecessor, the war on poverty received his highest priority. In his 1964 State of the Union message, Johnson declared his unequivocal "war on poverty." By August, the Economic Opportunity Act had been signed into law.

The Limited Effort

In important respects, the influence of New Deal liberalism still had an important hold on the conduct of the war on poverty. J. David Greenstone and Paul E. Peterson (1973) have identified two philosophical approaches in the antipoverty program which conform to traditional liberalism and one which diverges from that tradition. One approach sought to ensure stable employment, a goal of the New Deal, but to attack the employment problems of the poor by trying to eliminate their educational deficiencies and wipe away the social barriers that kept them from job opportunities through such programs as the Job Corps, the Neighborhood Youth Corps,

State of the Union Message, 1964: Launching the war on poverty. *(United Press International.)*

and Head Start. A second traditional approach utilized the existing government agencies but tried to coordinate them and improve the access of the poor to their services through neighborhood service centers of the Community Action Agencies. In both of these traditional approaches, the attack was directed at *economic* poverty. What other kind of poverty is there? In a sense, there is more to being poor than simply being without money. A poor person is also without power, and so he or she suffers from *political* poverty. One may, of course, be the cause of the other, and the third and nontraditional approach made a direct attack on the political side. By calling for the "maximum feasible participation" among the poor in local antipoverty programs, the new law went beyond New Deal liberalism to legitimize a direct attack by the powerless poor on the ruling big city coalitions. The threat to these existing coalitions was made real by provisions to bypass state and local governments in the funding for many of the programs and forge a direct link between the federal government and the urban poor.

Evaluating the Outcome

Money spent on the war on poverty was widely scattered on programs that were put together in an effort at compromise which resulted in the adoption of "not a choice among policies so much as a collection of them [Moynihan, p. xv]." Funding never exceeded $2 billion a year. The space program got nearly six times as much money, the war in Vietnam ten times as much. "The war on poverty," said Michael Harrington (1969), "was never more than a skirmish . . . [p. 35]." In a moral sense, things had become worse because the nonpoor majority could no longer claim ignorance of poverty. Despite the attention paid to the problem, Harrington said in 1969, "tens of millions of Americans still live in a social underworld and an even larger number are only one recession, one illness, one accident removed from it [p. 35]."

The number of persons living in poverty was reduced during the Johnson administration but began to climb again in the Nixon years. This change was not traceable to the poverty policies of the two presidents so much as to the general economic climate. Johnson presided over a business upturn, Nixon over a frustrating period of inflation and recession. The political power of the poor was likewise not visibly enhanced in the long run. The program did have its political beneficiaries, but they tended to be interests that had held political power in the first place. In the midst of the Vietnam war, President Johnson assured the nation that his Great Society programs would continue; it was possible to have "guns and butter" at the same time. Ironically, he turned out to be right. Although the war drained funds from the poverty programs, it fueled an expanded economy and created more jobs. The war thus raised "the income of millions of families who would otherwise have fallen below the poverty line [Friedlander and Apte, p. 301]." The poverty program began in 1965 with an appropriation

Table 15-1   The Shrinking Poverty Population

YEAR	NUMBER OF POOR PEOPLE (millions)	PERCENT OF TOTAL POPULATION
1959	39.5	22.4
1960	39.9	22.2
1961	39.6	21.9
1962	38.6	21.0
1963	36.4	19.5
1964	36.1	19.0
1965	33.2	17.3
1966	28.5	14.7
1967	27.8	14.2
1968	25.4	12.8
1969	24.1	12.1
1970	25.4	12.6
1971	25.6	12.5
1972	24.5	11.9
1973	23.0	11.1

Source: Bureau of the Census, Current Population Surveys.
Note: Much of the decrease from 1965 to 1966 reflects an improved method of processing income data. Number of poor people calculated by the old method for 1966 would have been 30.4 million.

of $800 million, reaching its peak of $2 billion in 1970. But William C. Mitchell (1971) has estimated that to match the welfare efforts of most European countries, the United States would have had to spend about three times as much. Even when Social Security, VA pensions, and food programs administered by the Department of Agriculture were added to the war on poverty, the total, he estimated, came to less than 5 percent of the national income. James Tobin (1968) estimated that to raise the poor to the standard of living represented by the Department of Agriculture's "emergency food plan" would have required at least $11 billion in direct payments. A more ambitious program, not only to raise the poor above the poverty level but to give them an incentive to remain in the labor force, would have cost, according to Sar Levitan (1969), between $20 billion and $25 billion.

The largest program was Head Start, a preschool-training project designed to help poor children overcome their social and cultural deficiencies and start public school on a more equal footing with their nonpoor classmates. In 1969, its full-year programs reached less than 16 percent of the group for which it was targeted. According to Levitan's estimate, the government would have had to spend more than the total OEO budget in its first four years just to reach all of the eligible children in one year. Obviously, the war against poverty was lost due to insufficient funding. That defeat was closely linked to the other side of that war, the war against political poverty.

The Participation Problem

Poverty, as we have seen, is more than a lack of money. It is also a lack of options, an absence of control over one's chances in life. The failure to gain funding for the war on poverty reflected the political reality of the poor and their lack of power. This danger had been recognized at the outset, and commitment to "maximum feasible participation" in the 1964 law implied that the goal was for the poor to gain both power and money. The poor in America tend to vote less, to be unorganized, and to lack representation in the places where decisions are made. The desire to correct this lack may have seemed at the time to be a harmless reassertion of grass-roots democracy. But when the Office of Economic Opportunity took the first steps to carry it out, a clash of interests was revealed. Public officials in local communities, many of them there because they had risen to power by helping to establish workers' rights in the 1930s, correctly saw this provision as a threat to their usual power base. In many places, the issue was complicated by racial antagonism with the black poor challenging white officialdom for a share in local decision making. Greenstone and Peterson (1973) assessed what happened:

> In most places OEO had to settle for little more than formal representation of the poor on local boards and agencies. In the decentralized American political system, the impact of federal policy can be blunted by established local elites, political, economic, and bureaucratic, unless the latter are themselves committed to its program. OEO's own grass roots rhetoric of community action only provided these elites with a federal mandate for shaping the program to their own needs . . . [p. 5].

In some cases, the balance of power did shift in a direction favorable to the poor, but for the most part local officials were successful in keeping

A Harlem Family in 1970: Besides a lack of money, a lack of options. *(United Press International.)*

control of the purse strings and using that economic power to maintain the existing patterns of voter allegiance. The hope of waging an effective battle against political poverty was lost when Congress amended the Economic Opportunity Act to specify that members of local Community Action Agencies would be chosen by local election. Although fair and democratic on its face, this plan usually meant that the selection of board members was bound to existing patterns of power distribution. In 1967, Congress amended the law again to provide that the requirement of maximum feasible participation could be met by a board that had one-third of its membership from poor neighbors and the remainder from local officials and community leaders. Local agencies became instruments of state and local government, preserving the influence of those already in power over those who were not. The final dismantling of the effort came in the Nixon administration when funding was reduced and major poverty programs were transferred out of OEO and placed in established federal agencies whose clientele was not limited to low-income groups.

Why did the antipoverty efforts of the 1960s fail? Frances Fox Piven and Richard A. Cloward (1971) have a pessimistic hypothesis. They argue that welfare policies in capitalist societies are intended to reinforce the work ethic and penalize those who cannot work except in times of political unrest. In times of instability, such as the depression-haunted 1930s and the riot-stricken 1960s, welfare policies are made more liberal to pacify the unruly masses. The implication of that thesis is that the antipoverty efforts stopped because the rioting had stopped, but that may not be the entire explanation. A more basic problem is that no political system can cope very well with an issue that is not clearly defined. This lack of definition makes the poor relatively invisible to society in general as well as to one another. They can form no cohesive pressure group, no clear bloc of votes at which politicians can aim except when special circumstances create an incentive for others to see them and recognize their needs. Kennedy's search for the city vote in the early 1960s was such a special case. So were the urban riots of the mid 1960s. There will be other government efforts against poverty, but they will take different forms as the dimensions of the problem are reevaluated.

TOWARD A DEFINITION OF POVERTY

The Numbers Game

If, as Angus Campbell has said, nothing makes a problem come alive like a quantitative definition, the poor owe a good deal to Mollie Orshansky and her colleagues at the Social Security Administration who produced the first generally accepted dollar definition of poverty. Tracking the number of poor by this definition from year to year can show the trend, but it fails to demonstrate the real magnitude of the problem. If the official definition were a literal description, wiping out poverty would be a straightforward task. The Bureau of the Census (1973) calculated that it would have taken only $12 billion in 1972 to bring each poor family up to the official poverty line. Such an effort would be relatively modest; the sum is no greater than that expended to assist war veterans who get their payments as a matter of right.

But such direct payments could be made, and we would still have a poverty problem. The official definition is based on the amount of money a well-managed and fully informed family needs to maintain a minimum standard of nutrition. It does not reflect the costs to the poor that are solely the result of their isolation and lack of skills and information. It ignores regional differences. It fails to take into account the extraordinary expenses the poor may have for health needs as the result of past deprivation. Most important of all, it does not reach the problem of the relative nature of poverty.

This problem is very difficult to face. Given an unequal distribution of incomes, we shall always have people who are relatively poor. Herman Miller (1971) has noted that even Tunica County, Mississippi, the poorest county in the poorest state in 1960, has a surprising number of automobiles, television sets, and washing machines—enough wealth in short to make Tunica County seem wealthy in other contexts such as the America of an earlier century or other parts of the world today. But these are residents of the United States in the twentieth century, and so they are poor.

The trouble with taking the relativity of poverty into account is that it tends to make the problem permanent. If we define poverty as being in the bottom five percent of economic resources, then we must face the fact that there will always be a bottom 5 percent. The problem then might be reduced to one of finding ways to make people happy at being there— perhaps along the lines of Aldous Huxley's *Brave New World*. Few current students of the problem find anything to gain by such a definition, although some come close. Bruno Stein (1971) has suggested that the poverty line be set at half the median income. This definition has several advantages. It is self-compensating for both inflation and improved standards of well-being. And it is not entirely a relative definition. If the way income is distributed were to change—if we were to take from the rich and give to the poor—then the number who had less than half the median income would decrease.

Visibility

The printing of comparative statistics of infant mortality is often followed by a reduction of the death rate of babies. Municipal officials and voters did not have, before publication, a place in their picture of the environment for those babies. The statistics made them visible, as visible as if the babies had elected an alderman to air their grievances.

—Walter Lippman in *Public Opinion*, Free Press, New York, 1922, 1965.

Given, however, a situation in which the pattern of income distribution is fairly constant—and that has been the case since World War II—then the Stein definition shows no progress being made at all. For the past generation, the proportion of the population with less than half the median income has remained very close to 20 percent. Income distribution has changed hardly at all in that period (see Table 13-2).

Slicing the Pie

The question to be faced, then, is this: Is it enough for the pie to get bigger so that everyone gets a larger piece while maintaining the same proportionate share? Or should the proportionate shares be changed as well? Making the same splits in a bigger pie is politically easy. The political costs of changing the proportions is always quite high. The history of the issue indicates that established leaders would want to pay those costs in only the rarest of circumstances.

Yet another way to look at the problem of defining the poor is based on a procedure that the Bureau of Labor Statistics uses for tracking changes in the cost of living. The statisticians at the Bureau change the market basket on which the index is based from time to time to reflect the changes in living standards. The index reflects such things as the fact that the price difference between a new car purchased in 1975 and the same make purchased in 1935 is not entirely a result of inflation. The 1975 model has comfort, speed, safety, and pollution-abatement features that could not have been bought at any price in 1935. Conversely (disregarding antique value), a buyer would not be as satisfied with a brand new 1935 model car in 1975 as he would have been in the year of its issue. In addition to the Consumer Price Index, the Bureau maintains and updates three hypothetical but quite specific family budgets for low-, intermediate-, and higher-income families. These budgets include food, housing, transportation, clothing, personal care, medical care, taxes, and other items at three different standards of living. These items, priced separately in thirty-nine metropolitan areas and four nonmetropolitan regions so that geographical comparisons can be made, are for a rather precisely defined family of four. Given that kind of statistical sophistication, it ought to be possible to develop a market-basket approach to a poverty definition, with the contents of the market basket upgraded from time to time to reflect changing standards. Edward S. Greenberg (1973) has suggested that the Bureau's middle budget be adopted as the poverty definition. The effect on what would be considered poverty under such a definition is impossible to evaluate exactly because it has been worked out only for the specific four-person family. But in the fall of 1972, that particular market basket would have cost $11,446. Since that is slightly above the median family income for 1972, such a definition would put a majority of Americans in officially defined poverty—and perhaps that majority would agree with the definition. Whether one is poor or affluent may be largely a matter of aspiration.

The Road Ahead

Those who have moved out of the official poverty population have not moved far. The Bureau of the Census keeps track of those who live on the margin between 100 and 125 percent of the poverty income and who could therefore easily fall back into the poverty category. In 1972, about 10 million people were in that category—enough to set antipoverty efforts back by a decade if they should slip below the line. A reversal of the economic improvement of the 1960s could have that effect. Stein (1971) has suggested that existing economic and welfare policies tend to create a permanent underclass that moves in and out of poverty with fluctuations in economic activity and technological developments.

This situation is not likely to change until a redistribution of income gives those at the bottom a larger slice of the pie. We see no trend in that direction. A reverse trend, in fact, began to appear after 1969. The proportion of the population in the $7,000 to $15,000 income bracket began to decline, while the proportion with incomes below $7,000 or above $15,000 increased. If such a trend were sustained over a long period of time, the problem of relative poverty could greatly increase.

Indeed, the economic pressures of the 1970s served to demonstrate just how tenuous the heralded gains of the poor in the previous decade had been. With inflation (especially in food) and the dollar crisis abroad, the nation faced something novel for this generation, a scramble for shares of a *smaller* pie. The interests of the poor and the rich are always in conflict, but the conflict can be masked and ameliorated when everyone's share is increasing in good times. In hard times, the conflict is abrasive. If pressure for economy in government causes welfare expenditures to be cut, there is little the poor can do about it. Monetary and fiscal policies that will stem inflation do so at the cost of raising unemployment. When unemployment goes up, the poor and the near poor are the first to be laid off.

Disillusionment over the innovative efforts begun with the Economic Opportunity Act of 1964 may not be totally justified by the performance. That performance was damaged primarily by weak financial commitment and poor administration and secondarily by weaknesses in the scope, philosophy, and method of the programs themselves. Nevertheless, the antipoverty programs of the future may be heavily influenced by the lack of better results from the programmatic approach. The next round of reforms, when and if it comes, may find some more direct method of helping the poor, such as a children's allowance, a negative income tax, or a guaranteed annual income. Such a direct payment could counter the regressive nature of most of our tax systems and reach those substantial segments of the poor which are untouched by the traditional public assistance programs.

Such measures have the virtue of simplicity, but they might still leave the root causes of poverty untouched. If the poor remained dependent on the government for their life needs, their ability to compete for political power might be worsened. The political and economic forces that caused or allowed their poverty would remain undisturbed. Such programs would work in the sense of reducing the number of persons with incomes below the poverty line, however defined, but there would be no political incentive for the nonpoor to maintain such a program in times of economic difficulty. The psychology of poverty, which grows out of dependency, might be left intact. Liberals generally approve of income-maintenance proposals for humanitarian reasons, and conservatives sometimes like them as well because they would mollify the powerless without changing existing institutions. The long-term effects are not so easy to predict.

THE ECONOMIC STATUS OF BLACKS

The Fruits of Access

Most poor people are not black. Most blacks are not poor. Nevertheless, the problems of racism and poverty are closely interlocked, and the efforts of blacks to improve their status represent a special case of the problem of defining an issue and making it visible. Black Americans constitute a visible interest group which has, after many years of arduous effort, gained access to government for the redress of historic grievances. Legislative, judicial, and executive action on behalf of blacks has been the result of some of the most dramatic and unconventional inputs in the nation's political history. One such action was the Civil Rights Act of 1964, which Thomas Dye and Harmon Ziegler (1970) have ranked with "the Emancipation Proclamation, the Fourteenth Amendment, and *Brown v. Board of Education of Topeka* as one of the most important steps toward full equality for the Negro in America [p. 300]." While its long-term importance remains to be seen, the act led to progress in several areas: voting and political participation, public accommodations, education, housing, employment, and, indirectly, general socioeconomic status. The implicit assumption was that legal equality would lead to equality in other areas, so that blacks, like other minority groups before them, could share in the benefits of American affluence. To some extent, the hope was borne out, and to some extent it was not. The case demonstrates both some possibilities and some limitations of traditional government power.

Political Participation.   The voting rights section was the key. If blacks could make the political system respond in proportion to their numbers, other problems would be solved more easily, it was believed. In fact, voter registration of blacks, and especially registration in the South, increased sharply by 1966. The act, as augmented in 1965, gave the federal government strong coercive powers to use against state and local governments, and they were applied. But estimates of the immediate power of the ballot box proved to have been exaggerated. Harrell R. Rodgers, Jr., and Charles S. Bullock III (1972), reviewed black progress since 1964 and concluded that increased black voting made a difference in the outcome of close elections in many localities and brought about changes in the provision of services for many black communities, but it did not contribute to the achievement of integration. The number of black officeholders increased sharply, but black registration peaked in 1968 after failing to match the proportion of white registration. And the 2,556 blacks who held public office in 1974 were still only a fraction of the number which would have been elected if blacks were proportionately represented. Even though there can be no questioning the increase in black political consciousness and power in recent years, its material effects have been limited.

Public Accommodations.   Because lunch counters were the sites for much of the unconventional political activity of blacks in the late 1950s and early 1960s, the equal access of blacks to public accommodations was given heavy symbolic importance. The 1964 Civil Rights Act's mandate and its aggressive enforcement largely removed racial barriers in public places, but the benefit may be of marginal value. For lower-income blacks, the problem

Mississippi Blacks Registering to Vote, 1966: The power of the ballot box was exaggerated. *(United Press International.)*

of getting the money to spend at the lunch counter continues to be more pressing.

Education.   Just as access to the ballot box was to bring blacks political equality, so equal access to education was expected to bring them economic equality. As indicated in Chapter 2, the problem has since been perceived as more complicated and the efficacy of education itself has been called into serious question. Meanwhile, segregation in schools persists, chiefly as the result of segregated housing patterns. Thomas F. Pettigrew (1971) has noted that in 1965, more than 75 percent of all whites attended schools that were predominately (more than 90 percent) white while 65 percent of all blacks attended schools that were predominantly black. Rodgers and Bullock believe that the failure to integrate is even greater than the statistics indicate. "In many of the schools that have been integrated in the South," they report, "the most invidious kinds of racial discrimination persist. In these schools, the potential for alienation and confrontation seems to be rising [p. 69]." Resistance to busing to overcome segregation caused by housing patterns has further slowed the progress of integration.

Housing.   Behind the school segregation problem is, of course, a housing segregation problem, especially in the North. The Civil Rights Act of 1964 outlawed discrimination in public housing and urban renewal projects, and the Open Housing Act of 1968 covered private sale or rental of housing, but the success of these efforts has been meager. The social forces in this area are persistent and difficult to handle. A few neighborhoods have succeeded in achieving a stable pattern of integration, but they are rare. Enforcement of the fair-housing rules has not had the sustained and widespread citizen support that is needed for it to be effective. Said Rodgers and Bullock (1972):

> The crucial players in the housing industry continue to evade the law at will. Whites remain unconvinced that integrated living is a permanent phenomenon and flee contact with blacks, moving further from the urban hub. . . . So far there has been no follow-up to the Open Housing Act of 1968. Experience leads us to conclude that early edicts may be largely symbolic, and that in the absence of renewed initiative few changes will be forthcoming [p. 157].

Pettigrew argues that segregation in housing actually increased in the 1960s despite a decline outside the South in the 1950s. Survey research suggests that interracial sociability within integrated housing has diminished as well so that the effect of what integration there is has been minimal. Home ownership by blacks has increased—from 38 percent in 1960 to 42 percent in 1970—but Pettigrew says this is largely a function of the increase in the supply of owner-occupied housing available to blacks as the result of the white flight to the suburbs. Census data show that the quality of black housing has improved, but that housing occupied by blacks is still more likely to be substandard than that occupied by whites (Bureau of the Census, 1972).

Employment and Income.   More directly tied to income than any other factor, employment is the most basic problem area attacked by the Civil Rights Act of 1964. It is also an area where there has been visible improvement, with women and young men making most of the gains. In 1959, the median income of black workers was between 57 and 58 percent of white workers. By the 1970s, black women, who are less likely to interrupt careers for child care, had earnings as high as or higher than comparable white women; young black male college graduates earned as much as their white classmates. For all young men, the ratio of black to white income had reached 85 percent, an important gain but still well short of equality. Moreover, the black gains are at least in large part attributable to general economic improvement of the 1960s. The economic downturn in the early 1970s jeopardized these gains. Unemployment rates for blacks in the early 1970s were about twice as high as those for whites, and rising.

Poverty among Blacks.   The poverty population continues to have an overrepresentation of blacks. In a relative sense, the disparity is getting worse. In 1959, the risk of being poor was three times as great for blacks as for whites; in 1972, it was three and a half times as great. Nine percent of whites and 32 percent of blacks were below the official poverty line in 1972.

Table 15-2   Median Family Income by Race of Head
(In 1973 dollars)

YEAR	WHITE	NEGRO AND OTHER RACES	RATIO (Negro and other races to white)
1947	6,285	3,212	.51
1950	6,405	3,449	.54
1955	7,673	4,236	.55
1960	8,758	4,848	.55
1963	9,502	5,033	.53
1964	9,827	5,510	.56
1965	10,210	5,677	.56
1966	10,670	6,394	.60
1967	10,960	6,777	.62
1968	11,425	7,145	.63
1969	11,869	7,513	.63
1970	11,671	7,454	.64
1971	11,628	7,361	.63
1972	12,273	7,534	.61
1973	12,595	7,596	.60

Source: Bureau of the Census.

This shift was caused by an absolute gain in the number of poor blacks while the number of poor whites was decreasing, and it reflects the middle-class bias in response to worsening economic conditions. Social Security payments increased and welfare payments decreased. More whites depend on the former, more blacks on the latter.

The situation of urban blacks is somewhat better than that of rural blacks. In 1972, 41 percent of black families outside the major metropolitan areas were poor, compared with 25.7 percent of those inside. The difference illustrates a cause of the seemingly conflicting statistical supports for arguments over the status of blacks in the 1970s. Blacks were doing well or doing poorly, depending on where one looked. If one looked at the young, urban, and Northern, the picture was bright. If one looked at older, rural blacks, the picture was grimmer. The *Washington Post* (1973) noted this phenomenon with some justifiable alarm:

> . . . our social policies and our economy are creating two quite distinct groups in black America: the almost equal and the abandoned. America has a great penchant for savoring the good news about race relations while ignoring the hard realities tucked away in ghettoes which are both out of sight and out of mind. . . . The visible progress made by some black Americans tends to support the positions of those who, consciously or unconsciously, want or need to ignore the plight of the poor. But the progress of some makes the plight of the abandoned no less brutal and no less threatening to the society as a whole [p. A18].

A Black Middle Class?

Ben J. Wattenberg and Richard M. Scammon (1973) have argued that as a result of the government programs of the 1960s a majority of blacks may now be categorized as middle class. The argument depends, as always, on one's definition of "middle class." To Wattenberg and Scammon, being middle class means

> . . . first, to have enough to eat, to have adequate, if not necessarily expensive, clothes to wear, and to be able to afford housing that is safe and sanitary. But that is only the beginning. The advent of a majority of blacks into the middle-income class has triggered a domino-like movement throughout American society. Once the necessities of food, shelter, and clothing are provided for, a vast flow of secondary desires follows. A middle-income family wants . . . a safe and sanitary neighborhood . . . good schools . . . better jobs . . . [p. 35].

These things are possible, Wattenberg and Scammon estimate, for families whose incomes are no more than $3,000 to $5,000 below the national median (with the lower figure applying to the South). If that definition is accepted, then just over half the blacks in the country are, indeed, in the middle class. Such a definition is, of course, as arbitrary and objectively meaningless as the official poverty definition. But it at least illustrates that blacks, on the whole, have made some progress in the 1960s. Scammon and Wattenberg also use it to make another point. It is that conventional liberals have become so accustomed to complaining about black deprivation that they have ignored the progress that has been made. Scammon and Wattenberg view this as harmful for blacks:

> By refusing to acknowledge the facts of success, liberals give further currency to the old stereotypes of black poverty—slums, rat-infested dwellings, a self-perpetuating welfare culture—and thereby help to confer legitimacy on the policies of those who would shirk the hard task of social and economic integration. . . . Integration, still the only realistic solution to the race problem, will proceed only as economic class gaps narrow, and are publicly acknowledged to be narrowing [p. 44].

The converse danger also holds: that the nation will applaud the successes of the black subgroups that have achieved or approached parity with their white counterparts and ignore the underclass which is as entrapped as ever. For that underclass, the relative deprivation may be greater as the gap between aspirations and reality becomes ever wider and more apparent. Moreover, this class still has no stable and continuing means of influencing the political system. The unconventional inputs of the 1960s produced some gains, but such inputs are extremely costly to the participants and incapable of being sustained. If the trend toward polarization of black society into "the almost equal and the abandoned" continues, the black poor are in danger of becoming a permanent minority of a minority and a continuing rebuke to the democratic system, their problems left undefined and off the agenda.

tenBroek, Jacobus (ed.). *The Law of the Poor.* Chandler, 1966. An exhaustive compilation of articles reviewing the legal status of poor persons and how their legal rights are affected by their economic position.

Caplovitz, David. *The Poor Pay More.* New York: Free Press, 1967. A hard-hitting examination of how low-income citizens end up paying higher rates for consumer goods.

Downs, Anthony. *Opening up the Suburbs.* New Haven, Conn.: Yale, 1973. A detailed analysis of how movement to the suburbs has intensified the problems of the poor in inner cities and a prescription for making economic benefits of the suburbs available to the poor.

Gans, Herbert J. *More Equality.* New York: Pantheon, 1968. Starting from the position of social egalitarianism, this book argues that the social harmony that most Americans desire can be achieved through policies that encourage greater social and political equality.

Moynihan, Daniel P. *Maximum Feasible Misunderstanding.* New York: Free Press, 1969. A highly critical review of the origins, appropriateness, and underlying liberal social philosophy of the "maximum feasible participation" clause of the 1964 Economic Opportunity Act.

Moynihan, Daniel P. (ed.). *On Understanding Poverty.* New York: Basic Books, 1968. A book of readings devoted to the lack of systematic knowledge on the nature, causes and cures of poverty.

Sundquist, James L. (ed.). *On Fighting Poverty.* New York: Basic Books, 1969. An edited volume of readings on how the war on poverty was fought, with what effect, and what might be learned from this attempt to end poverty.

Chapter 16

Politics and Economic Policy

HOW TO ORGANIZE AN ECONOMY

A Continuing Debate

The relationship of government to the economy has been a central issue, perhaps even *the* central issue, of American political debate. That this should be so is not surprising. The way the economy performs determines how well the nation's citizens live, and governmental decisions which affect that performance become political questions. Attempts to answer these questions are usually based on some general theories of economic organization. An understanding of some of these basic theories is helpful in seeing the relationship of government actions to the American economy.

It has been said that the United States is the last haven of unfettered capitalism, but a comparison of the classic laissez faire model with our current arrangements reveals a considerable difference between the two. It has also been said that "creeping socialism" has engulfed us. A careful examination of the nature of socialism would show that this view is also unrealistic. Both models are worth studying, however, because reality, however elusive, lies somewhere between.

Laissez Faire Capitalism

The central element of the capitalist economy is the private ownership of
the means of production and distribution of goods and services. Those who
make, serve, transport, and store these goods and services offer consumers
a choice—to buy or not to buy and, if to buy, which goods and services to
select. This exchange is governed by laws of supply and demand. If

New York Stock Ex-
change: Many private de-
cisions. *(Staffan Wennberg,
Black Star.)*

consumers are conscious of cost and quality and producers are free to compete and unconstrained by shortages of natural resources, the economy will be self-regulating in a way that maximizes the general well-being. Efforts of producers to sell more than their competitors will hold prices down. Efforts to maximize the profit margin—the difference between the cost of production and the sale price—will encourage efficiency. The quest for profit will stimulate new inventions, discoveries, and technological advances that benefit the whole society.

Because this regulation is the automatic result of many private decisions by producers and consumers, the role of government is limited to maintaining the conditions in which the market can operate: a monetary system, free trade, property rights, enforcement of contracts, and defense of the nation against foreign invasion. Government action that goes beyond these limited services and intervenes in the market system dislocates the efficient operation of the market's "invisible hand."

That is the theory. It has never been fully tested, for the kind of pure capitalism we have just described has never existed in the United States. From its earliest beginnings, the government has promoted and regulated business, and no party or group has held power without trying to use the government's powers of promotion and regulation for its own self-interest. However, the degree of government intervention in economic affairs has varied considerably over time, increasing and decreasing to meet changing patterns of production and distribution.

The Invisible Hand

Every individual endeavors to employ his capital so that its produce may be of greatest value. He generally neither intends to promote the public interest, nor knows how much he is promoting it. He intends only his own gain. And he is in this led by an invisible hand to promote an end which was no part of his intention. By pursuing his own interest he frequently promotes that of society more effectually than when he really intends it.

—Adam Smith, *The Wealth of Nations* (1776)

William A. Williams (1961) has noted three basic kinds of government involvement in the economic system since colonial times. From the colonial period through the early nineteenth century, a system with high government involvement, called *mercantilism,* was in effect. Corporations chartered by European monarchs received monopoly rights and subsidies to operate in the colonies. The taxes and regulations imposed by this system were a chief cause of the American Revolution. Nevertheless, the new nation quickly extended the previous mercantilist pattern by enacting tariffs, limiting foreign trade, and even inventing new forms of monopoly.

Around 1840, a policy of relative laissez faire began to emerge and lasted until the turn of the century. This was our closest approach to pure capitalism with its minimization of government protection and subsidization for business, but the relatively unregulated situation fostered the rise of the robber barons who replaced the previous public monopolies with their private monopolies. Instead of free and open market competition, trusts formed by the pooling of resources, cornering of markets, and fixing of prices substituted a different kind of regulated economy. This, too, was in violation of fundamental principles of capitalism.

The government response to the abuses of this period was to intervene through a host of regulatory agencies and establish what Williams calls "controlled capitalism." Because of its close affiliation with the government, this system also fell well short of pure capitalism.

Socialism

A socialist economic system is one in which the government owns the means of production and distribution of goods and services. The first step toward socialism is the nationalization of key industries, such as steel, coal, and the transportation system. With state ownership, government planning replaces the market system, and its hand is not hidden. Instead of ability to purchase, the criterion for distribution of the available goods and services is one of equity, however defined. Gaps between income levels are limited through redistribution, heavy taxes on the wealthy, and government aid for the needy. The role of the state is central as opposed to its minimal place as referee and housekeeper under capitalism.

The belief that the American economy is becoming socialized along these lines makes more or less sense depending on where you look, as Paul A. Samuelson (1970), the Nobel prize-winning economist, has suggested:

> Everyone notices how much the government does to control economic activity—tariff legislation, pure-food laws, utility and railroad regulations, minimum-wage regulations, fair labor-practice acts, social security, price ceilings and floors, public works, national defense, national and local taxation, police protection and judicial redress, zoning ordinances, municipal water or gas works, and so forth. What goes unnoted is how much of economic life proceeds *without* direct government intervention [p. 38].

The classification scheme suggested by Adolfe A. Berle (1963) is useful to sort the larger economy into three somewhat separate economies: private, controlled, and public. The private economy includes those industries and firms owned by private enterprise; the controlled economy consists of public utilities and privately owned enterprises which fall under government regulation; and the public economy covers the publicly owned and operated enterprises such as the Postal Service, libraries, schools, the Tennessee Valley Authority, and publicly sponsored social welfare programs. Only the public economy resembles socialism, and those who argue that our nation is becoming socialist usually confine their discussion to that sector while ignoring the rest.

The Mixed Economy

Because of the simultaneous existence of private, controlled, and public economies in the system, economists have labeled it a mixed economy. Government is required to play many different roles. It is responsible for the public economy and the goods and services produced and distributed. Government monitors and regulates the controlled economy, and it promotes the private economy by providing the market conditions that enable private enterprise to thrive.

One way to simplify the study of government policy in the mixed economy is to separate the various policies by their scope. Some policies are aimed at regulating behavior that is quite specific with narrow effects. Regulation of specific industries in the controlled economy, such as transportation or communication, fits this category. Other policies are much broader, including those which encourage free enterprise in the private economy and those which stimulate growth and maintain stability through manipulation of the instruments and controls in the public economy. The separation between these categories is not always neat, but it will serve to focus our discussion of how political factors affect economic performance.

REGULATING INDUSTRY

Reform through Regulation

The reaction to the abuses of the robber barons generated demands for new roles for government. In some Western nations, these new roles included governmental ownership of key industries. In the United States, the response was governmental regulation of private enterprise. Independent agencies and commissions were given authority over specific industries, beginning with the Interstate Commerce Commission (ICC) in 1887. After transportation, other industries followed. The Food and Drug Administration (FDA) was given the task of protecting the public from dangerous drugs and adulterated food. The Federal Communications Commission (FCC) was created to see that the limited number of broadcast channels were used in the public interest.

A common interpretation of the advent of such regulation is that it was intended to reduce concentrations of capital, reduce domination of markets, and curb abuses of the public welfare. The victims of the nineteenth-century patterns of industrial concentration were therefore the logical advocates of regulation. According to William Miller and Thomas Cochran (1960), these victims were

Wolfman Jack: The number of channels is limited. (Wide World Photos.)

... smaller industrialists and merchants and their white-collar workers, ... men who lived on modest inherited incomes and professional men—ministers, teachers, scholars, lawyers, doctors, writers, and artists, the educated and well born and their leisured wives . . .[p. 274].

These persons feared concentration of wealth and power in business organizations above them and the surge of socialism below. Through private associations and by alliance with the Progressives of the Republican party, these groups were able to effect legislation to regulate the conduct and employment practices of a number of industries. Opposition to such legislation by the affected industries is cited as evidence supporting this interpretation of middle-class-initiated reform.

Regulation as a Tool of Industry

But there is an opposite view about the source of regulatory policies. Gabriel Kolko in *The Triumph of Conservatism* (1967) argues that big-business resistance to regulation changed after the passage of the Interstate Commerce Act of 1887. From that time on, business was more of an advocate of regulation to counter pressure on two sides. One was from competition. Where it existed, prices and profits were forced down. The other was in the rising level of dissatisfaction among populist groups and labor unions.

The power of government, however, could be used to ease both these pressures. Agencies could be created to regulate the harmful competition and guarantee stability. The myth that the abuses of big business were thwarted by such actions could relieve the pressures of protest. Big business, according to this theory, was able to accomplish this because none of its opponents were powerful enough to defeat business measures or bring about other forms of governmental intervention.

Outcomes

What impact have regulatory agencies had? Different answers to this question parallel the competing views about the origin of regulation. Those who view regulation as an attempt to preserve or restore competition or to curb abuses have concluded that it has been relatively successful. Elmer Smead (1969) observes that the regulated industries do not always get their way. Their frustration suggests that to some degree the regulatory agency is serving the interest of some broader public. Asher Issacs and Reuben Slesinger (1964) concur and note that, ''On the whole, in view of the atmosphere in which it had to operate, the ICC has performed rather well [p. 335].''

But others, who represent a more widely accepted viewpoint, point to the numerous failures of regulatory agencies to achieve the objectives intended by their supposedly middle-class supporters. They cite decisions and acts by the agencies which appear to be aimed more at protecting and promoting the industries than at regulating them. The agencies serve industry, they say, because that is why they were created in the first place.

The Natural History of Regulatory Agencies

Most observers can agree that regardless of the original purpose of the regulatory agencies, they have tended, in time, to become the protectors and promoters of those industries. The older the agency, the more this tendency is likely to have surfaced. Marver Bernstein (1955) has outlined the processes of this change. He suggests that the transformation may be seen as a movement through four stages. The first stage, in the youth of the agency, is marked by heavy agitation for regulation. Before the formation of the ICC, numerous farm and shipping interest groups sought governmental action to halt rail abuses. Similarly, the collapse of the national financial markets brought pressures for the creation of the Securities Exchange Commission.

In the second phase of the agency's life, expectations about its regulatory aggressiveness remain high. But something new happens. To do its work, the agency must arrive at definitions and applications of the legislation which created it. Ideas that could be agreed upon in abstract theory become controversial when applied to specific cases, and bitter controversy and lengthy litigation result. The support of public-interest groups which helped create the agency begins to wane. This decline does not go unnoticed by the political leadership, which then withdraws its support for effective regulation. This particular stage in the process is worth pondering because it provides one of the clearest illuminations of the gap between democratic ideals and democratic practice. David Truman (1971) has noted that the broad problems which lead to the creation of regulatory agencies may affect collections of groups which, although adding up to a majority, are "essentially unstable" and have different objectives and different levels of interest. When these groups start to quibble over differences that had been papered over before the agency was created, some drop out, leaving the field to the more cohesive groups. Eventually, only the most interested minority is left, and this, of course, is the regulated industry itself. Those political leaders who are still paying attention are willing to ratify the agreements and adjustments worked out among the competing segments of the industry. Governmental authority is thereby

Symbiosis

> Administrative decision-makers on the regulatory commissions function in a setting in which they become in effect part of the management of the industry they are to regulate. . . . As the industry grows, so does their function and importance; if the industry dies, so does the agency. Symbiosis ripens into osmosis and digestion.
>
> —Murray Edelman, *The Symbolic Uses of Politics* (1964, p. 66).

delegated to the industry through the agency that was supposed to regulate it. Theodore Lowi (1969) has called this "interest group liberalism."

This development marks the beginning of Bernstein's third stage, the agency's maturity. Now the transformation from regulator to promoter of the industry is complete. Cut off from other sources of support, the agency comes to accept the standards and interests of the industry. Agency commissioners may be recruited from the regulated industries, which return the favor by hiring agency personnel when they finish their government service. Another structure has been created to support the status quo. For an example, we need look no further than the ICC, which, with the passage of time, came more and more to identify its interests with those of the railroad managers and their short-term needs, even when those needs were in conflict with the development of better transportation.

The last stage of a regulatory agency, its old age, finds it linked so closely to the regulated industry that it has no force at all. Other governmental institutions come to recognize this dependency and begin to withdraw their support. This loss of support forces the agency to rely still more on the industry, and its demise as an instrument to protect the public interest from industrial abuse is complete.

Competition and Concentration

The importance of free competitive enterprise is deeply engrained in the American belief system. Competition operates to accomplish the following:

1   Force business to give the consumer the best quality products and services at the lowest price

2   Eliminate the inefficient and unfit business operators

3   Ensure that resources will be used in the manner that customers prefer

4   Make the economy innovative and adaptable

5   Provide incentives and opportunities for the greatest number of people [Redford, 1966, p. 244]

Each of these benefits may not result from competition in all situations. One critical variable is the degree of competition. In earlier years, competition, or at least the absence of national industrial concentration, was generally the rule. The growth of railroads in the middle of the nineteenth century was a harbinger of change. Through the end of that century, the nation experienced a significant increase in industrial concentration. From 1880 to 1904, three hundred industrial combinations absorbed nearly 5,200 separate firms. Of these combinations, seventy-eight controlled 50 percent or more of the output in their industries (Reynolds, 1963).

Railroad Construction, 1868: Enlarging the markets. *(Wide World Photos.)*

Two forces were particularly significant in bringing about this concentration. One was a rapid change in technological development. New means of production were often more efficient when applied on a larger scale. Economies of scale led to bigger factories. New methods of transportation led to larger markets for those plants. Development in communications permitted greater coordination among them. Efficiency meant bigness.

A second factor reinforced the tendencies toward industrial concentration. A growing company could eventually dominate its industry. The more it dominated, the more it could approach exclusive control of production and inflate prices. This control could be exercised to provide both a lucrative and a stable environment. The benefits of such dominance intensified the motivation to seek concentration.

Responses to Concentration

When dominant firms abused their powers, prices were set at artificially high levels, supply was controlled to create artificial scarcity, and, not surprisingly, a reaction set in. Besides the obvious complainants, the agrarian-based Granger and Progressive organizations, and small businesses also began to feel threatened by the developing concentration and to protest against it. But historians disagree as to which groups were instrumental in bringing about governmental action. Some attribute the resulting legislation to the activities of disaffected middle-class reformers and businessmen (Faulker, 1954; Cochran and Miller, 1960). Others interpret the resulting legislative activity as an attempt by the new concentrations to consolidate and legitimize their gains (Kolko, 1967). That both views can be held by prominent observers is an indication of the ambiguity of the outcome.

Antitrust Legislation

Four legislative acts were particularly important in empowering the Justice Department and the Federal Trade Commission (FTC) to protect free market competition. The Sherman Antitrust Act of 1890 made it illegal to "monopolize trade" or engage in any "combination or conspiracy in restraint of trade." The act sought to prohibit monopolies and trusts from pooling resources to control an entire market, but as initially enforced by the Justice Department, it was largely ineffective for two reasons. First, the act's very general terms, such as "restraint of trade," required extended legal interpretation. The Supreme Court's initial interpretation of this phrase was enunciated in the "rule of reason" doctrine. Only "unreasonable" restraints of trade were forbidden, which meant that only companies engaged in *visible* coercion or attacks on others to gain a monopoly position were in violation of the law. The creation and existence of a monopoly was not per se illegal; only the creation of monopoly by certain behaviors was outlawed.

The government's unwillingness to enforce the law aggressively provided a second problem. Throughout the administrations of Harrison, Cleveland, and McKinley, the process of concentration went unimpeded. Only under Theodore Roosevelt and William Howard Taft were there any serious efforts at enforcement. By the time Wilson took office in 1913, the number of successful prosecutions was still quite small.

Two new laws were enacted in 1914 to strengthen the Sherman Act. One was the Clayton Act, which (1) outlawed price discrimination to lessen competition, (2) prohibited "tied" contracts that forced a buyer or seller to deal exclusively with one company, (3) limited interlocking directorates and mergers through stock acquisitions, and (4) permitted prevention of violations through court injunctions rather than merely providing for prosecution after the fact.

The other 1914 legislation created the Federal Trade Commission. This independent administrative agency was delegated the powers to investigate, hold hearings, and issue "cease and desist orders" in cases where "unfair methods of competition" were found. In 1938, it gained the additional authority to ban false and deceptive advertising.

The fourth and most recent step was the Celler-Kefauver Antimerger Act of 1950. This legislation dealt with a loophole in the Clayton Act which forbade merger by stock acquisition but permitted acquisition of direct assets. The 1950 legislation barred certain mergers achieved in this manner.

What Happened to Competition?

The success of any legislation depends on the vigor with which it is enforced. Smead (1969) notes that the commitment to enforce procompetition legislation has been independent of the party in power. Both Democratic and Republican administrations have been vigorous in some years and lax in other years. Two prominent economists, Samuelson (1970) and Reynolds (1963), maintain that the acts have generally been successful. "The Sherman and Clayton Acts and most of the antitrust laws," says Samuelson, "have contributed enormously toward improving the degree of competition in our system [p. 502]." Reynolds considers the achievements of the laws "certainly substantial [p. 253]." The evidence for this conclusion is drawn from several sources.

For one, they note that the Justice Department and the Federal Trade Commission have successfully prosecuted several cases. These include one decision which forced du Pont to sell its stock holdings in General Motors and another which prevented a merger in the shoe industry that would have resulted in one company controlling 5 percent of the market, a small amount, yet enough to constitute the oligopoly Congress sought to avoid. Another example is the prosecution which resulted in the jailing in 1961 of executives of two of the largest electrical companies, Westinghouse and General Electric, for collusion in setting prices.

As further evidence, Reynolds notes that businesses have shied away from attempting to create single-firm monopolies. He also claims that large firms no longer engage in predatory tactics against small competitors. Price-fixing agreements have, in the most obvious areas, been driven underground, and thus, he concludes, their scope and effectiveness have been reduced.

But not all observers are as convinced. Emmette Redford (1966) argues that many forces operate to limit the application of the government's competition-sustaining powers. No clear and interested constituency offers continuing political support for either the Department of Justice's antitrust division or the Federal Trade Commission. Instead, corporate power is able to array substantial political power and legal resources against the agencies. The low level of support is reflected in the difficulty these agencies have in obtaining funds to enforce the law. Other impediments include the severe limits on the agencies' powers to compel the production of information in the investigative stages of inquiry. And they still face the burden, despite decades of Supreme Court interpretations, of unclear statutes.

Further limits on the effectiveness of agencies to foster competition stem from protective tariff policies. These tariffs exclude foreign competition and subsidize domestic monopolies that are less efficient than their foreign competitors. Patent laws grant exclusive rights to some businesses, and legislative exemptions sometimes lead to further concentration.

One of the fundamental sources of failure of the antitrust laws, according to Redford, is the past policy emphasis of looking at conduct within an industry rather than the structure of the market as a whole. He is supported in this point by both Samuelson and Reynolds. Reynolds notes that nearly one-half of the antitrust suits which have been initiated have involved just three industries: food processing, building industries, and service trades, all of which are already characterized by a high degree of competition. Yet there has been little activity in fields of high concentration, such as steel, automobiles, electrical equipment, chemicals, and nonferrous metals. Why should there be such bias? From the viewpoint of the antitrust division of the Justice Department and the Federal Trade Commission, one of the continuing problems is sustaining public interest in what they are doing. It is easier to win public attention and support when they direct their activity at industries which have regular contact with consumers. Food, building, and service industries have this contact. Sellers of electrical turbines do not (Reynolds, 1963).

Second, larger firms are tougher to beat in a court fight. Pursuing cases against them is more costly and involves a higher risk of losing. With limited funds and a desire for a high success record, the agencies are tempted to seek out their weakest adversaries.

In sum, perhaps the main consequence of the antitrust laws has been to ensure the continued existence of private enterprise and the private ownership of industry. Although examples can be found where industry has not gotten its way, the burden of evidence appears to be that industry itself has been a primary beneficiary of regulatory policies and the enforcement of antitrust laws. Patterns of industrial concentration have proved sufficiently immune from public intervention to raise the question of whether governmental agencies responsible for overseeing industrial practices have the capability, let alone the disposition, to ensure competitive market structures and prevent industry abuses.

MAINTAINING ECONOMIC STABILITY AND GROWTH

Enhancing the Pie

The concerns of government go beyond promoting the health of specific industries, maintaining competition, and preventing abuses. Government is also vitally interested in the overall performance of the economy. That performance is the major determinant of how poor or affluent the nation's citizens will be. And the way their poverty or affluence is increased, diminished, and distributed has, as seen in earlier chapters, an important influence on the type and direction of a number of political activities.

Any assessment of government's role in affecting the performance of the American economy must seek to answer several questions: How has the economy performed? What have the policies been and how have they contributed to that performance? What effects have these policies had upon the distribution of resources among the citizens?

Defining Performance

Economic performance is usually judged by two trends: growth in output and price stability. Output may be measured in several ways. A common indicator is the gross national product (GNP), which is the total consumption and investment expenditure of the economy. It is not a truly objective indicator of economic well-being, however; two nations may have the same level of gross national product but different size populations and therefore different per capita output. That problem is easily adjusted. Other aspects of the GNP are more difficult to handle. For one thing, the raw number tells nothing about how the output is being used. If the government, business, or exports take a large portion of the GNP, the citizens will have less private income. Unless the government and business portions are returned to the population in the form of goods and services, the citizens will be less affluent than they would under other possible divisions of GNP. To use an ironic example, the tonnage of bombs dropped by American aircraft on Southeast Asia was counted as part of the gross national product.

For better indicators of economic well-being, economists sometimes turn to measures of the output available for private consumption: personal income and disposable income. Like gross national product, these measures are expressed in terms of the dollar value of goods and services. Goods and services are not in themselves a complete indicator of well-being and affluence. They ignore the problem of equitable distribution, and they fail to consider how hard the citizenry must work to get these goods and services. Better measures would therefore take into account the level of unemployment as an indicator of equitable distribution, and they would note the average number of hours worked per week as an indicator of the amount of leisure time available to citizens. Finally, there is the problem of stability. Steady, predictable income is worth more than income that reacts to every fluctuation in the business cycle with its ups, downs, and uncertainties. Psychological anxiety can be a form of economic cost. When prices are unstable and there are periods of inflation—when money becomes worth less because of spiraling prices—or deflation—when money becomes more valuable—a person's fortunes can change very dramatically for better or worse depending on his situation. Inflation, to cite just one example, can be good for someone who is in debt because he or she can repay the loan with cheaper dollars, but it can be devastating for a pensioner who is living on a fixed income because his money buys much less.

How Has the U.S. Economy Performed?

To measure performance, we need a standard of comparison. By taking measures at different points in time, trends can be identified. Or the American economy can be compared with those of other nations at the same point in time.

The general trend of the American economy over time has been an increase in output. Reynolds (1963) observes that any country experiencing

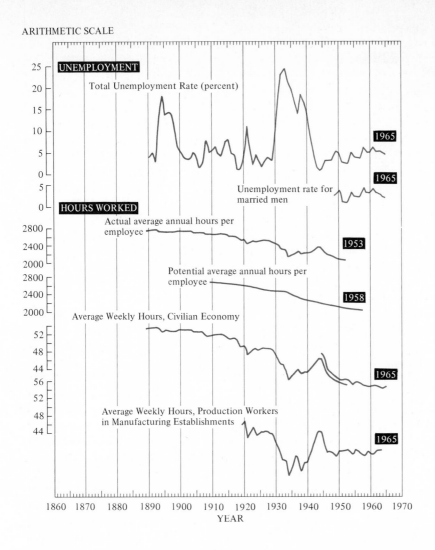

Figure 16-1 Processes
Related to Economic
Growth: Utilization of
Labor and Capital

economic development will have a period of a rapidly increasing growth rate. For the United States that period was from 1830 to 1860. Since that time, growth has continued, although not as rapidly.

In unemployment, no such long-term trend is evident, but there have been periods when there were sharp and unpleasant deviations (see Figure 16-1). The rate exceeded 15 percent in 1894 and reached 25 percent in the early 1930s. Another measure, average work hours per week, does indicate a long-term trend; a decline from 54 hours in 1889 to approximately 37 hours in 1972. But this indicator does not always measure a choice of leisure over work, as the correspondence between the diminished work week and lowered production and income of the 1930s indicates. One clearly favorable long-term trend is the rise of wages, from about 50 cents to $3.57

RATIO SCALE

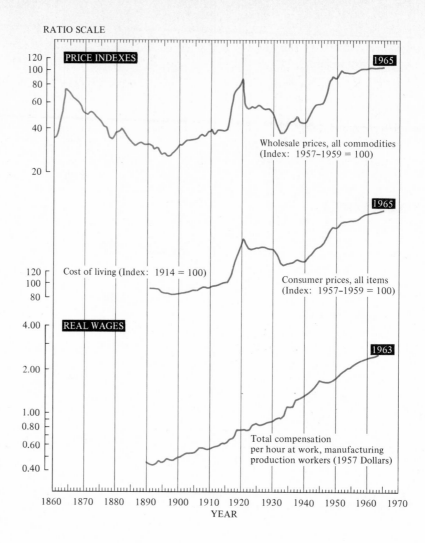

PRICE INDEXES

1965

Wholesale prices, all commodities
(Index: 1957–1959 = 100)

1965

Cost of living (Index: 1914 = 100)

Consumer prices, all items
(Index: 1957–1959 = 100)

REAL WAGES

1963

Total compensation
per hour at work, manufacturing
production workers (1957 Dollars)

YEAR

Figure 16-2 Processes Related to Economic Growth: Background Economic Variables

an hour between 1889 and the 1960s (expressed in constant dollars to correct for inflation).

Wholesale and retail prices have both shown similar movement through time. Although the rate and direction of change has not been constant, prices today are higher than at any time in the past, and have escalated sharply in the early 1970s. Figure 16-2 shows the fluctuations in the general upward movement. A comparison of the economy of the United States with that of other nations reveals that its overall output is higher; however, some other nations, especially Japan and West Germany, have a much higher rate of increase which, if sustained, will put their output above ours in the United States.

Much of the growth in the United States economy occurred before the 1930s, before government attempted any consistent or coordinated role in improving economic performance. Some take this as evidence that government intervention is unnecessary, unwise, and injurious to healthy economic performance. Yet Figure 16-1 shows dramatic fluctuations in basic measures of economic health for the same time period, reflecting the good times that prosperity brought and the severe problems that were introduced by periodic economic collapse. Alternating between business "booms" and depression, the business cycle proved to be much more unstable in the absence of government intervention, and the fluctuations took place at considerable costs. Economic downturns meant that the productive capacity of the nation was underused. Perhaps the most costly impact, in personal and social terms, was the massive unemployment the cycle periodically produced. When production declined, the "hidden hand" could be painfully slow to return it to a state of growth without government intervention. Price fluctuations also encourage inequities because some populations are more disadvantaged by them than others.

Instability in business cycles and the problems it created, particularly during the extreme depression of the 1930s, contributed to the demand for the use of governmental powers to smooth out fluctuations in economic performance. Increased knowledge about the operation of the industrial economy facilitated government's ability to act. When downturns occur, the government now responds by manipulating the money supply, interest rates, credit policies, taxes, and government spending. In theory, these devices can be very effective tools. In practice, putting them into effect often involves hard choices about which tools to implement, when, and with how much intensity. Because of the different interests which advocate the use of some tools but not others and the varying consequences which flow from their use, it is at this point that government intervention in the economy becomes a highly political subject.

The Economic Arsenal

One important means for stabilizing economic performance is through fiscal policy: the government's power to tax and spend, to plan a budget deficit or a surplus. Samuelson (1970) explains fiscal policy as

> the process of shaping taxation and public expenditures in order (1) to help dampen down the swings of the business cycle and (2) to contribute toward the maintenance of a growing, high-employment economy free from excessive inflation or deflation [p. 331].

The theory is straightforward. Consider what happens in the business cycle. In an industrial economy, the different sectors are interdependent. When one firm or a group of firms or an entire sector changes its behavior, there are consequences for others, and they change their behavior, setting off further reactions. In a recession, something happens at some point in the interactive chain to reduce the demand for a product. This reduction in demand is passed back to the suppliers of the materials and services for that product. The Arab oil embargo in 1973, for example, reduced the supply of gasoline and made motorists reluctant to buy big cars. Auto companies cut production and laid off workers. Without jobs, the workers were unable to spend and demand as much.

Reversing this downward spiral requires behavior changes. To turn the economy around, demand must be stimulated and production must go up. If firms produce more, they will spend more, hire more workers, and buy more materials. The employed workers will demand and spend more. But when the economy is declining, no one wants to do these things. It is not rational for a firm to increase production when it already has a surplus that it cannot sell, to spend money that will result in a loss. Nor is it rational for a worker who has been laid off to buy products for which he may not be able to pay.

In the opposite case, the spiral goes upward as demand outraces supply. The economy has only a finite number of raw materials, machines, and workers. If there is enough money in circulation to keep demand for the economy's products in excess of what the economy can produce, then prices must rise. Inflation sets in. Higher prices create pressures for higher wages, which in turn create more demand which boosts prices still higher.

This case, too, can be solved only by a change in behavior. If consumers would reduce their demand and stop bidding against one another, prices would go down. But it is not rational for any one consumer, whether an individual or a business, to seek to reverse the spiral on his own. A consumer who has a demand plus the money to satisfy it will spend the money and contribute to the upward spiral of prices.

The common thread in both these cases is that what is good for the economy in general may not be good or rational for the individual spending or buying unit. Indeed, what the economy needs is just the opposite of what the individual units need: spending when money is short and demand is declining and not spending when money is plentiful and demand is rising. This is the kind of problem which the government can confront through fiscal policy.

Deficit Spending.   The cure for recession is, in theory, quite simple: The government should spend money it does not have. By cutting taxes and increasing spending—making up the difference by increasing the national debt—the government does what individual actors in the economic system cannot do. The tax cut allows consumers to spend more so that demand rises. The increased demand stimulates producers to keep their machinery operating, hire workers, and expand the productive capacity. Because the government is also a consumer, its increased spending also expands demand (its own), stimulates production, and creates jobs.

The key element in this equation is the federal deficit. If the government balanced its budget by increasing taxes to support the increased spending, then the decline in personal consumption would offset the expansion of government consumption. So, in seeming contravention of the Puritan ethic, fiscal policy aimed at stimulating a lagging economy involves the conscious, deliberate planning of a deficit in the federal budget.

Budgeting a Surplus.   The reverse situation occurs when consumption demands exceed the capacity of the economy and inflation results. The strategy then is to create a budget surplus by increasing taxes and reducing government spending. The tax increase will leave fewer dollars to chase the limited supply of goods, so prices will be forced down. Reduced government spending will have the same effect. Again, it is important not to cancel the effect of the shift in government spending with a compensating tax adjustment. If reduced spending were offset with a tax cut, the net effect would be wiped out. The budget surplus is what makes the anti-inflation strategy work.

In its ideal application, fiscal policy would not offend the Puritan ethic because the budget deficits and surpluses would cancel each other out over time and the government's budget would be balanced in the long run. This is the classic Keynesian theory. In practice, the ideal is difficult, if not impossible, to achieve because policymakers find it so much easier to gain acceptance for a deficit than for a surplus. (See Table 16-1.) Another problem is figuring out when to do what. Instead of reacting to inflation or recession after they have set in, the hardest job for economists is to know what inflationary or recessionary trends are incipient so that they may be anticipated and combated before they occur.

Perhaps the finest hour of what used to be called "the new economics" (even though by then it was neoclassic) came early in the Kennedy administration when the President accepted the advice of the Council of Economics Advisors headed by Dr. Walter Heller. The nation had grown accustomed to periodic recessions, and the Council's advice was to try to skip the next recession by planning a moderate deficit to stimulate demand and keep the economy running close to full capacity. Kennedy accepted the advice, obtained the necessary tax cut from Congress, and the strategy worked. The periodic recession did not happen. That part was politically easy, because it involved a tax cut. To follow through, however, the next step should have been a tax increase or a cut in government spending to create a surplus as soon as the economy began to heat up. By that time, however, Kennedy was dead and the Johnson administration had set for itself the impossible task of boosting consumer comforts at home and

Table 16-1 Budget Receipts and Outlays, 1951–1975
(Millions of dollars)

FISCAL YEAR	RECEIPTS	OUTLAYS	SURPLUS (+) OR DEFICIT (−)
1951	53,390	45,797	+7,593
1952	68,011	67,962	+49
1953	71,495	76,769	−5,274
1954	69,719	70,890	−1,170
1955	65,469	68,509	−3,041
1956	74,547	70,460	+4,087
1957	79,990	76,741	+3,249
1958	79,636	82,575	−2,939
1959	79,249	92,104	−12,855
1960	92,492	92,223	+269
1961	94,389	97,795	−3,406
1962	99,676	106,813	−7,137
1963	106,560	111,311	−4,751
1964	112,662	118,584	−5,922
1965	116,833	118,430	−1,596
1966	130,856	134,652	−3,796
1967	149,552	158,254	−8,702
1968	153,671	178,833	−25,161
1969	187,784	184,548	−3,236
1970	193,743	196,588	−2,845
1971	188,392	211,425	−23,033
1972	208,649	231,876	−23,227
1973	232,225	246,526	−14,301
1974 est.	270,000	274,660	−4,660
1975 est.	295,000	304,445	−9,445

Source: The Budget of the United States Government, Fiscal Year 1975.

fighting an expensive war in Southeast Asia. The tax increase was too late, and the stabilizing surplus never came. The sword of fiscal policy has two edges and one can be very difficult to wield. The inflationary problems of the 1970s can be traced directly to President Johnson's attempt in the 1960s to eat his fiscal cake and have it too.

Monetary Policy. The other main economic tool, monetary policy, is more complicated. Because it is hard for citizens to understand, politicians have considerably more freedom to manipulate it. But its effectiveness tends to be erratic and uncertain, partly because monetary policy-making lacks coordination. Yet the basic concept is simple enough. Monetary policy is simply that government action which affects the supply and cost of money. It is managed through two basic means: through the creation of money by the banking system and through the control of the cost of money. One way banks are able to create money is through what is called the "fractional reserve system." Bankers know from experience that the

Kennedy and Heller: The
advice was accepted.
(United Press International.)

probability of all depositors claiming all their money at once is infinitesimal-
ly small. A bank needs therefore to hold in reserve only part of the money
that is obligated in checking accounts and demand-deposit savings accounts.
The rest of the money can be loaned out at interest, and that is how the
bank makes its profit. The size of the nation's money supply depends on the
federal government's reserve requirements, after a multiplier effect is taken
into account. Here is how it works:

Suppose that you deposit $1,000 with your friendly neighborhood
banker. He keeps a 20 percent reserve against possible withdrawals. That
means he now has $800 to loan. He loans this $800 to your neighbor. The
neighbor pays interest on this money, so he is not going to leave it idle in
the bank. He is going to spend it, perhaps investing it in equipment or
buying a secondhand car. Either way, that $800 moves to someone else and
becomes a deposit in another bank. If this bank has the same 20 percent
reserve policy, it will hold $160 in reserve and loan $640. (See Table 16-2.)
If you follow this process through to the practical limit, you find that the
original $1,000 can become about $5,000. If the reserve requirement were
smaller, the money would have increased more. With a larger reserve
requirement, the money would have expanded less.

There are other ways of expanding or contracting the money supply
short of speeding up or slowing down the printing presses at the Bureau of

Table 16-2 Creating Money Through the Multiplier Effect
(Of bank deposits and loans)

Starting with an original deposit of $1,000 with banks holding 20 percent in reserve:

CYCLE	LOANED	DEPOSITS	HELD IN RESERVE	TOTAL DEPOSITS*
1	$ 0.00	$1,000.00	$200.00	$1,000.00
2	800.00	800.00	160.00	1,800.00
3	640.00	640.00	128.00	2,440.00
4	512.00	512.00	102.40	2,952.00
5	409.60	409.60	81.92	3,361.60

*Money available for economy.

Engraving and Printing. One way is through the purchase and sale of government securities. A government agency, the Federal Reserve System, known as the Fed, has the authority to buy and sell these securities. Its buy and sell decisions put money into the economy or take it out. Another way is by manipulating interest rates through the "rediscount rate," the rate at which the Fed loans money to member banks. The ups and downs in the interest rate are passed on to the ultimate borrowers. When interest is low, borrowing is encouraged and more money gets into circulation. When interest is high, borrowing is discouraged, and the amount of money in circulation should decrease.

Regardless of how the money supply is manipulated, the effect is usually straightforward. Decreasing the money supply cools down the economy, whereas increasing the money supply heats up the economy. However, paradoxical effects will occur. When the government tried to cool the inflation of the 1970s by restricting the money supply, the scarcity of money drove interest rates up. The high cost of capital in turn boosted the prices of goods and services which depend on large amounts of borrowed money, such as housing and electric power, and inflation got worse to that extent. On the other hand, demand for housing was reduced by the high prices, and new building activity slowed down.

Finally, the Federal Reserve has some minor weapons which it can apply to try to find the optimum balance in the money supply. One is moral suasion. If a bank raises its interest rates beyond what the Fed thinks is good for the economy, the Fed may tell the bank so. Often, the offending bank will change its mind. Another tool is the power to apply selective controls over certain transactions. The "margin requirement"—the amount of borrowed money that one can use to buy stock—can be regulated. Ceilings can be set on the interest rates which banks will pay on various kinds of deposits. The Fed has the authority to set limits on installment contracts. This authority was last applied during the Korean war when installment purchasers were required to make a minimum down payment of one-third of the purchase price. A similar power has also been applied in the past to home mortgages.

Printing the Money:
There are other ways.
(United Press International.)

Automatic Stabilizers

The stabilizing devices we have discussed so far—deficit spending, budget surpluses, manipulating the money supply—all require policymakers to decide to do things and then do them. In a turbulence of cross-pressures, that requirement can be a disadvantage. Happily, some things built into our system provide a measure of automatic equilibrating force. The income tax is one. Federal income tax is progressive—graduated to take a larger share of larger incomes—in theory, if not always in effect. So when production and income go up, more people move into the higher tax brackets, and the federal budget moves in the direction of surplus without anybody's conscious direction. This happened in fiscal 1973, and although the effect was not as strong as a consciously preplanned surplus would have been, it was at least of some help. Conversely, if production and income fall, people move into lower tax brackets and the fiscal situation automatically moves toward the deficit that will help get things moving again.

The unemployment and welfare systems are also stabilizing forces. In hard times, more people get this money. In good times, fewer get it. Either way, spending is encouraged or depressed in a way that smooths out the up-and-down cycles.

Wage and Price Controls

Efforts to influence wages and prices directly have one strong advantage. They are politically cheap. The Kennedy and Johnson administrations tried to influence the level of wages with persuasion by setting out guidelines which would keep wage increases growing no faster than overall productivity. The guidelines did not have the force of law and they were not very effective. A more drastic measure is to impose direct wage and price controls. The process is costly, cumbersome, and difficult to enforce. It also risks being counterproductive. Direct controls were imposed during World War I, World War II, and the Korean war. They were also employed by the Nixon administration in an effort to straighten out the economic distortions resulting from the Vietnam war. President Nixon instituted them prior to the 1972 election after warning that they would not work, and his warning proved to be right. An extreme example of the distortions that resulted came when prices were frozen on food products but not on the things that farmers had to buy. Farmers quickly calculated that they would lose less money by not producing at all, and so the price control program actually aggravated the shortages which had created the original high prices, which postponed the solution.

Inflation and Depression

The state of the art of managing the U.S. economy has come a long way since the Great Depression of the early 1930s. That disaster could have been ended much sooner with strong fiscal policy involving heavy deficit financing, but the notion of purposeful deficit was so politically repugnant that it took World War II to force the United States into the deficit that primed the economy and brought it back to health. Problems of that era, painful as they were, now seem relatively simple to manage. But present-day problems have some complications that do not lend themselves to such obvious solutions. One is that the nature of inflation has changed. Inflation used to generally be of the kind that economists call "demand-pull" inflation, which is simply too much money chasing too few goods. The remedy is to step up the productive capacity of the economy to meet the demand. But today there is a new kind of inflation based on the interactions of powerful business and labor groups which operates relatively independent of the supply and demand situation. It is called "cost-push" inflation. Labor leaders press for higher wages while business wants higher profits. Management pays the higher wages and passes the cost to the consumers. The higher prices stimulate demands for higher wages. The result is a self-fueled spiral which is very difficult to control. Since it can operate independently of the degree to which the economy is operating at capacity, it can lead to a paradoxical situation in which a business recession—with much of the available productive capacity going unused—exists while prices continue to rise. In short, the worst aspects of recession and inflation exist side by side in cost-pull inflation. This problem was first clearly distinguished during the Kennedy administration when the wage-price guidelines were promoted to fight cost-push inflation at the same time

Apple Vendors, 1930:
Deficit spending was po-
litically repugnant. *(Wide
World Photos.)*

that a tax cut was passed to avoid a recession. The attempts at solution were
disappointing, and the problems were aggravated by the Johnson administration's guns-and-butter policy which sought to finance a war and social
programs at home at a time when classic economic theory would have
dictated restraint in government spending. The Nixon administration was
also reluctant to apply the classic fiscal medicine of a tax increase—in
deference to the 1972 campaign promise that there would be no tax
increase—and relied instead on the politically cheap wage and price
controls plus the less visible effects of monetary policy. "The rules of
economics," lamented Federal Reserve Chairman Arthur Burns, "are not
working in quite the way they used to [Knight, 1972, p. 411]." One of
the most disturbing questions of the 1970s is whether the economic
problems of the post-Vietnam period can be managed at all. Much of the
difficulty lies in the political constraints inherent in economic policymaking.

Arthur Burns: Somebody
changed the rules. *(Wide
World Photos.)*

ECONOMIC THEORY AND POLITICAL REALITY

Living in the Real World

Most citizens want economic growth, high employment, and stable prices.
Economic theory seems to reveal the procedures for attaining these things,
but applying these procedures in the real world is not so simple. In the
first place, experts in economics have honest disagreements about the

usefulness of fiscal and monetary policy. They argue about whether to adjust the taxing side or the spending side of fiscal policy. They do not agree about the timing for action even when it is clear that action will be necessary. These debates do not occur in an atmosphere of scientific detachment, for noneconomic issues often underlie them. For example, an argument for a cutback in expenditures may be an expression of opposition to the substantive policy for which the money is being spent rather than an objective evaluation of the economic situation. Economics—the most exact social science—is less exact than many of its practitioners acknowledge.

Monetarism versus Fine Tuning

A core debate turns on the relative merits of fiscal and monetary policies. One group of economists, led by Milton Friedman of the University of Chicago, argues that fiscal policy has no predictable effect on business cycles. Friedman claims, on the basis of a study of the history of money in several nations, including the United States, that money supply alone shapes economic fluctuations. Fiscal policy, he says, determines only how much of the nation's production is controlled by government and how much by the private sector.

Most economists, however, see uses for both fiscal and monetary policy. Some of them cite the 1964 tax cut as an example of economic growth and increased employment resulting from a planned deficit. In their view, timely adjustments in fiscal policies, along with monetary changes, can be used to fine-tune the economy and dampen the fluctuations of the business cycle. These debates are not strictly academic. Policymakers have to decide which economists to listen to, and their choices may serve differing values and beliefs that go beyond the economic questions. For example, if, as Friedman claims, fiscal policy is ineffective in controlling recession or inflation, the need for an active role by government is reduced. It is therefore not surprising to find that many of the supporters of a strict reliance on monetary policy favor limited government. Correspondingly, many of the advocates of fine tuning through fiscal policy are also proponents of active government. Moreover, even those who favor planned deficits or surpluses to head off recession or inflation will differ on how to go about it, depending on their view of government's proper role. If a surplus is called for, those who favor a limited government role will call for reducing expenditures. Those who want to expand the role of government will prefer raising taxes instead.

The Dilemma of Incompatible Goals

Many complications arise along the path toward full employment, economic growth, and stable prices. The goals are not strictly compatible. For example, as the economy moves toward fuller employment and maximum

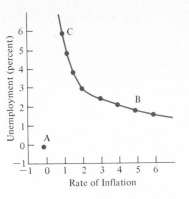

Figure 16-3 Hypothetical "Possibility Curve"

utilization of the machinery of production, it becomes less efficient. Factories will hire less qualified workers or pay overtime. Farmers will put marginal land into production. Obsolescent machinery that stood idle when production was low will be put back into service. The result is that the added increments of production will be more costly. As production costs rise, prices rise, and cost-push inflation is stimulated. But if the demand-reducing remedies are employed, the least efficient workers will be laid off, the marginal land and equipment will be idled, and the economy will operate at less than full capacity with increased unemployment.

The upshot is that policymakers have to decide how much unemployment to put up with and how much inflation. This range of choices is represented in a hypothetical "possibility curve" shown in Figure 16-3. The ideal situation is represented by point A where inflation and unemployment are both zero, but the available choices lie along the curve from point C to point B. Which choice one prefers will depend on his situation and his values. Those who are particularly vulnerable to unemployment will prefer a point near B. Those with fixed incomes and no danger of joblessness will be happier near point C.

Economic Decision Making

Who decides? The government's economic forecasters, particularly those in the Council of Economic Advisors and the Office of Management and Budget, play an important role, but the ultimate decision belongs to Congress and the President. Traditionally, the initiative in reconciling competing claims and formulating a policy belongs to the executive. Edward Flash (1965) argues that all the presidents from Franklin Roosevelt to Lyndon Johnson began their terms of office as fiscal conservatives. They favored a balanced budget as a primary goal, and they were reluctant to use fiscal policy to achieve such goals as high employment and growth. All changed. Eisenhower remained the most reluctant to adopt fiscal activism.

Kennedy was persuaded by Walter Heller. Johnson belatedly sought a 10 percent income tax surcharge and accepted a reduction in government expenditures to fight inflation in 1967. Nixon and Ford acted similarly.

Some of the constraints are brought about by conflicts between economic and other goals. Tax cuts to fight a recession, for example, may require reduction or elimination of programs favored by groups on whom the President relies for support, or the competing noneconomic goals may simply be more important. Conducting a war requires large expenditures, and inflation often follows. But if national security is judged to be threatened more by the enemy in battle than by inflation, then the economic goals must yield.

Another constraint upon the President is the limited nature of his authority. He can propose that spending and taxing levels be changed to promote his economic goals, but congressional assent is required to enact his proposals. This congressional support may be unavailable or available only at a cost. President Johnson wanted his surtax early in 1966. Congress did not enact it until late summer of 1967. President Nixon tried to impound money to reduce spending. Congress compelled him to spend it.

Other constraints include past commitments. Ongoing programs, such as Social Security, are large and inflexible. Finally there is the constraint imposed by uncertainty. Economic forecasting is still not an exact science, and the uncertainty leads policymakers to be hesitant at times when action may be required or active when hesitation would be better. Whatever they do exposes them to question and further conflict.

The Role of Congress

The new congressional budgeting procedure, to be implemented in the 1977 fiscal year, may resolve some of the conflicts which impede decisive economic policy making. By setting its budget targets in advance, Congress may gain support for fine-tuning measures before the specifics are worked out. The traditional piecemeal approach has given maximum consideration to the demands of limited and specific interest groups at the expense of the economy as a whole. Interest groups will still be heard, but the new procedure will make it easier for Congress to evaluate their claims against the needs of the larger society. (See Chapter 9.)

The Federal Reserve

In shaping monetary policy, the Federal Reserve System has an institutional bias, stemming from its structure and membership, favoring price stability over full employment and growth. The Federal Reserve Board has seven members appointed by the President for fourteen-year terms. Since 1950, the membership has included one person from the banking industry, two from business schools, and one from a government career. Although this membership reflects the Board's original purpose to serve the banking interests and commerce and industry, its current role in economic policy is, of course, much broader. Such groups as labor or consumer interests are excluded. Because of the fourteen-year term, the President cannot exercise very much control over the board's composition. Moreover, congressional oversight activity is not effective in this relatively closed operation. Most observers conclude, therefore, that the Fed is most responsive to the interests of the banking and financial community.

A case can be made, of course, that such insulation from political pressures is necessary. Policies needed to fight inflation are often politically unpopular. But there is no very good mechanism for coordinating the Fed's economic policies with those of the rest of the government.

SUGGESTED READINGS

Black, Angus. *A Radical's Guide to Economic Reality.* New York: Holt, Rinehart and Winston, 1970. A short and spicy critique of business dominance of most aspects of American life.

Brenner, Philip, Robert Borosage, and Bethany Weidner (eds.). *Exploring Contradictions.* New York: McKay, 1974. A series of essays on the relationship between government and the economy with particular attention devoted to the dominant position established by the modern corporation.

Epstein, Edwin M. *The Corporation in American Politics.* Englewood Cliffs, N.J.: Prentice-Hall, 1969. An examination of the political behavior of business corporations and the legal policies affecting corporate involvement in politics.

Heilbroner, Robert L., and Peter L. Bernstein. *A Primer on Government Spending.* New York: Vintage, 1963. This layman's guide to fiscal policy was a hit when it came out, perhaps because it coincided with the Kennedy tax cut. Fiscal policy seems more complicated now, but you have to start somewhere.

Parkin, Frank. *Class Inequality and Political Order.* New York: Praeger, 1971. Casting a wide net, this is a comparative analysis of the social and material inequalities in modern industrial societies and the belief systems which sustain such inequalities.

Schultze, Charles L. *The Politics and Economics of Public Spending.* Washington: The Brookings Institution, 1968. A cogent analysis of dilemmas which government officials face in trying to reconcile and balance group demands and program expenditures, with particular attention to how this is done in the budgetary process.

Sundquist, James L. *Politics and Policy: The Eisenhower, Kennedy, and Johnson Years.* Washington: The Brookings Institution, 1968. Includes an important discussion of the different approaches to manipulating fiscal and monetary policies by recent national administrations.

Chapter 17
Foreign Policy

THE FOREIGN POLICY PROCESS

Goals and Purposes

A primary function of government is to protect the interests of the nation with respect to the rest of the world. There is an aphorism, ''Politics stops at the water's edge,'' which, in one of its many meanings, indicates a fundamental difference between domestic and foreign policy making. Domestic issues involve the clash of interests, the struggle to determine who gets what, the sorting of many actors into winners and losers. In foreign policy, more mutuality of interests is perceived where basic issues are concerned. Presumably, everyone can unite behind what is best for the country, provided all can perceive just what the best policy is. It is not quite that simple, of course, and there is division of opinion over foreign policy. But the division is less likely to form along party lines than are disputes over domestic issues. Both Republican and Democratic parties are dominated by internationalists, and it is this coalition that keeps America's stance toward the rest of the world relatively united.

The foreign policy of the United States is a complex set of national aims and activities. The programs, postures, relationships, and stated purposes of the nation, as formed by different leaders over time, constitute the backdrop for wide sets of national actions. In the 1970s the Nixon

Doctrine recast the general directions of American diplomacy and the new posture the nation would assume in world politics.

An essential problem in analyzing American foreign policy is understanding what is meant by national interests. During the last decade the Vietnam war precipitated an unusual but useful nationwide debate on the subject. Henry Kissinger (1968), writing in a Brookings Institution volume on the urgent public policy issues confronting the new administration, stated that "it is necessary to undertake an inquiry, from which we have historically shied away, into the essence of our national interest and into the premises of our foreign policy [p. 610]." As an instrument of political action, the concept of national interest has served as a means for justifying, denouncing, and proposing policies. Although the concept has won a prominent place in the dialogue of public affairs, it remains a very vague and elusive concept.

This elusiveness has a number of sources. First, there is the ambiguity of specifying whose interest is encompassed. Some analysts argue that the national interest is whatever the national leaders seek to promote and preserve. There is some justification for this line of reasoning, for political leaders do tend to perceive and discuss their goals in terms of the national interest. At the same time, they are apt to make the automatic claim that their goals *are* the national interest, even when they may not be so. A second problem involving this concept arises when we attempt to determine the existence of interests and to trace their presence in substantive policies. This dilemma is very apparent in the process of foreign policy making. Often the President, cabinet members, other executive officials, and the leaders and committees in Congress pursue conflicting policy goals and values. The ensuing policies reflect this complex political process.

Confusion about goals may be disquieting, but the process of policy making is politics. The procedures for making national decisions are not orderly. Participants in the process do not have precisely defined roles and powers. Roger Hilsman (1967), who served as director of the Bureau of Intelligence and Research in the State Department during the Kennedy years, describes the inherently political nature of foreign policy making:

> Policy faces inward as much as outward, seeking to reconcile conflicting goals, to adjust aspirations to available means, and to accommodate the different advocates of these competing goals and aspirations to one another. It is here that the essence of policy-making seems to lie, in a process that is in its deepest sense political [p. 13].

Although the foreign policy process is a mechanism which attempts to satisfy interests, there is no definitive, objectively discoverable national interest. The national interests of a political system are not self-interpreting, but they are the subjective perceptions which exist in the minds of policymakers and citizens.

The Ideal Policy-making Machine

Foreign policy making is a process in which it is extremely hard to recognize sharp beginnings and decisive endings. In theory policy making should be the result of conscious and deliberate reasoning, including the analysis of problems and the systematic examination of alternatives. John Lovell (1970) has described what an ideal foreign policy system would do. He calls it IIMMP, for Imaginary Ideal Machine for Making Policy, but he is nevertheless serious. Such a machine would proceed through eight basic steps:

Scanning. The geographical-political interactions of the rest of the world have to be watched for events that might affect us.

Coding. Information that is gathered in the scanning process must be evaluated and classified.

Transmission. The scanners and coders have to get their information to headquarters in a way that is clear, understandable, and usable.

Storage and Recall. Data have to be held against the day when they might be needed; they must be kept in a form that permits them to be quickly retrieved when necessary.

Recognition of Options. There is usually more than one way to handle a situation. It is important not to overlook any possibilities.

Decision making. There has to be a mechanism for deciding what problem to solve and how to do it.

Implementation. Once it is decided what to do, somebody has to do it.

Feedback. Results of the action have to be watched to see if they are working so that corrections can be made when they are not [pp. 208–210].

Such a fanciful design has some use because real-world problems can be measured against it. Like any machine, its performance depends upon those who operate the machine. Although the possibility of a perfect machine exists, it must inevitably be manned by imperfect humans. Their scanning for information is fragmentary and spotty. Their coding is biased and subject to blind spots. Information gets lost, delayed, and distorted in transmission. The most important information is sometimes forgotten just when its retrieval is most vital. Limitations of human imagination leave many possible options off the decision agenda altogether. Decisions are often based on emotion and other nonrational factors. Putting them into effect is often done too slowly, inefficiently, and without sufficient coordination. Sometimes the foreign policy-making machinery is plagued by rivalries between different government agencies participating in the policy process. The State Department, CIA, and military each do intelligence work, at times trying to discredit each other's reliability. Jealousy between government agencies, if not controlled, can cripple the policy-making apparatus. When things go wrong, the trouble may not be detected until it is too late.

Yet the machine is not entirely capricious and beyond management. Some of its peculiarities involve items that voters can control: choice of a

President, for example. The personalities of officials like Wilson, Kennedy, and Nixon had a strong influence over the outcomes of foreign affairs policy. The political culture—the set of norms, beliefs, and institutional linkages that affect attitudes toward the international community—is subject to change and manipulation. The way in which key policymakers are recruited, socialized, and organized can make a difference in the decisions.

But because few foreign affairs issues get the kind of citizen attention that domestic matters usually do, the effectiveness of popular control at making the system work is limited. Inertia and inattention have made the system rather slow and stodgy. President Kennedy, frustrated by inaction at the State Department, once called it "a bowl of jelly." Journalist Joseph Kraft said the place was "run as a fudge factory [Campbell, 1971, p. 6]." In part, problems of this sort are the product of the organization of the policy-making system, and this organization is the result of a series of historical accidents more than conscious planning.

Growth of Foreign Policy Machinery

John Campbell (1971) notes that most of the foreign policy institutions are less than a generation old, dating from the National Security Act of 1947. Formed hastily in response to what seemed to be an emergency situation, they are based on a world view which he describes as "globalism," the notion that we could control and manipulate the great geopolitical forces of change that sweep the world and make them work to our advantage. Fueled by what has been called the myth of American omnipotence, it got us into several different kinds of trouble. Its costs were high, both economically and psychologically. Even when the manipulations seemed to work, the end result was not very effective. It ignored traditions of international law by impelling us to interfere with the internal affairs of other nations. It was pretentious, anxiety-provoking to other countries, and caused us to take positions that were not always credible to friends or foes. Perhaps worst of all was the internal effect: the creation of a national emergency psychology at a time when it was difficult to make a case for the existence of a clear and present foreign threat.

The year 1947, when the National Security Council and the Office of Special Assistant to the President for National Security Affairs were established, also marked the development of national security as a policy objective. The striking deficiencies that were discovered in the administrative machinery during World War II demonstrated the need for coordination and long-range planning. The notion of "national security," in some respects a reformulation of the concept of national interest, set the mood for America's postwar thinking. National security, that is, "the ability of a nation to protect its internal values from external threats [Berkowitz and Bock, 1968]," has provided the framework upon which important decision-making positions are based. The rise of national security as a

President Kennedy: Influencing a bowl of jelly.
(Dick Halstead, Black Star.)

guideline to policy objectives was due to its seemingly substantive nature. Recommendations for policy decisions and strategic problems could be more easily operationalized. National leaders began to approach problems in a new way. Policy issues were viewed from the perspective of allocating and balancing resources needed for protecting internal values from external threats.

The concept of national security was strengthened as a policy guideline by America's military establishment. From the end of World War II to the end of the conflict in Vietnam, American thinking in matters of foreign policy was militaristic. During the long years in which a cold war consensus existed within the United States, the military was successful in keeping national security high on the agenda of foreign policy objectives. Adam Yarmolinsky (1971), who served in the Pentagon as a Deputy Assistant of Defense for International Security Affairs, notes that "American statesmanship became preoccupied with military security, with the capabilities of the potential foe, and readiness for the worst contingencies [p. 123]." The ascendency of national security as a policy determinant was accompanied by a corresponding growth in the institutions that fostered its primacy.

Groups with the most interest in a given policy field tend, over time, to work themselves into positions where their power matches their interest. World War II left us with a variety of interest groups whose concerns were related to war and preparation for war. Richard J. Barnet (1972) has pointed out how the federal bureaucracy changed radically under the impact of World War II. First, government agencies came to control the creation and disposition of a significant share of the national wealth. Second, the balance of power within the bureaucracy shifted to those agencies concerned with foreign and military affairs. In 1939, the federal government had about 800,000 civilian employees, about 10 percent of whom worked for national security agencies. At war's end, the government had 4 million workers and 75 percent of them were in national security activities. The last premobilization defense budget represented about 1.4 percent of the gross national product (Bureau of the Budget, 1946). The lowest postwar defense budget, in that happy interlude between the Japanese surrender and the remobilization for the cold war, took 4.7 percent of the GNP. Once postwar remobilization was under way, defense spending climbed rapidly and has averaged about 8 percent of the GNP since 1964 (Office of Management and Budget, 1974). So two things were happening. There was a phenomenal increase in size in the defense establishment, and there was an ascendancy of a new generation of policymakers schooled in war. This new generation of policymakers, both civilian and military, made the problem of the nation's security the highest priority. Perceiving the globe as a potential battleground between ideologically opposed forces, policymakers adopted military staff habits of thinking. It became more important to plan contingencies on the basis of the foes' capabilities instead of their intentions. Barnet (1972) observes how the worldwide U.S. military presence created by World War II lingered on. By his count, there were 1.2 million men manning 299 major overseas installations and 1,930 minor installations. "The effect," he says, "has been that military officers have outnumbered all other representatives of the United States around the world. The personal relationships they have made have had an important impact on the direction of U.S. policy [p. 30]." Meanwhile, the authority of Congress was diminishing in relation to the executive branch, causing an important check on the foreign policy bureaucracy to lapse.

American foreign policy is no longer premised on the fear of the global menace of encroaching communism with monolithic and conspiratorial threats. It is no longer founded on the belief that we can manipulate and manage everything in the world. But as in other aspects of government, there has been a certain amount of lag in putting the new premises into effect. Campbell (1971) says

> . . . the Washington bureaucracies have not yet gotten this message. Rigidities of size and structure built into the process of bureaucratic action make it hard to change foreign policy, even when the changes have been announced by the President. In the present system, national purpose can easily become mired in a swamp of "interagency coordination," while expert advice from the lower working levels of government rarely reaches the place it is most needed—the top. Organization, in other words, undercuts policy. Until policy makers change the structure of the organizations, they will have great difficulty in changing the shape of their policies [pp. 12, 13].

Stanley Hoffman (1968) has called the problems of organization "elephantiasis and fragmentation." Campbell calls them dispersal and gigantism. Whatever the language, they agree that the foreign affairs policy system is so large, diffuse, and disorganized that presidents have often been forced to abandon it for their own informal and closed circle of advisors. We have already seen, from our examination of the Presidency in Chapter 10, what kind of trouble that can cause.

THE FORMAL STRUCTURE

The President

The Constitution, while vague in granting specific powers over foreign policy, does set guidelines. In particular, it divides certain powers between the President and Congress. The resulting formal structure brings a multiplicity of actors into the process who do have an effect on the decisions so that the result is not wholly dominated by a bureaucratic elite.

The President has, of course, the power to negotiate treaties and executive agreements, to begin or terminate recognition of foreign governments, to hire and fire officials in foreign policy jobs, and to decide military policy down to tactical decisions. All this makes him the focal point in the process. His is the final political responsibility for the successes and failures. He is the ultimate coordinator and the ultimate persuader. If politics is to stop at the water's edge, he must build the consensus that will make that possible.

Being at the apex of the foreign policy bureaucracy, the President is also entrusted with the responsibility of final decision making and the implementation of policies. President Truman knew perfectly well what the role of the Presidency meant when he said, "The buck stops here." Truman alone had to make the final decision whether to drop the bomb on Hiroshima and whether to send troops to Korea. The President also has the enormous task of making sure that the numerous government agencies connected with foreign policy perform the functions they are supposed to. Dean Acheson, former Secretary of State, often told a story about Chief Justice Taft. Taft had just finished a conversation with an eminent man about the "machinery" of government. "And you know," said Taft with a touch of wonder in his voice, "he really does believe it *is* machinery." [Related in Hilsman 1967, p. 17]." In fact, presidents are often hindered in the implementation of policies by a recalcitrant bureaucracy.

John Marshall in 1799 described the Presidency as "the sole organ of the nation in its external relations, and its sole representative with foreign nations." Harry Truman said in 1948, "I make American foreign policy." But the President's influence increases and diminishes with different circumstances. His power is greatest in times of crisis when action must be taken quickly. Not only his subordinates but the general public will rally to his support—as when approval of President Kennedy reached its zenith despite the disastrous failure of the Bay of Pigs invasion. When events unfold less swiftly, however, the President is limited by public opinion, the press, Congress, interest groups, and his own subordinates. The institutional limits—the Senate's power over confirming appointments and treaty ratification and the congressional appropriation process—have been only minor obstacles through most of our recent history. Even the congressional ban on funds for bombing of Cambodia in 1973 was more of a political than an institutional limitation. It told the President that he had to take the wishes of the legislative branch and the body of public opinion behind it into account.

A President's ability to manipulate public attitudes toward other nations can be one of his strongest foreign policy tools. It is often accepted as a truism that only a Republican President with a strong anticommunist record–such as Mr. Nixon–could have effected the rapproachment with mainland China. A Democrat would have been accused of selling out to the communists. Earlier Presidents might have liked to ease the tensions with China but were restricted by the attitudes set by their cold war predecessors.

Below the President

Different presidents have different ways of spreading the work around. The men who constitute the "administration" are secretaries of departments, undersecretaries, assistant secretaries, the White House staff, directors of the Central Intelligence Agency and the Agency for International Development. Roger Hilsman (1967) calls them the "front men" and describes their function as

> . . . to be the advocates of policy and to represent the different bureaucratic constituencies inside the government and the public constituencies, special interests, and attentive publics outside the government [p. 35].

Within the foreign policy-making process the "front men" also serve to transmit information to the President. It is their job to present the President with concise, yet thorough, reports on topics of importance to him. More importantly, the "front men" form a select advisory body. In this capacity they assist the President in the recognition and formulation of policy options. The President is still free to reject policy recommendations. In 1954, when the French were under siege from the Vietnamese forces, Eisenhower declined to follow the recommendation of his advisors to intervene in Indochina.

The President traditionally has three main foreign policy advisors: the Secretary of Defense, the Secretary of State, and the Assistant to the President for National Security Affairs. He also has the National Security Council, established in 1947 to include the President, Vice President, Secretary of Defense, Secretary of State, the director of the Office of Emergency Preparedness, and some ad hoc appointees who vary over time. The Joint Chiefs of Staff, consisting of a chairman and the military commanders of the Army, Navy, and Air Force, was also established in 1947. Its strength lies in its wide constituency, including veterans, industrialists, portions of the press, and Congress. Yet another outgrowth of the same period was the creation of the CIA as an independent organization reporting to the NSC. Although it is supposed to be a coordinating and interpreting device for intelligence work, it has been criticized for becoming an independent force. In 1974 Congress moved to apply checks on the CIA's covert operations, after revelations of its clandestine involvement in the fall of Salvator Allende's regime in Chile in 1973.

The Department of State

The State Department's job is to amass information, analyze it, recommend policy, and carry out day-to-day operations in the field. In 1938, it had 5,692 employees. It now has more than 40,000. Most of the jobs, both abroad and in Washington, are filled by career foreign service officers who tend to develop rather narrow technical and geographic specialities. The Department carves the world into five regions: Europe, East Asia and the Pacific, Africa, Latin America, and Near East and South Asia. An assistant secretary is in charge of each region and his operations are further divided into individual "desks," generally one per country. Hilsman (1967) notes that

> each of the five regional assistant secretaries is important precisely because he is the President's appointee, and as such is the junction at which all strands of policy—political, military, economic, and diplomatic—first come together. His is the *first* level in government that can begin to apply these broad political considerations to policy and the management of foreign affairs [p. 34].

The Department of State, while one of the smallest executive departments, has responsibilities which are worldwide. The daily communications traffic between the Department and its hundreds of overseas posts stream back and forth without end. As much as the Department of State has been criticized, it must be remembered that it has the difficult task of carrying out a great deal of the functions so necessary to the foreign policy-making process—scanning, coding, transmission, storage and recall, and feedback. Although the Department of State does the lion's share of the tedious and endless daily operations, it receives little glory.

Congress

Although Congress as a whole is relatively weak in the foreign policy field, individual members and certain committees may have considerable influence. But the obstacles to congressional initiative are several. Foreign policy work is detail work, so by its nature it is to a large extent beyond congressional control. Members do not have the information they need to compete with the President in exercising initiative, and there are not very many foreign policy interest groups which find it advantageous to work with Congress. So there are fewer occasions when Congress is stimulated to disagree with the President.

Although the paramount position of the President in foreign affairs is now a well-established maxim, the lack of congressional initiative partly reflects the temper of the times. Within a consensual atmosphere, presidential policies were likely to meet little resistance. Since Vietnam the consensus on foreign policy has been undermined, and the willingness of Congress to be more critical and assertive has increased. The repeal of the Gulf of Tonkin resolution, the questioning of defense budgets, and the reexamination of the wisdom of stationing 2 million troops in Europe are all indicators of this new attitude. Historically, many of the major foreign policy decisions have been executive decisions: the wartime agreements at Tehran, Yalta and Potsdam, the Korean war, the 1965 Dominican intervention, and Vietnam. Congress, if it is to participate more fully in the making of policy, cannot afford to allow its role to be merely that of conducting

Yalta Conference, 1945:
For Congress, a minor
role. *(Wide World Photos.)*

consultations or ratifying resolutions after the fact. Although there is a need at times for swift executive action, the necessity for immediate presidential action may have been exaggerated. The Senate, hoping to bring about a new balance between the executive and the legislature, passed the National Commitments resolution in 1969. By a vote of 70 to 16, it was resolved by the Senate that any national commitment involving either the use or potential use of troops would be valid only if approved by Congress through treaty, statute, or concurrent resolution.

Traditionally, Congress has provided for foreign affairs an important platform for public debate. In the past this function has declined. The near unanimity of the Gulf of Tonkin resolution on August 7, 1964, is an example. Reaction to the events of the second Nixon administration may, however, serve to effect a long-term restoration of the tradition of Congressional debate over foreign affairs. A revived Congress, while it may not be able to prevent drastic and costly mistakes, can take steps to improve the functioning of the foreign policy process. Such improvement could increase its investigatory role, serving to keep a critical eye on the whole range of the policy process, including the parts played by the Pentagon, CIA, and other government agencies.

General Stilwell in
China: From the field, a
voice in foreign policy.
(Wide World Photos.)

The Military

Since World War II, the military has exerted a significant influence on the making of American foreign policy. During and immediately following the war it was evident that military leaders had a voice in determining foreign policy. Field commanders such as General MacArthur, General Joseph Stilwell, and General Albert Wedemeyer acted as the ranking American representatives in their dealings with the British Dominions, the Republic of China, and the Chinese Communists. During the 1950s and 1960s American military leaders participating in the NATO command were very successful in formulating foreign policy issues and in championing the choice of specific policies. A good indicator of the military's influence has been the aid funds earmarked for military purposes. During the period between 1950 and 1968 aid funds in the form of military assistance constituted almost half the total foreign assistance program (Yarmolinsky, 1971, p. 114).

Military influence is the result of two key factors. On matters of strategic interest it is the military that has the upper hand in determining what foreign policy issues will be heard in Washington. Additionally, the military's unique status in the foreign policy process ensures that its voice is heard. Morton Halperin (1972) points out this special relationship by noting that "the military . . . has a virtual monopoly on providing information to the President about the readiness and capabilities of U.S. or even allied forces [p. 310]." The military's role in the preparation of national intelligence reports guarantees its influence on the options which come before the President will be felt.

In general, our presidents have not been content with their relations with the military. President Johnson, becoming increasingly weary of

Percent of Foreign Assistance Program 1950–1969 Represented by Military Assistance, in Millions of Dollars (**Yarmolinsky**, 1971, p. 114.)

FISCAL YEAR	TOTAL FOREIGN ASSISTANCE PROGRAM	ECONOMIC ASSISTANCE	MILITARY ASSISTANCE	% OF PROGRAM FOR MILITARY ASSISTANCE
1950	$ 5,042.4	$ 3,728.4	$ 1,314.0	26.1
1951	7,485.0	2,262.5	5,222.5	69.8
1952	7,284.4	1,540.4	5,744.0	78.9
1953	6,001.9	1,782.1	4,219.8	70.3
1954	4,531.5	1,301.5	3,230.0	71.3
1955	2,781.5	1,588.8	1,192.7	42.9
1956	2,703.3	1,681.1	1,022.2	37.8
1957	3,766.6	1,749.1	2,017.5	53.6
1958	2,768.9	1,428.9	1,340.0	48.4
1959	3,448.1	1,933.1	1,515.0	43.9
1960	3,225.8	1,925.8	1,300.0	40.3
1961	4,431.4	2,631.4	1,800.0	40.6
1962	3,914.6	2,314.6	1,600.0	40.9
1963	3,928.9	2,603.9	1,325.0	33.7
1964	3,000.0	2,000.0	1,000.0	33.3
1965	3,325.0	2,195.0	1,055.0	31.8
1966	3,933.0	2,463.0	1,545.0	39.5
1967	2,935.5	2,143.5	792.0	26.8
1968	2,295.6	1,895.6	400.0	17.4
1969	1,974.1	1,599.1	375.0	19.1
Total	$78,777.5	$40,767.8	$38,009.7	Avg. 48.6

military advice, once remarked that "the generals know only two words—spend and bomb [Yarmolinsky, 1971, p. 31]." The reaction by presidents has been to seek alternative sources of information and advice, including civilian advisors, the Secretary of State, Secretary of Defense, and scientists. President Nixon used the strategy of reorganization. His appointment of the President's Blue Ribbon Panel on Defense Reorganization, the Fitzhugh Panel, reflected his desire to widen his sources of information and advice.

Recently the military establishment has been widely criticized, both by Congress and by private citizens. Yet most of the criticism might be misdirected. Cost overruns, influence peddling, and the inefficiencies of poor policies are relatively minor compared to the task of finding a way to attain the appropriate contribution the Pentagon should be making to the development of foreign policy. In the past the Pentagon's excessive influence was due to its huge political weight. Providing counterweights to the Pentagon will ultimately involve drawing new arrangements of institutional and interagency relationships.

THE FOREIGN POLICYMAKERS

The National Security Establishment

When John F. Kennedy was President-elect and organizing his foreign policy staff, he turned for advice to Robert Lovett, a member of the foreign policy establishment which David Halberstam (1972) has described as the guiding force behind postwar developments:

> They knew one another, were linked to one another, and they guided America's national security in those years, men like James Forrestal, Douglas Dillon, and Allen Dulles. . . . They were men linked more to one another, their schools, their own social class and their own concerns than they were linked to the country [p. 6].

They propounded the global view, the need for toughness, the belief in their own efficacy. Barnet (1972) holds that the definition of the foreign policy elite can be extended to include some four hundred persons at first- and second-level posts who rotate in and out of government and from one policy job to another. Like Halberstam, he is impressed by their uniformity:

> The temporary civilian managers who come to Washington to run America's wars and preparations for wars, the national security managers, were so like one another in occupation, religion, and social status that, apart from a few Washington lawyers, Texans, and mavericks, it was possible to locate the offices of all of them within 15 city blocks in New York, Boston, and Detroit. Most of their biographies in Who's Who read like minor variations on a single

theme—wealthy parents, Ivy-league education, leading law firm or bank (or entrepreneur in a war industry), introduction to government in World War II [pp. 48–49].

These are the men who defined the problems, proposed the solutions, and ensured access for businessmen, lawyers, bankers, and industrialists to the policy-making circles. Their association outside of public life is not entirely informal. A private organization, the Council on Foreign Relations (CFR), headquartered in New York, keeps them in touch with one another. Its membership, reports Laurence I. Radway (1969), "constitutes a significant fraction of any national listing of Americans whose opinions on foreign affairs carry great weight [p. 126]." It publishes a quarterly journal, *Foreign Affairs*, which serves as a useful record of what the foreign policy establishment is thinking.

William Domhoff (1969), in a study of the CFR, has delineated the influence of corporations on the composition and functioning of the Council. Besides the significant funding by corporations, its membership is also drawn from corporate leaders. Domhoff also notes that of the 509 committee members participating in the Council's nationwide-sponsored Committee on Foreign Relations, some 41 percent were either bankers or corporate executives, with an additional 21 percent being lawyers, half of whom were also corporate directors. Although these data are not definitive, they do indicate a strong relationship between the top levels of foreign policy leadership and the highest circles of the business world.

Richard Barnet (1971), who labels the foreign policy elite the "National Security Managers," argues that these are the men whose role has been to interpret the national interest. He contends that "it is their collective picture of the outside world which has formed the basis for official judgments of the national interest." As the National Security Managers they "defined the threats to the national interest, made the commitments that were supposed to meet the threats, and, in most cases, have been the sole judges of their own performances [p. 258]."

The Munitions Makers

Those who profit from war and preparation for war through the manufacture and sale of military equipment are so traditionally suspect that to cite their influence in urging a belligerent foreign policy is almost a cliche. Behind the $80 billion defense budgets have been businessmen, industrialists, their lawyers, and others who have a personal, psychological, and economic stake in belligerence. Associated with them are scientists, educational institutions, and research organizations who develop their own shares in these interests. Between 1967 and 1969, the National Science Foundation reported that 85 percent of the government's expenditures on research and development was spent on "national security"—including

Prime Military Contract Awards 1960–1967 to U.S. Companies   (Pursell, 1972, p. 322.)

FISCAL YEAR	1961	1962	1963	1964	1965	1966	1967	7-YEAR TOTAL	PERCENT OF TOTAL SALES
1. Lockheed Aircraft	1,175	1,419	1,517	1,455	1,715	1,531	1,807	10,619	88
2. General Dynamics	1,460	1,197	1,033	987	1,179	1,136	1,832	8,824	67
3. McDonnell Douglas	527	779	863	1,360	1,026	1,001	2,125	7,681	75
4. Boeing Co.	920	1,133	1,365	1,356	583	914	912	7,183	54
5. General Electric	875	976	1,021	893	824	1,187	1,290	7,066	19
6. No. American-Rockwell	1,197	1,032	1,062	1,019	746	520	689	6,265	57
7. United Aircraft	625	663	530	625	632	1,139	1,097	5,311	57
8. American Tel. & Tel	551	468	579	636	588	672	673	4,167	9
9. Martin-Marietta	692	803	767	476	316	338	290	3,682	62
10. Sperry-Rand	408	466	446	374	318	427	484	2,923	35
11. General Motors	282	449	444	256	254	508	625	2,818	2
12. Grumman Aircraft	238	304	390	396	353	323	488	2,492	67
13. General Tire	290	366	425	364	302	327	273	2,347	37
14. Raytheon	305	407	295	253	293	368	403	2,324	55
15. AVCO	251	323	253	279	234	506	449	2,295	75
16. Hughes	331	234	312	289	278	337	419	2,200	u
17. Westinghouse Electric	308	246	323	237	261	349	453	2,177	13
18. Ford (Philco)	200	269	228	211	312	440	404	2,064	3
19. RCA	392	340	329	234	214	242	268	2,019	16
20. Bendix	269	286	290	257	235	282	296	1,915	42
21. Textron	66	117	151	216	196	555	497	1,798	36
22. Ling-Temco-Vought	47	133	206	247	265	311	535	1,744	70
23. Internat. Tel. & Tel.	202	244	266	256	207	220	255	1,650	19
24. I.B.M.	330	155	203	332	186	182	195	1,583	7
25. Raymond International	46	61	84	196	71	548	462	1,568	u
26. Newport News Shipbuilding	290	185	221	400	185	51	188	1,520	90+
27. Northrop	156	152	223	165	256	276	306	1,434	61
28. Thiokol	210	178	239	254	136	111	173	1,301	96
29. Std. Oil of N.J.	168	180	155	161	164	214	235	1,277	2
30. Kaiser Industries	–	87	49	152	219	441	306	1,255	45
31. Honeywell	86	127	170	107	82	251	306	1,129	24
32. General Tel.	61	116	162	229	232	196	138	1,124	25
33. Collins Radio	94	150	144	129	141	245	202	1,105	65
34. Chrysler	158	181	186	170	81	150	165	1,091	4
35. Litton	–	88	198	210	190	219	180	1,085	25
36. Pan Am. World Air.	127	147	155	164	158	170	115	1,046	44
37. F.M.C.	88	160	199	141	124	163	170	1,045	21
38. Hercules	117	182	183	137	101	120	195	1,035	31

u-unavailable.

defense, space, and nuclear programs. Think tanks supported by the Pentagon have achieved a key role in the shaping of U.S. foreign and military policy through their work on weapons systems, tactics, and technology advances.

The increasingly complex technical aspects of the cold war created, in the words of Kenneth M. Dolbeare and Murray J. Edelman (1971), a "link of mutual dependency and shared interest between particular types of industries," especially electronics, aviation, nuclear energy, and rocket propulsion. There has developed a sizable portion of the economy whose concern is exclusively military and which is not now and never has been involved in "production for civilian needs or competitive consumer sales [p. 88]." Insulated from the rigors of competition, they tend to make a lot of money.

Although these industries have their detractors and are not unassailable, they have been on the whole successful in maintaining their positions in recent years through a network of mutual supports. The pattern is not unfamiliar: part of the defense cost is spent on public relations activity to maintain public support for military endeavor; certain members of Congress prosper in a symbiotic relationship with the military; and the industrial suppliers look out for the interests of, and are protected by, both.

The term "military-industrial complex" has been used in many ways, often misleading and oversimplified. The phrase itself is merely descriptive, depicting a set of commonly shared interests between the military and some major corporations. Almost all writers on the subject focus on one striking feature: the interchange between the military and their corporate suppliers. Critics of the term like to point out that the tracing of the exercise of power to the motivation of private interests, usually defined in economic terms, is problematic. Whether their criticisms are valid or not, it does not nullify the effects of their actions. Even if the munitions makers truly acted in accord with what they believed to be the national interest, the interchange of personnel did build into the operations of the foreign policy-making machinery a commitment to military spending and an escalating arms race.

Multinational Corporations

Multinational corporations provide an interesting example of the connection between the national security management and the munitions makers. Anthony Sampson (1973), in his book on the history of ITT, has attempted to show how a multinational corporation has become an independent force in the making of foreign policy. His study, entitled *The Sovereign State*, describes how ITT in its negotiations with foreign countries acted as if it were a separate state. Sampson focused in particular on ITT's independence of governments, its self-contained organization, and its conducting of private diplomacy and communications.

A more analytic examination of multinational corporations by Dennis

M. Ray (1972) has identified three avenues of influence that corporations may use: "(1) their capacity to take independent action in the international arena through foreign investment; (2) their direct and indirect influence on foreign policy decision-making; and (3) their capacity to shape public opinion in such a way as to legitimize government action in favor of business interests abroad [p. 83]." These avenues are depicted in Figure 17-1. Although special economic interests may or may not represent the true national interests, corporate influence has undoubtedly been a factor in defining what the national interest has come to mean.

There are many points of access for corporate influence in the foreign policy-making process, but the most direct and perhaps most effective is the pattern of recruitment of national security officials. The Council on Foreign Relations, as discussed earlier, has, in the words of Joseph Kraft (1958), served as a "school of statesmen" for young corporate executives. Other studies show the same pattern of recruitment. Barnet (1971), in his study of top-level officials between 1940 and 1967, noted that out of ninety-one of the very top positions—the director of the CIA, the chairman of the AEC, the secretaries and undersecretaries of the Defense and State Departments, and the secretaries of the three services—seventy came from major corporations and investment concerns. Gabriel Kolko (1969), examining 234 top foreign policy officials, discovered that "men who came from big business, investment and law held 59.6 percent of the posts [p. 19]." Kolko then concludes that "at every level of the administration of the American state, domestically and internationally, business serves as the fount of

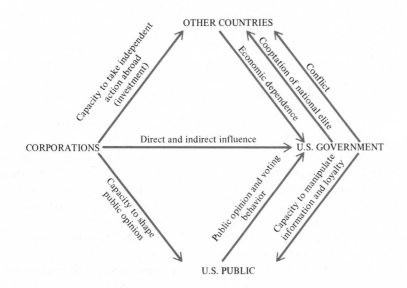

Figure 17-1 The Influence of National and Multinational Corporations on American Foreign Relations (Ray, 1972, p. 83)

critical assumptions or goals and strategically placed personnel [p. 26]."
What is surprising is not the fact that national goals may be equated by some
with business goals, but the extent of business influence in creating the
general consensus from which the foreign and security policies are drawn.

A Case of Crisis: The Cuban Missiles

John Scali, later U.S. ambassador to the UN, was the State Department
correspondent for ABC during the Cuban missile crisis. On October 26,
1962, in the midst of the crisis, he was contacted on the telephone by
Aleksander Fomin, a senior Soviet official. Scali had been contacted on that
fateful Friday to relay an important message to high-level friends in the
State Department. The informal exchanges between these two men concerned new Soviet initiatives aimed at solving the crisis. Scali, after
reporting the Soviet's willingness to negotiate, returned to the State
Department. That evening, Dean Rusk, the Secretary of State, related to
Scali the significance of his information: "John, you have served your
country well. Remember when you report this—that, eyeball to eyeball,
they blinked first [Hilsman, 1967, p. 219]." For thirteen days in October of
1962 the United States and the Soviet Union faced each other in the world's
first nuclear crisis. They were thirteen days of tension and waiting, in which
two powers, each possessing weapons of mass destruction, sought to
outmaneuver the other.

In retrospect, the Cuban missile crisis provides a good example of how
the men, machinery, and decision-making process of American foreign
policy operates. The flaws as well as the strengths of both men and their
institutions became the object of public debate following that eventful
October.

Measuring 59.6 feet in length and 5.4 feet in diameter, the first Soviet
missiles reached Cuba in September. But it was not until October 14 that
American intelligence first learned that nuclear missiles existed in Cuba.
Ironically, on that Sunday, at the same time a U-2 was photographing the
presence of offensive missiles in Cuba, Presidential Assistant McGeorge
Bundy was appearing before ABC's "Issues and Answers" denying that
any nuclear missiles were housed on Cuban soil.

On September 19, the United States Intelligence Board released its
now notorious "September estimate." In this report, it was stated that the
emplacement of Soviet offensive missiles was highly unlikely. With the
discovery of missiles in October, the U.S. government was shocked and
surprised. Today these events only help to show how incredibly complex
the job of intelligence is. The process of reviewing and evaluating endless
files of reports and information presents only one aspect of the problem.
The coordination of numerous individuals and agencies provides another
obstacle to the smooth operation of the intelligence community. At the
time of the crisis the United States had four major sources of information:

(1) shipping intelligence, (2) refugee reports, (3) intelligence agents within Cuba, and (4) U-2 overflights. Intelligence reports had to be sorted, classified, and evaluated. These reports also had to be checked and documented. All this involved time pressures as well. Agent reports took ten days between the time something was noticed in Cuba and the time the information arrived in Washington. U-2 flights were subject to weather conditions as well as strategic considerations. The successful U-2 flight of October 14 had been delayed on account of an organizational dispute between the CIA and the Defense Department. In the vagueness of jurisdiction, each agency had claimed responsibility.

The instruments of information gathering, evaluation, and transmission contained weaknesses, but in the end the intelligence community had fulfilled its functions. The missiles had been discovered before they were made operational. The work done by the intelligence community allowed the government to assess the situation, arrive at a policy, and decide on appropriate actions. As Sen. Hubert H. Humphrey said, we caught the Soviets "with their rockets down and their missile showing [Hilsman, 1967, p. 191]."

On the morning of October 15, Bundy briefed President Kennedy, still dressed in his bathrobe and slippers. At 11:45 the Executive Committee of the National Security Council met in the west wing of the White House. During that first meeting of the ExCom most of the major issues that the government had to resolve were discussed. Roger Hilsman (1967), in his account of the Cuban missile crisis, identifies four issues that were taken up by the ExCom. First, it was necessary to understand the motivations and objectives behind the Soviet's decision. Next, it was important to estimate what the Soviet's move would mean in terms of our national security interests. Third, in light of a possible new strategic shift of Soviet nuclear strength, the objective of what American policy would be had to be discussed in full. Finally, the actual mechanics of how any objective was to be accomplished were debated. At the end of the meeting four alternative courses of action were formulated: (1) do nothing, (2) pursue political and diplomatic action, (3) employ some kind of military move, and (4) set up a naval blockade. Throughout the week these issues and alternatives were examined and questioned. In each case it was important to investigate all the implications of any possible move. All the participants in the foreign policy-making process were tapped for their advice and recommendations.

The question of what course of action to take involved long hours of conflicting debate. The Joint Chiefs of Staff had been opposed to a blockade, preferring instead a more aggressive course of action. Within ExCom meetings the possibility of a "surgical air strike," that is, a quick air operation knocking out the missile installations in a single blow, received much attention. Military capabilities were subjected to close examination, as well as the consequences of any military action. In the end the President decided against such a "surgical operation." In the midst of the discussion it was Robert F. Kennedy, the Attorney General, who provided the persuasive argument against a military attack. Using moral arguments from the past, he reminded the ExCom of the reaction to Pearl Harbor: "For the United States to attack a small country without warning would irreparably hurt our reputation in the world—and our own conscience [Hilsman, 1967, p. 203]."

President Kennedy, desiring to gain control of events, knew the value of managing each move, allowing the Soviets time to review the consequences of their actions as well. But the President was also subject to outside influences. There were considerable political pressures to be kept in mind. Various government officials, especially Senators Keating and Goldwater, had criticized the administration's attitude toward Cuba as a "do-nothing" policy. The pressure to take strong actions could not be taken lightly. The Cuban missile crisis was something new in international politics. Both sides realized that they would be setting precedents. Similarly, each realized that in a nuclear confrontation neither side could afford reckless action. This attitude was felt throughout the government. In the State Department briefing room this point was conveyed by a scribbled sign which someone had posted— "In a Nuclear Age nations must make war as porcupines make love—carefully [Hilsman, 1967, p. 215]." Because of the care that was taken, the Soviets had the opportunity to back down, and they did. "If anybody is around to write this," President Kennedy told his brother, Robert Kennedy (1959), "they are going to understand that we made every effort to find peace and every effort to give our adversary room to move [p. 127]."

EUROPE

A President's Journey

In February of 1969, a month after his first inauguration, President Nixon made a journey to Europe, visiting Brussels, London, Paris, Bonn, Berlin, and Rome. On February 18, 1970, he sent to Congress a 40,000-word document entitled "United States Foreign Policy for the 1970s: A New Strategy for Peace." It was the first annual report on foreign policy by the administration, and its purpose was to set forth the objectives for the new decade. The first section on regional policies was devoted to Western Europe. It covered three issues: a genuine partnership should be created with less domination by the United States; American security commitments should be maintained; and the United States would be ready to negotiate with the Soviet Union and Eastern Europe to ease tensions.

This priority position for Europe was not something new in U.S. foreign policy, but rather a new commitment to one of its oldest concerns. Secretary of State William P. Rogers (1972) has said, "In each of the permanent interests of United States foreign policy—security, economic

well-being, peace—Europe continues to play a central role [p. 21]."
McGeorge Bundy (1970), a long-time career expert in foreign policy, sees
four enduring links with Europe: the gradual search for and emergence of
detente—the urge to get along, in other words; the continuous presence of
American military forces; the gradual withdrawal of Europe from involvement in the geopolitical conflicts of other continents; and the gradual
interpenetration of the economies of the Atlantic world.

World War II was the event that drew America out of its long isolation
into a position of power. Hans Morgenthau (1969) cites three ways in which
the United States has been connected to Europe:

> Throughout its history, the United States has consistently pursued three
> interconnected interests with regard to Europe: not to get involved in the
> conflicts of European powers; to prevent European powers from interfering in
> the affairs of the Western Hemisphere; and to maintain or, if need be, to
> restore the balance of power in Europe [p. 157].

Morgenthau contends that the need to foster a balance of power in
Europe required an active foreign policy beyond the limits of the Western
Hemisphere. World War II was the event that capped that objective.
Europe, since the War, has become a key link in U.S. foreign policy. It has
been a central site of the cold war, and it has defined critical areas of conflict
faced by the United States. U.S. policies, all marked by the necessity of
reformulating the postwar arrangements, have been directed at three goals:
rebuilding Europe, integrating it politically and economically, and giving it
a secure military capacity.

These goals were developed in the context of the policy of contain-
ment and alliance building that was forged in the immediate postwar period.
Concretely, American efforts can be seen in the Marshall Plan, the Brussels
Treaty, the Vandenburg resolution, and NATO. The efforts to promote
European unity bore fruit in the European Recovery Program, the North
Atlantic Alliance, and after many frustrations, the emergence of the
Common Market. But some basic goals remain unrealized, and present
policy represents the continuing effort to achieve those goals.

President Nixon declared 1973 to be the year of Europe. It was to be a
year in which the United States renewed its commitments to its closest
allies. During 1972 the United States and its Western allies concluded a
number of significant agreements, including SALT, the Quadripartite
Declaration on Germany, and various bilateral understandings. In the
hopes of easing East-West tensions two major sets of negotiations were
begun in 1973—talks on mutual and balanced force reductions and a
conference on security and cooperation in Europe.

Yet underlying the new American interest in trans-Atlantic unity,
there remained a veiled sense of undiscovered conflicts of interest existing
on each side of the Atlantic. President Nixon in a report submitted to

Congress in May of 1973 even admitted that our alliance was not on as solid ground as we had always supposed. As President Nixon (1973) said, "We assumed, perhaps too uncritically, that our basic interests would be assured by our long history of cooperation, by our common cultures and our political similarities [p. 295]." Now, American foreign policy leaders began emphasizing themes of reciprocity. For instance, while the United States reaffirmed that it would not withdraw its forces from Europe unilaterally, it also reiterated that all its allies would have to contribute to the common defense effort. Historically, the assumption of an identity of interests between the United States and Europe was an axiom of American foreign policy. This is no longer true. Fear of the Soviet Union created the Atlantic Alliance over a generation ago. Today the consensus which supported the Atlantic security arrangements of the past has been shattered. This situation brings out a seldom-mentioned feature of the nature of foreign policy. In order to pursue a successful foreign policy, a nation must be able to build a working consensus with the countries with which it hopes to deal. A conception of partnership cannot work unless it can gain widespread support, bridging international boundaries.

Attitudes toward Europe

The postwar generation of policymakers was influenced by certain American attitudes. Stanley Hoffman (1968) points out one factor which is typically American:

> Another important effect of the various layers of American attitudes toward Europe is that they have left behind a legacy of impatience—in fact, of varieties of impatience. They can perhaps be summarized, unfair as it may sound, as impatience with, and sometimes ignorance of, the intricacy of European history [p. 98].

One form of impatience distinguished by Hoffman is the "impatience with various political forms associated with Europe's historical experience." In particular, the United States has misunderstood the European experience of balance-of-power factors and nationalism. Another form of impatience reflects a more serious flaw. It shows itself, says Hoffman (1968), "in the tendency to look at Europe as a whole—to see in it a basket of eels, perhaps, but one basket all the same [p. 103]." This impatience has produced two troublesome American attitudes. One is the dismay and frustration over European nationalism. The other is the belief that we can apply the recipes of past American history to the European problems of today, as exemplified by our pressing for a commercial market and a federal political structure. If the United States were omnipotent, those solutions might not be overly simple. In the real world, the limits on U.S. policy toward Europe arise from in its blindness to the power of the political and social forces of individual countries.

American insensitivity to the autonomy of European nations has been the result of clouded perceptions on the part of its policy leaders. Consequently the policies reflect misconceptions of European as well as our own interests. To a European, the idea of a politically integrated Europe in close partnership with the United States "is too much like sharing a bath with a genial elephant [Barbard Ward, in Kermit Gordon, 1969, p. 344]."

THE THIRD WORLD

A New Stage

Before World War II, the U.S. concern with Asia, Africa, and Latin America was marginal, but postwar developments changed all of that. The new attitude was a response to the Third World's setting as the stage for numerous international crises—Korea, Suez, the Congo, Dominican Republic, Rhodesia, and Vietnam. The Third World became the principal arena for new adventures in the cold war.

Frantz Fanon (1968), the Algerian writer, labelled the newly emerging nations with the French phrase, *le Tiers Monde*—the Third World. His terminology is by now familiar and widely used, but the term is rather broad and includes a divergent range of nations with varying characteristics. Irving Louis Horowitz (1966) has identified a common set of traits:

> First it tends to be independent of both power centers, the United States-NATO complex and the Soviet Warsaw-Pact group. Second, the bulk of the Third World was in a colonial condition until World War Two. Third, it draws its technology from the First World while drawing its ideology from the Second World. Thus, the Third World is non-America, ex-colonial, and thoroughly dedicated to becoming industrialized [p. 17].

Between World War II and 1968, sixty-six new states were born. They constitute about two-thirds of the total number of Third World countries. Together, those sixty-six new states cover about one-fourth of the surface of the world and contain about 40 percent of its population. Although these new nations, as well as the rest of the Third World, display a wide range of political structures, they share a common problem—the process of nation building. They face such problems as creating a workable political structure, ways of choosing their leaders, creating an efficient administration, and the protection of the rights of their citizens. One trouble with these evolving conditions is that they foster political instability, especially when contrasted to the rigid control of prior colonial systems. The crises and problems of the Third World countries invite intervention by the superpowers in competition for their loyalties in international affairs.

These conditions are aggravated by relative and absolute poverty. "Despite their many geographical, political, and cultural differences," says Willard Thorp (1971), "what the less-developed countries have in common, whether recently independent or not, is that they are poor [p. 33]." The contrast between the rich nations of the world and the poor has now become a significant issue in international relations. The contrast is vividly illustrated in Table 17-1.

Table 17-1 Per Capita Income of Developed and Less Developed Countries, 1968

	POPULATION MID-1968 (MILLIONS)	GNP (IN BILLIONS OF DOLLARS)	PER CAPITA GNP, IN DOLLARS
Developed Countries	648	1,699	2,622
Less Developed Countries	1,695	342	202

The communist countries, including Cuba and Yugoslavia, are omitted.
Source: AID, *Reports Control No. 137*. Washington, March 27, 1970.

For Third World countries, Table 17-1 confirms "the omnipresence of illiteracy and ignorance, the widespread incidence of disease, the lack of decent housing, and the barest minimum of consumer goods which will permit human survival [Thorp, 1971, p. 34]." These conditions are often aggravated by the desire of the less developed countries to modernize. Instability results from population growth, shift of the population to cities, rising unemployment, and the transition from an agricultural to an industrial society. Moreover, all this is likely to take place against the background of a low potential for economic production, the result of a lack of natural resources or the lack of a market in which to sell goods or both.

How They See It

As a modern, affluent society, the United States presents itself as a possible model for development, but the rude fit of that model is not always appreciated. Although having a tradition of anticolonialism and noninvolvement in the internal affairs of other nations, postwar U.S. globalism—both in terms of foreign policy and the influence of the military and business establishments—has changed that image. Horowitz (1966) observes that "Third World identification with the origins of the American Revolution contrasts markedly with its rejection of the present conduct of American nationalism [p. 117]." Third World countries also tend to be irritated by the U.S. stance of equating neutralism with betrayal—the old if-you're-not-with-us-you're-against-us attitude. To Third Worlders, nonalignment has seemed the proper position.

Then there is the economic problem. The Third World leaders figure, not without some reason, that U.S. dealings with them are tainted by a preoccupation with its own economic self-interest. "Although Third World industries are nominally free," says Horowitz (1966), "American business firms often control the major branches of production and technology, which means they can influence the political structure and the internal social life of each nation [p. 120]." And, although developments beginning in 1973 threatened to change this pattern, the U.S. has dominated the international money market, gaining the power to manipulate world prices and lower the prices received by Third World countries for their products. Another form of U.S. economic power which is often perceived by less developed countries as being used against their interests is its control of a significant share of the world's transportation and communications facilities. These can be used as political weapons. All this tends to make the Third Worlders suspicious. As Horowitz (1966) puts it, "Until the United States puts its own interests ahead of the protection of private American business overseas, the Third World will remain suspicious that the first New Nation seeks to establish a claim to being the only New Nation [p. 125]."

One aggravating factor is a variation of the old sample-of-one problem. We cannot understand why everyone does not think and act like us. United States policy toward the Third World has attempted to export American economic theory and strategies. When we negotiate grants and loans, we try to use them to exercise some control over the recipient country. Such strings may specify, for example, that the country must widen the scope of public participation in its government. As admirable as these democratic and Western ideals may seem to be, sociocultural and political values make awkward exports. And U.S. domestic problems are severe and visible enough (racism, poverty, and corruption, for example) to have a cooling effect on whatever desire there might be to emulate the U.S. model.

Although the United States has the power and capabilities to conduct policies in the interest of the Third World—if it so desired and was willing to accept the consequences—it remains hindered by its own image. U.S. relations with the Third World have suffered from one crucial failure. The foreign policy bureaucracy has not been able to judge the political and cultural elements at work which shape Third World reactions and responses to U.S. policy. The information gathered on the Third World did not accurately reflect its attitudes toward the United States.

Patronizing the Third World

The essence of postwar U.S. policy toward the Third World was foreign aid. Between 1948 and 1967, the total in loans and grants authorized to be administered by the Agency for International Development and its predecessors was $44.8 million. Before World War II, American assistance to less developed countries was almost entirely a private matter. That changed in 1948 with the European Recovery Program, better known as the Marshall Plan. When President Truman outlined its initial stages in his inaugural address, he mentioned Point Four, the program of assistance to less developed nations of the world. Congress formalized the Point Four approach in 1950 with the Act of International Development. However, the stress began to shift from economic assistance to military aid with the establishment of the North Atlantic Treaty Organization and the Korean war. The Truman-Acheson policy of containment pushed foreign aid appropriations, dominated by military assistance, to $7.5 billion in fiscal 1951. Then as Europe got moving under its own power, after the Korean Armistice, the completion of NATO, the death of Stalin, and a gradual reduction in East-West tensions, the foreign aid program diminished. It took a brief upward turn in the Kennedy administration. President Kennedy, declaring the 1960s to be the decade of development, promoted the Foreign Assistance Act of 1961 to create the Agency for International Development. He established the Peace Corps, instituted the Alliance for Progress to aid Latin America, and obtained increased funding for the Food for Peace Program (Public Law 480), but the resurgence was temporary. In the beginning, foreign aid was sold to the public as a way of building allies and influencing friends. By the 1960s it was hard to find anybody who was noticeably friendlier as a result of that aid. Consequently, over the years foreign aid became a smaller share of the Gross National Product, declining from 2 percent at its peak to less than one-third of a percent in 1974.

Meanwhile, the futility of containment was becoming apparent, and less need was seen for military aid. An unforeseen complication was recognized. Modernization produced political upheaval, and by promoting economic development, the United States was helping to generate disorder. The resulting distress may have been somewhat akin to Southern nostalgia for the old plantation, but it was nonetheless a product of prior policies.

What Next?

A variety of motives has been advanced for foreign aid, including charity, commercial and strategic interests, and patronizing self-interests. Even the altruistic motives, of course, have some measure of self-interest behind them.

United States aid has had varied objectives: a humanitarian interest in helping the less developed, promoting world order, attempting to build greater respect for U.S. principles and purposes, and expanding world growth and trade. What complicates all this is that there is often a conflict between long-range goals and short-range interests. In one of the most intense conflicts of all, we often face a choice between fostering long-term democratic ideals and short-term stability within countries where we do business. The question of whether to support a Latin American dictatorship is a good example of this. Not surprisingly, a confusion of policy goals can result from these unavoidable problems, and in the internal bargaining and compromising process, we often emerge with a patchwork of inconsistent policies toward the Third World. To that extent, our Third World policy has been short-sighted. It is not clear that it has been an avoidable failure. It is not even clear that things will change very much. One rather ominous possibility, however, is seen by C. Fred Bergsten (1973); that America could become increasingly vulnerable to the manipulations of the increasingly sophisticated Third World powers. They might learn such old-fashioned tricks as price gouging by manipulating the supply of natural resources which we need and they control. The oil situation in the Middle East may be only the prototype of this kind of leverage. They might decide to limit or even confiscate American investments within their boundaries. They might welsh on the money loaned to them. How they behave toward us will depend a lot on their attitudes and, given our past policies, the prospect is bleak.

EMERGING POWERS

A World of Change

The problem of cultural lag is always with us. The world changes faster than the policies we make to cope with it. Henry Kissinger (1968) has cited three main currents of change. The number of participants in the international order has increased to the point where foreign policy must now be global. Not too long ago, different segments of the world could act in relative isolation; what happened in Asia did not make much difference in Europe. Secondly, the technical capacity of one nation to affect another has changed. Technology has made the world, in effect, smaller and more crowded. The probability of getting elbowed in the ribs is, through no one's fault, much greater now. Finally, says Kissinger (1968), the scope of the purposes of the participants in international change has necessarily expanded:

> Whenever the participants of the international system change, a period of profound dislocation is inevitable. They can change because new states enter the political system or because there is a change in values as to what constitutes legitimate rule, or finally, because of the reduction in influence of some of the traditional units. In our period, all of these factors have combined. . . . Our age has yet to find a structure which matches the responsibilities of the new nations to their aspirations [p. 586].

Kissinger also emphasizes the consequences of the end of what he calls "military bipolarity," that is, domination of the world by two great superpowers. This situation of two giants facing off causes rigidity and anxiety. Any gain by one is seen as a loss by the other. Opportunities for mutual benefit tend to be overlooked. Now that we are approaching a situation where there will be a multiplicity of major powers, conditions will become more flexible, but they could also get more complicated and harder to manage. What is needed, in Kissinger's view (1968), is a clearer philosophy about our national interests, taking into account ''the wide-spread interest in stability and peaceful change [p. 611].'' Perhaps nothing illustrates his points as well as the Vietnam war. The policy assumptions that led to it were based on a global, bipolar view of the world that was out of date. In one sense, it marked the end of the cold war—at least its competitive and aggressive period. And it has forced the United States to seek new directions in foreign policy. It was a tragic way to gain that awareness, but it may have contained some lessons. Although U.S. military participation in the conflict in Vietnam has ceased, that corner of the world still persists as a key area in international relations. In East Asia, the interests of the four major powers of the world—China, the Soviet Union, Japan, and the United States—converge.

China

In the spring of 1971, they called it ''ping-pong diplomacy.'' An American table tennis team participating in an international tournament in Japan was invited to mainland China, shortly after the Nixon administration announced that all special restrictions on travel to the People's Republic were ended. Premier Chou En-lai received the American team on April 14 and said the visit ''opened a new page in relations between Chinese and American peoples [Barnet, 1972, p. xiv].'' On the same day, President Nixon announced new relaxations in our longstanding hostility toward China by revising travel, trade, and shipping rules.

It was a dramatic turnabout. Since 1941, the Sino-American relationship had been marked by an atmosphere of mutual fear and hostile interaction. The Korean war made it worse. For the next twenty years, the two nations were frozen by rigid ideological considerations which made it very difficult to think about practical realities. The United States, says Barnet (1972),

> declared in its view the Chinese Communist regime was illegitimate, that Communism in China should be viewed as ''a passing and not a perpetual state,'' that Peking was both aggressive and expansionist, that it was an integral part of ''monolithic world Communism'' subordinate to Moscow, and that it should be militarily contained, diplomatically and politically isolated, and subjected to economic and other pressures designed to limit its power and influence, weaken it, and help bring about its ultimate demise [p. 11].

Few elected officials dared question that blindness to China as a new and important participant in the international system. (Ohio Senator Stephen Young was a notable exception.) The fear of being stereotyped as a Communist sympathizer was too strong. Nixon's actions, from the ping-pong exchange to his own visit to Peking, changed all that. Now it is accepted that it is in our national interest to welcome ideologically motivated regimes as participants in the world scene (Niemeyer, 1971).

Ping-Pong Diplomacy:
Escape from fear and hos-
tility. *(Wide World Photos.)*

As a result, a number of things are bound to happen. We shall
pay less attention to the anti-Communist government on Taiwan and more
toward the Communist government on the mainland. China's neighbors
will rely less on us for protection from the power center in Peking. In fact,
our whole network of alliances, cemented in the past by fear of Communism, may change. And we may be less anxious to commit ourselves to a high
state of military preparedness, on the theory that there is less to be afraid
of. That could lead to further changes in the distribution of world power.

Behind our new relationship with China is a long history of fear and
ignorance. More than any other factor, public opinion was the dominant
force shaping our relationship during the 1950s and 1960s. The term
"China Lobby" is used rather loosely to refer to numerous organizations
and individuals which, during the past two decades, attempted to influence
public opinion and official government attitudes toward opposing the

Chinese Communists and supporting the Chinese Nationalists. All these different groups constituted not one China Lobby but several.

During 1971, while President Nixon was developing a new China policy, many lobby groups were actively working against any change. One organization, the Committee of One Million, had been a long-time veteran in the struggle to keep U.S. policy towards China unchanged. The organization—founded in 1953—gained widespread public support as well as endorsement from prominent public officials of both parties. Besides the Committee of One Million, many other influential groups, such as the American Legion, AFL-CIO, American Security Council, and VFW, had worked against the opening of the door to Peking.

These lobbies used a number of methods to maintain support of an anti-China policy. In particular, they concentrated on influencing important individuals and groups instrumental in shaping China policy—the Congress, political parties, the administration, and public opinion leaders. Recognizing the power of public opinion, these groups sought to play upon the anti-Communist hysteria in America. For over two decades the interplay between various pressure groups, public opinion, the administration, and Congress formed a vicious circle. Congressional leaders had always been fearful that any change in policy would provoke a hostile public reaction. Yet, at the same time, congressional attitudes served to reaffirm already existing public sentiments. Numerous resolutions, such as the Taiwan resolution of 1955 adopted by the Senate by a vote of 85 to 3 and by the House by 409 to 3, served to institutionalize China policy to such an extent that any flexibility on the part of Congress in solving the China problem was greatly curbed.

Senator J. W. Fulbright, chairman of the Senate Foreign Relations Committee, in a speech in 1964 criticized congressional inertia. Seeking a reevaluation of policy, he realized that the major obstacle to change was "the fear of many government officials, *undoubtedly well-founded*, that even the suggestion of new policies toward China and Viet-Nam would provoke a vehement public outcry [Steele, 1966, p. 213–214]."

But underneath the outward public stance on China, there had been greater elasticity than generally assumed. American attitudes toward China never polarized around specific viewpoints. The "liberal-conservative" dichotomy was an oversimplification. Attitudes were the composite of complex sets of considerations, including economic, nationalistic loyalties, and even race. In his study for the Council on Foreign Relations, published in 1966, A. T. Steele discovered that public opinion was not entirely rigid and cemented to firm positions on policy. In the examination of public reaction to presidential initiatives, he found that opinion ranged significantly on specific policy issues.

By 1971 the conditions for presidential initiative had improved considerably. There was now a new Republican president. The lobbies opposing China had weakened and were now opposed by lobbies working toward a reconciliation with China. Major U.S. businesses, such as Xerox, Monsanto, and General Motors, were seeking to begin trade with mainland China. The Communists had been in control of the mainland for more than twenty years, and nonrecognition of China seemed foolhardy.

Attitudes toward China in the 1960s
"Now the President of the United States might decide that it was in our best interests to take certain new actions with regard to Communist China. For each thing I mention, would you tell me how you would feel about it if the President suggested that action?"
(Asked only of persons who know that most of China is ruled by a Communist government)

"Suppose the President suggested visits between Americans and people from Communist China—like newspapermen from each country visiting the other?"

Definitely in favor	41%	73%
Probably in favor	32	
Probably against	6	16
Definitely against	10	
No opinion		10
Not ascertained		1
Total		100%
	(Number of persons, 1088)	

"Suppose the President suggested that we exchange ambassadors with Communist China the way we do with other countries?"

Definitely in favor	24%	51%
Probably in favor	27	
Probably against	11	34
Definitely against	23	
No opinion		14
Not ascertained		1
Total		100%
	(Number of persons, 1088)	

"Suppose the President suggested that we talk over problems of Asia with Communist China and try to come to some agreements with them?"

Definitely in favor	37%	71%
Probably in favor	34	
Probably against	7	19
Definitely against	12	
No opinion		9
Not ascertained		1
Total		100%
	(Number of persons, 1088)	

Source: Steele, 1966, p. 281.

The Soviet Union

On May 22, 1972, exactly twenty-five years after President Truman signed a bill committing the United States to support Greece and Turkey against communism, President Nixon landed in Moscow. His message to the Soviet leaders was this: "We meet at a moment when we can make peaceful

Nixon in Moscow, 1972: A moment for cooperation. *(Wide World Photos.)*

cooperation a reality [Brzezinski, 1972, p. 181].'' Several bilateral agreements were signed at that meeting, including trade and cultural accords, and the Strategic Arms Limitation Treaty agreement was made. U.S.-Soviet relations had traveled a long way.

The policy of containment of Soviet communism dates from about 1947 when the cold war became a Soviet-American affair. The domination of the world by the two superpowers illustrated Kissinger's point about military bipolarity as a source of rigidity in foreign policy. Each side experimented with alternating offensive and defensive moves—the Berlin airlift is an example—but, as Brzezinski (1972) notes, ''neither side (was) demonstrating the will or the capacity for sustained political momentum [p. 202].'' The relationship was marked by miscues and misunderstandings, but it did reach a kind of stability. The two powers accepted military parity. It made no sense for each side to outgun the other, ad infinitum. But it has been a precarious stability because of the difficulty of the two powers to maintain prolonged communication.

But there were worse problems. Anatol Rapoport (1971) has argued that all the emphasis on military relationships has been a major mistake. It put all of the concern on means, not goals, as has been so splendidly satirizied in such literary works as *Dr. Strangelove*, *Fail-Safe*, and *We Bombed in New Haven*. The military framework also contributed to the tendency to leave foreign policy making to a dominant elite. Policy toward the Soviet Union in particular reflected control by the military, whose interests did not necessarily coincide with those of the nation.

American foreign policy toward the Soviet Union demonstrates several important points about the decision-making process. The role of the military in shaping policy on both sides is clearly evident in the cold war history. The military's effect on patterns of policy thinking runs throughout U.S. postwar relation with the Soviet Union. The cost of these factors led to an increasing military budget and arms race. Adam Yarmolinsky (1971) described how these factors interacted to affect the nature of the policy decisions:

> Although the foreign policies of the United States might have been rationalized in military terms in any case, the actual involvement of the Pentagon and military commands in the policy-making process has had the effect of intertwining with the rationale for certain foreign policies a rationale for increased spending. It has also entailed an increase in the number and variety of military options available to Presidents in crises, probably at the expense of making other kinds of options either less available or less visible [p. 124].

The failure of the policymakers to perceive the actual intentions of the Soviet Union often led to policies which the leaders did not fully comprehend or see all the consequences. Both the United States and the Soviet Union often miscalculated in their estimations of how the other would respond to global situations. Only recently have the two superpowers begun to seriously discuss the business of arms control. But even in this vital matter, American thinking has not yet assigned the needed priority to arms control and disarmament. In 1971 the government's research budget for this area of concern amounted to only one two-thousandths of the weapons research budget (Paul Dickson, 1971, p. 38). Instead of dwelling entirely on the enemy's capabilities, political dialogue needed to be given emphasis.

Japan

On May 15, 1972, the United States and Japan signed a treaty for the return of Okinawa to Japanese control, thus ending twenty-seven years of American occupation. Like the relaxation of China policy and President Nixon's trip to Moscow, it marked a new stage in postwar relations. Unlike the Soviet Union and China, however, Japan has had very close ties to the United States since the end of World War II. First, the two countries have been tied by a mutual security relationship. Secondly, they became economically interdependent. However, our interests have not always been identical.

In this period of transition it is not clear how U.S.-Japanese relations will develop. Japan has been reluctant to strike at a new assertive role in world politics. Yet Japan is eager to end its client-state relationship with the United States. Facing a new role in global politics, Japan is hesitant. Knowing that it is an economic giant, yet a military pygmy, Japan is unsure of the consequence of attempting to be a power in international politics.

Increasing Japanese productivity has led to a situation where we now buy from them more than we sell. Today's U.S.-Japan economic relations involve goods and capital in the billions of dollars. Japan is America's largest business partner. In 1972 Japan bought $4.9 billion worth of goods from the United States. At the same time Japanese exports continue to grow at a rate higher than our exports. This situation has resulted in a major problem, a U.S.-Japanese trade deficit of $4.2 billion.

Japan's postwar economic miracle has challenged the U.S. economy. But the problem of an unfavorable balance of trade is only a surface indication of more serious existing problems. The fundamental issue is whether American-Japanese economic relations will lead to the reestablishment of a prosperous and strong American economy. Although the available data show that such American industries as textiles, metal and machinery, and electrical equipment are increasingly becoming less profitable, the problem may not necessarily be the result of Japanese exports. Japanese exports have had an impact on major industries in the United States, but part of our troubles also stem from internal problems of the domestic economy.

But the biggest problem between the two countries has been the restoration of Japanese independence following the unconditional surrender of 1945. The reversion of Okinawa symbolized the last step in gaining that independence. The new problems, summarized by John K. Emmerson (1972), are based mainly on economic difficulties and Japanese concern over new U.S. friendship with China. "Already the Japanese may believe that American actions indicate that China is to take precedence over Japan in foreign policy," he says (p. 634). A related problem is the extent of America's commitment to helping Japan maintain military security. Economic and political pressures have compelled the U.S. to reduce its forces in Asia, and that event may or may not coincide with Japanese wishes. The Nixon administration's policy called for reducing the U.S. military presence in and around Japan but without any changes in the basic commitments to Japanese security.

The Nixon Doctrine had as one of its key elements the desire to build a cooperative relationship between America and the countries of East Asia, in which all would share the responsibilities of peace. The Shanghai Communique of February 28, 1972, and the Agreement of January 27, 1973, to cease hostilities in Vietnam attest to this new era of security. Japan, if it is to play a role in this endeavor, must be concerned with the capacities of its armed forces. The central question that remains to be answered is whether Japan can act as a major power, particularly if it lacks military power. The reversion of Okinawa has not fundamentally affected U.S. security arrangements. But from the Japanese perspective the U.S.-Japanese Treaty of Mutual Cooperation and Security of 1960 has a new significance. The Japanese Self Defense Force does not provide the means for Japan to take up the strategic vacuum created by U.S. withdrawal.

The effect of the emerging relationship might be to reduce the role of the United States in the Pacific and to enhance the role of Japan. The U.S. aim, in short, is to initiate Japan into a role of active participant in the world order. And it may be an indication of American recognition that a new constellation of powers is emerging in the world and that the United States is attaining new realism in its appraisal of its national interests.

SUGGESTED READINGS

Almond, Gabriel A. *The American People and Foreign Policy.* New York: Harcourt, Brace, 1950.   A valuable and useful study of the role of public opinion in the formulation of foreign policy and the conduct of overseas policy.

Barnet, Richard J. *The Roots of War.* New York: Atheneum, 1972.   A revealing analysis of the growth of the military-industrial complex and how this change has affected the nature of American foreign policy.

Carleton, William. *The Revolution in American Foreign Policy.* 2d ed. New York: Random House, 1967.   An extensive account of the development and changes in foreign policy during the postwar era.

Hilsman, Roger. *The Politics of Policy-Making in Defense and Foreign Affairs.* New York: Harper & Row, 1971.   An excellent overview of the institutions and processes by which foreign and military policy are formulated.

Magdoff, Harry. *The Age of Imperialism: The Economics of United States Foreign Policy.* New York: Monthly Review Press, 1969.   A critical review of American foreign policy from the perspective of its economic policies. Examines the impact and consequences of our economic policy both at home and abroad.

Morris, Bernard S. *International Communism and American Policy.* New York: Atherton, 1966.   Analytically discusses the premises of United States foreign policy toward communist nations and the rest of the international community in light of a communist presence.

Robinson, James A. *Congress and Foreign Policy-Making.* rev. ed. Homewood, Ill.: Dorsey, 1967.   A comprehensive treatment of the role of Congress in the foreign policy-making process, pointing out its powers and limitations.

Yarmolinsky, Adam. *The Military Establishment: Its Impact on American Society.* New York: Harper & Row, 1971.   Historical and analytical discussion of the growth of the military and its influence on the direction of foreign and domestic policy.

Afterword

Afterword

And so this is how we are governed. If you hoped to see the machinery of government unwrapped, you are by now disappointed. If you searched for direct links between cause and effect, between specific input and predictable output, you are wiser for not having found them. Your uncertainty is not unique. Walter Lippman (1973), in the twilight of his years, was asked whether President Nixon's challenge to the authority of Congress exceeded the rules that had been set down for presidents by the Constitution. In his answer, Lippman was poignant as a schoolboy, accurate as a sage: "Nobody knows the theoretical answer to that. When I was a student in college, we knew that the problem existed, and we knew there was no answer [p. 18]."

Such answers as may be discovered are situational, not universal. When different branches of government tug at one another, the outcomes will be determined by prevailing power relationships at least as much as by fidelity to codes of the past. And so government exists in a state of perpetual uncertainty.

Learning to live with uncertainty may be the central skill, the key to survival. It is no new thing. The native Americans who occupied this land before us lived with the uncertainties of drought and flood, plentiful or scarce game, all the vagaries of nature. People can live with uncertainty and even turn it into an asset. If this year's crop fails, we shall have the will to plant next year's because we know that weather changes. A political interest group or political party that loses one election or battle for legislation can still hope for victory another time. "Uncertainty," said Nelson Polsby (1971), "is the glue that holds together many of the disparate parts of a complex, stable democracy [p. 10]."

The existence of uncertainty does not, of course, imply an absence of rules. There are rules of the game, and to violate them invites disaster—as the Watergate case so dramatically illustrated. But uncertainty is also necessary to enforce the rules. The people who blew the whistle on Watergate knew the outcome was uncertain, but they opted for the most favorable chance as they saw it. We are a nation of risk-takers. Ours is a risky world.

The Republic survived the turmoil of the late 1960s, and it survived Watergate. Given a slightly different turn of events, it might not have done so. In the long run, we make our own luck, and we roll our own dice. On the day set for the final signing of the Constitution, Benjamin Franklin, who knew the uncertainties of keeping the Republic, rose and asked for the floor so that his carefully prepared remarks could be read for him. He was seeking unanimity; he was asking the other delegates to trust a little to luck:

> In these sentiments, Sir, I agree to this Constitution, with all its Faults, if they are such; because I think a General Government necessary for us, and there is no *Form* of Government but what may be a Blessing to the People if well administered; and I believe farther that this is likely to be well administered for a Course of Years, and can only end in Despotism as other Forms have done before it, when the People shall become so corrupted as to need Despotic Government, being incapable of any other . . . Thus I consent, Sir, to this Constitution because I am not sure that it is not the best [Boorstin, 1968, p. 97].

He was not sure then, nor are we today. It is only the best that we know about. We can keep it only as long as we keep our public virtue, our tolerance for uncertainty, our hope for the future. That is how it was and how it will be.

Bibliography

Abraham, Henry J.: *The Judicial Process*, 2d ed. Oxford University Press, New York, 1968.

Abramson, Paul R.: "Political Efficacy and Political Trust Among Black Schoolchildren: Two Explanations," *Journal of Politics*, vol. 34, no. 4, 1972.

Ackland, Len: "Anti-crime Politics," Hearings, Subcommittee No. 5, Committee on the Judiciary, U.S. House of Representatives, 1973.

Adams, Charles Francis: *The Works of John Adams*, Little, Brown, Boston, 1856, vol. X.

Adams, John: "Letter to Hezekiah Niles," in Daniel J. Boorstin (ed.), *An American Primer*, New American Library, New York, 1968. Original, owned by the Maryland Historical Society, is dated Feb. 13, 1818.

Adams, Sherman: *Firsthand Report*, Popular, New York, 1962.

Adelson, Joseph: "What Generation Gap?" *New York Times Magazine*, Jan. 18, 1970. Reprinted in Benjamin A. Kogan (ed.), *Readings in Health Science*, Harcourt Brace Jovanovich, New York, 1971.

Agnew, Spiro T.: quoted in *New York Times*, Oct. 14, 1968.

Ahern, James F.: *Police in Trouble: Our Frightening Crisis in Law Enforcement*, Hawthorn Books, New York, 1970.

Alexander, Herbert: *Financing the 1968 Election*, Heath, Lexington, Mass., 1971.

American Civil Liberties Union: *Annual Report*, July 1971–June 1972.

American Civil Liberties Union: *Mayday 1971: Order without Liberty*, Washington, 1972.

American Farm Bureau Federation: "Farm Policies for 1973," Los Angeles, December, 1972.

American Political Science Association: *Toward a More Responsible Two-party System*, Rinehart, New York, 1950.

Anderson, Jack: "The Washington Merry-Go-Round," *Washington Post*, Feb. 15, 1973.

Apple, R. W., Jr.: "Haldeman the Fierce, Haldeman the Faithful, Haldeman the Fallen," *New York Times Magazine*, May 6, 1973.

Archibald, Samuel J.: "A Brief History of Dirty Politics," in Ray Hiebert, Robert Jones, John Lorenz, and Ernest Lotito (eds.), *The Political Image Merchants*, Acropolis, Washington, 1971.

Asch, Sidney H.: *Police Authority and the Rights of the Individual*, 3d ed., ARCO Publishing Co., New York, 1973.

Bachrach, Peter, and Morton Baratz: *Power and Poverty*, Oxford University Press, New York, 1970.

Bagdikian, Ben H.: "Mr. Nixon and the Press: A 27-Year Conflict," *The New York Times*, Nov. 1, 1973.

Bailey, Harry A., Jr.: "Presidential Tenure and the Two-term Tradition," *Publius: The Journal of Federalism*, vol. 2, fall, 1972.

Bailey, Thomas A.: *Presidential Greatness*, Appleton-Century, New York, 1966.

Bailyn, Bernard: *The Ideological Origins of the American Revolution*, Harvard, Cambridge, Mass., 1967.

Bailyn, Bernard: *The Origins of American Politics*, Knopf, New York, 1968.

Baldwin, James: "A Report from Occupied Territory," *The Nation*, July 11, 1963.

Baldwin, Leland D.: *Reframing the Constitution: An Imperative for Modern America*, American Bibliographical Center, Santa Barbara, Calif., 1972.

Balk, Alfred: *The Free List*, Russell Sage, New York, 1971.

Banfield, Edward C.: *The Unheavenly City Revisited*, 2d ed., Little, Brown, Boston, 1974.

Banfield, Edward C., and James Q. Wilson: *City Politics*, Vintage Books, New York, 1963.

Barber, James David: "Choosing Our Leaders," *The Washington Post*, Aug. 18, 1974.

Barber, James David: *The Presidential Character*, Prentice-Hall, Englewood Cliffs, N.J., 1972.

Barger, Harold: *Money, Banking and Public Policy*, Rand McNally, Chicago, 1962.

Barlett, Donald L., and James B. Steele: "Crime and Injustice," reprint, *The Philadelphia Inquirer*, 1973.

Barnet, Richard J.: "The National Security Managers and the National Interest," *Politics and Society*, vol. 1, no. 2, February 1971.

Barnet, Richard J.: *Roots of War*, Atheneum, New York, 1972.

Barnett, A. Doak: *A New U.S. Policy toward China*, Brookings, Washington, 1971.

Bauer, Raymond A., and Fenn, Dan H., Jr.: *The Corporate Social Audit*, Russell Sage, New York, 1972.

Beard, Charles A.: *An Economic Interpretation of the Constitution of the United States*, Macmillan, New York, 1913.

Becker, Carl: *The Declaration of Independence; A Study in the History of Political Ideas*, Vintage Books, New York, 1922.

Becker, Carl: *The Heavenly City of the Eighteenth Century Philosophers*, Yale, New Haven, 1932.

Bell, Daniel: *The End of Ideology*, Free Press, Glencoe, Ill., 1960.

Bendix, Reinhard: *Max Weber: An Intellectual Portrait*, Doubleday, Garden City, N.Y., 1960.

Bennett, James V.: "A Cool Look at the Crime Crisis," *Harper's Magazine*, April 1964.

Berelson, Bernard R., Paul F. Lazarsfeld, and William N. McPhee: *Voting*, The University of Chicago Press, Chicago, 1954.

Berger, Raoul: *Impeachment: The Constitutional Problems,* Harvard, Cambridge, Mass., 1973.

Bergsten, C. Fred: "The Threat from the Third World," *Foreign Policy*, summer, 1973.

Berkowitz, Morton, and P. G. Bock: "National Security," in David L. Sills (ed.), *International Encyclopedia of the Social Sciences*, Crowell, Collier and Macmillan, New York, 1968.

Berle, Adolf A.: *The American Economic Republic*, Harcourt, Brace, & World, New York, 1963.

Bernays, Edward L.: *Propaganda*, Horace Livewright, New York, 1928.

Bernstein, Marver: *Regulating Business by Independent Commission*, Princeton University Press, Princeton, N.J., 1955.

Biderman, Albert D., and Albert J. Reiss, Jr.: "On Exploring the 'Dark Figure' of Crime," *The Annals of the American Academy of Political and Social Science*, vol. 374, November 1967.

Birkby, Robert H.: "Politics of Accommodation: The Origin of the Supremacy Clause," *The Western Political Quarterly*, vol. 19, March 1966.

Bishop, Robert L.: "The Rush to Chain Ownership," *Columbia Journalism Review*, vol. 11, no. 4, November–December 1972.

Black, Charles L.: *The People and the Court*, Macmillan, New York, 1960.

Black, Donald F.: "Production of Crime Rates," *American Sociological Review*, vol. 35, 1970.

Blackwell, G. W.: "Community Analysis," in Roland Young (ed.), *Approaches to the Study of Politics*, Northwestern University Press, Evanston, Ill., 1950.

Block, Herbert Aaron, and Gilbert Geis: *Man, Crime and Society*, 2d ed., Random House, New York, 1970.

Bogart, Leo: *Silent Politics*, Wiley, New York, 1972.

Bone, Hugh A., and Austin Ranney: *Politics and Voters*, 3d ed., McGraw-Hill, New York, 1971. Originally published in 1963.

Boorstin, Daniel J.: *An American Primer*, The University of Chicago Press, Chicago, 1966. Mentor paperback edition, 1968.

Bopp, William J.: *The Police Rebellion*, Charles C Thomas, Springfield, Ill., 1971.

Borins, Sanford: "The Political Economy of 'The Fed,'" *Public Policy*, vol. 20, 1972.

Brandeis, Louis D.: "Decision Rules of the Court," in Aaron Wildavsky and Nelson W. Polsby (eds.), *American Governmental Institutions*, Rand McNally, Chicago, 1968. From *Ashwander v. Tennessee Valley Authority*, 80 L. ED. 710 (1936).

Broder, David S.: "And What about a Hitler?" in Ray Heibert, Robert Jones, John Lorenz, and Ernest Lotito (eds.), *The Political Image Merchants*, Acropolis, Washington, 1971.

Broder, David S.: *The Party's Over*, Harper & Row, New York, 1971.

Brzezinski, Zbigniew: "How the Cold War Was Played," *Foreign Affairs*, vol. 51, no. 1, October 1972.

Buchanan, Patrick J.: "Excerpts from the Buchanan Testimony," *New York Times*, Sept. 27, 1973.

Bundy, McGeorge: "America's Enduring Links with Europe," *The Atlantic Community Quarterly*, vol. 8, spring, 1970.

Burdick, Eugene: *The 480*, Dell, New York, 1964.

Bureau of the Budget: *The U.S. at War*, Government Printing Office, Washington, 1946.

Bureau of the Census: "Characteristics of the Low-income Population: 1972," series P-60, no. 88, Government Printing Office, Washington, June 1973.

Bureau of the Census: "Current Population Reports," P-23, no. 42, Government Printing Office, Washington, 1972.

Bureau of the Census: *Statistical Abstracts of the United States*, 1966, 1972, Government Printing Office, Washington.

Bureau of Executive Manpower, U.S. Civil Service Commission: "Executive Manpower in the Federal Service," Government Printing Office, Washington, 1972.

Burke, Edmund: *The Works of Edmund Burke*, vol. 1, Somerset Press, London, 1896.

Burnham, Walter Dean: "The Changing Shape of the American Political Universe," *American Political Science Review*, vol. 59, no. 1, March 1965.

Burnham, Walter Dean: "Party Systems and the Political Process," in William Nisbet Chambers and Walter Dean Burnham (eds.), *The American Party Systems: Stages of Political Development*, Oxford University Press, New York, 1967.

Burns, James MacGregor: *Presidential Government*, Sentry ed., Houghton Mifflin, Boston, 1973.

Burns, John, and the Citizens Conference on State Legislatures: *The Sometime Governments: A Critical Study of the 50 American Legislatures*, Bantam, New York, 1971.

Calhoun, John C.: "A Disquisition on Government," in Richard K. Cralle (ed.), *The Works of John C. Calhoun*, D. Appelton and Co., New York, 1854, vol. 1.

Campbell, Angus, Philip E. Converse, Warren E. Miller, and Donald E. Stokes: *The American Voter*, Wiley, New York, 1960.

Campbell, Angus: "A Classification of the Presidential Elections," in Angus Campbell, Philip E. Converse, Warren E. Miller, and Donald E. Stokes, *Elections and the Political Order*, Wiley, New York, 1966.

Campbell, Angus: *White Attitudes toward Black People*, Institute for Social Research, Ann Arbor, Mich., 1971.

Campbell, Angus, Gerald Gurin, and Warren E. Miller: *The Voter Decides*, Row, Peterson, Evanston, Ill., 1954.

Campbell, Angus, and Howard Schuman: "Racial Attitudes in Fifteen American Cities," in *Supplemental Studies for the National Advisory Commission of Civil Disorders*, Government Printing Office, Washington, July 1968.

Campbell, Donald: "Reforms as Experiments," *American Psychologist*, vol. 24, April 1969.

Campbell, John F.: *The Foreign Affairs Fudge Factory*, Basic Books, New York, 1971.

Campbell, James S., Joseph R. Sahid, and David P. Stang: *Law and Order Reconsidered: A Staff Report to the National Commission on the Causes and Prevention of Violence*, The New York Times Co., New York, 1970.

Camus, Albert: *The Rebel: An Essay on Man in Revolt*, Vintage, New York, 1951.

Capron, William: "Development of Cost Effectiveness Systems in the Federal Government," in Robert L. Chartrand, Kenneth Janda, and Michael Hugo (eds.), *Information Support, Program Budgeting, and the Congress*, Spartan, New York, 1968.

Carpenter, W. S.: *Introduction to Locke's "Two Treatises of Government,"* Everyman's Library edition, J. M. Dent & Sons, London, 1924, p. xii.

Cater, Douglass: *Power in Washington*, Vintage, New York, 1964.

Chambliss, William J., and Robert B. Seidman: *Law, Order, and Power*, Addison-Wesley, Reading, Mass., 1971.

Chase, Harold W.: *Federal Judges: The Appointing Process*, University of Minnesota Press, Minneapolis, 1972.

Chrysler Corporation: "Facts about the 1975–76 Federal Emissions Standards," *Washington Post*, Mar. 13, 1973.

The Citizens Conference on State Legislatures: *State Legislatures: An Evaluation of Their Effectiveness*, Praeger, New York, 1971.

Clapp, Charles L.: *The Congressman: His Work as He Sees It*, Brookings, Washington, 1973.

Clark, Paul Gordon: *American Aid for Development*, Praeger, New York, 1972.

Clark, Timothy B., John K. Iglehart, and William Lilley, III: "New Federalism Report," *National Journal*, vol. 4, 1972.

Clotfeler, James: "Senate Voting and Constituency Stake in Defense Spending," *Journal of Politics*, vol. 32, November 1970.

Coles, Robert: "God and the Rural-Poor," *Psychology Today*, vol. 5, January 1972.

Commager, Henry Steele: *Testimony before the Senate Foreign Relations Committee*, March 1971. Quoted in *Guide to the Congress of the United States*, Congressional Quarterly, Washington, 1971.

Commager, Henry Steele: "How Long Should a President Serve?" *Parade*, Sept. 16, 1973.

Commission on Party Structure and Delegate Selection: "Mandate for Reform," Democratic National Committee, Washington, April 1970.

Congressional Quarterly: *Civil Rights: Progress Report, 1970*, Washington, 1971.

Congressional Quarterly: *Guide to the Congress of the United States*, Washington, 1971.

Congressional Quarterly: *'72 Campaign Trends: More Computers, Fewer TV Spots*, Apr. 15, 1972.

Congressional Quarterly: *The U.S. Economy: Challenge in the '70s*, Washington, 1972.

Converse, Philip E.: "Attitudes and Non-Attitudes," paper read at 17th International Congress of Psychology, 1963.

Converse, Philip E.: "Changes in the American Electorate," in Angus Campbell and Philip E. Converse (eds.), *The Human Meaning of Social Change*, Russell Sage, New York, 1972.

Converse, Philip E.: "The Concept of a Normal Vote," in Angus Campbell, Philip E. Converse, Warren E. Miller, and Donald E. Stokes, *Elections and the Political Order*, Wiley, New York, 1966.

Converse, Philip E.: "The Nature of Belief Systems in Mass Publics," in David E. Apter (ed.), *Ideology and Discontent*, Free Press, New York, 1964.

Converse, Philip E., Aage R. Clausen, and Warren E. Miller: "Electoral Myth and Reality: The 1964 Election," *American Political Science Review*, vol. 59, no. 2, June 1965.

Converse, Philip E., Warren E. Miller, Jerrold G. Rusk, and Arthur C. Wolfe: "Continuity and Change in American Politics: Parties and Issues in the 1968 Election," *American Political Science Review*, vol. 68, December 1969.

Cook, Fred J.: "There's Always a Crime Wave," in Donald R. Cressey (ed.), *Crime and Criminal Justice*, Quadrangle, Chicago, 1971. Originally appeared in *The New York Times Magazine*, Oct. 6, 1968.

Corwin, Edward S.: *The Constitution and What It Means Today*, Atheneum, New York, 1963.

Cox, Archibald: *The Warren Court*, Harvard, Cambridge, Mass., 1968.

Crenson, Matthew A.: *The Un-Politics of Air Pollution*, Johns Hopkins, Baltimore, 1971.

Cressey, Donald R.: *Theft of the Nation*, Harper & Row, New York, 1969.

Cronin, Thomas E.: "'Everybody Believes in Democracy Until He Gets to the White House . . .': An Examination of White House Departmental Relations," *Law and Contemporary Problems*, vol. 35, summer, 1970.

Cronin, Thomas E.: "The Swelling of the Presidency," *The Society*, vol. 1, February 1973.

Currie, Elliott: "Toward a Sociology of Repression," Conference on Violence and Political Change, Drury College, Springfield, Missouri, 1970.

Dahl, Robert A.: "Decision-Making in a Democracy: The Supreme Court as a National Policy Maker," *Journal of Public Law*, vol. 6, 1958.

Dahl, Robert A.: *Modern Political Analysis*, 2d ed., Prentice-Hall, Englewood Cliffs, N.J., 1970.

Dahl, Robert A.: *Pluralist Democracy in the United States: Conflict and Consent*, Rand McNally, Chicago, 1967.

Daniels, Jonathan: *Frontier on the Potomac*, Macmillan, New York, 1946.

David, Paul T., Ralph M. Goldman, and Richard C. Bain: *The Politics of National Party Conventions*, Brookings, Washington, 1960.

Davis, James W.: *National Conventions*, Barron's Educational Series, Woodbury, N.Y., 1972.

Davis, Kenneth S.: *River on the Rampage*, Doubleday, Garden City, N.Y., 1953.

Davis, Otto A., M. A. H. Dempster, and Aaron Wildavsky: "A Theory of the Budgetary Process," *American Political Science Review*, vol. 60, September 1966.

de Grazia, Edward: "Congressional Liaison," in Alfred de Grazia (ed.), *Congress: The First Branch of Government*, American Enterprise Institute, Washington, 1966.

DeGrove, John M.: "Help or Hindrance to State Action? The National Government," in Alan K. Campbell (ed.), *The States and the Urban Crisis*, Prentice-Hall, Englewood Cliffs, N.J., 1970.

de Tocqueville, Alexis: *Democracy in America*, New American Library, New York, 1956. Originally published 1835.

De Vries, Walter, and Lance Tarrance, Jr.: *The Ticket-Splitter*, Eerdmans, Grand Rapids, Mich., 1972.

Dickson, Paul: *Think Tanks*, Atheneum, New York, 1971.

Dixon, Robert G., Jr.: "The Court, the People, and 'One Man, One Vote,'" in Nelson W. Polsby (ed.), *Reapportionment in the 1970s*, University of California Press, Berkeley, 1971.

Dolbeare, Kenneth M., and Murray J. Edelman: *American Politics*, Heath, Lexington, Mass., 1971.

Domhoff, G. William: "Who Made American Foreign Policy, 1945–1963?" in

David Horowitz (ed.), *Corporations and the Cold War*, Monthly Review Press, New York, 1969.

Domhoff, G. William: *Who Rules America?* Prentice-Hall, Englewood Cliffs, N.J., 1967.

Donovan, John C.: *The Politics of Poverty*, Western Publishing Co. Inc., New York, 1967.

Duff, Elizabeth: "Protestors Fail to Woo TV Cameras from Hall," *The Miami Herald*, Aug. 27, 1972.

Duffy, LaVern J.: Statement to the Permanent Subcommittee on Investigations of the Committee on Government Operations, United States Senate, Dec. 13, 1973.

Dunn, Delmar D.: *Financing Presidential Campaigns*, Brookings, Washington, 1972.

Durbin, E. F. M.: *The Politics of Democratic Socialism*, Routledge, London, 1940.

Dye, Thomas R.: *Politics in States and Communities*, Prentice-Hall, Englewood Cliffs, N.J., 1969.

Dye, Thomas R.: *Politics, Economics, and the Public: Policy Outcomes in the American States*, Rand McNally, Chicago, 1966.

Dye, Thomas R.: *The Politics of Equality*, Bobbs-Merrill, Indianapolis, 1971.

Dye, Thomas, and Harmon Ziegler: *The Irony of Democracy*, Wadsworth, Belmont, Calif., 1970.

Easton, David, and Robert D. Hess: "The Child's Political World," *Midwest Journal of Political Science*, vol. 6, 1962.

Eccles, Marriner S.: *Beckoning Frontiers*, Knopf, New York, 1951.

Eisenhower, Dwight D.: *Public Papers of the Presidents of the United States, Dwight D. Eisenhower*, Government Printing Office, Washington, 1957.

Elazer, Daniel J.: *American Federalism: A View from the States,* Thomas Y. Crowell, New York, 1966.

Elkins, Stanley, and Eric McKitrick: "Founding Fathers; Young Men of the Revolution," *Political Science Quarterly*, vol. 76, June 1961.

Ellul, Jacques: *The Theological Foundations of Law*, The Seabury Press, New York, 1960.

Ennis, Philip H.: "Crimes, Victims, and the Police," *Trans-Action*, June 1967.

Etzioni, Amitai: *The Active Society*, Free Press, New York, 1968.

Etzioni, Amitai: "The Kennedy Experiment," *Western Political Quarterly*, vol. 20, no. 2, June 1967.

Fanon, Frantz: *The Wretched of the Earth*, Grove Press, Inc., New York, 1968.

Faulkner, Harold Underwood: *American Economic History*, 7th ed., Harper, New York, 1954.

Federal Bureau of Investigation: *Uniform Crime Reports*, Government Printing Office, Washington, 1966.

The Federalist, Putnam, New York, 1888.

Feer, Robert A: "Shay's Rebellion and the Constitution: A Study in Causation," *New England Quarterly*, vol. 42, September 1969.

Fenno, Richard F., Jr.: "The House Appropriations Committee," *The American Political Science Review*, vol. 56, June 1962.

Fenno, Richard F., Jr.: *The Power of the Purse*, Little, Brown, Boston, 1966.

Festinger, Leon: "Cognitive Dissonance," *Scientific American*, October 1962.

Filler, Louis, and Allen Guttmann: *The Removal of the Cherokee Nation: Manifest Destiny or National Dishonor?* Heath, Boston, 1962.

Flaherty, Joe: *Managing Mailer*, Coward-McCann, New York, 1970.

Flash, Edward, Jr.: *Economic Advice and Presidential Leadership*, Columbia University Press, New York, 1965.

Fogelson, Robert M., and Robert B. Hill: "Who Riots?" in *Supplemental Studies for the National Advisory Commission on Civil Disorders*, Government Printing Office, Washington, 1968.

Frank, John P.: *Marble Palace: The Supreme Court in American Life*, Knopf, New York, 1958.

Frankel, Charles: "Is It Ever Right to Break the Law?" in Thomas R. Dye and Brett W. Hawkins (eds.), *Politics in the Metropolis*, Bobbs-Merrill, Indianapolis, 1967. Originally published in *The New York Times*, Jan. 12, 1964.

Franklin, Ben: "Election Contributions Pose Awkward Queries for Nixon," *The New York Times*, Jan. 7, 1973.

Freeman, Richard B.: "Changes in the Labor Market for Black Americans, 1948–72," Brookings Papers on Economic Activity, no. 1, 1973.

Friedlander, Walter A., and Robert Z. Apte: *Introduction to Social Welfare*, 4th ed., Prentice-Hall, Englewood Cliffs, N.J., 1974.

Froman, Lewis A., Jr.: *People and Politics*, Prentice-Hall, Englewood Cliffs, N.J., 1962.

Galbraith, John Kenneth: *The Affluent Society*, Houghton Mifflin, Boston, 1958.

Galbraith, John Kenneth: *American Capitalism; The Concept of Countervailing Power*, Houghton Mifflin, Boston, 1952.

Gallup, George: *The Sophisticated Poll Watcher's Guide*, Princeton University Press, Princeton, N.J., 1972.

The Gallup Opinion Index, Princeton, N.J., 1963–74.

The Gallup Opinion Index, Report No. 40, October 1968.

The Gallup Opinion Index, Report No. 84, June 1972.

The Gallup Opinion Index, Report No. 90, December 1972.

The Gallup Opinion Index, Report No. 97, July 1973.

Glazer, Nathan: "The Good Society," *Commentary*, vol. 36, September 1963.

Goldman, Sheldon: "Voting Behavior on U.S. Courts of Appeals, 1961–64," *American Political Science Review*, vol. 60, June 1966.

Gould, Leroy C.: "Crime and Its Impact in an Affluent Society," in Jack D. Douglas (ed.), *Crime and Justice in American Society*, Bobbs-Merrill, Indianapolis, 1971.

Graham, Hugh Davis, and Ted Robert Gurr (eds.): *The History of Violence in America*, A Report to the National Commission on the Causes and Prevention of Violence, Bantam, New York, 1969.

Grant, Daniel R.: "Urban Needs and State Response: Local Government Reorganization," in Alan K. Campbell (ed.), *The States and the Urban Crisis*, Prentice-Hall, Englewood Cliffs, N.J., 1970.

Grant, Daniel R., and H. C. Nixon: *State and Local Government in America*, 2d ed, Allyn & Bacon, Boston, 1968.

Green, Mark J., James Fallows, and David R. Zwick: *Who Runs Congress?* Bantam, New York, 1972.

Greenberg, Edward S. (ed.): *Political Socialization*, Atherton, New York, 1970.

Greenberg, Edward S.: "The Welfare State and Benefit Distribution," in Edward S. Greenberg and Richard Young (eds.), *American Politics Reconsidered*, Wadsworth, Belmont, Calif., 1973.

Greenfield, Meg: "Why Are You Calling Me, Son?" *The Reporter*, Aug. 16, 1962.

Greenstein, Fred I.: "The Benevolent Leader: Children's Images of Political Authority," *American Political Science Review*, vol. 54, no. 4, December 1960.

Greenstone, J. David, and Paul E. Peterson: *Race and Authority in Urban Politics*, Russell Sage, New York, 1973.

Grodzins, Morton, and Daniel Elazar: "Centralization and Decentralization in the American Federal System," in Robert A. Goldwin (ed.), *A Nation of States*, Rand McNally, Chicago, 1961.

Grosse, Robert N.: "Cost-Effectiveness as a Tool for Decision Makers in the Executive Branch," in Robert L. Chartrand, Kenneth Janda, and Michael Hugo (eds.), *Information Support, Program Budgeting, and the Congress*, Spartan, New York, 1968.

Grotta, Gerald L.: "Consolidation of Newspapers: What Happens to the Consumer?" *Journalism Quarterly*, vol. 78, summer, 1971.

Gulick, Luther: "Reorganization of the State," *Civil Engineering*, vol. III, August 1933.

Halberstam, David: *The Best and the Brightest*, Random House, New York, 1972.

Hallowell, John H.: *Main Currents in Modern Political Thought*, Holt, New York, 1950.

Halperin, Morton H.: "The President and the Military," *Foreign Affairs*, vol. 50, no. 2, January 1972.

Hamill, Pete: "When the Client Is a Candidate," *The New York Times Magazine*, Oct. 25, 1964.

Hamilton, Alexander: "The Federalist, No. 65," *The New York Packet*, March 7, 1788. Reprinted in Henry Cabot Lodge (ed.), *The Federalist*, Putnam, New York, 1888.

Hamilton, Alexander: "The Federalist, No. 78," in Henry Cabot Lodge (ed.), *The Federalist*, Putnam, New York, 1923. Originally published in 1888.

Hamilton, Richard F.: *Class and Politics in the United States*, Wiley, New York, 1972.

Harrington, Michael: *The Other America*, Macmillan, New York, 1962.

Harrington, Michael: "The Other America Revisited," *The Center Magazine*, January 1969.

Harris, Louis: *Confidence and Concern: Citizens View American Government*. Subcommittee on Intergovernmental Relations, Committee on Government Operations, U.S. Senate, Government Printing Office, Washington, 1973.

Harris, Richard: *The Fear of Crime*, Praeger, New York, 1969.

Heard, Alexander: *The Costs of Democracy*, The University of North Carolina Press, Chapel Hill, 1960.

Heller, Joseph: *Catch-22*, Dell, New York, 1961.

Heller, Walter W.: *New Dimensions of Political Economy*, Norton, New York, 1967.

Hesseltine, William B.: *Third Party Movements in the United States,* Van Nostrand Reinhold, New York, 1962.

Hilsman, Roger: *To Move a Nation*, Doubleday, Garden City, N.Y., 1967.

Hodgson, Godfrey: "Do Schools Make a Difference?" *The Atlantic*, vol. 231, no. 3, March 1973.

Hofferbert, Richard I.: "Classification of American State Party Systems," *Journal of Politics*, vol. 26, August 1964.

Hoffman, Stanley: *Gulliver's Troubles*, McGraw-Hill, New York, 1968.

Hook, Sidney: "Violence," in Edwin R. A. Seligman and Alvin Johnson (eds.), *Encyclopedia of the Social Sciences*, Macmillan, New York, 1935.

Horowitz, Irving Louis: *Three Worlds of Development*, Oxford University Press, New York, 1966.

Huckshorn, Robert J., and Robert C. Spencer: *The Politics of Defeat*, University of Massachusetts Press, Amherst, 1971.

Hudson, Winthrop S. (ed.): *Nationalism and Religion in America*, Harper & Row, New York, 1970.

Huitt, Ralph K.: "The Outsider in the Senate," *American Political Science Review*, vol. 55, September 1961.

Hunter, Marjorie: "Congressman Finds Instant Pressure," *The New York Times*, Feb. 2, 1973.

Hyman, H. H., and Sheatsley, Paul B.: "Some Reasons Why Information Campaigns Fail," *Public Opinion Quarterly*, vol. 11, fall, 1947.

Ianni, Frances A. J.: *A Family Business: Kinship and Social Control in Organized Crime*, Russell Sage, New York, 1972.

Irwin, John, and Lewis Yablonsky: "The New Criminal: A View of the Contemporary Offender," in Bruce J. Cohen (ed.), *Crime in America*, F. C. Peacock Publishers, Inc., Itasca, 1970.

Isaacs, Asher, and Reuben Slesinger: *Business, Government and Public Policy*, Van Nostrand, Princeton, N.J., 1964.

Jacob, Herbert: *Justice in America*, 2d ed., Little, Brown, Boston, 1972.

Janis, Irving L.: "Groupthink," *Psychology Today*, vol. 5, November 1971.

Jennings, M. Kent, and Harmon Zeigler: "The Salience of American State Politics," *American Political Science Review*, vol. 64, June 1970.

Jennings, M. Kent, and Richard G. Neimi: "Patterns of Political Learning," in Edward C. Dreyer and Walter A. Rosenbaum (eds.), *Political Opinion and Behavior*, Wadsworth, Belmont, Calif., 1970. From *Harvard Educational Review*, vol. 38, 1968.

Johnson, Lyndon B.: *The Vantage Point; Perspectives of the Presidency 1963–1969*, Holt, New York, 1971.

Jones, Charles O.: *Every Second Year*, Brookings, Washington, D.C., 1967.

Kahn, Robert L.: "The Justification of Violence," *The Journal of Social Issues*, vol. 28, no. 1, 1972.

Kariel, Henry S.: *The Decline of American Pluralism*, Stanford, Stanford, Calif., 1961.

Delmar, Karlen: *The Citizen in Court*, Holt, New York, 1964.

Katz, Stanley Nider (ed.): *A Brief Narrative of the Case and Trial of John Peter Zenger*, Harvard, Cambridge, Mass., 1963.

Kelley, Stanley, Jr.: *Professional Public Relations and Political Power*, Johns Hopkins, Baltimore, 1956.

Kelly, Alfred H., and Winfred A. Harbison: *The American Constitution; Its Origins and Development*, Norton, New York, 1955.

Kennedy, John F.: *Public Papers of the Presidents of the United States, John F. Kennedy, 1962*, Government Printing Office, Washington, 1973.

Kennedy, Robert F.: *Thirteen Days: A Memoir of the Cuban Missile Crisis*, Norton, New York, 1969.

Key, V. O., Jr.: *Public Opinion and American Democracy*, Knopf, New York, 1961.

Key, V. O., Jr.: *The Responsible Electorate*, Harvard, Cambridge, Mass., 1966.

Kilpatrick, Franklin P., Milton Cummings, and M. Kent Jennings: *The Image of the Federal Service*, Brookings, Washington, 1964.

King, Seth S.: "Mother of Special Interests," *The New York Times*, Dec. 17, 1972.

Kingdon, John W.: "Politicians' Beliefs about Voters," *American Political Science Review*, vol. 61, March 1967.

Kirkpatrick, Evron M.: "Toward a More Responsible Two-Party System: Political Science, Policy Science, or Pseudo-Science?" *American Political Science Review*, vol. 65, December 1971.

Kissinger, Henry A.: "Central Issues of American Foreign Policy," in Kermit Gordon (ed.), *Agenda for the Nation*, Brookings, Washington, 1968.

Klein, Milton M.: "American Revolution in the Twentieth Century," *Historian*, vol. 34, February, 1972.

Knight, Edward: "Economic Policy and Inflation in the United States: A Survey of Developments from the Enactment of the Employment Act of 1946 through 1972," *Price and Wage Control: An Evaluation of Current Policies* (Part 2, Studies of Selected Aspects), Hearings before the Joint Economic Committee, 92nd Congress, 1972, pp. 362–435.

Knowles, Louis L., and Kenneth Prewitt (eds.): *Institutional Racism in America*, Prentice-Hall, Englewood Cliffs, N.J., 1969.

Kolko, Gabriel: *The Roots of American Foreign Policy*, Beacon Press, Boston, 1969.

Kolko, Gabriel: *The Triumph of Conservatism*, Free Press, New York, 1967.

Kraft, Joseph: "School for Statesmen," *Harper's Magazine*, July 1958.

Krislov, Samuel: *The Supreme Court in the Political Process*, Macmillan, New York, 1965.

Landau, Jack C.: "Free at Last, at Least," *Quill*, vol. 59, no. 8, August 1971.

Landis, Paul H.: *Social Control*, Lippincott, Philadelphia, 1939.

Lane, Robert E.: *Political Life*, Free Press, New York, 1959.

Langton, Kenneth P.: "Peer Group and School and the Political Socialization Process," *American Political Science Review*, vol. 61, no. 3, September 1967.

Lardner, George: "$5,000 in Dairymen's Funds Financed Ellsberg Burglary," *The Washington Post*, Oct. 11, 1973.

Large, Arlen J.: "The Shock Treatment for Congress," *The Wall Street Journal*, Apr. 13, 1973.

Lasswell, Harold D., and Arnold A. Rogow: *Power, Corruption and Rectitude*, Prentice-Hall, Englewood Cliffs, N.J., 1963.

Lazarsfeld, Paul F., Bernard Berelson, and Hazel Gaudet: *The People's Choice*, Duell, Sloan & Pearce, New York, 1944.

Levin, Murray B.: *Kennedy Campaigning*, Beacon Press, Boston, 1965.

Levitan, Sar: *The Great Society's Poor Law*, Johns Hopkins, Baltimore, 1969.

Levitin, Teresa E., and Warren E. Miller: "The New Politics and Partisan Realignment," paper presented at the meeting of the American Political Science Association, Washington, September 1972.

Lewis, Anthony: *Gideon's Trumpet*, Knopf, New York, 1964.

Lewis, Eugene: *The Urban Political System*, The Dryden Press, Inc., New York, 1973.

Lingeman, Richard R.: *Don't You Know There's a War On?* Putnam, New York, 1970.

Link, Arthur S.: *American Epoch*, Knopf, New York, 1955.

Lippmann, Walter: "An Interview with Ronald Steel," *The New Republic*, Apr. 14, 1973.

Lippman, Walter: *Public Opinion*, Free Press, New York, 1922, 1965.

Lipset, Seymour Martin: *Political Man: The Social Bases of Politics*, Doubleday, Garden City, N.Y., 1960.

Lipset, Seymour Martin: "Social Mobility and Equal Opportunity," *The Public Interest*, no. 29, fall, 1972.

Lockard, Duane: *The Perverted Priorities of American Politics*, Macmillan, New York, 1971.

Lodge, Henry Cabot, (ed.): *The Federalist: A Commentary on the Constitution of the United States*, from the original text of Alexander Hamilton, John Jay, and James Madison, Putnam, New York, 1888.

Lomax, Louis: *The Negro Revolt*, Harper & Row, New York, 1962.

Longley, Lawrence D., and Alan G. Braun: *The Politics of Electoral College Reform*, Yale, New Haven, Conn., 1972.

Loory, Stuart H.: "The Adversaries," *The New York Times*, May 10, 1973.

Lovell, John P.: *Foreign Policy in Perspective*, Holt, New York, 1970.

Lowi, Theodore J.: *The End of Liberalism*, Norton, New York, 1969.

Lowi, Theodore J.: "Machine Politics Old and New," in Harold F. Gosnell, *Machine Politics: Chicago Model*, 2d. ed., The University of Chicago Press, Chicago, 1968.

Lundberg, Ferdinand: *The Rich and the Super-Rich*, Bantam, New York, 1968.

Lynd, Robert S., and Helen M. Lynd: *Middletown in Transition*, Harcourt, Brace, New York, 1937.

Lyons, Eugene: *Herbert Hoover: A Biography*, Doubleday, New York, 1964.

Maas, Arthur: *Muddy Waters: The Army Engineers and the Nation's Rivers*, Harvard, Cambridge, Mass., 1951.

MacDonald, Dwight: "Our Invisible Poor," *The New Yorker*, vol. 38, Jan. 19, 1963.

MacIver, R. M.: *The Web of Government*, Macmillan, New York, 1947.

Madison, James: *Letter to W. T. Barry, Aug. 4, 1822*, in Saul K. Padover (ed.), *The Complete Madison*, Kraus Reprint Co., Millwood, N.Y., 1953.

Madison, James: "Selections from Notes of the Debates in the Federal Convention at Philadelphia," in Samuel Eliot Morison (ed.), *Sources and Documents Illustrating the American Revolution*, Oxford University Press, New York, 1928. Galaxy Book edition, 1965.

Manley, John F.: *The Politics of Finance*, Little, Brown, Boston, 1970.

Mann, Dean E.: *The Assistant Secretaries*, Brookings, Washington, 1965.

Mao Tse-Tung, "Problems of War and Strategy," *Selected Works*, vol. II, November 6, 1938. Quoted in *Quotations from Chairman Mao Tse-Tung*, Foreign Languages Press, Peking, 1966.

Marmor, Theodore R.: *Poverty Policy*, Aldine-Atherton, Chicago, 1971.

Marx, Gary T.: *Protest and Prejudice: A Study of Belief in the Black Community*, Harper & Row, New York, 1967.

Mason, Edward S. (ed.): *The Corporation in Modern Society*, Harvard, Cambridge, Mass., 1959.

Masters, Nicholas A.: "House Committee Assignments," *American Political Science Review*, vol. 55, June 1961.

Matthews, Donald R.: *U.S. Senators and Their World*, The University of North Carolina Press, Chapel Hill, 1960.

Matthews, Donald R., and James W. Prothro: *Negroes and the New Southern Politics*, Harcourt, Brace, New York, 1966.

Matthews, Linda: "The Newest Trial Tactic: Avoid the Supreme Court," *The Louisville Courier-Journal*, Oct. 8, 1973.

Maynard, Robert C.: "Must Protests Be Violent to Attract News Coverage?" *Washington Post*, Feb. 14, 1973.

McCartney, James: "Must the Media Be Used?" *Columbia Journalism Review*, vol. 8, no. 4, winter, 1969–70.

McCloskey, Herbert: "Political Participation," in David L. Sills (ed.), *International Encyclopedia of the Social Sciences*, Crowell, Collier and Macmillan, New York, 1968.

McClosky, Robert: *The American Supreme Court*, The University of Chicago Press, Chicago, 1960.

McGinnis, Joe: *The Selling of the President, 1968*, Trident Press, New York, 1969.

Merrill, John C.: *The Elite Press*, Pitman, New York, 1968.

Meyer, Philip: "Flashy GOP 'Selling' Reflects Confidence," *The Miami Herald*, Aug. 22, 1972.

Meyer, Philip: "If Hitler Asked You to Electrocute a Stranger, Would You?" *Esquire*, February 1970. Reprinted in Richard Greenbaum and Harvey A. Tilker (eds.): *The Challenge of Psychology*, Prentice-Hall, Englewood Cliffs, N.J., 1972.

Meyer, Philip: "Plot against TV-Watchers Launched by Tire Makers," *Chicago Daily News*, May 13, 1965.

Milbrath, Lester W.: *Political Participation*, Rand McNally, Chicago, 1965.

Miller, Arthur H., Warren E. Miller, Alden S. Raine, and Thad A. Brown: "A Majority Party in Disarray: Policy Polarization in the 1972 Election," paper delivered at the 1973 annual meeting of the American Political Science Association.

Miller, Herman: *Rich Man, Poor Man*, Crowell-Collier, New York, 1971.

Miller, Warren E.: "Presidential Coattails: A Study in Political Myth and Methodology." *Public Opinion Quarterly*, vol. 19, winter, 1955–56.

Miller, Warren E., and Donald E. Stokes: "Constituency Influence in Congress," *American Political Science Review*, vol. 57, March 1963.

Miller, William, and Thomas Cochran: *The Age of Enterprise*, Macmillan, New York, 1960.

Mills, C. Wright: *The Power Elite*, Oxford University Press, New York, 1957.

Milton, John: *Complete Poetry and Selected Prose of John Milton*, Modern Library, New York, 1950.

Mintz, Morton, and Jerry S. Cohen: *America, Inc.*, Dial, New York, 1971.

Mitchell, William C.: *Public Choice in America*, Markham, Chicago, 1971.

Montesquieu, Charles Louis de Secondat: *The Spirit of the Laws*, Heffner, New York, 1966. Originally published in 1748.

Moos, Malcom: *Politics, Presidents, and Coattails*, Johns Hopkins, Baltimore, 1952.

Morgenthau, Hans J.: *A New Foreign Policy for the United States*, Praeger, New York, 1969.

Morgenthau, Hans J.: *The Purpose of American Politics*, Knopf, New York, 1960.

Morison, Samuel Eliot, Henry Steele Commager, and William E. Leuchtenburg: *The Growth of the American Republic*, vol. I, Oxford University Press, New York, 1969.

Mosteller, Frederick, Herbert Hyman, Philip J. McCarthy, Eli S. Marks, and David B. Truman: *The Pre-Election Polls of 1948*, Social Science Research Council, New York, 1949.

Mosteller, Frederick, and Daniel P. Moynihan (eds.): *On Equality of Educational Opportunity*, Random House, New York, 1972.

Mott, Frank Luther: *American Journalism*, Macmillan, New York, 1941.

Moynihan, Daniel P.: *Maximum Feasible Misunderstanding*, Free Press, New York, 1969.

Murphy, Walter F.: *Elements of Judicial Strategy*, The University of Chicago Press, Chicago, 1964.

Murphy, Walter F., and Joseph Tanenhaus: "Public Opinion and the United States Supreme Court," in Joe B. Grossman and Joseph Tanenhaus (eds.), *Frontiers of Judicial Research*, Wiley, New York, 1969.

Murray, J. Edward: "4000 Miles Across China," *Detroit Free Press* reprint, 1972.

Nader, Ralph: *Unsafe at Any Speed*, Grossman, New York, 1965.

Nagel, Stuart S.: "Court-Curbing Periods in American History," in Theodore L. Becker (ed.), *The Impact of Supreme Court Decisions*, Oxford University Press, New York, 1969.

Natchez, Peter B., and Irvin C. Bupp: "Candidates, Issues, and Voters," *Public Policy*, vol. XVII, 1968.

National Advisory Commission on Civil Disorders: *Report*, Bantam, New York, 1968.

National Advisory Commission on Criminal Justice Standards and Goals: *Community Crime Prevention*, Government Printing Office, Washington, 1973.

Nettels, Curtis P.: *The Roots of American Civilization*, Appleton-Century-Crofts, New York, 1963.

Neustadt, Richard E.: "Approaches to Staffing the Presidency: Notes on FDR and JFK," *American Political Science Review*, vol. 57, December 1963.

Neustadt, Richard E.: "Politicians and Bureaucrats," in David B. Truman (ed.), *The Congress and America's Future*, 2d ed., Prentice-Hall, Englewood Cliffs, N.J., 1973.

Neustadt, Richard E.: *Presidential Power*, Wiley, New York, 1962. Originally published in 1960.

New York Times Company: "Tomorrow's Markets Today: An Interpretation of a Study of the New York Times Reader," New York, 1968.

Niemeyer, Gerhart: "Ideological Dimensions of the New China Policy," *Orbis*, vol. 15, fall, 1971.

Nixon, Richard M.: "Europe and the Atlantic Alliance," *Atlantic Community*, vol. 11, no. 3, fall, 1973.

Nixon, Richard M.: "Statement by the President upon Signing the Bill Providing State and Local Fiscal Assistance," in Office of the Federal Register, *Weekly Compilation of Presidential Documents*, vol. 8, no. 43, 1972.

Norton, Thomas James: *The Constitution of the United States: Its Sources and Applications*, Little, Brown, Boston, 1925.

Oakeshott, Michael (ed.): *Leviathan* (by Thomas Hobbes), Oxford, New York, 1947.

Oberdorfer, Don: "Political Polling and Electoral Strategy: The 1968 Election," in Edward C. Dreyer and Walter A. Rosenbaum (eds.), *Political Opinion and Behavior*, Wadsworth, Belmont, Calif., 1970.

Oberdorfer, Don: *Tet!* Doubleday, New York, 1971; Avon, 1972.

O'Dea, Thomas F.: *The Sociology of Religion*, Prentice-Hall, Englewood Cliffs, N.J., 1966.

Office of Management and Budget: *The United States Budget in Brief, Fiscal Year 1974*, Government Printing Office, Washington, 1973.

Olsen, Marvin L. (ed.): *Power in Societies*, Macmillan, New York, 1970.

Opperman, Leonard: "Aid for the States: Is Revenue Sharing the Answer?" *The Review of Politics*, vol. 30, January 1968.

Ostrogorski, M.: *Democracy and the Organization of Political Parties*, vol. II, Macmillan, New York, 1902.

Paine, Thomas: "Letter to the Abbe Raynal" (1782), in Moncure D. Conway (ed.), *The Writings of Thomas Paine*, vol. II, Burt Franklin, New York, 1969.

Paletz, David L.: "Perspectives on the Presidency," *Law and Contemporary Problems*, vol. 35, summer, 1970.

Parris, Judith H.: *The Convention Problem*, Brookings, Washington, 1972.

Pechman, Joseph A., and Benjamin A. Okner: *Who Bears the Tax Burden?* Brookings, Washington, 1974.

Peirce, Neal R.: *The People's President*, Simon and Schuster, New York, 1968.

Peltason, Jack: *Federal Courts in the Political Process*, Random House, New York, 1955.

Perry, James M.: *The New Politics*, Clarkson N. Potter, New York, 1968.

Pettigrew, Thomas F.: "Negro American Crime," in Marvin R. Summers and Thomas E. Barth (eds.), *Law and Order in a Democratic Society*, Charles E. Merrill Books, Inc., Columbus, Ohio, 1970.

Pettigrew, Thomas F.: *Racially Separate or Together?* McGraw-Hill, New York, 1971.

Pierce, Lawrence C.: *The Politics of Fiscal Policy Formation*, Goodyear Publishing Co., Pacific Palisades, Calif., 1971.

Piven, Francis Fox, and Richard A. Cloward: *Regulating the Poor: The Functions of Public Welfare*, Random House, New York, 1971.

Plato, *The Republic*, English translation by Benjamin Jowett, Clarendon Press, Oxford, 1908.

Polk, James: "100 Donors Gave Nixon's Campaign $14 Million," *Washington Star-News*, Feb. 25, 1973.

Polk, James: "3 Companies, 2 Officials Charged in Nixon Gifts," *Washington Star-News*, Oct. 17, 1973.

Polsby, Nelson W.: *Congress and the Presidency*, 2d. ed., Prentice-Hall, Englewood Cliffs, N.J., 1971.

Polsby, Nelson: "The Trial of President Nixon," *Washington Post*, June 3, 1973. Also in Nelson Polsby, *Political Promises: Essays and Commentary on American Politics*, Oxford University Press, New York, 1974.

Polsby, Nelson, and Aaron Wildavsky: *Presidential Elections*, 3d ed., Scribners, New York, 1971.

Pomper, Gerald M.: *Elections in America*, Dodd, Mead, New York, 1971.

Pomper, Gerald M.: "Nixon and the End of Presidential Politics," *Society*, vol. 10, no. 3, March–April 1973.

Pool, Ithiel de Sola: "What Will be New in the New Politics?" in Ray E. Hiebert, Robert Jones, Ernest Lotito, John Lorenz (eds.), *The Political Image Merchants*, Acropolis, Washington, 1971.

Pool, Ithiel de Sola, Robert P. Abelson, and Samuel L. Popkin: *Candidates, Issues, and Strategies*, M. I. T., Cambridge, Mass., 1965.

Potter, David M.: "A House Divided," in *The Democratic Experience*, Scott, Foresman, Glenview, Ill., 1963.

President's Commission on Law Enforcement and the Administration of Justice: *The Challenge of Crime in a Free Society*, Government Printing Office, Washington, 1967.

President's Commission on Law Enforcement and Administration of Justice: *Task Force Report: Organized Crime*, Government Printing Office, Washington, 1967.

Pursell, Carroll W., Jr.: *The Military-Industrial Complex*, Harper & Row, New York, 1972.

Quayle, Oliver: Remarks to meeting of the American Association for Public Opinion Research, Bolton's Landing, New York, May 1967. Quoted in Philip Meyer, *Precision Journalism*, Indiana University Press, Bloomington, 1973.

Quinney, Richard: *The Social Reality of Crime*, Little, Brown, Boston, 1970.

Radway, Laurence I.: *Foreign Policy and National Defense*, Scott, Foresman, Glenview, Ill., 1969.

Rae, Douglas W.: *The Political Consequences of Electoral Laws*, rev. ed., Yale Univ. Press, New Haven, Conn., 1971.

Randall, John Herman, Jr.: *The Making of the Modern Mind*, Houghton Mifflin, Boston, 1940.

Ranney, Austin: "Parties in State Politics," in Herbert Jacob and Kenneth N. Vines (eds.), *Politics in the American States: A Comparative Analysis*, 2d ed., Little, Brown, Boston, 1971.

Ranney, Austin, and Willmoore Kendall: *Democracy and the American Party System*, Harcourt, Brace, New York, 1956.

Rapoport, Anatol: *The Big Two: Soviet American Perceptions of Foreign Policy*, Pegasus, New York, 1971.

Ray, Dennis M.: "Corporations and American Foreign Relations," *The Annals of the American Academy of Political and Social Science*, vol. 403, September 1972.

Reagan, Michael D.: *The Managed Economy*, Oxford University Press, New York, 1963.

Reagan, Michael L.: "The Political Structure of the Federal Reserve System," *American Political Science Review*, vol. 55, no. 1, 1961.

Redford, Emmette Shelburn: *The Role of Government in the American Economy*, Macmillan, New York, 1966.

Reedy, George E.: *The Twilight of the Presidency*, New American Library, New York, 1970.

Reese, Matthew: "Locating the 'Switch-Split' Vote," in Ray Hiebert, Robert Jones, John Lorenz, and Ernest Lotito (eds.), *The Political Image Merchants*, Acropolis, Washington, 1971.

Reiselbach, Leroy N.: *Congressional Politics*, McGraw-Hill, New York, 1973.

Reston, James: *The Artillery of the Press*, Harper & Row, New York, 1967.

Reuss, Henry S.: *Revenue-Sharing*, Praeger, New York, 1970.

Reynolds, Lloyd G.: *Economics: A General Introduction*, Irwin, Homewood, Ill., 1963.

Rice, Robert: *The Challenge of Crime*, Public Affairs Committee, Washington, 1968.

Robinson, John P.: "The Audience for National TV News Programs," *Public Opinion Quarterly*, vol. 35, no. 3, fall, 1971.

Robinson, John P.: *Public Information about World Affairs*, Survey Research Center, University of Michigan, Ann Arbor, 1967.

Robinson, John P., Jerrold G. Rusk, and Kendra B. Head: *Measures of Political Attitudes*, Institute for Social Research, Ann Arbor, Mich., 1968.

Robson, Eric: *The American Revolution*, Archon Shoe String, Hamden, Conn., 1965.

Roche, John P.: "The Founding Fathers: A Reform Caucus in Action," *American Political Science Review*, vol. 55, December 1961.

Roche, John P.: "Judicial Self-Restraint," *American Political Science Review*, vol. 49, September 1955.

Rodgers, Harrell R., Jr., and Charles S. Bullock, III: *Law and Social Change*, McGraw-Hill, New York, 1972.

Rogers, William P.: "Our Permanent Interests in Europe," *The Atlantic Community Quarterly*, vol. 10, no. 1, spring, 1972.

Roper, Bernard: "A Ten-year View of Public Attitudes toward Television and Other Mass Media, 1959–1968," Television Information Office, New York, 1969.

Rose, Stephen M.: *The Betrayal of the Poor*, Schenkman, Cambridge, Mass., 1972.

Rossiter, Clinton: *The American Presidency*, New American Library, New York, 1956.

Rossiter, Clinton: *1787: The Grand Convention*, Macmillan, New York, 1966.

Rossiter, Clinton: "Impact of Mobilization of the Constitutional System," Academy of Political Science *Proceedings*, vol. 30, May 1971. Previously published in vol. 24, May 1951.

Rothchild, John: "Finding the Facts Bureaucrats Hide," *Washington Monthly*, vol. 3, January 1972.

Rourke, Francis E.: "Bureaucratic Secrecy and Its Constituents," *Bureaucrat*, vol. 1, summer, 1972.

Royko, Mike: *Boss: Richard J. Daley of Chicago*, Dutton, New York, 1971.

Rubin, Jesse: "Police Identity and the Police Role," in Robert F. Steadman (ed.), *The Police and the Community*, Johns Hopkins, Baltimore, 1972.

Russell, Bertrand: *The Impact of Science on Society*, Simon & Schuster, New York, 1953.

Russell, Mary: "Albert Presses House Reform Drive," *Washington Post*, May 3, 1973.

Sabine, George H.: "The Two Democratic Traditions," *The Philosophical Review*, vol. 61, October 1952.

Safire, William: *The New Language of Politics*, 2d. ed., Collier Books, The Macmillan Company, New York, 1972. Originally published by Random House in 1968.

Saloma, John S., III: *Congress and the New Politics*, Little, Brown, Boston, 1969.

Salter, John T.: *Boss Rule: Portraits in City Politics*, McGraw-Hill, New York, 1935.

Sampson, Anthony: *The Sovereign State*, Hodder, London, 1973; Stein and Day, New York, 1973.

Samuelson, Paul A.: *Economics*, 8th ed., McGraw-Hill, New York, 1970.

Sanford, Terry: *Storm Over the States*, McGraw-Hill, New York, 1967.

Sayre, Wallace S., and Judith H. Parris: *Voting for President: The Electoral College and the American Political System*, Brookings, Washington, 1970.

Schattschneider, E. E.: *Party Government*, Holt, New York, 1942.

Schattschneider, E. E.: *The Semi-Sovereign People*, Holt, New York, 1960.

Schattschneider, E. E.: *Two-Hundred Million Americans in Search of a Government*, Holt, New York, 1969.

Schechter, Alan H.: *Contemporary Constitutional Issues*, McGraw-Hill, New York, 1972.

Schelling, Thomas C.: *The Strategy of Conflict*, Oxford University Press, New York, 1963. Originally published in 1960.

Schlesinger, Arthur, Jr.: "The Dark Heart of American History," *Saturday Review*, Oct. 19, 1968.

Schlesinger, Arthur, Jr.: "How to Save the Presidency," *The Wall Street Journal*, June 1, 1973.

Schlesinger, Arthur, Jr.: *A Thousand Days*, Houghton Mifflin, Boston, 1965.

Schmidhauser, John R.: *The Supreme Court: Its Politics, Personalities, and Procedures*, Holt, New York, 1960.

Schmidhauser, John: "The Supreme Court: A Collective Portrait," *Midwest Journal of Political Science*, vol. III, 1959.

Schubert, Glendon: *Judicial Policy-making*, Scott, Foresman, Glenview, Ill., 1965.

Schuman, Howard: "Two Sources of Antiwar Sentiment in America," *The American Journal of Sociology*, vol. 78, no. 3, November 1972.

Schumpeter, Joseph A.: *Capitalism, Socialism, and Democracy*, 3d. ed., Harper & Row, New York, 1950.

Scoble, Harry M.: "Access to Politics," in David Sills (ed.), *International Encyclopedia of the Social Sciences*, vol. I, Macmillan, New York, 1968.

Seidman, Harold: *Politics, Position & Power: The Dynamics of Federal Organization*, Oxford University Press, New York, 1970.

Serrin, William: *The Company and the Union*, Knopf, New York, 1973.

Sethi, S. Prakash: *Up Against the Corporate Wall*, Prentice-Hall, Englewood Cliffs, N.J., 1971.

Sharkansky, Ira: *The Maligned States*, McGraw-Hill, New York, 1972.

Shepsle, Kenneth A.: "The Strategy of Ambiguity: Uncertainty and Electoral Competition," *American Political Science Review*, vol. 66, June 1972.

Sherrill, Robert: *The Accidental President*, Grossman, New York, 1967.

Sherrill, Robert: "Instant Electorate," *Playboy*, vol. 15, November 1968.

Simmel, Georg: *Conflict and the Web of Group Affiliations*, Free Press, New York, 1955.

Smead, Elmer: *Governmental Promotion and Regulation of Business*, Appleton-Century-Crofts, New York, 1969.

Smith, Bob: *They Closed Their Schools*, The University of North Carolina Press, Chapel Hill, 1965.

Society: "How the West Is Being Won," January–February 1973.

Sorauf, Frank J.: *Party Politics in America*, Little, Brown, Boston, 1968.

Statistical Abstract: Government Printing Office, Washington, 1972, 1973.

Steele, A. T.: *The American People and China*, McGraw-Hill, New York, 1966.

Stein, Bruno: *On Relief: The Economics of Poverty and Public Welfare*, Basic Books, New York, 1971.

Stokes, Donald E.: "Some Dynamic Flements of Contests for the Presidency," *American Political Science Review*, vol. 60, no. 1, March 1966.

Sundquist, James L.: *Politics and Policy*, Brookings, Washington, 1968.

Swanson, Charles E.: "What They Read in 130 Daily Newspapers," *Journalism Quarterly*, vol. 32, fall, 1965.

Taft, William Howard: "A Restricted View of the Office," in Sidney Warren (ed.), *The American President*, Prentice-Hall, Englewood Cliffs, N.J., 1967. Originally published in 1916.

Thomas, William F.: "How Did We Get into This Terrible Fix?" *Bulletin of the American Society of Newspaper Editors*, no. 566, February 1973.

Thoreau, Henry David: "Civil Disobedience," in Brooks Atkinson (ed.), *Walden and Other Writings of Henry David Thoreau*, Modern Library, New York, 1950. Originally published in 1849.

Thorp, Willard: *The Reality of Foreign Aid*, Praeger, New York, 1971.

Tilly, Charles: "Collective Violence in European Perspective," in Hugh Davis Graham & Ted Robert Gurr, *The History of Violence in America*, Bantam, New York, 1969.

Tobin, James: "Raising the Income of the Poor," in Kermit Gordon (ed.), *Agenda for the Nation*, Doubleday, Garden City, N.Y., 1968.

Toffler, Alvin: *Future Shock*, Bantam, New York, 1970.

Truman, David B.: *The Governmental Process*, Knopf, New York, 1951, 1960, 1971.

Truman, Harry S.: "Lobbyist for All the People," *The New York Times*, May 9, 1954. Reprinted in Sidney Warren (ed.), *The American President*, Prentice-Hall, Englewood Cliffs, N.J., 1967.

Truman, Harry S.: *Year of Decisions*, Doubleday, Garden City, N.Y., 1955.

Tuchman, Barbara W.: "Should We Abolish the Presidency?" *The New York Times*, Feb. 12, 1973.

Tuchman, Sam, and Coffin, Thomas E.: "The Influence of Election Night Television Broadcasts in a Close Election," *Public Opinion Quarterly*, vol. 35, fall, 1971.

Tuck, Richard: "Corrupting the Political Prank," *The Washington Post*, Mar. 29, 1973.

Tugwell, Rexford, G.: "The Presidency: Who Measured Up?" *The Center Magazine*, vol. 51, March–April 1973.

Uniform Crime Reports for the United States: Government Printing Office, Washington, 1972, 1973.

U.S. Commission on Civil Rights: *The Federal Civil Rights Enforcement Effort—A Reassessment*, Government Printing Office, Washington, 1973.

U.S. Department of Commerce: *The Social and Economic Status of Negroes in the United States*, 1970, BLS Report No. 394, Government Printing Office, Washington, 1971.

United States Committee on Government Operations, Subcommittee on Intergovernmental Relations: *Confidence and Concern: Citizens View American Government*, Government Printing Office, Washington, 1973.

Van Doren, Carl: *The Great Rehearsal*, Viking, New York, 1961. Originally published in 1948.

Vose, Clement E.: "Litigation as a Form of Pressure Group Activity," *The Annals of the American Academy of Political and Social Science*, vol. 319, September 1958.

Walzer, Michael: "Civil Disobedience and Corporate Authority," in Philip Green and Sanford Levinson (eds.), *Power and Community*, Pantheon, New York, 1970.

Washington Post: "Black Income: Delusion and Reality," July 5, 1973.

Wattenberg, Ben J., and Richard M. Scammon: "Black Progress and Liberal Rhetoric," *Commentary*, April 1973.

Weaver, Warren, Jr.: "White House Expected to Cite Legal Backing for President's Refusal to Spend Funds Congress Voted," *New York Times*, Feb. 6, 1973.

Weber, Max: *The Theory of Social and Economic Organization*, Talcott Parsons (ed.), Free Press, New York, 1964.

Weber, Ronald E.: "The Political Responsiveness of the American States and Their Local Governments," in Leroy N. Rieselbach (ed.), *People vs. Government: The Responsiveness of American Institutions*, Indiana University Press, Bloomington, 1975.

Weschler, Herbert: "The Nationalization of Civil Liberties and Civil Rights," *Texas Quarterly*, vol. 12, 3d Supp., summer, 1969.

Wheeler, Stanton (ed.): *On Record: Files and Dossiers in American Life*, Russell Sage, New York, 1969.

The White House Transcripts: The Full Text of the Submission of Recorded Presidential

Conversations to the Committee on the Judiciary of the House of Representatives by President Richard M. Nixon, Bantam, New York, 1974.

White, Ralph, K.: *Nobody Wanted War*, Doubleday, Garden City, N.Y., 1968.

White, Theodore: *The Making of the President 1960*, Pocket Books, New York, 1961, Atheneum, New York, 1961; Giant Cardinal Edition, 1961.

White, Theodore: *The Making of the President 1972*, Atheneum, New York, 1973.

White, Wilbur W.: *White's Political Dictionary*, World Publishing, Cleveland, 1947.

White, William S.: *Citadel: The Story of the U.S. Senate*, Harper & Row, New York, 1957.

Whiting, John W., and Irvin L. Child: *Child Training and Personality: A Cross Cultural Study*, Yale, New Haven, Conn., 1963.

Whitley, Oliver R.: *Religious Behavior: Where Sociology and Religion Meet*, Prentice-Hall, Englewood Cliffs, N.J., 1964.

Wildavsky, Aaron: "The Political Economy of Efficiency: Cost-Benefit Analysis, Systems Analysis and Program Budgeting," *Public Administration Review*, vol. 26, Dec. 1966.

Wildavsky, Aaron: "Toward a Radical Incrementalism: A Proposal to Aid Congress in Reform of the Budgetary Process," in Alfred de Grazia (ed.), *Congress: The First Branch of Government*, American Enterprise Institute, Washington, 1966.

Williams, William Appleman: *The Contours of American History*, World Publishing, Cleveland, 1961.

Wilson, James Q.: "The Strategy of Protest: Problems of Negro Civil Action," *Journal of Conflict Resolution*, vol. 5, September 1961.

Wilson, Woodrow: *Congressional Government*, Houghton Mifflin, Boston, 1891.

Wise, David: *The Politics of Lying: Government Deception, Secrecy, and Power*, Random House, New York, 1973.

Wise, David, and Thomas B. Ross: *The Invisible Government*, Random House, New York, 1965.

Witcover, Jules: "November Group Suffers Discontent," *Washington Post*, June 24, 1973.

Woll, Peter: *American Bureaucracy*, Norton, New York, 1963.

Woll, Peter, and Robert Binstock: *America's Political System: State and Local*, Random House, New York, 1972.

Woll, Peter, and Rochelle Jones: "The Bureaucracy: A Brake on Presidential Power," *The National Observer*, Oct. 13, 1973.

Wood, Gordon S.: "Rhetoric and Reality in the American Revolution," *William and Mary Quarterly*, series 3, vol. 23, January 1966.

Woodward, C. Vann: *Reunion & Reaction*, Doubleday, Garden City, N.Y., 1956.

Yarmolinsky, Adam: *The Military Establishment*, Harper & Row, New York, 1971.

Index

nonviolence by, 280
political participation by, 480
poverty among, 482–483
and public accommodations, 480–481
in public office, 70
and religion, 441
riots of, in the 1960s, 264, 273–274
and slavery, 68–70
urban, 483
voting by, 71, 79, 92, 184, 208, 221, 470, 479–480
Blackstone, 60
Blaine, James G., 219
Blanton, Thomas L., 300
Blue Ribbon Panel on Defense Reorganization, 525
Blue Valley Study Association, 161, 166
Bogart, Leo, 149
Bolivar, Simon, 20
Bolling v. Sharpe, 72
Bolton, Frances P., 305–306
Bolton, Oliver, 221
Bone, Hugh A., 252
Booms, 501
Bootleggers, 375
Boston, 117, 470
Boston *Globe*, 60
Boston Tea Party, 14, 16
Boycotts, 281
Boyle, W. A. (Tony), 229
Brandeis, Louis, 59, 381
Brave New World (Huxley), 476
Brearley, David, 33
Brennan, William J., 53, 61
Broder, David, 180, 196
Brooke, Edward, 305
Brown, John, 267, 275–276
Brown, Linda, 72–73, 77, 376–377
Brown, Rap, 265, 276
Brown, Robert E., 29
Brown, Thad A., 254
Brown v. Board of Education, 72–82, 361, 376–377, 381, 387, 430, 479
Brownlow, Louis, 340
Brussels Treaty, 533
Brzezinski, 544
Buchanan. Patrick J., 214, 223, 349
Budget and Accounting Procedures Act of 1950, 398
Budget and Impoundment Control Act of 1974, 292, 335
Budget Office, 293
Budget Reform Act of 1974, 320
Budget of the United States Government, The, 405
Budgets:
defense, 520
family, 477
federal, 404–405
agencies and, 406
method of making, 406
and planning, 409–410
and politics of budgeting, 405
Bullock, Charles S., III, 480–481
Bundy, McGeorge, 528, 531, 533
Burdick, Eugene, 207
Bureau of the Budget, 341

Bureau of the Census, 397, 453, 464, 476
Bureau of Engraving and Printing, 505–506
Bureau of Executive Manpower, 404
Bureau of Labor Statistics, 477
Bureaucracy, 389–417, 519
agencies, and congressional committees, 411–413
and career executives, 403–404
conflict between bureaus in, 396
county and city, 115, 122
divisions for apportioning work in, 397–399
employees in, 392–393, 401–404
as an enemy, 390–391
executive branch and, 394–395
foreign policy, 519–520
and information, 413–416
and merit system, 393–394
national security, 391
origins of, 392–393
and policy making, 390
political executives in, 401–403
power of, 391
private, 421–422
private organizations in, 400
and the public, 400
recent developments in, 399–400
reduction of, 320
shifts in, 518
and spoils system, 393
structure of, 395–396
Bureaucrats, 394, 396, 411, 415–416
and need for information, 413
Burger, George, 159–160, 163–164
Burger, Warren E., 51, 374, 381
Burger Court, 51–54, 58, 74
Burglary, 464
Burke, Edmund, 147
Burlington, Vermont, 100
Burnham, Walter Dean, 181, 253, 258
Burns, Arthur, 509
Burns, James MacGregor, 355–356
Burton, Harold, 371
Business:
with Communist China, 543
government and, 486–489
Business cycles, 501
Busing, 74, 76–77, 481
Butler, Pierce, 113
Byrd, Harry, Sr., 233, 239n.

Cabinet, the, 327, 338
Calhoun, John C., 89–90
California, 198–199, 204, 222, 237, 240–241
King's River project in, 411
legislature of, 107
University of, 49, 280
Cambodia, bombing of, 520
Campaigns (*see* Political campaigns)
Campaigns, Inc., 198
Campbell, Angus, 82, 256, 465–466, 475
Campbell, John, 517, 519
Camus, Albert, 268

Capitalism:
laissez faire, 487–489
in U.S., 486
Capron, William M., 406
Cardoza, Benjamin N., 44–45, 49, 52
Carnegie Foundation, 438
Carswell, G. Harrold, 294, 370
Castro, Fidel, 324
Catch 22 (Heller), 382, 422
Cater, Douglass, 344
Catholic Archdiocese of Hartford, Connecticut, 439–440
Catholics, 251
Celler, Emanuel, 318
Celler-Kefauver Antimerger Act of 1950, 495
Censorship, 60
Central Intelligence Agency (CIA), 324, 339, 395, 529, 531
and foreign policy, 516, 521, 523
Centrism, 89, 94
Chase, Harold W., 366
Chase, Samuel, 297
Checks and balances, 23
Cherokee Indian Nation, 8
Chicago, 120–121, 123, 138–139, 245
Child, Irvin L., 132
Children:
black, 138–139
effect of Watergate on, 135
middle-class, 136–140
political socialization of, 129–140
president evaluated by, table, 138
upper-class white, 136–137, 140
working-class, 138–139
Chile, 521
China, 129–130, 155–157, 356, 520
as emerging power, 540–543
trade with, 543
U.S. and, 540
China Lobby, 540–541
Chinese Nationalists, 542
Chisholm, Shirley, 310
Chou En-lai, 540
Chrysler Corporation, 172
Church and state, separation of, 62
Churches:
power of, 439–441
tax exemption for, 63, 439–440
Churchill, Winston, 157
Cities:
and federal government, 97
increase in, 114
politicians and organized crime in, 282
problems of, 112, 119
states and, 112
Citizens:
apathy of, 263–264, 275
Congress as representative of, 303–305
and obedience to law, 269
political involvement of, 264–265
and political parties, 181
protection of: from each other, 67–82
from government, 39–46
Citizens Conference on State Legislatures, 107
Citizens' Research Foundation, 226

574

and nonvoters, 146
on professions for young people, 401
and public opinion on Nixon, 141–142
on spending taxpayers money, 105
Galveston, Texas, 118
Gamson, William, 178, 281
Garfield, James, 357, 393
Garment, Leonard, 59
Gary, Indiana, 282
General Accounting Office, 398
General Allotment Act of 1887, 84
General Electric, 496
General Motors, 419, 423, 432, 443, 496
General Reserve Sharing Act of 1972, 99–100
General Services Administration, 395, 399, 412
Generation gap, 137
George III, King, 13, 18, 25, 69
Georgia, 16, 19, 80
Germany, 533
  Nazi, 131
  West, output of, 500
Gerry, Elbridge, 29, 33, 247–248
Gerrymander, the, 247–248
Gibbons v. Ogden, 92
Gideon, Clarence, 376, 387
Gideon case, 51, 387
Ginn, Rosemary, 217
Ginzburg, Ralph, 53
Gitlow, 46, 56
Gitlow v. New York, 48
Glazer, Nathan, 421–422
Glenn, John, 220
Godfather, The (Puzo), 282
Goldfarb, Lewis, 439
Goldman, Ralph M., 210
Goldman, Sheldon, 372
Goldwater, Barry, 196, 229, 233, 240, 252, 254, 281, 457–458, 532
Goods and services, 498
Government, 132–133
  alternative forms of, 282–283
  antidote to rigidity in, 283–285
  authority of, 267–268
  bigness and diversity in, 88–89
  business and, 486–489
  confederate system of, 87
  corruption in, 101
  factions in, 101
  federal (*see* United States government)
  first concern of, 419
  ideal system of, 394–395
  justice in, 267
  layers of, 87–88, 94–96
  in mixed economy, 490
  need for, 420–421
  and the people, 10
  and the poor, 468–475
  power of, 7
    conflicts with, 54–58
  primary function of, 514
  protection of citizens from, 39–46
  purpose of, 18–19
  purposeful procrastination by, 275
  and society, 4
  and technology, 428

unitary system of, 87
United States (*see* United States government)
Government agencies, 339, 398–400, 406, 410
  bureaucracy and, 411–413
  and control of national wealth, 518
  regulatory, 490
    history of, 492–493
    impact of, 491–492
Government Corporation Control Act of 1945, 398
Government documents, secret, 413–417
Government employees, 518, 521–522
Government services, 419
Government spending, 283–284, 501
  Congress and, 292–293
  deficit, 502–503, 518
  on foreign aid, 524
  military, 406
Governors:
  executive authority of, 106–107
  limited powers of, 105–106
Graft, 283
  (*See also* Corruption)
Graham, Hugh Davis, 278
Graham, James, 196
Grant, Ulysses S., 350
Grant programs, 95–97, 99
  decline in, 101
  history of, 96
  impounding funds for, 101
  from states to localities, 113
  strings attached to, 97–98
Gray, Patrick, 295
Great Depression, the, 398, 501, 508
  poverty during, 469
Great Society, 472
Greenberg, Edward S., 132, 140, 477
Greenstone, J. David, 471, 474
Grodzins, Martin, 95, 98
Gross national product (GNP):
  defense budget and, 518
  economic performance and, 498
  and foreign aid, 538
Grosse, Robert N., 406–408
Grotta, Gerald L., 145
Guerilla tactics, 275
Gulick, Luther, 103
Gurr, Ted Robert, 278
Guy, William, 227

Habeas corpus, writ of, 41, 45
Halberstam, David, 525
Haldeman, H. R., 201, 344–345
Hallowell, 8
Halperin, Morton, 524
Hamilton, Alexander, 26, 29, 35, 45, 87–89, 184, 296, 367
Hamilton, Richard, 176
Hancock, John, 17–18, 45
Hand, Learned, 56, 366
Harbison, 34, 92
Harding, Warren G., 197*n.*, 299
Hargis, Billy James, 169–170
Harlan, John Marshall, 57, 71

Harper's Ferry, 267, 275
Harrington, Michael, 470, 472
Harris, Louis, 143
Harris Survey, 151, 156
  on confidence: in executive branch, 401
    in government, 103–104
  on Supreme Court, 385–386
Harrison, Benjamin, 238
Harrison, William Henry, 184, 197*n.*
Harrison administration, 495
Hart, Gary, 190
Hart, Philip, 460
Hartke, Vance, 214, 223
Hatch Act, 225, 229, 393
Hatcher, Richard, 282
Hayes, Rutherford B., 232, 238
Hayes-Tilden election, 70, 238
Haynesworth, Clement F., Jr., 294, 370
Hays, Brooks, 253
Head Start, 472–473
Health Services, 397
Heller, Joseph, 382, 422
Heller, Walter, 98, 503, 505
Henry, Patrick, 28–29
Hesburgh, Reverend Theodore M., 81
Hess, Karl, 281
Hess, Robert D., 136–137
Hill family, the, 59
Hilsman, Roger, 515, 521–522, 531
Hobbes, Thomas, 10, 267, 420
Hodgson, Godfrey, 71
Hoffman, Stanley, 519, 534
Holmes, Oliver Wendell, 56–57, 378
Home rule, local governments and, 113–114
Hook, Stanley, 278
Hoover, Herbert, 184, 339, 350–351
Horowitz, Irving Louis, 535–537
Housing:
  for blacks, 481–482
  public, segregation in, 77–78, 81
Huckshorn, Robert J., 153
Hughes, Charles Evans, 48, 72, 297
Hughes, Howard, 223
Huitt, Ralph K., 315
Humphrey, Hubert, 152–153, 202–205, 222–223, 233, 237, 459, 531
Huxley, Aldous, 476
Hyman, Herbert H., 146–147

Illinois, legislature of, 107, 245
Imaginary Ideal Machine for Making Policy (IIMMP), 516
Impeachment, Congress and, 296–297
Import duties, 14
Income:
  of blacks, 482
  distribution of, unequal, 476–478
  median family, table, 482
  personal and disposable, economy and, 498
  redistribution of, 478
Income groups, crime and, 464–465
Independent Journal, 87
Indian Removal Act of 1830, 84
Indian Reorganization Act of 1934, 84

Minorities:
in Congress, 304
government and, 272
political, 179–180, 243
Minton, Sherman, 371
Mintz, Morton, 435
Miranda rule, 51, 383–384, 387
Miscegenation, 71
Mississippi, 80, 100, 377, 476
Mississippi Freedom Democrats, 216, 300
Missouri, 69, 72, 113, 246
Missouri Compromise, 69–70, 387
Mitchell, John, 190, 202
Mitchell, William C., 473
MITRE Corporation, 400
Mobilization for Youth (MFY), 470–471
Model Cities program, 335
Mohbat, Joseph, 343
Monarchy, presidency and, 325–326
Monetary policy, 504–506, 510
Money supply, 505–506
decrease in, 506
Monopoly, 92, 496
Monroe, James, 91
Montana, 105
Montesquieu, Baron de, 32, 86–87
Montgomery, Alabama, 77, 281
Morgenthau, Hans J., 437, 441, 532
Morison, Samuel Eliot, 28
Mormons, 62
Morris, Gouverneur, 34
Moss, John, 415
Mott, Stewart, 423
Moyers, Bill, 337
Moynihan, Daniel P., 75
Mueller, Willard F., 424–425
Mundt, Karl, 241
Municipal government:
corruption in, 121–122
forms of, 117–119
Munitions makers, foreign policy and, 526–528
Murphy, Walter F., 386
Murray, J. Edward, 129
Muskie, Edmund, 214–215, 224

Nader, Ralph, 171–172, 191, 368, 395, 418, 435–436, 441, 443
Nagel, Stuart S., 380, 384–385
Napolitan, Joseph, 205
Nation, Carrie, 277
Nation:
definition of, 8
state and, 8
Nation building, 8
National Advisory Commission on Civil Disorders, 264, 278, 284–285
National Advisory Commission on Criminal Justice, Standards, and Goals, 282–283
National Aeronautics and Space Administration, 399, 412
National Association for the Advancement of Colored People, 72, 77, 79, 169, 376–377

National Association of Manufacturers, 167
National Association of State Universities and Land Grant Colleges, 424
National Commission on the Causes and Prevention of Violence, 465
National Commission on Law Observance and Enforcement, 282
National Commitments resolution, 523
National committee chairmen, 190
National Committee for an Effective Congress, 191
National Committee for Fairness to the President, 162
National Council of Churches, 423
National Federation of Independent Businesses, 160
National Guard, the, 74
National Home Ownership Foundation, 400
National Labor Relations Board, 399
National Labor Relations (Wagner) Act of 1935, 271, 297–298, 430
National Republican party, 184
National Rifle Association, 160, 167
National Right to Work Committee, 167
National Rivers and Harbors Congress, 395, 411
National Science Foundation, 526
National security, 413, 452, 519–520
money spent on, 526, 528
National Security Council, 341, 519
Executive Committee of, 531–532
National security establishment, as foreign policymaker, 525–526
National sovereignty, 92–93
Nationalism, 20
Algerian, 268
Nationhood, 13
NATO, 524, 533, 538
Navajos, the, 8
Near v. Minnesota, 48, 60
Nebraska, 93
Neighborhood Youth Corps, 471
Netherlands, the, 26
Neustadt, Richard E., 331–332, 340, 411–412
New Britain, Connecticut, 439–440
New Deal, the, 150, 297, 352, 380, 469, 471–472
New Echota, Treaty of, 8
New England River Basin Commission, 400
New England states, 63
New Hampshire, 25, 63
and presidential primary, 214, 271
New Haven, Connecticut, 134–135, 470
New Industrial State, The, Galbraith, 442
New Jersey, 63
New Jersey Plan, the, 31–32, 35
New Orleans, 47
New Rochelle, New York, 75
New York City, 189, 283
New York State, 29, 32, 37, 48, 56, 58, 92, 246
legislature of, 107
opponents of Constitution in, 86–87

and presidential primary, 213
New York Stock Exchange, 487
New York Times, 40, 60, 66, 144–145, 224, 378
N.Y. Times Co. v. Sullivan, 55
New York Times Magazine, 144
New York Weekly Journal, 55
New Yorker, 470
Newark, 278, 282
Newfield, Jack, 219
News management:
and leak of information, 154–155
public opinion and, 153–155
News media, 415
(See also Media)
Newspapers:
group ownership of, 145
and public affairs information, 144–145
Newton, Sir Isaac, 18
Ney, Edward N., 202
Niemi, Richard G., 140
1984 (Orwell), 7
Nixon, Richard, 3, 54, 59, 66, 81, 90, 99–101, 135, 144–146, 149, 155–156, 172, 185, 190, 199–202, 205, 211, 217, 221–224, 226, 228, 232–233, 237, 239n., 241, 255, 283, 290, 294, 296–297, 299, 325, 327–328, 333–339, 347–354, 357, 391, 402, 413, 449–451, 459, 461, 466, 472
and China, 540, 542
and executive privilege, 416
and foreign policy, 517, 520, 525, 533–534
journey to Europe by, 532–534
popularity of, 1973, table, 142
public opinion on, 141
reelection campaign of, 325
and Soviet Union, 543–544
Nixon administration, 80, 98, 162, 290, 292, 298, 318, 321, 334, 353, 365, 370, 391, 461, 509, 523
Nixon Doctrine, 514–515, 546
Nonpartisanship, 122
Nonviolence, 274
black, 280
North, the, 16, 34, 41, 69–70, 184, 275
blacks in, 74–75
busing in, 76
segregation in, 74
North Atlantic Alliance, 533–534
NATO, 524, 533, 538
North Carolina, 37, 63, 74, 80, 247–248
North Vietnam, 294
bombing of, 324–325
Northwest Ordinance, 27
November Group, the, 201–202, 224
Nuclear missiles, Soviet, 530–532
Nuremberg trials, 268–269

Oakland, California, 470
Oberdorfer, Don, 154
O'Brian, David Paul, 57–58
O'Brien, Lawrence, 190
Obscenity, 53–54
O'Donnell, Ken, 343

587